ORDNANCE SURVEY

STREET ATLAS
Cardiff, Swansea & Glamorgan *E.C.L*

Contents

IV *Key to maps*

VI *Administrative boundaries*

1 *Street maps*

228 *Index explanation and abbreviations*

229 *Index of towns, villages and rural localities*

230 *Index of street names*

PHILIP'S

First edition published 1995 by

Ordnance Survey   and   Philip's
Romsey Road   an imprint of Reed Books
Maybush   Michelin House, 81 Fulham Road, London, SW3 6RB
Southampton SO16 4GU   and Auckland, Melbourne, Singapore and Toronto

ISBN 0-540-06186-7 (Philip's, hardback)
ISBN 0-540-06187-5 (Philip's, softback)
ISBN 0-319-00805-3 (Ordnance Survey, hardback)
ISBN 0-319-00806-1 (Ordnance Survey, softback)

To the best of the Publishers' knowledge, the information in this atlas was correct at
the time of going to press. No responsibility can be accepted for any errors or their
consequences.

The representation in this atlas of a road, track or path is no evidence of the existence
of a right of way.

Printed and bound in Great Britain by
Bath Press, Bath

Gorsaf Rheilffyrdd Brydeinig	British Rail station
Gorsaf rheilffyrdd breifat	Private railway station
Gorsaf fysiau	Bus or coach station
(H) Maes hofrenyddion	(H) Heliport
Gorsaf Heddlu (nid yn sicr o fod a'r agor 24awr)	Police station (may not be open 24 hours)
Ysbyti gyda cyfleusterau damweiniol (nid yn sicr o fod a'r agor 24 awr)	Hospital with casualty facilities (may not be open 24 hours)
Swyddfa'r Post	Post office
Lle o addoliad	Place of worship
Adeilad Pwysig	Important building
P Parcio	P Parking
174 Dangosydd tudalen cyffwrdd	E.C.L P 174 Adjoining page indicator
Dim tudalen cyffwrdd	No adjoining page
Traffordd	Motorway
Ffordd ddeuol	Dual carriageway
Priffordd neu ffordd trwodd	Main or through road
A27 Rhifau Ffordd (Adran Trafnidiaeth)	A27 Road numbers (Department of Transport)
Gât, Clwyd neu rhwystir i drafnidiaeth (ni gymhwysir gyfyngiadau bob amser nac i bob cerbyd)	Gate or obstruction to traffic (restrictions may not apply at all times or to all vehicles)
Llwybrau, Llwybrau march, BOAT'S RUPP'S, rheilffyrdd segur	All paths, bridleways, BOAT's, RUPP's, dismantled railways, etc.
Trac	Track

Nid yw ymddangosiad unrhyw ffordd arall neu drac neu lwybr ar yr atlas hwn yn tystio fod hawl tramwy ar hyd-ddynt	The representation in this atlas of a road, track or path is no evidence of the existence of a right of way

Amb Sta	Gorsaf Ambiwlans	LC	Croesfan wastad	Amb Sta	Ambulance Station	LC	Level Crossing
Coll	Coleg	Liby	Llyfrgell	Coll	College	Liby	Library
FB	Pompren	Mus	Amgueddfa	FB	Footbridge	Mus	Museum
F Sta	Gorsaf Dân	Sch	Ysgol	F Sta	Fire Station	Sch	School
Hospl	Ysbyti	TH	Neuadd y Dref	Hospl	Hospital	TH	Town Hall

0	¼	½	¾	1 mile/milltir

0	250 m	500 m	250 m	1 Kilometre/Kilometr

Graddfa y map yw 5.52 cm i'r km
(3½ modfedd i'r filltir)
Y mae'r rhifau bach o amgylch y mapiau yn cyduabod
y llinellau Grid cenedlaethol 1 Kilometr

The scale of the maps is 5.52 cm to 1 km
(3½ inches to 1 mile)
The small numbers around the edges of the maps
identify the 1 kilometre National Grid lines

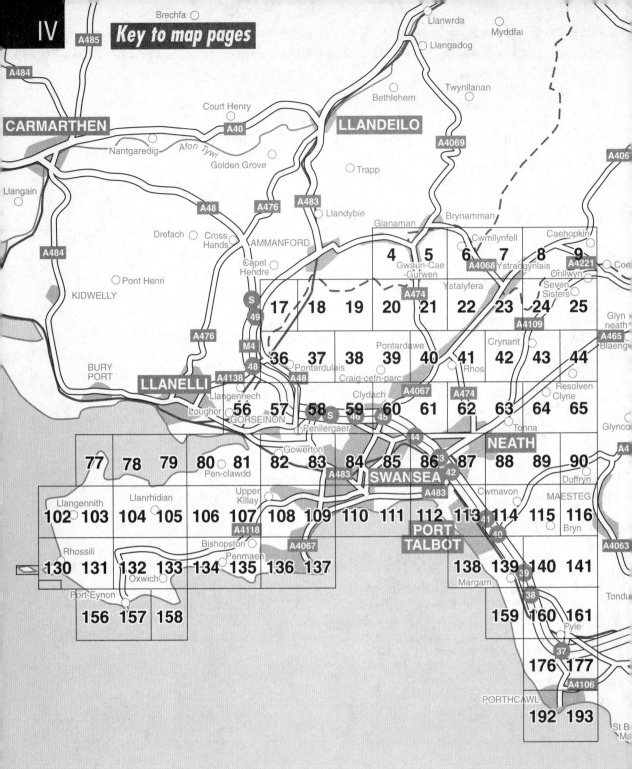

A485

Key to map pages

A484

CARMARTHEN

Brechfa ○

○ Llanwrda

○ Llangadog

Myddfai ○

A406

A484

Llangain ○

Court Henry

A40

LLANDEILO

A4069

Bethlehem ○

Twynllanan ○

Nantgaredig

Afon Tywi

Golden Grove ○

○ Trapp

Drefach

Cross Hands

A48

A476

A483

○ Llandybie

Glanaman

Brynamman

Caehopkin ○

Coe

AMMANFORD

4 **5** **6** **7** **8** **9**

Cwmllynfell ○

A4068 Ystradgynlais

A4221

Capel Hendre

Gwaun-Cae -Gurwen

Ystalyfera

Onllwyn ○

Pont Henri ○

KIDWELLY

A474

17 **18** **19** **20** **21** **22** **23** **24** **25**

Seven Sisters

Glyn neath

A4109

A476

M4

Pontardawe

Crynant

A465

Blaeng

36 **37** **38** **39** **40** **41** **42** **43** **44**

BURY PORT

A4138

A48

Pontardulais

Craig-cefn-parc

Rhos

Resolven

Clyne

LLANELLI

Llangennech

A4067

A474

Clydach

56 **57** **58** **59** **60** **61** **62** **63** **64** **65**

Loughor

GORSEINON

Penllergaer

Tonna

Glynco

77 **78** **79** **80** **81** **82** **83** **84** **85** **86** **87** **88** **89** **90**

NEATH

A4

Gowerton

Pen-clawdd ○

A483

SWANSEA

Duffryn

Llangennith

Llanrhidian

Upper Killay

Cwmavon

MAESTEG

102 **103** **104** **105** **106** **107** **108** **109** **110** **111** **112** **113** **114** **115** **116**

A4118

A4067

Bishopston ○

Bryn

A4063

Rhossili

Penmaen

PORT TALBOT

130 **131** **132** **133** **134** **135** **136** **137** **138** **139** **140** **141**

Port-Eynon

Oxwich ○

Margam

Tondu

156 **157** **158** **159** **160** **161**

Pyle ○

176 **177**

A4106

PORTHCAWL

192 **193**

St B

Ma

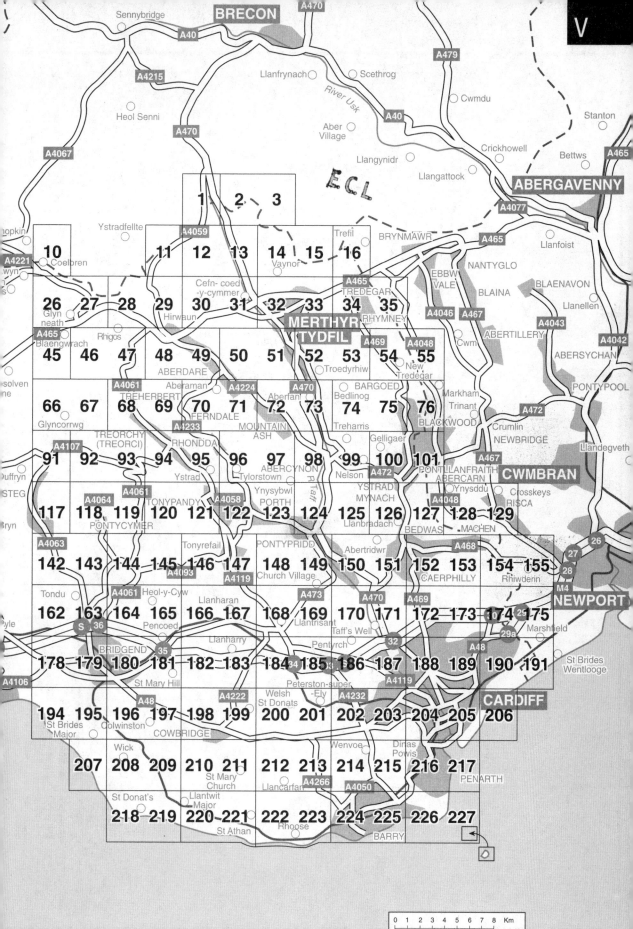

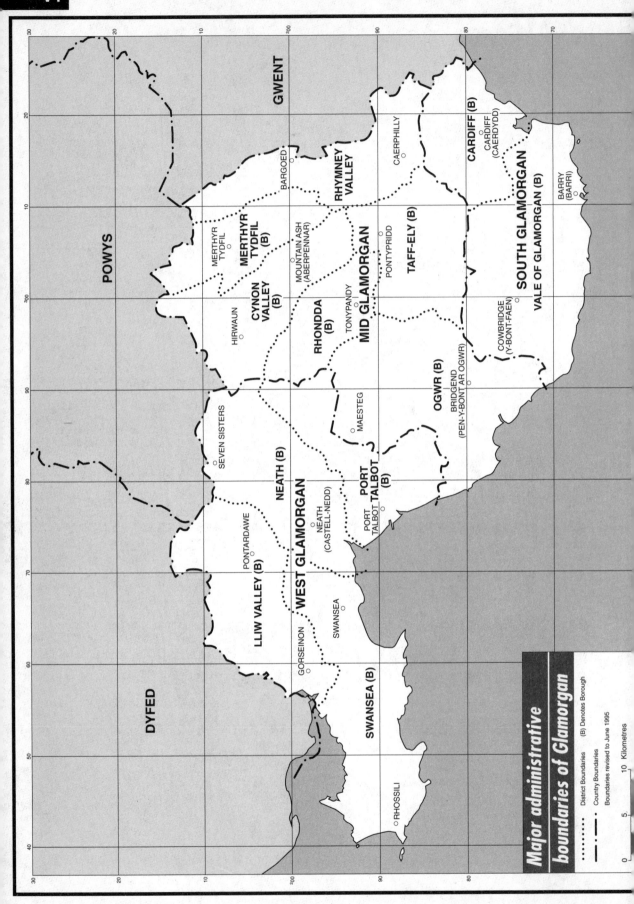

Major administrative boundaries of Glamorgan

.... District Boundaries

—·—·— County Boundaries

(B) Denotes Borough

Boundaries revised to June 1995

0   5   10   Kilometres

GWENT

POWYS

DYFED

CARDIFF (B)

CARDIFF
(CAERDYDD)

SOUTH GLAMORGAN

VALE OF GLAMORGAN (B)

BARRY
(BARRI)

CAERPHILLY

RHYMNEY
VALLEY

BARGOED

MERTHYR
TYDFIL

MERTHYR
TYDFIL
(B)

MOUNTAIN ASH
(ABERPENNAR)

TAFF-ELY (B)

PONTYPRIDD

CYNON
VALLEY
(B)

HIRWAUN

RHONDDA
(B)

TONYPANDY

MID GLAMORGAN

COWBRIDGE
(Y-BONT-FAEN)

SEVEN SISTERS

OGWR (B)

BRIDGEND
(PEN-Y-BONT AR OGWR)

MAESTEG

NEATH (B)

PORT
TALBOT

PORT
TALBOT (B)

NEATH
(CASTELL-NEDD)

PONTARDAWE

WEST GLAMORGAN

LLIW VALLEY (B)

GORSEINON

SWANSEA

SWANSEA (B)

RHOSSILI

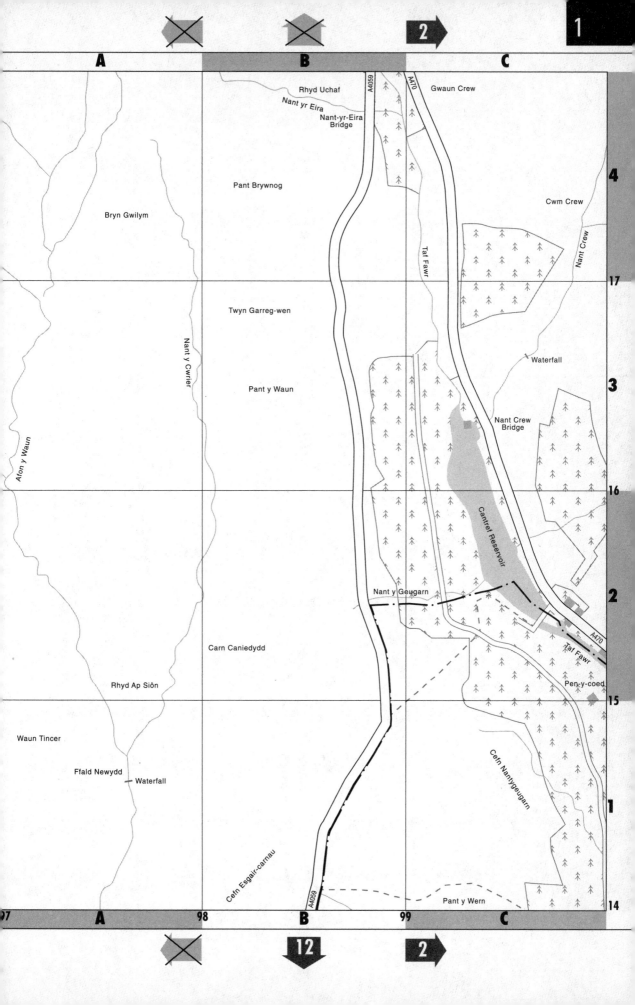

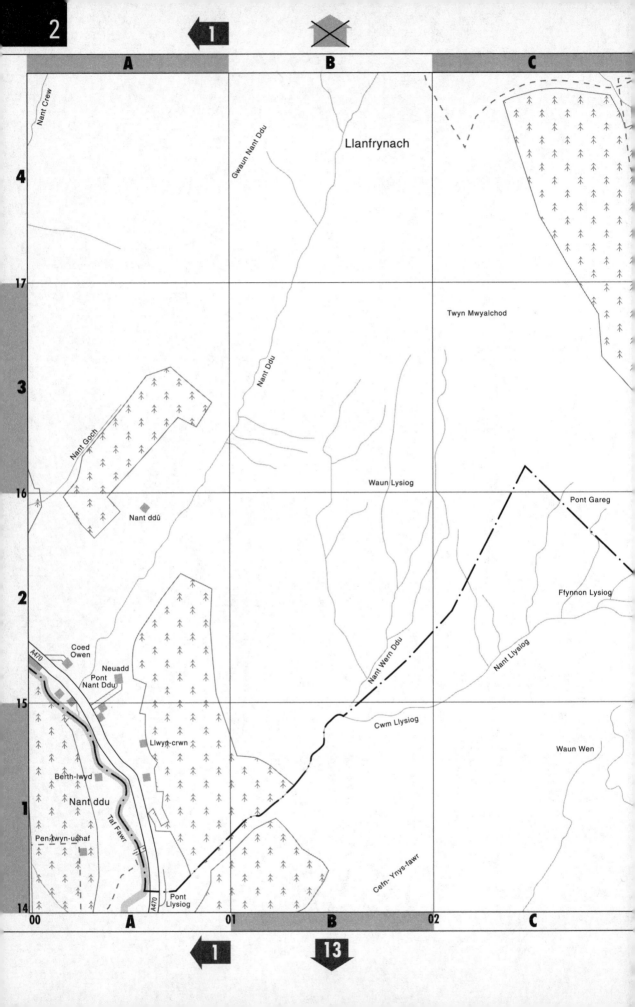

A
B
C

4

17

Llanfrynach

Gwaun Nant Ddu

Nant Crew

Twyn Mwyalchod

3

Nant Ddu

Nant Goch

16

Nant ddû

Waun Lysiog

Pont Gareg

2

Ffynnon Lysiog

Nant Wern Ddu

Nant Llysiog

Coed
Owen

A470

Neuadd
Pont
Nant Ddu

15

Cwm Llysiog

Llwyn-crwn

Waun Wen

Berth-lwyd

Nant ddu

1

Taf Fawr

Pen-twyn-uchaf

Cefn- Ynys-fawr

A470

Pont
Llysiog

14

00
A
01
B
02
C

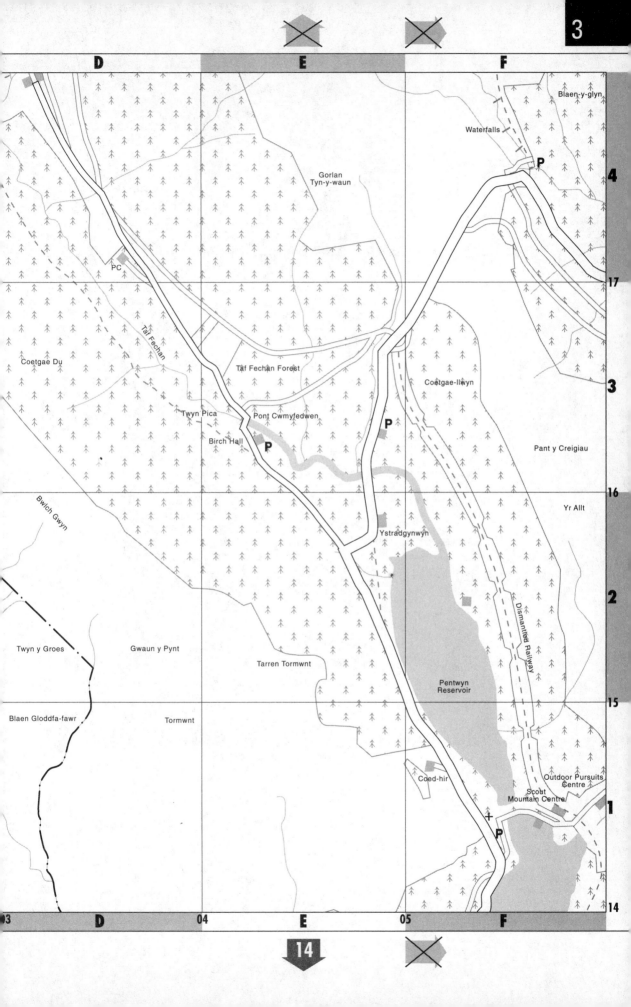

TABERNACLE RD
Berach
TIRYCOED RD
Hospl
FOLLAND RD
HEOL FELEN
Hendre-fawr
LLANDEILO RD
LLANDEILO RD
Cefngoleu
Twyn
MAESYBEDD
HENDRE RD
OAKFIELD RD
HIGHFIELD RD
MAESYRHENDRE
TAN-Y-GELLI
Glan-yr-afon
River Amman (Afon Aman)
STATION RD
GER YR AFON
LC
LC
PH
PC
Sch
HIGH ST
P
PC
A474
SCHOOL RD
BRYN-LLO
RHYDWEN
ED RYAN
Glanaman
CWM AMMAN RD
CADE TERR
MAES Y FRON
PH
NEW CEIDRIM RD
WERN RD
NEW SCHOOL RD
Sch
Garnant
CORPORATION RD
Sch
CHURCH ROW
VICARAGE RD
GREENFIELD RD
P
UPPER STATION RD
LOWER STATION RD
NANT GWINEU RD
Tir Syr Walter
Cwm Aman
Dismtd Rly
LC
LC
BISHOP RD
PC
Liby
TREVOR RD
STEPNEY RD
PC
NEUADD RD
AMMANFORD RD
Cwm Garnant
COWELL RD
MAESYWERN RD
Cemy
Gelli-caedrum-isaf
Maes-y-deri
Pistyll-llwyd-isaf
Nant Main
Pen-rhiw
PENYRALLT
PENYRALLT
Cwm drysien
GRAIG RD
GRAIG RD
A47
Cwm Gafenig
Nant Gafenig
Hafod
Cnap-llwyd
Opencast Workings
Nan y Gath
BRYNCETHIN RD
Hill Crest
Hendy
GRENIG RD
Pant -bryn-henydd
Bryn-cethen -bâch
Goleufryn
Bryn-y-cynydd
Banwen
Gellyceidrim Fach
Bryn-cethen
Crud-yr -awel
Pen-y-bwnsion
Ty'n-domen
Pen-y-waun
Pen-y-waun
Ty-mawr
Trum-yr-hŵch
Foel
Banc Cwmhelen
Gelli-fawr
Mynydd y Betws
Bancbryn
Nantricket
Henrhyd

A | **B** | **C**

4

River Giedd (Afon Giedd)

Giedd Forest

Nant Ceiliog

Tir-y-cwm

Nant Cyw

Pen-rhiw-llwythau

Maes-y-fron

Garth

13

Fforch-orllwyn

Cefn Garth

Llwyn-Turnor

Abercrave
(Aber-craf)

P

Gwern-gafaeliau

TANYRALLT

TANYGARTH

KENFIGUARD

F Sta
Sch

DAN-Y-FRON

MAESYCWM

HEOL TAWE

3

Neuadd-lwyd

Nant Gwinau

Bridgend
Cottage

LAMB AND FLAG
COTTS

A4067

Pant-y-Cwrt

Cae'r-Lan

TAN-Y-GRAIG

YNYS-BYDAFAU

TROED-Y-RHIW

BRECON RD

River Tawe (Afon Tawe)

Gwaun-clawdd

Gwern-y-gilfach

Castle Hotel
(PH)

BRICKYARD
COTTS

LITTLE LONDON

12

Castle
Bridge

Cae'r-bont

ISYRHOS

CAER BONT
IND EST

Glyn-yr-hebog

WATKINS TERR

BANK COTTS

JAMES ST

WINDSAF COTTS

BALA COTTS

B4599

Nant Pen-rhos

Metz Cotts

Ynys-Isaf

Cwm-Tawe

CANNON ST

LONG ST

CROSS ST

Ynys-uchaf

2

Penrhos

Sch

CWM TAWE RD

TANYWAUN

MAIN CWM-GYRLAIS

Dismantled Railway

11

HEOL GIEDD

PEN-Y-BRYN

MILL-Y-BRYN

AEL-Y-BRYN

DOL FAWR

DOL FACH

BRECON RD

Amb Sta
Community
Centre

Gwern-Gerlais

Mynydd y Drum

A4067

LLUEST

LLUEST

TY'R WAUN

HEDRA CADUR

RICARDSMOOR

Garn Goch

Ystradgynlais

Hendra-ladis

1

BRYNHEULOG

Nant Gyrlais

BRYNAWEL VILLAS

B4599

YSTRAD-FAWR VILLAS

Blaen-nant-têg

STATION RD

10

79 | **A** | 80 | **B** | 81 | **C**

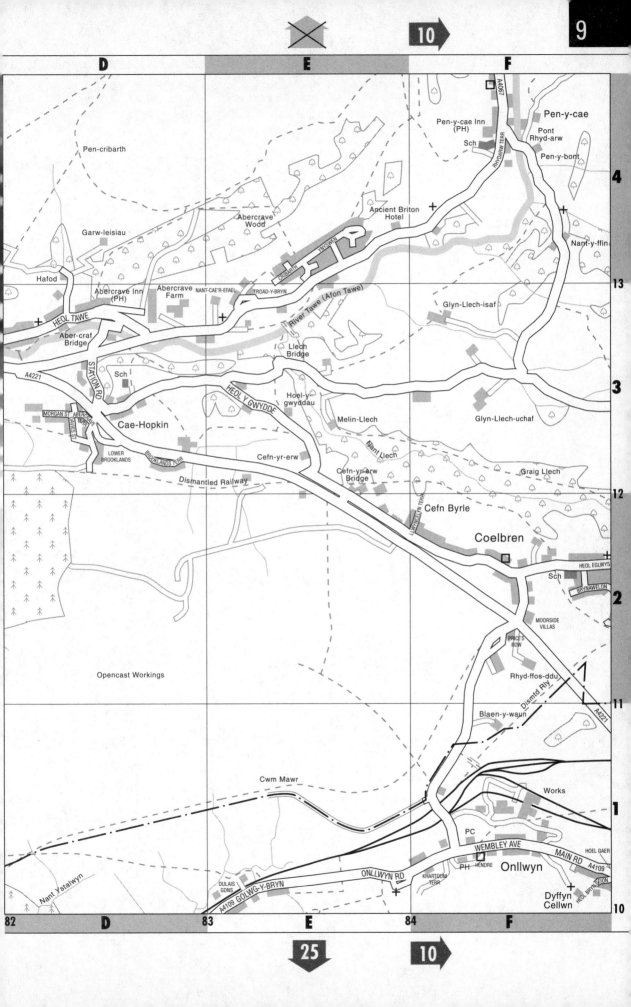

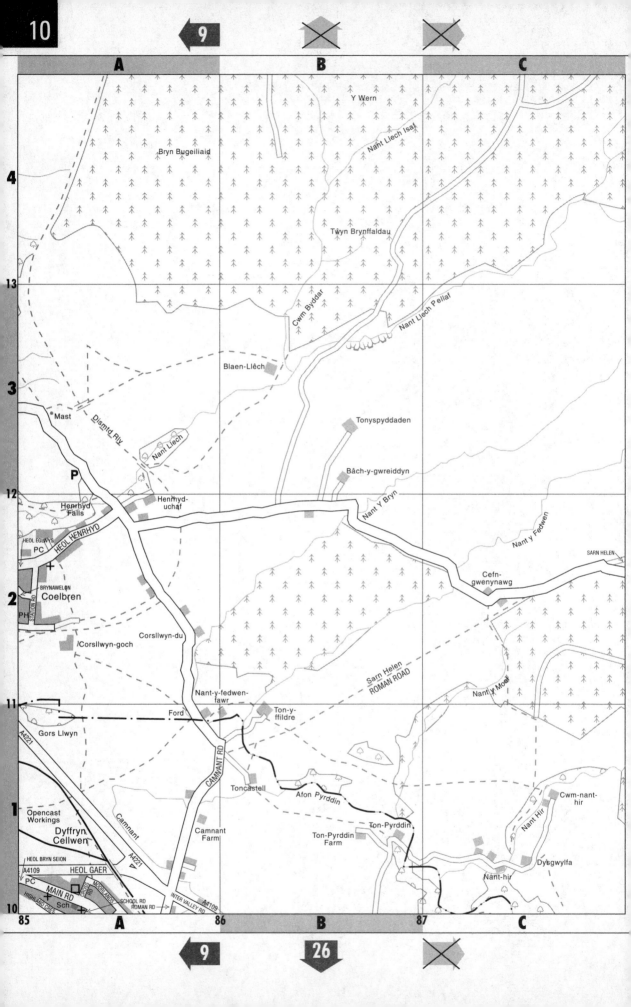

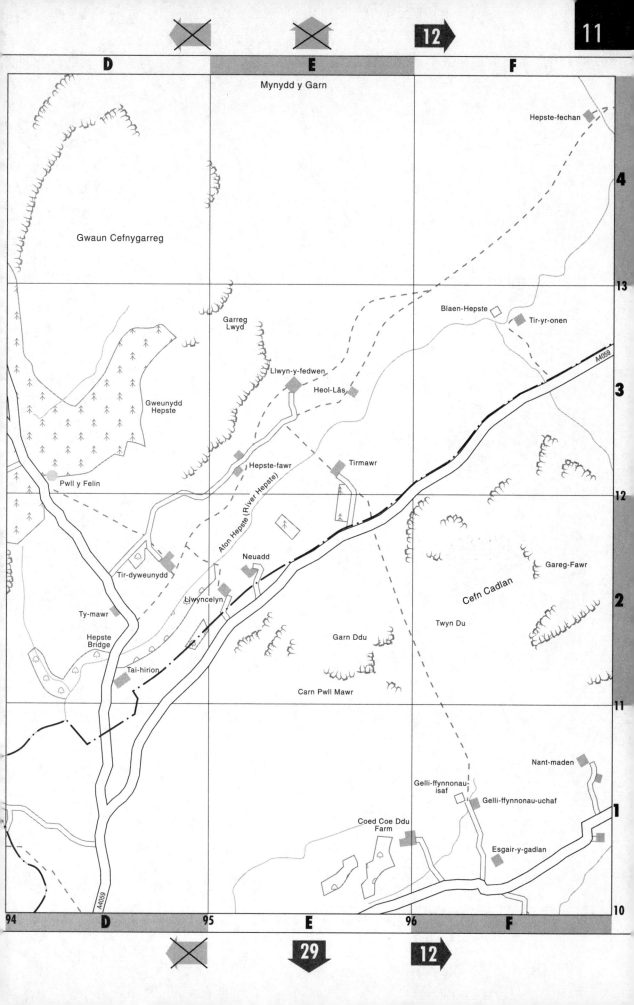

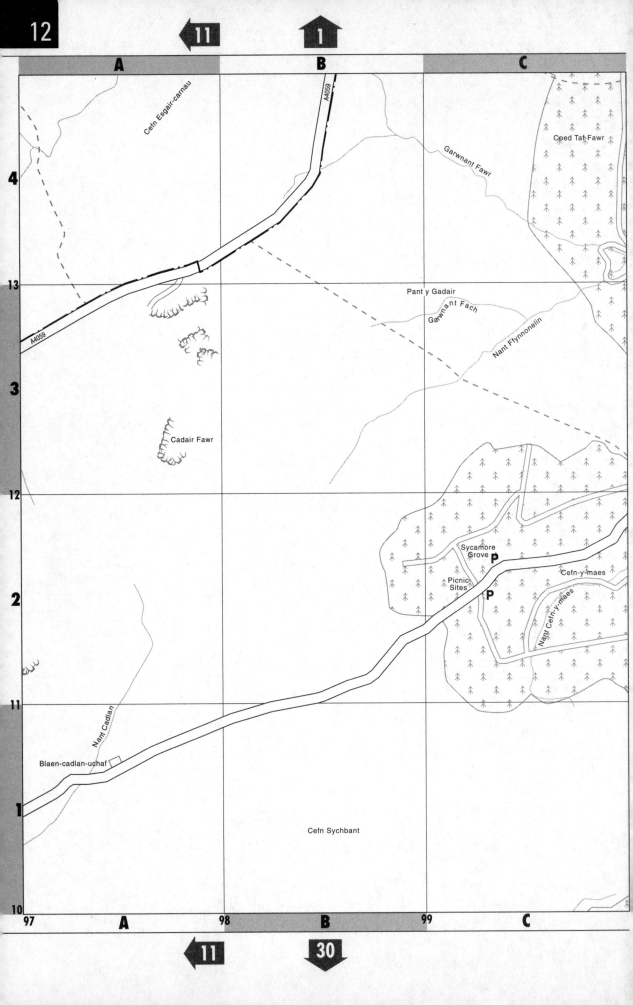

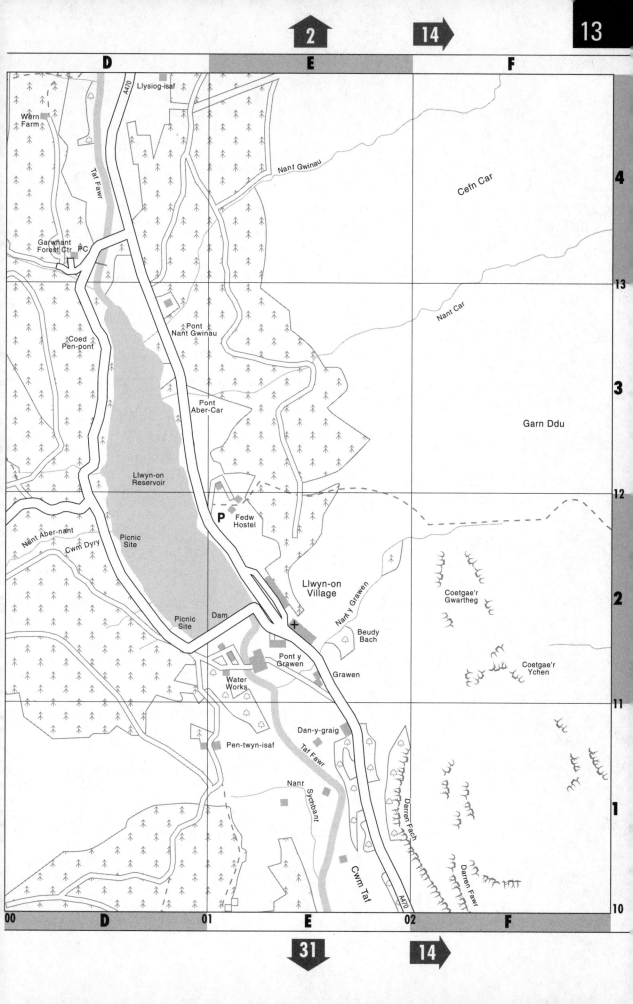

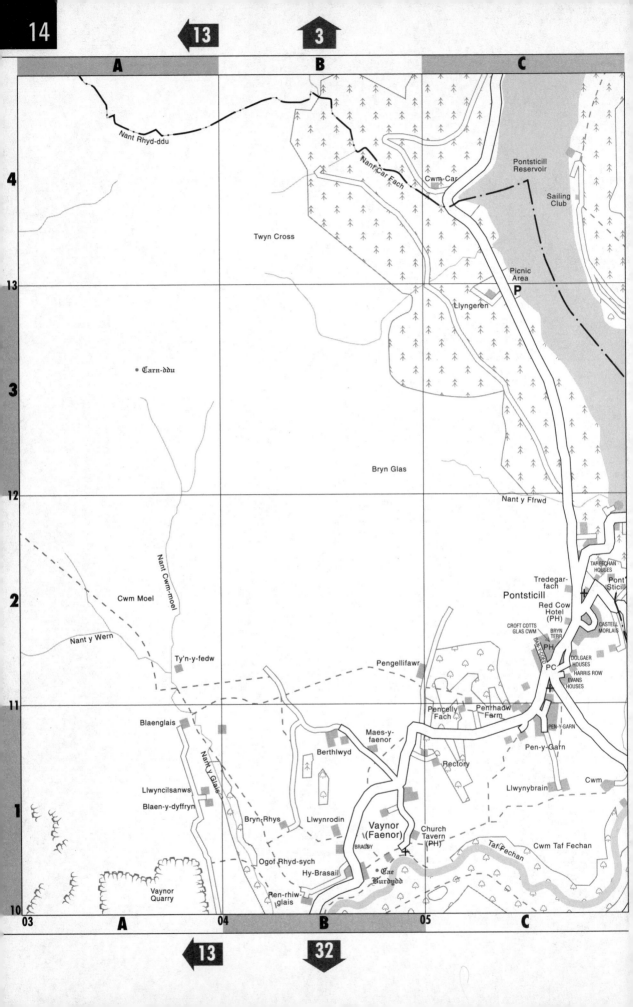

A   B   C

Nant Rhyd-ddu

Nant Car Fach

Cwm-Car

4

Pontsticill
Reservoir

Sailing
Club

Twyn Cross

Picnic
Area

P

13

Llyngeren

Carn-ddu

3

Bryn Glas

Nant y Ffrwd

12

Nant Cwm-moel

Cwm Moel

TAF FECHAN
HOUSES

Tredegar-
fach

Pont
Sticill

Pontsticill

Nant y Wern

2

Red Cow
Hotel
(PH)

CROFT COTTS
GLAS CWM

BRYN
TERR

CASTELL
MORLAIS

Ty'n-y-fedw

PH

DAN-Y-COED

DOLGAER
HOUSES

PC

HARRIS ROW

Pengellifawr

EVANS
HOUSES

11

Pencelly
Fach

Penrhadw
Farm

Blaenglais

PEN-Y-GARN

Maes-y-
faenor

Pen-y-Garn

Berthlwyd

Cwm

Rectory

Llwyncilsanws

Llwynybrain

Blaen-y-dyffryn

1

Bryn-Rhys

Llwynrodin

Vaynor
(Faenor)

Church
Tavern
(PH)

BRAGBY

Cwm Taf Fechan

Ogof Rhyd-sych

Taf Fechan

Hy-Brasail

Cae
Burdydd

Vaynor
Quarry

Pen-rhiw-
glais

10

03   A   04   B   05   C

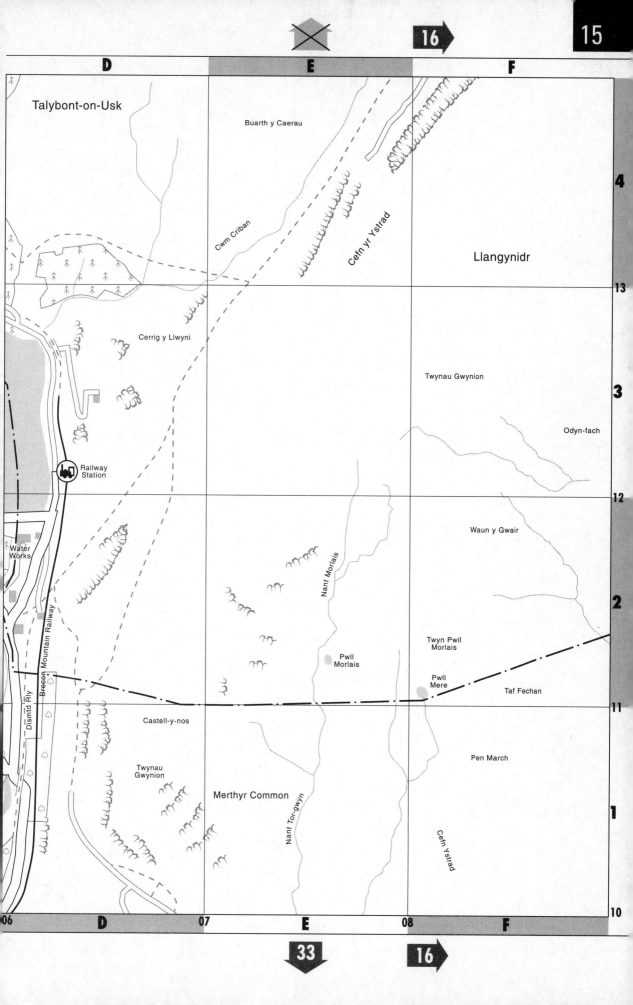

D · E · F

4

13

3

12

2

11

1

10

Talybont-on-Usk

Buarth y Caerau

Cwm Criban

Cefn yr Ystrad

Llangynidr

Cerrig y Llwyni

Twynau Gwynion

Odyn-fach

Railway Station

Water Works

Waun y Gwair

Nant Morlais

Twyn Pwll Morlais

Pwll Morlais

Pwll Mere

Taf Fechan

Breon Mountain Railway

Dismtd Rly

Castell-y-nos

Pen March

Twynau Gwynion

Merthyr Common

Nant Tor-gwyn

Cefn Ystrad

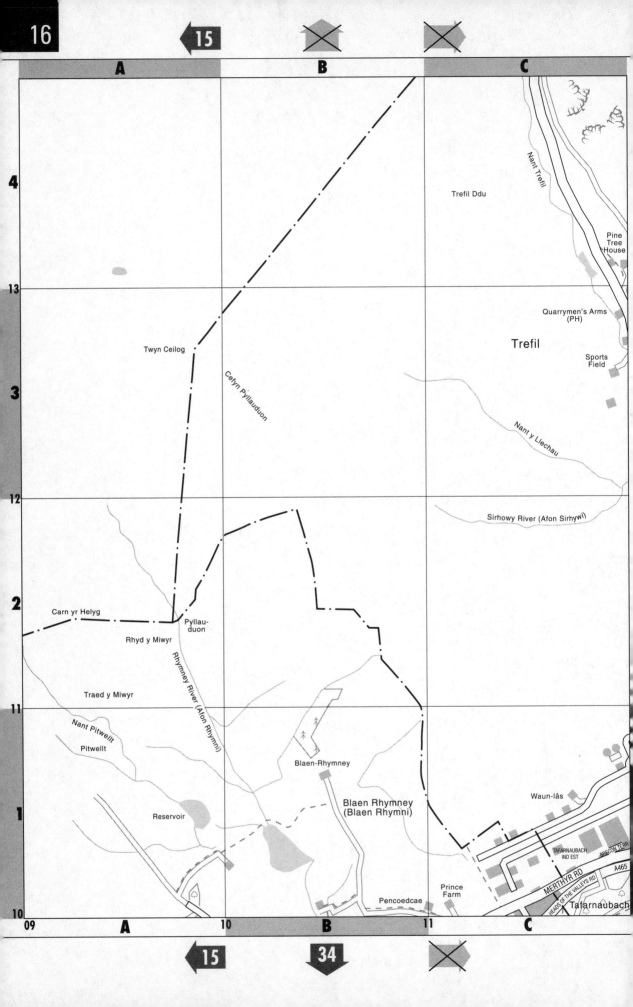

A

B

C

4

Trefil Ddu

Nant Trefil

Pine Tree House

13

Quarrymen's Arms (PH)

Twyn Ceilog

Trefil

Cefyn Pyllauduon

Sports Field

3

Nant y Llechau

12

Sirhowy River (Afon Sirhywi)

2

Carn yr Helyg

Pyllau-duon

Rhyd y Miwyr

Rhymney River (Afon Rhymni)

Traed y Miwyr

11

Nant Pitwellt

Pitwellt

Blaen-Rhymney

Waun-lâs

1

Reservoir

Blaen Rhymney (Blaen Rhymni)

Tafarnaubach Ind Est

Brecon Terr

Merthyr Rd

A465

Prince Farm

Heads of the Valleys Rd

10

Pencoedcae

Tafarnaubach

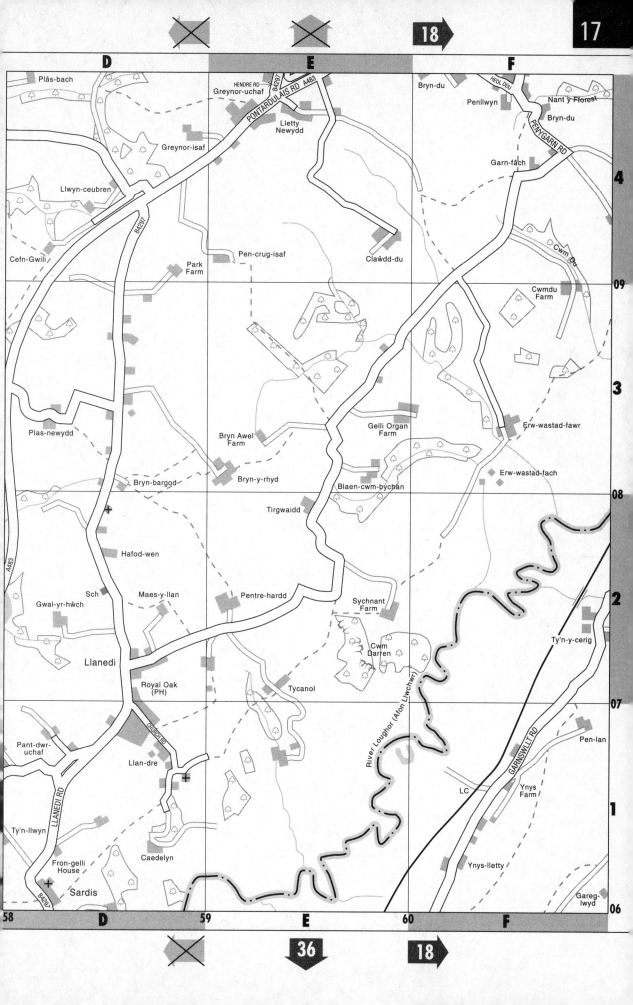

Plâs-bach

HENDRE RD
Greynor-uchaf
PONTARDULAIS RD
B4297
A483
Lletty Newydd

Greynor-isaf

Bryn-du
Penllwyn
HEOL DDU
Nant y Fforest
Bryn-du
PENYGARN RD

Llwyn-ceubren

Garn-fâch

4

Cefn-Gwili

Pen-crug-isaf

Clawdd-du

Cwm Ddu

Cwmdu Farm

09

Park Farm

B4297

A483

Plas-newydd

Bryn Awel Farm

Gelli Organ Farm

Erw-wastad-fawr

3

Bryn-bargod

Bryn-y-rhyd

Blaen-cwm-bychan

Erw-wastad-fach

08

Tirgwaidd

Hafod-wen

Sch
Maes-y-llan

Pentre-hardd

Sychnant Farm

Ty'n-y-cerig

2

Gwal-yr-hwch

Llanedi

Cwm Darren

Royal Oak (PH)

Tycanol

River Loughor (Afon Llwchwr)

GARNSWLLT RD

Pen-lan

07

CHURCH RD

Pant-dwr-uchaf

Llan-dre

LC

Ynys Farm

LLANEDI RD

Ty'n-llwyn

Ynys-lletty

1

Fron-gelli House

Caedelyn

B4297

Sardis

Gareg-lwyd

06

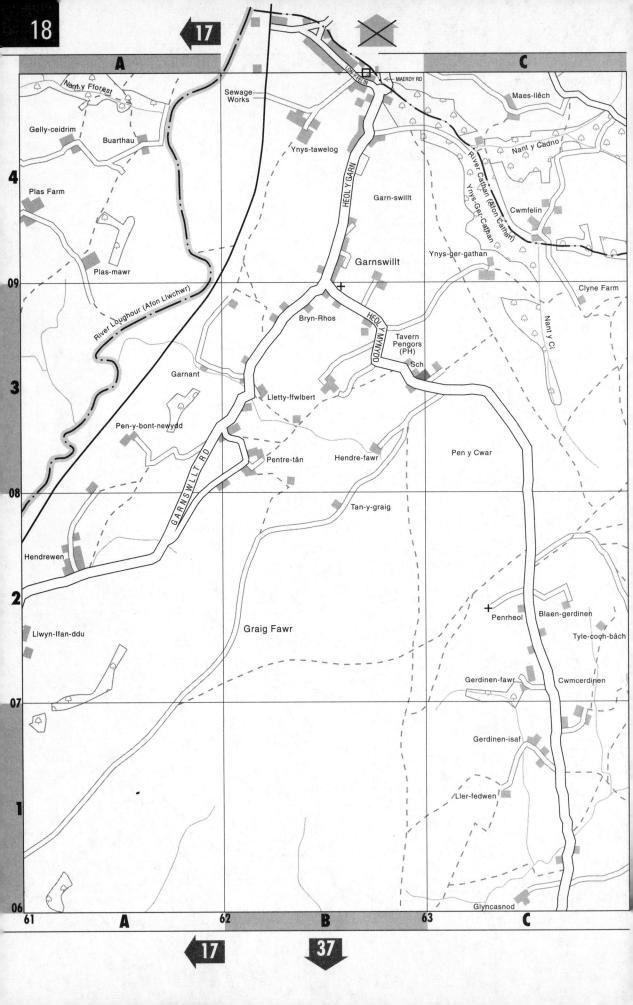

17

A B C

Nant y Fforest
Sewage Works
MAERDY RD
Maes-llêch
Gelly-ceidrim
Buarthau
Ynys-tawelog
Nant y Cadno
HEOL Y GARN
River Cathan (Afon Cathan)
Garn-swillt
Cwmfelin
4
Plas Farm
Ynys-Ger-Cathan
Garnswillt
Ynys-ger-gathan
Plas-mawr
Clyne Farm
09
River Loughour (Afon Llwchwr)
Bryn-Rhos
Nant y Ci
HEOL Y MYNYDD
Tavern Pengors (PH)
Garnant
Sch
3
Lletty-ffwlbert
Pen-y-bont-newydd
GARNSWLLT RD
Hendre-fawr
Pen y Cwar
Pentre-tân
08
Tan-y-graig
Hendrewen
2
Penrheol
Blaen-gerdinen
Llwyn-Ifan-ddu
Graig Fawr
Tyle-coch-bâch
Gerdinen-fawr
Cwmcerdinen
07
Gerdinen-isaf
1
Ller-fedwen
06
Glyncasnod
61 A 62 B 63 C

17 37

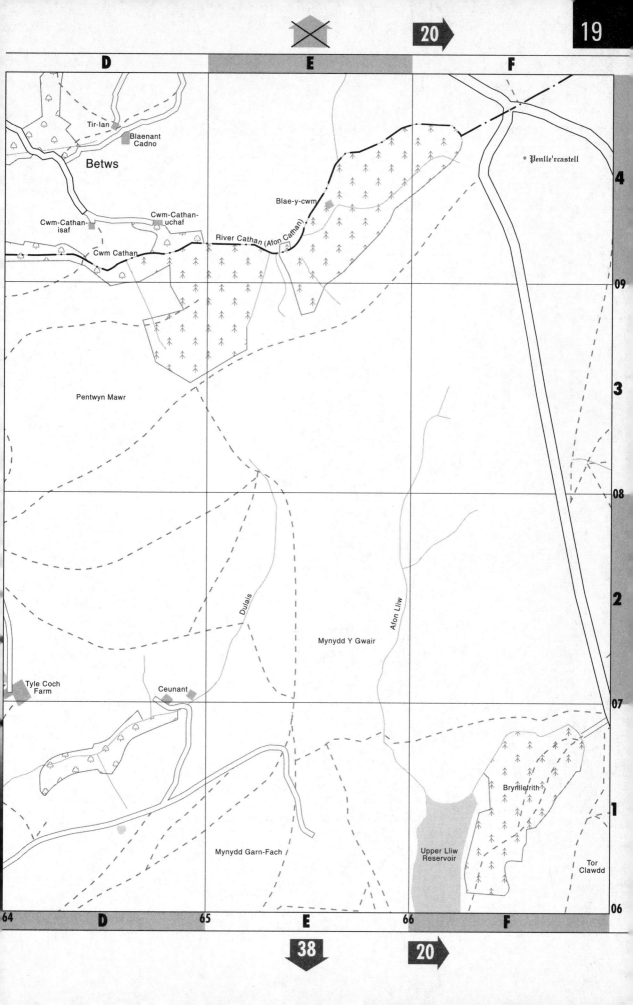

D

E

F

Tir-lan

Blaenant
Cadno

Betws

Blae-y-cwm

Penlle'rcastell

Cwm-Cathan-
uchaf

Cwm-Cathan-
isaf

River Cathan (Afon Cathan)

Cwm Cathan

09

Pentwyn Mawr

3

08

Dulais

Afon Lliw

2

Mynydd Y Gwair

Tyle Coch
Farm

Ceunant

07

Brynllefrith

1

Mynydd Garn-Fach

Upper Lliw
Reservoir

Tor
Clawdd

06

64

D

65

E

66

F

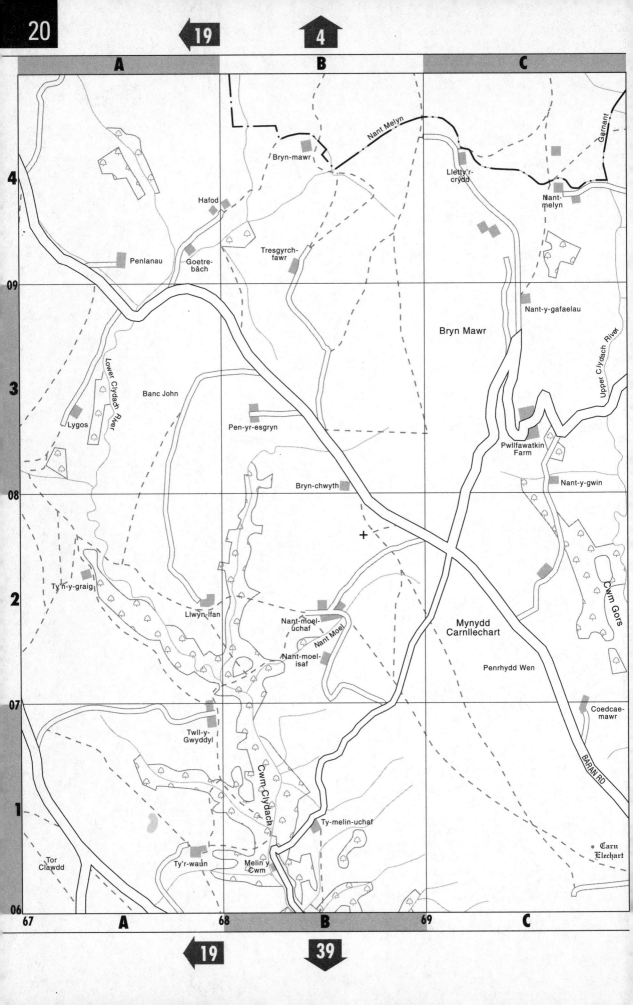

A   B   C

4

Garnant

Nant Melyn

Bryn-mawr

Lletty'r-
crÿdd

Nant-
melyn

Hafod

Penlanau

Goetre-
bâch

Tresgyrch-
fawr

09

Nant-y-gafaelau

Bryn Mawr

Upper Clydach River

Banc John

Lower Clydach River

3

Lygos

Pen-yr-esgryn

Pwllfawatkin
Farm

Bryn-chwyth

Nant-y-gwin

08

+

Ty'n-y-graig

Cwm Gors

2

Llwyn-ifan

Nant-moel-
uchaf

Nant Moel

Mynydd
Carnllechart

Penrhydd Wen

Nant-moel-
isaf

07

Coedcae-
mawr

Twll-y-
Gwyddyl

BARAN RD

Cwm Clydach

1

Ty-melin-uchaf

Carn
Elechart

Tor
Clawdd

Ty'r-waun

Melin y
Cwm

06

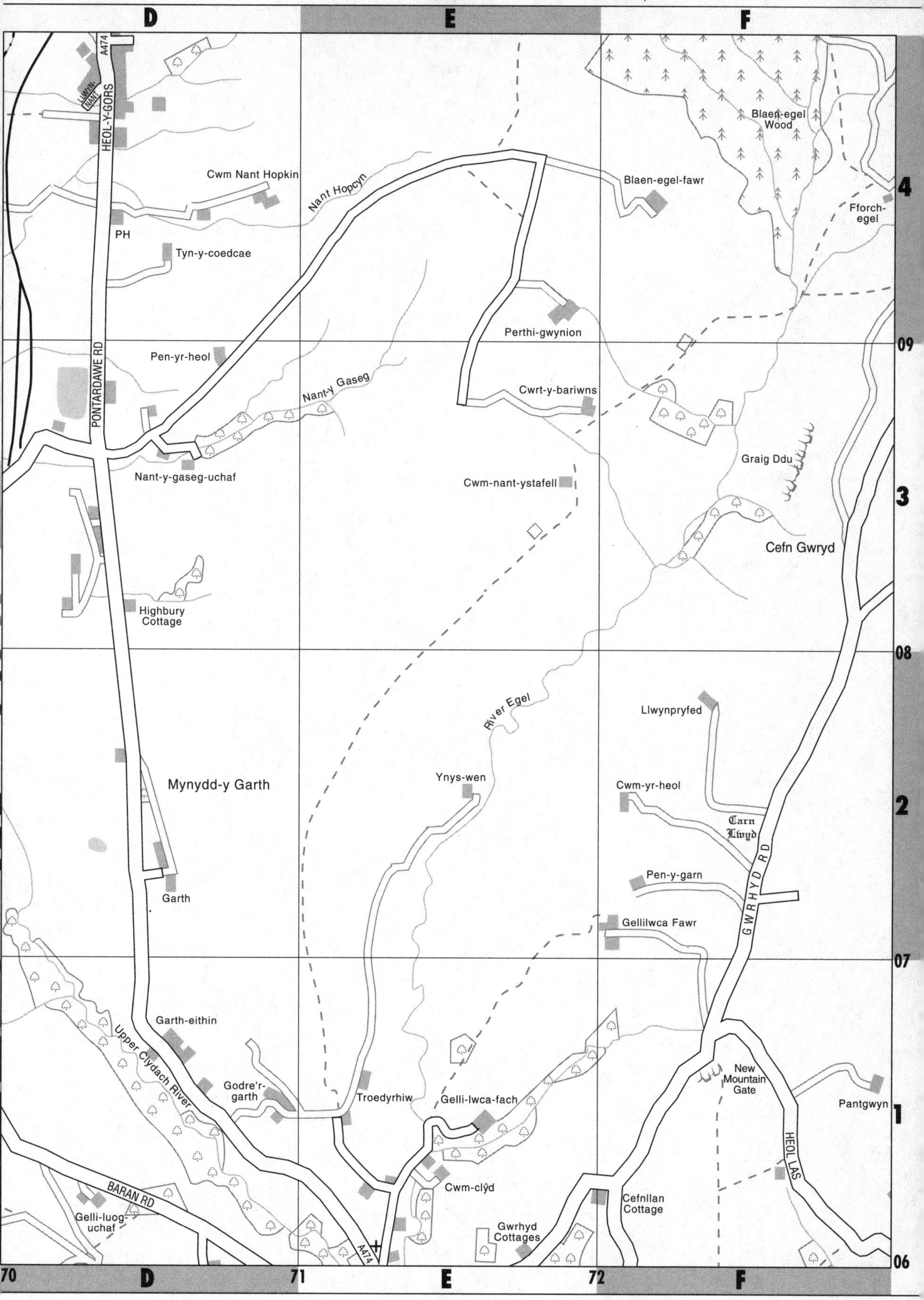

D **E** **F**

A474

LLWYN NANT

HEOL-Y-GORS

PONTARDAWE RD

Cwm Nant Hopkin

Nant Hopcyn

PH

Tyn-y-coedcae

Pen-yr-heol

Nant-y Gaseg

Perthi-gwynion

Blaen-egel Wood

Blaen-egel-fawr

Fforch-egel

4

Cwrt-y-bariwns

09

Nant-y-gaseg-uchaf

Cwm-nant-ystafell

Graig Ddu

Cefn Gwryd

3

Highbury Cottage

08

River Egel

Llwynpryfed

Mynydd-y Garth

Ynys-wen

Cwm-yr-heol

Carn Llwyd

2

Garth

Pen-y-garn

GWRHYD RD

Gellilwca Fawr

07

Garth-eithin

Upper Clydach River

Godre'r-garth

Troedyrhiw

Gelli-lwca-fach

New Mountain Gate

Pantgwyn

1

BARAN RD

Cwm-clŷd

Cefnllan Cottage

HEOL LAS

Gelli-luog-uchaf

Gwrhyd Cottages

A474

06

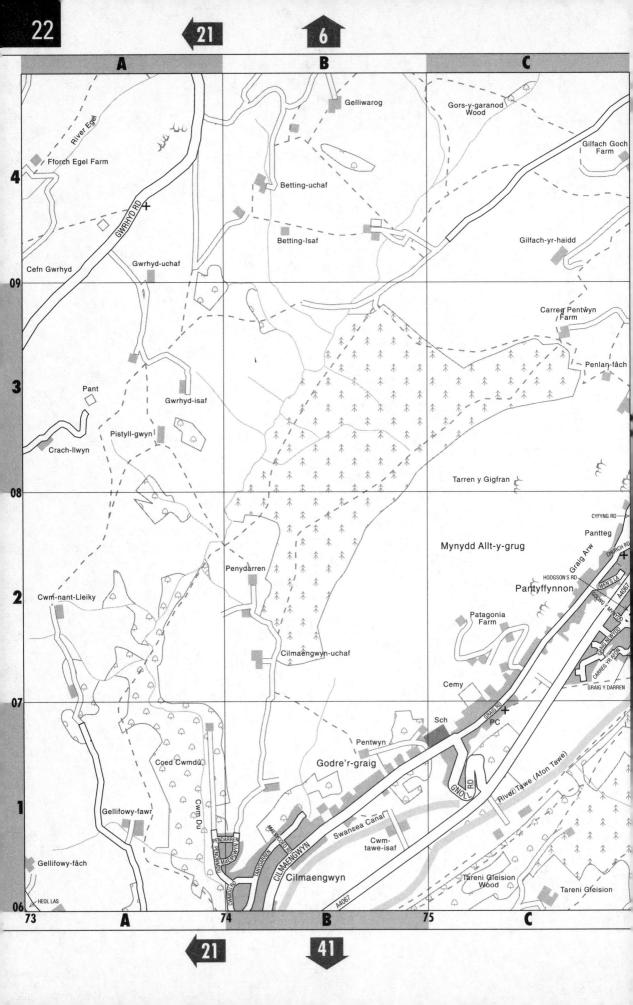

A   B   C

River Egel

Fforch Egel Farm

Gelliwarog

Gors-y-garanod Wood

Gilfach Goch Farm

4

Betting-uchaf

Gilfach-yr-haidd

GWRHYD RD

Cefn Gwrhyd

Gwrhyd-uchaf

Betting-Isaf

09

Carreg Pentwyn Farm

Penlan-fâch

Pant

3

Gwrhyd-isaf

Pistyll-gwyn

Crach-llwyn

Tarren y Gigfran

08

Cwm-nant-Lleiky

Penydarren

Mynydd Allt-y-grug

CYFYNG RD

Pantteg

Graig Arw

CHURCH RD

HODGSON'S RD

Pantyffynnon

2

Patagonia Farm

OWEN'S LA

GELLWG MAWR DD

A4067

GELLWG

CARREG YR AFON

Cilmaengwyn-uchaf

Cemy

GRAIG Y DARREN

07

Sch

GRAIG RD

PC

River Tawe (Afon Tawe)

Pentwyn

Coed Cwmdû

Godre'r-graig

GINOL RD

Gellifowy-fawr

1

Cwm Dû

Swansea Canal

PENDARREN

MAESYDDERREN

Cwm-tawe-isaf

MAESYDERREN

CWMDU RD

TANYDARREN

CILMAENGWYN

Gellifowy-fâch

Tareni Gleision Wood

Tareni Gleision

Cilmaengwyn

HEOL LAS

A4067

06

73   A   74   B   75   C

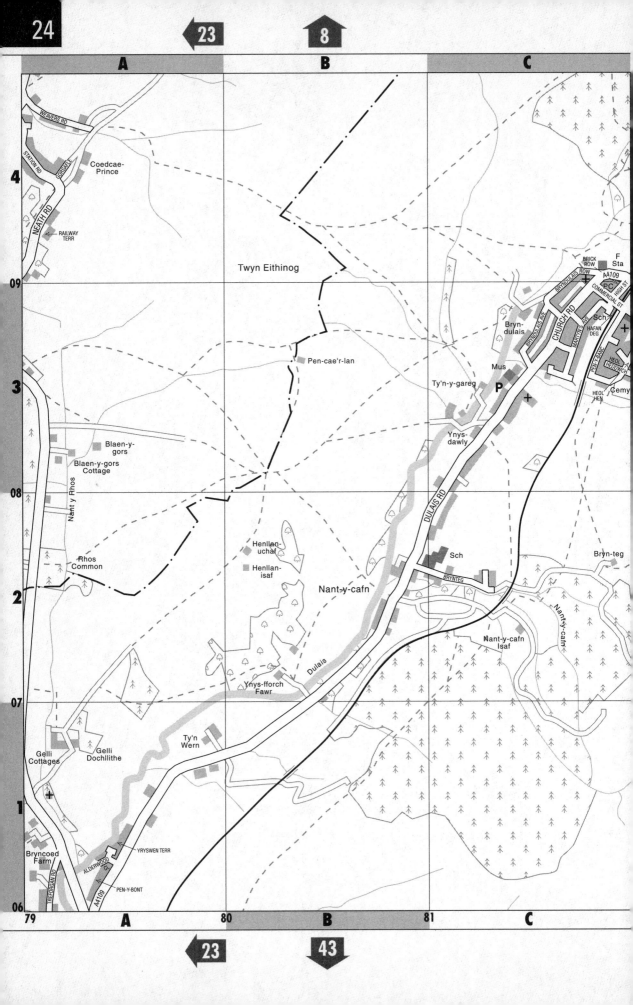

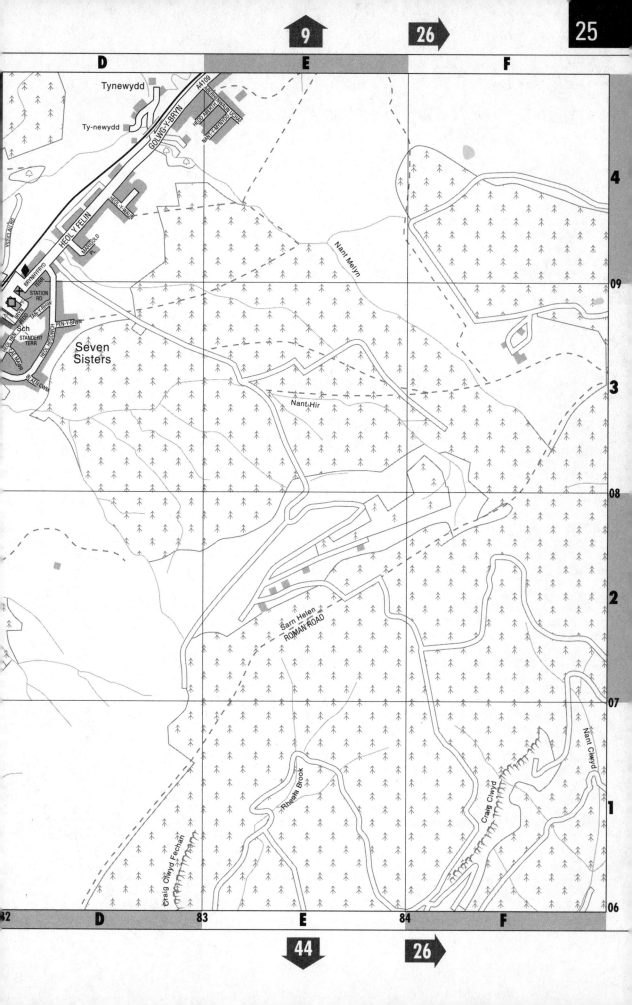

A

B

C

HIGHLAND CRES
SCHOOL RD
MOORLANDS
Sch
MAIN RD
Cemy
ROMAN RD
Amb
Sta
Maple
House
Banwen
A4109

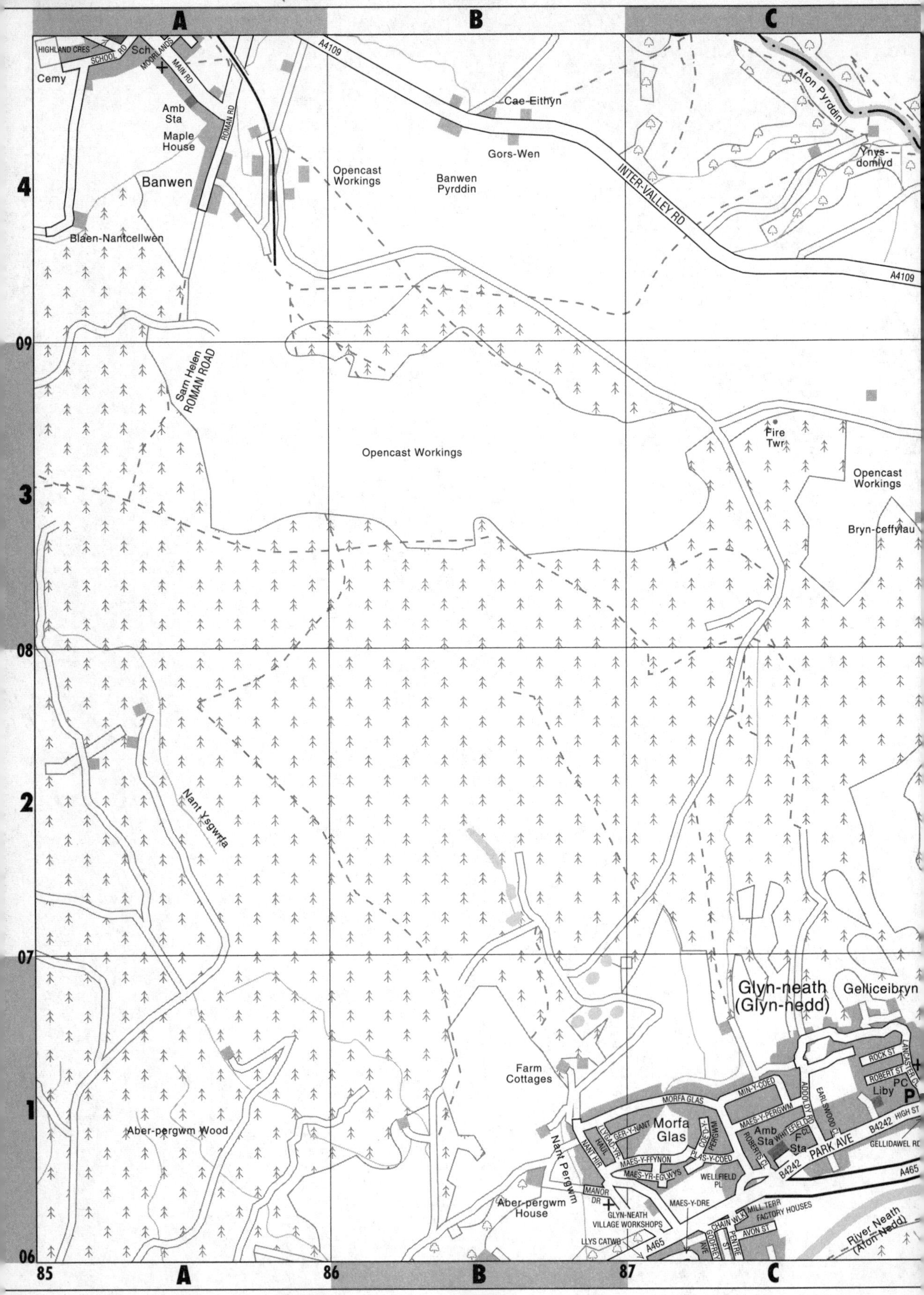

Cae-Eithyn

Gors-Wen

Banwen
Pyrddin

Opencast
Workings

INTER-VALLEY RD

Ynys-
domlyd

Afon Pyrddin

4

Blaen-Nantcellwen

A4109

Sam Helen
ROMAN ROAD

09

Opencast Workings

Fire
Twr

Opencast
Workings

Bryn-ceffylau

3

08

Nant Ysgwrfa

2

07

Glyn-neath
(Glyn-nedd)

Gelliceibryn

Farm
Cottages

ROCK ST
ROBERT ST
LANCASTER RD
PC
Liby
P

MORFA GLAS
MILL-Y-COED
EARL SWOOD
ADDOLDY RD
HIGH ST
Morfa
Glas
Amb
Sta
Sta
WHITEFIELDS
PARK AVE
B4242
GELLIDAWEL RD

1

Aber-pergwm Wood

Nant Pergwm
Nant Thir
MAES-Y-FFYNON
LLWYN-ONN
ABER-Y-NANT
MAES-Y-PERGWM
PLAS-Y-COED
MAES-YR-EGLWYS
WELLFIELD
PL
MAES-Y-DRE

Aber-pergwm
House
MANOR
DR
GLYN-NEATH
VILLAGE WORKSHOPS
LLYS CATWG
A465
MILL TERR
FACTORY HOUSES
CHAIN WK
GOUREY
POINTE
AVON ST
A465
River Neath
(Afon Nedd)

06

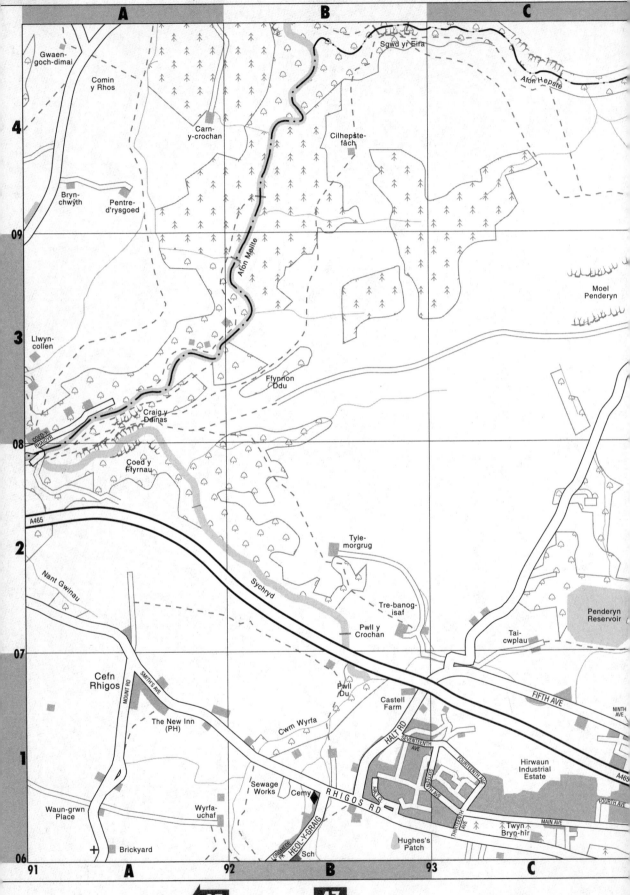

A · B · C

Gwaen-
goch-dimai

Comin
y Rhos

Sgwd yr Eira

Afon Hepste

Carn-
y-crochan

Cilhepste-
fâch

4

Bryn-
chwŷth

Pentre-
d'rysgoed

09

Moel
Penderyn

Afon Mellte

Llwyn-
collen

3

Ffynnon
Ddu

Craig y
Ddinas

COED Y RHAIDYR

08

Coed y
Ffyrnau

A465

Tyle-
morgrug

2

Nant Gwinau

Sychryd

Tre-banog-
isaf

Penderyn
Reservoir

Pwll y
Crochan

Tai-
cwplau

07

Cefn
Rhigos

MOUNT RD

SMITH'S AVE

FIFTH AVE

NINTH AVE

Pwll
Du

Castell
Farm

The New Inn
(PH)

Cwm Wyrfa

HALT RD

SEVENTEENTH AVE

Hirwaun
Industrial
Estate

1

A465

Sewage
Works

Cemy

RHIGOS RD

FOURTH AVE

Waun-grwn
Place

Wyrfa-
uchaf

LONGMEAD PK

HEOL-Y-GRAIG

Sch

Hughes's
Patch

Twyn
Bryn-hir

MAIN AVE

THIRTEENTH AVE

06

Brickyard

91 · A · 92 · B · 93 · C

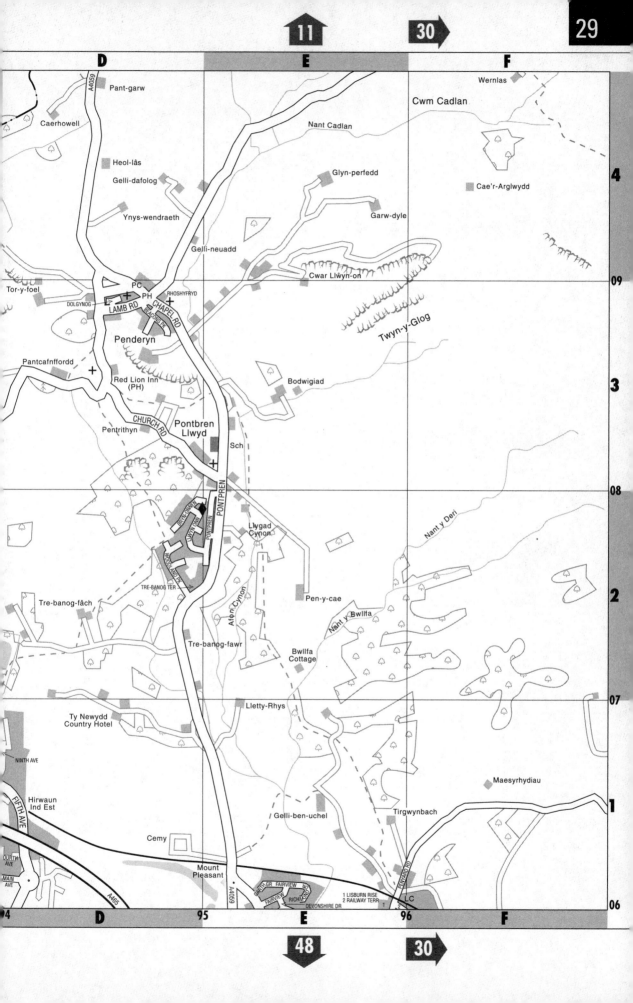

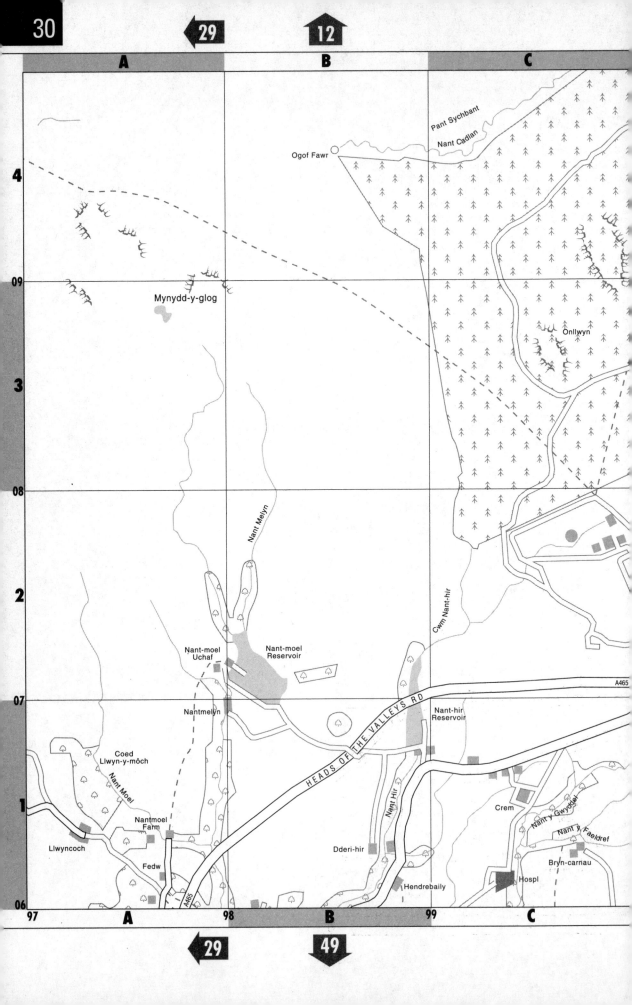

A   B   C

4

Pant Sychbant

Nant Cadlan

Ogof Fawr

09

Mynydd-y-glog

Onllwyn

3

08

Nant Melyn

Cwm Nant-hir

2

Nant-moel
Uchaf

Nant-moel
Reservoir

A465

07

Nantmelyn

Nant-hir
Reservoir

Coed
Llwyn-y-môch

HEADS OF THE VALLEYS RD

Nant Moel

Nant Hir

1

Crem

Nant y Gwyddel

Nant y Faeldref

Nantmoel
Farm

Llwyncoch

Dderi-hir

Bryn-carnau

Fedw

Hendrebaily

Hospl

06

97   A   98   B   99   C

A   B   C

Glais Bridge
Vaynor Quarry
Pontsarn Hotel (PH)
Pont-sarn
Brecon Mountain Railway
Station

Aberglais (PH)
Morlais Hill
Golf Course
CH
Castle Farm
Cemy

4

Coed Llaindir

Golf Course

Sewage Works

POPLAR PL
SWEETWATER PK
HIGH TREES
THE COPSE
SYCAMORE CRES
HAWTHORN HILL
BEECHWOOD RD
ROWAN RISE
LINDEN WAY
MAPLE CRES
CRABTREE WALK
THE BROADWAY
THE GREEN

09

Trefechan

Bryniau
BRYNIAU RD
Ind Est

Gurnos Farm
Rough Ground

1 HEOL-Y-MYNYDD
2 GERSANWS
3 CIL-SANWS LA
4 PEARCE'S CT

CH

Cwm Taf Fechan
Taf Fechan

HEADS OF THE VALLEYS RD
A465

3

Hornbeam Cl
Pen Gurnos
Pen-y-dre
Sch

Galon Uchaf
ROCKY RD

Lupin Cl
Forsythia Cl
Heather Rd
Honeysuckle Cl
Marigold Cl
Jasmine Cl
Lavender Rd
Clover Rd
Birch Gr
Pine Cl
Blackthorn Willow

EIGHTH AVE
ELEVENTH AVE
SIXTH AVE
FIFTH AVE
TENTH AVE
NINTH AVE

Magnolia Cl

Hospl
Gurnos

P
PC

Penbryn
HILLCREST

VAYNOR RD

SOMERSET ST
GOTH HALL
SOMERSET
Sch
TRIANGLE
HIGH ST
DAN-Y-DERI

08

Prince Charles Hospl
GURNOS RD
Almond Gr

GARDEN CITY 1
AWELFRYN VILLAS 2
PENBRYN VILLAS 3
BRYNMORLAIS ST 4
BRYN-ONEN TERR 5
NIBLOE TERR 6
AMBERTON PL 7
SUMMERFIELD TERR 8
BRYNMAIR TERR 9

Sch
Rowan Way

Cyfarthfa Park

GALON UCHAF RD

ROYAL CRES 10
PEMBROKE CL 11
GWLADYS ST 12
TYNYCOED TERR 13
FRONWEN TERR 14
TYLLWYD ST 15

BANK TERR
BRYNHYFRD TERR
OLD CHURCH ST
Ind Est

Pont y Cefn

Cyfarthfa Castle (Sch and Mus)

Chase View
Rookwood Cl

HIRWAUN TERR
GILLINGHAM CRES

ALEXANDRA AVE
ALEXANDRA CL

HIGH ST
A4102
NORTH ST

2

Taf Fawr

5 HEOL BRYCHAN
6 HEOL TWYN DU
7 HEOL LLWYN DERI
8 HEOL LLWYN ONNEN
9 HEOL LLWYN GRYSI
10 HEOL LLWYN GOLLEN
11 HEOL BRYN-Y-GWYDDYL
12 HEOL PARC-Y-LAN

E F I IND EST

CASTLE SQ 1
MARGARET ST 2
CROSS MARGARET ST 3
PLEASANTVIEW ST 4
CHURCH ST 5
MILES ST 6
MOUNT ST 7
CARADOC ST 8
MORGAN ST 9
CROSS MORGAN ST 10
KING EDWARD ST 11
STUART ST 12
BRYCHAN PL 13
FFYNNON TUDFUL 14
SUNNYBANK 15

PC

BRECON RD

Gellideg

Pont y Cafnau

PARK ROW GDNS

Tydfil's Well

Pen y Darren

16 TYGWYN ST
17 LEWIS TERR
18 TALBOT SQ
19 ST JOHN'S ST
20 HOREB CL

HEOL SOWRFA
HEOL LANSBURY
HEOL NANTGARU
A4102

Sch

07

Williamstown

CFARTHFA IND EST
Williamstown

River Taff (Afon Taf)

GWAELODYGARTH RD
TRAMROAD LA

The Quar
The Rink
Incline Top
MODERN COTTS

BRUNSWICK ST
PENYDARREN RD

Penyard

SWANSEA RD
GELLI-DEG

Georgetown
A4102

Morgan Town
Mus

GLYNN TERR
FOTHERGILL CRES

CAMBRIAN ST 16
WILLIAM ST 17
UPPER EDWARD ST 18
DAVID ST 19
SAND ST 20
LOWER EDWARD ST 21
MORIAH ST 22
GARTH ST 23

BETHESDA ST
PONTMORLAIS W

Hospl
GORSEDD TERR
Schs

1

Heolgerrig

MARTIN CL
FARM TERR
SIX BELLS ST

PANTYCELYNEN

COFFINS ROW
F Sta

Off
Lby
New Castle St

CAE
MARI
CAE MAWR

1 TRAMROAD TR
2 UNION TR
3 SMRSET TR
4 CTLAND TR

Thomas Town

1 WINCH FAWR RD
2 CHESTER CL
3 WORCESTER CL
MOUNT PLEASANT

SHIRLEY DR
HEOL GERRIG
CORONATION TERR
LEWIS TERR
THE HOLLIES

CAPEL BETHLEHEM
CADLAN BETHEL

HIGH STREET ARC 24
GRAHAM WAY 25
NEWMARKET WLK 26
RIVER WLK 27

Glebeland
Wheatsheaf
Coll
Mkt

Victoria St
AVE DE CLYDY AFON

5 WOODLAND PL
6 KINGSLEY TERR

THE PARADE
BRYNTEG

WOODLAND
Schs

Sta

06

03   A   04   B   05   C

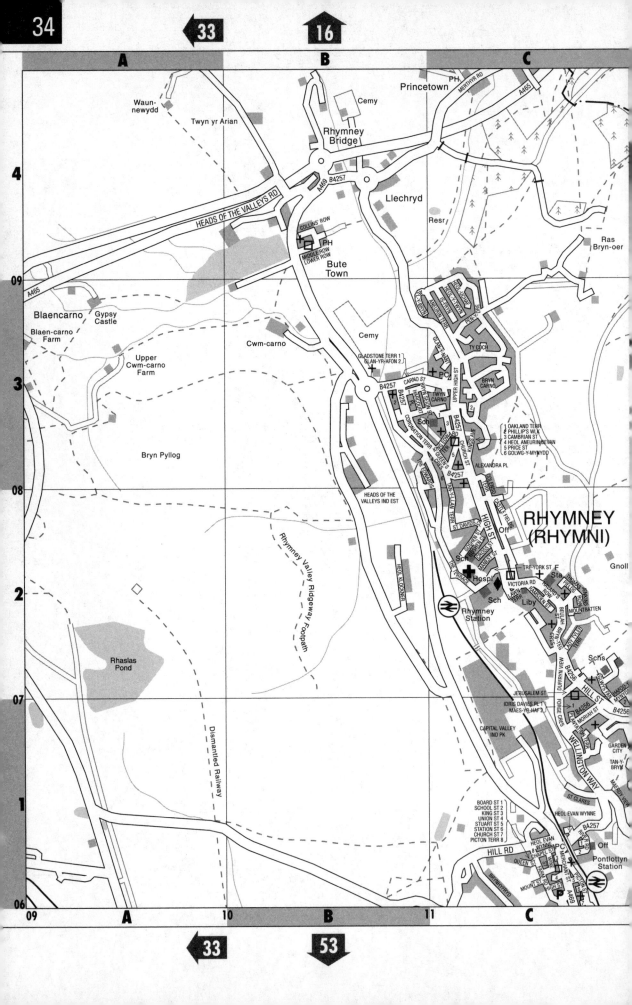

PONTARDULAIS

A | B | C

4

Pen-y-wern
Tal-y-cynllwyn
Tynewydd
Ty'r-gôf
Tal-y-fan-fawr
Works
GARNSWLLT RD
Pentrebach
HEOL DWR

05

Fforest Hall
Graig-Fawr
Tal-y-fan-fâch
Glyn-y-fid
BLAEN-Y-FFOREST
HEOL-Y-PLAS
PONTARDULAIS IND EST
Glanffrwd Rd
GLANFFRWD RD
A48
CARMARTHEN RD
PANT-Y-FELIN RD
GLYNHIR RD
Ty'n-y-bonau
B4297
Fforest
HEOL Y FELIN
GLAN LLWYD
PONTARDULAIS WORKSHOPS
Bryn-du

3

HEOL FFOREST
RHODA'R WIWER
HEOL BRONALLT
Ty'n-y-coed
Tycamffrwd Bridge
Tan-y-graig
Works
WOODVILLE ST
TY'N-Y-BONAU RD
MYRTLE HILL
MAES TEG
HEOL-Y-CAE
HIGH ST
HEOL-Y-WAUN
HEOL-Y-COED
Llettygariad
HEOL BRONALLT
CLAYTON RD
STATION RD
GLYN TEG RD
DAN TWYN RD
MAES-GWYN TERR
GLANFFRWD

04

Sch
MAES-Y-CAE
CAE-GWYN
Cefn-drum
PC
Works
Liby
WILLIAMS ST
Plasgwyn
HEOL WYLLT
WATER ST
A4138
ST MICHAEL'S DR
CAE-CERRIG RD
UPPER MILL RD
STATION RD
FFOS-YR-EFAIL TERR
DULAIS RD
WYNCELYN
PONTARDULAIS
River Loughor (Afon Llwchwr)
HEOL ISCOED
Sch
WATER ST
Dulais
GER Y PANT
CUSTISS
GLANYRAFON RD
PANTIAGO RD
BRYNGWILI RD
BRYN RD
NEW RD
CROSS ST
ALLT-IAGO RD
BRYNAFON

2

Hendy
A4138
CAE-FERRO
Afon Gwili
Liby Ind Est
TRINITY CL
CAMBRIAN PL
ST TEILO
ST BRIDES
OAKFIELD ST
Schs
TWYNIAGO
Goppa Hill
BLAENMORFA
YSTNITY PL
MAYTAFANN
JAMES ST
Sch
GOPPA RD
GLASFRYN RD
WYNDHAM CL
Schs
HIGHLAND TERR
Bolgoed-uchaf
PARK CL
BWYNWYLL RD
B4296
CHURCH RD
Coedbach Park
LLYS GER Y LLAN
CEFN RD

03

M4
PARK TERR
BOLGOED RD
Bolgoed Farm
HEOL Y BARNA
Bolgoed-ganol

1

PENTRE RD
Cemy
Cil-yr-ystarn
BRINTIRION RD
Castell-ddu
CASTELL DDU RD
B4296
PH
A48
Hazeldene
Waungron
M4
ALLT-Y-GRABAN RD

02

58 | A | 59 | B | 60 | C

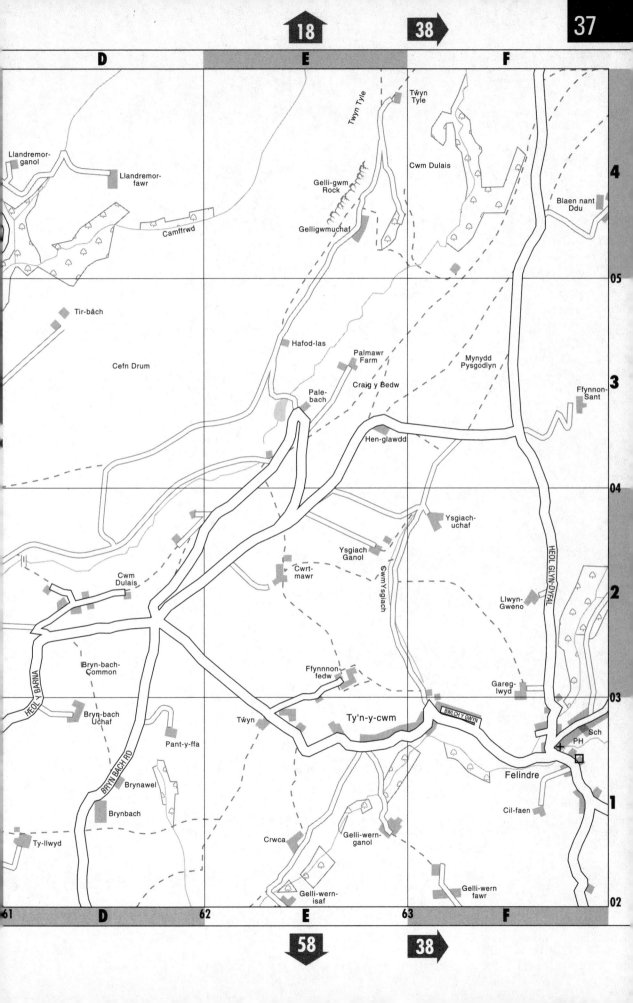

D
E
F

4

Llandremor-ganol

Llandremor-fawr

Camffrwd

Twyn Tyle

Tŵyn Tyle

Cwm Dulais

Gelli-gwm Rock

Gelligwmuchaf

Blaen nant Ddu

05

Tir-bâch

Cefn Drum

Hafod-las

Palmawr Farm

Mynydd Pysgodlyn

Ffynnon-Sant

3

Pale-bach

Craig y Bedw

Hen-glawdd

04

Ysgiach-uchaf

Ysgiach Ganol

Cwrt-mawr

Cwm Ysgiach

Llwyn-Gweno

HEOL GLYN-DYFAL

2

Cwm Dulais

Bryn-bach-Common

Ffynnnon-fedw

Gareg-lwyd

HEOL Y BARNA

Bryn-bach Uchaf

Pant-y-ffa

Tŵyn

Ty'n-y-cwm

BWLCH Y GWYN

03

Sch

PH

Felindre

BRYN BACH RD

Brynawel

Brynbach

Cil-faen

Ty-llwyd

Crwca

Gelli-wern-ganol

1

Gelli-wern-isaf

Gelli-wern-fawr

02

61
D
62
E
63
F

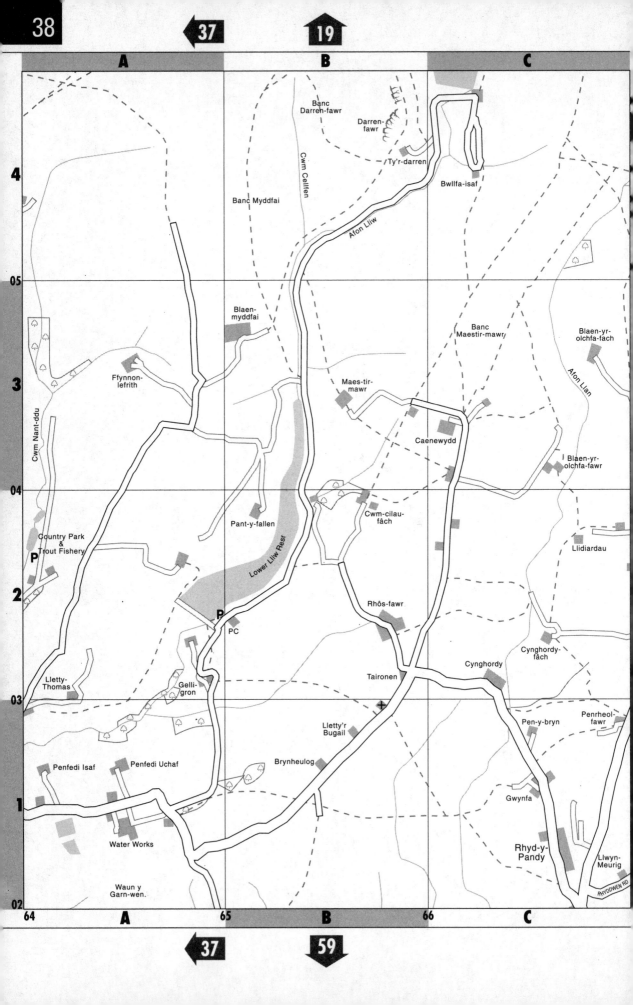

A   B   C

4

Banc
Darren-fawr

Darren-
fawr

Cwm Cellfen

Ty'r-darren

Bwllfa-isaf

Banc Myddfai

Afon Lliw

05

Blaen-
myddfai

Banc
Maestir-mawr

Blaen-yr-
olchfa-fách

3

Ffynnon-
lefrith

Maes-tir-
mawr

Afon Llan

Caenewydd

Blaen-yr-
olchfa-fawr

04

Cwm-cilau-
fách

Cwm Nant-ddu

Pant-y-fallen

Llidiardau

Country Park
&
Trout Fishery

Lower Lliw Resr

P

Rhôs-fawr

Cynghordy-
fách

2

P

PC

Cynghordy

Lletty-
Thomas

Gelli-
gron

Taironen

Penrheol-
fawr

03

Lletty'r
Bugail

Pen-y-bryn

Penfedi Isaf   Penfedi Uchaf

Brynheulog

Gwynfa

1

Water Works

Rhyd-y-
Pandy

Llwyn-
Meurig

Waun y
Garn-wen.

RHYDWEN RD

02

64   A   65   B   66   C

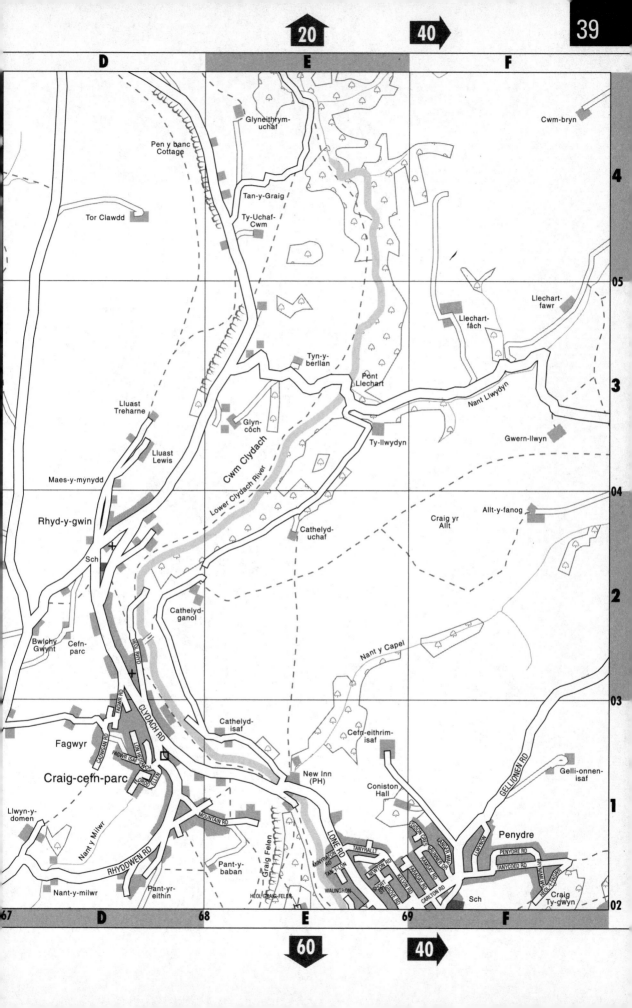

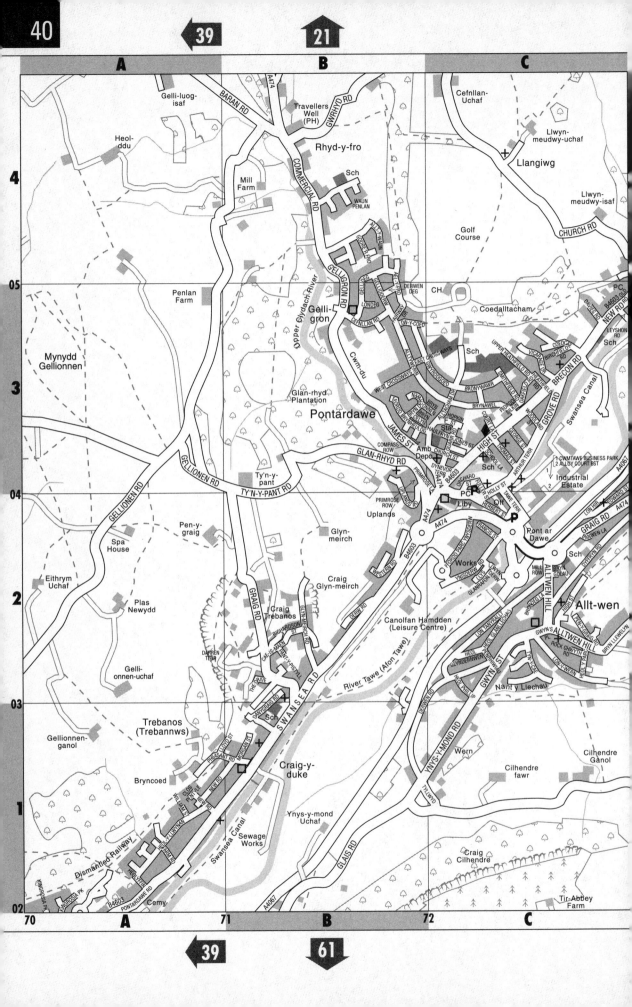

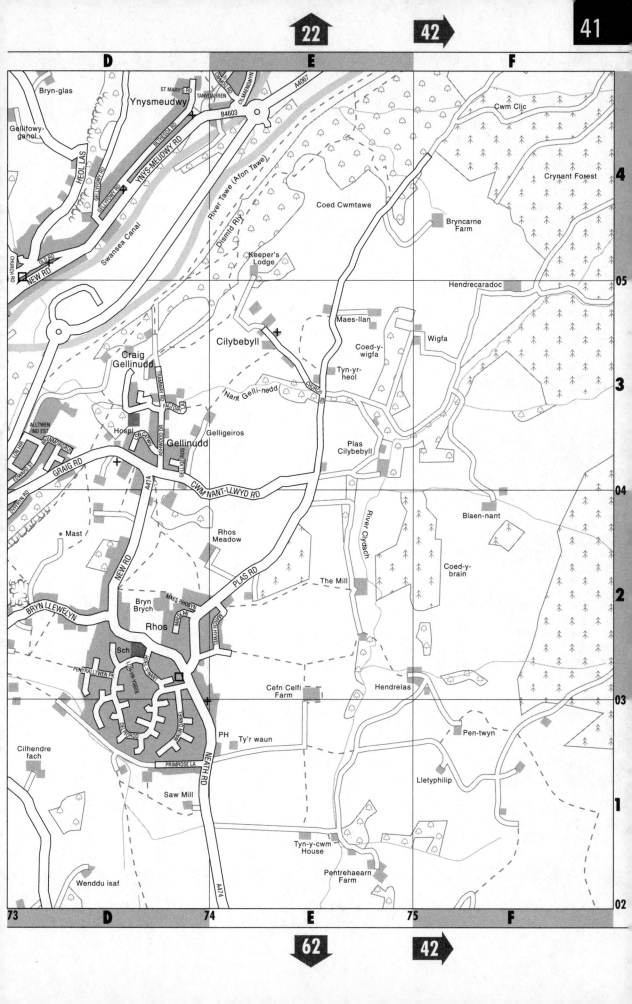

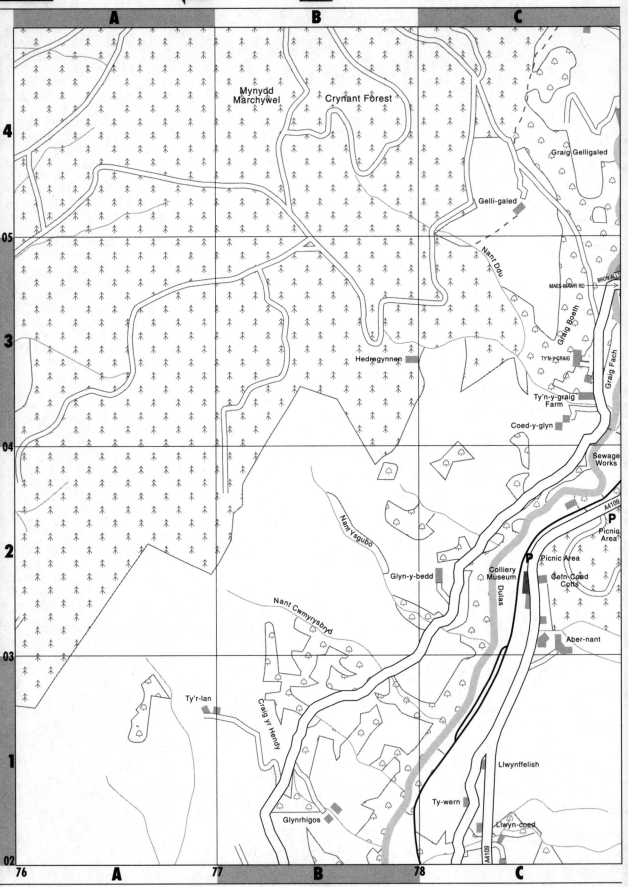

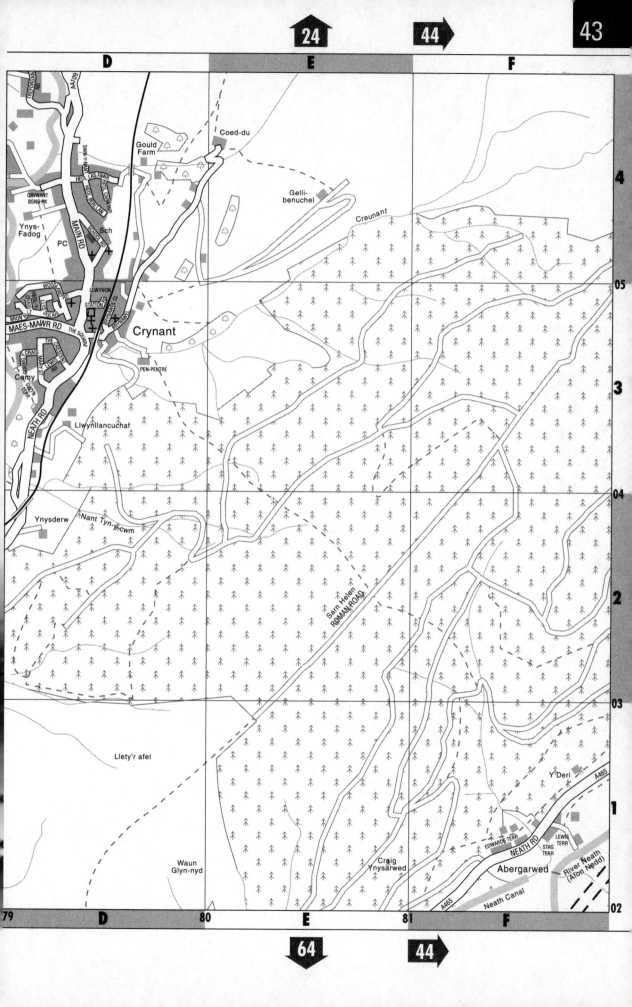

D E F

4

Coed-du

Gould
Farm

TREFORGAN
RD
A4109

Gelli-
benuchel

Creunant

SWN-Y-NANT
HEOL LAS FAWR
HEOL BERLLAN
HEOL CAE HIR

CRYNANT
BSNS PK

05

Sch
SCHOOL RD

Ynys-
Fadog

PC

MAIN RD

Llwynon
STATION
BRYNAWEL CL
BRYNAWEL

Crynant

WOODLAND RD
BRON
LWSYN
CILAS

MAES-MAWR RD
THE SQUARE

PEN-PENTRE

3

THE
CRESCENT
A CRAIG
MARY ST.
LEWIS ST.

GLYNN TERR
CEFN
CAMY
NEATH RD

Llwynllancuchaf

04

Ynysderw

Nant Tyn-y-cwm

2

Sarn Helen
ROMAN ROAD

03

Llety'r afel

Y Deri
A465

1

EDWARDS TERR
NEATH RD
LEWIS
TERR
STAG
TERR

Waun
Glyn-nyd

Craig
Ynysarwed

Abergarwed

River Neath
(Afon Nedd)

A465
Neath Canal

02

79 D 80 E 81 F

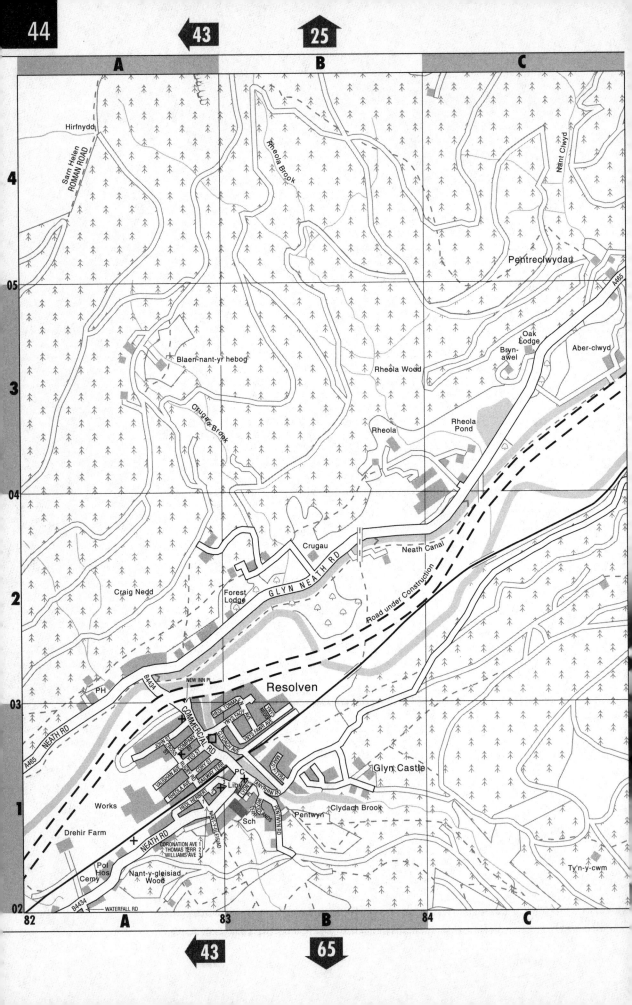

A   B   C

Hirfnydd

Sarn Helen
ROMAN ROAD

4

Pentreclwydau

A465

05

Oak
Lodge

Bryn-
awel

Aber-clwyd

Blaen-nant-yr hebog

Rheola Wood

3

Crugau Brook

Rheola

Rheola
Pond

04

Crugau

Neath Canal

GLYN NEATH RD

Road under Construction

Craig Nedd

Forest
Lodge

2

New Inn Pl

Resolven

03

PH

B4434

COMMERCIAL RD

HEOL TONMAS

YNYS FACH AVE

YNYS FAWR AVE

NEATH RD

A465

JOHN ST
CROSS ST
THEO ST

GLYNCASTLE AVE

Glyn Castle

VAUGHAN AVE
RHEOLA AVE
RAILWAY TERR

PC

Library

HEOL HERBERT

TANYRHIW RD

LLWYN

GLYNDALE AVE

1

Works

Clydach Brook

Sch

Pentwyn

PENTWYN RD

WOODLANDS TERR

NANT-Y-GLEISIAD

Drehir Farm

NEATH RD

CORONATION AVE 1
THOMAS TERR 2
WILLIAMS AVE 3

Pol
Hos
Cemy

Nant-y-gleisiad
Wood

Ty'n-y-cwm

02

82   A   83   B   84   C

B4434

WATERFALL RD

Rheola Brook

Nant Clwyd

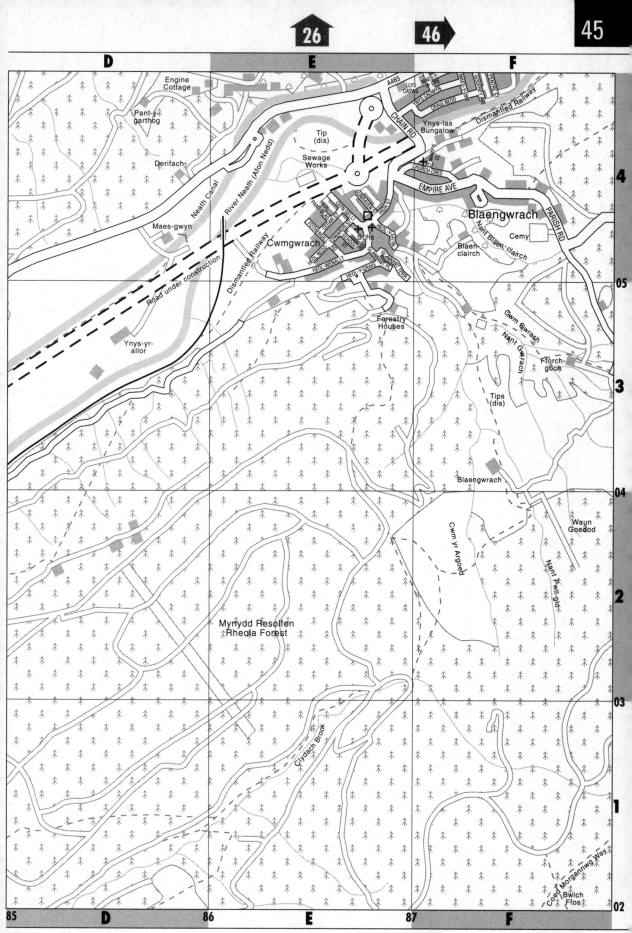

D
E
F

Engine Cottage

Pant-y-garthog

Derifach

A465

LLYS
CATWG

MAES-Y-
FFRE

MAES-YDRE

PENTRE ST

Dismantled Railway

Ynys-las Bungalow

YNYS CADWYN

CRAIG NEDD

Tip
(dis)

CHAIN RD

Sewage Works

ST MARYS CL

CHURCH CRES

EMPIRE AVE

PARISH RD

4

Maes-gwyn

Neath Canal

River Neath (Afon Nedd)

Dismantled Railway

Cwmgwrach

FOTHERBELL

HEOL NEDD

PANT GLAS RD

EDWARDS RD

SCHOOL ST

PEN-Y-BELL

HIGH ST

Schs

HEOL-Y-FELIN

Blaengwrach

Cemy

Blaen-clairch

Nant Blaen-clairch

HEOL-WENALLT

GRAWEN TERR

GWAUN-GWYN PL

HEOL-Y-GRAIG

05

Road under construction

Ynys-yr-allor

Forestry Houses

Cwm Gwrach

Nant Gwrach

Fforch-goch

3

Tips
(dis)

Blaengwrach

04

Waun Goedod

Cwm yr Argoed

Nant Pwll-glo

2

Mynydd Resolfen
Rheola Forest

03

Clydach Brook

1

Coed Morgannwg Way

Bwlch Ffos

02

85
D
86
E
87
F

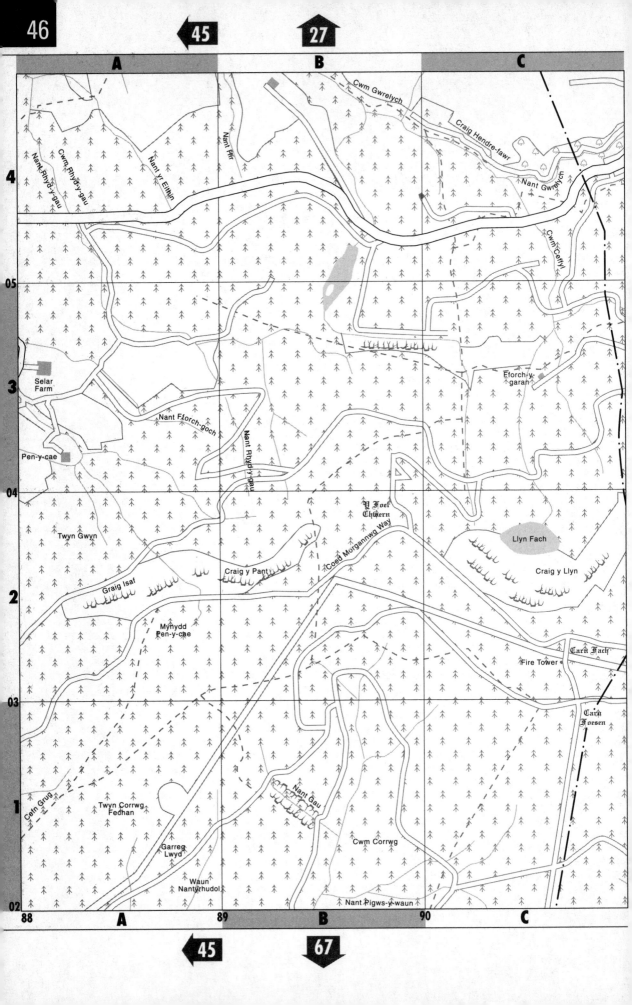

A B C

4

05

3

04

2

03

1

02

Selar Farm

Pen-y-cae

Cwm Rhyd-y-gau

Nant Rhyd-y-gau

Nant yr Eithin

Nant Ffir

Cwm Gwrelych

Craig Hendre-fawr

Nant Gwrelych

Cwm Ceftyl

Fforch-y-garan

Nant Fforch-goch

Nant Rhyd-y-gau

Twyn Gwyn

Y Foel Chwern

Coed Morgannwg Way

Llyn Fach

Craig y Pant

Craig y Llyn

Graig Isaf

Mynydd Pen-y-cae

Carn Fach

Fire Tower

Carn Foesen

Cefn Grug

Twyn Corrwg Fechan

Nant Gau

Cwm Corrwg

Garreg Lwyd

Waun Nantyrhudol

Nant Pigws-y-waun

88 A 89 B 90 C

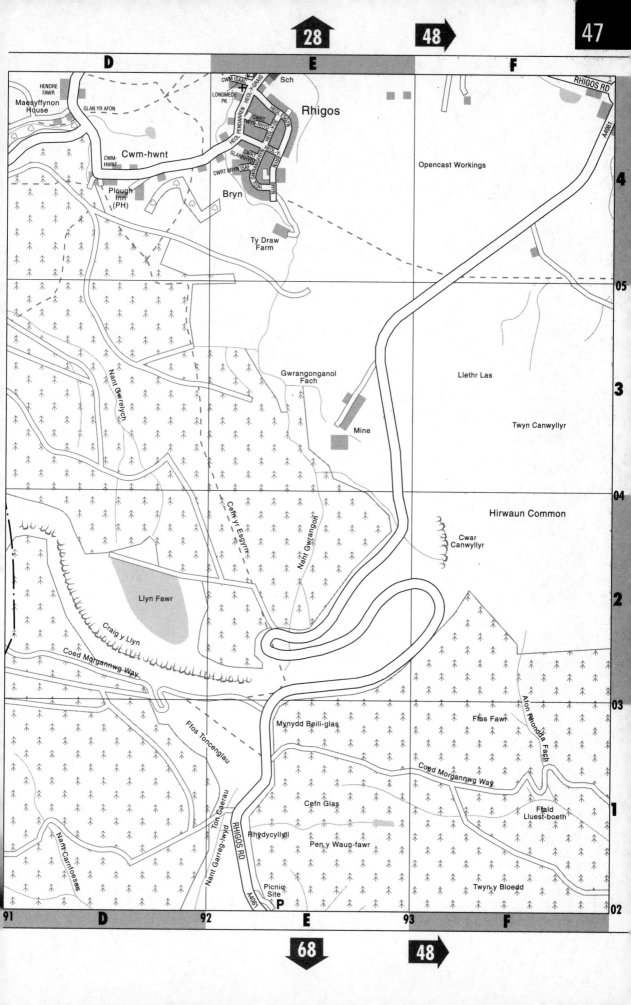

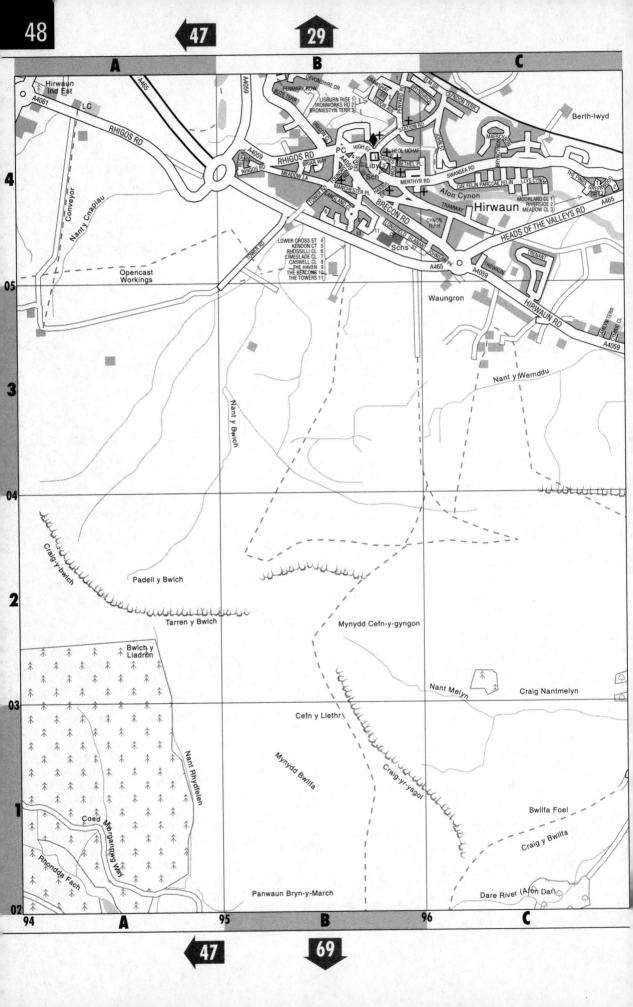

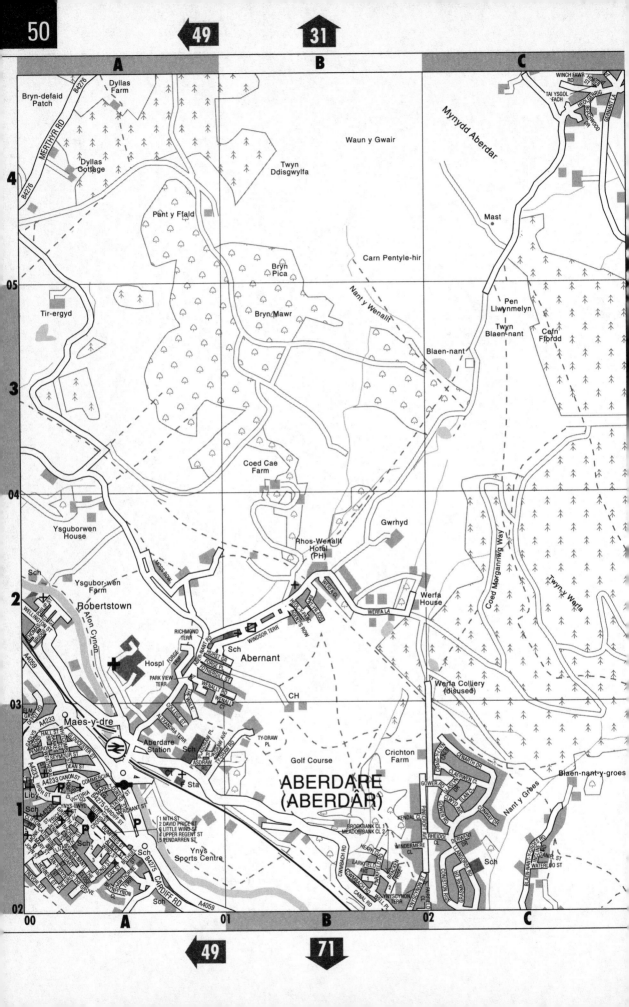

A
B
C

4

05

3

04

2

03

1

02

00
A
01
B
02
C

Bryn-defaid Patch
Dyllas Farm
MERTHYR RD
B4276
Dyllas Cottage
Pant y Ffald
Tir-ergyd

Waun y Gwair
Twyn Ddisgwylfa
Carn Pentyle-hir
Bryn Pica
Bryn Mawr
Nant y Wenallt
Coed Cae Farm

Mynydd Aberdâr
WINCH FAWR RD
HEOL SERIG
TAI YSGOL FACH
HEOL BEECHWOOD
GERMAIN LA
Mast
Pen Llwynmelyn
Twyn Blaen-nant
Cefn Ffordd
Blaen-nant

Ysguborwen House
Sch
Ysgubor-wen Farm
MOSS ROW
Robertstown
Afon Cynon
WELLINGTON ST
Richmond Terr
Hospl
Forge PL
Park View Terr
The Walk
College St
Alexandra Terr

Rhos-Wenallt Hotel (PH)
Gwrhyd
WERFA LA
Werfa House
WERFA LA
HEOL-NANT RD
HURST GR
FOTHERGILL ST
WENALLT RD
WENALLT CT
Windsor Terr
Sch
Abernant
CH

Coed Morgannwg Way
Twyn y Werfa
Werfa Colliery (disused)

Maes-y-dre
Aberdare Station
Sch
ASDRAW
TY-DRAW PL
Golf Course
Crichton Farm
CRAIG-Y-LLYN
CENARTH DR
CLAERWEN CL
GOWER RD
CLWYD
PLAN CL
GOWER RD
Blaen-nant-y-groes
Nant y Groes

Liby
Sch
Sch
1 NITH ST
2 DAVID PRICE ST
3 LITTLE WIND ST
4 UPPER REGENT ST
5 PENDARREN ST
P
ABERDARE (ABERDÂR)
KENDAL PL
PINECROFT AVE
RHEIDOL AVE
WINDERMERE CL
DERWENT DR
Sch
DANIEL ST
WATERLOO ST
CONISTON RISE
LLANGOWER RD
CONWAY DR
BLAEN-NANT-Y-GROES RD

Ynys Sports Centre
Sch
B4275 CARDIFF RD
A4059
BROCKBANK CL 1
MEADOWBANK CL 2
CWMBACH RD
HEATH CT
LARKFIELD AVE
CANAL RD
BRACKEN RISE
CWMBACH RD
YNYSCYNON TERR
FAIRFIELD

D

E

F

Sch
WS
HEOLGERRIG

Ynys-fach
Cae'r WERN
LLWYN-CELYN-WEN
PEN-AN-VIEW
WERN LA

Wern
Farm

Cwm Glo

Rhyd-y-car

THREE
SALMON
CELENDAR RD

Cae-
Draw

HIGH ST

SWAN ST

COURT

A470

HIGH ST

BROAD ST 1
GILAR ST 2
MASONIC ST 3

A470

TRAMROAD SIDE N 4
CROSS THOMAS ST 5
LOWER THOMAS ST 6
COEDCAE'R CWRT 7
COURT TERR 8
UNION ST 9
MILTON PL 10
BRYNTIRION RD 11
WINDSOR TERR 12
ALEXANDRA TERR 13
MORRELL ST 14
ARFRYN TERR 15
ST TYDFIL'S AVE 16

ALMA ST
ROCKFIELD
CRES
TWYNYRODYN RD
GILFACH-CYNON
WALKER'S TERR

PENHEOLFERTHYR

BRYONY
CL Sch

AERON
TERR

Sch

Twynyrodyn

GLYNCOED
TERR

PLYMOUTH ST

WESTBOURNE

RAILWAY

PENTREBACH RD

MARDY TERR 1
GLADSTONE TERR 2

MARDY ST

HANKEY

ANEURIN CRES

Ysgubor
Newydd
Hospl

MERTHYR RD

4

05

3

Blaen-canaid

Blaencanaid

Disused Rly

Road under construction

Glyndyrus
House

Upper Abercanaid

LEWIS SCL

River Taff (Afon Taf)

Triangle Bsns Pk

P

A4060

A4060

A470

Coed Morgannwg Way

GRAIG
CL

GRAIG RD

ANTHONY GR

ANTHONY CL

WYN-Y-EOS

Pentrebach
Station

04

Pen-y-lan Hill

Nant Graig

Graig Gethin

Sch

HIGH ST

CARDIFF ST

BUCKINGHAM PL

CHAPEL ST

GETHIN ST

NEWTON

Abercanaid

Gethin

1 ALEXANDRA PL
2 DONALD ST

2

Craig
y Gilfach

Carn
Castellymeibion

03

Penwaun Iago

Twyn
Ddisgwylfa Fawr

Cefnpennar Road

Gwaun Helen

Mynydd Gethin

1

Tyle Robert

Bryn Pica

Tarren y Gafr

Cefn-pennar-uchaf

CEFN PENNAR RD

Cefn Pwlldwr

02

03

D

04

E

05

F

A | B | C

BOGEY RD

Incline Top Ho

Tip

INCLINE SIDE

PENHEOL FERTHYR

Fros y frân

Pen-coedcae

Cwm Golau

Nant Gyra Wa

4

Garth Fawr

Cwmblacks Farm

Bargod Taf

05

Merthyr Common

Opencast Workings

Bryn Caerau

3

Factory

MERTHYR RD

PH

Pentrebach

1 CHAPEL CL
2 MORLAIS ST

GREENFIELD GDNS

DYFFRYN RD

CASTLE

HAMILTON

Schs

HICKMAN ST

3 CEREDIG ST
4 ARTHUR ST

04

TAI BACH

PERLAN

MAESTEG ST

Ski Slope

2

RHYD-GARN

Merthyr Tydfil Ind Pk

MERTHYR RD

Mynydd Cilfach-yr-encil

Craig Penddeugae

Bargod Taf

03

Pen-rhiw- 'ronen

River Taff (Afon Taf)

FURNACE ROW

HOLLY TERR 1
HAZEL TERR 2
LABURNAM TERR 3

4 TYDFIL TERR
5 RHODFA TERR
6 TALDWYN TERR
7 PHYLLIS ST

SOUTH VIEW

PEMBROKE

ARCHER ST

Troedyrhiw

Cwm Bargod

ENOCH MORRELL CL

PC

1

Schs

SCHOOL RD

Liby

TYNTALDWYN RD

CHAPEL ST

Pont Rhun

B4285

BRIDGE ST

HARRIET TOWN

FERNDALE RD

LOWER MOUNT

WINDSOR ST

GLANTAF RD

ELM ST

POPLAR ST

WYCHAM ST

CARDIFF RD A4054

DIANA ST 1
ANGUS ST 2
CHURCH ST 3
CARLTON TERR 4

SHILL ST

HAWEN

Mount Pleasant

MOUNT PLEASANT

1 BRYNHYFRYD VILLAS
2 HENRY RICHARD ST

CWMDU RD

B4285

A470

Sch

NANT

02

A4060
A470
A4054
MERTHYR RD

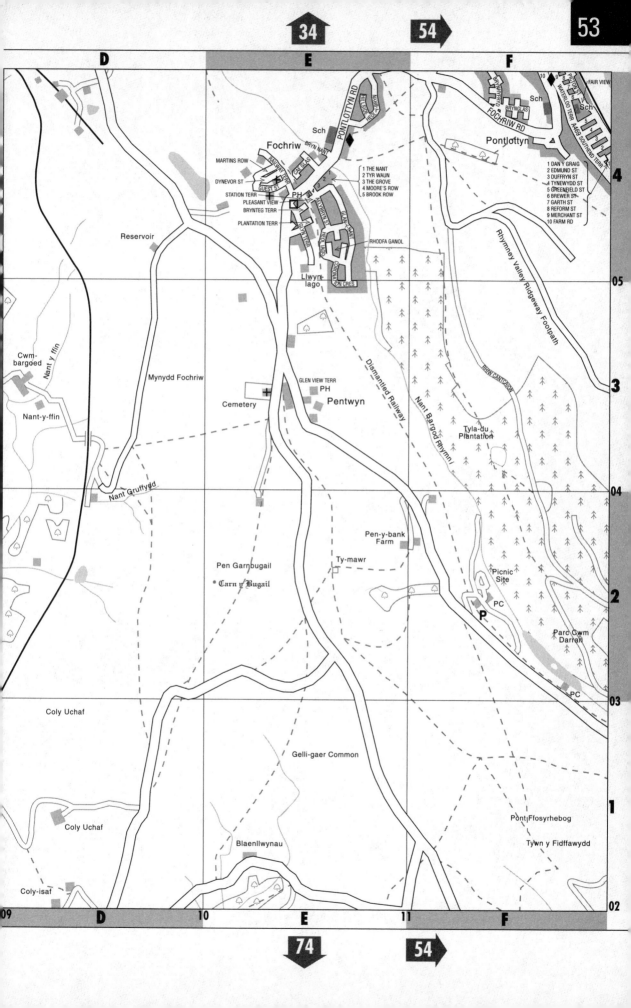

D
E
F

PONTLOTTYN RD

Sch

Fochriw

BRYN NANT

MARTINS ROW

DYNEVOR ST

STATION TERR

PLEASANT VIEW

BRYNTEG TERR

PLANTATION TERR

RAILWAY TERR

CAE GLAS

GUEST ST

PH

AELYBRYN TERR

GLAN TERR

GLAN Y NANT

CORONATION CRES

RHODFA GANOL

1 THE NANT
2 TYR WAUN
3 THE GROVE
4 MOORE'S ROW
5 BROOK ROW

Llwyn-
Iago

FOCHRIW RD

BRYNFFRWD

BRYNGLAS

PICTON ST

WATERLOO TERR

FAIR VIEW

A469 SOUTHERN TERR

Sch

Pontlottyn

1 DAN Y GRAIG
2 EDMUND ST
3 DUFFRYN ST
4 TYNEWYDD ST
5 GREENFIELD ST
6 BREWER ST
7 GARTH ST
8 REFORM ST
9 MERCHANT ST
10 FARM RD

4

Reservoir

Mynydd Fochriw

Cwm-
bargoed

Nant-y-ffin

Nant y ffin

Rhymney Valley Ridgeway Footpath

05

3

GLEN VIEW TERR

PH

Pentwyn

Cemetery

Dismantled Railway

Nant Bargod Rhymni

TRUW CANTCBON

Tyla-du
Plantation

Pen-y-bank
Farm

Ty-mawr

Pen Garnbugail

Carn y Bugail

04

Picnic
Site

PC

P

Parc Cwm
Darran

2

PC

03

Coly Uchaf

Gelli-gaer Common

1

Pont Ffosyrhebog

Tywn y Fidffawydd

Coly Uchaf

Blaenllwynau

Coly-isaf

09
D
10
E
11
F
02

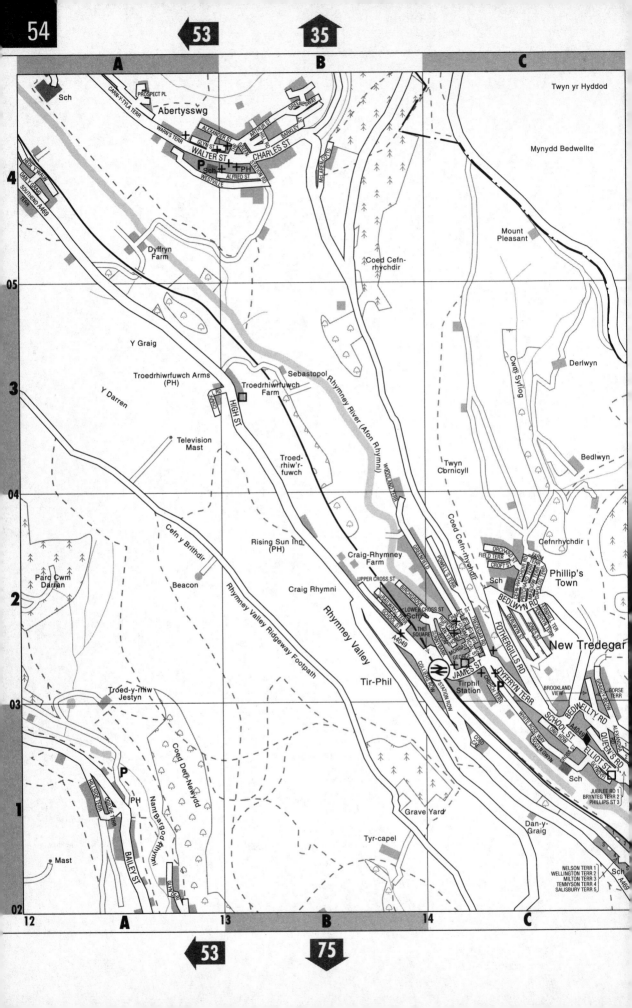

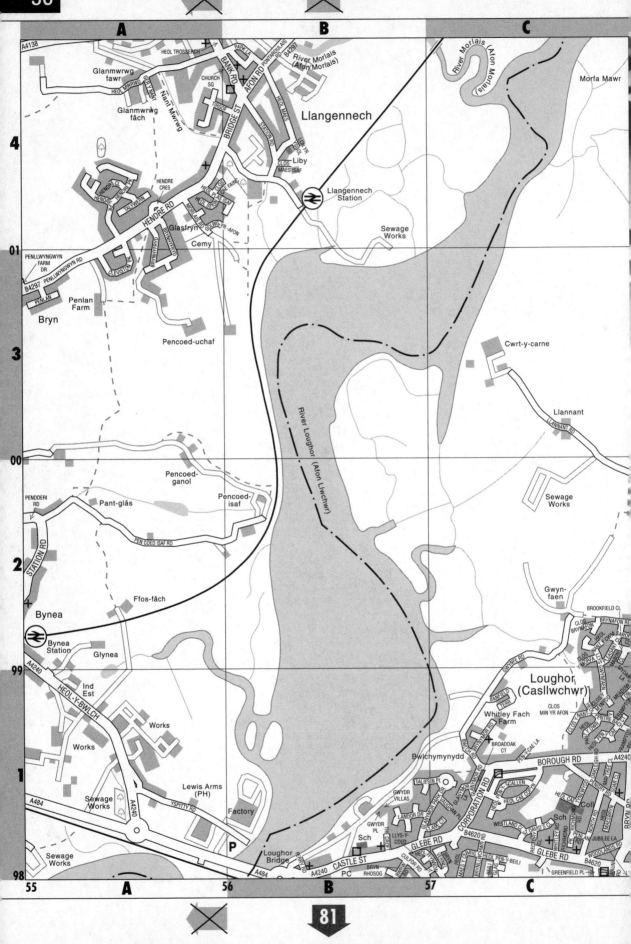

A4138

HEOL TROSSERCH

Glanmwrwg
fawr

PARK LA

HEOL MWRWG

GLER Y MYNT

Glanmwrwg
fâch

BANK RD

AFON RD

CHURCH
SQ

TIRGOF

BRIDGE ST

Nant Mwrwg

PONTARDULAIS RD

B4297

River Morlais
(Afon Morlais)

HEOL MAES

STATION RD

Llangennech

LON YR

Liby

HENDRE CL

HENDRE RD

HENDRE CRES

TALWERN

CLOS FAINC

HEOL PLAS ISAF

MORLAIS RD

CLOS
MAES ISAF

Llangennech
Station

Sewage
Works

HEOL SECSI

BRYNFFRWD

BRYNHYFRYD

CLEVISTON

LON YR

Glasfryn

SOLWG YR AFON

Cemy

4

01

PENLLWYNGWYN
FARM
DR

B4297

PENLLWYNGWYN RD

PENLAN

Penlan
Farm

Bryn

Pencoed-uchaf

River Loughor (Afon Llwchwr)

3

PENDDERI
RD

STATION RD

Pant-glâs

Pencoed-
ganol

Pencoed-
isaf

PEN COED ISAF RD

00

2

Ffos-fâch

Bynea

Bynea
Station

Glynea

A4240

99

HEOL-Y-BWLCH

Ind
Est

Works

Works

A484

Sewage
Works

A4240

Lewis Arms
(PH)

YSPITTY RD

Factory

River Morlais (Afon Morlais)

Morfa Mawr

Cwrt-y-carne

Llannant

LLANNANT RD

Sewage
Works

Gwyn-
faen

BROOKFIELD CL

BRYNAFON CL

CLOS
BRYNAFON

GWYNFE RD

Loughor
(Casllwchwr)

CLOS
MIN YR AFON

Whitley Fach
Farm

BROADOAK
CT

PEN-Y-CAE LA

Bwlchymynydd

BOROUGH RD

A4240

BORO

CORPORATION RD

GWYDR
VILLAS

TALIESIN PL

LANDOR DR

GWYDR
PL

LLYS-Y-
COED

Sch

THE CROFT

BRYN
RHOSOG

B4620

GLEBE RD

GLEBE RD

B4620

GREENFIELD PL

1

P

Loughor
Bridge

A484

CASTLE ST

PC

A4240

98

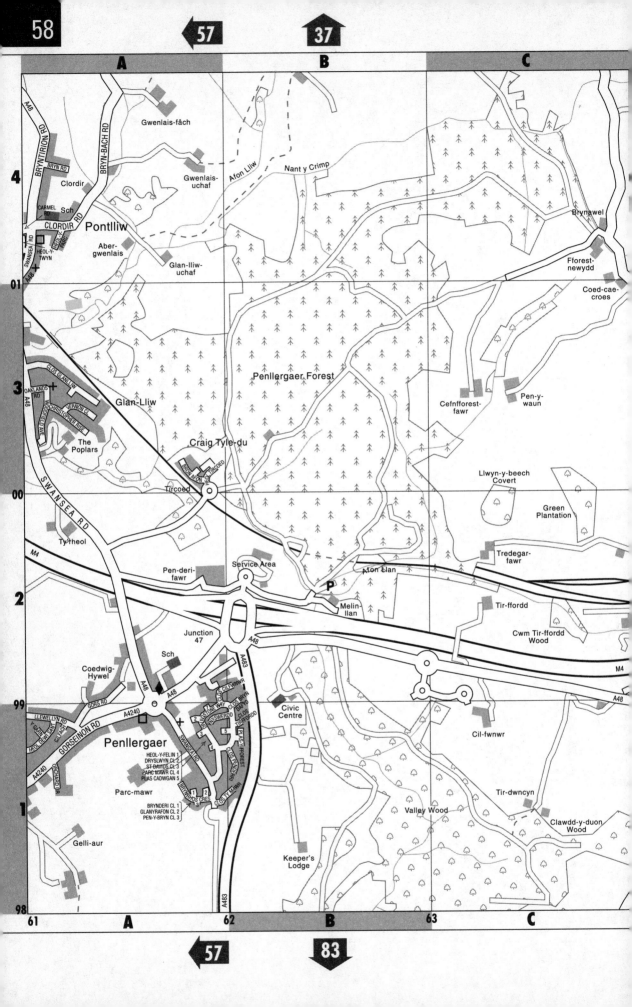

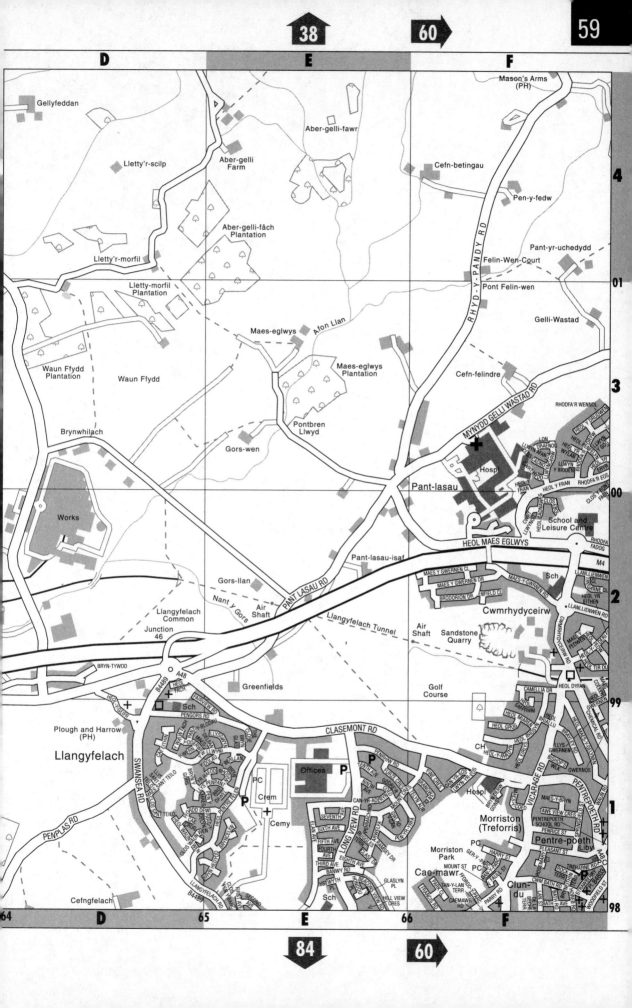

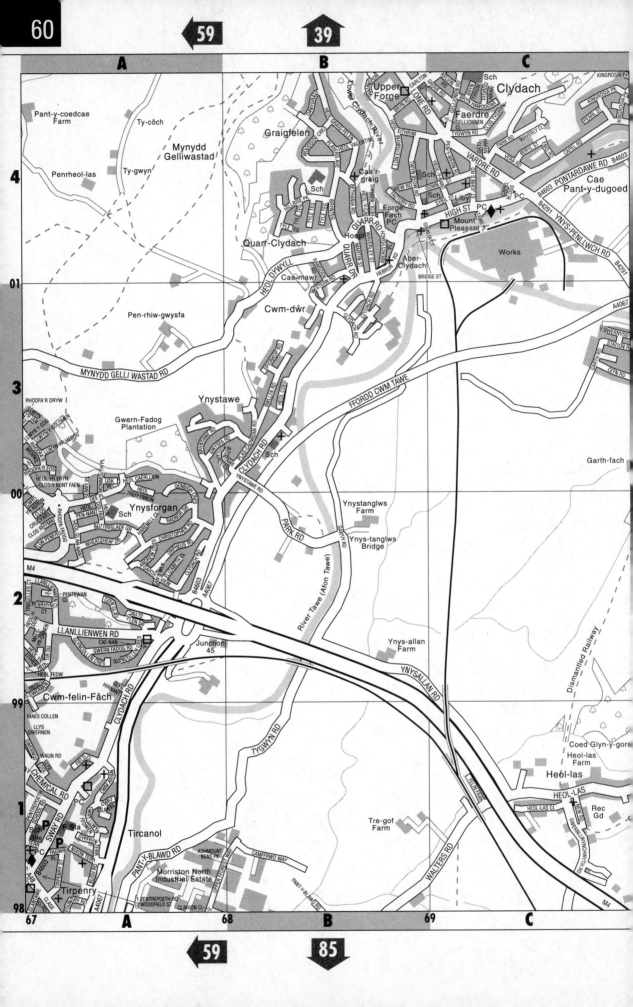

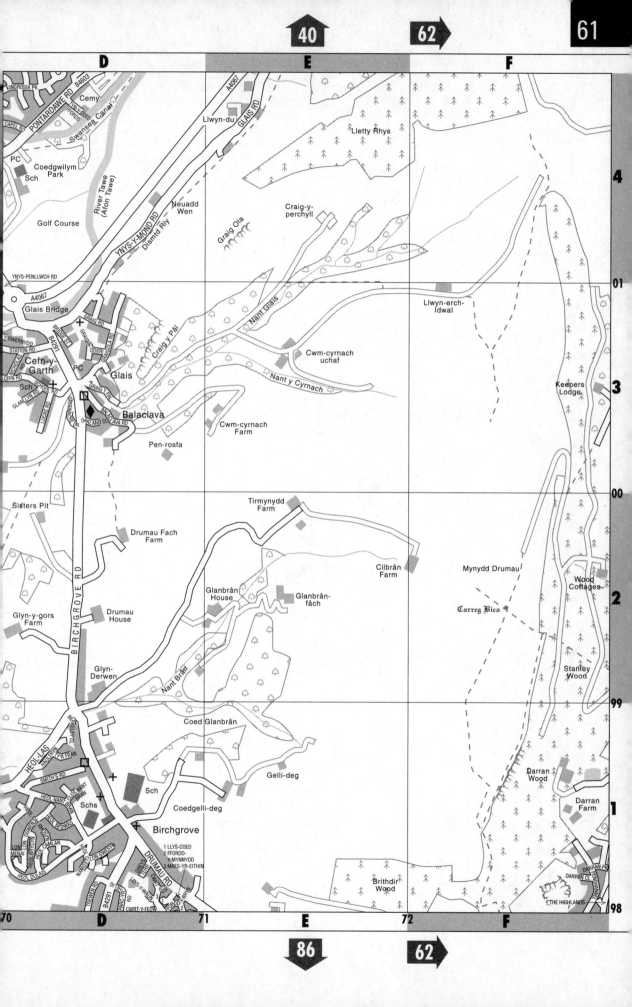

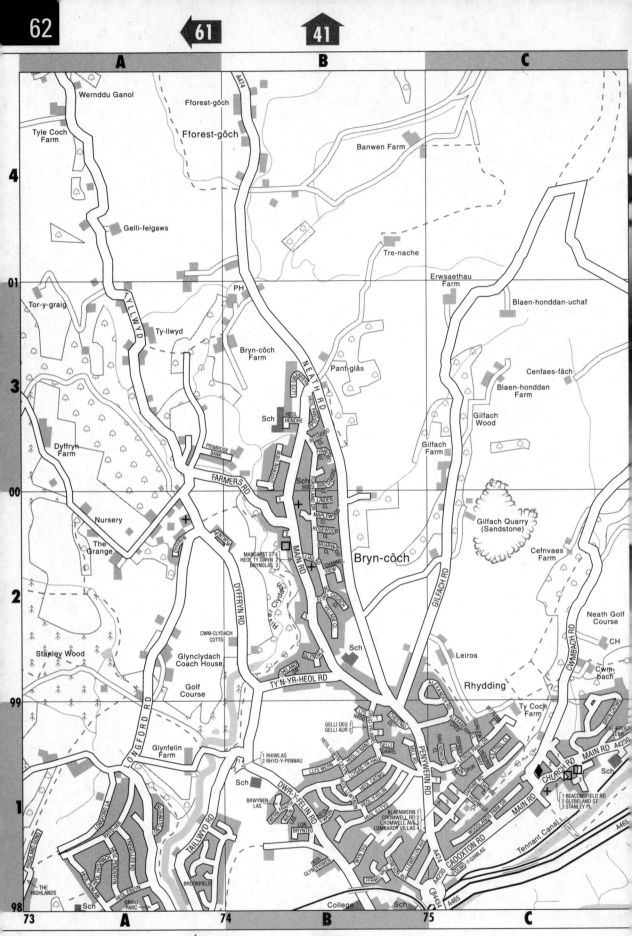

A B C

4

01

3

00

2

99

1

98

73 A 74 B 75 C

Wernddu Ganol

Fforest-gôch

Fforest-gôch

Banwen Farm

Tyle Coch Farm

Gelli-felgaws

Tre-nache

Erwsaethau Farm

Tor-y-graig

PH

Blaen-honddan-uchaf

Ty-llwyd

Bryn-côch Farm

Pant-glâs

Cenfaes-fâch

Blaen-honddan Farm

Gilfach Wood

Dyffryn Farm

PRIMROSE BANK

Sch
HEOL HENDRE

Gilfach Farm

FARMERS RD

Sch

BIRCH CL
LINDEN CL
MAPLEWOOD CL
ROSEWOOD CL
BRIARW CL
FIRZLAND CL
REDWOOD CL
FIRWD CL
DYFFRYN VIEW
LLYS GOLAU
NEATH RD
HEOL PRIVACY

Gilfach Quarry
(Sandstone)

Nursery

The Grange

MARGARET ST 1
HEOL TY GWYN 2
BRYNGLAS 3

ELIAS RD
CHANNEL VIEW

Bryn-côch

Cefnvaes Farm

DYFFRYN RD

River Clydach

CWM-CLYDACH COTTS

ELIAS RD
CHURCH
VILLAGE CL

Neath Golf Course

CH

Stanley Wood

Glynclydach Coach House

Golf Course

Sch

Leiros

Cwm-bach

GLENDALE

OAKLAND DR

TY'N-YR-HEOL RD

Rhydding

Ty Coch Farm

LONGFORD RD

Glynfelin Farm

1 RHIWLAS
2 RHYD-Y-PENNAU

LLYS WERN

LLYS DDU

CHESTNUT

GELLI DAWEL

HILL RD

ALEXANDER CRES

GELLI DEG 1
GELLI AUR 2

PENWERN RD

DAPHNE RD
HIGHFIELD

CAE BROES TERR

BRYN CAWR

Sch

Sch

BRWYNEN LAS

DWR-Y-FELIN RD

HEOL CATWG

BLAENWERN 1
CROMWELL RD 2
CROMWELL AVE 3
LOMBARDY VILLAS 4

WOODLANDS PARK DR

CHURCH RD
MAIN RD A4230

1 BEACONSFIELD RD
2 GLEBELAND ST
3 STANLEY PL

TAILLWYD RD

CADOXTON RD

MAIN RD

Tennant Canal

THE HIGHLANDS

Sch

GRAIG PARC

BROOKFIELD

HEOL GLYNDERWEN

GOLEG-Y-GAMLAS

A474 A4230 B4434

A465

College

Sch

Tennant Canal

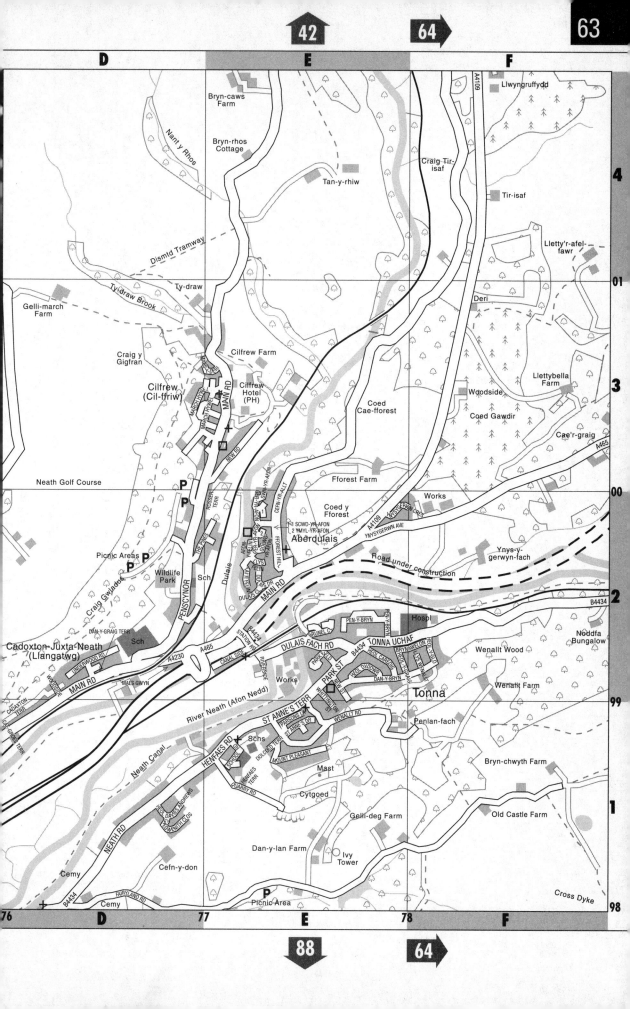

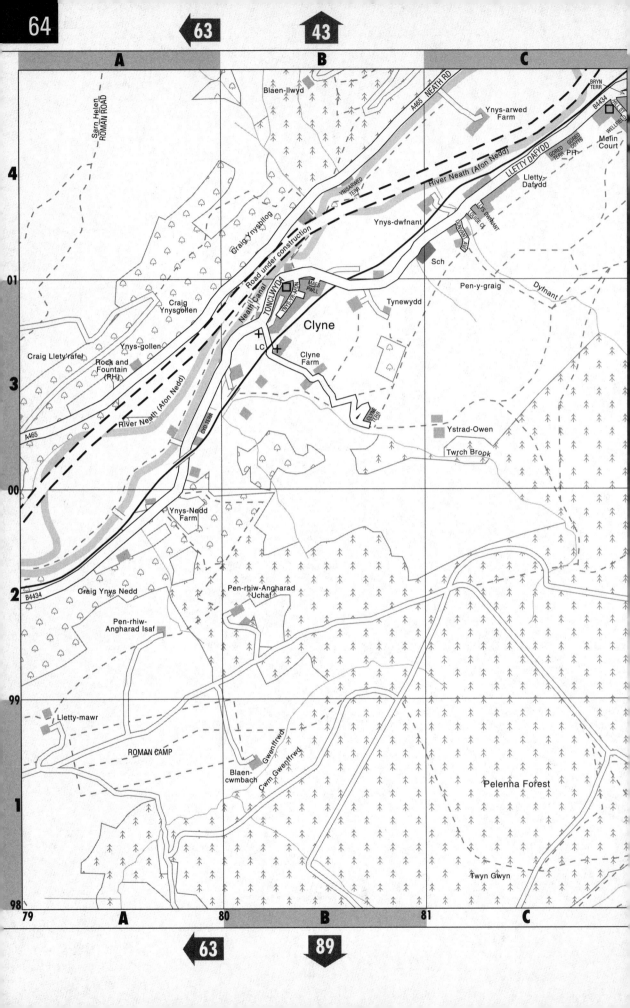

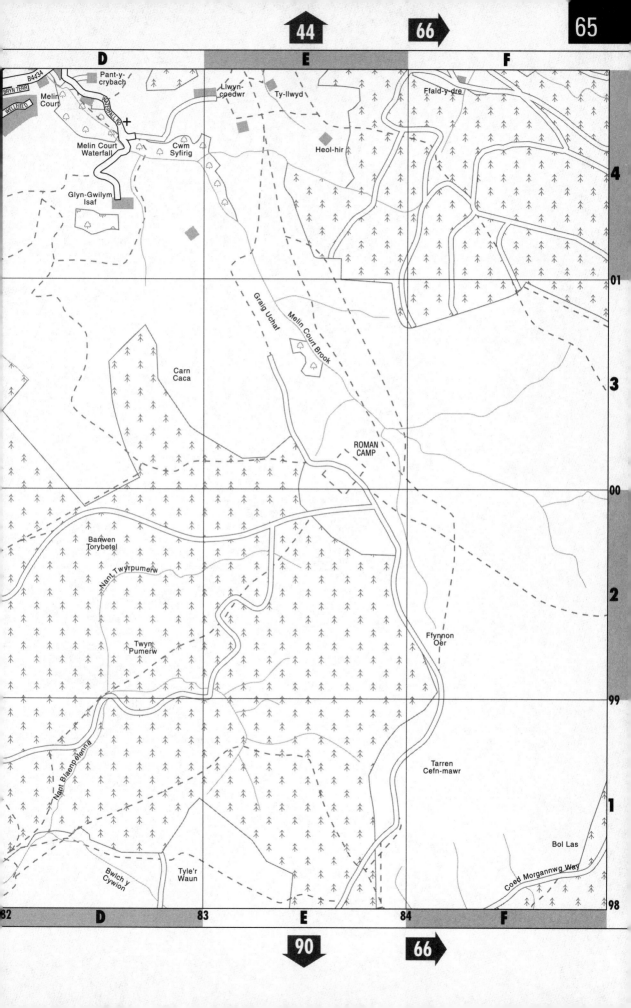

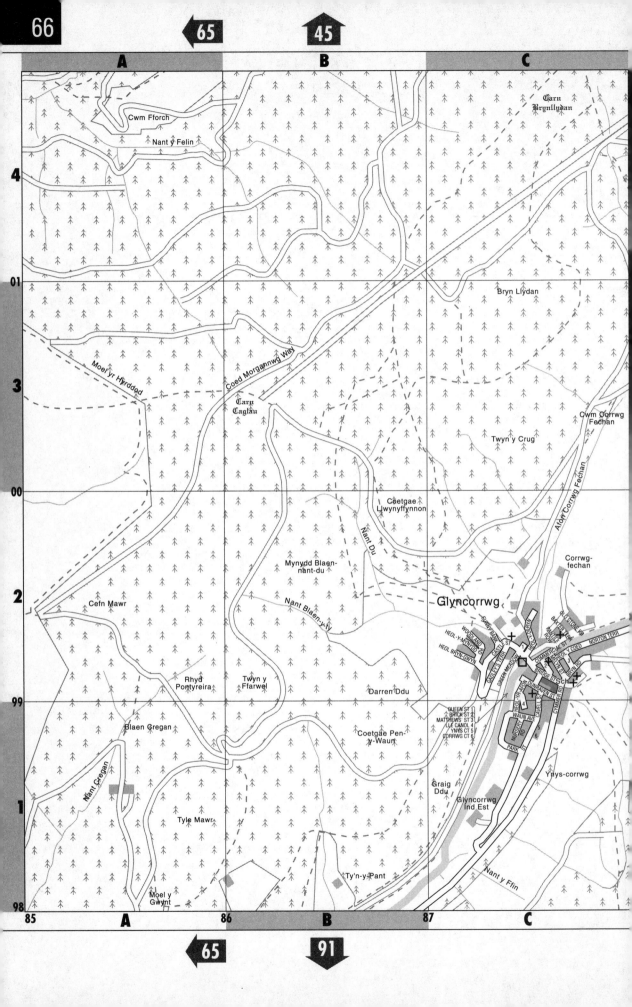

A **B** **C**

Carn
Brynllydan

Cwm Fforch

Nant y Felin

4

01

Moel yr Hyrddod

Coed Morgannwg Way

Bryn Llydan

3

Caru
Caglau

Cwm Corrwg
Fechan

Twyn y Crug

Afon Corrwg Fechan

00

Coetgae
Llwynyffynnon

Corrwg-
fechan

Nant Du

Cefn Mawr

Mynydd Blaen-
nant-du

Glyncorrwg

2

Nant Blaen-y-ty

SUNNY BANK
WOODLAND RD
HEOL-Y-MYNYDD RD
CASTLE ST
HEOL BRYN-GWYN
GRO VEY TERR
GREEN MEADOW
COMMERCIAL ST
HEOL-Y-COED
BRIDGE ST SCH
OLD STONE RD
BAPTIST TERR
PARK TERR
NORTON TERR
BRYN RD

Rhyd
Pontyreira

Twyn y
Ffarwel

Darren Ddu

HEOL-YR-AFON
DUNRAVEN ST
CYMMER RD
KAVELL ST

99

Blaen Cregan

Coetgae Pen-
y-Waun

QUEEN ST 1
BRICK ST 2
MATTHEWS ST 3
LLE CANOL 4
YNYS CT 5
CORRWG CT 6
WAUN AVE
NURSERY RD
PARK ST

Nant Cregan

Graig
Ddu

Ynys-corrwg

1

Glyncorrwg
Ind Est

Tyle Mawr

Nant y Ffin

Ty'n-y-Pant

98

Moel y
Gwynt

A **B** **C**

85 86 87

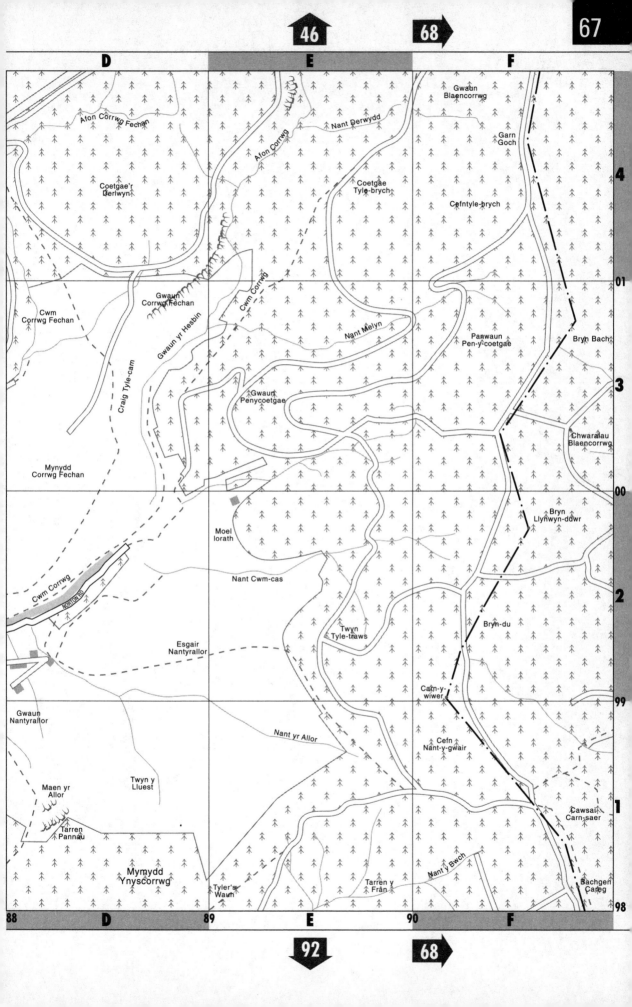

Gwaun
Blaencorrwg

Afon Corrwg Fechan

Nant Derwydd

Garn
Goch

Coetgae'r
Derlwyn

Afon Corrwg

Coetgae
Tyle-brych

Cefntyle-brych

4

01

Gwaun
Corrwg Fechan

Cwm Corrwg

Cwm
Corrwg Fechan

Gwaun yr Hesbin

Nant Melyn

Panwaun
Pen-y-coetgae

Bryn Bach

3

Craig Tyle-cam

Gwaun
Penycoetgae

Chwaralau
Blaencorrwg

Mynydd
Corrwg Fechan

00

Moel
Iorath

Bryn
Llynwyn-ddwr

Cwm Corrwg

NORTON RD

Nant Cwm-cas

2

Esgair
Nantyrallor

Twyn
Tyle-traws

Bryn-du

Carn-y-
wiwer

99

Gwaun
Nantyrallor

Nant yr Allor

Cefn
Nant-y-gwair

Maen yr
Allor

Twyn y
Lluest

Cawsai
Carn-saer

1

Tarren
Pannau

Mymydd
Ynyscorrwg

Tyler's
Waun

Tarren y
Frân

Nant y Bwch

Bachgen
Careg

98

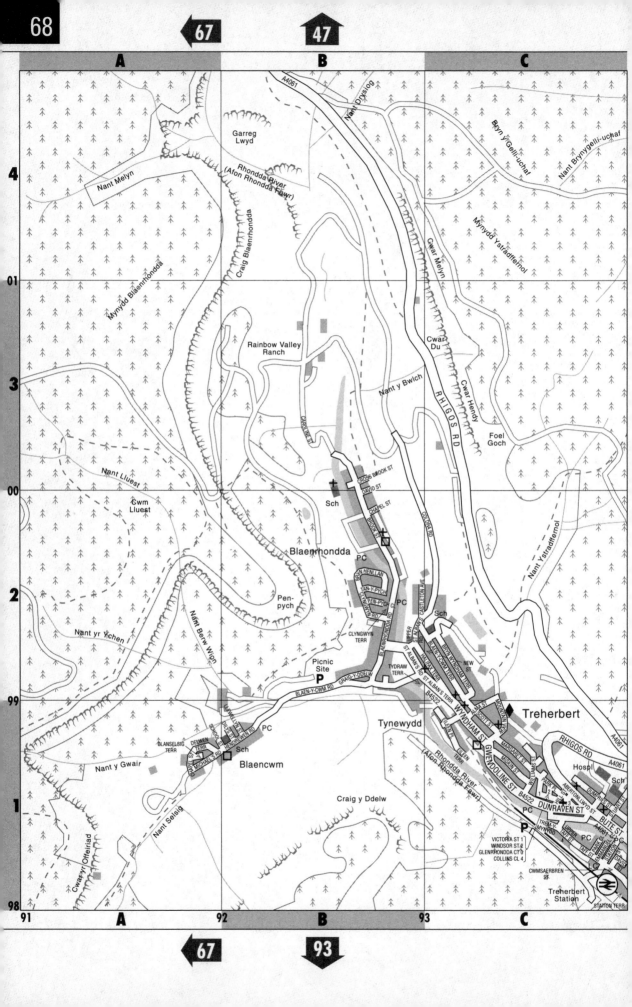

A **B** **C**

4

01

3

2

99

1

98

91 **A** 92 **B** 93 **C**

Garreg
Lwyd

Nant Dryslog

A4061

Bryn-y-Gelli-uchaf

Nant Brynygelli-uchaf

Nant Melyn

Rhondda River
(Afon Rhondda Fawr)

Craig Blaenrhondda

Mynydd Blaenrhondda

Mynydd Ystradffernol

Cwar Melyn

Rainbow Valley
Ranch

Cwar
Du

Nant y Bwlch

RHIGOS RD

Cwar Hendy

Foel
Goch

Nant Lluest

CAROLINE ST

Cwm
Lluest

Sch

CROSS BROOK ST

DAVID ST

CHAPEL ST

BRICK ST

COLBRA RD

Nant Ystradffernol

Blaenrhondda

PC

BRON HENLLAN

TAN-Y-PYCH

CAE MARTEN RD

PEN-PYCH

Pen-pych

BLAENRHONDDA RD

PC

CASTLETON AVE

UPPER

Sch

Nant yr Ychen

Nant Berw Wion

CLYNGWYN
TERR

ST ALBAN'S

BRON WYNDHAM TERR

NEW
ST

Picnic
Site

P

GRAIG-Y-DDELW

TYDRAW
TERR

ST ALBAN'S TERR

HALIFAX TERR

MOUNTAIN ST

B4522

Tynewydd

Treherbert

BLAEN-Y-CWM RD

PC

WYNDHAM ST

SCOTT ST

BAPTIST ST

Nant y Gwair

UPPER INST RD

HENDREWEN RD

SCHOOL ST

CHAPEL ST

ST MICHAEL'S RD

DELWEN
TERR

GLANSELSIG
TERR

Sch

Blaencwm

PC

Rhondda River
(Afon Rhondda Fawr)

GWENDOLINE ST

B4522

MARGARET ST

MISKIN ST

WM LLYWS ST

ELFEN
ST

DUNRAVEN ST

Craig y Ddelw

Nant Selsig

Hospl

RHIGOS RD

A4061

A4061

Sch

ABERTONLLWYD ST

PC

TREM-Y-
MYNYDD

UPPER
TAFF ST

BUTE ST

PARK ST

DUMFRIES ST

TAFF ST

PC

P

VICTORIA ST 1
WINDSOR ST 2
GLENRHONDDA CT 3
COLLINS CL 4

CWMSAERBREN ST

Nant y Gwair

Cwar yr Offeiriad

Treherbert
Station

STATION TERR

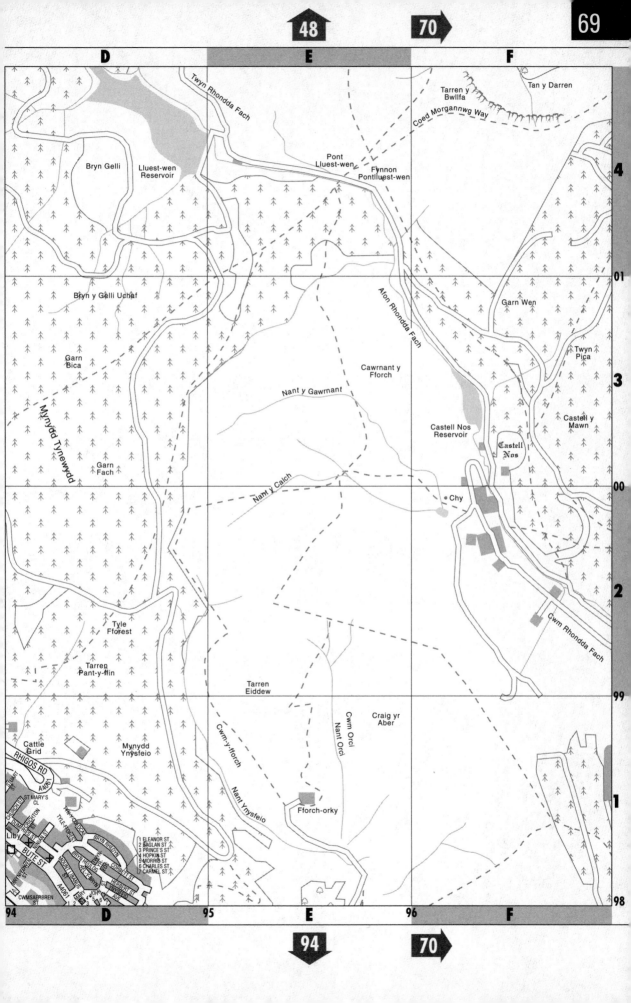

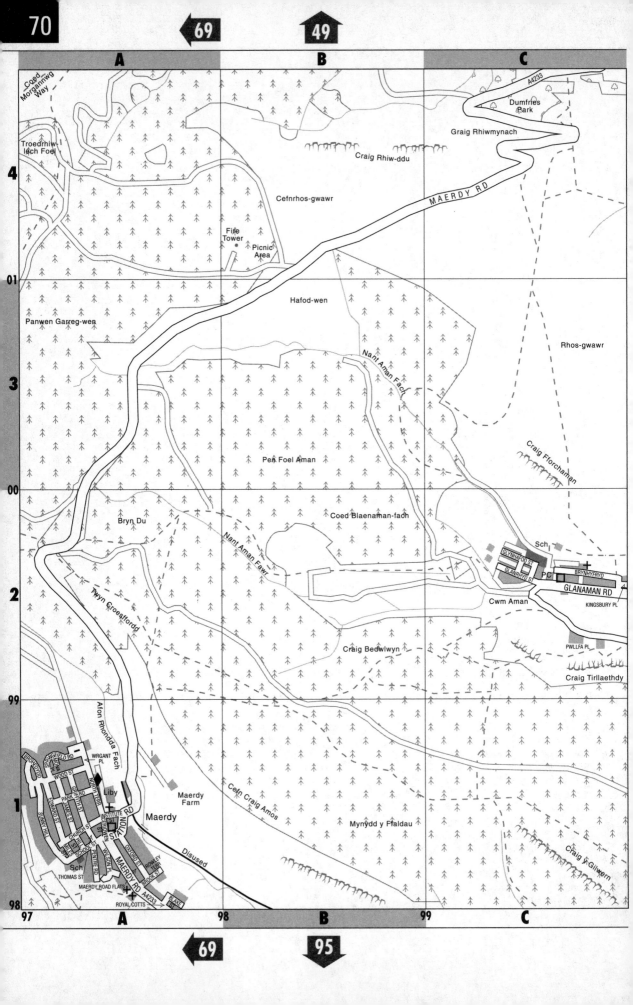

A B C

Coed Morgannwg Way

Troedrhiw-llech Foel

4

Fire Tower
Picnic Area

Cefnrhos-gwawr

Craig Rhiw-ddu

MAERDY RD

Graig Rhiwmynach

Dumfries Park

A4233

01

Panwen Garreg-wen

Hafod-wen

Rhos-gwawr

Nant Aman Fach

3

Craig Fforchaman

Pen Foel Aman

00

Bryn Du

Coed Blaenaman-fach

Nant Aman Fawr

GLYN HAFOD ST
GLANRHYD ST
Sch
PC
BRYNHYFRYD

Twyn Croesffordd

GLANAMAN RD

2

Cwm Aman

KINGSBURY PL

Craig Bedwlwyn

PWLLFA PL

Craig Tirllaethdy

99

Afon Rhondda Fach

WRGANT PL

SPRINGFIELD RD
WOOD ST
PARK TERR
GREY PL
BROOKLYN
JAMES ST
NORTH TERR
Liby

Maerdy Farm

Cefn Craig Amos

1

EDWARD ST
SUNNY HILL
CHURCH ST
PENTRE RD
SCHOOL ST
WILSON PL
INSTITUTE RD
STATION
OXFORD ST
ROWLEY TERR
BROOK ST
Maerdy

Disused

Mynydd y Ffaldau

Craig y Gilwern

Sch
THOMAS ST
MAERDY RD A4233
MAERDY ROAD FLATS
ROYAL COTTS
BLAKE ST

98

97 A 98 B 99 C

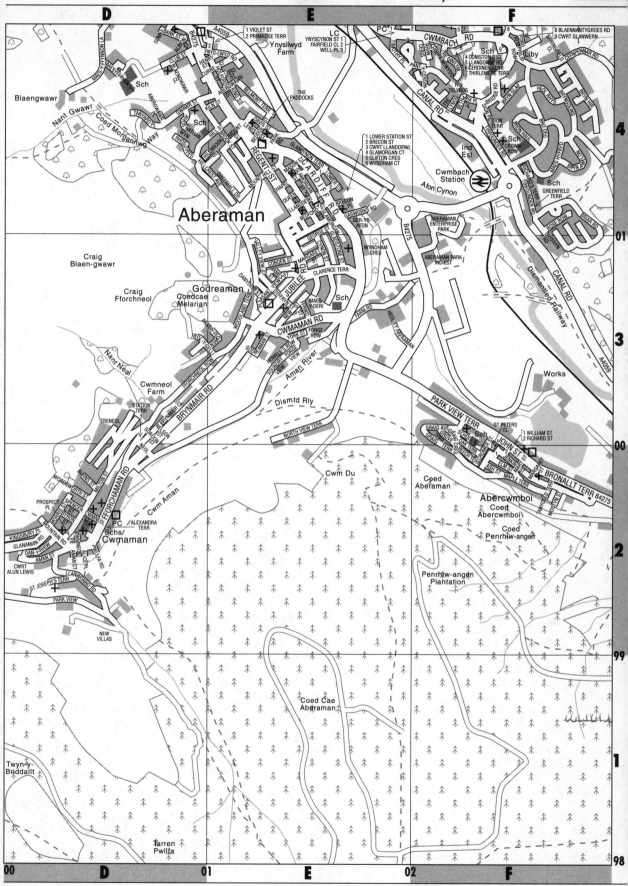

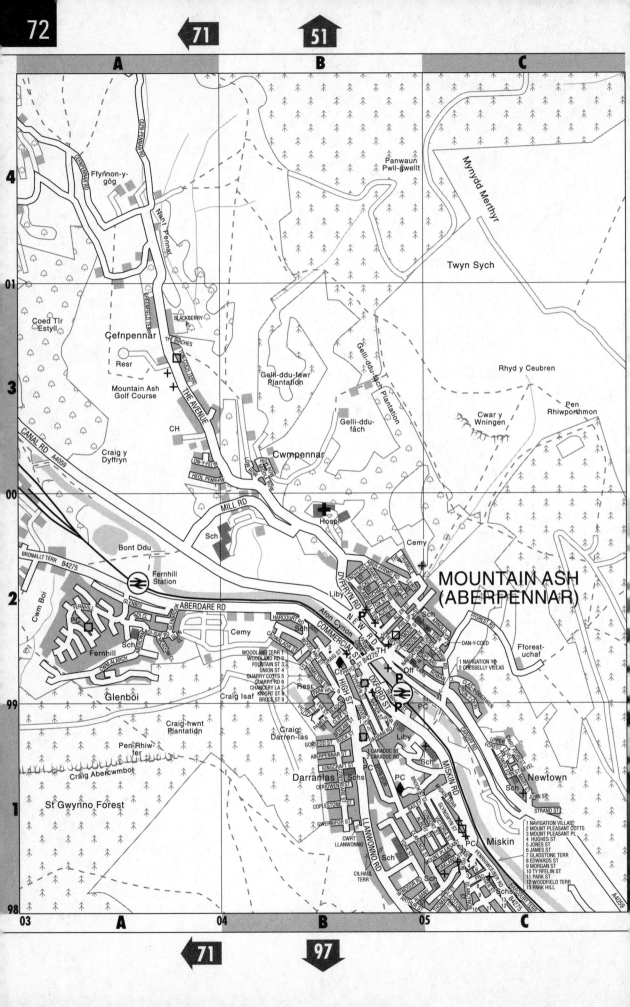

A   B   C

4

01

Coed Tir Estyll

Cefnpennar

Resr

Mountain Ash Golf Course

3

Craig y Dyffryn

CANAL RD A4059

CH

THE CROCKETTERR

THE BIRCHES

GREENFIELD TERR

PEN PENNAR RD

Nant Pennar

Ffynnon-y-gôg

BLACKBERRY PL

THE AVENUE

LON-Y-FELIN

HEOL PENRHIW

Cwmpennar

Gelli-ddu-fawr Plantation

Gelli-ddu-fâch

Gelli-ddu-fâch Plantation

HIGH MOW

LOW MOW

Panwaun Pwll-gwellt

Mynydd Merthyr

Twyn Sych

Rhyd y Ceubren

Pen Rhiwporthmon

Cwar y Wningen

MILL RD

Sch

Hospl

Cemy

00

Bont Ddu

BRONALLT TERR B4275

Fernhill Station

2

Cwm Boi

FERNHILL

PC

Sch

Fernhill

GLENBOI

ABERCWMBOI-ISAF RD

GLENBROOK

GLENBOI CL

GLEN

MEADOW

PL

ABERDARE RD

Cemy

Craig Isaf

Afon Cynon

DYFFRYN RD

Liby

NEW RD

MOUNTAIN ASH
(ABERPENNAR)

Sch

FFOREST RD

Ffforest-uchaf

DAN-Y-COED

CLAS-Y-DERWEN

1 NAVIGATION YD
2 CRESSELLY VILLAS

Glenboi

Craig-hwnt Plantation

Pen Rhiw-fer

Craig Abercwmboi

St Gwynno Forest

99

Craig Darren-las

WOODLAND TERR 1
WOODLAND RD 2
FOUNTAIN ST 3
UNION ST 4
QUARRY COTTS 5
QUARRY RD 6
CHANCERY LA 7
KNIGHT ST 8
BRUCE ST 9

HARCOURT RD

COMMERCIAL ST

HIGH ST

Resr

Ctr

PRYCE ST

PARK HILL

DARRAN RD

OXFORD ST

B4275

Off

PC

Liby

Sch

UPPER FOREST

LEVEL

Newtown

JOHN ST

STRAND ST

GORSEDD ST

ROCK ST

ABERPENNAR ST

KINGCRAFT ST

COPLESTONE ST

GWERNIFOR ST

Darranlas

Schs

1 CARADOC ST
2 CARADOC RD

PC

MISKIN RD

LLANWONNO RD

Sch

Miskin

CWRT LLANWONNO

CILHAUL TERR

WINDSOR RD

ALBANY

ARTHUR ST

PENRHIWCEIBR RD

Schs

B4275

A4059

1 NAVIGATION VILLAS
2 MOUNT PLEASANT COTTS
3 MOUNT PLEASANT PL
4 HUGHES ST
5 JONES ST
6 JAMES ST
7 GLADSTONE TERR
8 EDWARDS ST
9 MORGAN ST
10 TY RFELIN ST
11 PARK ST
12 WOODFIELD TERR
13 PARK HILL

1

98

03   A   04   B   05   C

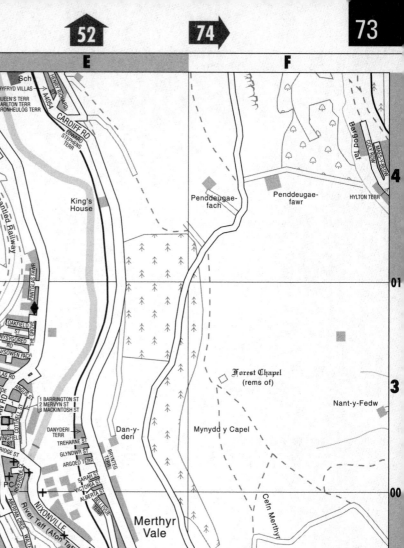
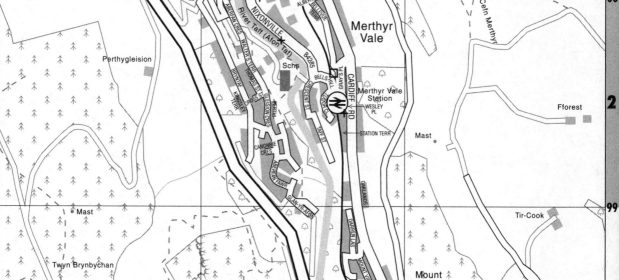

A B C

4

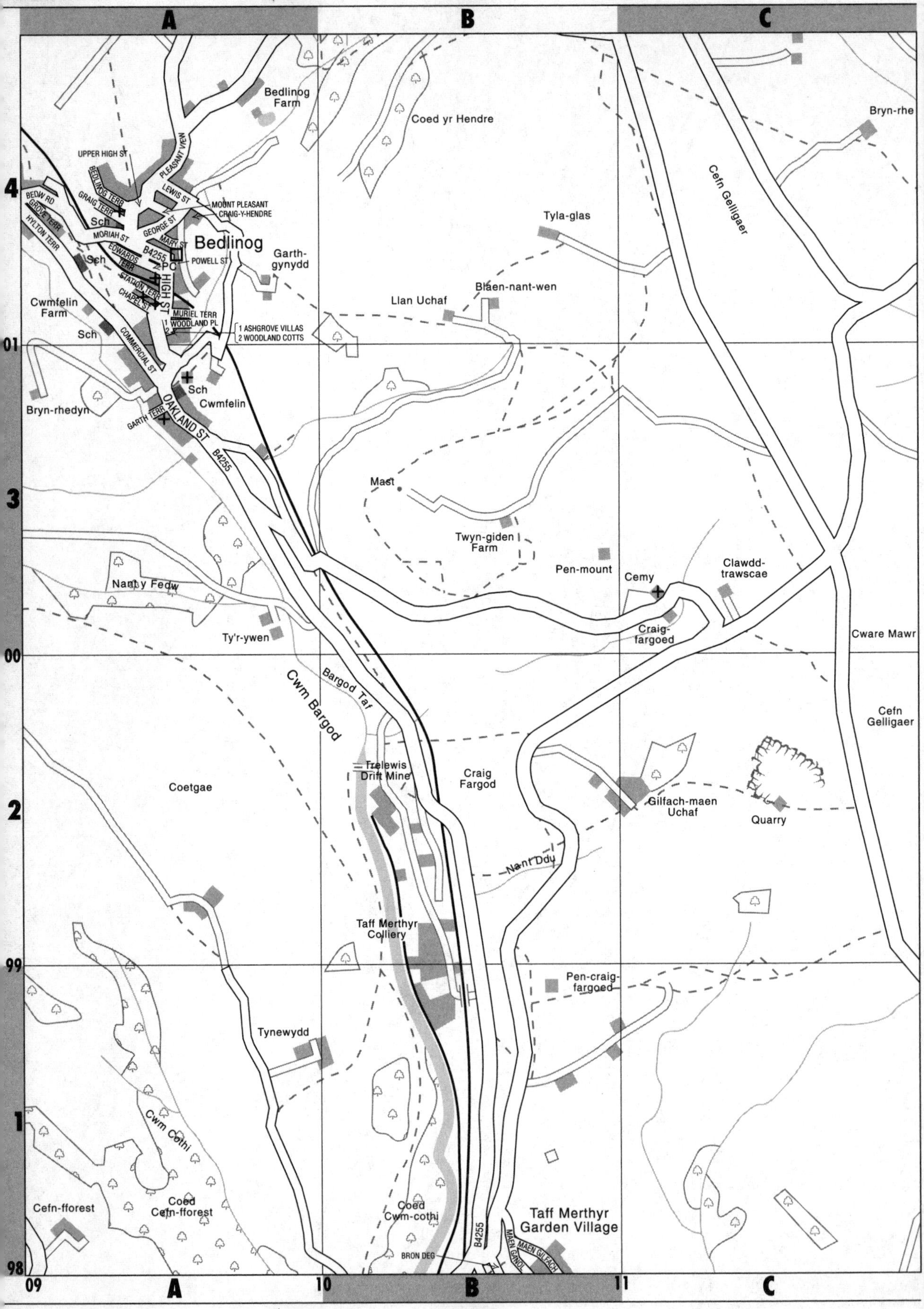

Bedlinog Farm

Coed yr Hendre

Cefn Gelligaer

Bryn-rhe

UPPER HIGH ST
BEDLINOG TERR
GRAIG TERR
PLEASANT VIEW
LEWIS ST
Sch
BEDW RD
GROVE TERR
HYLTON TERR
GEORGE ST
MOUNT PLEASANT
CRAIG-Y-HENDRE
MORIAH ST
EDWARDS TERR
Sch
MARY ST
B4255
POWELL ST
STATION TERR
CHAPEL ST
HIGH ST
PO
COMMERCIAL ST
Cwmfelin Farm
Sch
MURIEL TERR
WOODLAND PL

Tyla-glas

Blaen-nant-wen

Bedlinog

Garth-gynydd

Llan Uchaf

1 ASHGROVE VILLAS
2 WOODLAND COTTS

01

Bryn-rhedyn

GARTH TERR
OAKLAND ST
B4255

Sch Cwmfelin

Mast

3

Twyn-giden Farm

Pen-mount

Cemy

Clawdd-trawscae

Cware Mawr

Nant y Fedw

Craig-fargoed

Ty'r-ywen

00

Cwm Bargod

Bargod Taf

Cefn Gelligaer

Coetgae

Trelewis Drift Mine

Craig Fargod

Gilfach-maen Uchaf

Quarry

2

Nant Ddu

Taff Merthyr Colliery

99

Pen-craig-fargoed

Tynewydd

Cwm Cothi

1

Cefn-fforest

Coed Cefn-fforest

Coed Cwm-cothi

Taff Merthyr Garden Village

B4255
MAEN GILFACH
BRON DEG

98

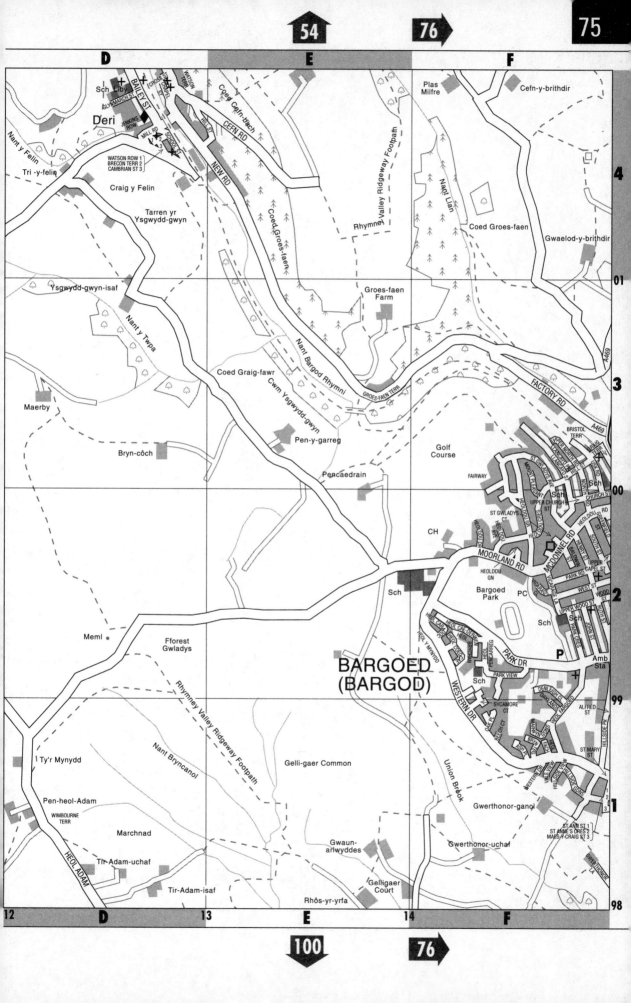

Plas
Milfre
Cefn-y-brithdir

Sch Lby
Deri

Nant y Felin

Tri-y-felin

Craig y Felin

WATSON ROW 1
BRECON TERR 2
CAMBRIAN ST 3

Tarren yr
Ysgwydd-gwyn

Coed Cefn-bach

CEFN RD

NEW RD

Coed Groes-faen

Rhymney Valley Ridgeway Footpath

Nant Llan

Coed Groes-faen

Gwaelod-y-brithdir

4

Ysgwydd-gwyn-isaf

Nant y Twpa

Coed Graig-fawr

Nant Bargod Rhymni

Groes-faen
Farm

GROES-FAEN TERR

01

Maerby

Bryn-côch

Cwm Ysgwydd-gwyn

Pen-y-garreg

Pencaedrain

Golf
Course

FAIRWAY

FACTORY RD

A469

BRISTOL
TERR

A469

3

CH

MOORLAND RD

HEOLDDU
GN

Bargoed
Park

PC

Sch

UPPER NORTH ST
ST GWLADYS AVE
MOUNT PLEASANT
UPPER CHURCH ST
ST GWLADYS
CT
HEOLDDU RD
HEOLDDU AVE
NORTH CHURCH ST
Sch

HEOL
PENCARREG

00

Meml

Fforest
Gwladys

Sch

HEOL CAE-DERW
HEOL CAE-DERW
HEOL MYNYDD
VICARAGE
VICARAGE TERR
WEST ST
PARK RD
PARK CRES
UPPER WOOD ST
JOHN ST
RUTH ST
PARK CRES
UPPER
CAPEL ST
HENRY ST
BALDWIN
SOUTH ST
MACDONNEL RD

P
Amb
Sta

2

PARK DR

WESTERN DR

Sch

PARK VIEW

Sch

OAK PL
BEECH CT
DEMLEIGH CT
OAK LAND
SYCAMORE
CT
ST MARY
ST

ALFRED
ST

HILLSIDE PK

99

BARGOED
(BARGOD)

Rhymney Valley Ridgeway Footpath

Ty'r Mynydd

Nant Bryncanol

Gelli-gaer Common

Union Brook

WESTERN DR
HILLSIDE VIEW
VALE VIEW
BERW RD
WILSON GDNS

Gwerthonor-ganol

1

Pen-heol-Adam

WIMBOURNE
TERR

Marchnad

HEOL ADAM

Tir-Adam-uchaf

Tir-Adam-isaf

Rhôs-yr-yrfa

Gwaun-
arlwyddes

Gelligaer
Court

Gwerthonor-uchaf

ST ANN ST 1
ST ANNE'S CRES 2
MAES-Y-CRAIG ST 3

GWERTHONOR LA

98

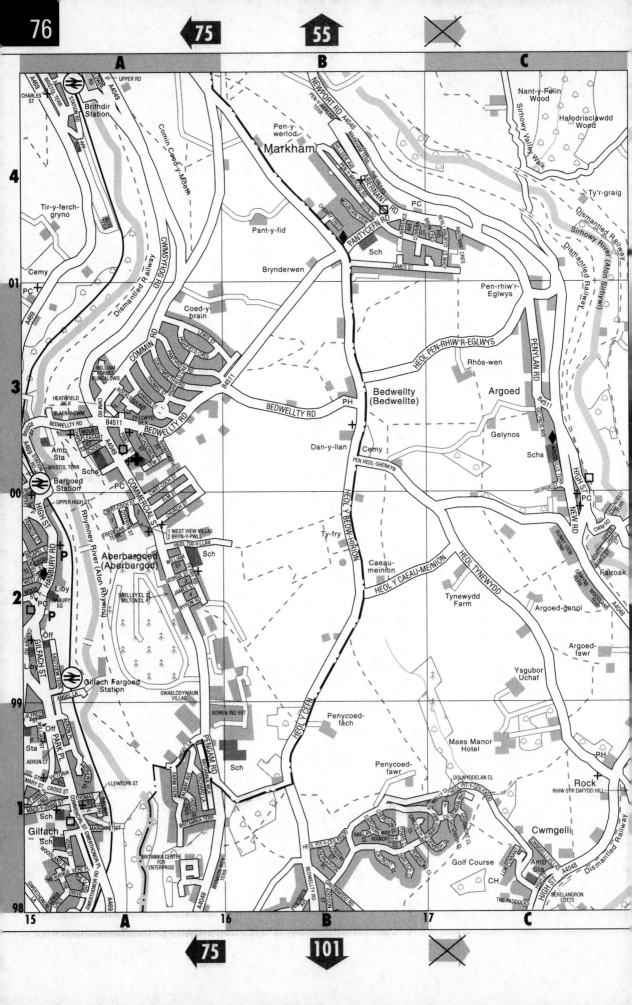

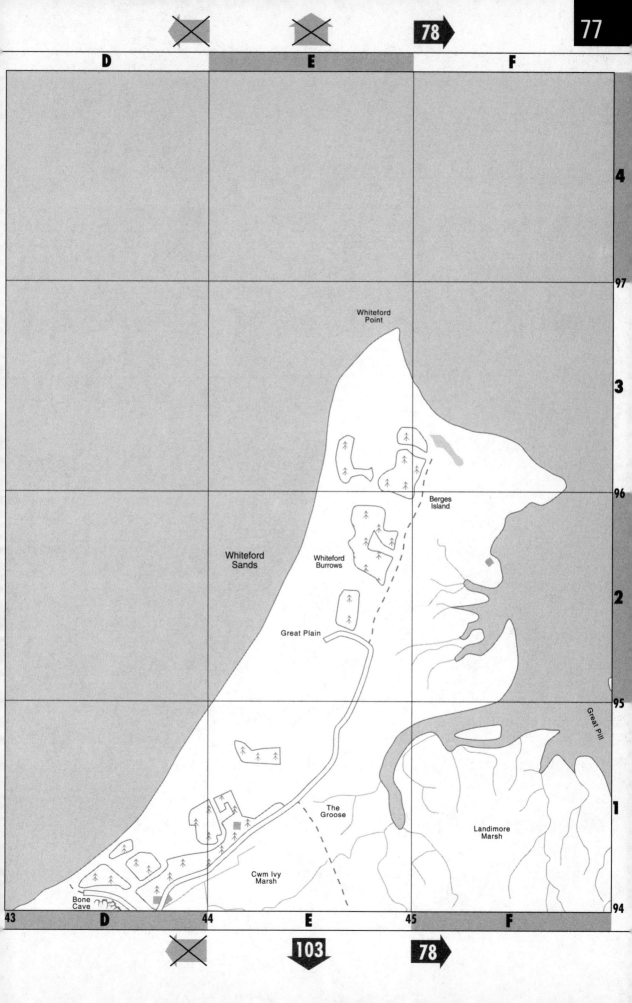

Whiteford
Point

Berges
Island

Whiteford
Sands

Whiteford
Burrows

Great Plain

Great Pill

The
Groose

Landimore
Marsh

Cwm Ivy
Marsh

Bone
Cave

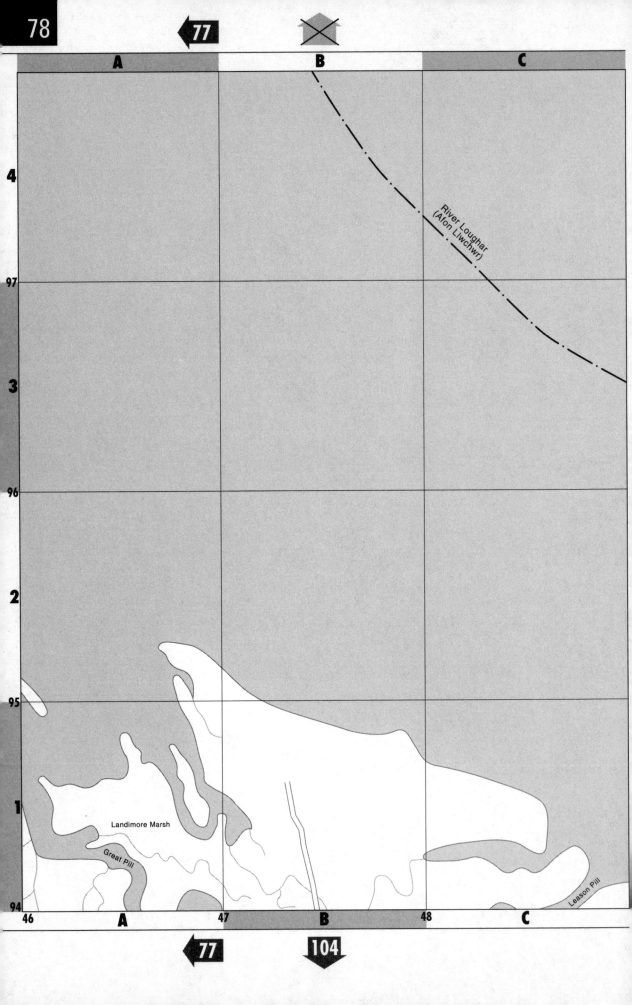

A B C

4

97

3

96

2

95

1

Landimore Marsh

Great Pill

94

46 47 48

A B C

River Loughar
(Afon Llwchwr)

Leason Pill

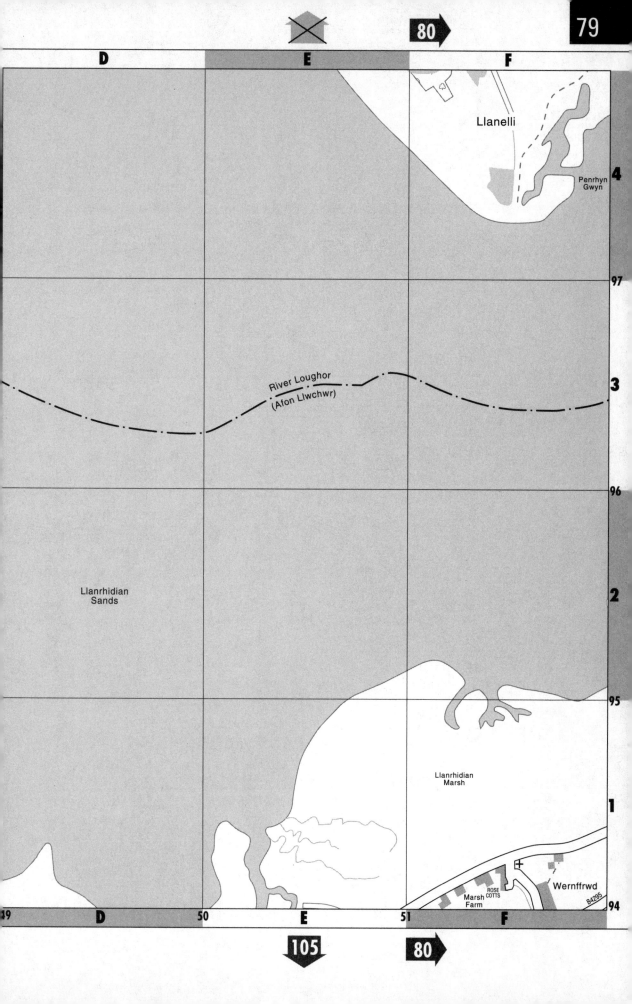

Llanelli

Penrhyn
Gwyn

4

97

River Loughor

(Afon Llwchwr)

3

96

Llanrhidian
Sands

2

95

Llanrhidian
Marsh

1

Wernffrwd

ROSE
COTTS
Marsh
Farm

B4295

94

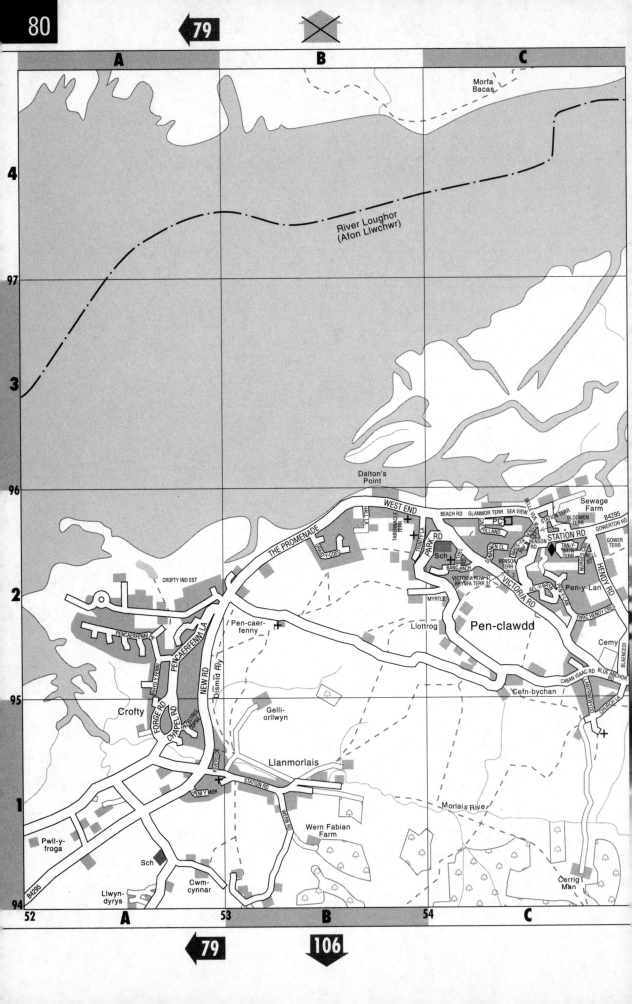

A B C

4

River Loughor
(Afon Llwchwr)

Morfa
Bacas

97

3

Dalton's
Point

96

WEST END

THE PROMENADE

BEACH RD GLANMOR TERR SEA VIEW

PC

STATION TERR

BLODWEN TERR

Sewage
Farm

B4295

STATION RD

GOWERTON RD

GOWER TERR

TABERNACLE TERR

TRINITY LA

PARK RD

Sch

BETHEL

CAPEL HOLLAND

PEN CL

BENSON TERR

BENSON TERR

TAN-Y-BRYN TERR

MILL ST

CROFTY IND EST

GRAIG-Y-COED

HALL LA

BANC BACH

VICTORIA ROW 1
BRYNFA TERR 2

NEL-Y-BRYN

VICTORIA RD

PEN-Y-CLAN

Pen-y-Lan

HENDY RD

2

PENCAERFENNI LA

Pen-caer-
fenny

MYRTLE

Llottrog

Pen-clawdd

PARC HENDY CRES

Cemy

BLAENCEDI

PENCAERFENNI LA

NEW RD

Dismtd Rly

Gelli-
orllwyn

Cefn-bychan

CABAN ISAAC RD

BLUE ANCHOR RD

95

Crofty

FORGE RD

CHAPEL RD

RHYD Y FENNI

MALLTREE COPSE

RIVERSIDE

LLANRHEWYDD

CHURCH LA

Llanmorlais

STATION RD

PEN Y MOR

1

WERN RD

Wern Fabian
Farm

Morlais River

Pwll-y-
froga

B4295

Sch

Cwm-
cynnar

Cerrig
Man

Llwyn-
dyrys

94

52 A 53 B 54 C

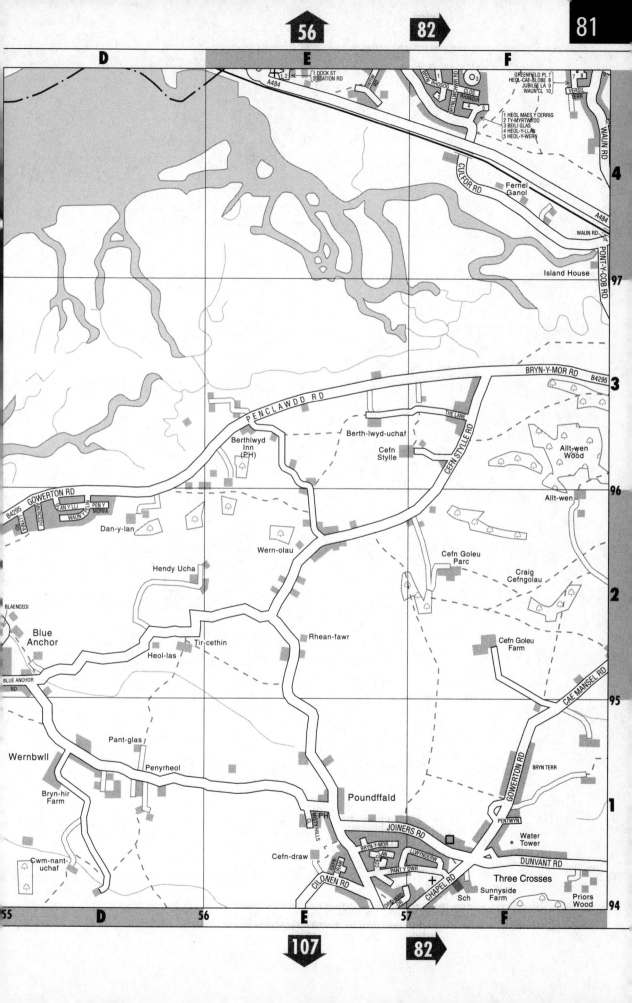

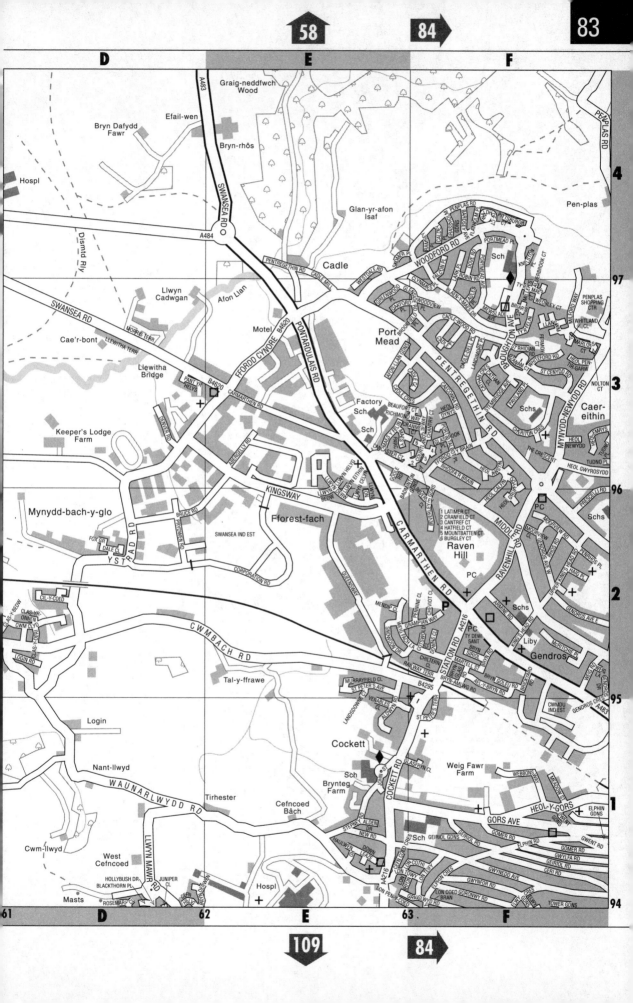

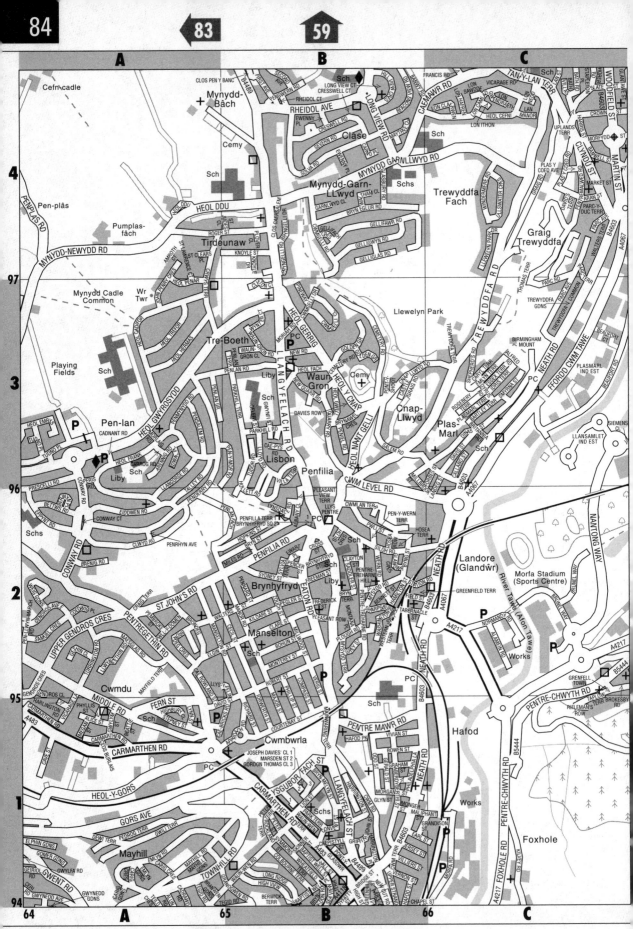

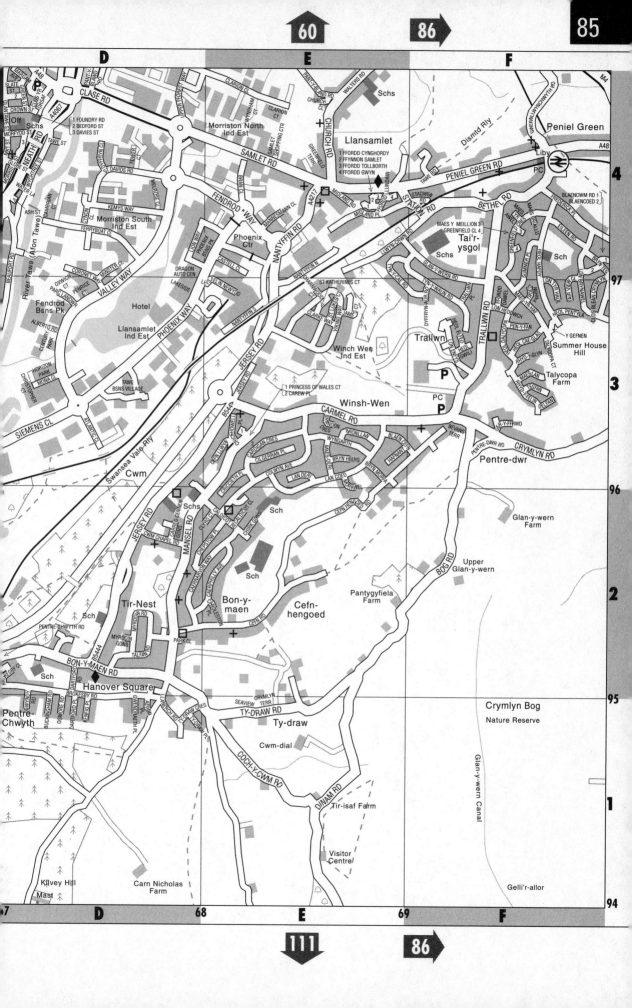

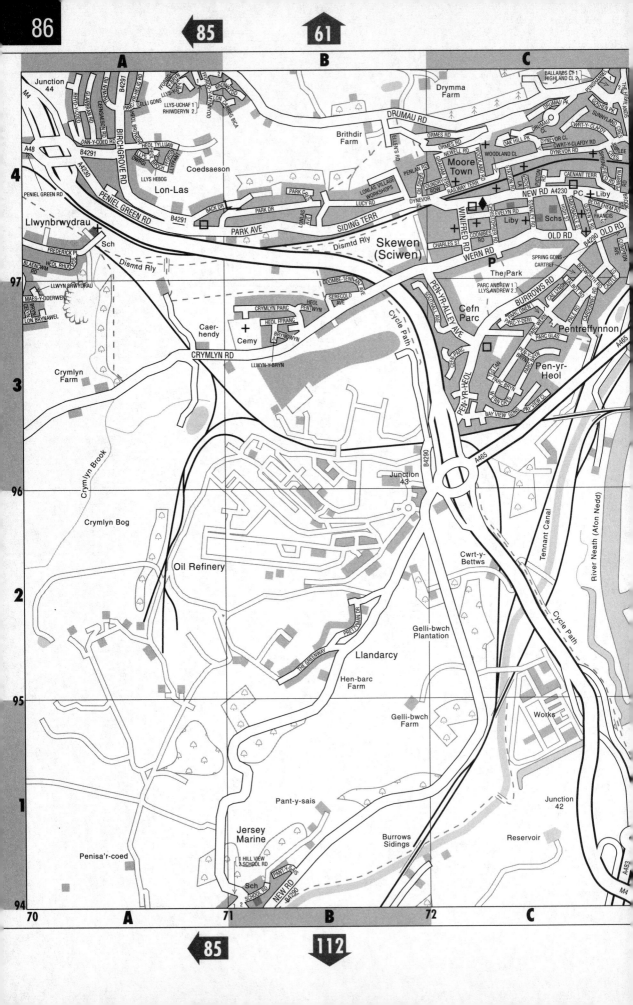

NEATH
(CASTELL-NEDD)

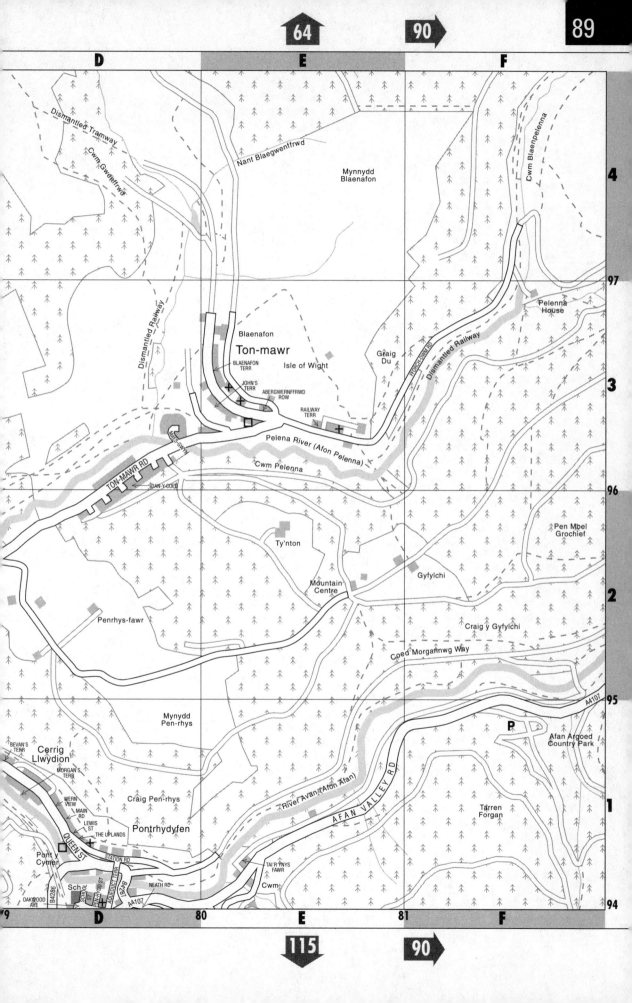

D
E
F

4

97

Dismantled Tramway

Cwm Gwenffrwd

Nant Blaegwenffrwd

Mynnydd
Blaenafon

Cwm Blaenpelenna

Pelenna
House

Dismantled Railway

PORTCHENNA RD

Dismantled Railway

Blaenafon

Ton-mawr

Isle of Wight

Graig
Du

BLAENAFON
TERR

JOHN'S
TERR

ABERGWERNFFRWD
ROW

RAILWAY
TERR

3

MAES-GWYN

TON-MAWR RD

DAN-Y-COED

Pelena River (Afon Pelenna)

Cwm Pelenna

96

Ty'nton

Pen Moel
Grochief

Mountain
Centre

Gyfylchi

2

Penrhys-fawr

Craig y Gyfylchi

Coed Morgannwg Way

95

Mynydd
Pen-rhys

P

Afan Argoed
Country Park

BEVAN'S
TERR

Cerrig
Llwydion

MORGAN'S
TERR

WERN
VIEW

MAIN
RD

LEWIS
ST

Craig Pen-rhys

River Avan (Afon Afan)

AFAN VALLEY RD

Tarren
Forgan

1

THE UPLANDS

Pontrhydyfen

QUEEN ST

Pont y
Cymer

STATION RD

SCHOOL
ST

PENTYLD ST

AQUEDUCT TERR

B4287

NEATH RD

TAI'R YNYS
FAWR

Cwm

OAKWOOD
AVE

B4286

A4107

94

'9
D
80
E
81
F

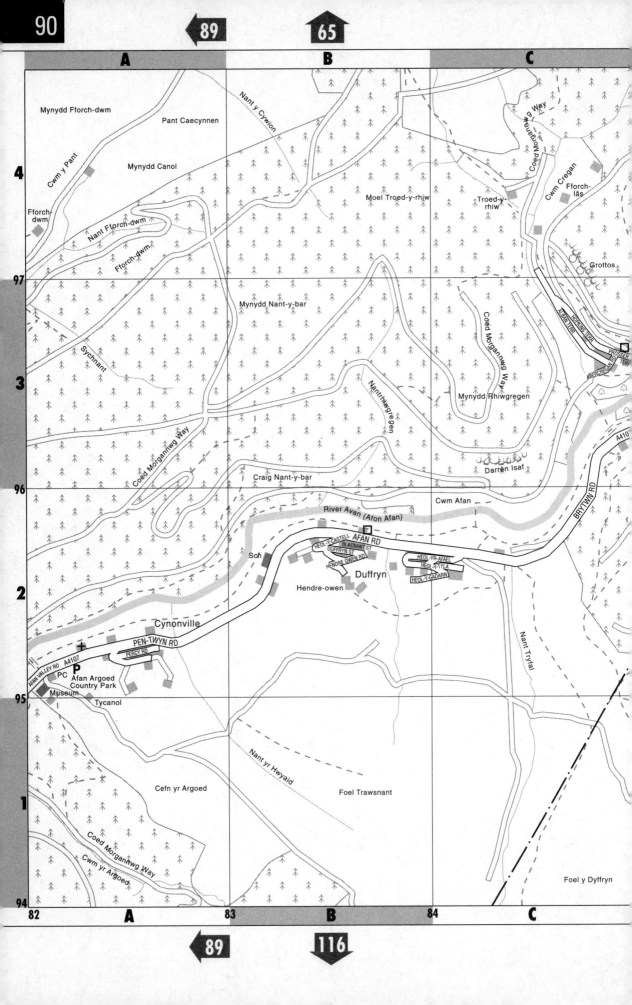

A

B

C

4

Mynydd Fforch-dwm

Pant Caecynnen

Cwm y Pant

Mynydd Canol

Nant y Cywion

Moel Troed-y-rhiw

Troed-y-rhiw

Cwm Cregan

Fforch-lâs

Coed Morgannwg Way

Fforch-dwm

Nant Fforch-dwm

Fforch-dwm

Grottos

97

Sychnant

Mynydd Nant-y-bar

Coed Morgannwg Way

Mynydd Rhiwgregen

HOPKINS TERR

AFAN TERR

PROSSER TERR

ABERCREGAN

3

Coed Morgannwg Way

Nantrhiwgregen

Darren Isaf

A410

BRYTWN RD

96

Craig Nant-y-bar

River Avan (Afon Afan)

Cwm Afan

AFAN RD

HEOL-Y-CASTELL

BLAENANT ST

DUFFRYN ST

HENDRE OWEN RD

Sch

Duffryn

HEOL-YR-AFAEL

HEOL-Y-TYLA

HEOL-Y-GADARN

2

Cynonville

Hendre-owen

Nant Tryfal

PEN-TWYN RD

PERCY RD

AFAN VALLEY RD   A4107

PC

P

Afan Argoed
Country Park

95

Museum

Tycanol

Cefn yr Argoed

Nant yr Hwyaid

Foel Trawsnant

1

Coed Morgannwg Way

Cwm yr Argoed

Foel y Dyffryn

94

82

A

83

B

84

C

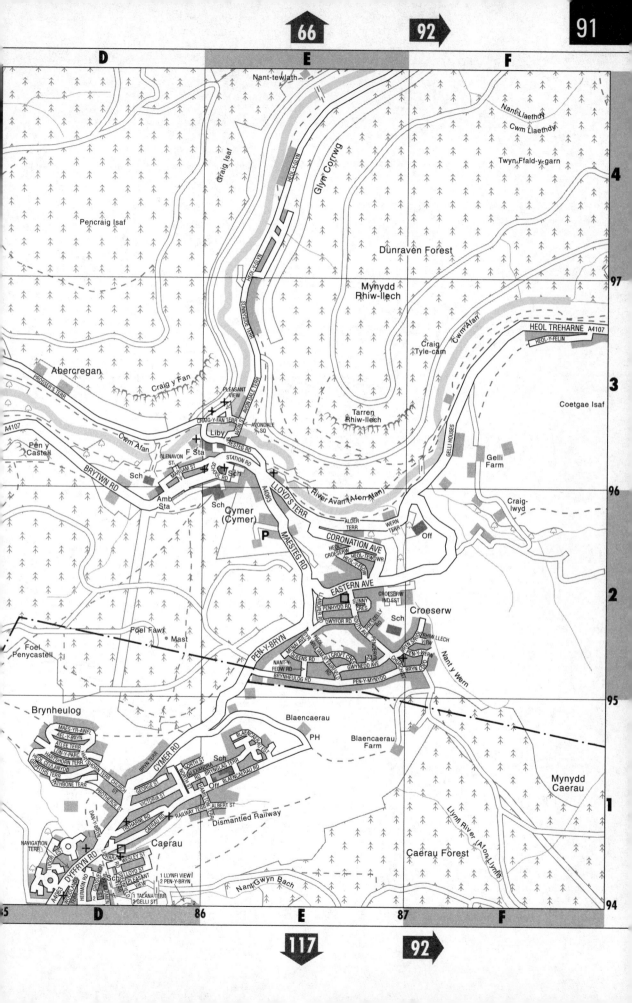

Nant-tewlath

Nant Llaethdy
Cwm Llaethdy

Twyn Ffald-y-garn

4

Dunraven Forest

Mynydd
Rhiw-llech
97

Glyn Corrwg

Cwm Afan

HEOL TREHARNE A4107
HEOL-Y-FELIN

Craig
Tyle-cam

Coetgae Isaf

3

Abercregan
Craig y Fan

PLEASANT VIEW

PROSSER'S TERR

Gelli Houses

Gelli
Farm

Liby

Cwm Afan
CRAIG-Y-FAN TERR
AVONDALE SQ

Craig-
Iwyd

A4107

Pen y
Castell
GLENAVON ST

F Sta

STATION RD

River Avan (Afon Afan)

96

BRYTWN RD

Sch

MARGAM ST

OXFORD RD

Sch

Amb
Sta

Sch

Cymer
(Cymer)

MAESTEG RD

LLOYD'S TERR

A4063

ALDER
TERR

WERN
TERR

Off

CORONATION AVE

HEOL
CROESERW

HEOL-TEWDWR

HEOL-Y-FFLOYW

P

EASTERN AVE

CROESERW
IND EST

PENHYDD RD

SUNNY
CRES

Sch

Croeserw

2

Foel Fawr
Mast

PEN-Y-BRYN

LLANDDER RD

MENAI AVE

SOUTH AVE

PRYSGELLY

PENDERYN

RHIW LLECH
VIEW

BRYN SAVO
CHURCH ST

PEN-Y-WERN

Foel
Penycastell

NANT-Y-
FEOW RD

QUEENS RD

HILLCROFT CRES

GWYNEDD AVE

BRYN CAE

Nant y Wern

BRYNHEULOG RD

DWYFOR RD

PEN-Y-MYNYDD

95

Brynheulog

Blaencaerau

MAES-YR-AWEL
AEL-Y-BRYN

BLAEN TERR

PH

Blaencaerau
Farm

HEOL-Y-PARC
HANTSHORN TERR
GRIFFITHS TERR
RATHBONE TERR

ONLY-PARC

CYMER RD

NORTH ST

Sch

Mynydd
Caerau

BRYN TERR

GEORGE ST

ALEXANDRA ST

BRYNGLAS TERR

BLAENCAERAU RD

1

VICTORIA ST

Off

PROTHEROE ST

TREHARNE RD

CAERAU RD

ALBERT ST

Dismantled Railway

Navigation
Terr

DYFFRYN RD

RAILWAY TERR

Caerau Forest

Llynfi River (Afon Llynfi)

Caerau

PLEASANT ST

Sch

HERMON RD

1 LLYNFI VIEW
2 PEN-Y-BRYN

A4063

Nant Gwyn Bach

1 TALANA TERR
2 GELLI ST

94

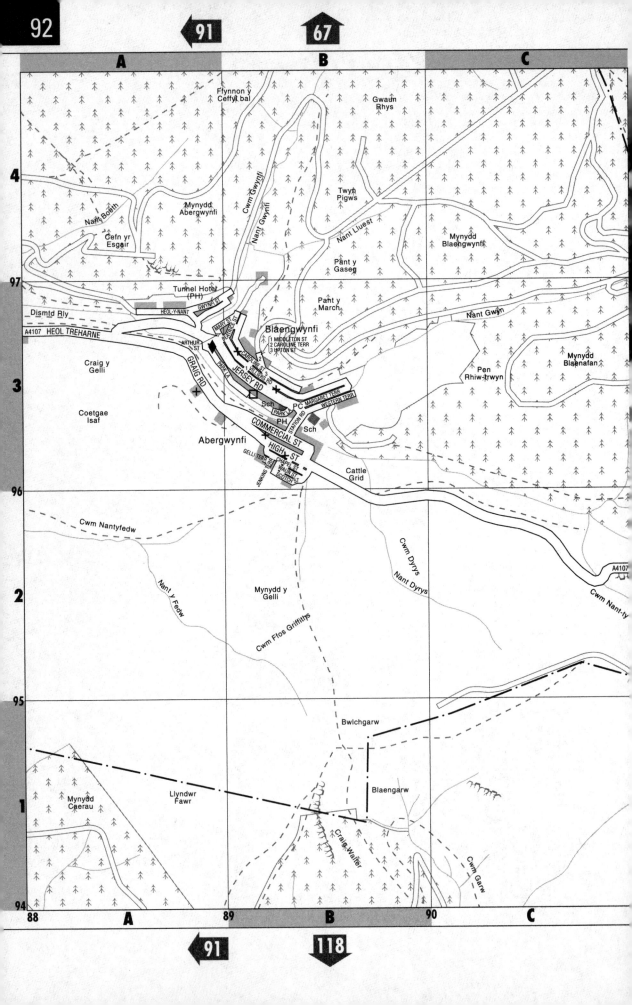

A B C

4

Ffynnon y
Ceffyl bal

Gwaun
Rhys

Cwm Gwynfi

Mynydd
Abergwynfi

Nant Gwynfi

Twyn
Pigws

Nant y Boeth

Mynydd
Blaengwynfi

Cefn yr
Esgair

Nant Lluest

97

Pant y
Gaseg

Tunnel Hotel
(PH)

Pant y
March

GWYN ST

Dismtd Rly

HEOL-Y-NANT

Nant Gwyn

A4107 HEOL TREHARNE

MAEN ST

BEATRICE ST

Blaengwynfi

1 MIDDLETON ST
2 CAROLINE TERR
3 UPTON ST

ARTHUR
ST

Craig y
Gelli

PARK LA

CAROLINE ST

3

GRAIG RD

JERSEY RD

HILL TERR

Pen
Rhiw-trwyn

Mynydd
Blaenafan

Coetgae
Isaf

PARK

MARGARET TERR

WESTERN TERR

STATION RD

PC

PH

Sch

Abergwynfi

COMMERCIAL ST

Sch

HIGH ST

GELLI TERR

CHAPEL ST

Cattle
Grid

JENKINS TERR

MAUN ST

SCOTCH ST

96

Cwm Nantyfedw

Cwm Dyrys

Nant Dyrys

A4107

Cwm Nant-ty

2

Nant y Fedw

Mynydd y
Gelli

Cwm Ffos Griffiths

95

Bwlchgarw

Blaengarw

1

Mynydd
Caerau

Llyndwr
Fawr

Craig Walter

Cwm Garw

94

88 A 89 B 90 C

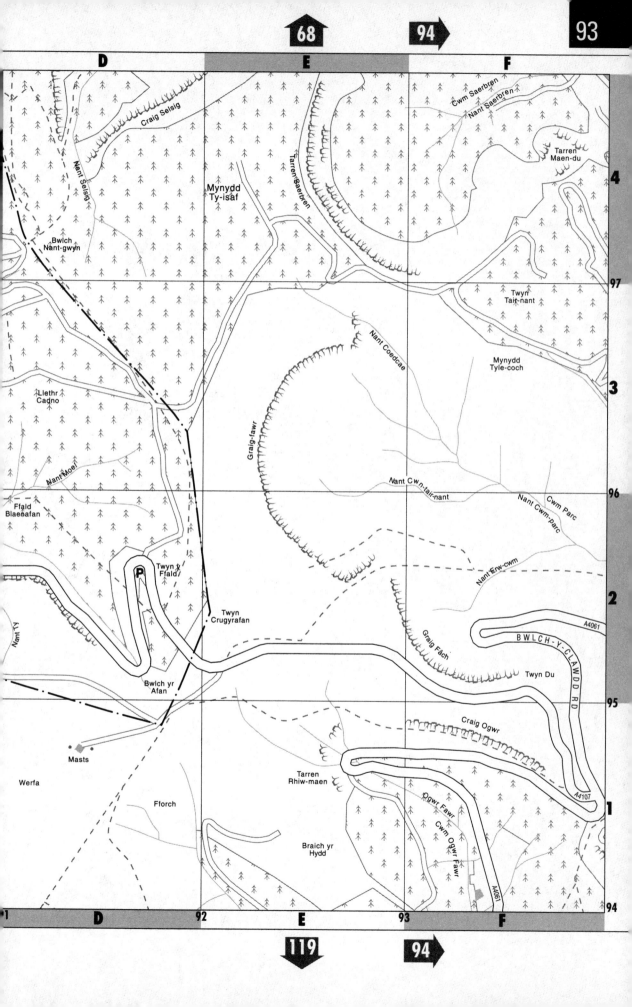

D
E
F

Cwm Saerbren
Nant Saerbren

Craig Selsig

Tarren Maen-du

Nant Selsig

4

Mynydd
Ty-isaf

Tarren Saerbren

Bwlch
Nant-gwyn

97

Twyn
Tait-nant

Nant Coedcae

Mynydd
Tyle-coch

Llethr
Cadno

3

Graig-fawr

Nant Cwm-fair-nant

Nant Moel

Cwm Parc

96

Nant Cwm-parc

Ffald
Blaenafan

Nant Erw-cwm

P

Twyn y
Ffald

2

A4061

Graig Fách

BWLCH-Y-CLAWDD RD

Nant Ty

Twyn
Crugyrafan

Twyn Du

Bwlch yr
Afan

95

Craig Ogwr

Masts

Werfa

Tarren
Rhiw-maen

A4107

Fforch

Ogwr Fawr

1

Cwm Ogwr Fawr

Braich yr
Hydd

A4061

D
92
E
93
F
94

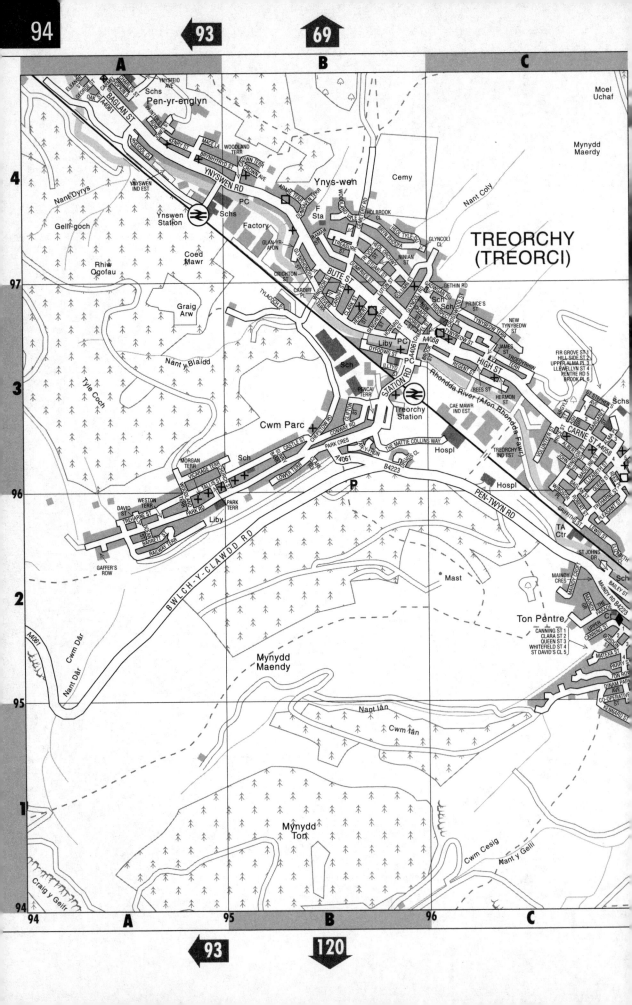

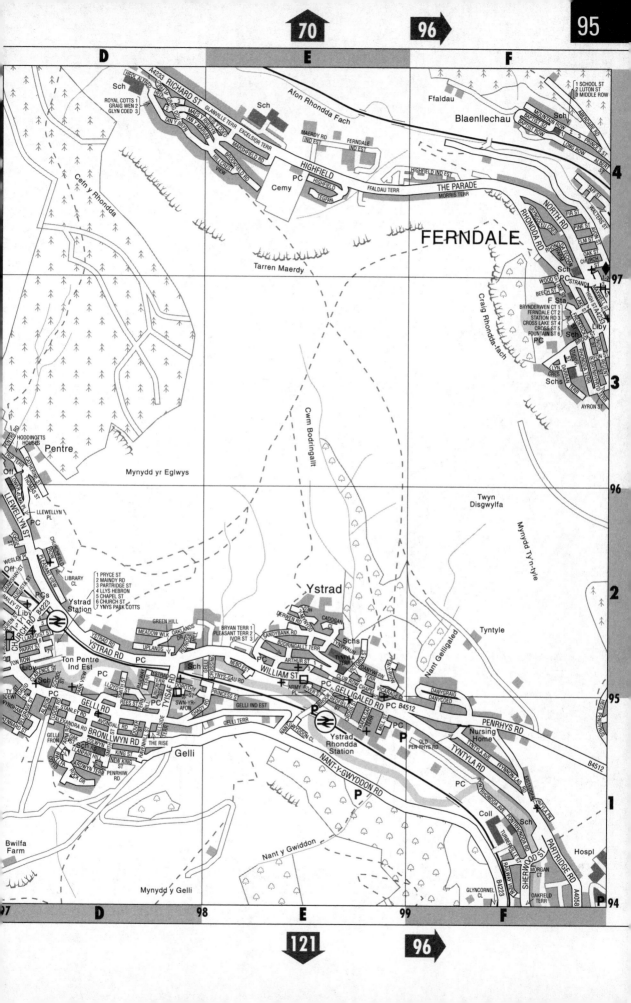

D
E
F

RICHARD ST
A4233

Sch
ROYAL COTTS 1
GRAIG WEN 2
GLYN COED 3

HIROL ALFRED
CHERRY HILL

Afon Rhondda Fach
Ffaldau
Blaenllechau

1 SCHOOL ST
2 LUTON ST
3 MIDDLE ROW

MOUNTAIN ROW
BAPTIST SQ
BAPTIST ROW
LONG ROW
ALBERT ST
PRINCE'S ST
ABERDARE RD
Sch

GLANVILLE TERR
EXCELSIOR TERR
Sch
MAERDY RD
IND EST
FERNDALE
IND EST

MARSHFIELD RD
BROOKFIELD RD
HILLCREST
VIEW

MAES Y TALWRN
TAN Y BRYN
TAN Y MARIAN

HIGHFIELD
PC
Cemy
HIGHFIELD
TEGFAN

FFALDAU TERR
MORRIS TERR
THE PARADE
HIGHFIELD IND EST

FERNDALE

NORTH RD
RHONDDA RD
BAKERS ELL CRES
FIR ST
PINE ST
ELM ST
OAK ST
CHURCH ST
WALTERS RD
TAFF ST
4

Cefn y Rhondda

Tarren Maerdy

Cwm Bodringallt

Craig Rhondda-fach

WOOD ST
BEECH ST
F Sta
BRYNDERWEN CT 1
FERNDALE CT 2
STATION RD 3
CROSS LAKE ST 4
CROSS ST 5
FOUNTAIN ST 6
PC
Sch
Sch
Liby
97

LLYN
CRES
DYFFRYN TERR
IRFON TERR
RHONDDA TERR
UNION ST
Schs
AYRON ST
3

Pentre
PENTRE RD
HODDINOTTS
HOUSES
Off
RIP TERR
CATHERINE ST
THOMAS ST

Mynydd yr Eglwys

LLEWELLYN ST
LLEWELLYN PL
PC

Twyn
Disgwylfa

Mynydd Ty'n-tyle

96

LIBRARY CL
CHURCHFIELD
ROW
1 PRYCE ST
2 MAINDY RD
3 PARTRIDGE ST
4 LLYS HEBRON
5 CHAPEL ST
6 CHURCH ST
7 YNYS PARK COTTS

WESLEY ST
Off

Ystrad Station

Ystrad

Tyntyle

Nant Gelligaled

2

RAILEY ST
PCs
Liby
CHURCH RD
B4223

LLANTOIST ST
TON ROW
Liby

YSTRAD RD
STRAD RD
GREEN HILL
MEADOW WLK
OAKLANDS
DRI
UPLANDS

BRYAN TERR 1
PLEASANT TERR 2
IVOR ST 3
SANDYBANK RD
DERWEN RD
MARIAN
BODRINGALLT TERR
CADOGAN
CL
TYN'YWAUN

Schs
TYN'LA
TERR
DANYWERN
PC
DANYGRAIG
DANYCOED

PENRHYS RD
Nursing
Home
B4512
95

Ton Pentre
Ind Est
PC
Sch
GELLI RD
PC
PC

CROSSING
YNYS-GAU RD
NERO EST
PC
WILLIAM ST
ARTHUR ST
1
2
ARMY
PL
RIVER ST
GELLIGALED RD
PC B4512
CLUB ROW
CHAPEL ST
VICARAGE

TYNTYLA RD
FFYNNON CAS
FFYNNONAU
TYNTYLA AVE
B4512

TY
DEWI
GELLI RD
STANLEY RD
ALBION ST
ALEXANDRA RD
OAK ST
COLWYN
LLOYD ST
SMITH ST
REES ST
TYISAF RD
DOROTHY
SWN-YR-
AFON
PRINCESS ST
SHOP ST
GELLI IND EST

Gelli
GELLI
FRON
WYNDHAM
GELLI TERR
THE RISE
BRONLLWYN RD

CAE'R ODYN
NANT-Y-GWYDDON CL
Ystrad
Rhondda Station
P
P
OLD
PEN-RHYS RD

PON RHONDDA AVE
PONTRHONDDA RD
ESTERHY ST
DANYCOED

Sch
1

Bwilfa
Farm

Mynydd y Gelli

Nant y Gwiddon

NANT-Y-GWYDDON RD
P

Coll
Sch
PC

SHERWOOD ST
RAILWAY VIEW
TURBERVILLE ST
MORGAN
CT
GLYNCORNEL
CL
OAKFIELD
TERR
B4223
PARTRIDGE RD
A4058
Hospl
P
94

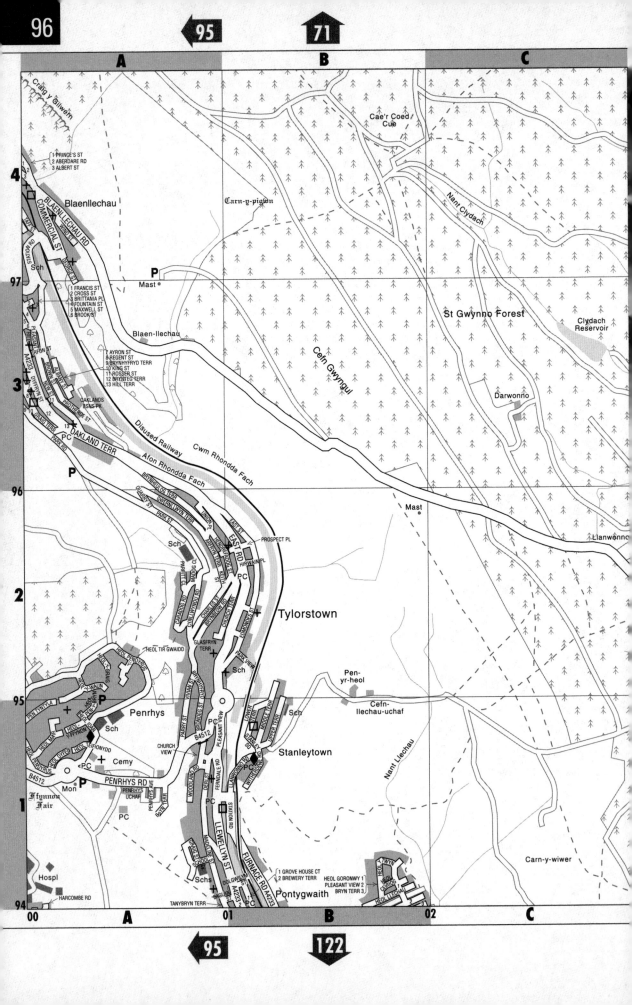

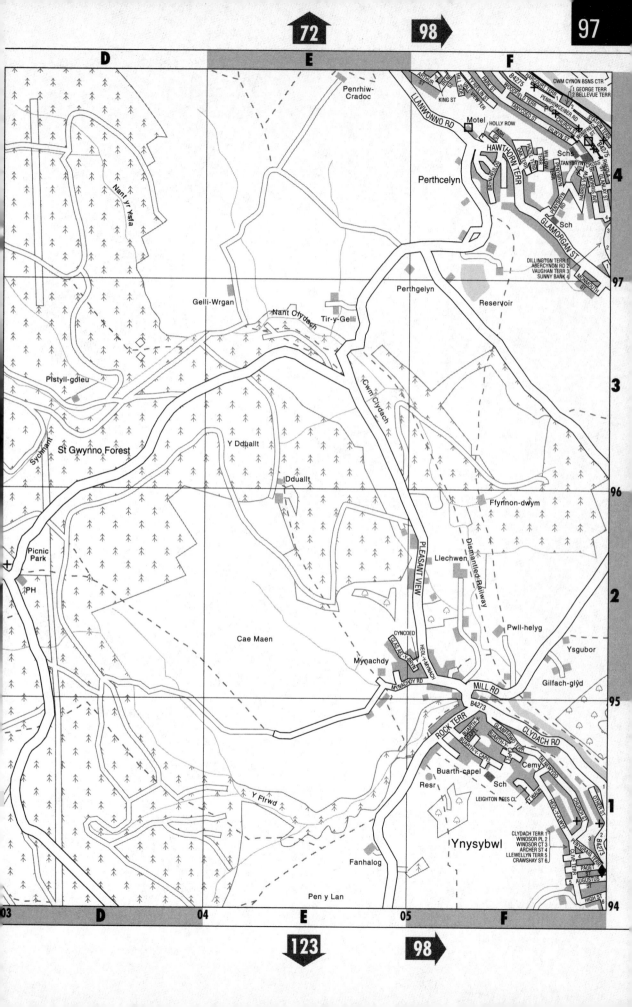

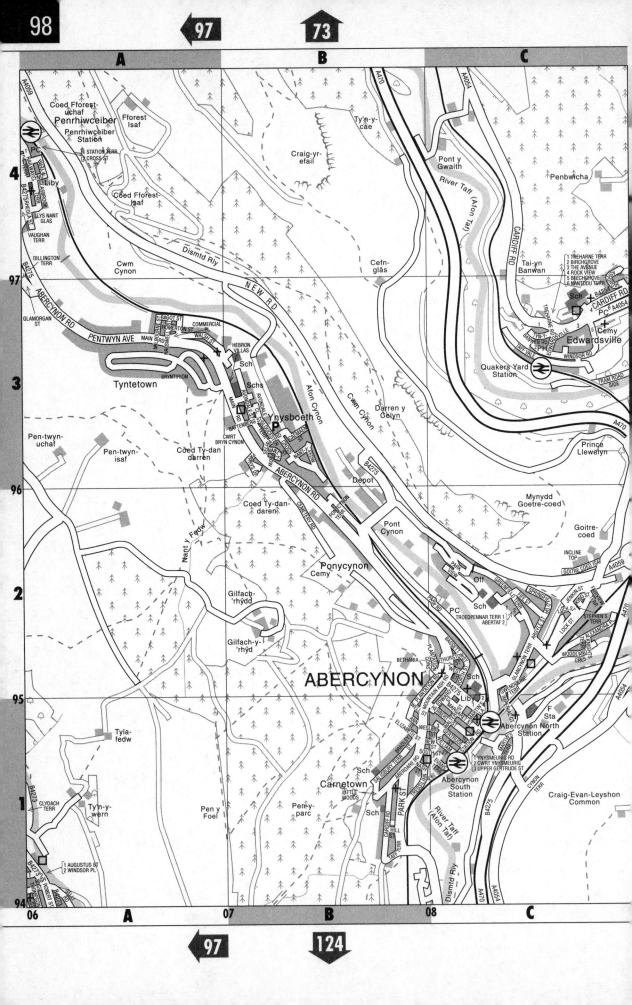

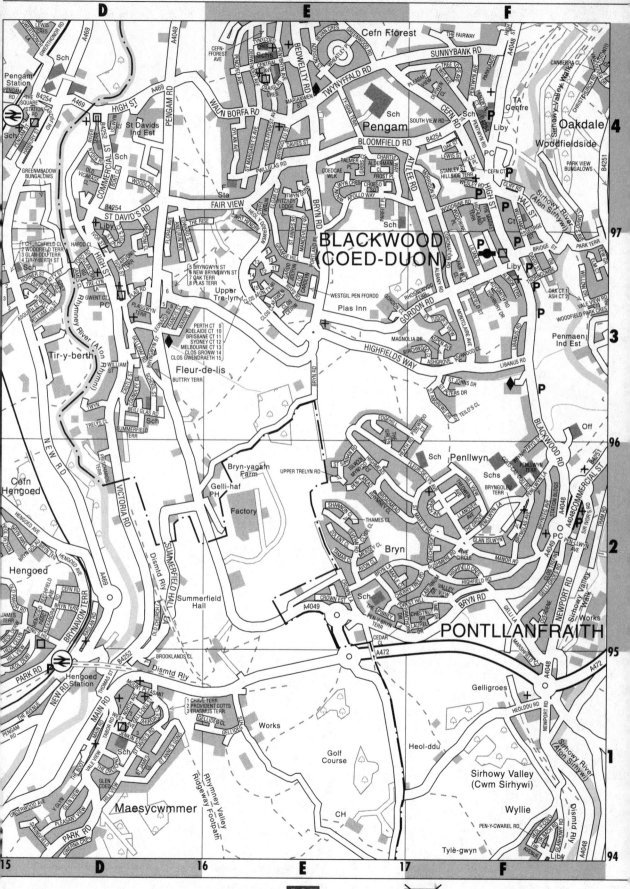

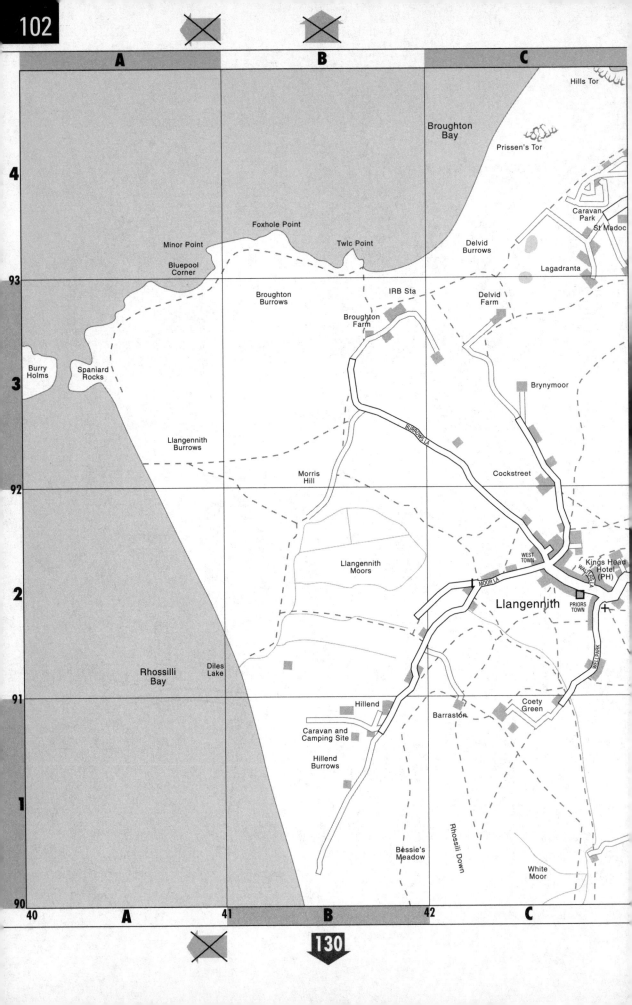

A   B   C

4

Hills Tor

Broughton
Bay

Prissen's Tor

Caravan
Park
St Madoc

Foxhole Point

Minor Point

Twlc Point

Delvid
Burrows

Lagadranta

Bluepool
Corner

93

Broughton
Burrows

IRB Sta

Delvid
Farm

Broughton
Farm

Burry
Holms

Spaniard
Rocks

3

Brynymoor

BURROWS LA

Llangennith
Burrows

Morris
Hill

Cockstreet

92

Llangennith
Moors

WEST
TOWN

Kings Head
Hotel
(PH)

WALTERS LA

2

MOOR LA

Llangennith

PRIORS
TOWN

Rhossilli
Bay

Diles
Lake

WELL PARK

91

Hillend

Coety
Green

Barraston

Caravan and
Camping Site

Hillend
Burrows

1

Bessie's
Meadow

Rhossili Down

White
Moor

90

40   A   41   B   42   C

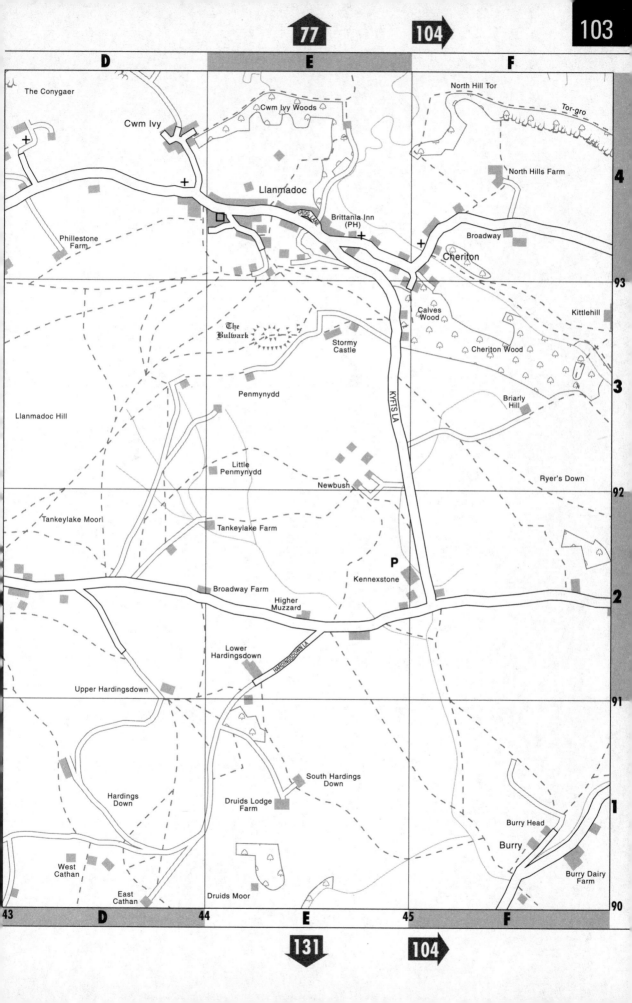

The Conygaer

Cwm Ivy

Cwm Ivy Woods

North Hill Tor

Tor-gro

North Hills Farm

4

Llanmadoc

FROG LANE

Brittania Inn
(PH)

Broadway

Cheriton

Phillestone
Farm

93

Calves
Wood

Kittlehill

The Bulwark

Stormy
Castle

Cheriton Wood

3

Penmynydd

KYFTS LA

Briarly
Hill

Llanmadoc Hill

Little
Penmynydd

Ryer's Down

Newbush

92

Tankeylake Moor

Tankeylake Farm

Broadway Farm

P

Kennexstone

2

Higher
Muzzard

Lower
Hardingsdown

HARDINGSDOWN LA

Upper Hardingsdown

91

South Hardings
Down

Hardings
Down

Druids Lodge
Farm

Burry Head

1

Burry

West
Cathan

Burry Dairy
Farm

East
Cathan

Druids Moor

90

103

78

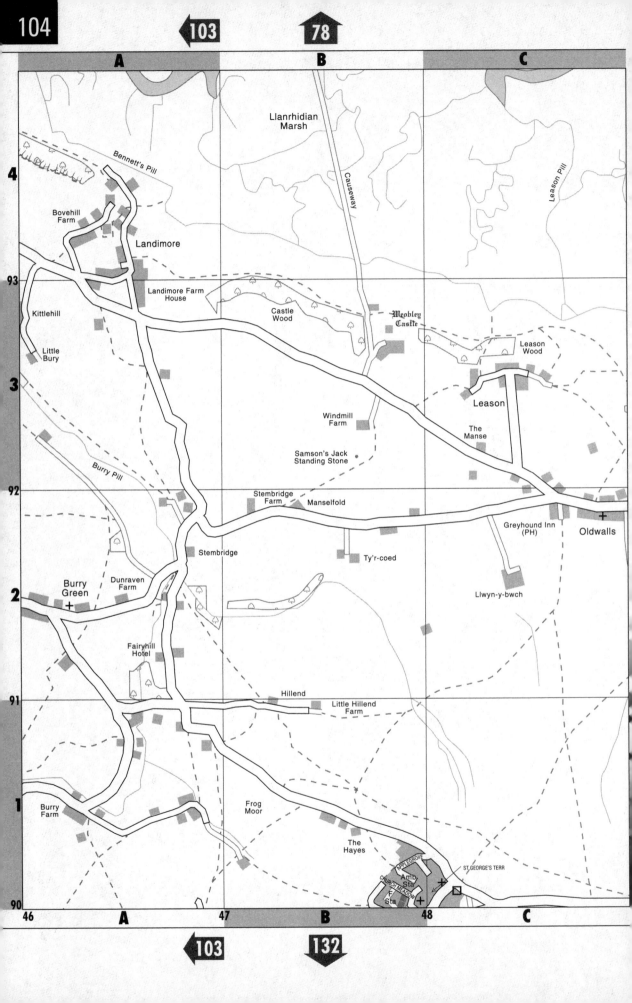

103

132

79
106

D
E
F
ORCHARD TERR
B4295
Aber-Login
4
Llanallen
Caravan Site
Welsh Moor Farm
Little Wern-Halog
Nant y wrach
Wern-halog Farm
Wern-halog Wood
93
The Common
Welsh Moor
3
Staffal Haegr
Llanrhidian
Woodfield House
Cilifor Top
Dolphin Inn (PH)
MILL LA
Pen-yr-allt
Penrhallt Farm
Prysg
Cae Ifor Farm
MALT HALL
B4295
92
Sch
THE CROSS
B4271
Parc-y-rhedyn
Black Park Farm
Crickton
Cillibion Park Farm
Little Cillibion
2
Stonyford
Cae-Morgan
B4271
Pen-y-crug
Cillibion
Moormills
Freedown
Broad Pool
91
Decoy Wood
Little Bryngwyn
Arthur's Stone
1
Water Works
90
49
D
50
E
51
F

133
106

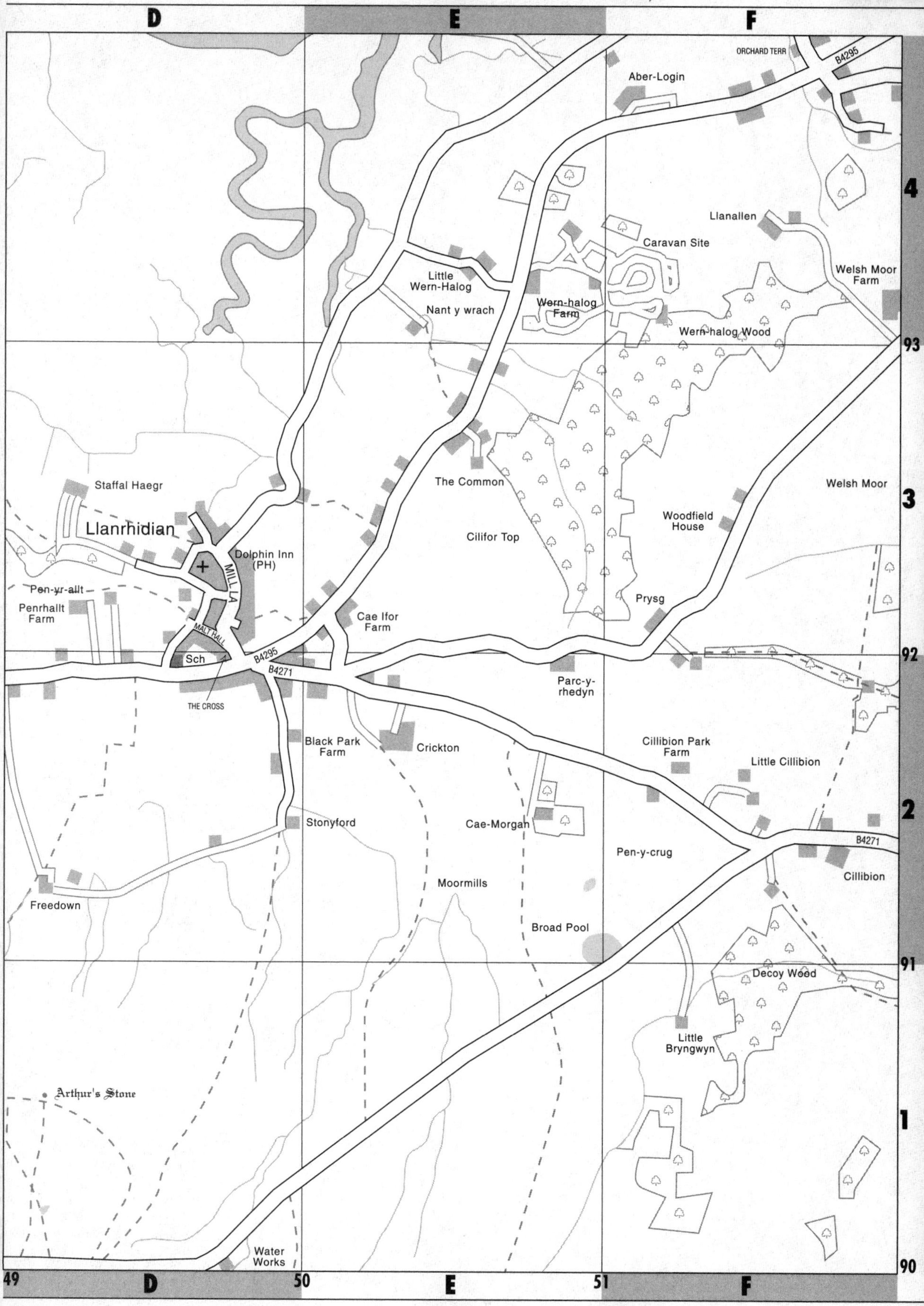

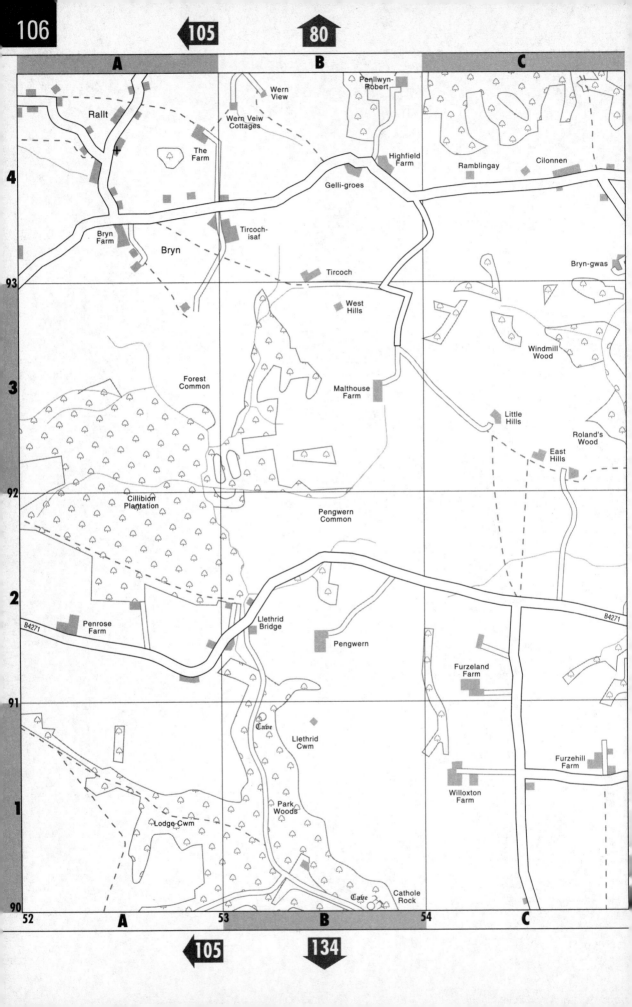

A   B   C

Rallt

Wern View

Wern Veiw Cottages

Penllwyn-Robert

The Farm

Highfield Farm

Ramblingay

Cilonnen

4

Gelli-groes

Bryn Farm

Tircoch-isaf

Bryn

Tircoch

Bryn-gwas

93

West Hills

Windmill Wood

Forest Common

Malthouse Farm

Little Hills

Roland's Wood

3

East Hills

92

Cillibion Plantation

Pengwern Common

B4271

2

Penrose Farm

Llethrid Bridge

Pengwern

Furzeland Farm

B4271

91

Cave

Llethrid Cwm

Furzehill Farm

1

Park Woods

Lodge Cwm

Willoxton Farm

90

Cave

Cathole Rock

52   A   53   B   54   C

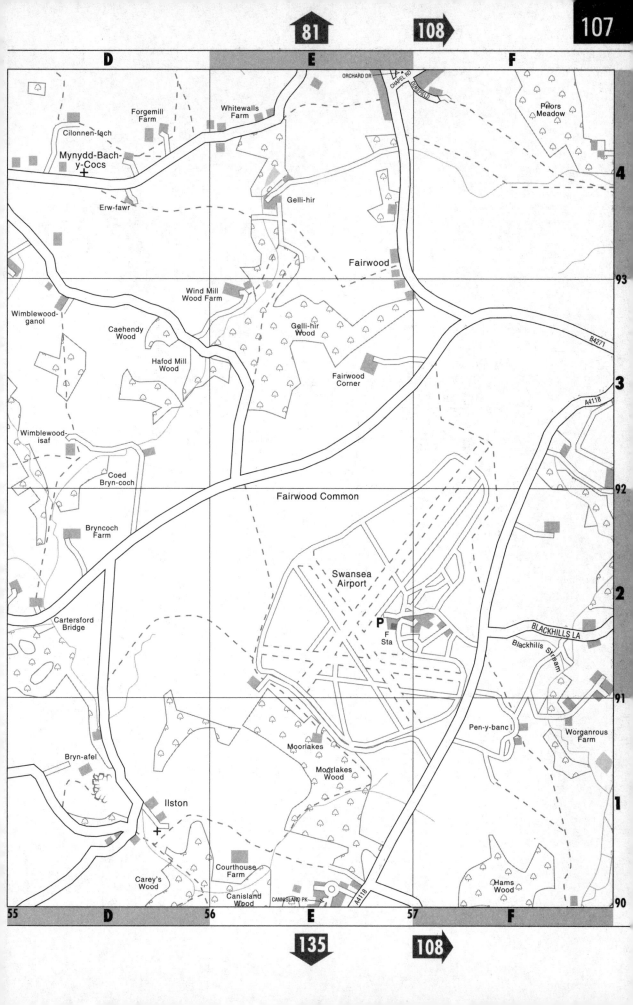

D

E

F

ORCHARD DR
CHAPEL RD
LAKEFIELD

Priors
Meadow

Cilonnen-fach

Forgemill
Farm

Whitewalls
Farm

Mynydd-Bach-
y-Cocs

Erw-fawr

Gelli-hir

4

Fairwood

93

B4271

Wimblewood-
ganol

Wind Mill
Wood Farm

Caehendy
Wood

Gelli-hir
Wood

A4118

Hafod Mill
Wood

Fairwood
Corner

3

Wimblewood-
isaf

Coed
Bryn-coch

Fairwood Common

92

Bryncoch
Farm

Swansea
Airport

Cartersford
Bridge

P
F
Sta

BLACKHILLS LA

Blackhills Stream

2

91

Pen-y-banc l

Worganrous
Farm

Bryn-afel

Moorlakes

Moorlakes
Wood

Ilston

1

Carey's
Wood

Courthouse
Farm

Hams
Wood

Canisland
Wood

CANNISLAND PK

A4118

90

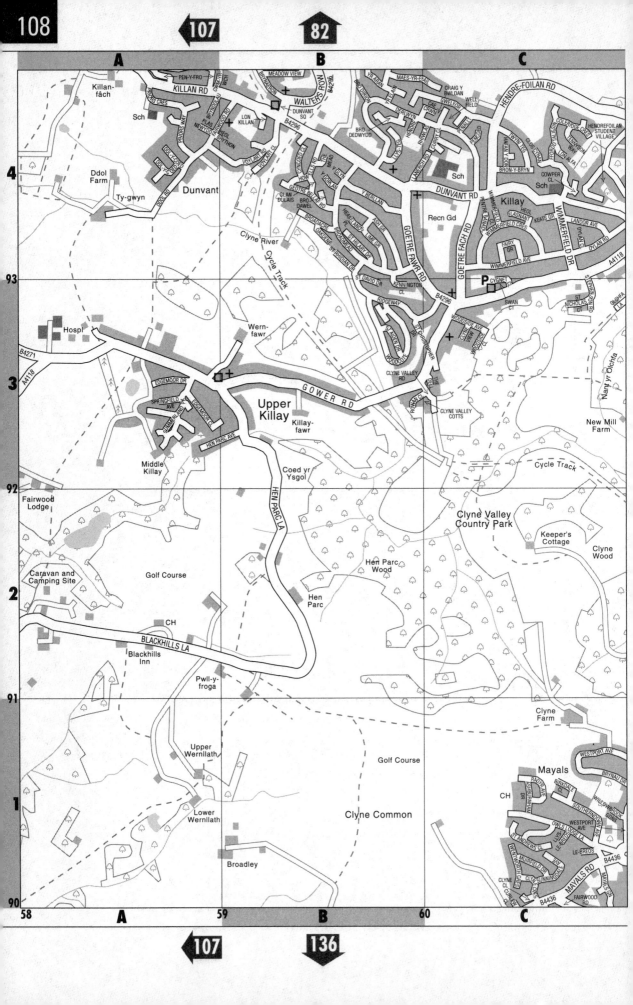

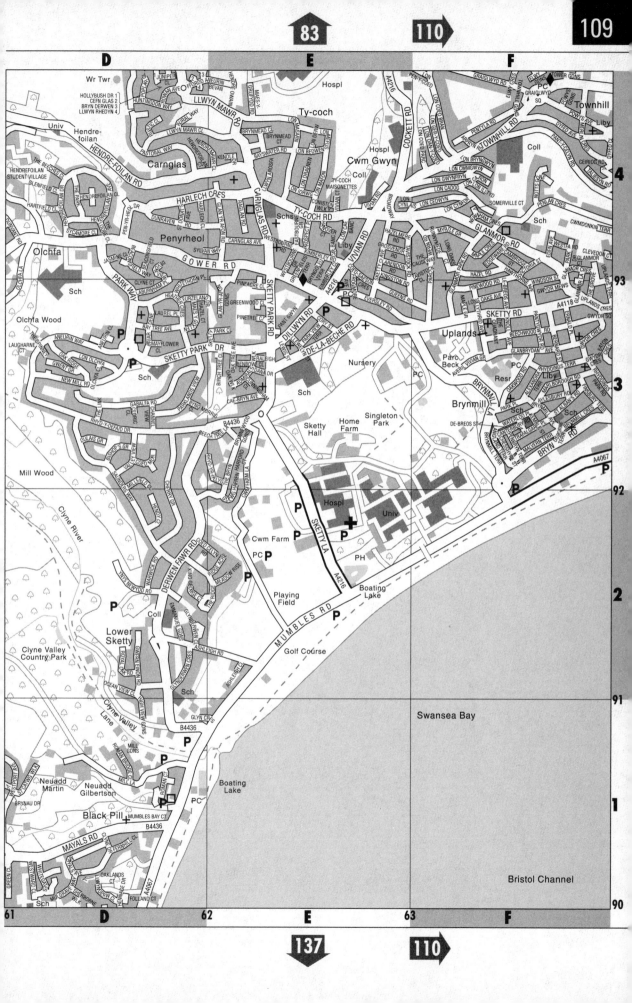

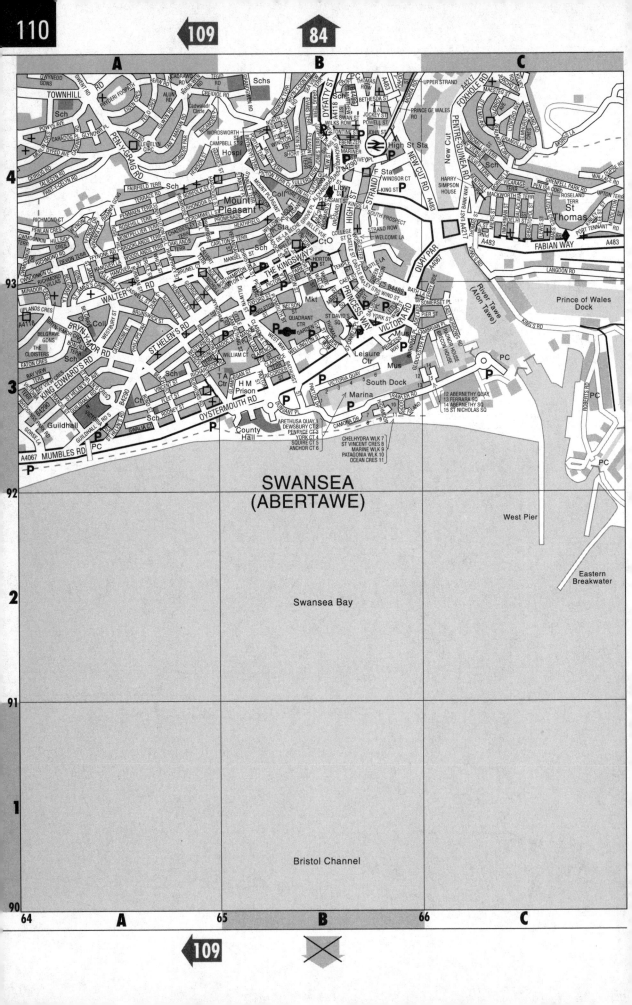

SWANSEA
(ABERTAWE)

Swansea Bay

Bristol Channel

Prince of Wales
Dock

West Pier

Eastern
Breakwater

TOWNHILL

Mount
Pleasant

THE KINGSWAY

PRINCESS WAY

Guildhall

County
Hall

Marina

South Dock

Leisure
Ctr

St
Thomas

FABIAN WAY

Prince of Wales
Dock

ARETHUSA QUAY 1
DEWSBURY CT 2
PENRYCE CT 3
YORK CT 4
SQUIRE CT 5
ANCHOR CT 6

CHELHYDRA WLK 7
ST VINCENT CRES 8
MARINE WLK 9
PATAGONIA WLK 10
OCEAN CRES 11

12 ABERNETHY QUAY
13 FERRARA SQ
14 ABERNETHY SQ
15 ST NICHOLAS SQ

85
112

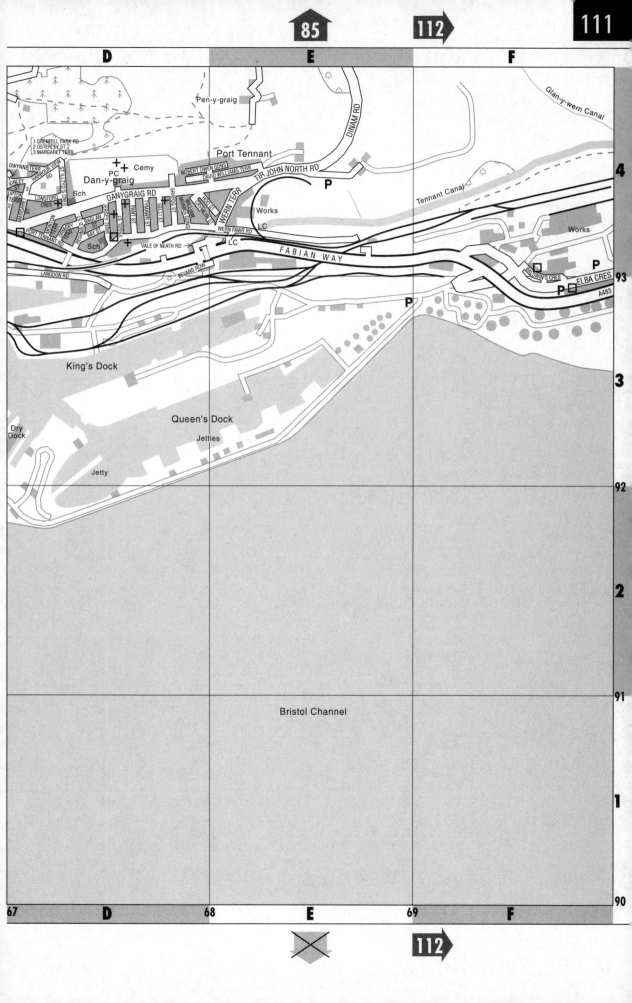

D **E** **F**

Pen-y-graig

Glan-y-wern Canal

DINAM RD

Port Tennant

1 GRENFELL PARK RD
2 OSTERLEY ST
3 MARGARET TERR

ROBERT OWEN GDNS

DAVID WILLIAMS TERR

TIR JOHN NORTH RD

4

GWYNNE TERR

HARBOUR VIEW RD

KINLEY ST

UPTON TERR

MARGARET ST

LONGFORD CRES

Cemy

PC

Dan-y-graig

Sch

DANYGRAIG RD

SILLTYDS CRES

TONTON TERR

HEORNIS

CRASBY ST

BAGLAN ST

BAY ST

JERSEY TERR

GRABOG ST

MORRIS GDNS

WILLIAM

PANT ST

YMAWR ST

DOCK ST

BRYN ST

WERN TERR

GELLI ST

S TOSA

BRYN NEWT

Works

Tennant Canal

Works

P

P

Port Tennant RD

Sch

VALE OF NEATH RD

LC

WERN FAWR RD

LC

F A B I A N   W A Y

P

BALDWIN'S CRES

ELBA CRES

93

LANGDON RD

BEVANS ROW

P

A483

King's Dock

P

3

Dry
Dock

Queen's Dock

Jetties

92

Jetty

2

91

Bristol Channel

1

90

67 **D** **68** **E** **69** **F** **90**

A   **B**   **C**

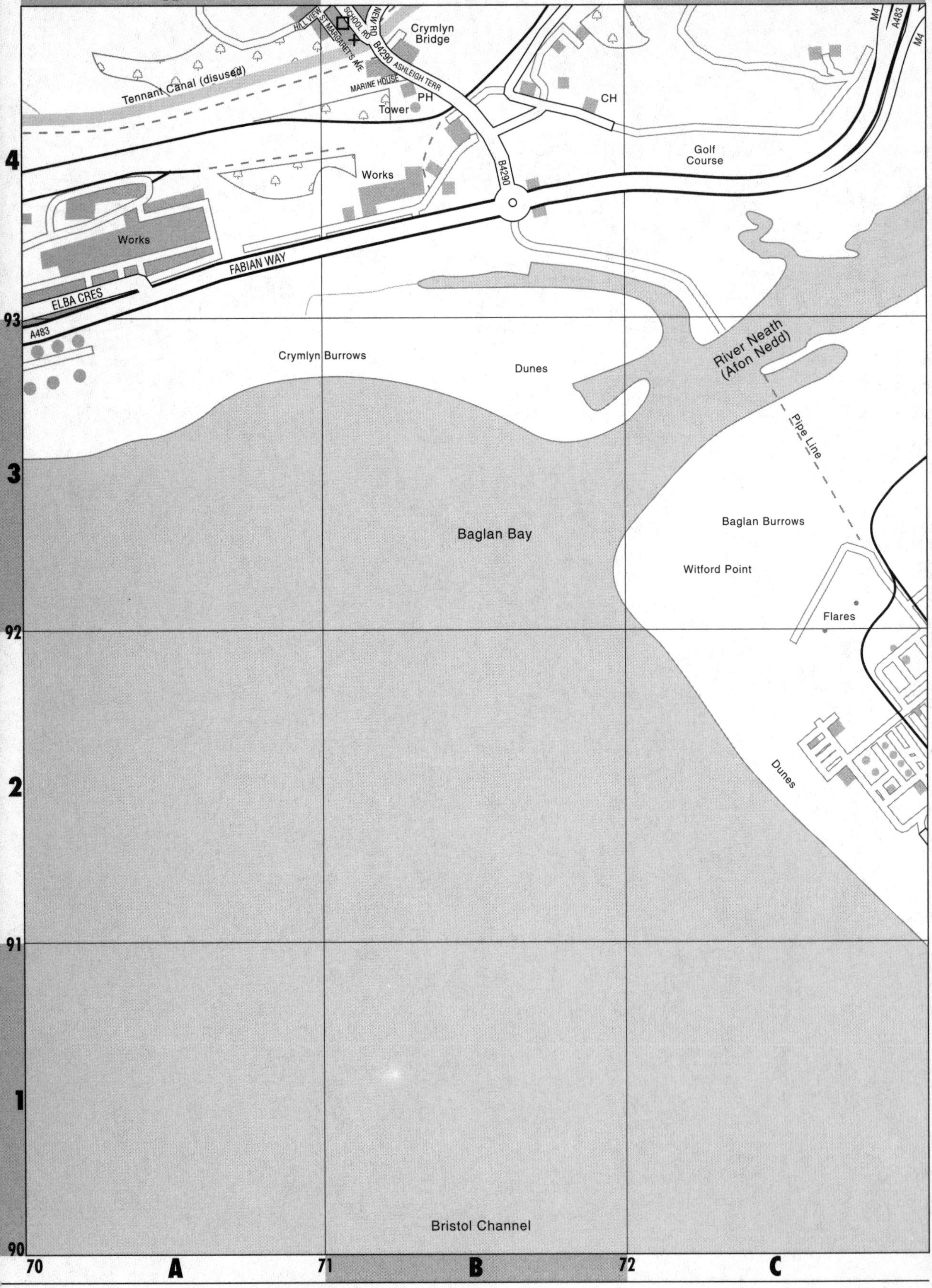

HILL VIEW
ST MARGARET'S AVE
NEW RD
SCHOOL RD
B4290
ASHLEIGH TERR

Crymlyn
Bridge

Tennant Canal (disused)

MARINE HOUSE

PH

Tower

CH

Golf
Course

4

Works

B4290

M4
A483
M4

Works

FABIAN WAY

ELBA CRES

93

A483

Crymlyn Burrows

Dunes

River Neath
(Afon Nedd)

Pipe Line

3

Baglan Bay

Baglan Burrows

Witford Point

Flares

92

Dunes

2

91

1

Bristol Channel

90

70   **A**   71   **B**   72   **C**

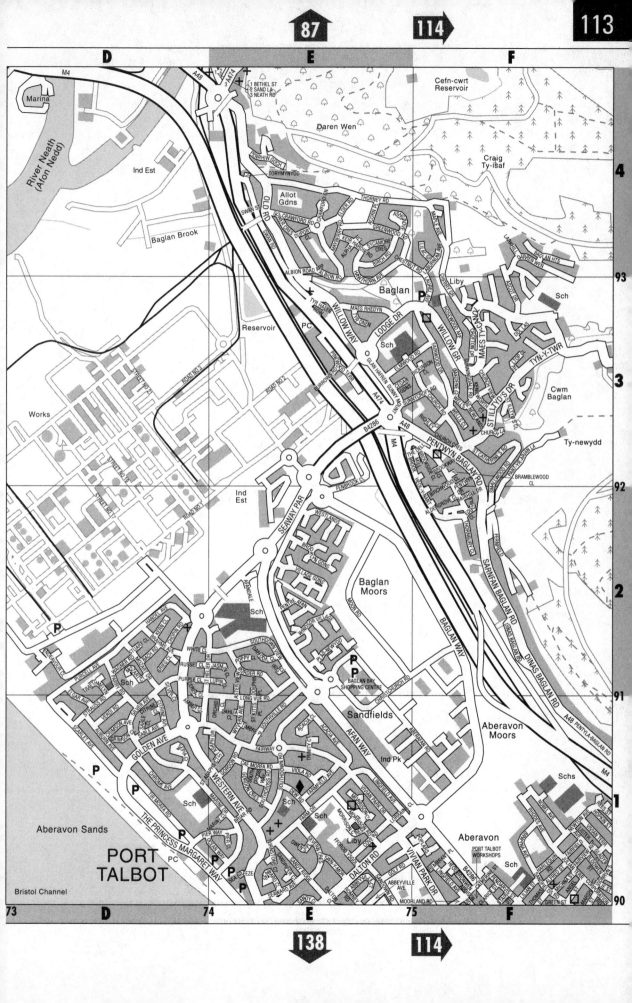

M4
Marina

River Neath
(Afon Nedd)

Ind Est

A48

3 A474
1 BETHEL ST
2 SAND LA
3 NEATH RD

Cefn-cwrt
Reservoir

Daren Wen

Craig
Ty-isaf

4

Baglan Brook

PENRHIW ROCH
TORYMYNYDD

Allot
Gdns

THORNEY RD

ASHGROVE
GREENWOOD

LARWILL
DARREL WEN
BAGLAN HTS

MAPLE AVE

Reservoir

PC

ALBION ROAD   ALBION RD

Baglan

P

Liby

Sch

93

Road No.3

Works

ROAD NO 2

Road No.2

STREET NO 2A

STREET NO 19

WILLOW WAY

TYR HALEN
ROW

GLAN HAFREN SUNNY MOR

MAES RHEDYN

LODGE DR

Sch

A474

ELMWOOD RD

A48

B4286

WILLOW GR

MAES TY-CANO

ST ILLTYD'S DR

TYN-Y-TWR

Cwm
Baglan

CHURCH LA
CHURCH

PENTWYN BAGLAN RD
Baglan

Ty-newydd

3

STREET NO 17

Ind
Est

Road No.1

SEAWAY PAR

WESTLANDS

FENBROOK CL

BROO

BROOKSIDE

BINCHWOOD

SARNFAN BAGLAN RD

BRAMBLEWOOD
CL

FERNBED

92

VILLAGE GDNS

AFANDALE

PENTRE AFAN

WINDSOR VILLAGE

Sch

Baglan
Moors

MOOR RD

BAGLAN WAY

DINAS BAGLAN RD

A48 PENTYLA-BAGLAN RD

2

P

HANDEL AVE

WAGNER RD
BACH RD
ELGAR AVE
KERRY CL
WHITE CL

BURCELL CL

SOUTHDOWN VIEW

POPPY CL
DAFFODIL CL
RUSSET CL
JASM
PURPLE CL
LUPIN

PRIMROSE CL

ORCHID

PL NEWYDD

DAHLIA AVE

LONG VUE RD

ASTER WK

CHRISTCHURCH RD

Baglan Bay
SHOPPING CENTRE

Sandfields

Ind Pk

A48

Aberavon
Moors

ABERAVON PL

Schs

M4

91

Sch

VERDI RD
CRIMSON AVE
SCARLET AVE
GOLDEN AVE

SILVER AVE
ST KITTS
LIMBRE

FAIRWAY

ACACIA CL
ACACIA AVE

VIVIAN PARK DR

Aberavon

1

P

Aberavon Sands

THE PRINCESS MARGARET WAY

PC

PIER WAY
PIER CL

WESTERN AVE
MARINE CL

Sch

CAE MORFA RD

VIOLA RD
FARMFIELD AVE

Sch

MORRISTON
MORRISTON RD

Sch
Liby

LINGFIELD AVE

VIVIAN PARK DR

B4286

GREEN ST

Port Talbot
WORKSHOPS

Sch

90

**PORT
TALBOT**

Bristol Channel

SEA BREEZE
SEAWARD AVE
SANDY RIDGE

DALTON RD

ABBEYVILLE
AVE
MOORLAND RD

D   **E**   **F**

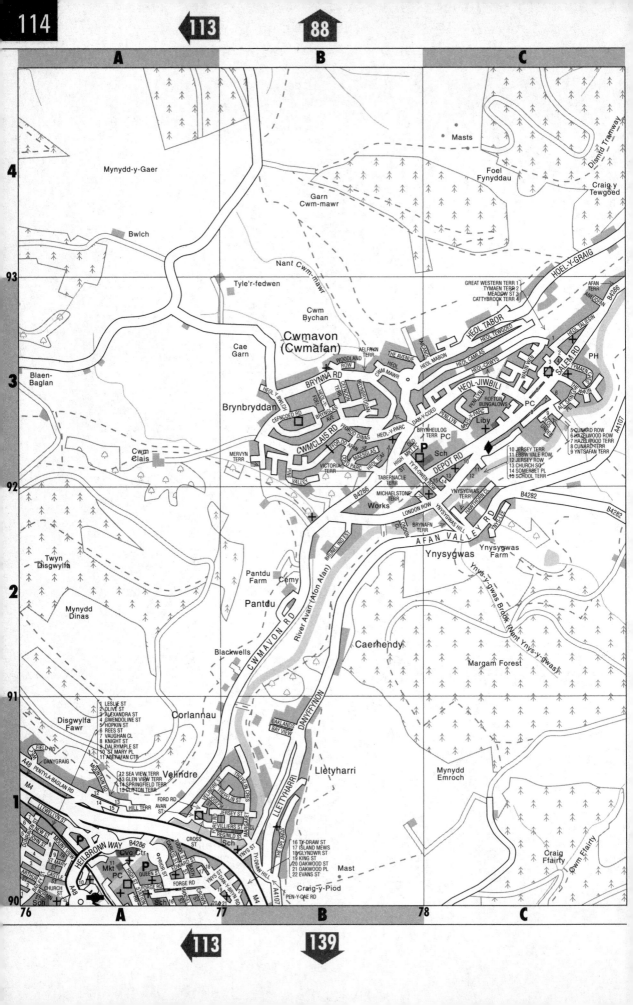

D   E   F

4

93

3

Bryn

Sch   Bryn Cotts

MAESTEG RD

ROWLANDS COTTS

92

2

91

1

B4286
OAKWOOD RD
A4107
Bwlch-y-gwynt
1 PENHYDD HOUSE
2 OAKWOOD HOUSE

Penhydd-fach

Craig y Tewgoed
Mast
Myndd Pen-hydd

Cwm Ifan-bach

MAES-Y-BETWS

HEOL-Y-GRAIG
ROCK TERR
TWYN-Y-COED
PWLL-Y-GLAW
AFON TYWYS VILLAS
AFON TERR
SALEM RD
TARREN TERR

Moel y Fen
NEATH RD
Pen-hydd-fawr

AFON VALLEY RD
River Avon (Afon Afan)

Pwll-y-glaw

Cwm Nanto
Cilcarn

Mynydd Bychan

Patch Mawr

Penhydd-waelod

PENHYDD-WAELOD COTTS

LLWYNHELYG GDNS
BRYNHELIG
MYNYDD VIEW
WELFARE AVE
HEOL PENHYDD
BRYNGYRNOS ST
CHAPEL TERR

FARTEG RD

PH
B4282
CWM FARTEG
ALL CWM TERR
STATION TERR
Coed Morgannwg Way

Bryngyrnos

Penycastell

Twyn Penycastell

Cil-y-gofid

Ffrwd Wyllt
Dismantled Railway

NANT-Y-BODA

Penrhiw Bungalow

Cwm Nant-y-boda

Nant-y-boda

Gallt-y-cwm

Cwm Dyffryn

Moel Gallt-y-cwm

Craig Einroch

Afon Wen Farm

Cwm Wernderi

Nant Cwmwernderi

Cwmwernderi Reservoir

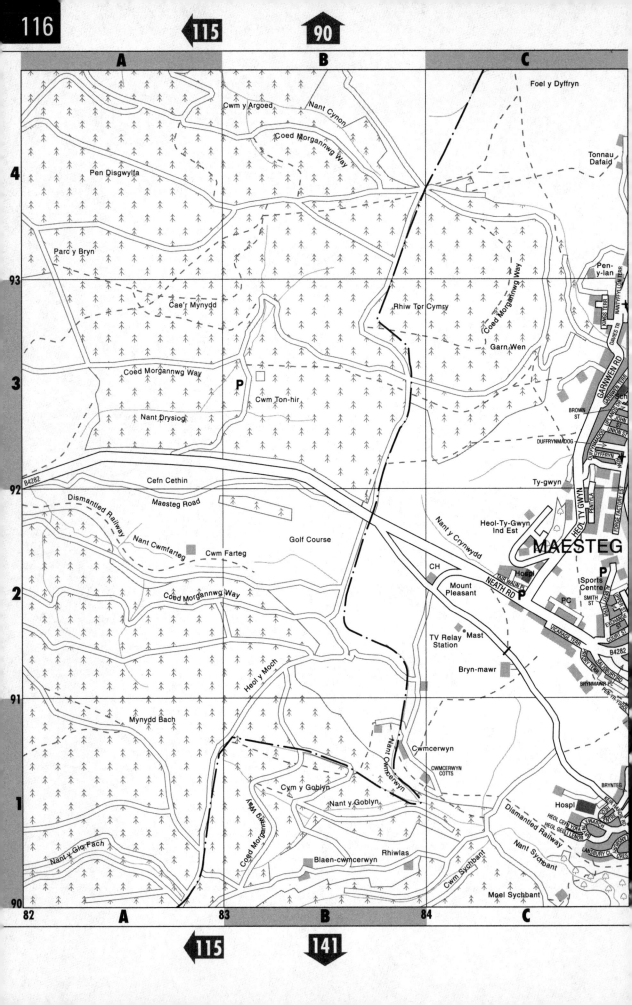

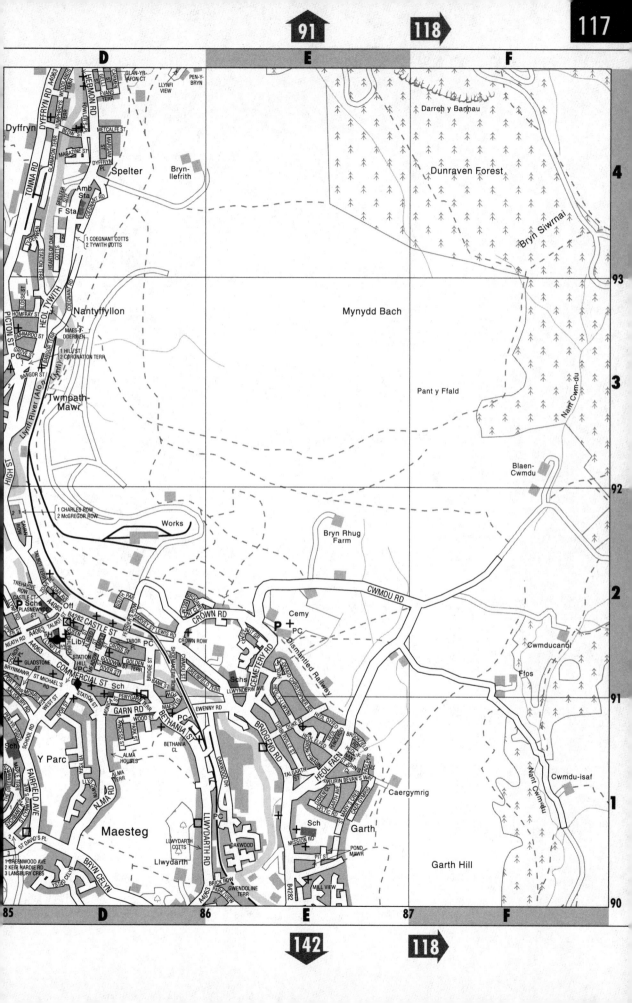

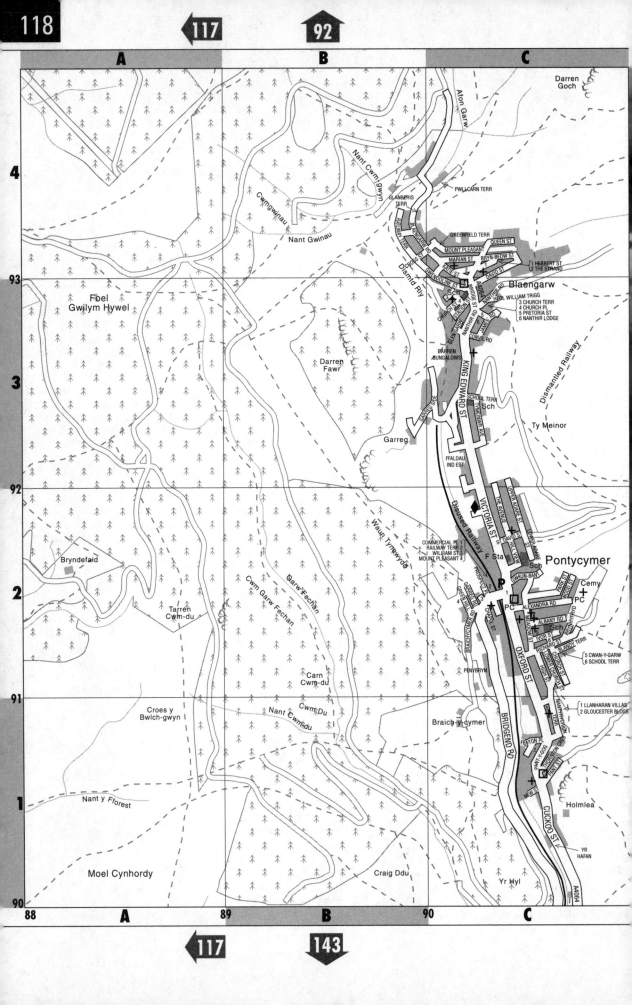

A   B   C

4

Darren
Goch

Afon Garw

Nant Cwm-gwyn

Cwmgwinau

Nant Gwinau

PWLLCARN TERR

GLANPERIS
TERR

RAILWAY TERR

GREENFIELD TERR

QUEEN ST

RAINBOW RD

MOUNT PLEASANT

DEROS ST

GWENDOLINE ST

MARIAN ST

BRYN-BEDW ST

KATE ST

DAVID ST

1 HERBERT ST
2 THE STRAND

93

Disdd Rly

Blaengarw

Foel
Gwilym Hywel

Sch

CHURCH ST

BRIDGE ST

STATION RD

NANTHIR RD

AUBREY RD

HEOL WILLIAM TRIGG

3 CHURCH TERR
4 CHURCH PL
5 PRETORIA ST
6 NANTHIR LODGE

GLENGARW RD

BRITHDIR TERR

JAMES RD

CONVIL RD

DARREN
BUNGALOWS

Darren
Fawr

CAMBRIS SIDE

KING EDWARD ST

SCHOOL TERR

Sch

TY-MENWR AVE

Ty Meinor

3

Dismantled Railway

Garreg

FFALDAU
IND EST

92

Waun Tynewydd

UPPER ADARE ST

VICTORIA ST

THE AVENUE

ST DAVID'S

LOWER ADARE ST

Disused Railway

COMMERCIAL PL 1
RAILWAY TERR 2
WILLIAM ST 3
MOUNT PLEASANT 4

HILL VIEW

F Sta

Pontycymer

Bryndefaid

CROSS PL

P

SWAUN-BAN

PARK RD

WOOD ST

Cemy

PC

2

Tarren
Cwm-du

Cwm Garw Fechan

Garw Fechan

Cwm Garw Fechan

CHAPEL ST

PC

GREEN TERR

GARDEN ST

BRIDGEND RD MACHEN

ALEXANDRA RD

ALBANY RD

MEADOW ST

IVOR ST

RICHARD ST

CHURCH ST

BLANDY TERR

Sch

5 CWAN-Y-GARW
6 SCHOOL TERR

Carn
Cwm-du

PENYBRYN

OXFORD ST

1 LLANHARAN VILLAS
2 GLOUCESTER BLDGS

NANT-Y-FEDWEN

91

Croes y
Bwlch-gwyn

Nant Cwm-du

Cwm Du

Braich-y-cymer

BRIDGEND RD

FENTON PL

Nant Y Fforest

PANT-Y-SONS

ROBERTON TERR

NEW ST

PRIM ST

Holmlea

1

CUCKOO ST

YR
HAFAN

Moel Cynhordy

Craig Ddu

Yr Hyl

A4064

90

88   A   89   B   90   C

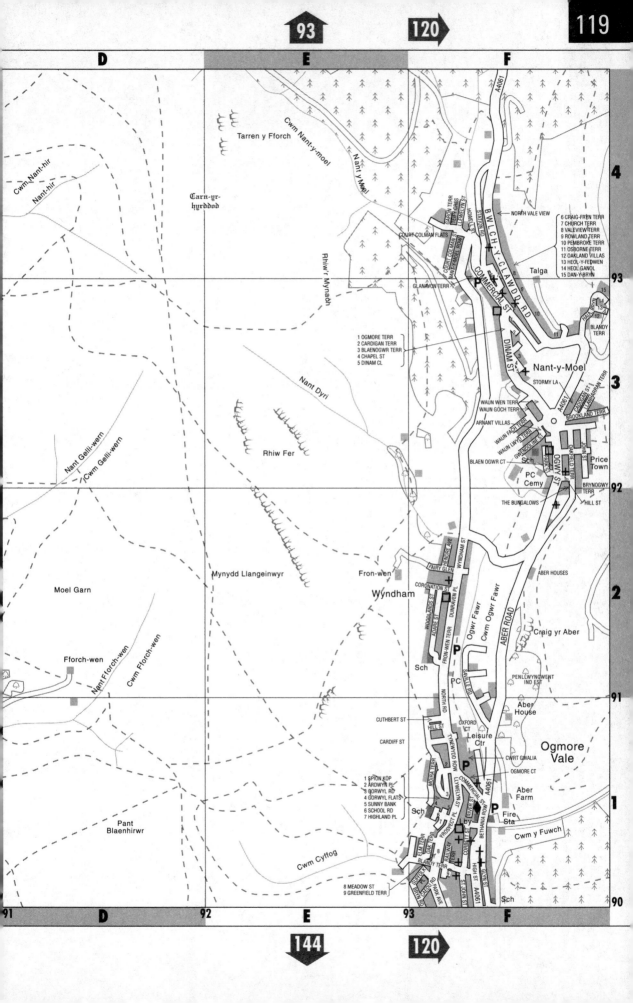

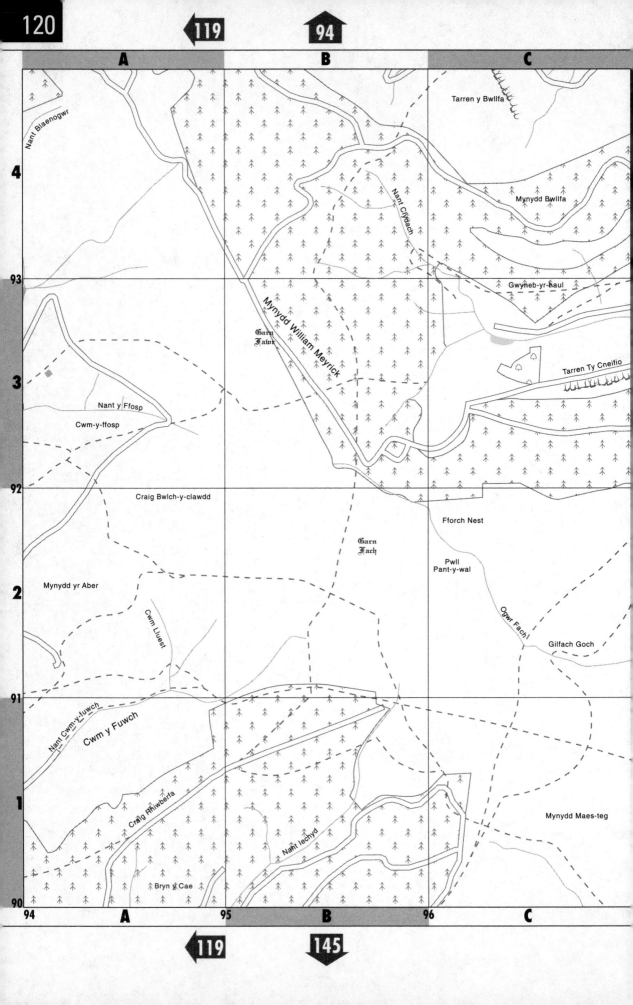

Tarren y Bwllfa

Nant Clydach

Mynydd Bwllfa

Nant Blaenogwr

Mynydd William Meyrick

Gwyneb-yr-haul

Garn
Fawr

Tarren Ty Cneifio

Nant y Ffosp

Cwm-y-ffosp

Craig Bwlch-y-clawdd

Fforch Nest

Garn
Fach

Pwll
Pant-y-wal

Mynydd yr Aber

Cwm Lluest

Ogwr Fach

Gilfach Goch

Nant Cwm-y-fuwch

Cwm y Fuwch

Craig Rhiwberfa

Mynydd Maes-teg

Nant Iechyd

Bryn y Cae

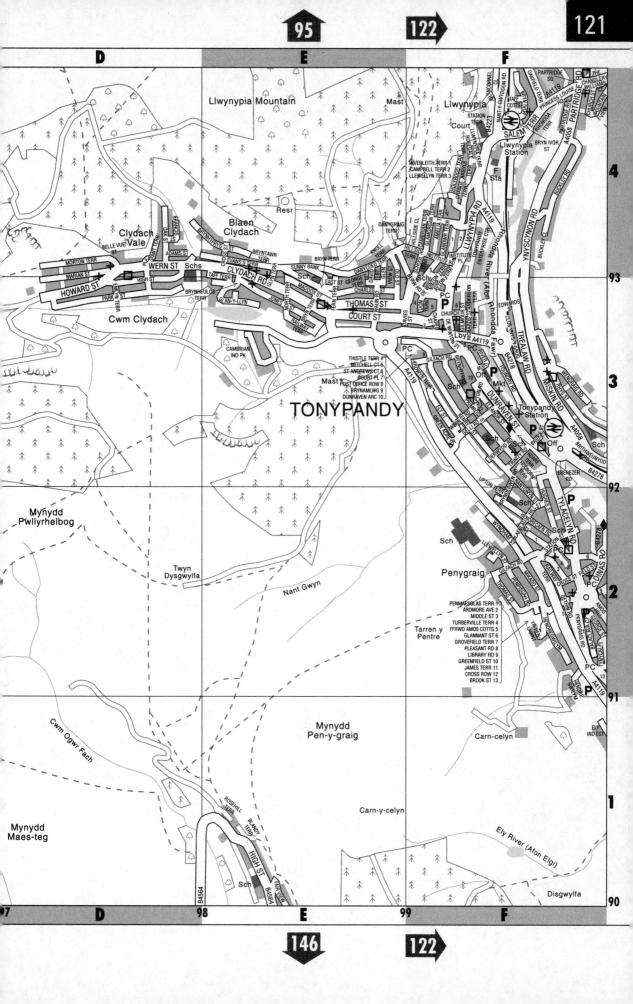

D E F

Llwynypia Mountain

Mast

Llwynypia

Court

Resr

Clydach Vale

Blaen Clydach

JAVERLEITH TERR 1
CAMPBELL TERR 2
LLEWELLYN TERR 3

DANYGRAIG TERR

WERN ST

HOWARD ST

Cwm Clydach

CLYDACH RD

Schs

SUNNY BANK

BRYN TERR

THISTLE TERR 4
MITCHELL CT 5
ST ANDREWS CT 6
COURT PL 7
POST OFFICE ROW 8
BRYNAMLWG 9
DUNRAVEN ARC 10

CAMBRIAN IND PK

Mast

THOMAS ST

COURT ST

TONYPANDY

Llwynypia Station

SALEM TERR

BRYN IVOR ST

CYNSCYNON RD

BUCKLEY RD

DUNRAVEN ST

Tonypandy Station

MISKIN RD

TREALAW RD

EBENEZER RD

Mynydd Pwllyrhelbog

Twyn Dysgwylfa

Nant Gwyn

Tarren y Pentre

Penygraig

PENMAESGLAS TERR 1
ARDMORE AVE 2
MIDDLE ST 3
TURBERVILLE TERR 4
FFRWD AMOS COTTS 5
GLANNANT ST 6
GROVEFIELD TERR 7
PLEASANT RD 8
LIBRARY RD 9
GREENFIELD ST 10
JAMES TERR 11
CROSS ROW 12
BROOK ST 13

TYLACELYN RD

DINAS RD

PENYGRAIG RD

Mynydd Pen-y-graig

Carn-celyn

ELY IND EST

Carn-y-celyn

Mynydd Maes-teg

Cwm Ogwr Fach

ROSEHILL TERR

BLANDY TERR

HIGH ST

FAIRVIEW

Sch

Ely River (Afon Elgi)

Disgwylfa

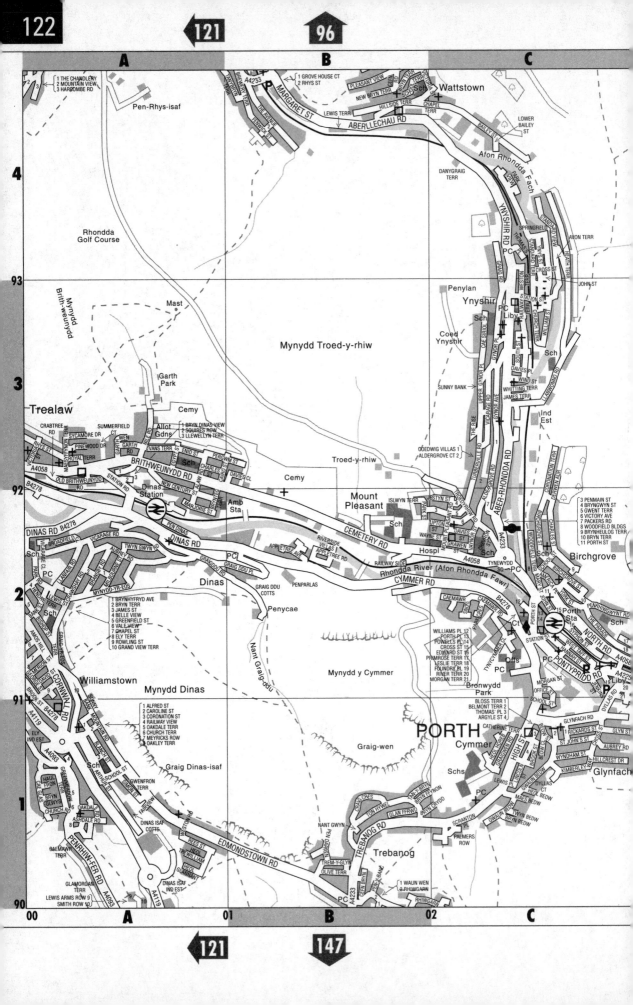

D E F

CRAWSHAY ST

Llwynperdid

Llys-Nant

Cribyn-du

Llysnant

4

Twyn y glog

Glog

Cae-Crwn

93

Cyrnau

Berth Fawr

3

Nant Blaenhenwysg

Pen-y-wal

Nant Hafod

92

Blaenhenwysg

Llwyncelyn

Cwm Hafod

Rhiw-yr-uchain

Bryngoleu

Nyth-brân House

Hafod-ganol

Coed yr Hafod Fawr-uchaf

2

HOLLYBUSH CR

LEWIS TERR

GETHIN TERR

Hafod Fawr

ST LUKE'S RD

MAGNA

CHURCH WALK

NYTHBRAN TERR

Sch

ORCHARD CLO

HEATH CLO

LLWYNCELYN PARK

Llwyncelyn

Heritage Centre

PRIMROSE TERR

LESLIE TERR

LLWYNCELYN CT

F Sta

BRIDGE ST

Trehafod Station

MARGARET ST

Trehafod

HAFOD LA

Troedrhiw-Trwyn

GYFEILLON RD

C

EIRW RD

LLWYNCELYN RD

A4225

COEDCAE RD

Phillips TERR

TREHAFOD RD

COLLIERY ST

FOUNTAIN ST

TROEDRHIW-TRWYN

TY-MAWR RD

LEYSHON TERR

1 RIVER TERR

2 MORGAN TERR

BRITANNIA RD

CLIFTON ROW

PLEASANT VIEW

SOVEREIGN TERR

WOODLEA TERR

RHEOL-Y TERR

PO

Sch

AEL-Y-BRYN

LEWIS STREET

IVOR ST

WEST AND EAST

WINE ST

COURT ST

TY-MAWR PARK

Mine

91

Britannia

KENSINGTON DR

RHONDALE RD

GLYN ST

THE WALK

MOUNT PLEASANT

Rhondda River (Afon Rhondda)

TYPICA COTTS F

MARGARET ST 2

DISTILLERY ROAD LA 3

HENWYSG CL 4

HOPKINSTOWN RD

A4058

Hopkinstown

Oaklands

LLANDRAW CT

1

Mynydd y Glyn

Mynydd Gelliwion

90

3 D 04 E 05 F

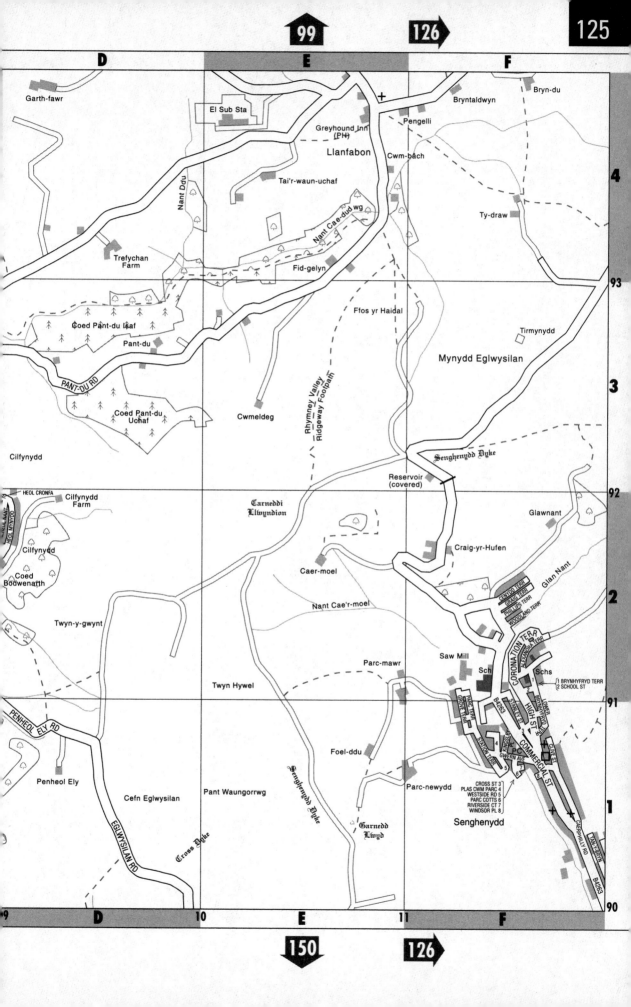

Garth-fawr

El Sub Sta

Greyhound Inn
(PH)

Bryntaldwyn

Bryn-du

Pengelli

Llanfabon

Cwm-bach

Nant Ddu

Tai'r-waun-uchaf

Ty-draw

Nant Cae-dud wg

Trefychan
Farm

Fid-gelyn

Coed Pant-du Isaf

Ffos yr Haidal

Tirmynydd

Pant-du

Mynydd Eglwysilan

PANT-DU RD

Coed Pant-du
Uchaf

Cwmeldeg

Rhymney Valley
Ridgeway Footpath

Senghenydd Dyke

Cilfynydd

Reservoir
(covered)

HEOL CRONFA

Cilfynydd
Farm

92

Carneddi
Llwyndion

Glawnant

HEOL MYNYDD

Cilfynydd

Craig-yr-Hufen

Coed
Bodwenarth

Caer-moel

Glan Nant

CENYDD TERR
CRAIG TERR
PHILLIPS TERR
WOODLAND TERR

Twyn-y-gwynt

Nant Cae'r-moel

Saw Mill

CORONATION TERR
ALEXANDRA TERR

Parc-mawr

Sch

Schs

1 BRYNHYFRYD TERR
2 SCHOOL ST

Twyn Hywel

PARC TERR
GROVE TERR

B4263

STANLEY'S ST

LOWER
BRYNHYFRYD TERR

HIGH ST

PENHEOL ELY RD

Foel-ddu

STATION TERR

CATE ST

COMMERCIAL ST

PC

GWERN AVE

Penheol Ely

Parc-newydd

CROSS ST 3
PLAS CWM PARC 4
WESTSIDE RD 5
PARC COTTS 6
RIVERSIDE CT 7
WINDSOR PL 8

Cefn Eglwysilan

Pant Waungorrwg

Senghenydd Dyke

Senghenydd

CAERPHILLY RD

TAN-Y-BRYN

B4263

EGLWYSILAN RD

Garnedd
Llwyd

Cross Dyke

Cwm-du

Gwernau-fawr

Nant y Twyn

Gwernau-ganol

Twyn-Shôn-Ifan

Gwernau Hall

Ty'r-ywen

Pen-y-cwarel

Ffynnon-y-gwaed

PEN-Y-CWAREL RD

GLANDWYN RD

Dismtd Rly

Sirhowy River (Afon Sirhywi)

A4048

PONTGAM TERR

CAE'R-LLWYN TERR

Sirhowy Valley Walk

ALEXANDRA RD

GREENFIELD TERR 1
GLENVIEW TERR 2
THE GARDENS 3

ISLWYN C A4048

93

4

Pant-y-ffawydden

Bryn-ysgawen

Ty'n-y-coed

Nant y Ffrwd

Cae-brith

Mast

Craig y Prisiad

Dismtd Rly

BRIDGE ST

HIGH ST

JOHN ST

Sch

3

TAN-Y-COED-UCHA

BRYNGWENNOL

TELOR
DAR-Y-DERI

GWTIAN

CEDR-Y-DERI

Ffrwd

Wern Cae-brith

Rhymney Valley Ridgeway Footpath

Tyle-crwth

Mynydd Bach

Coed Cae-Hugh

92

Glyn River (Afon Rhymni)

Dismtd Rly

Pen-y-rhiw

Coed Ochr-ddu

Nant Cwm Kenfelin

Ffos yr Hebog

Twyn Cae-Hugh

2

GLYN COLLEN
GLYN BEDW
GLYN LLWYD
GLYN ONDREW
GLYN Y DERWEN

Sch

Coed Margaret-Shôn

Tŷ-gwyn

PANT GLAS

HEOL TY-GWYN

VICTORIA ST
OAKFIELD ST

WINGFIELD CRES

PLASTURTWYN

LON-YR-AFON

Mynydd y Grug

91

GLENVIEW TERR
GARDENS 3
MONMOUTH VIEW
TŶ AVENUE

A469

Tŷ-isaf

Cwm-y-bwch

Nant y Bwch

MOUNTAIN RD

1

Mynydd Dimlaith

PANT-Y-MAWR RD

Cwm

Pen-y-waun

Dyffryn Isaf

90

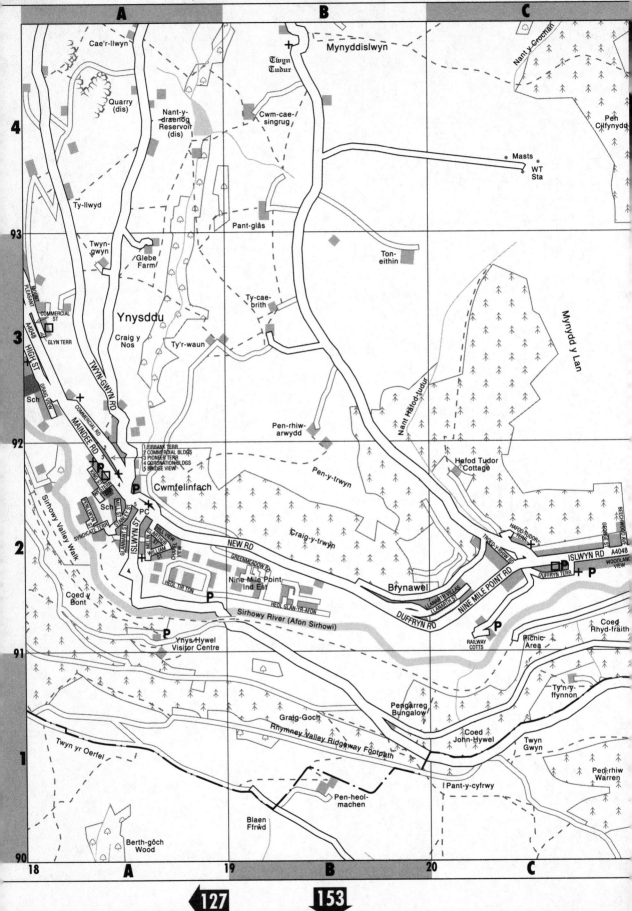

A · B · C

Cae'r-llwyn

Mynyddislwyn

Twyn Tudur

Nant y Crochan

Quarry (dis)

Nant-y-draenog Reservoir (dis)

Cwm-cae-singrug

Pen Cilfynydd

Masts
WT Sta

Ty-llwyd

Pant-glâs

Ton-eithin

93

Twyn-gwyn

Glebe Farm

Ty-cae-brith

Mynydd y Lan

MOUNT PLEASANT

COMMERCIAL ST

GLYN TERR

Ynysddu

HIGH ST A4048

Craig y Nos

Ty'r-waun

Pen-rhiw-arwydd

Nant Hafod-Tudur

Sch
CRAIG VIEW

3

TWYN-GWYN RD

COMMERCIAL RD

MAINDEE RD

92

1 FIRBANK TERR
2 COMMERCIAL BLDGS
3 PIONEER TERR
4 CORONATION BLDGS
5 BRIDGE VIEW

Pen-y-trwyn

Hafod Tudor Cottage

WESTERN TERR
KING ST

P

Cwmfelinfach

BEECHWOOD AVE

GEORGE ST

PENLLWYN TERR
SYNDICATE TERR
GLANNANT ST
STANLEY ST
MILL ST
ISLWYN ST
WILLIAM ST
ARTHUR ST
HEOL NANT
HILL VIEW
CHAPEL VIEW

Sch
PC

Craig-y-trwyn

HAFOD TUDOR TERR

TROED-Y-RHIW RD

2

NEW RD

GREENMEADOW RD

HEOL TIR TON

Nine Mile Point Ind Est

HEOL GLAN-YR-AFON

Brynawel

LLANARTH VILLAS
LLANARTH ST

NINE MILE POINT RD

ISLWYN RD A4048
WOODLAND VIEW

DUFFRYN TERR

P

Coed y Bont

P

Sirhowy River (Afon Sirhowi)

DUFFRYN RD

RAILWAY COTTS

P

Picnic Area

Coed Rhyd-fraith

91

P

Ynys Hywel Visitor Centre

Pengarreg Bungalow

Ty'n-y-ffynnon

Craig-Goch

Coed John-Hywel

Twyn Gwyn

Twyn yr Oerfel

Rhymney Valley Ridgeway Footpath

1

Pant-y-cyfrwy

Pen-rhiw Warren

Pen-heol-machen

Blaen Ffrwd

Berth-gôch Wood

90

18   A   19   B   20   C

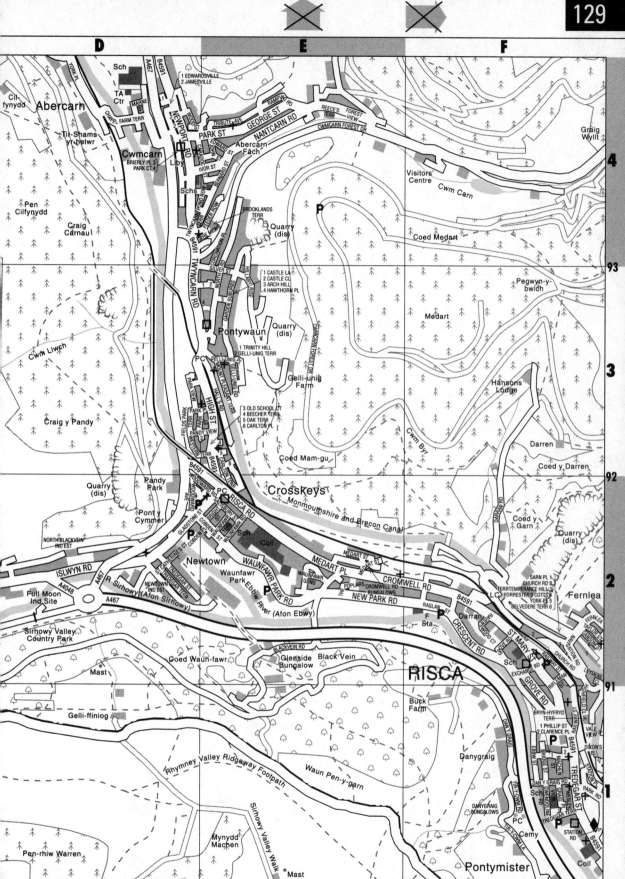

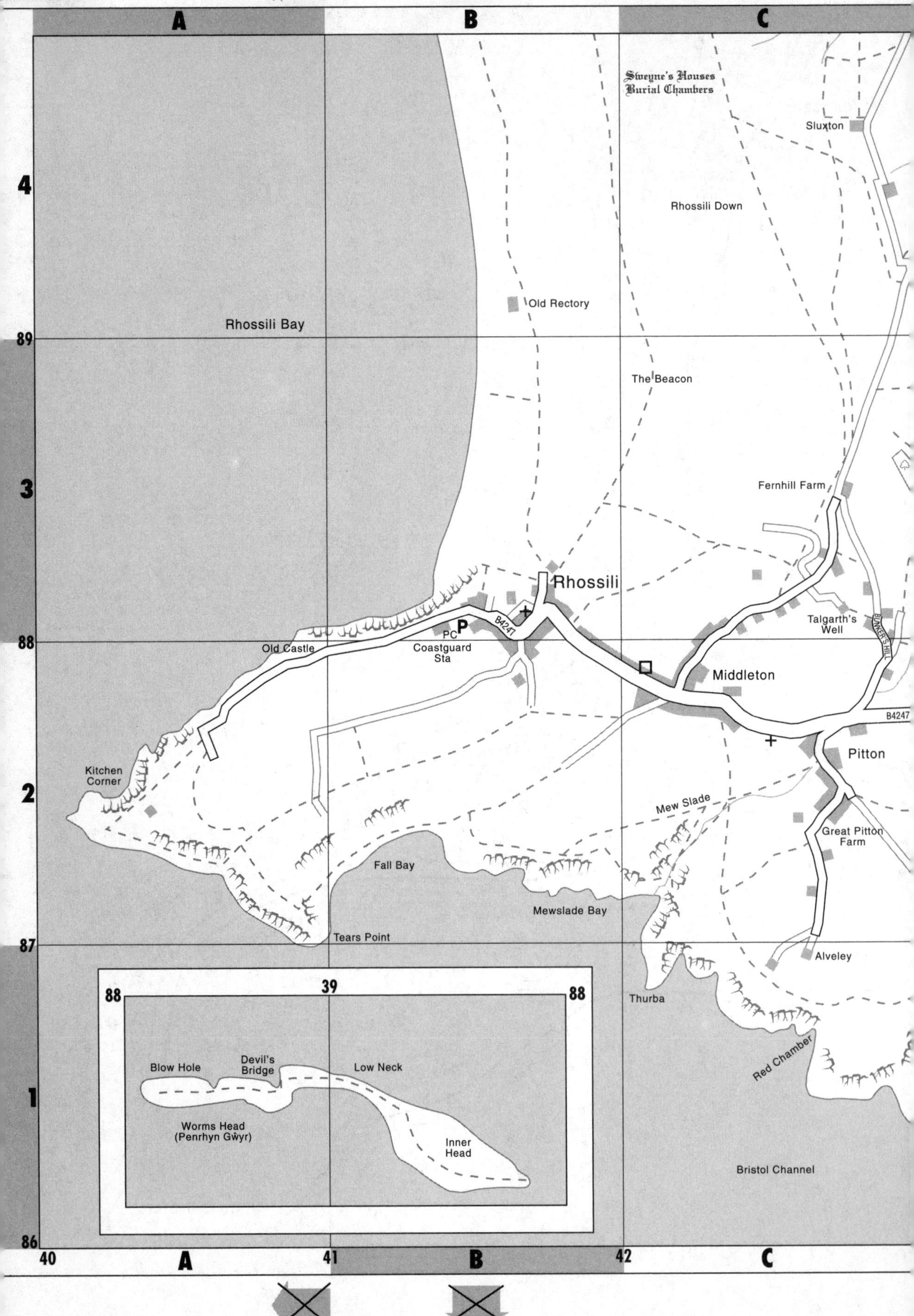

A   B   C

4

Sweyne's Houses
Burial Chambers

Sluxton

Rhossili Down

Old Rectory

Rhossili Bay

89

The Beacon

Fernhill Farm

3

Rhossili

Talgarth's
Well

P

PC
Coastguard
Sta

Old Castle

88

B4247

Middleton

Pitton

B4247

Kitchen
Corner

2

Mew Slade

Great Pitton
Farm

Fall Bay

Mewslade Bay

Tears Point

87

Alveley

Thurba

88   39   88

Red Chamber

Devil's
Bridge

Blow Hole

Low Neck

1

Worms Head
(Penrhyn Gŵyr)

Inner
Head

Bristol Channel

86
40   A   41   B   42   C

102

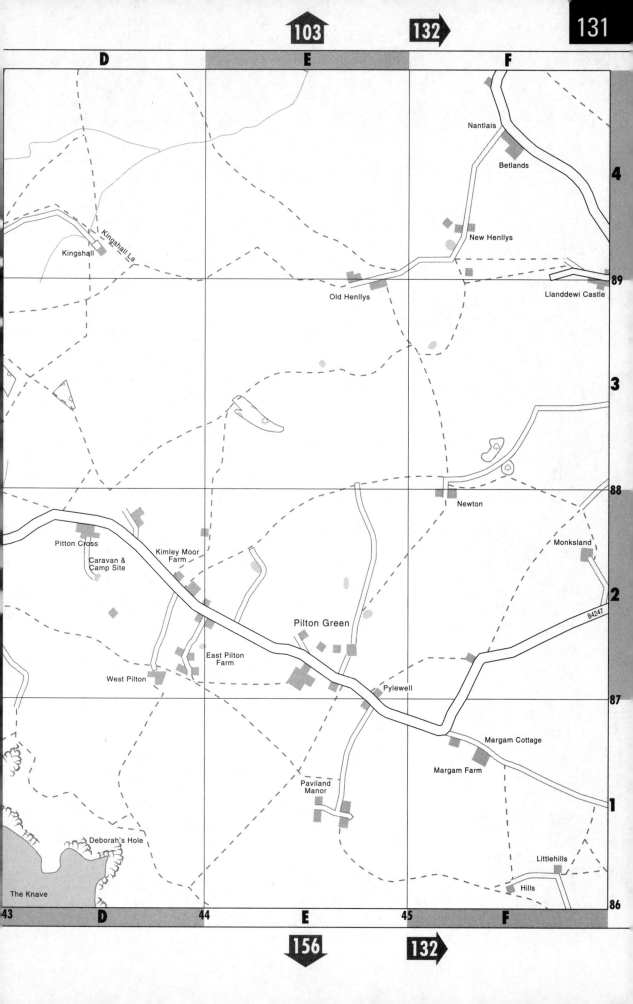

D E F

4

Nantlais

Betlands

New Henllys

89

Old Henllys

Llanddewi Castle

3

88

Newton

Monksland

Pitton Cross

Kimley Moor
Farm

Caravan &
Camp Site

Pilton Green

2

B4247

East Pilton
Farm

West Pilton

Pylewell

87

Margam Cottage

Margam Farm

Paviland
Manor

1

Deborah's Hole

Littlehills

The Knave

Hills

86

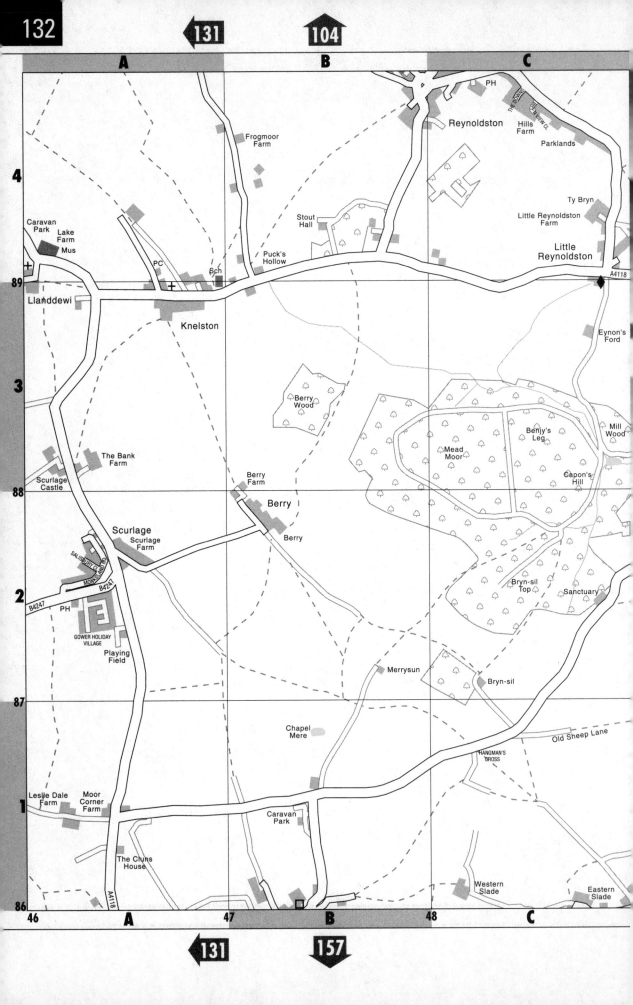

A

B

C

4

Frogmoor
Farm

Reynoldston

PH

THE DOWNS

Hills
Farm

Parklands

Ty Bryn

Little Reynoldston
Farm

Stout
Hall

Little
Reynoldston

Caravan
Park

Lake
Farm

Mus

PC

Sch

Puck's
Hollow

A4118

89

Llanddewi

Knelston

Eynon's
Ford

Berry
Wood

3

Mill
Wood

Benjy's
Leg

Mead
Moor

Capon's
Hill

The Bank
Farm

Scurlage
Castle

Berry
Farm

Berry

88

Berry

Bryn-sil
Top

Sanctuary

Scurlage

Scurlage
Farm

SALISBURY PLANT RD

MONKS LAND RD

B4247

2

B4247

PH

GOWER HOLIDAY
VILLAGE

Merrysun

Bryn-sil

Playing
Field

87

Chapel
Mere

Old Sheep Lane

HANGMAN'S
CROSS

Leslie Dale
Farm

Moor
Corner
Farm

1

Caravan
Park

The Cluns
House

A4118

Western
Slade

Eastern
Slade

86

46

A

47

B

48

C

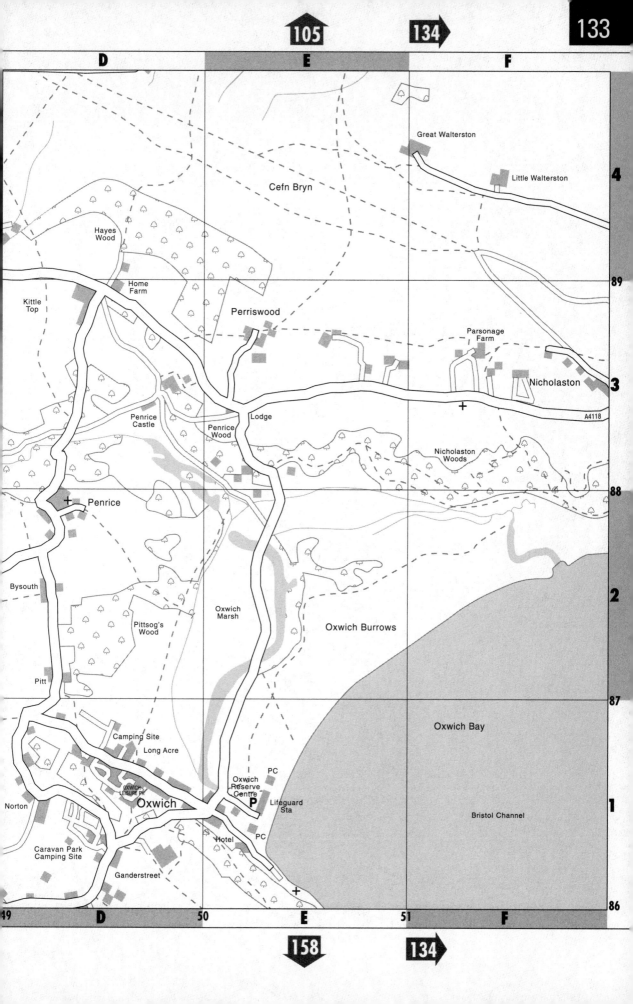

D
E
F

Great Walterston

Cefn Bryn

Little Walterston

4

Hayes
Wood

89

Home
Farm

Kittle
Top

Perriswood

Parsonage
Farm

Nicholaston

3

Penrice
Castle

Lodge

Penrice
Wood

A4118

Nicholaston
Woods

88

+ Penrice

Bysouth

Oxwich
Marsh

Oxwich Burrows

2

Pittsog's
Wood

Pitt

87

Oxwich Bay

Camping Site

Long Acre

PC

Oxwich
Reserve
Centre

Norton

OXWICH
LEISURE PK

Oxwich

P

Lifeguard
Sta

Bristol Channel

1

Caravan Park
Camping Site

Hotel

PC

Ganderstreet

+

86

49

D

50

E

51

F

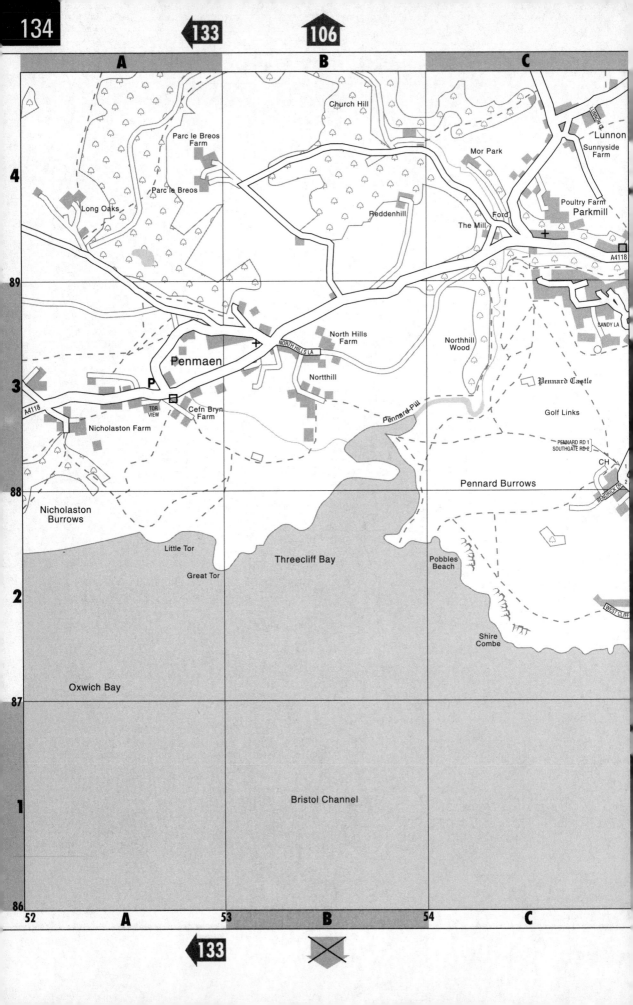

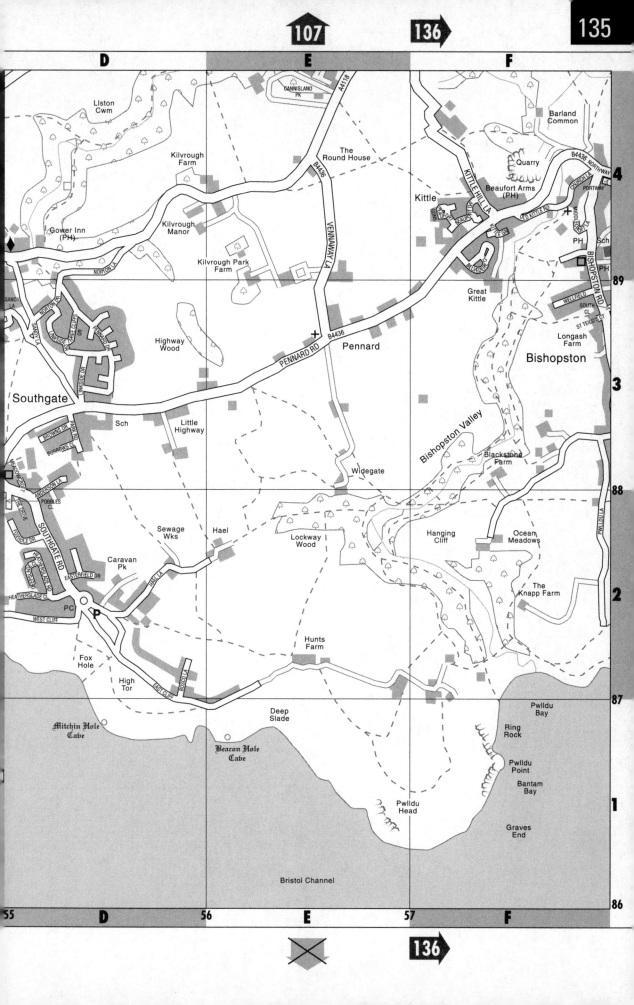

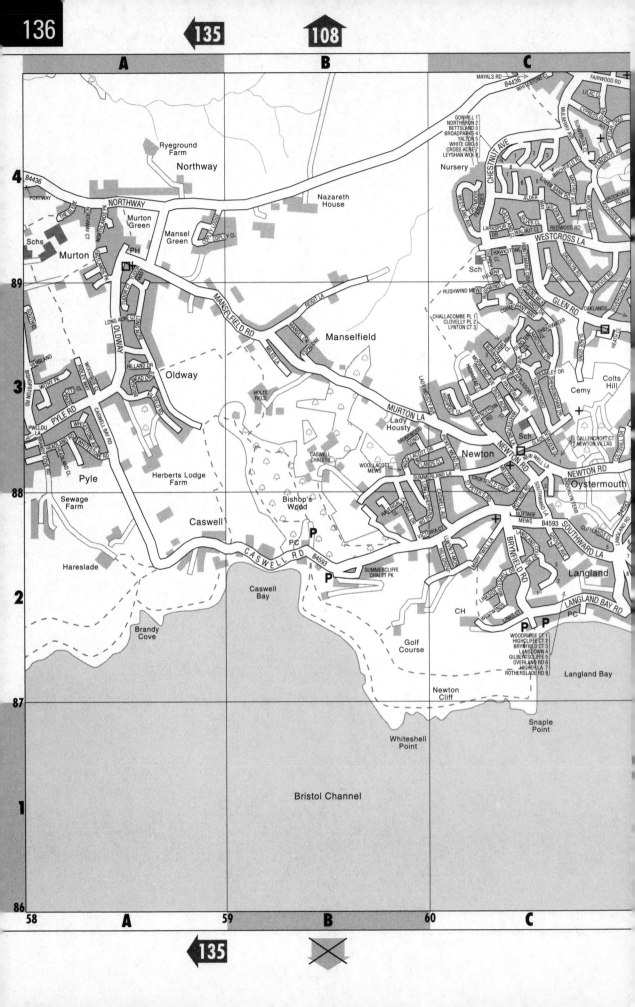

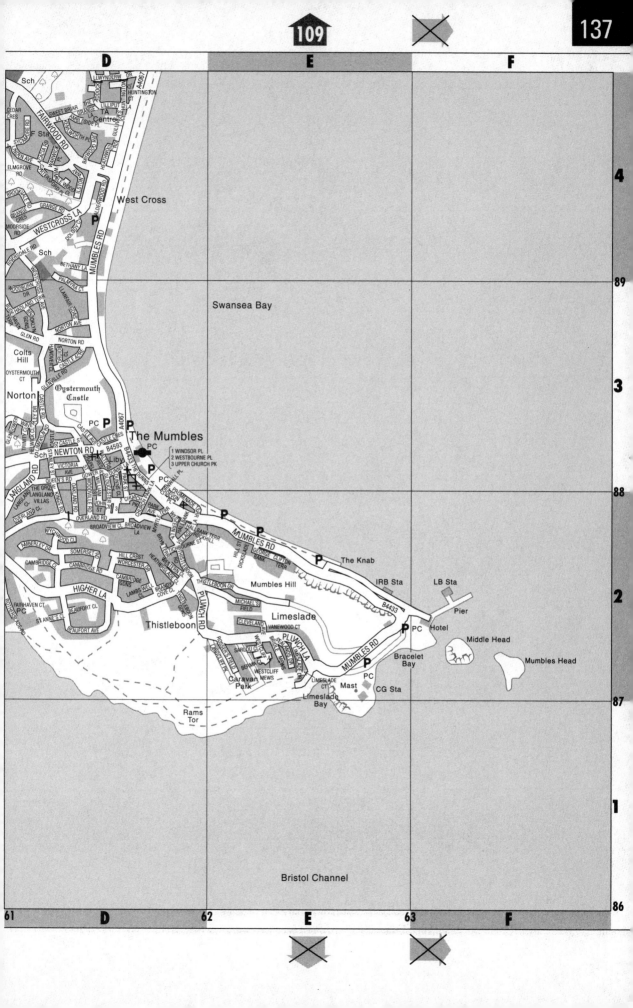

D
E
F

4

89

Swansea Bay

3

Colts
Hill
OYSTERMOUTH
CT
Norton

Oystermouth
Castle

PC P P
The Mumbles
PC
NEWTON RD B4593
Liby
1 WINDSOR PL
2 WESTBOURNE PL
3 UPPER CHURCH PK
PC P
PC

88

P
P
P
The Knab

IRB Sta
LB Sta

Mumbles Hill
B4433

Pier

2

Limeslade
Hotel
P PC
Thistleboon
Middle Head
Mumbles Head
P
Bracelet
Bay
PC
Caravan
Park
Mast
CG Sta
Limeslade
Bay

Rams
Tor

87

1

Bristol Channel

86

West Cross

WESTCROSS LA

Sch

Thistleboon

Langland

113

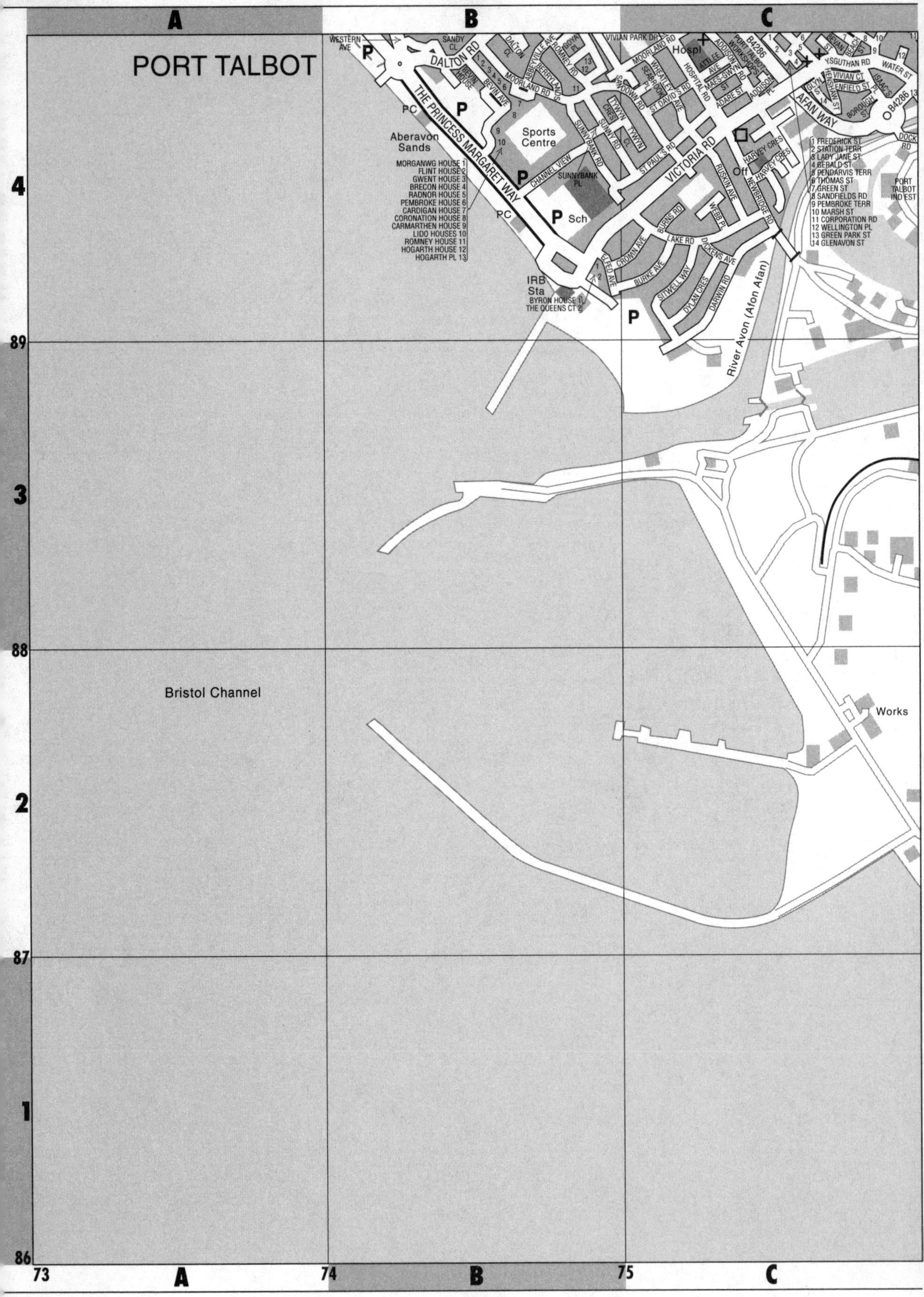

A
B
C
PORT TALBOT
WESTERN AVE
SANDY CL
DALTON RD
DALTON CL
ABBEYVILLE AVE
GOYA PL
ROMNEY RD
BERRYLANDS
MOORLAND RD
BEVIN HOUSE
BEVIN AVE
THE PRINCESS MARGARET WAY
PC
Aberavon Sands
MORGANWG HOUSE 1
FLINT HOUSE 2
GWENT HOUSE 3
BRECON HOUSE 4
RADNOR HOUSE 5
PEMBROKE HOUSE 6
CARDIGAN HOUSE 7
CORONATION HOUSE 8
CARMARTHEN HOUSE 9
LIDO HOUSES 10
ROMNEY HOUSE 11
HOGARTH HOUSE 12
HOGARTH PL 13
Sports Centre
CHANNEL VIEW
SUNNYBANK RD
SUNNYBANK PL
SUNNY RD
Sch
VIVIAN PARK DR
MOORLAND RD
SEABROOK
WHEATLEY
ST DAVID'S RD
TYWYN CRES
TYWYN CL
ST PAUL'S RD
VICTORIA RD
Hospl
ATTLEE AVE
ADDISON
HOSPITAL RD
MAES-GWYN RD
ADARE ST
PORT TALBOT WORKSHOPS
B4286
ADDISON PL
HARVEY CRES
Off
RUSKIN AVE
NEWBRIDGE RD
WEBB PL
BURNS RD
LAKE RD
DICKENS AVE
CROWN AVE
ELFED AVE
BURKE AVE
SITWELL WAY
DYLAN CRES
DARWIN RD
IRB Sta
BYRON HOUSE 1
THE QUEENS CT 2
River Avon (Afon Afan)
YSGUTHAN RD
WATER ST
VIVIAN CT
ENFIELD ST
HENSHAW ST
ISAACS PL
BOROUGH ST
AFAN WAY
B4286
DOCK RD
PORT TALBOT IND EST
1 FREDERICK ST
2 STATION TERR
3 LADY JANE ST
4 GERALD ST
5 PENDARVIS TERR
6 THOMAS ST
7 GREEN ST
8 SANDFIELDS RD
9 PEMBROKE TERR
10 MARSH ST
11 CORPORATION RD
12 WELLINGTON PL
13 GREEN PARK ST
14 GLENAVON ST
4
89
3
88
Bristol Channel
Works
2
87
1
86
73
74
75
A
B
C

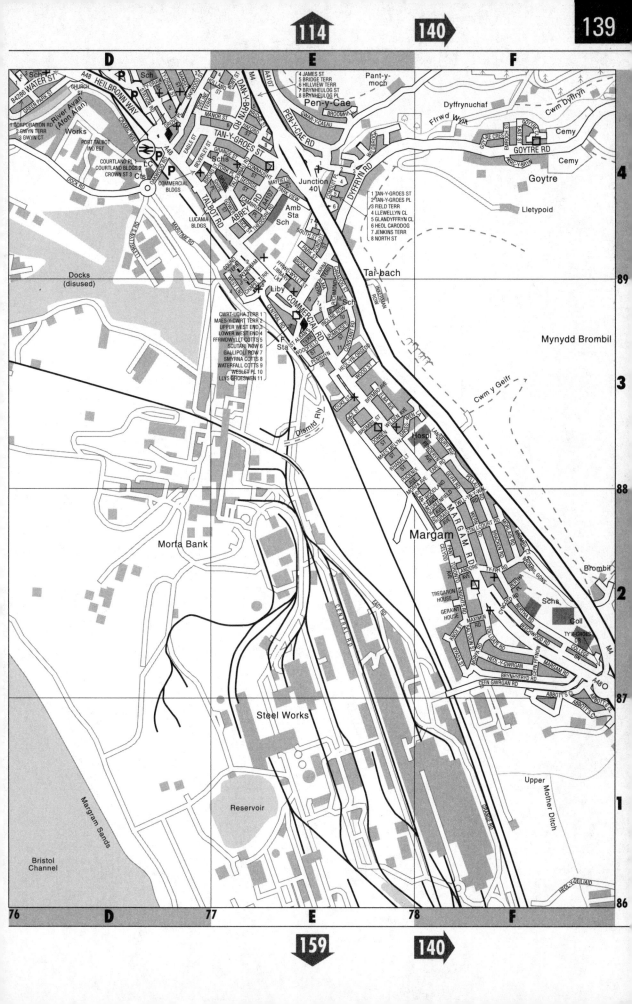

139
115

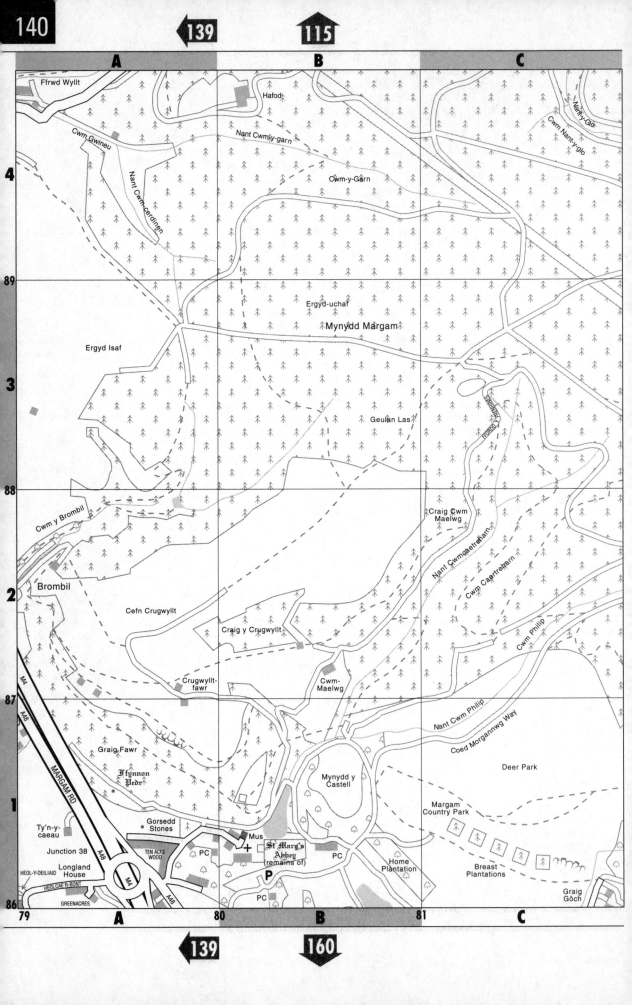

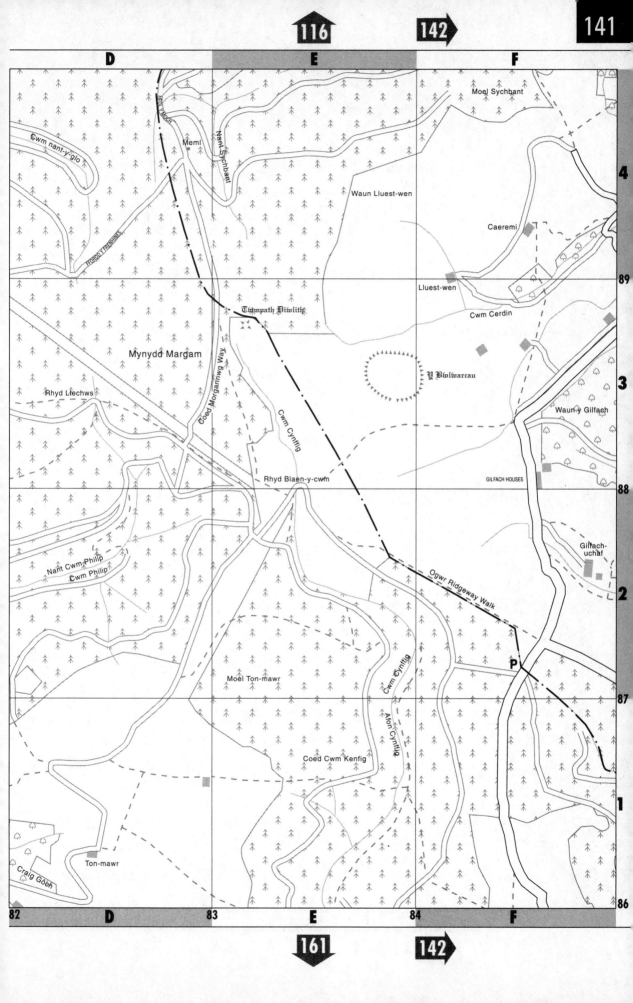

Moel Sychbant

Cwm nant-y-glo

Heol y Moch

Meml

Nant Sychbant

Waun Lluest-wen

Caeremi

4

Ffordd y Trenghines

89

Lluest-wen

Trumpath Diwlith

Cwm Cerdin

Coed Morganinwg Way

Mynydd Margam

Y Bwlwarcau

3

Rhyd Llechws

Cwm Cynffig

Waun-y Gilfach

Rhyd Blaen-y-cwm

GILFACH HOUSES

88

Nant Cwm Philip

Gilfach-uchaf

Cwm Philip

Ogwr Ridgeway Walk

2

Moel Ton-mawr

Cwm Cynffig

P

87

Afon Cynffig

Coed Cwm Kenfig

1

Ton-mawr

Craig Goch

86

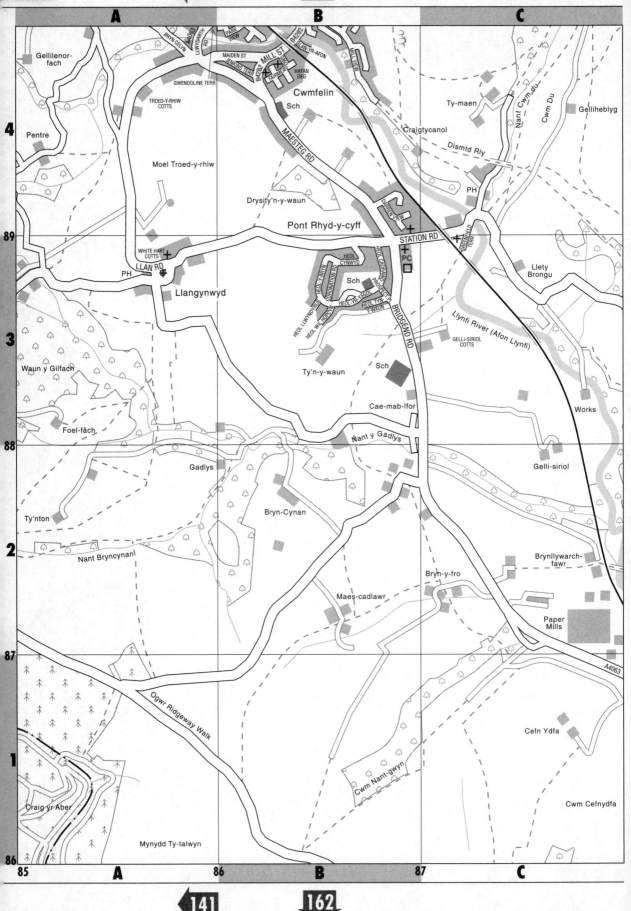

118
144

D   E   F

Lluest

Mynydd
Moelgeila

Cwmogwr
Forest

Pont-y-
rhyl

Lluest

4

Cynhordy

WEST RHONDDA

Aton Garw

A4064

89

Cynhordy
Farm

Craig yr
Hudol

Tor-y-fron

Cwmcedfyw

Mast

Craig-yr-hudol

Capel-bâch

MOEL GILAU

Lletty
Brongu

BRYN TERR

3

Dismantled Railway

Brithdir

Llynfi Valley

Moelgilau

88

Celfyddifan

Cwm Cedfyw

Llangeinor
House

2

Gwern-llwyn-
fawr

Tyle-coch

Shwt-Uchaf

Afon Llynfi

Ty Isaf

HEOL RICHARD PRICE

87

Green Field
Terr

ROSE
TERR

Bettws

Shwt

East
Side

1

Sewage
Works

BRYN BACH
COTTS

Schs

Gelli-las
Fawr

Nantmwth Fach
Farm

Bryn Siriol

BETTWS RD

Coedpentwyn

WEST
VIEW

WOODLAND
CL

TYN-Y-BETTWS

TUDOR
DR

Pen-twyn

A4063

Ogwr Ridgeway Walk

A4064

86

88   D   89   E   90   F

163
144

Nant Llwyncria

Pen y Foel

Craig Cae-du

Nant y Ci

Cwm Nant-y-ci

Ffawyddog

4

VALE VIEW

THE BUNGALOWS

PARK AVE

ST JOHN ST

FERN ST

A4061 HIGH ST

BRIDGE RD

BEYN RD

WALTERS RD

WATER ST

ALMA TERR

P

PC

Sch

RHIWGLYN RD

RIVERSIDE FLATS

SUNNYSIDE

CEMETERY RD

RHIWGLYN RD

Ogmore Forest

Mast

Craig Llyscwmllorwg

PC

Cemy

Llyscwmllorwg

89

Graig Wen

A4064

WEST RHONNOR

THE BUNGALOWS

Tylagwyn

Dismantled Railway

Disused

Ffynnon-dwym

3

1 DANYGRAIG

2 MIN Y COED

LLANGEINOR TERR

PENTRE-BELL

PENTREBELL TER

PC

Lewistown

Cwm Ogwr Fawr

Dismantled Railway

YSTRAD IFOR

PEN Y PANT

SWN YR AFON

LYNN DAVIES AVE

Mount Pleasant Cotts

Cae Forgan Cotts

Cefngelli

THE CROFT

GREEN MEADOW TERR

PH

1 ROSE COTTS

2 OLD TAVERN

3 CWM COTTS

A4093

Cae Abbot

The Llangeinor Arms (PH)

HILLSIDE

HILLSIDE TERR

WOODLAND TERR

PANT-YR-AWEL

HEOL AE EERYN

PAN YR HEOL

Ogwr Fawr

Pantyrawel

HEOL PANT-YR-AWEL

A4093

88

Cefngelli

LC Afon Gawr

HEOL LLANGEINOR

HEOL TY NANT

PC

Sch

Llangeinor

HEOL-Y-NANT

HEOL NANTDON

HEOL LLWYN Y FYNNON

Llwynffynnon

A4064

HEOL PANDY

CAE RHOCK

GRAIGLAS

Cefnmachen-uchaf

IFOR TERR

Dolau-Ifan-ddu

EBENEZER TERR

OAK RIDGE

DOLAU IFAN DDU TERR

A4093

ISFRYN IND EST

GRAIG TERR

Ogwr Fach

A4093

87

Bryn y Wrach

PC

PH

MEADOW VIEW

Blackmill

OLD PARISH RD

Blaenclydwyn

Tal-y-fan Farm

Mast

DAN Y OCHEN

Nant Cwm-dwr

Lan Farm

1

Cefnmachen-isaf

Ogwr Ridgeway Walk

Ogmore Valley (Cwm Ogwr)

Graig Tal-y-fan

Ogmore River

(Afon Ogwr)

A4061

Cwm Dŵr

86

91 **A** 92 **B** 93 **C**

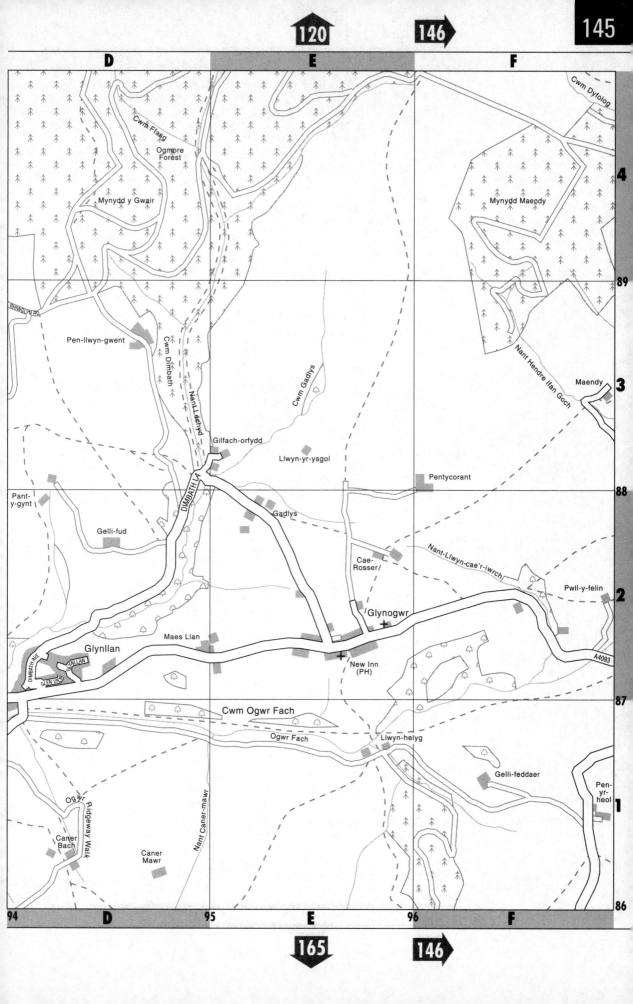

120
146

D E F

Cwm Dyfolog

4

Mynydd Maendy

Cwm Ffasg

Ogmore
Forest

Mynydd y Gwair

89

RHIWGLYN RD.

Nant Hendre Ifan Goch

Pen-llwyn-gwent

Cwm Dimbath

Nant Llechyd

Cwm Gadlys

Maendy 3

Gilfach-orfydd

Llwyn-yr-ysgol

Pentycorant

88

Panty-y-gynt

DIMBATH LA

Gadlys

Gelli-fud

Cae-Rosser/

Nant-Llwyn-cae'r-iwrch

Pwll-y-felin

2

Glynogwr

A4093

Maes Llan

Glynllan

DIMBATH AVE

GLYN LLAN

GLEN VIEW

New Inn
(PH)

87

Cwm Ogwr Fach

Ogwr Fach

Llwyn-helyg

Gelli-feddaer

Ogwr

Ridgeway Walk

Pen-yr-heol 1

Caner
Bach

Caner
Mawr

Nant Caner-mawr

86

165
146

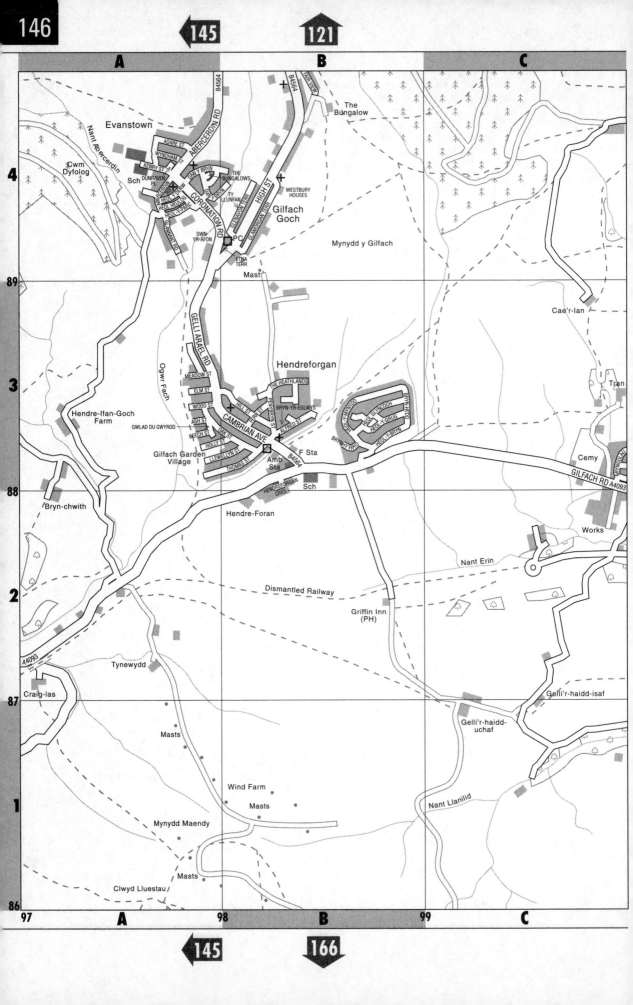

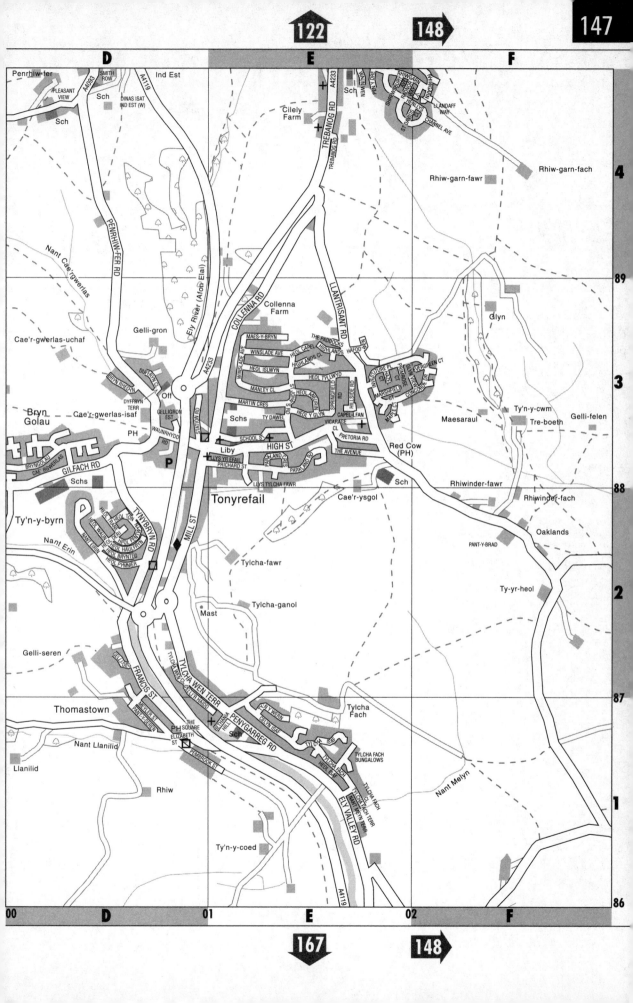

D
E
F

Penrhiw-fer
SMITH ROW
Ind Est
PLEASANT VIEW
Sch
A4093
A4119
DINAS ISAT IND EST (W)
Sch
Trebanog Rd
A4233
Sch
Cilely Farm
 RHIWBRYN
ST DAVIDS CL
HENLLYS
HENLLYS CT
Landaff Way
Rhiw-garn-fach
CHANNEL AVE
Rhiw-garn-fawr

4

Nant Cae'rgwerlas
PENRHIW-FER RD
Ely River (Afon Elai)
COLLENNA RD
LLANTRISANT RD
Glyn

89

Cae'r-gwerlas-uchaf
Gelli-gron
Collenna Farm
MAES-Y-BRYN
WINSLADE AVE
WINSLADE AVE
HEOL CAPEL
THE PADDOCKS
HIGHLANDS
HAFOD
Ty'n-y-cwm
Gelli-felen
Tre-boeth

3

Bryn Golau
BRYN RHEDYN
DUFFRYN CL
DYFFRYN TERR
Cae'r-gwerlas-isaf
GELLIGRON EST
WAUNRHYDD RD
Off
STATION RD
HEOL ISLWYN
MANLEY CL
MARTIN CRES
Schs
TY DAWEL
HEOL AMLWCH
HEOL TY'LLWYD
HILLSIDE RD
SPRINGFIELD
ST JOHN'S RD
HEOL Y GLYN
VICARAGE CL
CAPEL Y FAN
PRETORIA RD
MARSHFIELD
GLYN-THFC
EVERGREEN CT
CONCORDE CT
Maesaraul

PH
BRYNGOLAU
CAE ROWERLAS
GILFACH RD
Schs
SCHOOL S*
HIGH ST
Liby
LLYS YR EFAIL
PARK LAND
PRICHARD ST
PARKLAND
THE AVENUE
Red Cow (PH)
Rhiwinder-fawr
Rhiwinder-fach

88

Ty'n-y-byrn
Schs
LLYS TYLCHA FAWR
Tonyrefail
Cae'r-ysgol
Sch
Oaklands

Nant Erin
HEOL TON
HEOL PENTRE
HEOL HAULFRYN
HEOL BRYNTEG
HEOL PYMMER
TY'N YBRYN RD
MILL ST
Tylcha-fawr
PANT-Y-BRAD
Ty-yr-heol

2

Gelli-seren
Thomastown
BRAEDES
FRANCIS ST
PANT-Y-SEREN
PANT-Y-SEREN
TYLCHA WEN TERR
TYLCHA WEN
CELYN HAROD
TYLCHA WEN TERR
PENYGARREG RD
CELYN Y WERN
CELYN ISAF
Tylcha Fach

87

Mast
Tylcha-ganol
BETHANIA MILL LANE
THE SQUARE
PH
ELIZABETH ST
Sch
TYLCHA ISAF
HEOL SAL
TYLCHA FACH BUNGALOWS
Nant Llanilid
PEMBROOK ST
HEOL SAL
TYLCHA FACH
TWANT MEYN TERR
Nant Melyn

Llanilid
Rhiw
ELY VALLEY RD
A4119

1

Ty'n-y-coed
A4119

86

00
D
01
E
02
F

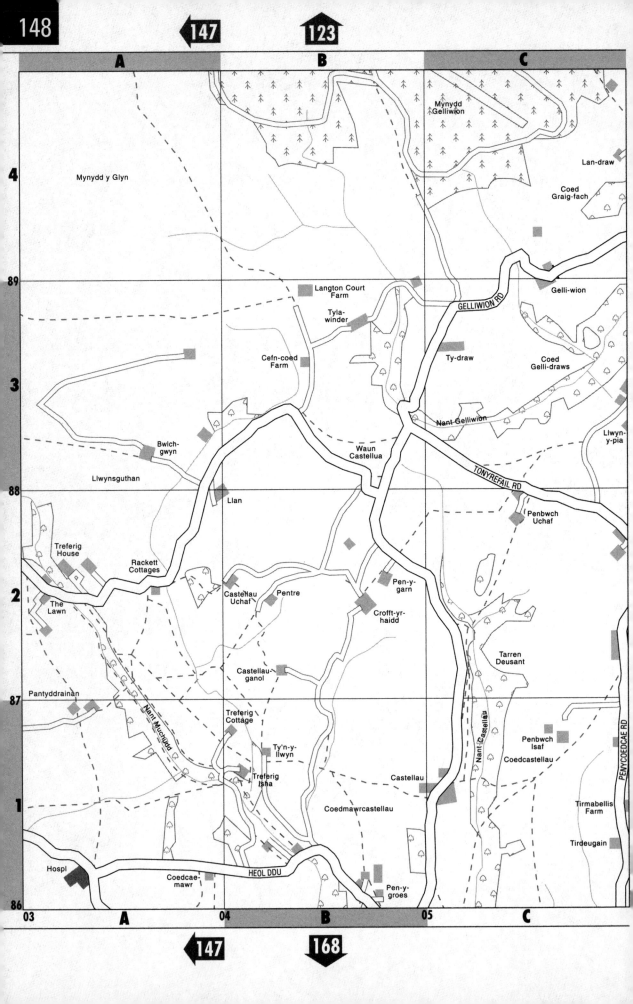

A B C

4

Mynydd y Glyn

Mynydd
Gelliwion

Lan-draw

Coed
Graig-fach

89

Langton Court
Farm

Tyla-
winder

GELLIWION RD

Gelli-wion

Cefn-coed
Farm

Ty-draw

Coed
Gelli-draws

3

Nant Gelliwion

Bwlch-
gwyn

Waun
Castellua

TONYREFAIL RD

Llwyn-
y-pia

Llwynsguthan

88

Llan

Penbwch
Uchaf

Treferig
House

Pen-y-
garn

Rackett
Cottages

Castellau
Uchaf

Pentre

Crofft-yr-
haidd

2

The
Lawn

Tarren
Deusant

Castellau-
ganol

87

Pantyddrainan

Nant Muchudd

Treferig
Cottage

Penbwch
Isaf

PENYCOEDCAE RD

Nant Castellau

Ty'n-y-
llwyn

Coedcastellau

Treferig
Isha

Castellau

Tirmabellis
Farm

1

Coedmawrcastellau

Tirdeugain

Hospl

HEOL DDU

Coedcae-
mawr

Pen-y-
groes

86

03

A

04

B

05

C

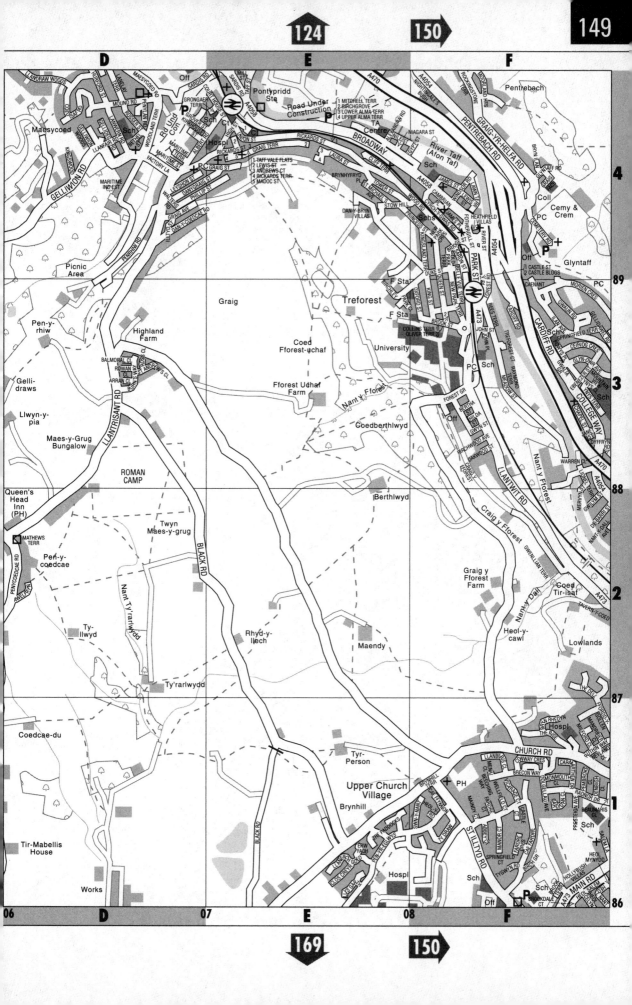

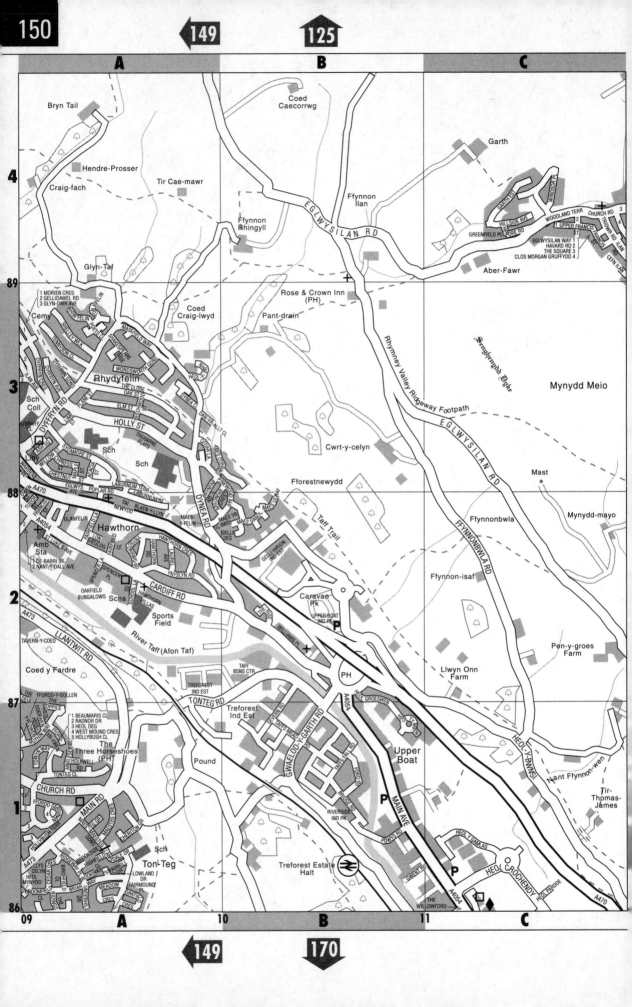

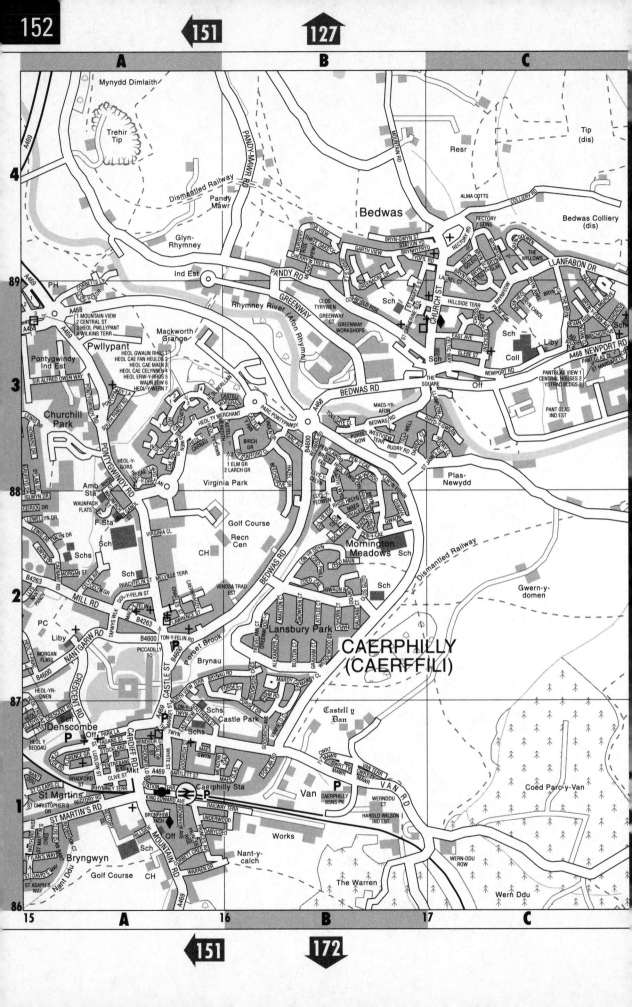

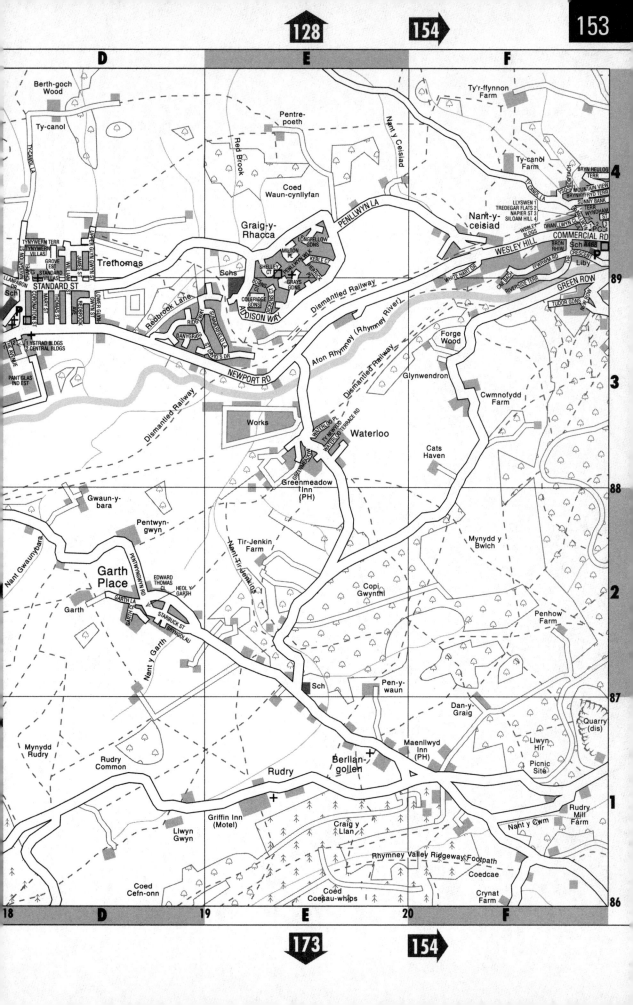

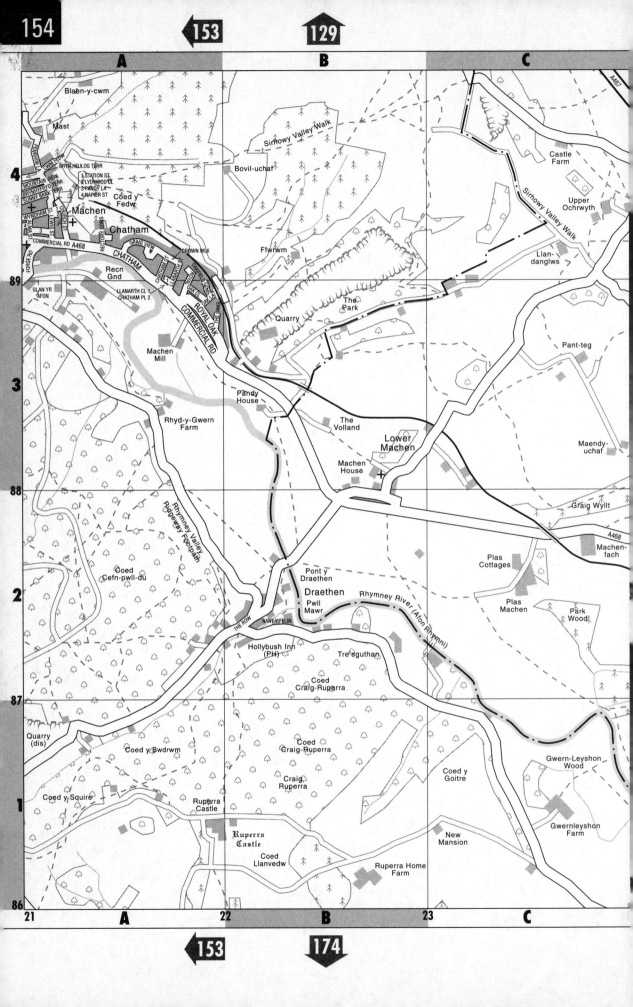

A B C

Blaen-y-cwm

Mast

BRYNHEULOG TERR
CWM TEDW
1 STATION ST
2 LYDWOOD CL
3 PANDY LA
4 NAPIER ST
MOUNTAIN VIEW
BRYNHYFRYD TERR
SUNNY BANK
Coed y Fedw

4

Bovil-uchaf

Sirhowy Valley Walk

Castle Farm

Upper Ochrwyth

Sirhowy Valley Walk

WYNDHAM ST
CHURCH ST
ALMA ST
LEWIS ST
Machen
Chatham
COMMERCIAL RD A468
FORGE RD
RECTORY GDNS
CRAIG VIEW
CROWN WLK

Ffwrwm

Llandanglws

GLAN YR AFON
Recn Gnd
CHATHAM
LLANARTH CL 1
CHATHAM PL 2
CHATHAM ST
LLANARTH ST
OAK CL 1
ROD CL 2
OAKFIELD TERR
ROYAL OAK
THE CWM

89

Quarry

The Park

Pant-teg

Machen Mill
COMMERCIAL RD

3

Pandy House

The Volland

Lower Machen

Maendy-uchaf

Rhyd-y-Gwern Farm

Machen House

Graig Wyllt

88

Rhymney Valley Ridgeway Footpath

A468

Machen-fach

Coed Cefn-pwll-du

Plas Cottages

2

Pont y Draethen

Draethen

Pwll Mawr

Rhymney River (Afon Rhymni)

Plas Machen

Park Wood

THE ROW
NANT Y FELIN

Hollybush Inn (PH)

Tre'sguthan

Coed Craig-Ruperra

87

Quarry (dis)

Coed y Bwdrwm

Coed Craig-Ruperra

Coed y Goitre

Gwern-Leyshon Wood

Coed y Squire

Craig Ruperra

Ruperra Castle

1

Ruperra Castle

Coed Llanvedw

New Mansion

Ruperra Home Farm

Gwernleyshon Farm

86

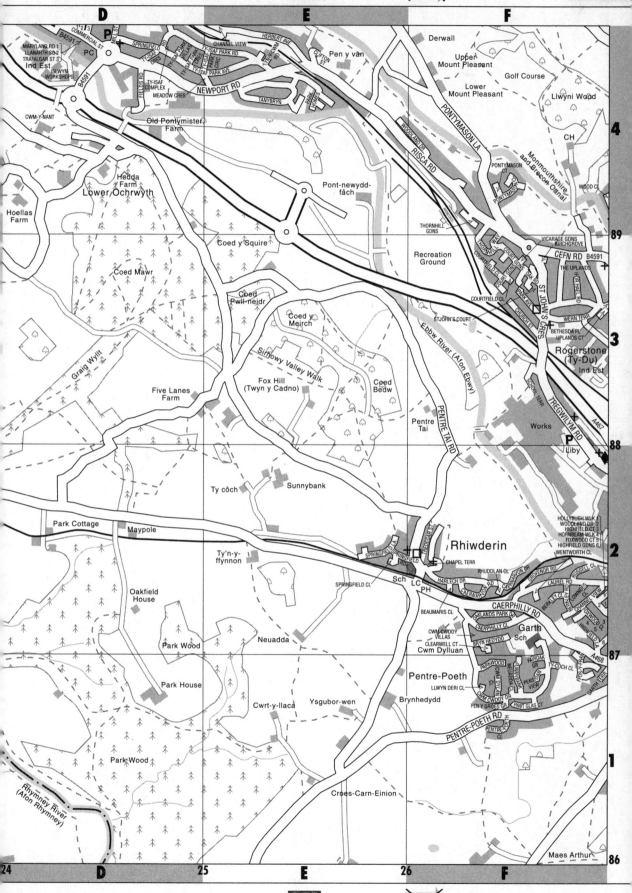

D **E** **F**

MARYLAND RD 1
LLANARTH SQ 2
TRAFALGAR ST 3
Ind Est
ISLWYN
WORKSHOPS
COMMERCIAL ST
MILL ST
B4591
PC
P
SPRINGFIELD
FIELDS RD
TY-ISAF
CRES
TY-ISAF PARK
PLACE
TY-ISAF PARK RD
TY-ISAF PARK ORC
TY-ISAF PARK AVE
HERBERT AVE
CHANNEL VIEW
CLIFTON ST
TY-Y-CWM RD
PARK HOMES
TANYBRYN
Pen y van
Derwall
Upper
Mount Pleasant
Golf Course
Lower
Mount Pleasant
Llwyni Wood
CH

CWM-Y-NANT
NEWPORT RD
MEADOW CRES
TY-ISAF
COMPLEX
PARK AVE

4

Old Pontymister
Farm
Hedda
Farm
Lower Ochrwyth
Hoellas
Farm
RISCA RD
WOODLAND DR
PONTYMASON LA
PONTYMASON
PONTYMASON
Monmouthshire
and Brecon Canal
WOOD CL

THORNHILL
GDNS
VICARAGE GDNS
BIRCHGROVE
CEFN RD
B4591
THE UPLANDS
IFOR HAEL RD

89

Coed y Squire
Pont-newydd-
fâch
Recreation
Ground
THORNHILL
COURT GDNS
COURTFIELD LA
ST JOHN'S CRES
WERN TERR
BETHESDA PL
UPLANDS CT

Coed Mawr
Coed
Pwll-neidr
COURTFIELD CL
ST JOHN'S COURT
PARK AVE
CHURCH ST
Rogerstone
(Ty-Du)
Ind Est

3

Graig Wyllt
Coed y
Meirch
Sirhowy Valley Walk
Fox Hill
(Twyn y Cadno)
Coed
Bedw
Ebbw River (Afon Ebbw)
Works
TREGWILYM RD
A467

Five Lanes
Farm
Pentre
Tai
PENTRE TAI RD
P
Liby

88

Ty côch
Sunnybank
HOLLYBUSH WLK
WOODLAND DR 2
HIGHFIELD CT 3
HORNBEAM WLK 4
FOXWOOD CT 5
HIGHFIELD GDNS 6
WENTWORTH CL

Park Cottage
Maypole
Ty'n-y-
ffynnon
Rhiwderin
SPRINGFIELD RD
SPRINGFIELD
TRECASTLE ST
Chapel Terr
RHUDDLAN CL
GROSVENOR RD
RUSSELL CL
LAUREL RD
CHANNEL VIEW
FOXWOOD CL 2
HIGH FIELD 3

2

SPRINGFIELD CL
Sch
LC
PH
HARLECH DR
CAERNARVON
BEAUMARIS CL
BERKELEY CL
BEAUFORT DR
CAERPHILLY RD
Garth
Sch

Oakfield
House
CWM CWDDY
VILLAS
CLEARWELL CT
Cwm Dylluan
CAERPHILLY CL
BRYN HEDYDD
OAKLANDS PARK DR
A468

Park Wood
Neuadda
Pentre-Poeth
LLWYN DERI CL
FAIROAK
GR
TY-COCH CL
PARK WOOD
PONTYMISTER
HEOL DYLAN
FRESHWATER RD
GARTH TERR

87

Park House
Cwrt-y-llaca
Ysgubor-wen
Brynhedydd
PEN Y GROES GR
CWM CWDDY DR
PANT GLAS CT
PENSARN
VIEW

Park Wood
Croes-Carn-Einion
PENTRE-POETH RD
PENTRE-POETH
CL

1

Rhymney River
(Afon Rhymney)
Maes Arthur

86

24 **D** **25** **E** **26** **F**

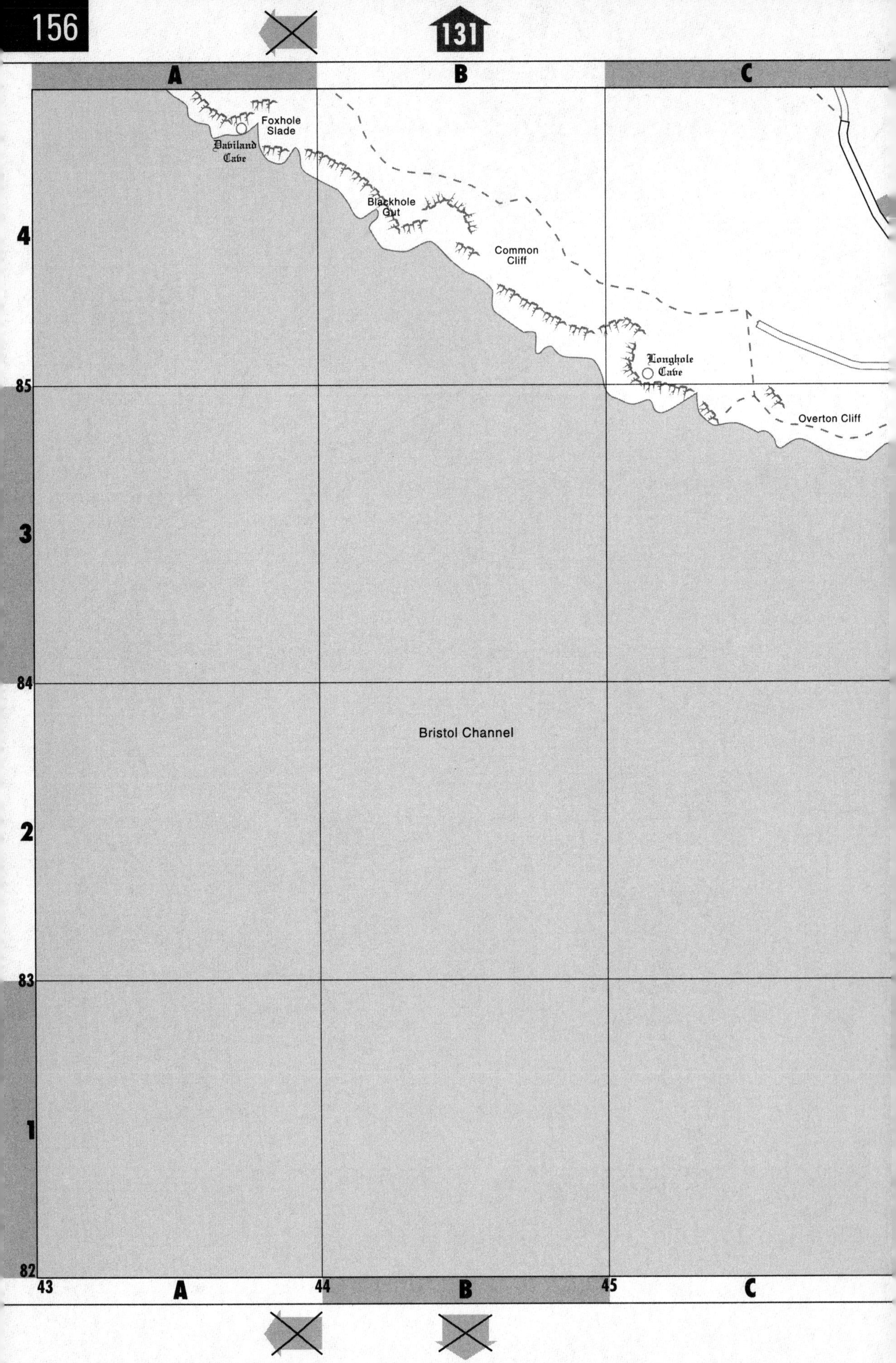

A B C

Foxhole
Slade

Daviland
Cave

Blackhole
Gut

Common
Cliff

4

Longhole
Cave

85

Overton Cliff

3

84

Bristol Channel

2

83

1

82

43 44 45

A B C

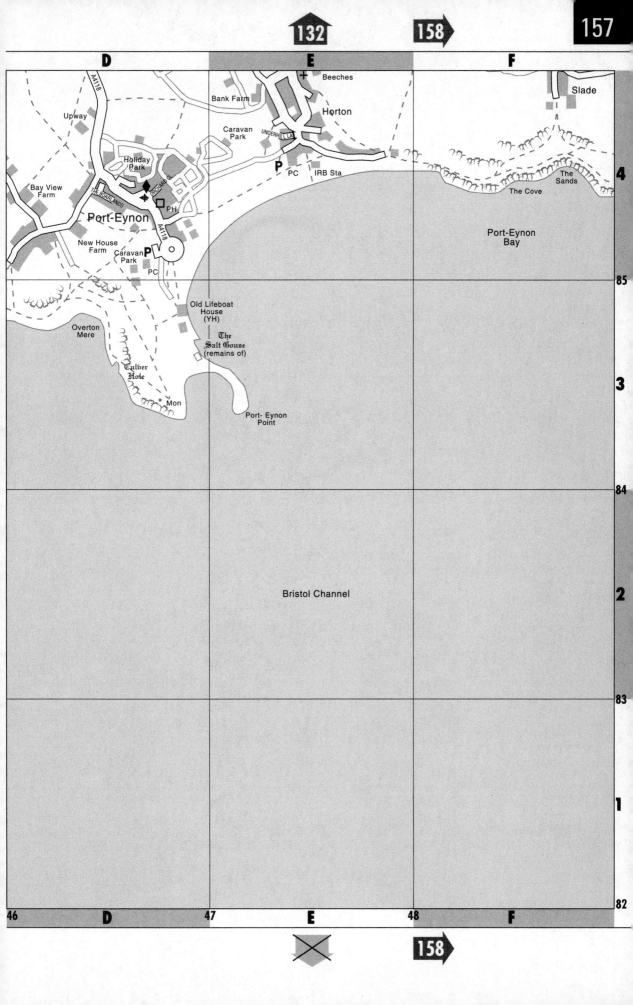

D

A4118

Upway

Bank Farm

+ Beeches

Horton

Caravan
Park

UNDERHILL LA.

Holiday
Park

ORCHARD CL

Bay View
Farm

THE BOARLANDS

Port-Eynon

□ PH

P

PC

IRB Sta

Slade

4

The
Sands

The Cove

New House
Farm

A4118

Caravan
Park

P

PC

O

Port-Eynon
Bay

85

Old Lifeboat
House
(YH)

Overton
Mere

The
Salt Gouse
(remains of)

Culver
Hole

• Mon

Port- Eynon
Point

3

84

Bristol Channel

2

83

1

82

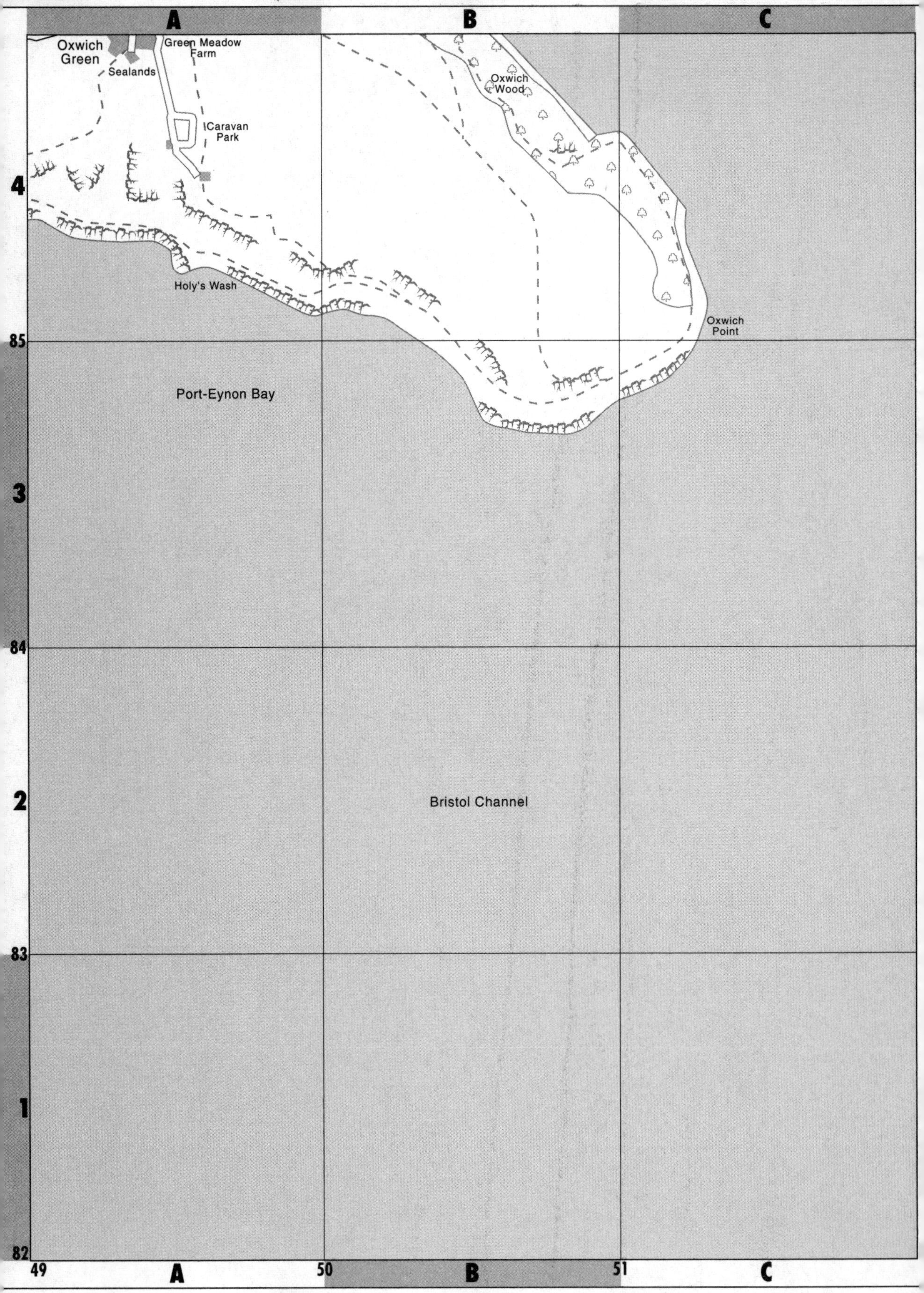

157

133

A

B

C

Oxwich
Green

Green Meadow
Farm

Sealands

Oxwich
Wood

Caravan
Park

4

Holy's Wash

85

Oxwich
Point

Port-Eynon Bay

3

84

2

Bristol Channel

83

1

82

49

50

51

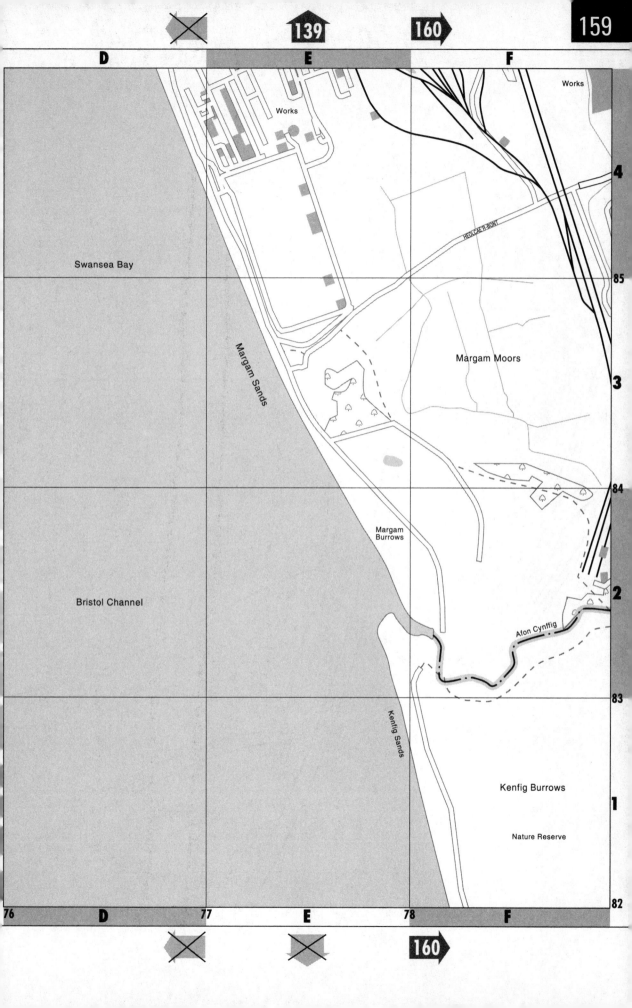

Works

Works

Swansea Bay

HEOLCAE R-BONT

Margam Moors

Margam Sands

Bristol Channel

Margam Burrows

Afon Cynffig

Kenfig Sands

Kenfig Burrows

Nature Reserve

159
140

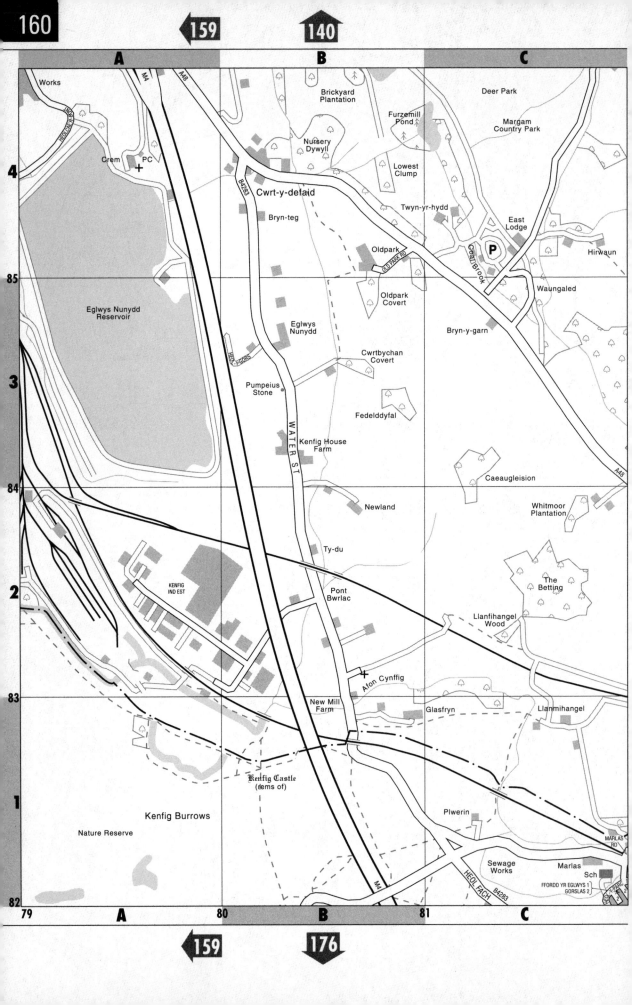

A   **B**   **C**

Works

Brickyard
Plantation

Deer Park

Furzemill
Pond

Margam
Country Park

Crem

PC

Nursery
Dywyll

Lowest
Clump

4

Cwrt-y-defaid

Twyn-yr-hydd

East
Lodge

Bryn-teg

Oldpark

Hirwaun

P

B4283

OLD PARK RD

Craig Brook

85

Oldpark
Covert

Waungaled

Eglwys Nunydd
Reservoir

Eglwys
Nunydd

Bryn-y-garn

Cwrtbychan
Covert

3

HEOL EGOBS

Pumpeius
Stone

Fedelddyfal

WATER ST

Kenfig House
Farm

Caeaugleision

A48

84

Newland

Whitmoor
Plantation

Ty-du

The
Betting

KENFIG
IND EST

2

Pont
Bwrlac

Llanfihangel
Wood

Afon Cynffig

Glasfryn

Llanmihangel

83

New Mill
Farm

Kenfig Castle
(rems of)

Plwerin

MARLAS
RD

1

Kenfig Burrows

Nature Reserve

Sewage
Works

Marlas

Sch

M4

HEOL FACH

B4283

FFORDD YR EGLWYS 1
GORSLAS 2

82

79   **A**   80   **B**   81   **C**

159
176

161 142

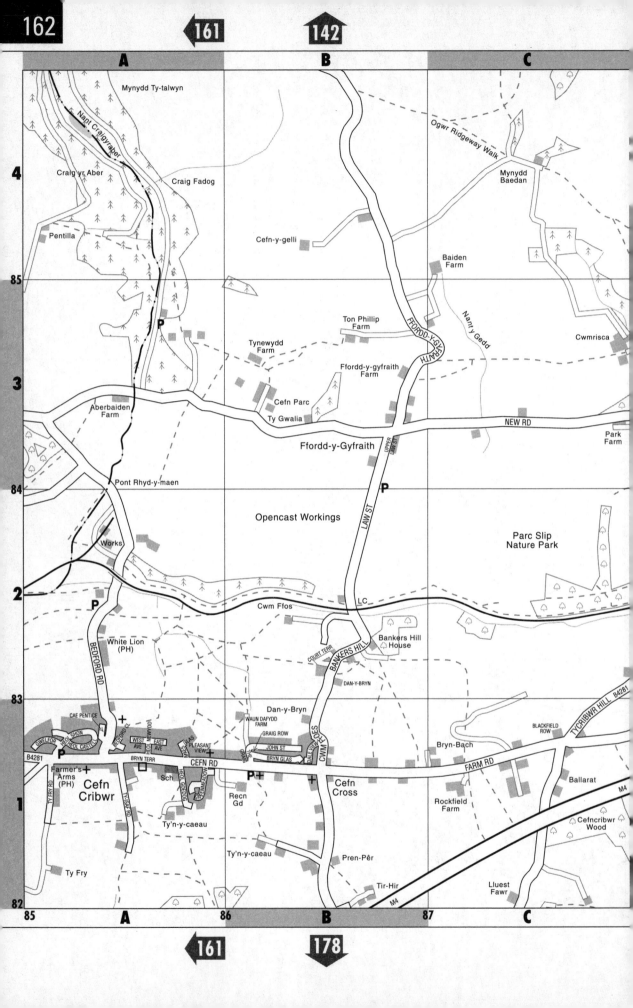

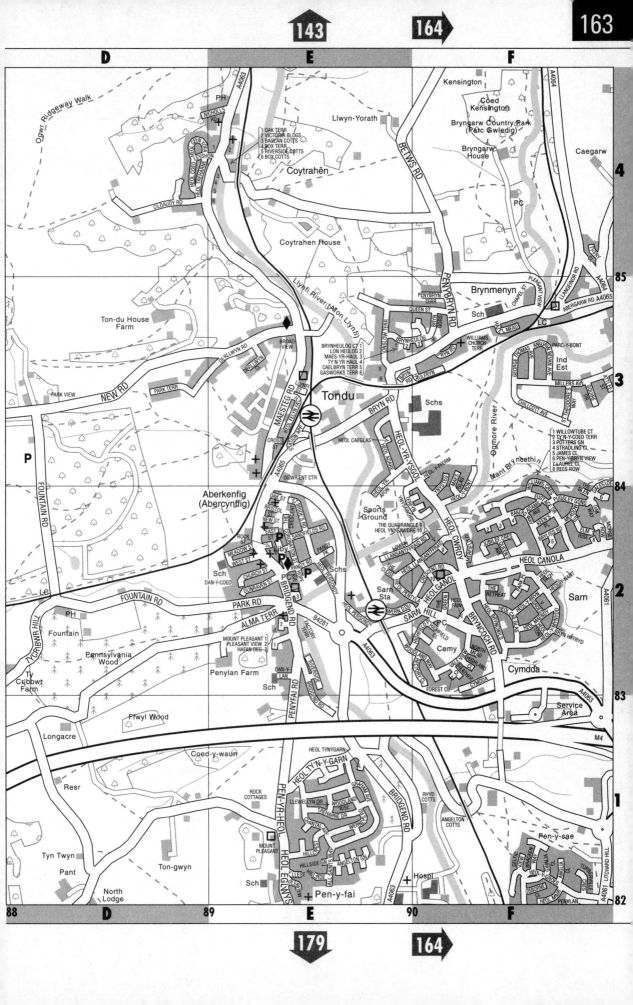

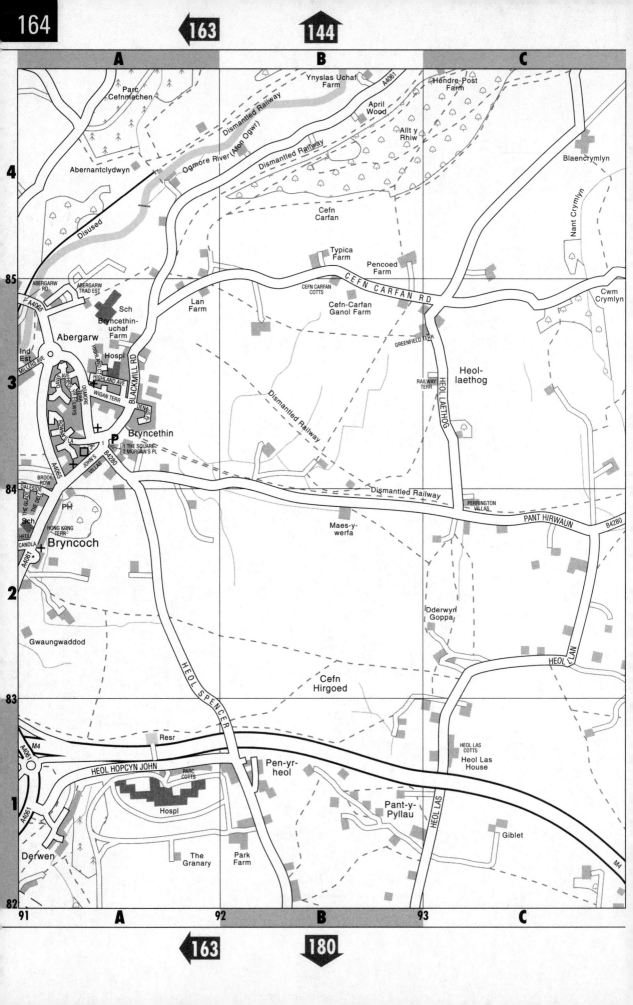

A   **B**   **C**

Parc Cefnmachen

Ynyslas Uchaf Farm

Hendre-Post Farm

April Wood

Dismantled Railway

Allt y Rhiw

Blaencrymlyn

4

Ogmore River (Afon Ogwr)

Dismantled Railway

Abernantclydwyn

Disused

Cefn Carfan

Nant Crymlyn

Typica Farm

Cwm Crymlyn

85

ABERGARW RD

ABERGARW TRAD EST

Sch

Lan Farm

CEFN CARFAN COTTS

Pencoed Farm

CEFN CARFAN RD

Abergarw

Bryncethin-uchaf Farm

Cefn-Carfan Ganol Farm

Greenfield Terr

Ind Est

MILLERS AVE

Hospl

HIGHLAND AVE

BLACKMILL RD

Heol-laethog

3

OGMORE TERR

WIGAN TERR

Dismantled Railway

RAILWAY TERR

HEOL LAETHOG

HEOL YR CLWYS

FOWLER LA

DERWAS LA

Bryncethin

1 THE SQUARE
2 MORGAN'S PL

P

A4065

JOHN'S VILLAS

B4280

84

BROOK ROW

DALESIDE

THE DELL

THE GLADE

PH

HONG KONG TERR

Dismantled Railway

PERRINGTON VILLAS

PANT HIRWAUN

B4280

Sch

HEOL

CANOLA

Bryncoch

Maes-y-werfa

A4061

2

Dderwyn Goppa

Gwaungwaddod

HEOL LAN

HEOL SPENCER

Cefn Hirgoed

83

Resr

M4

A4061

HEOL HOPCYN JOHN

PARC COTTS

Pen-yr-heol

Heol Las Cotts

Heol Las House

1

Hospl

Pant-y-Pyllau

HEOL LAS

Giblet

Derwen

The Granary

Park Farm

M4

82

91   **A**   **92**   **B**   **93**   **C**

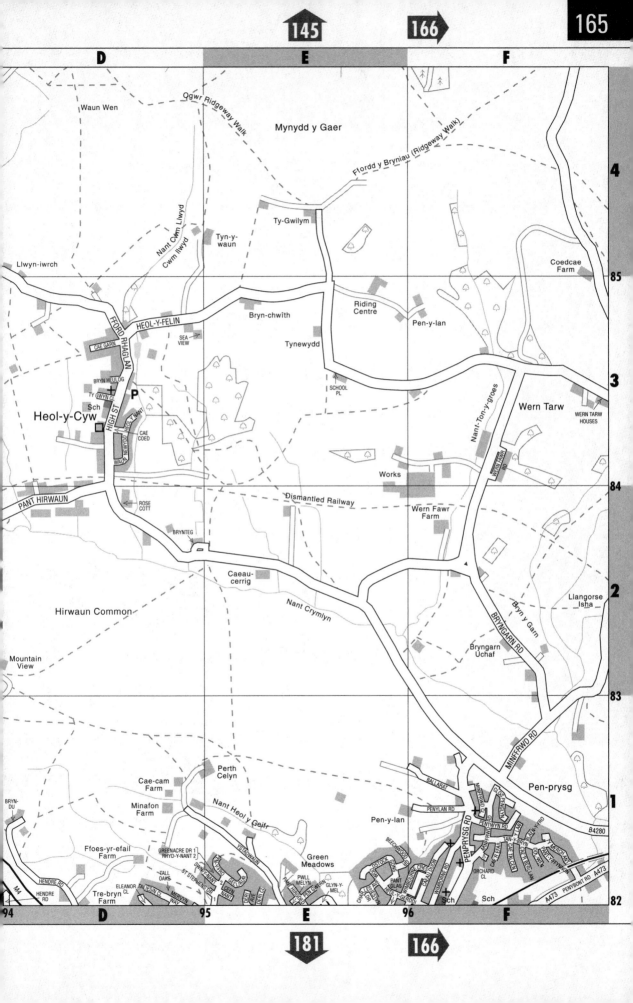

D
E
F

Waun Wen

Ogwr Ridgeway Walk

Mynydd y Gaer

Ffordd y Bryniau (Ridgeway Walk)

4

Nant Cwm Llwyd

Cwm llwyd

Tyn-y-waun

Ty-Gwilym

Ty-Gwilym

Coedcae Farm

85

Llwyn-iwrch

HEOL-Y-FELIN

Bryn-chwîth

Riding Centre

Pen-y-lan

FFORD RHAGLAN

CAE GARN

SEA VIEW

Tynewydd

BRYN HEULOG

TY GWYN CL

Heol-y-Cyw

Sch

P

HIGH ST

HEOL Y NANT

HEOL Y NANT

CAE COED

SCHOOL PL

Wern Tarw

WERN TARW HOUSES

3

WALK

Nant-Ton-y-groes

WERN FAWR RD

Works

84

PANT HIRWAUN

ROSE COTT

Dismantled Railway

Wern Fawr Farm

BRYNTEG

Caeau-cerrig

Nant Crymlyn

Hirwaun Common

Llangorse Isha

2

Bryn y Garn

BRYNGARN RD

Bryngarn Uchaf

Mountain View

83

MINFFRWD RD

Perth Celyn

Pen-prysg

BRYN-DU

Cae-cam Farm

Nant Heol y Geifr

BALLARAT

1

Minafon Farm

PENYLAN RD

Pen-y-lan

PENPRYSG RD

MINFFRWD RD

PENTWYN RD

B4280

Ffoes-yr-efail Farm

GREENACRE DR 1
RHYD-Y-NANT 2

YSTRADWAUN

BEECHWOOD

GLAS PENGWYN

TAN-Y-BRYN

CAE TEGAU

PARC-Y-FRO

ORCHARD CL

A473

HENDRE RD

TALL OAKS

ST STEPHENS DR

SWN-Y-NANT

PANT GLAS

Sch

PENYBONT RD A473

HENDRE RD

ELEANOR CL
TALIESIN CL

MERVYN WAY

CERI AVE

GREEN NANT

PANT HEOL

GLYN-Y-MEL

Green Meadows

PWLL MELYN

Sch

Tre-bryn Farm

94

D

95

E

96

F

82

A   B   C

4

85

3

Cwm Rhydymilwyr

Ty'n-yCwm

Nant Ciwc

Mynydd Maendy

Mynydd Hugh

Maendy

Ffordd y Bryniau (Ridgeway Walk)

Mynydd Portref

St Peter's Church (rems of)

Cadairfarch

Rhiwceiliog

Rhiw-ceiliog

Ty-Robert

Llanbad-fawr

Nant Llanbad

Cwm Llanbad

Mynydd Coedbychan

84

Ty'n-y-coed

BRYNHEULOG

Coed Bychan

2

Hendir-uchaf

Nant Ciwc

MILL COTTS

Brynna

CHURCH VIEW CL 1
MOSTYN CL 2
MELBOURNE TERR 3
BRYN HENLLAN 4

CHURCH ST

GELLIFED

TAN-Y-BRYN

CHURCH VIEW

LLANBAD

HILLCREST

HILLCREST

HILLCREST

BRYNNA RD

ST MARK'S CL
MEADOW RISE
TREDEGAR CL
ST PETER'S CL

Cemy

LLANBRYN GDNS

PC

ST AARONS

VALE VIEW

MEADOW CL

PENDER CRES

ST JULIUS CRES

COED BYCHAN CRES

GROVE TERR

PARK TERR

CHAPEL HILL CL

CHAPEL HILL

SCHOOL TERR

CHAPEL TERR

TREDEGAR AVE

SOUTHALL ST

WILLIAMS ST

HEOL DEW
TY CLOS
KES DERWEN

HAWTHORN

MAYWOOD

MAYWOOD

HAWTHORN PK

83

Sch

Dismantled Railway

1

Brynnau Gwynion

RED ROOFS CL

MANOR PK

BRYNNA RD

LC

Tre-nos-isaf

TRENOS GDNS

TRENOS PL

DUFFRYN CRES

HEATHERTON CRES

WOODFIELD ST

WESTBOURNE TERR

SOUTH VIEW

Bryncae

BRYNCAE IND EST

BRIDGEND RD

JUBILEE CL

ROBERT CL

HAVOD CL

A473

ROSE TERR

PC

HEOL CYNLLAN

BRYN-Y-CAE

BRYN-Y-CAE

Sch

B4280

A473

PENYBONT RD

Brynheulog

OLD LLANHARAN RD

NEW RD

82

97   98   99

A   B   C

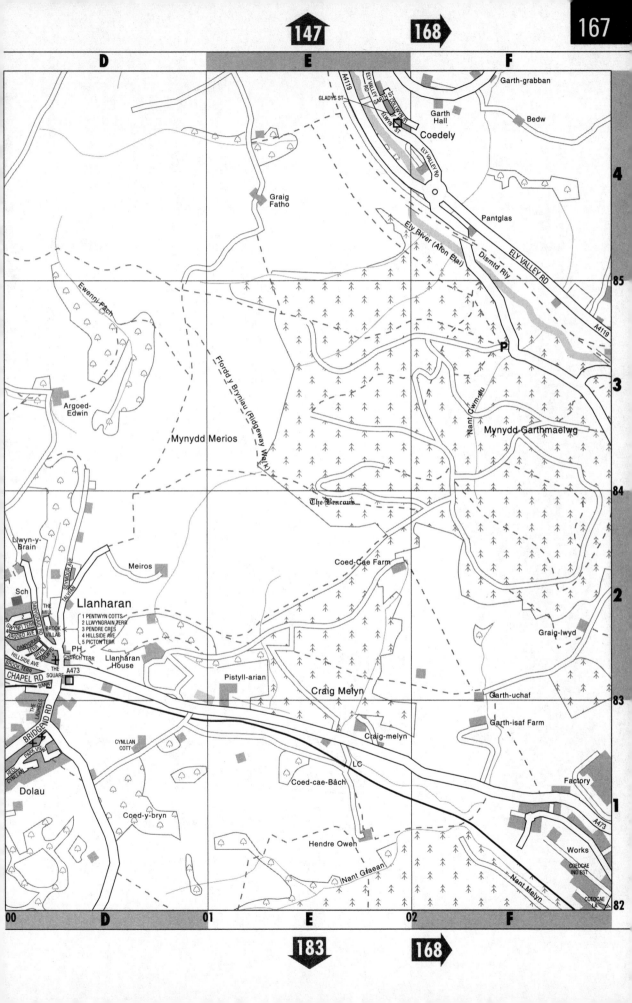

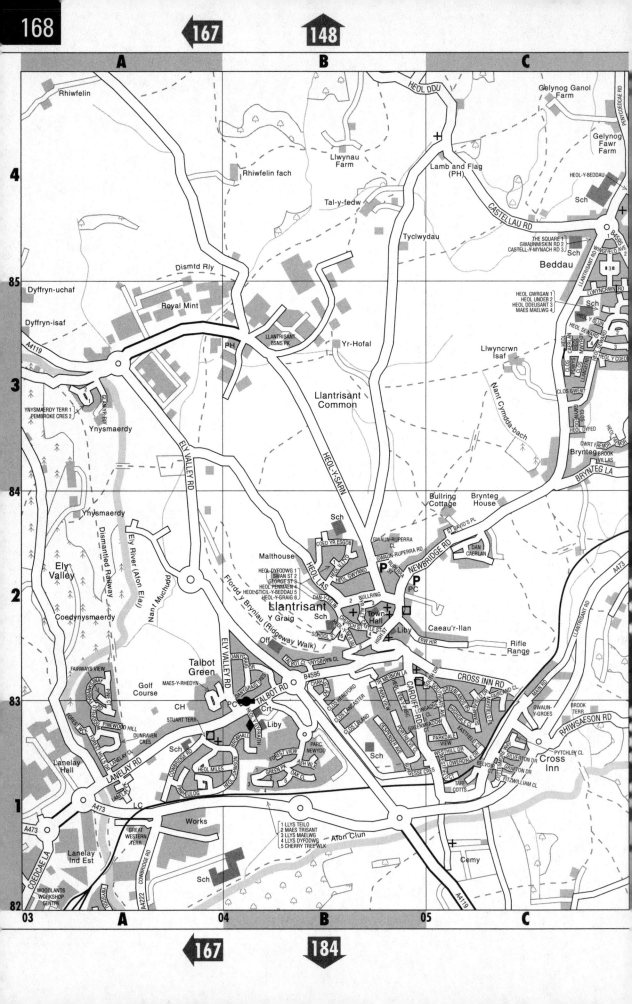

A B C

4

Rhiwfelin

Llwynau Farm

HEOL DDU

Gelynog Ganol Farm

Rhiwfelin fach

Lamb and Flag (PH)

Gelynog Fawr Farm

HEOL-Y-BEDDAU

Tal-y-fedw

CASTELLAU RD

Sch

Tyclwydau

THE SQUARE 1
GWAUNMISKIN RD 2
CASTELL-Y-MYNACH RD 3.

Sch

WINGFIELD AVE

Beddau

85

Dismtd Rly

Dyffryn-uchaf

Royal Mint

LLANTRISANT BSNS PK

Yr-Hofal

HEOL GWRGAN 1
HEOL UNDEB 2
HEOL DDEUSANT 3
MAES MAELWG 4.

Sch

LLWYNCRWN RD

Dyffryn-isaf

PH

A4119

3

YNYSMAERDY TERR 1
PEMBROKE CRES 2

Ynysmaerdy

Llantrisant Common

Llwyncrwn isaf

Nant Cymdda-bach

Brynteg

BROOK VILLAS

BRYNTEG LA

84

Ynysmaerdy

ELY VALLEY RD

HEOL-Y-SARN

Sch

Bullring Cottage

Brynteg House

Ely Valley

Dismantled Railway

Ely River (Afon Elái)

Coedynysmaerdy

Malthouse

COED YR ESGOB

HEOL LLWYD

Y GRAIG

HEOL GWYNNO

GWAUN-RUPERRA CL

GWAUN-RUPERRA RD

ST DAVID'S PL

NEWBRIDGE RD

DAN CAERLAN

2

Nant Muchudd

Ffordd y Bryniau (Ridgeway Walk)

Y Graig

HEOL-DYFODWG 1
SWAN ST 2
GEORGE ST 3
HEOL PENMAEN 4
HEOL STICIL-Y-BEDDAU 5
HEOL-Y-GRAIG 6

HEOL LAS

DAN-Y-FELIN

BULLRING

Llantrisant

Sch

CHURCH ST

Bullring

Town Hall

Liby

Caeau'r-Ilan

Rifle Range

Off

SCHOOL S

HIGH ST

ERW HIR

Fairways View

PINE CT

Golf Course

MAES-Y-RHEDYN

DANYGRAIG DR

DANYGRAIG CRES

TALBOT RD

YNYSBRYN CL

B4595

CHAR CL

CLOS HEREFORD

TIR MEIBION LA

CROSS INN RD

GWAUN-Y-GROES

RHIWSAESON RD

83

CH

Talbot Green

PC

Crt

Liby

Stuart Terr

HEOL Y FFRWD

FOREST VIEW

PARC NEWYDD

CLOS LANCASTER

CLOS LELAND

Sch

Cross Inn

Lanelay Hall

LANELAY RD

Sch

HEOL MILES

ASH WLK

GREEN PK

OAK CL

Cemy

1

A473

LC

Works

1 LLYS TEILO
2 MAES TRISANT
3 LLYS MAELWG
4 LLYS DYFODWG
5 CHERRY TREE WLK

Afon Clun

A4119

A473

COEDCAE LA

Lanelay Ind Est

GREAT WESTERN TERR

Sch

82

WOODLANDS WORKSHOP CENTRE

03 A 04 B 05 C

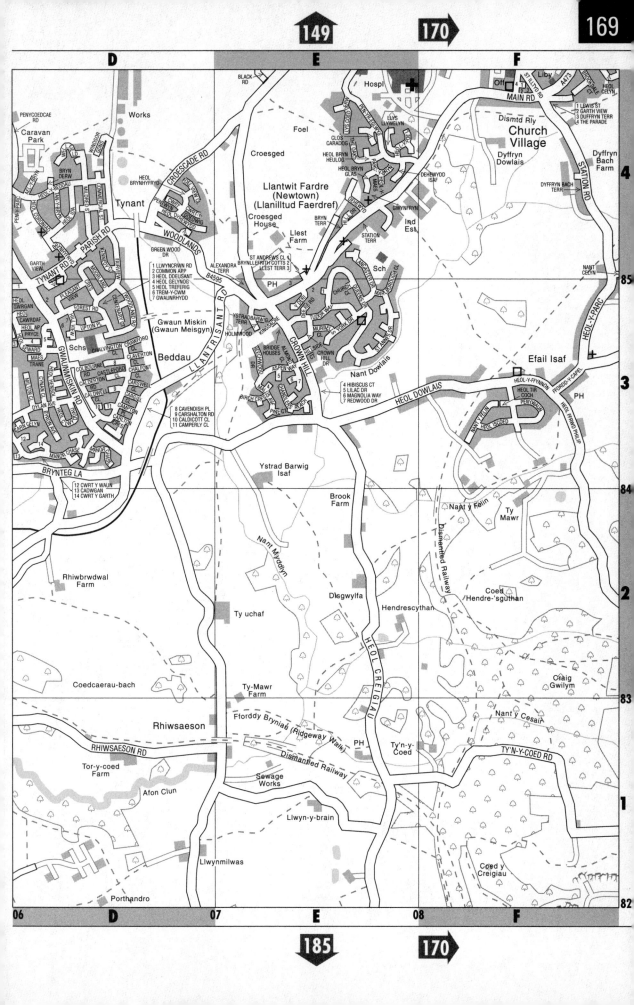

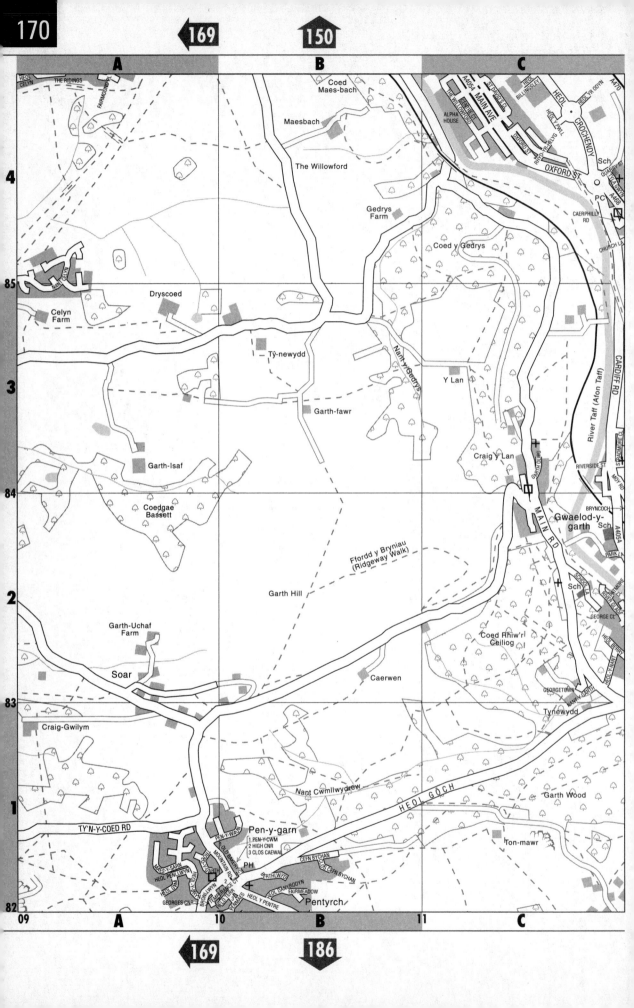

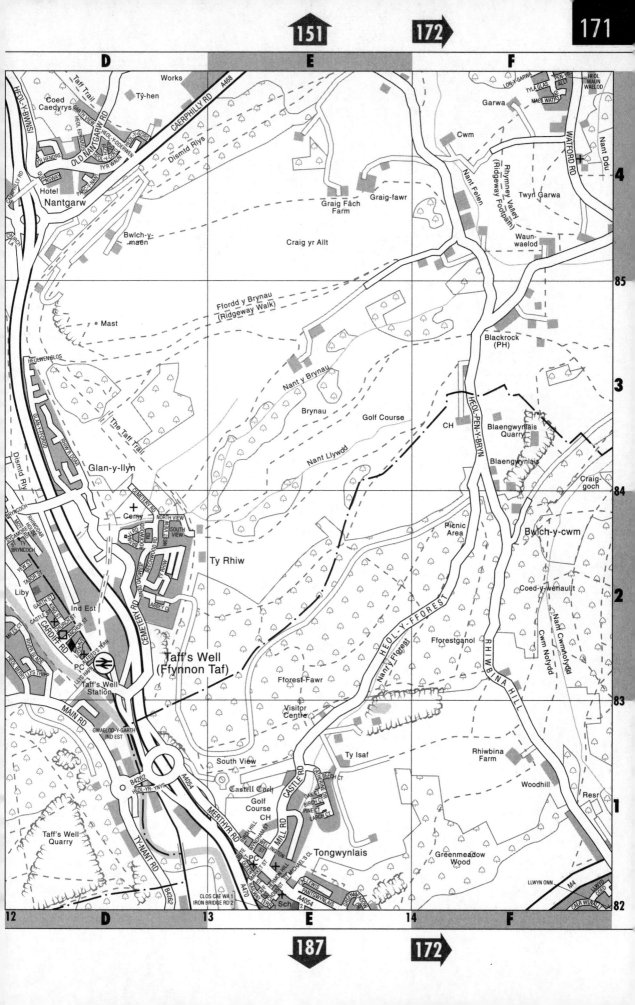

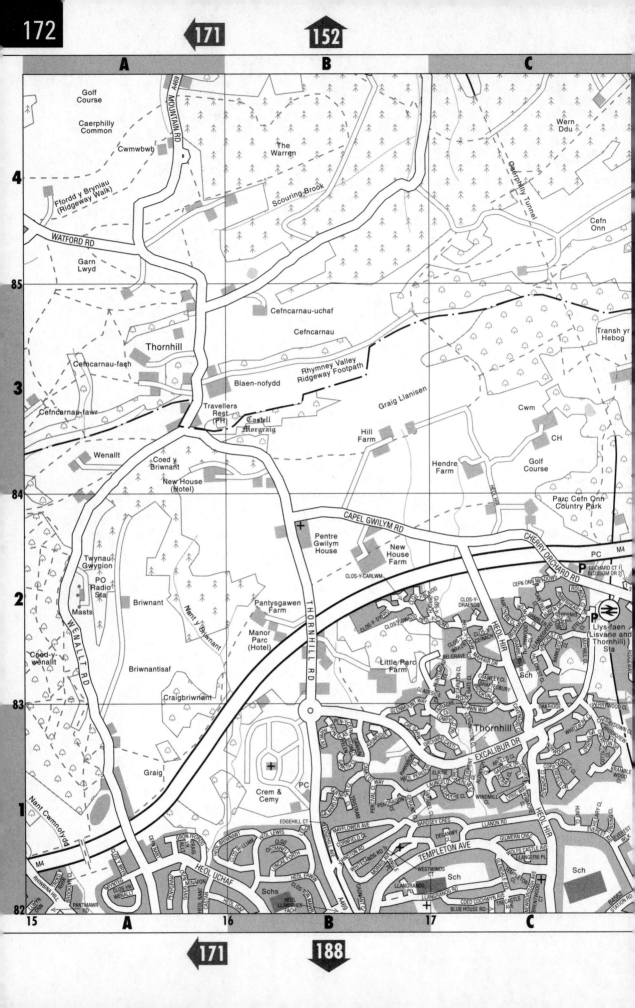

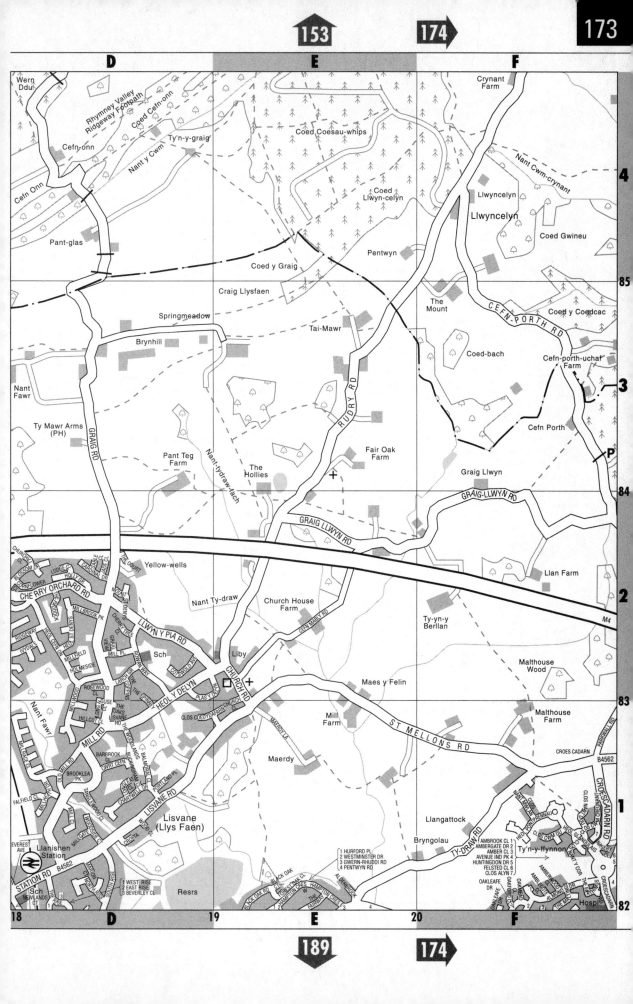

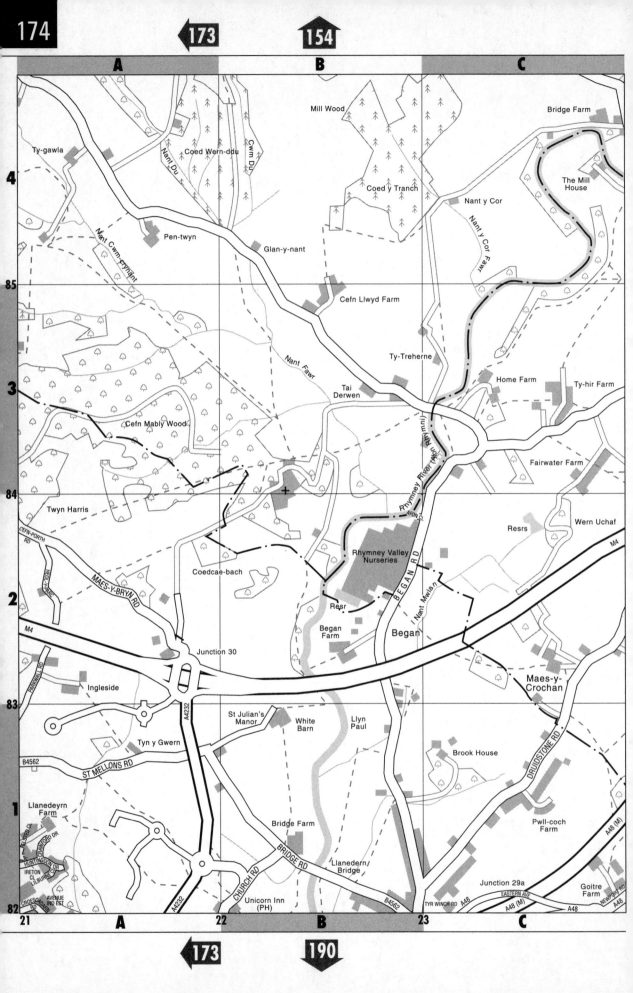

A B C

4

85

3

84

2

83

1

82

21 A 22 B 23 C

Mill Wood
Bridge Farm
Ty-gawla
Coed Wern-ddu
Cwm Du
Nant Du
Nant Cwm-grynant
Coed y Tranch
The Mill House
Nant y Cor
Pen-twyn
Glan-y-nant
Nant y Cor Fawr
Cefn Llwyd Farm
Nant Fawr
Ty-Treherne
Home Farm
Ty-hir Farm
Tai Derwen
Cefn Mably Wood
Rhymney River Afon Rhymni
Fairwater Farm
Twyn Harris
AFON CL
Resrs
Wern Uchaf
CEFN-PORTH RD
HOL-Y-GARE
Resrs
M4
Coedcae-bach
Rhymney Valley Nurseries
BEGAN RD
MAES-Y-BRYN RD
Resr
Nant Mwlan
M4
Began Farm
Began
Junction 30
Maes-y-Crochan
PARRWALL RD
Ingleside
St Julian's Manor
White Barn
Llyn Paul
DRUIDSTONE RD
Tyn y Gwern
Brook House
B4562
ST MELLONS RD
Llanedeyrn Farm
FIELSTED CL
Bridge Farm
Pwll-coch Farm
A48 (M)
HUNTINGDON DR
IRETON CL
LILBURN
CROESCADARN
BRIDGE RD
Llanedern Bridge
Junction 29a
Goitre Farm
AVENUE IND EST
Croescadarn RD
A4232
CHURCH RD
Unicorn Inn (PH)
B4562
TYR WINCH RD
A48
EASTERN AVE
A48 (M)
A48
NEWPORT RD
A4232

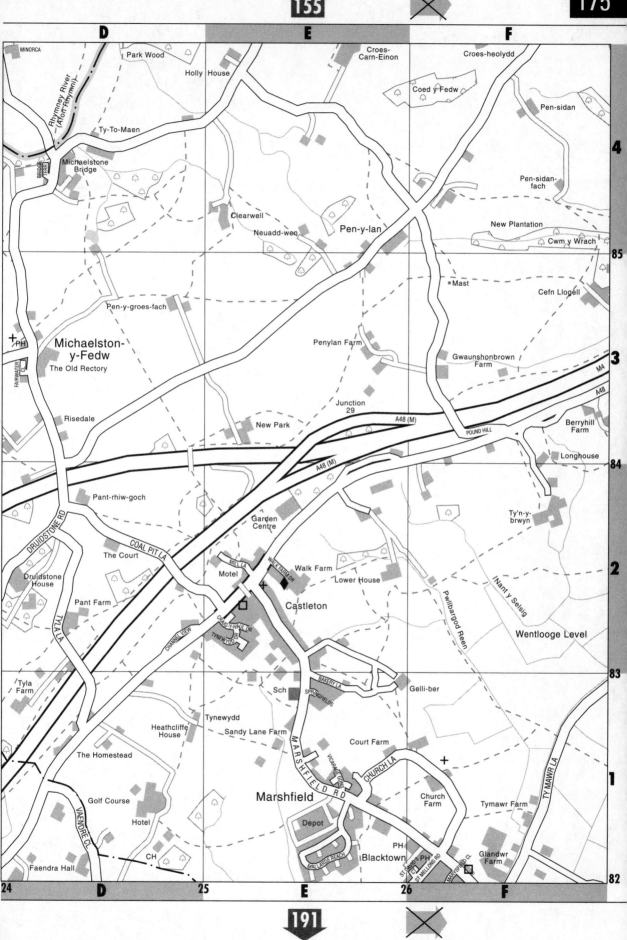

MINORCA

Park Wood

Holly House

Croes-Carn-Einon

Croes-heolydd

Coed y Fedw

Pen-sidan

Rhymney River (Afon Rhymni)

Ty-To-Maen

Michaelstone Bridge

BRIDGE FARM

Pen-sidan-fach

4

Clearwell

Neuadd-wen

Pen-y-lan

New Plantation

Cwm y Wrach

85

Mast

Cefn Llogell

PH

FAIRWATER CL

Pen-y-groes-fach

Michaelston-y-Fedw

The Old Rectory

Penylan Farm

Gwaunshonbrown Farm

M4

3

A48

Risedale

New Park

Junction 29

A48 (M)

POUND HILL

Berryhill Farm

Longhouse

84

A48 (M)

DRUIDSTONE RD

Pant-rhiw-goch

Ty'n-y-brwyn

Garden Centre

The Court

MILL LA

Motel

WALK FARM DR

Walk Farm

Lower House

l Nant y Selsig

Wentlooge Level

2

Druidstone House

Pant Farm

CHANNEL VIEW

CRAIG-Y-HAUL DR

TYNEWYDD

Castleton

Pwllbargod Reen

TYLA LA

BAKERY LA

SPRINGFIELDS

Gelli-ber

83

Tyla Farm

Sch

Tynewydd

Sandy Lane Farm

Court Farm

Heathcliffe House

The Homestead

MARSHFIELD RD

VICAREE GDNS

CHURCH LA

Church Farm

Tymawr Farm

TY MAWR LA

1

Golf Course

Hotel

Marshfield

Depot

PH

MALLARDS REACH

Blacktown

ST DAVIDS CT

ST DAVIDS RD

PH

ST MELLONS RD

MARSHFIELD CL

Glandwr Farm

CH

Faendra Hall

VAENDRE CL

24

25

26

82

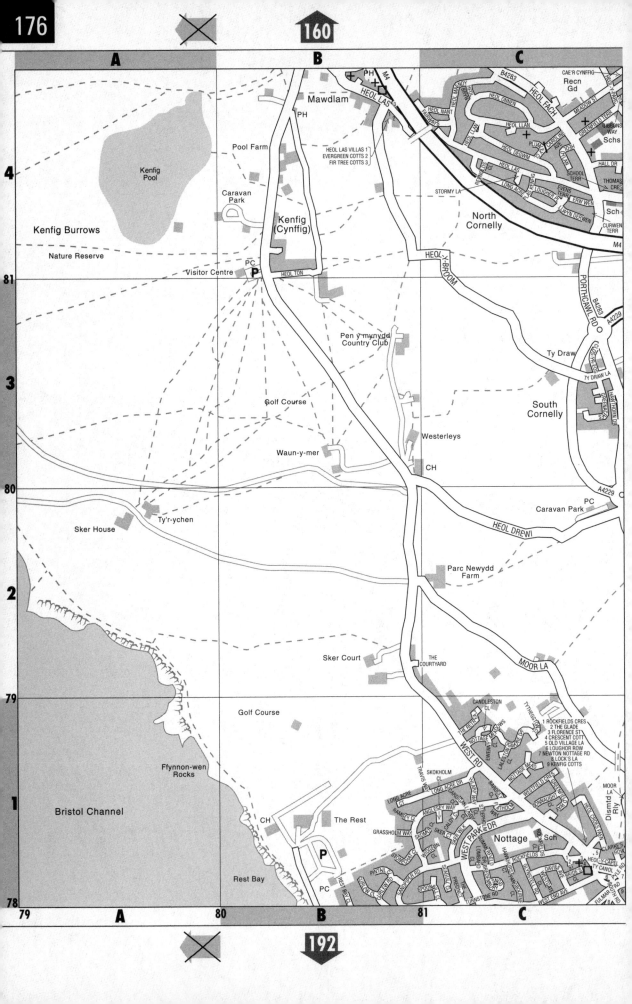

FFYNNON WEN
GIBBONS WAY
PIL-Y-CYNFFIG
A5 PIL-Y-BRYN
Industrial Estate
HEOL TYDRAW
VILLAGE FARM
HEOL MOSTYN
Village Farm Rd

Afon Fach

1 CAE R CYNFFIG
2 BRON-Y-WAWR
PLAS MORFA
HEOL YR EGLWYS
HEOL TYDRAW CRES
A48 PYLE RD
Factory
Dismantled Railway
Stormy

TIR NEWYDD
PLAS GLAS
Cemy
PLAS HEDDWCH
BRIXHAM
HALL DR
HEOL Y PARC

4

THOMAS CRES
HEOL FAWR
WASHINGTON WAY

81

1 SCHOOL TERR
2 FAIRFIELD
Junction 37
M4

Ty Tanglwyst Farm
HEOL-Y-SHEET
Ballas Cottage
Ballas Farm
Stormy Down
Stormy West Quarries (disused)

Old Ballas

3

PH
Cornelly Quarry
Pant-mawr Quarries (disused)
Stormy Down Quarry
A48

PORTHCAWL RD
RAILWAY TERR
HEOL-Y-SPLOT

Works
Cornelly Quarry

SOUTH CORNELLY IND EST

80

Grove Quarry
MOUNT PLEASANT RD
Mount Pleasant Farm

Grove
Tyllau Gro

Dismantled Railway
Tycoch Farm
Newton Down
The Beacons

2

Pant yr Hyl
Fir Wood

Ty'n-y-caeau

79

Orchard Farm
PYLE RD
JUBILEE GDNS
Pant yr Iards

St David's Well
Cemy
ZIG-ZAG RD
Tir Hapus

MOOR LA
MOOR LA
TYN-Y-CAEAU LA

1

A4106
Coedargraig
BRIDGEND RD
Wig-Fach Farm

Nottage Court
MARLPIT LA
Nottage
Manor Farm

NEWTON
NOTTAGE RD
M4229
A4106
The Lodge
A4106
ELDER DR
Danygraig

78

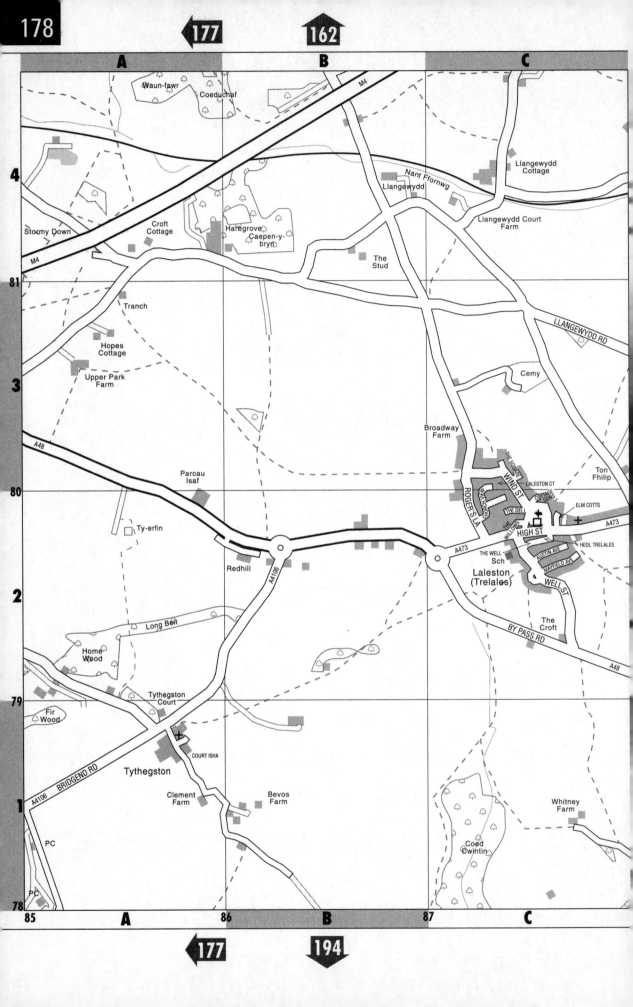

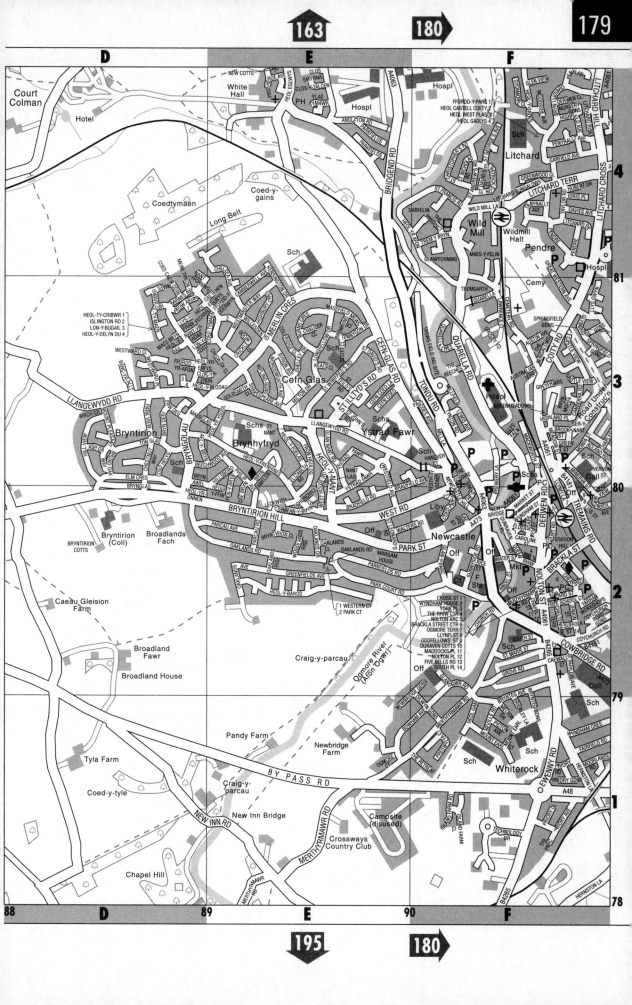

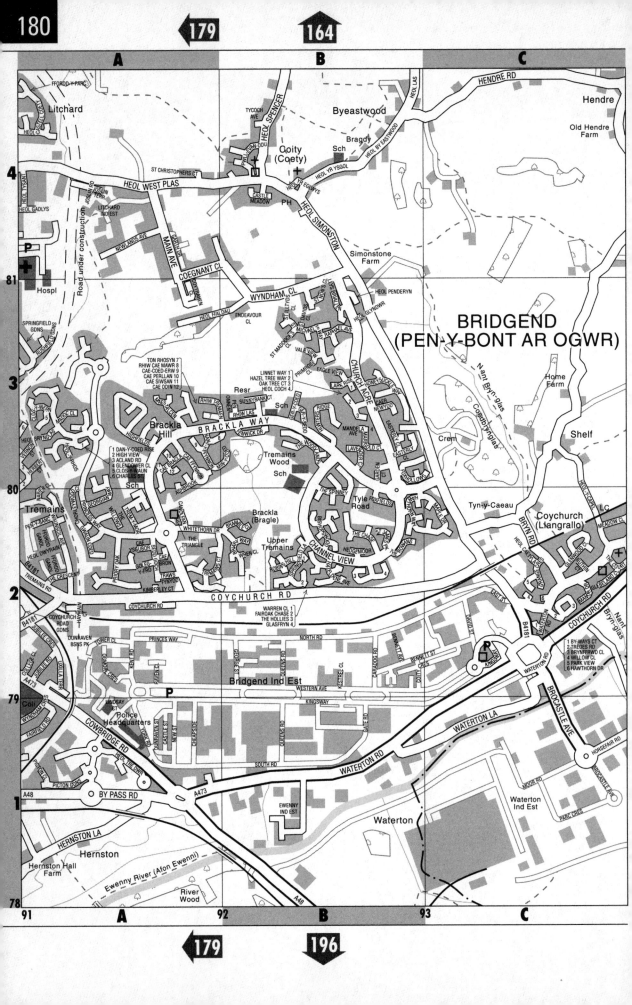

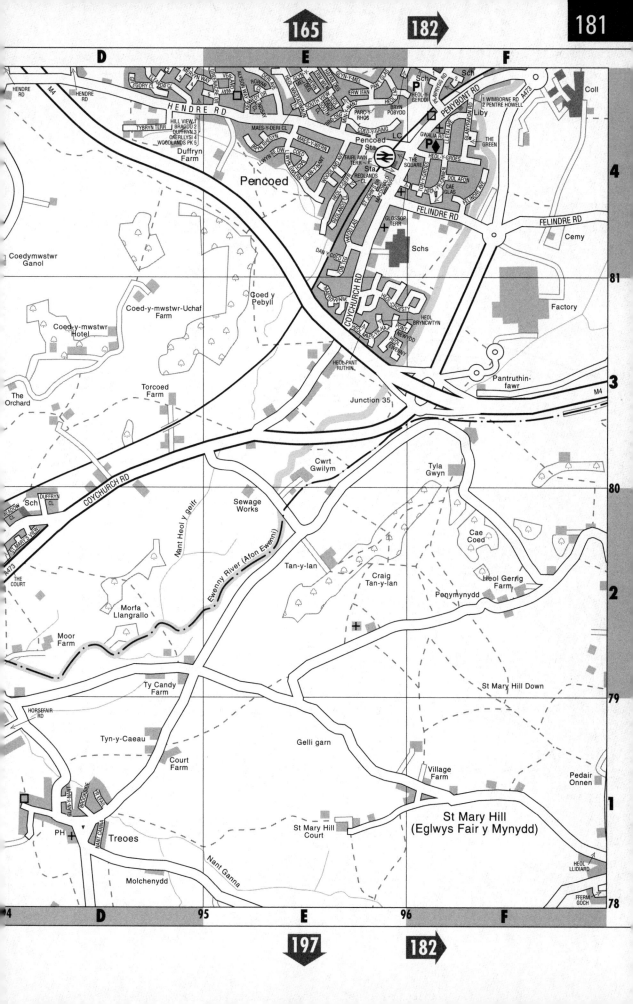

A B C

Tir-eithin

Mynydd Hywel
Deio

Ewenni Fach

4

Opencast
Workings

Llanilid

Felindre

Gelynog
Fâch

FELINDRE RD

Velindre
Farm

81

Tre-Frân

Coed-y-
wiw

M4

Coed y
Brynau

3

Craig-y-
Ruthin

CH

Fron-
wen
Farm

Golf
Course

M4

80

Ruthyn
Fawr

Brigam
Farm

Ruthin

Hillside
Farmhouse

Mynydd
Ruthin

Ton-
Breigam

Coed
Breigam

2

Argoed-ganol
Farm

Pant-y-lliwydd
Farm

River Thaw (Afon Ddawan)

79

Cae-Rhys-ddu

Windmill
Farm

Coed
Pant-Llywydd

Gelli-goll

Pedair
Onnen

1

Pont y
Rhyd

City

City Inn
(PH)

Is-y-coed
Farm

Rectory
Farm
House

FFERM GOCH

Graig

78

97 A 98 B 99 C

D
E
F

LC

Bryn
Awel
LLANHARRY RD
GWAUN
COTTS
Gwaun Llanhari

Cwm
Gran

Coed Trecastell

WOODLAND
TERR
ASH GR
PH
LLWYN ONN

Ty'n-y-waun

TYLAGARW TERR

TYLE GARW

4

Trecastell

Ty-du

Ty-draw

Torgelli

81

Nant Felin-fach

Sewage
Works

LLANHARRY RD

DANYBRYN

A4222

HIGH

Llanharry

Llechau
Farm

Brynsadler

Llwyna
Farm

BRYN TEREST

PADDOCKS

TAL-Y-GARN
OR

M4

PE PATCH

TRECASTLE

STATION TERR

Castell-y-
mwnws

TAL-Y-GARN CT

PH

Carreg Arwth

ADDISON AVE

TY ISAF
ELM RD
ALDER RD
BIRCH RD
TYLACOCH
GELLI RD
GELLI

The Elms
Farm

ST ANNES

3

Sch

HAZELDENE
ROWAN CT
LINDEN
CT
DROS COL
LAUR
LLDENE

MAPLE CL
BEECH RD
ASH GR
SYCAMORE RD
HAWTHORN RD
OLD MOTHIN
HEOL PANT GWYN

Tynewydd

Llwyn Gwyn

80

Degar
Farm

Cemy

FFOREST RD

Forest Wood
Quarry

Nant Rhydhalog

Rhydhalog

COWBRIDGE RD

2

Fforest-fawr

Fforest Fach

Tynytranch
Farm

79

Sch

Tymaen

Llwyn-
nwydog

Morfa Ystradowen

Newforest House
Farm

Crofta Farm

Mynydd y Fforest

Bryn-y-
fedwen

Dismantled Railway

Nant Dyfrgi

1

Coed Wern-fawr

Halifax

Ash Hall

A4222

78

00
D
01
E
02
F

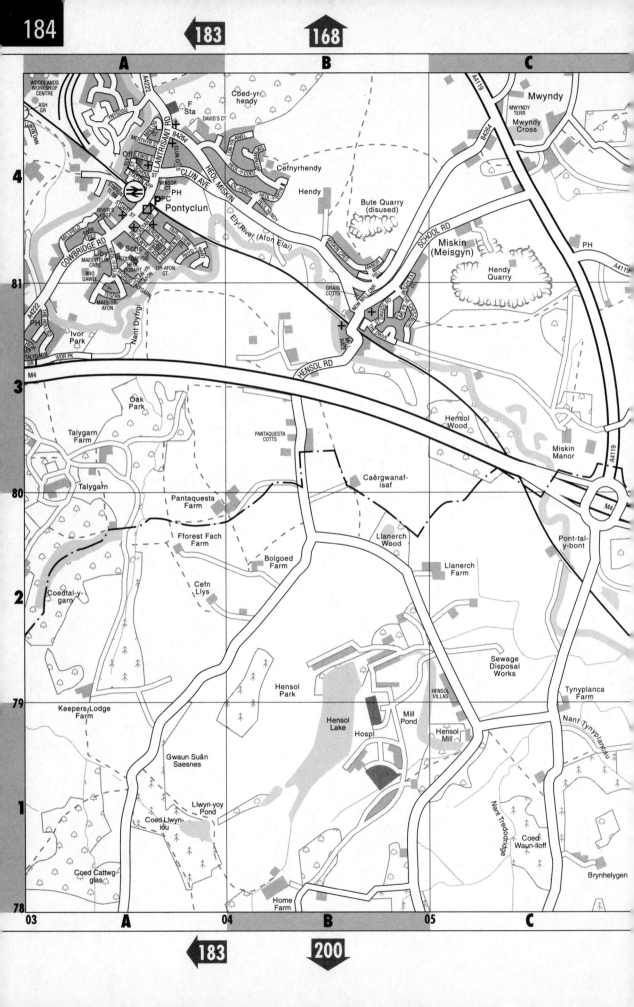

D E F

Llwyn-saer

Brofiscin Farm

Maendy Farm

Broviskin Fach

Golf Course

Creigiau Farm

PARC-Y-BRYN

HEOL CREIGIAU

CH

TREGARTH CL

TREGARTH CT

PARC CASTELL-Y-MYNACH

Sch

PARC CASTELL-Y-MYNACH

WOODLAND CRES

CASTLE CL

Creigiau

THE TERRACE

CLOS DARRAN LAS

PH

STATION HOUSES

OLD FARM LA

4

Brofiscin Quarry

Groes-Faen

GLAN CREIGIAU

BRYN CREIGIAU

HEOL-Y-HWL

HEOL BROFISCIN

PEN Y GROES

PARC LA

PARC

LLYS CARADOG

TYNANT RD

PARC-Y-COED

DÔL-Y-FELIN

PARC-Y-COED

GREEN ACRE

PARC-Y-COED

MAES-Y-GOLLEN

HEOL PANT-Y-GORED

81

Croffta

Maes Mawr

REDGATE TERR

PH

MAES-Y-HAFOD

CLOS LLEWELLYN

MAES-Y-DDERWEN

Dismantled Railway

QUEEN CHARLOTTE DR

BRUNWELL DRI

Llwyn-y-pennau House

LLWYNPENNAU COTTS

THE PADDOCKS

LLYS ILLTYD

LLYS DEWI

MAES-Y-RHEDYN

Robin Hill

CARDIFF RD

Dismantled Railway

Gadair-wen House

Gadairwen Farm

Nant Coslech

Henstaff Court

Llwynioli

A4119 LLANTRISANT RD

3

Gelli-wen

Ynysgarw

Llanfarach

80

Coed Gwernybwlau

Industrial Park

Llwyngibbon

Llanwensan-Fawr

2

M4

Crynallt

Tynewydd

Llanwensan-Fach

Nant Coslech

Gwern-y-gedrych

79

Parc Coed Machen

Dyffryn Bach

Ely River (Afon Elái)

Nant Criafol

1

Maendy Farm

Pont-sarn Crossing

Maes-Saeson

Allt Isaf

78

06 D 07 E 08 F

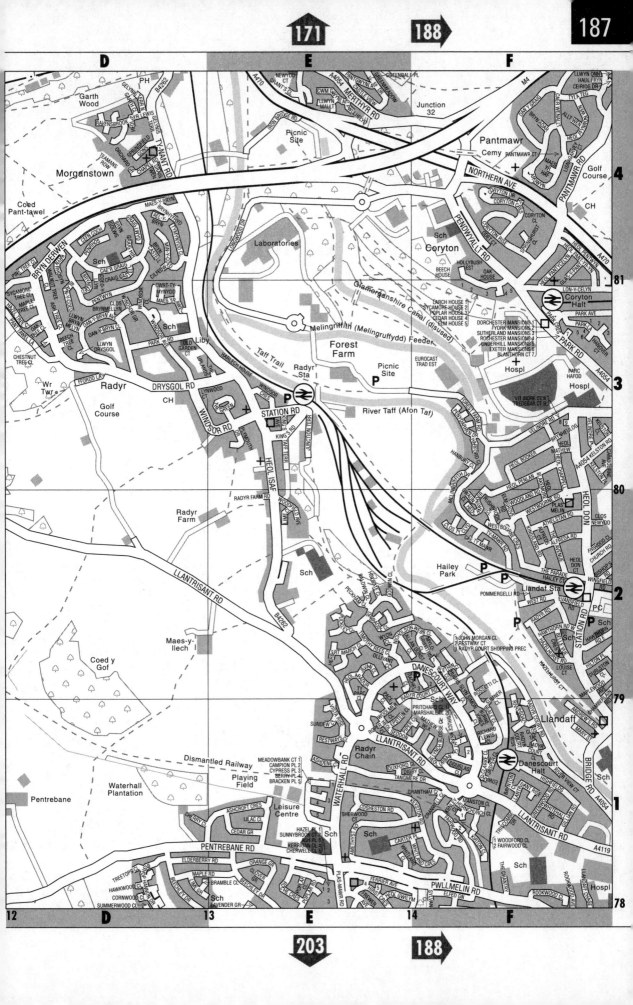

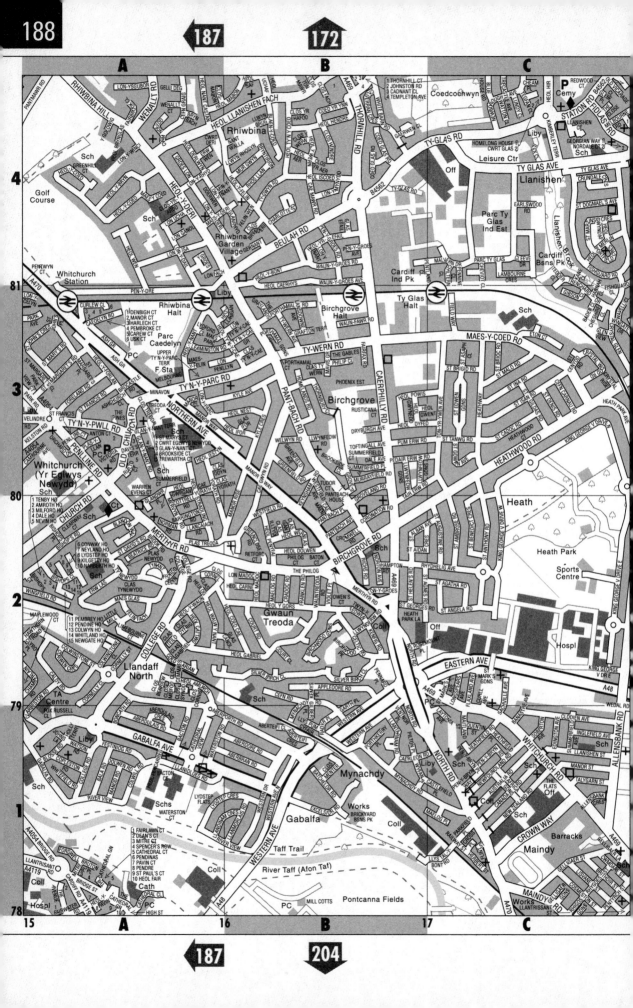

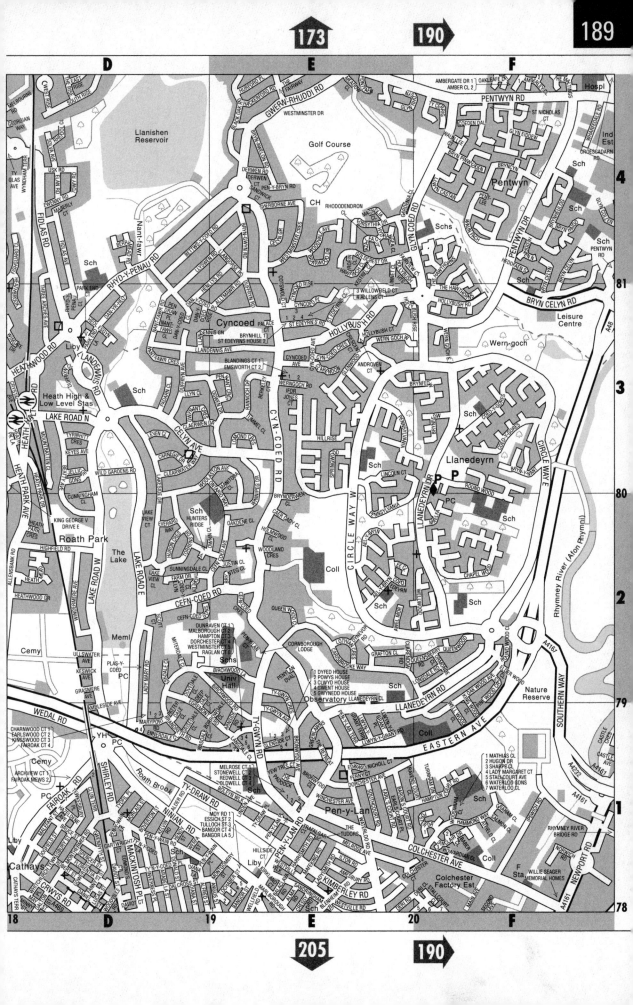

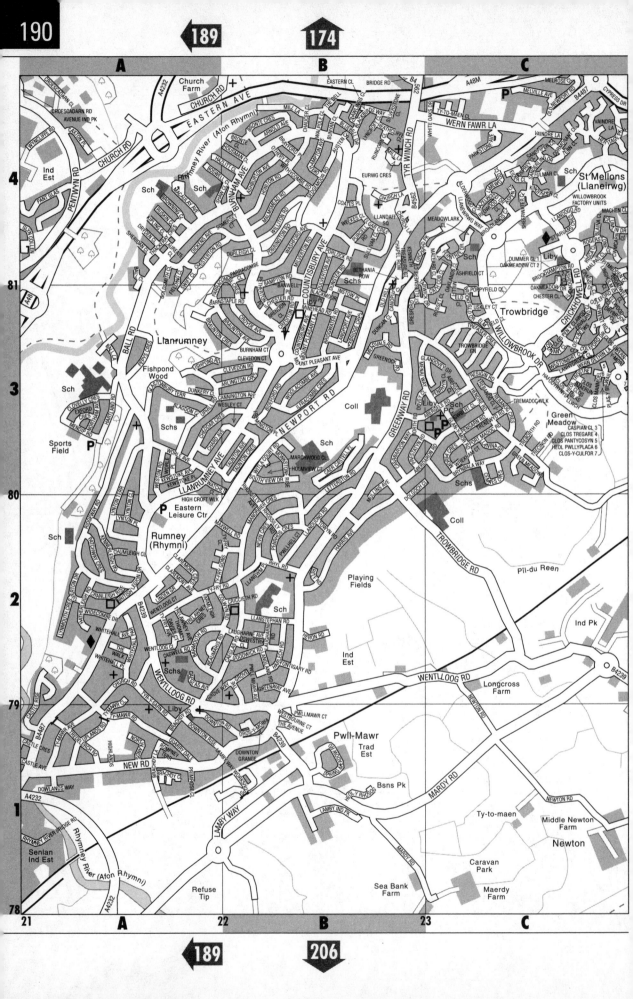

D | **E** | **F**

1 HERITAGE PK
2 ST PIERRE CL
3 VAINDRE CL
4 VAINDRE DR
5 CWRT PENTRE BACH

Golf Course

6 FAIRVIEW CL
7 FENNEL CL
8 OREGANO CL
9 CARAWAY CL
10 EUGENE CL

POST GWYNNE

Blacktown

MARSHFIELD

Pont Stone-Birch

CAE BRANDI
WELLFIELD CT
WELLFIELD RD
MARYSFIELD CL
HERBERT CL
THE HOLLIES
ORCHARD CL
PENTWYN TERR
BAKERS CT

1 PENTWYN COTTS
2 TY MAWR LA

PH

FOUNTAIN LA
CYPRESS DR
PASCAL CL
VAINDRE CL
VAINDRE LA
KOALE
WENTWORTH

FORTRAN RD
ST MELLONS BSNS PK
COBOL RD
EUGENE CL

ST MELLONS RD

CATHERINE DR

4

Rhubina Farm

Broadway Reen

11 BRYNMAWR CL
12 BLAENAVON CL
13 WINDFLOWER CL
14 WHINCHAT CL
15 CHARTLEY CL
16 ABERNETHY CL
17 STONECHAT CL

WILLOWBROOK DR

Faendre Reen

81

B4239

Sch

SANDBROOK RD
BULRUSH CL
FENVIOLET CL

18 CLOS-YR-GORNANT
19 WERN GETHIN LA
20 CLOS DYFNAINT
21 CLOS CAS-BACH
22 CLOS HAFREN
23 CLOS GWLAD-YR-HAF
24 CLOS MAES-Y-MOR

HEOL LAS

3

Peterstone Wentlooge
(Llanbedr Gwynllwg)

PH

MEADOW VIEW

CHURCH CL
Church Farm

VALARIAN CL
WATER AVENS CL

Pil-du-Reen

Pill du Farm

Wentlooge Level

Tarwick Reen

Swn-y-mor Farm

Ton-y-Pill Farm

80

Glan-y-Rhosog Farm

Rhosog Fawr Reen

Broadstreet Common

Peterstone Great Wharf

Sluice Farm

Sluice House Farm

Chapman's Farm

2

Wentloog Ind Pk

St Brides Wentlooge

New House Farm

Tŷ-du

WENTLLOOG RD

79

Rumney Great Wharf

Bristol Channel

1

NEWTON RD

Lower Newton Farm

78

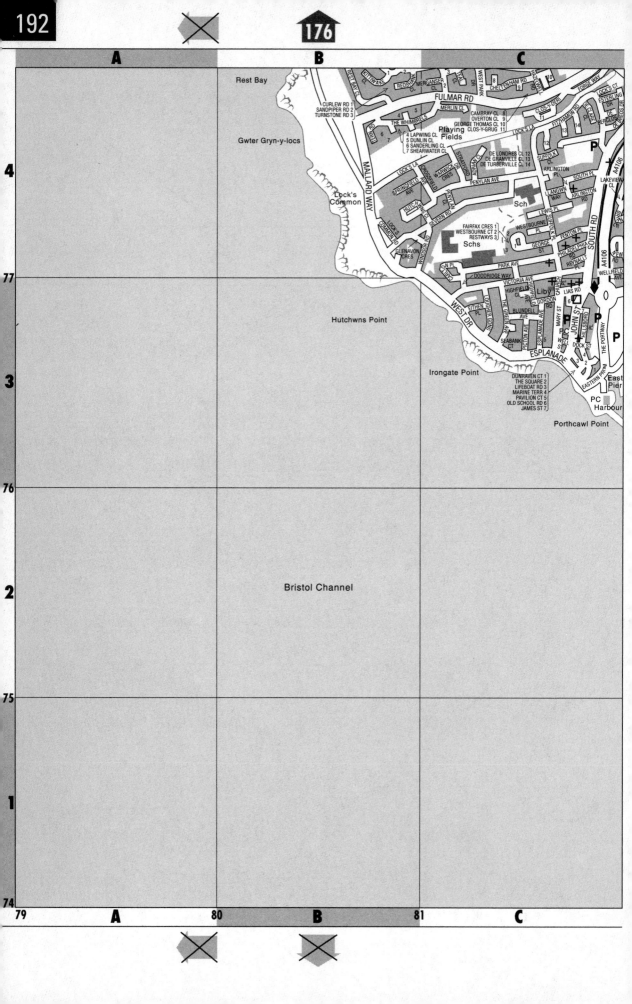

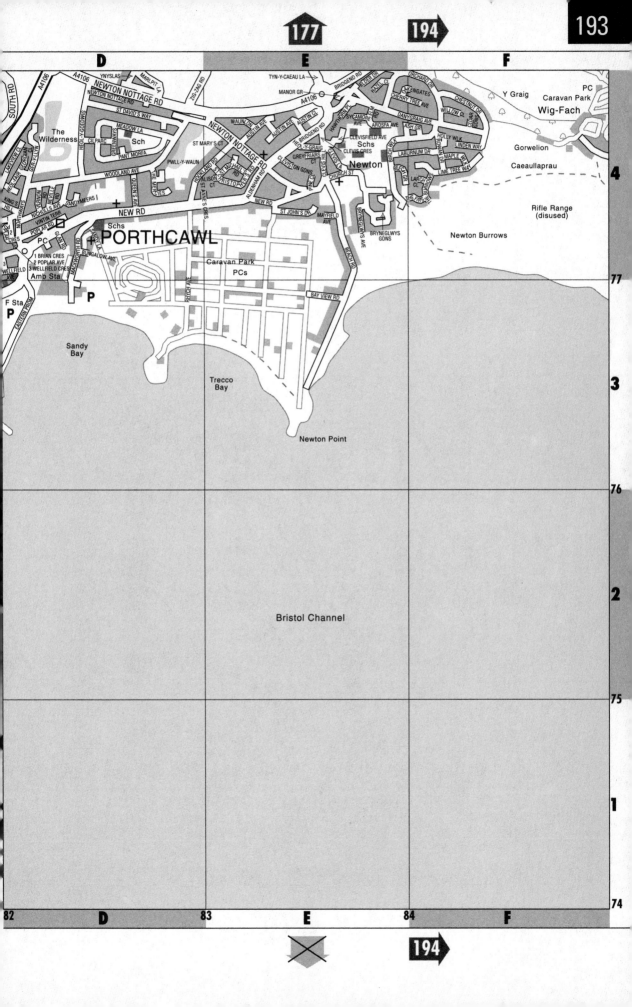

D **E** **F**

SOUTH RD
A4106
A4106
YNYSLAS
MARLPIT LA
NEWTON NOTTAGE RD
ZIG-ZAG RD
TYN-Y-CAEAU LA
MANOR GR
BRIDGEND RD
ELDER DR
HAZEL CL
ORCHARD DR
SKENGATES
CHERRY TREE AVE
Y Graig
PC
Caravan Park
NEWTON NOTTAGE RD
A4106
CHESTNUT DR
WILLOW CL
CEDAR GDNS
Wig-Fach
ST DAVID'S WAY
WAUN-ON AVE
AUSTIN AVE
AUSTIN AVE
AUSTIN CL
HAWTHORN LA
SYCAMORE AVE
AROSFA AVE
DANYGRAIG AVE
ASH GR
WILLOW CL
The
Wilderness
MEADOW LA
GREENWAYS
Sch
ST MARY'S CT
BRIDGEND RD
CLEVISFIELD AVE
Schs
HOLLY WLK
LINDEN WAY
Gorwelion
CILPARC
PANT MORFA
HEOL-Y-GOEWYD
PWLL-Y-WAUN
WOODLAND AVE
THE MEADES
QUEEN'S AVE
HOOK LAND RD
ST MICHAEL RD
HEOL-Y-GRAIG
GREYFRIARS CT
CLEVISTON GDNS
PINE CT
CLEVIS CRES
Newton
BIRCH WLK
LABURNUM DR
BEECH DR
MAPLE WLK
LIME TREE WAY
LARCH CL
Caeaullaprau
4
VERNON
NICHOLLS AVE
NEVILLE
SANDYMEERS
ALISON CT
ST ANNE'S CRES
ALDINHAM RD
BRISTOL RD
ST JOHN'S DR
CHURCH ST
THE FIRS
Rifle Range
(disused)
NEW RD
NEW RD
NEW RD
MAYFIELD AVE
77
VINTIN TERR
POPLAR RD
PC
GALL
MACKWORTH RD
BUNGALOW AVE
Schs
PORTHCAWL
RHYCH AVE
BRYNGLWYS AVE
BRYNEGLWYS GDNS
BEACH RD
Newton Burrows
1 BRIAN CRES
2 POPLAR AVE
3 WELLFIELD CRES
Amb Sta
P
Caravan Park
PCs
WELLFIELD AVE
F Sta
P
P
Sandy
Bay
BAY VIEW RD
Trecco
Bay
3
Newton Point
76
Bristol Channel
2
75
1
74

82 **D** 83 **E** 84 **F**

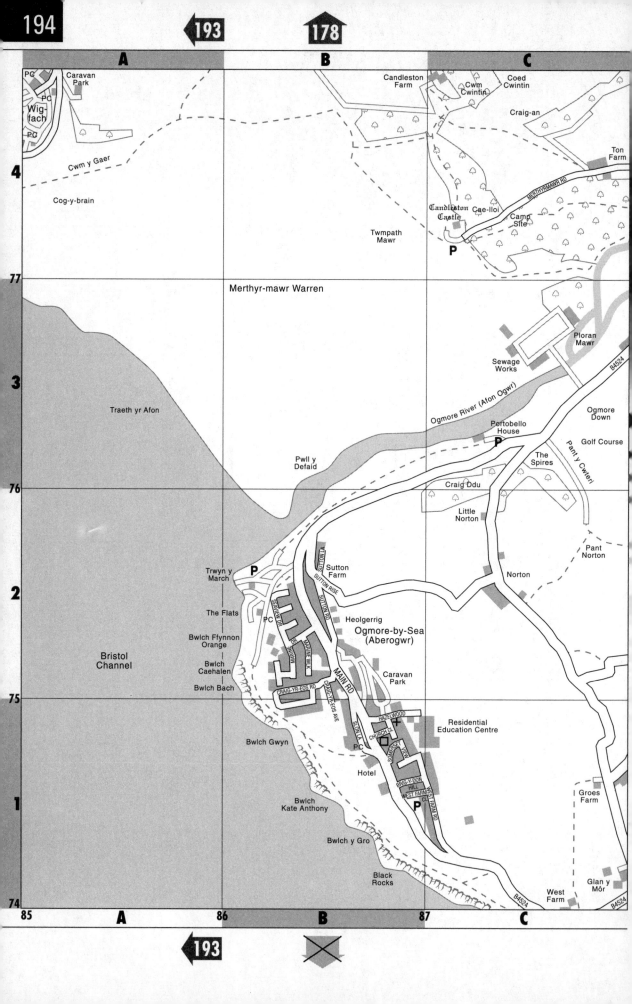

A B C

Wig-fach
PC
PC
PC
Caravan Park

Candleston Farm
Cwm Cwintin
Coed Cwintin
Craig-an

Cwm y Gaer

Ton Farm

4

Cog-y-brain

Candleston Castle
Cae-lloi
Camp Site

MERTHYR-MAWR RD

Twmpath Mawr

P

77

Merthyr-mawr Warren

Ploran Mawr

B4524

Sewage Works

3

Traeth yr Afon

Ogmore River (Afon Ogwr)

Ogmore Down

Portobello House
P

The Spires

Pant y Cwieri

Golf Course

Pwll y Defaid

Craig Ddu

76

Little Norton

Pant Norton

Trwyn y March
P

Norton

2

The Flats
PC
SEAVIEW DR
SUTTON RD
SUTTON RISE
SUTTON LN

Sutton Farm

Heolgerrig

Bwlch Ffynnon Orange
MARINE WALK

Ogmore-by-Sea (Aberogwr)

Bristol Channel

Bwlch Caehalen

Caravan Park

Bwlch Bach
CRAIG-YR-EOS RD

MAIN RD
CRAIG-YR-EOS AVE

75

SION LA

HAZELWOOD
CHURCH CL

Residential Education Centre

Bwlch Gwyn
PC

SOMERSET CL

Hotel

BRIG-Y-DON HILL
WEST FARM CL
WEST FARM RD

Groes Farm

1

Bwlch Kate Anthony

P

Bwlch y Gro

B452A

West Farm

Glan y Môr

B4524

Black Rocks

74

85 A 86 B 87 C

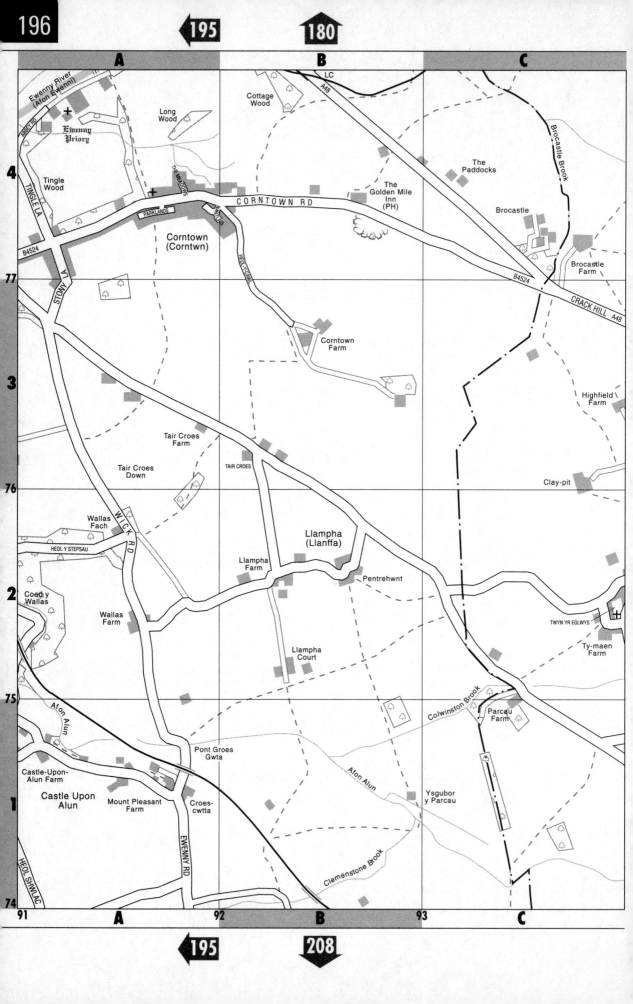

A B C

4

77

3

76

2

75

1

74

91 A 92 B 93 C

Ewenny River
(Afon Ewenni)

Ewenny Priory

Long Wood

Cottage Wood

LC

A48

The Paddocks

Brocastle Brook

ABBEY RD

Tingle Wood

TINGLE LA

THE MEADOWS

CORNTOWN RD

The Golden Mile Inn (PH)

Brocastle

Brocastle Farm

B4524

PARKLANDS

Corntown (Corntwn)

HEOL Y CANLL

STONY LA

B4524

CRACK HILL A48

Corntown Farm

Highfield Farm

Tair Croes Farm

TAIR CROES

Clay-pit

Tair Croes Down

WICK RD

Wallas Fach

Llampha (Llanffa)

HEOL Y STEPSAU

Llampha Farm

Pentrehwnt

TWYN YR EGLWYS

Coed y Wallas

Ty-maen Farm

Wallas Farm

Llampha Court

Afon Alun

Colwinston Brook

Parcau Farm

Castle-Upon-Alun Farm

Pont Groes Gwta

Afon Alun

Ysgubor y Parcau

Castle Upon Alun

Mount Pleasant Farm

Croes-cwtta

EWENNY RD

Clemenstone Brook

HEOL SIHWLAC

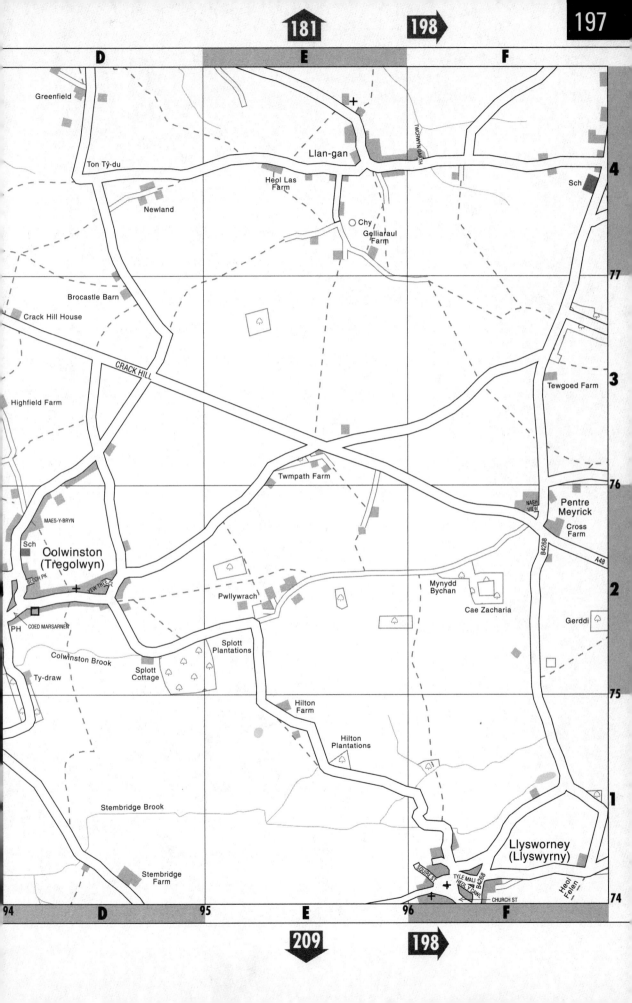

D · E · F

Greenfield

Ton Tŷ-du

Newland

Llan-gan

Heol Las Farm

TWCHWYN GWETH

Sch

4

Chy

Gelliaraul Farm

Brocastle Barn

Crack Hill House

77

CRACK HILL

Highfield Farm

Tewgoed Farm

3

Twmpath Farm

76

NASH VIEW

Pentre Meyrick

MAES-Y-BRYN

Cross Farm

Sch

Colwinston (Tregolwyn)

B4268

A48

BEECH PK

YEW TREE CL

Pwllywrach

Mynydd Bychan

Gerddi

2

PH

COED MARSARNEN

Cae Zacharia

Colwinston Brook

Splott Plantations

Ty-draw

Splott Cottage

Hilton Farm

75

Hilton Plantations

Stembridge Brook

1

Llysworney (Llyswyrny)

Stembridge Farm

SQUIRE ST

TYLE MALL

HEOL Y CAWL

B4268

Heol Felen

CHURCH ST

74

A   B   C

Red Farm

Bryn-Howell

Ham Farm

Coed y Graig

Ham Wood

Church Farm

Llansannor (Llansanwyr)

The Park

Court Farm

SALMONS WOOD

THE RHIW

Graig Penllyn

Coed y Stanby

Llansannor Court

4

Coed y Brain

PH

77

Court Farm

Vistla Farm

Black Meadow Plantation

Pen-y-lan

Penllyn Court

Moorlands Hall

Penlline Moor

Newton Farm

3

THE MEADOWS
Village Farm

Penllyne

PH

Trebettyn

Newton Moor

Great House Farm

Penllyn Castle

76

The Park

River Thaw (Afon Ddawan)

New Meads

A48

Beech Clump

Dre-fechan

2

Corrwg

Llwynhelig Farm

Mount Pleasant

75

GIBBET'S HILL

COWBRIDGE BY-PASS

WOODSTOCK MEWS

Leisure Centre

1 GRAYS WLK
2 SLADE CL
3 GREENSIDE

Darren Farm

DARREN HILL

A4222

THE BROAD SHOARD

COOPERS LA

TOWN HALL SQ

P

A48

WESTGATE

A4222

NORTH RD

EAGLE

MILLFIELD CL

TYLA'R HOSYB

B4270

WOODLANDS

BOWMAN'S WELL

GERAINT'S WAY

STIRLING CL

LA LINE CL

ST BLEDDIAN CL

WOLFE CL

GERAINT'S CL

HOPYARD MEADOW

THE BUTTS

West Village

Market

P

P

P

CHURCH ST

MILL PK

TH

Offices

THE LIMES
LIMES CT

Sch

CROFT ST
CROFT TERR

EASTGATE

A4222

DRUIDS

1

LLANTWIT MAJOR RD

TOWN MILL RD

RIVER WLK

4 CARDIFF RD
5 GEOFFREY ASHE CT
6 CLARE DR
7 HILL SIDE DR

CAE STUMPIE

Sch

Sch

ABERTHIN RD

CONSTITUTION HILL

CAE REX

East Village

ST JOHN'S CL

BROOK FIELD PARK

ST ATHAN RD

PH

COWBRIDGE (Y BONT-FAEN)

Llanblethian Castle

BROADWAY

LOVE LA

ST QUENTIN'S CL

Crossways Farm

B4270

CHURCH RD

CHURCH VIEW

STALL COURT CL

Llanblethian Hill

ST QUENTIN'S TERR

ST QUENTINS HILL

CASTLE HILL

PORTH-Y-GREEN LA

WINDMILL LA

PICCADILLY

GREENFIELD

BESSANT CL

LLANQUIAN CL
LAKE HILL DR
CRESCENT CL

97   A   98   B   99   C

74

197
210

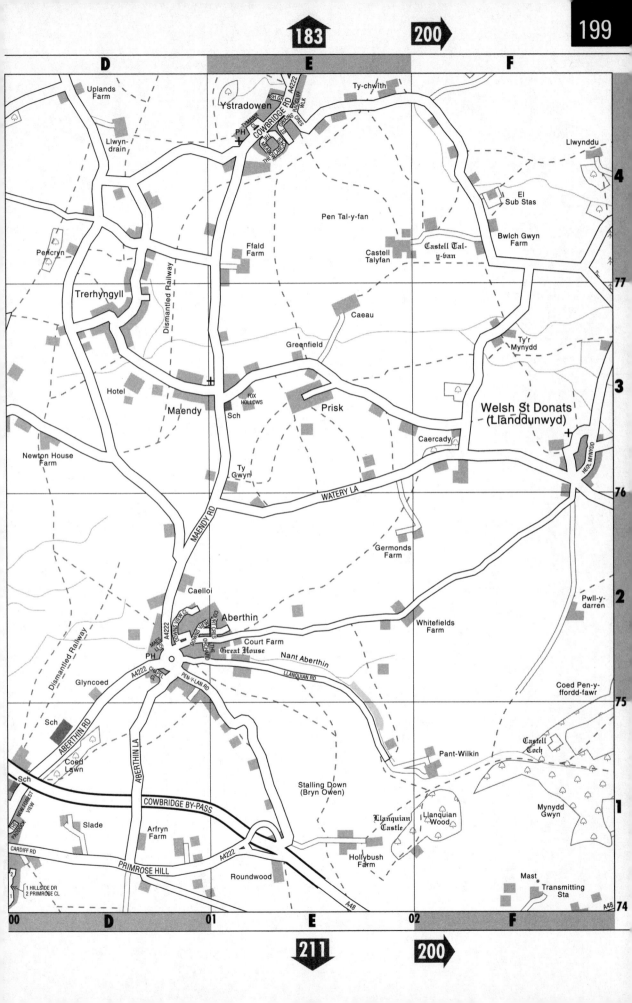

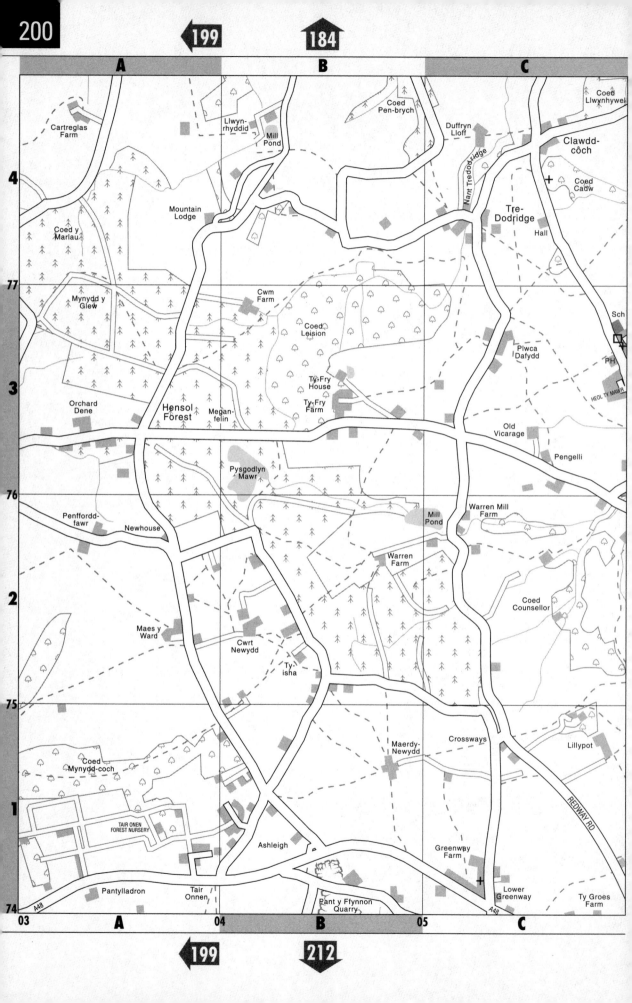

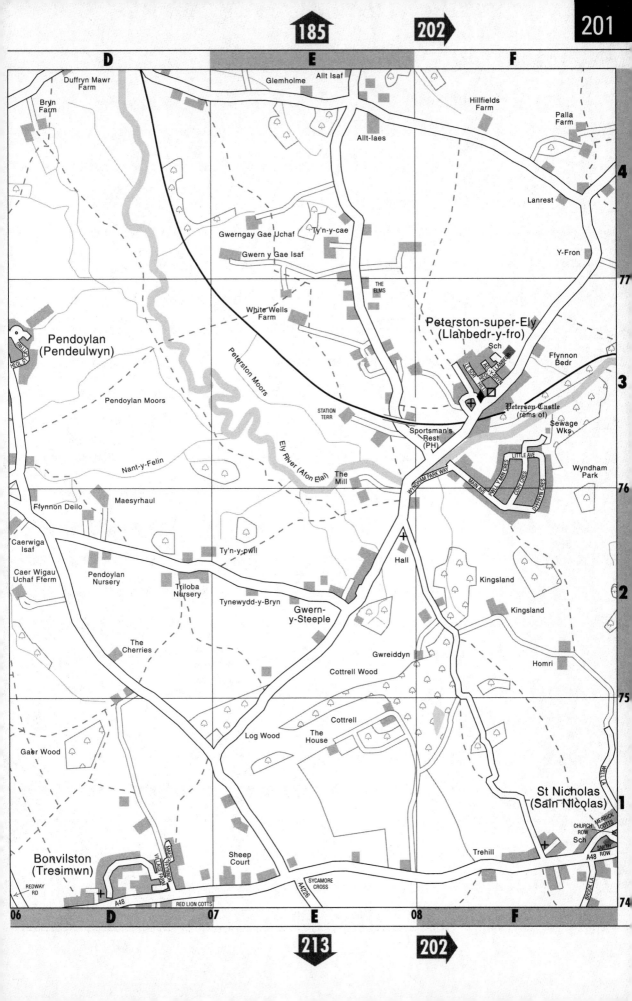

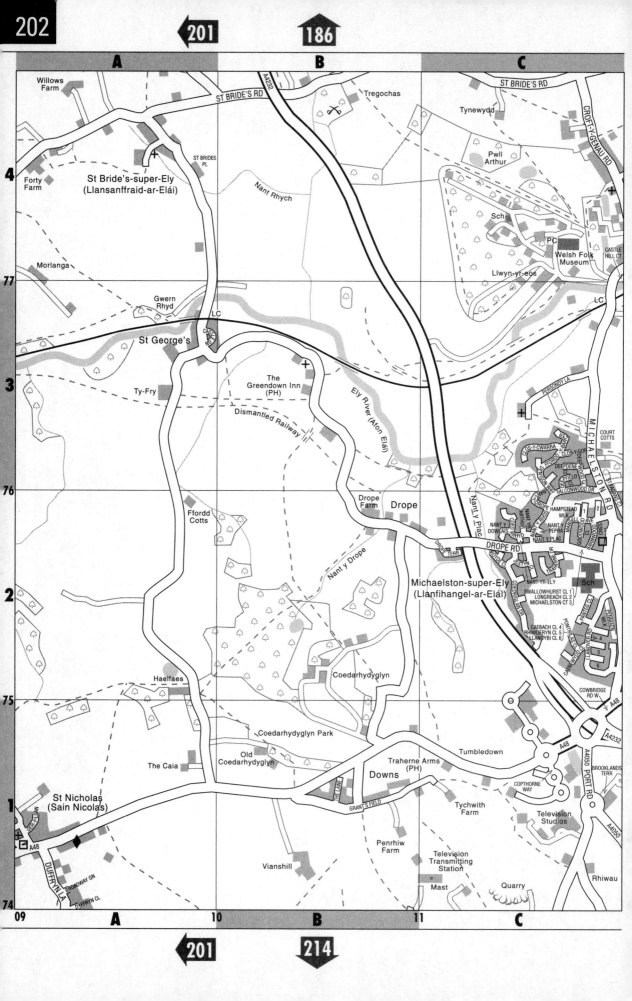

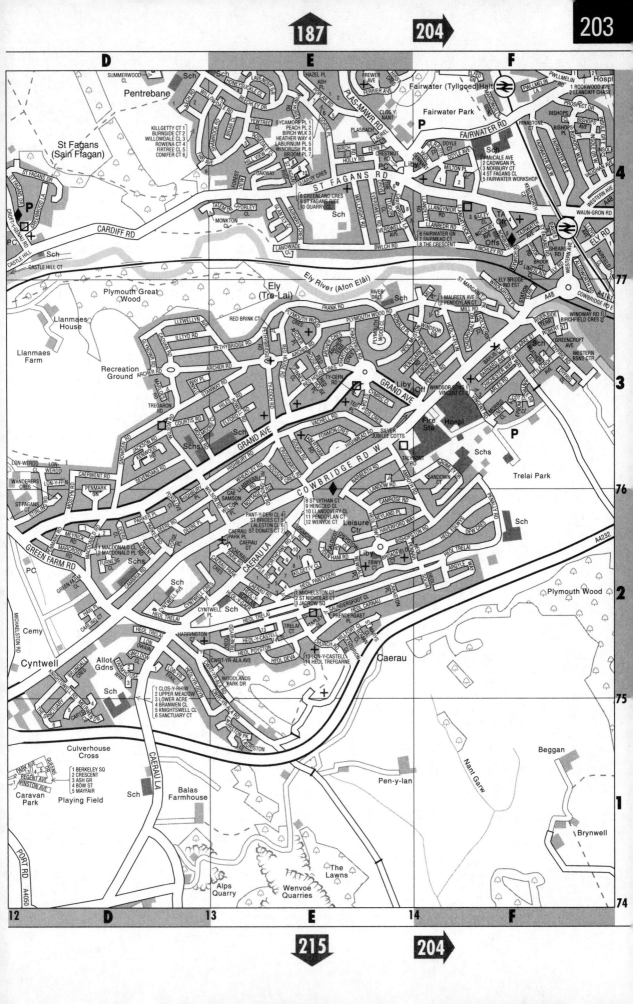

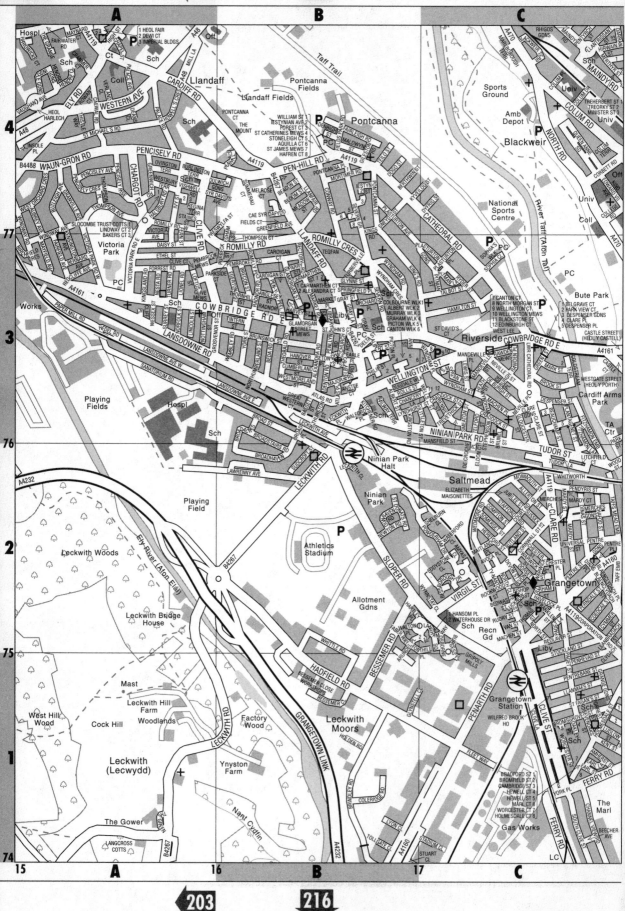

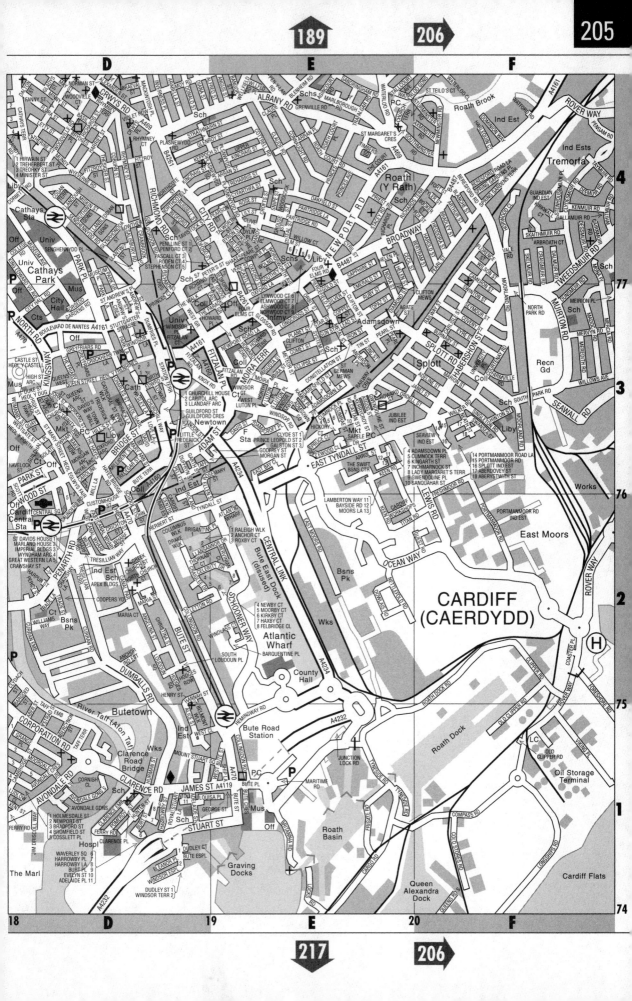

205
190

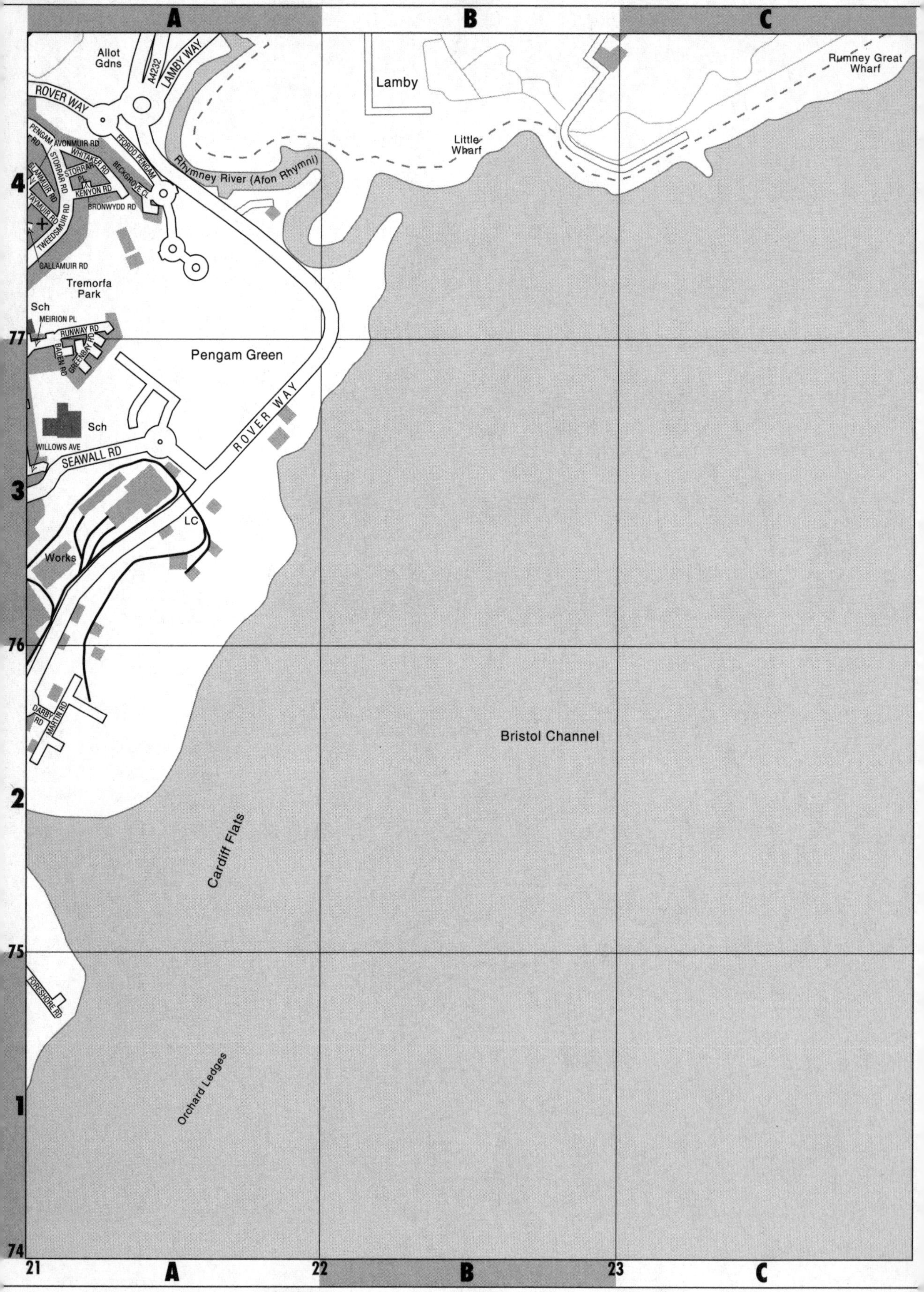

A

B

C

Allot
Gdns

ROVER WAY

LAMBY WAY

A4232

Lamby

Rumney Great
Wharf

Little
Wharf

PENGAM AVONMUIR RD
RD

WHITAKER RD

STORRAR RD

KENYON RD

BECKGROVE CL

FFORDD PENGAM

Rhymney River (Afon Rhymni)

BRONWYDD RD

4

LLANMUIR RD

TAYMUIR RD

TWEEDSMUIR RD

GALLAMUIR RD

Tremorfa
Park

Sch

MEIRION PL

RUNWAY RD

BADEN RD

GREEN WAY

77

Pengam Green

ROVER WAY

Sch

WILLOWS AVE

SEAWALL RD

3

LC

Works

76

Bristol Channel

2

Cardiff Flats

75

FORESHORE RD

1

Orchard Ledges

74

205

DARBY RD

MATHIR RD

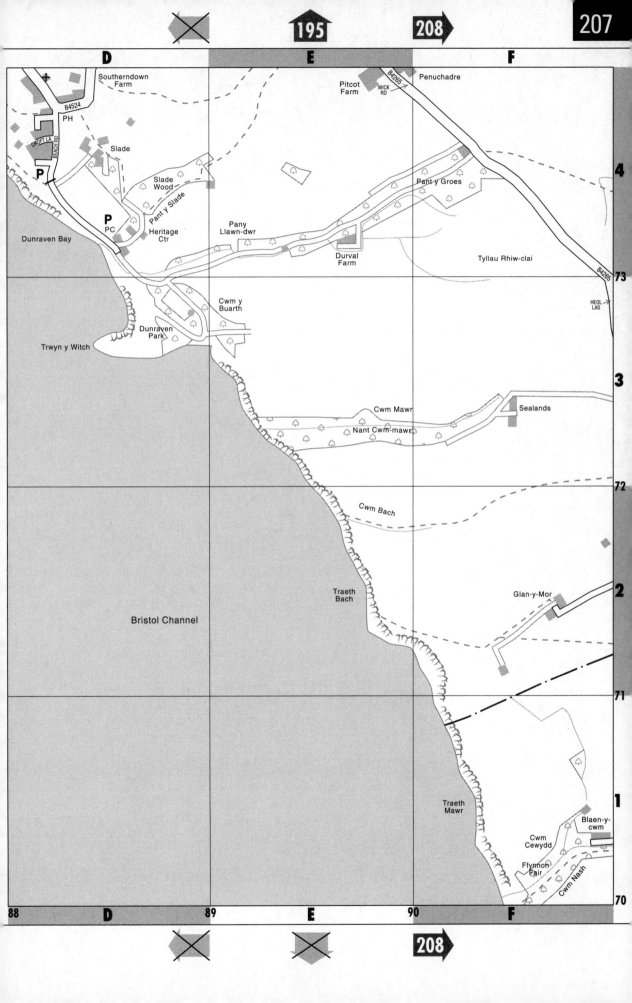

195
208

Southerndown Farm
Pitcot Farm
Penuchadre
WICK RD
B4265

PH
B4524
CROFT LA
BEACH RD
P
Slade
Slade Wood
Pant y Groes

P
PC
Heritage Ctr
Pant y Slade
Dunraven Bay
Pany Llawn-dwr
Durval Farm
Tyllau Rhiw-clai
B4265

4

73
HEOL LAS

Cwm y Buarth

Dunraven Park
Trwyn y Witch
Cwm Mawr
Nant Cwm-mawr
Sealands

3

72
Cwm Bach

Traeth Bach
Glan-y-Mor

Bristol Channel

2

71

Traeth Mawr
Blaen-y-cwm

1

Cwm Cewydd
Ffynnon Fair
Cwm Nash

70

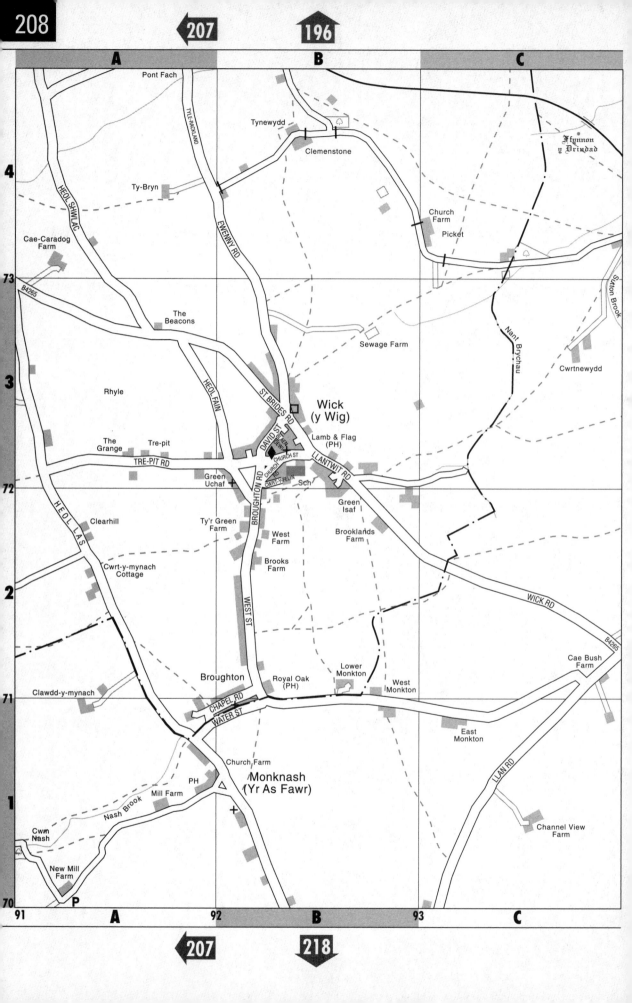

209
198

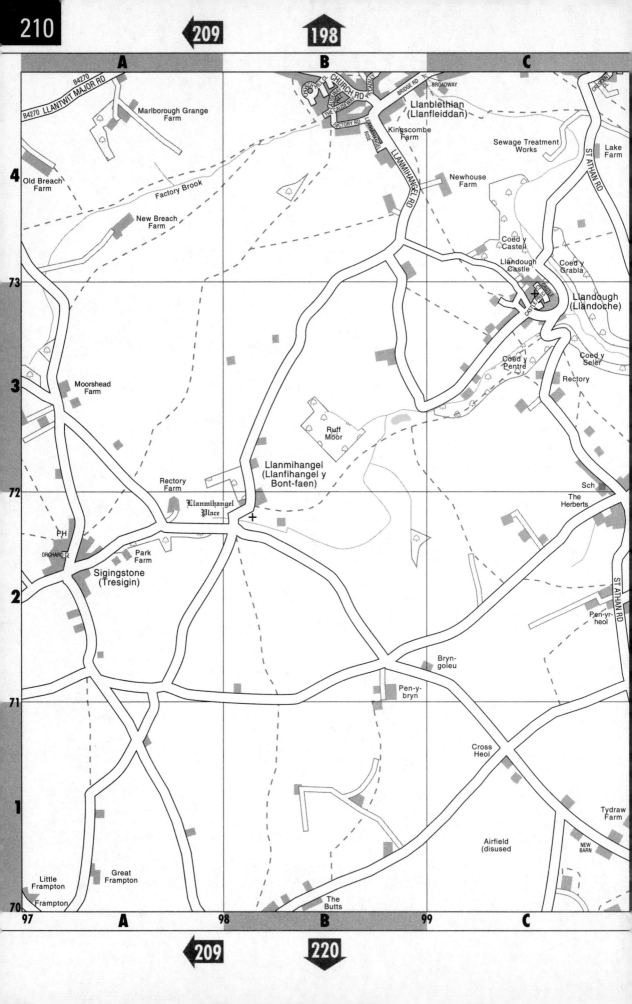

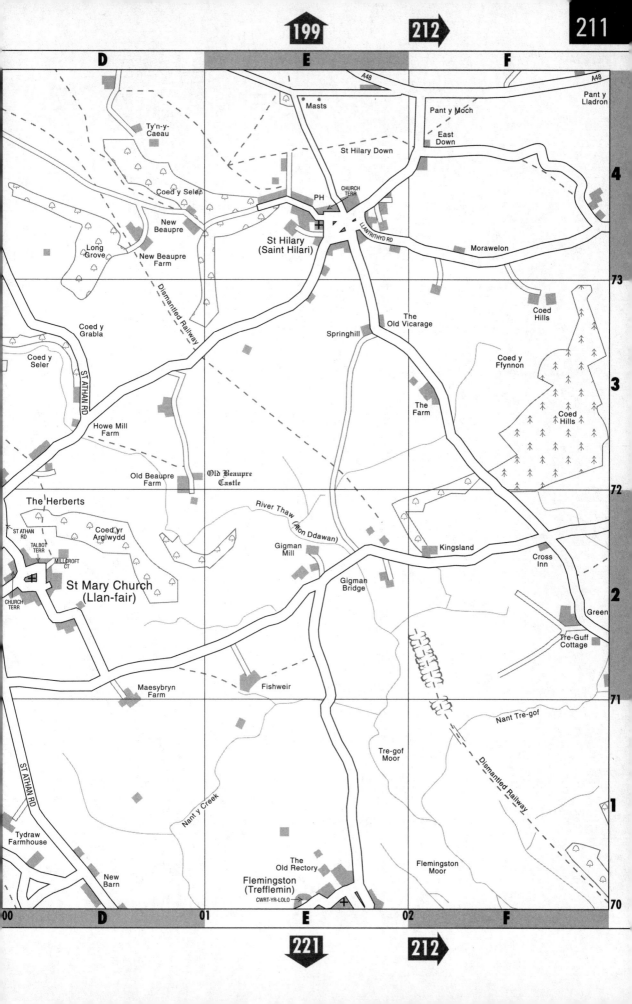

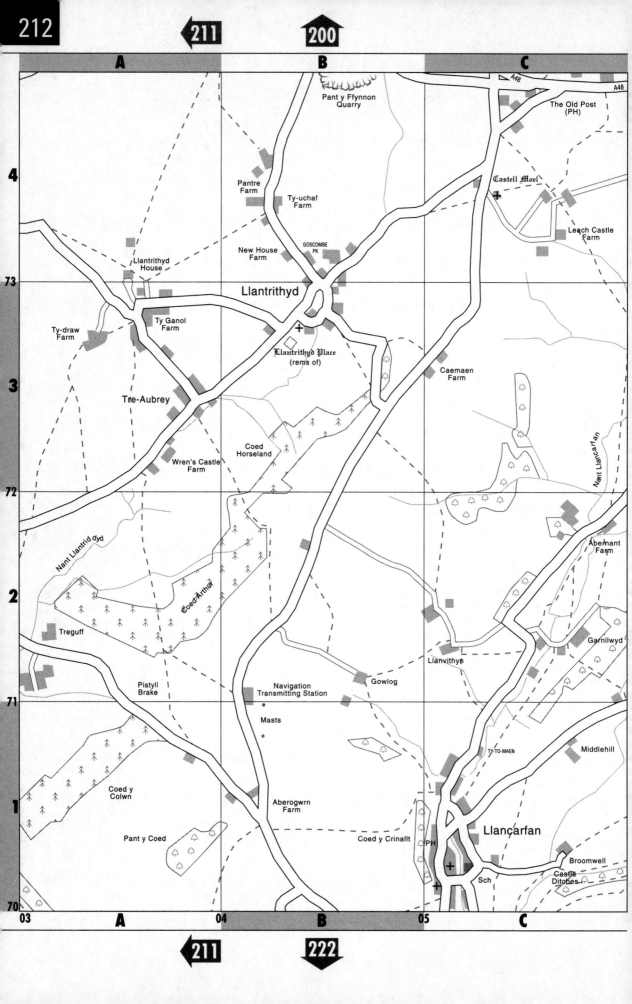

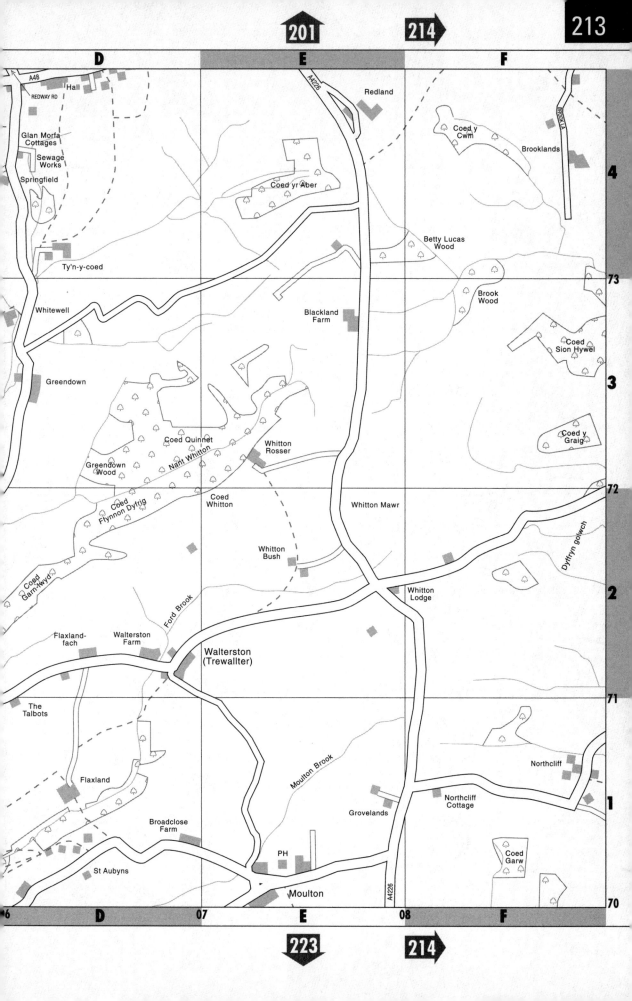

D
E
F

A48
Hall
REDWAY RD
Glan Morfa Cottages
Sewage Works
Springfield
Redland
Coed y Cwm
Brooklands
4
Coed yr Aber
Ty'n-y-coed
Betty Lucas Wood
73
Whitewell
Blackland Farm
Brook Wood
Greendown
Coed Sion Hywel
3
Coed Quinnet
Nant Whitton
Whitton Rosser
Coed y Graig
Greendown Wood
Coed Flynnon Dyfrig
Coed Whitton
Whitton Mawr
72
Whitton Bush
Dyffryn golwch
Coed Garn-lwyd
Whitton Lodge
2
Flaxland-fach
Walterston Farm
Ford Brook
Walterston (Trewallter)
The Talbots
71
Moulton Brook
Northcliff
Flaxland
Northcliff Cottage
1
Grovelands
Broadclose Farm
St Aubyns
PH
Coed Garw
Moulton
A4226
70

6
D
07
E
08
F

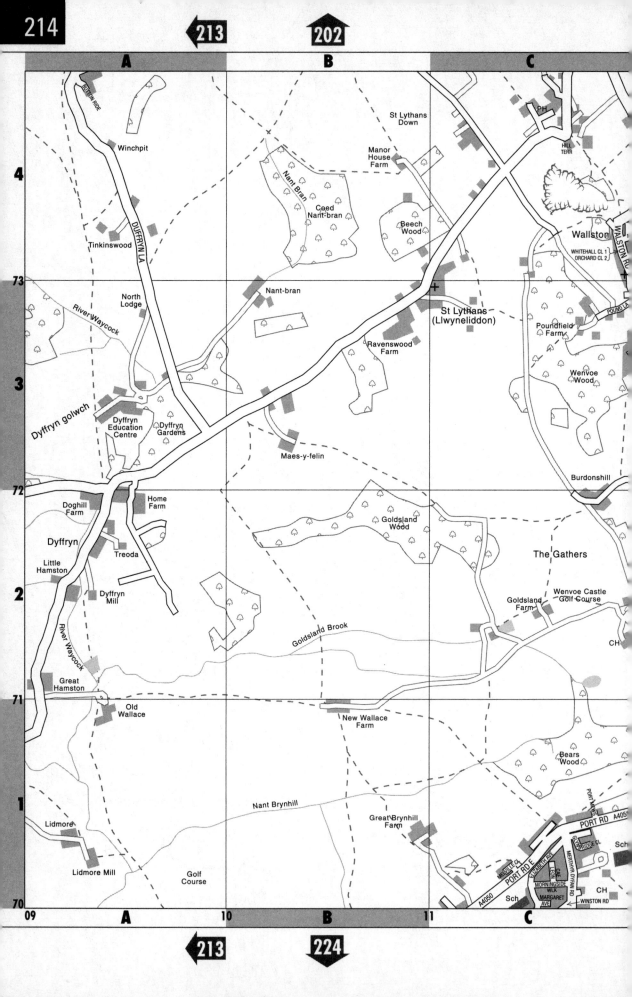

A B C

4

Bullrum Ride

Winchpit

St Lythans Down

Manor House Farm

PH

HILL TERR

Nant Bran

Coed Nant-bran

Beech Wood

Wallston

WHITEHALL CL 1
ORCHARD CL 2

WALSTON RD

DUFFRYN LA

Tinkinswood

73

River Waycock

North Lodge

Nant-bran

St Lythans (Llwyneliddon)

POUND LA

Poundfield Farm

Wenvoe Wood

Ravenswood Farm

3

Dyffryn golwch

Dyffryn Education Centre

Dyffryn Gardens

Maes-y-felin

Burdonshill

72

Doghill Farm

Home Farm

Goldsland Wood

Dyffryn

Little Hamston

Treoda

The Gathers

Wenvoe Castle Golf Course

Goldsland Farm

Dyffryn Mill

CH

River Waycock

Goldsland Brook

2

Great Hamston

71

Old Wallace

New Wallace Farm

Bears Wood

1

Lidmore

Nant Brynhill

Great Brynhill Farm

PORT MEWS

PORT RD A405

MELVILLE CL

PORT RD E

CLIVE BRIDGE CL

ELIZABETH AVE

MERTHYR DYFAN RD

OAK LEA

Sch

Lidmore Mill

Golf Course

A4050

Sch

MORNINGSIDE WLK

MARGARET AVE

CH

WINSTON RD

70

09 A 10 B 11 C

D E F

4

73

3

72

2

71

1

70

12 13 14

Twyn Bwmbegan
Alps Farm
Coed y Dyylluan
Coed y Cymdda
Bullcroft Brook
CAERAU LA
A4050
Greave
NANT ISAF
GREAVE CL
GRANGE CL
STATION RD E
WALSTON CL
Sch
Cwrt-yr-ala House
FAIRLEIGH
Wenvoe (Gwenfo)
STATION RD W
OLD MARKET
OLD PORT RD
WALSTON RD
CHURCH RISE
WENVOE CL
VENWOOD CL
SPRINGFIELD CL
CLOS LLANFAIR
ARCHWOOD
RECTORY CL
MORFA LA
Park Wood
Garden Ctr
Wrinstone Farm
Wrinstone Brook
Beauville Wood
Coed Clwyd-gwyn
Beauville Farm
Dinas Powis
Dismantled Railway
Vishwell Farm
VISHWELL RD
PORT RD
Golf Course
Ysguborgoch Farm
Waun Lawn
Garn
Coed Twyncyn
St Andrews Major (Saint Andras)
ST ANDREW'S RD
HIGHWALLS AVE
Twyncyn
KINGS RIDE
TWYNCYN
MEREVALE
Argae Farm
Nant yr Argae
Ty-draw
Sch
MOUNT RD
Wenvoe Castle Golf Course
Front Lawn
Crow Hill
Westra
Dinas Powis Common
Southra
SOUTHRA
WESTRA
A4231
PORT RD
A4050
Pencoetre Wood
Gilbert Manor
GILBERTS CROSS
GILBERT LA
ARGAE LA
Greenyard Farm
MOUNTBATTEN RD 1
FRANCIS RD 2
COLUMBUS CL 3
DOWNS CT 4
LLANDOW HOUSE 5
PENCOEDTRE RD
Pencoedtre Farm
Oakwood
Sch
BLYTH CL
COOK RD
SKOMER RD
Woodfield Farm
GILBERT LA
A4231
Cold Brook

A   B   C

4

Meadowvale
Farm

Langcross
Wood

Cwm
Cydfin

Llandough
Rectory

LECKWITH RD

WEST POINT
IND EST

Penarth
Moors

CHATTERTON SQ

Refuse
Tip

GRANGETOWN LINK

Ely River (Afon Elái)

Mast

Coed Twm-lw

Langcross
Farm

Llandough
(Llandochau)

GREENWAY CT

WILLOWMERE

PENARTH RD

LLANDOUGH HILL

B4267

Coed yr Eglwys

LEWIS RD

Sch

COGAN PILL RD

Cogan CT

Home
Farm

1 FAIRLEIGH
2 NORMAN COTTS
3 ST MICHAELS CL
4 CHURCH COTTS

73

Michaelston-le-Pit
(Llanfihangel-y-pwll)

PENLAN RD

SPENCER DR

Elizabethan CT

COGAN HILL

3

Hospl

Holms
Farm

Hospl

The
Merrie
Harrier
(PH)

East Brook

Corbett RD

A4055

B4267

BARRY RD

ANDREW RD

Cogan

Cogan
Station

Playing
Field

Leisure
Centre

Schs

WINDSOR RD

P

1 GAINSBOROUGH CT
2 ROWAN HOUSE
3 ROMNEY WLK

PEN-Y-TURNPIKE RD

Case Hill
Wood

Mill
Farm

GWYN
JAMES CT

BYRON CT

72

Eastbrook

SUNNYBANK

RAILWAY TERR

MATTHEW TERR

Sch

PENARTH

Sch

TENNYSON RD

MASEFIELD RD

Sch

Cadoxton River

Pen-y-turnpike
Cotts

Millbrook Hts

St David Ave

Chapel Cl

Georges
Row

P

Eastbrook
Station

Erw y
Delyn

SHAKESPEARE AVE

WORDSWORTH AVE

CHAUCER CL

COLERIDGE AVE

COWPER CL

REDLANDS RD

2

Golf
Course
CH

MILLBROOK RD

Sch

Brookside

CHAMBERLAIN ROW

CONWAY CL

DUNRAVEN CL

ERW-Y-DELYN

St CYRES RD

HASTINGS AVE

CORNERSWELL RD

ROSEBERY PL

Liby
Sch

1 THE PARADE
2 CASTLE CT
3 DUFFRYN HOUSE

Sch

ELM GROVE

CARDIFF RD

MILL RD

BRITWAY RD

MOUNT RD

Dinas
Powis
Station

YOULDON
HOUSE

1 ST GWYNNOS CL
2 ST NICHOLAS CL

CAMM'S
CNR

MURCH RD

MURCH CRES

Murch

Morristown

OAK CT

Sch

SULLY RD

MEADOWS LA

VICTORIA RD

LAVERNOCK RD

71

Dinas
Powis
Common

OLD
MALT
HOUSE

PC

A4055

ST JAMES
CT

F Sta

CARDIGAN
HOUSE

CARMARTHEN
HOUSE

RADNOR
HOUSE

BRECON RD

MONMOUT

SOUTHRA

ST WINIFREDS

HAWTHORN CL

Sch

Glascoed
Farm

HADLEY
HOUSE

1

Dinas Powis
(Dinas Powys)

CROSS COMMON RD

Cross
Common

Cadoxton River

A4055

Pop
Hill

The
Oxhams

Old Cogan
Hall Farm

Cosmeston
Country Park

Golf Course

Cemy

PC

70

15   16   17

A   B   C

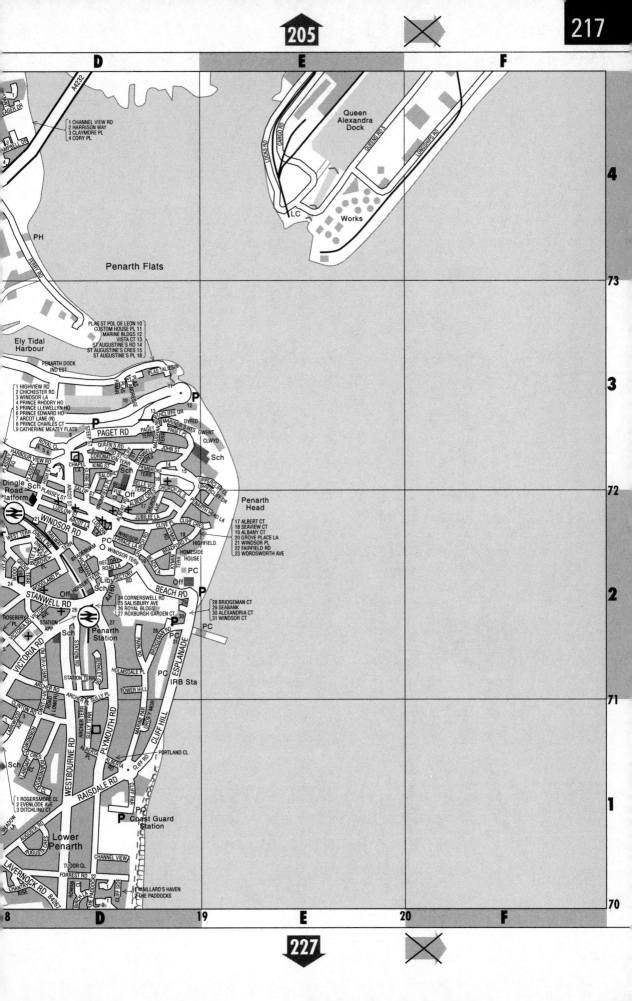

208

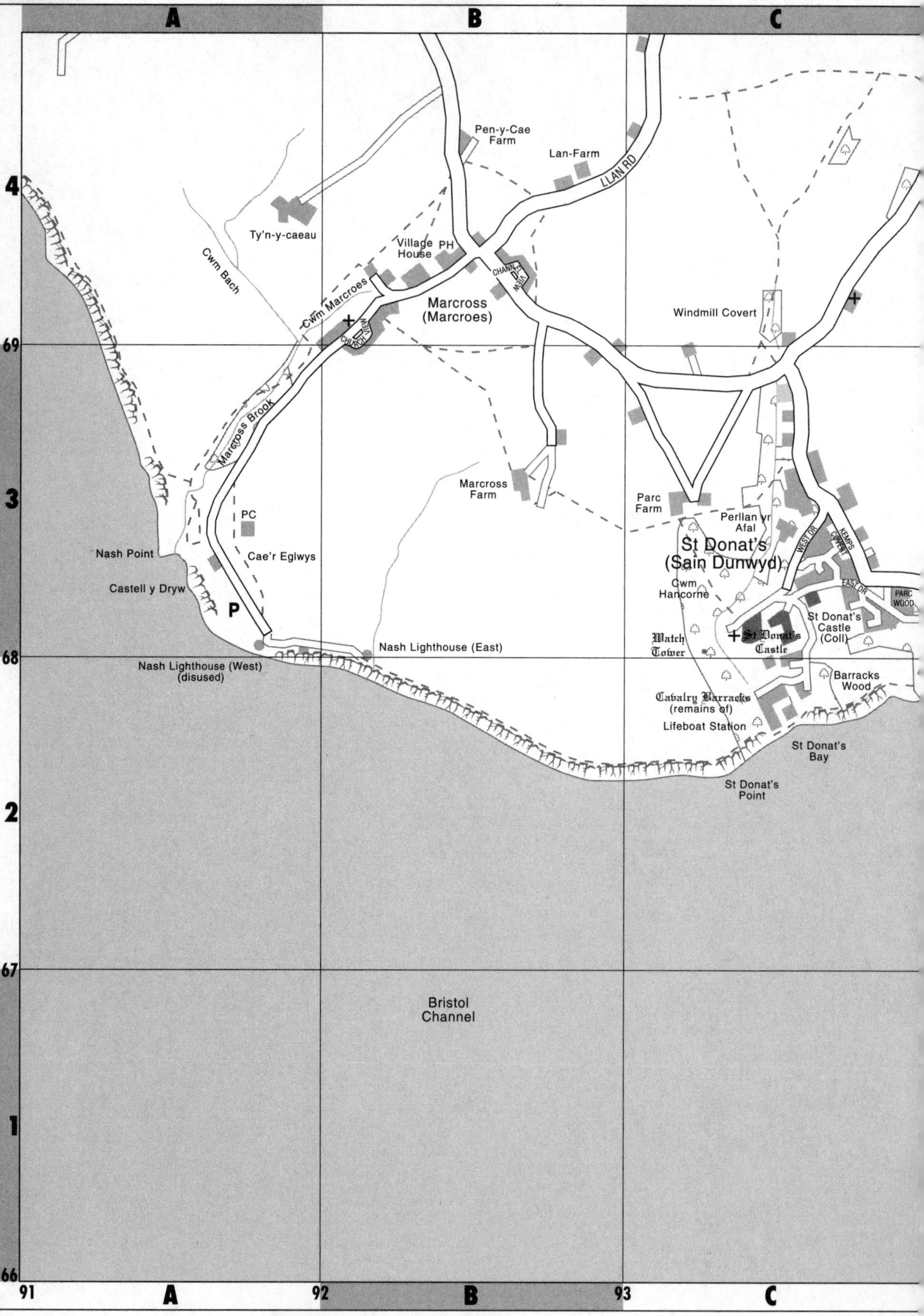

A   B   C

4

Pen-y-Cae
Farm

Lan-Farm

LLAN RD

Ty'n-y-caeau

Cwm Bach

Village PH
House

Windmill Covert

Cwm Marcroes

Marcross
(Marcroes)

CHANEL RD WEST

69

CHURCH RD

Marcross Brook

Marcross
Farm

Parc
Farm

Perllan yr
Afal

3

PC

WEST DR

KEMPS COVERT

Cae'r Eglwys

St Donat's
(Sain Dunwyd)

Nash Point

Cwm
Hancorne

EAST DR

PARC
WOOD

Castell y Dryw

Watch
Tower

St Donat's
Castle
(Coll)

P

+ St Donat's
Castle

68

Nash Lighthouse (East)

Barracks
Wood

Nash Lighthouse (West)
(disused)

Cavalry Barracks
(remains of)

Lifeboat Station

St Donat's
Bay

St Donat's
Point

2

67

Bristol
Channel

1

66

91   A   92   B   93   C

208

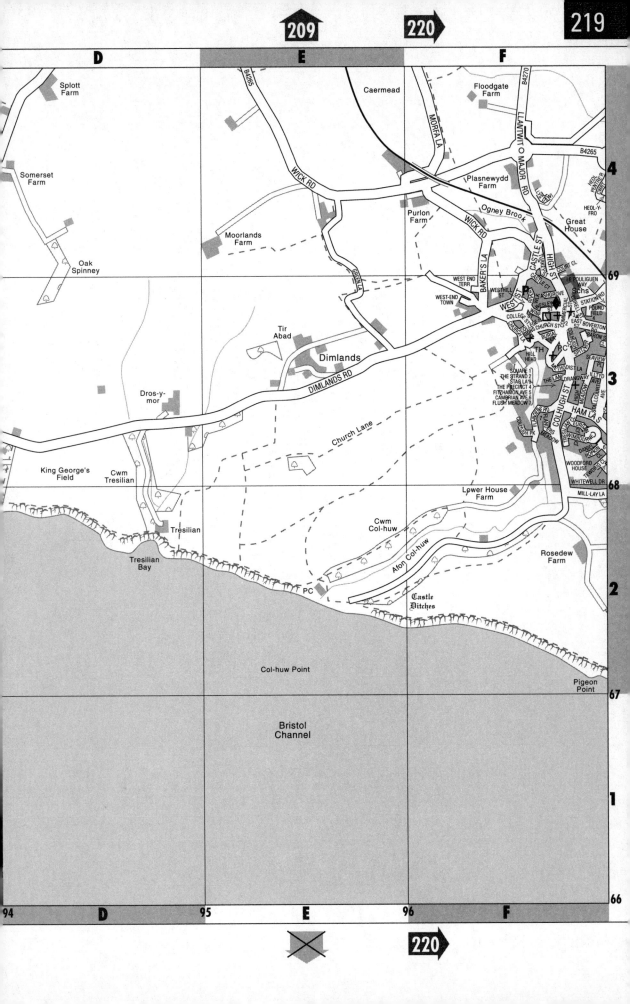

D | E | F

Splott
Farm

Caermead

Floodgate
Farm

B4265

MORFA LA

LLANTWIT O MAJOR RD

B4270

B4265

4

Somerset
Farm

Plasnewydd
Farm

HEOL PEBLERE DRIVE

HEOL-Y-
FRO

Great
House

Purlon
Farm

Ogney Brook

WICK RD

Oak
Spinney

Moorlands
Farm

GREEN LA

WICK RD

WEST END
TERR

BAKER'S LA

WESTHILL
ST

WEST-END
TOWN

WEST ST

COLLEGE

CHURCH ST

WING

WESLEY ST

CASTLE ST

COMMERCIAL

HIGH ST

COURT CL

LE POULIGUEN
WAY

Schs

STATION RD

POUND
FIELD

EAST BOVERTON

BARON'S CL

SEAVIEW
PL

69

Tir
Abad

Dimlands

DIMLANDS RD

BURIAL

HILL
HEAD

TH

BC

SQUARE 1
THE STRAND 2
STAG LA 3
THE PRECINCT 4
FITZHAMON AVE 5
CAMBRIAN AVE 6
FLUSH MEADOW 7

METHODIST LA
THE LANE
DRANGWAY

SPITZER

ILLTYD
AVE

HAM LA

3

Dros-y-
mor

Church Lane

FLANDERS RD

COLHUGH ST

COLHUGH PK

TREWMANS RD

PINERS

HIGH
MEADOW

WIMBOURNE
CL

DANIEL
HOPKIN

WOODFORD
HOUSE

WHITEWELL DR

WEWSTTED

King George's
Field

Cwm
Tresilian

Lower House
Farm

MILL-LAY LA

68

Tresilian

Cwm
Col-huw

Afon Col-huw

Rosedew
Farm

Tresilian
Bay

PC

Castle
Ditches

2

Col-huw Point

Pigeon
Point

67

Bristol
Channel

1

66

94 | D | 95 | E | 96 | F

A   B   C

Frampton Court
Farm

Brook Farm

WEST ACRE

Blacksmith's
Arms
(PH)

Heol Pentre'r
CWRT

Llanmaes

B4265

Windmill
(disused)

Great House
Farm

4

Tremains
Farm

Heol Pentre-Felin

Froglands
Farm

WINDMILL LA

LLANMAES RD

Sch

Millands
Farm

69

Windmill
CL

Amb
Sta
F Sta

Old Brewery
(PH)

RAF Station
St Athan

P

Liby

BOVERTON RD

HAM LA E

SEAVIEW PL

GLANYMOR

3

Boverton
(Trebefered)

Cemy

ORCHARD PL

Schs

TUDOR PL

STRADLING PL

BOVERTON BROOK

FITZHAMON AVE

Hoddnant

LLANTWIT RD

HAM LA S

Llantwit Major
(Llanilltud Fawr)

TREBEFERED

CASTLE CL

Nursery

68

MILL CAY LA

Ham Cott

Caravan
Park

Playing Field

B4265

2

Boverton Mill
Farm

New Way
Stair

67

Stout Bay

Stout Point

CG
Station

P

Hafod

1

Summerhouse
Point

Summerhouse
Bay

66

Bristol Channel

A

B

C

Ford Farm

Pant y Coed

Llanbethery Farm

The Wild Goose (PH)

PANT-Y-COED

Crosstown

Pantcross

Llanberthêry (Llanbydderi)

CATTWG COTTS

Redholme

Pen Onn Farm

4

Middlecross

Pen-Onn

69

Cliff House

Penmark (Pen-marc)

Barrenhill

Kenson Wood

Llancadle (Llancatal)

Llancadle Gorse

Kenson

Penmark Place

The Six Bells (PH)

KENSON HILL

Cwm

3

The Green Dragon (PH)

New Wood

Coed Llancadle

Lower Llancadle Farm

Kenson River

Castle Wood

B4265

Fonmon Castle

Ffwl-y-mwn Brook

Woodhouse

68

B4265

Rocks Head

CASTLE RD

Fonmon (Ffwl-y-mwn)

Burton

Home Farm

Fonmon Farmhouse

Highwayman Inn (PH)

2

Works

LC

PORT RD

Nurston

67

BURTON TERR

FONMON ROD

FONMON PARK RD

BEAULIEU WAY

Font-y-gary (Ffont-y-gari)

WELL RD

Upper House Farm

East Aberthaw

Blue Anchor Inn (PH)

STATION TERR

ADELFIELD WAY

NURSTON CL

MATTHEW RD

ST JOHN'S PL

SASSOON CL

ODYN'S FEE

WHITTANS

THAW CL

CELTIC WAY

MALBURIE CL

CHANNEL VW

LON CEFN MABLY

WESLEY AVE

1

WHARTON CL

SMEATON CL

KENSON CL

PH

FONTYGARY RD

P

RAILWAY HOUSES

SOUTH VIEW

66

Watch House Point

221

Ffontygari Bay

03

04

05

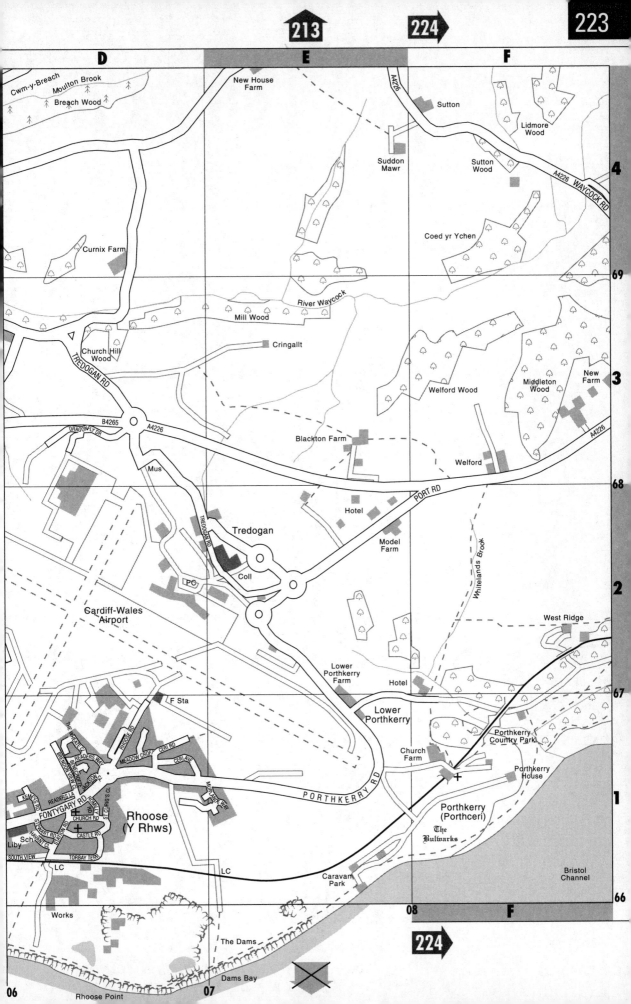

D
E
F

Cwm-y-Breach
Moulton Brook
Breach Wood

New House Farm

A4226

Sutton

Lidmore Wood

4

Curnix Farm

Suddon Mawr

Sutton Wood

Coed yr Ychen

A4226 WAYCOCK RD

69

River Waycock

Mill Wood

Cringallt

Church Hill Wood

TREDOGAN RD

Welford Wood

Middleton Wood

New Farm

3

B4265
DRAGON-FLY DR
A4226

Blackton Farm

Welford

A4226

Mus

68

TREDOGAN RD

Tredogan

Hotel

PORT RD

PC

Coll

Model Farm

Whitelands Brook

2

Cardiff-Wales Airport

West Ridge

Lower Porthkerry Farm

Hotel

67

F Sta

Lower Porthkerry

Porthkerry Country Park

READERS WAY
RHOOSE RD
MEADOW CROFT
CERI RD
CERI LANE

Church Farm

Porthkerry House

THE WHEATE CL
BRENDON VIEW
MOLSON CL

MILBAND WAY

PORTHKERRY RD

KEMEYS RD
READERS LA
FONTYGARY RD
STEWART RD
ST CHRIS'S CL
PENNANT

Rhoose
(Y Rhws)

Porthkerry
(Porthceri)

1

HAVANT CL
CASTLE RD
CHURCH RD

The Bulwarks

Liby
SOUTH VIEW
Sch
TORBAY TERR

LC

LC

Caravan Park

Bristol Channel

66

Works

08

F

The Dams

06

07

Rhoose Point

Dams Bay

A   B   C

4

69

3

68

2

67

1

66

Little Brynhill Farm
Golf Course

Highlight Farm

Welsh Hawking Centre

Coed Mawr

Coll

Middleton Plantation

Walters Farm

Waycock Cross

Green Farm

Hotel

Cwm-cidy Farm

Mill Wood

Cwm Barri

Porthkerry Country Park

Bull Cliff

Pebble Beach

Bristol Channel

The Knap

Cold Knap Point

Watch House Bay

Barry Harbour

Storehouse Point

Little Island

Whitmore Bay

Friars Point

PORT RD W

PORT RD

WAYCOCK RD

B4266

PONTYPRIDD RD

Cwm Talwg
Allot Gdns

COLCOT RD

BARRY (BARRI)

Cemy

Rec Gd

Hospl

Colcot

Merthyr Dyfan

SKOMER RD

BARRY RD

HOLTON RD

TY-NEWYDD RD

A4055

JENNER RD

BROAD ST

PARK RD

PARK CRES

ST NICHOLAS RD

ROMILLY PARK RD

HARBOUR RD

CHARLES DARWIN WAY

Barry Station

Barry Island Station

Barry Island

Holiday Camp

Oil Storage Terminal

Docks

Scrap Metal Yard

Romilly Park

The Parade

PROMENADE

CAERNARVON GDNS 1
ST MICHAELS GDNS 2
DOROTHY CL 3
DOROTHY AVE 4
WINIFRED AVE 5
CHAUCER RD 6
WINSTON SQ 7

ST GOVAN'S CL 8
ST CATHERINE S CT 9
TY FFYNNON 10
SLADE WOOD HOUSE 11
CRESSWELL CT 12
BITTERN WOOD HOUSE 13
NARBETH CT 14
LONG MEADOW DR 15

RADNOR GN 16
CARMARTHEN CL 17
DENBIGH WAY 18
MERIONETH PL 19

THE COTTAGES 1
HIGHFIELD CL 2
COURTLANDS 3
YEW TREE CT 4
ST NICHOLAS CT 5
BOWEN CT 6
HOLLY CT 7
LAUREL CT 8
PYRA CT 9
MULBERRY CT 10

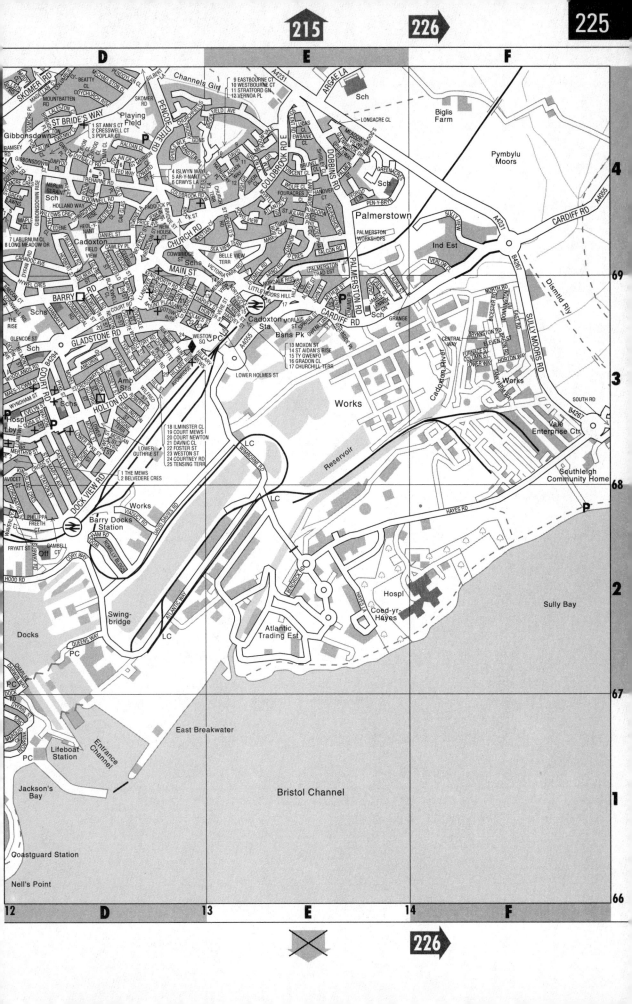

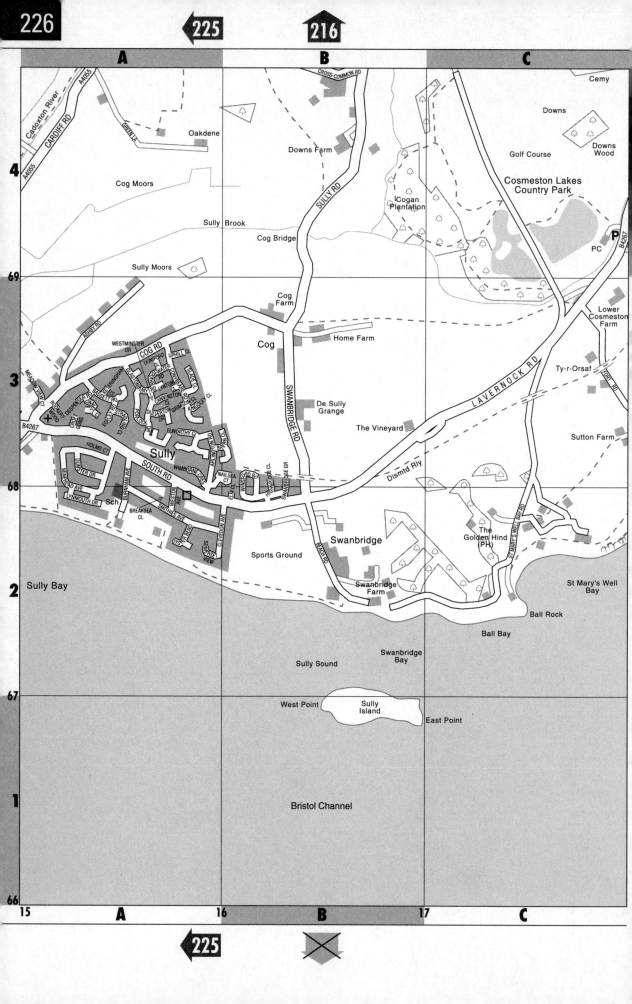

225

216

A B C

Cemy

Cadoxton River

CARDIFF RD

A4055

GREEN LA

Oakdene

Downs

Downs Farm

Downs Wood

Golf Course

4

A4055

Cog Moors

SULLY RD

Cogan Plantation

Cosmeston Lakes Country Park

P

Sully Brook

Cog Bridge

B4267

PC

69

Sully Moors

Cog Farm

Lower Cosmeston Farm

ASHBY RD

WESTMINSTER DR

COG RD

Cog

Home Farm

Ty-r-Orsaf

DONIFORD

UPHILL CL

3

MEADOW VIEW CT

GLASTONBURY

BASSETT RD

LYNTON CL

DE

De Sully Grange

LAVERNOCK RD

Sutton Farm

B4267

KETERINGHAM

DESPENSER

CAMINGTON CL

ELWORTHY CL

SWANBRIDGE RD

The Vineyard

CROFT GDNS

ECKLEY RD

STRADLING

PORLOCK RD

DULVERTON

GRIMSTON CL

KNEDLER CL

68

HOLMS CT

Sully

WIMBORNE CRES

ARLINGTON CL

Dismtd Rly

MINEAD AVE

LYNMOUTH DR

Sch

SOUTH RD

NAILSEA CT

BARRY RD

WINSBORO RD

HIGHBRIDGE CL

SWANBRIDGE GR

The Golden Hind (PH)

St Mary's Well Bay

BURNHAM AVE

BREAKSEA CL

SMITHIES AVE

CLEVEDON AVE

WESTON AVE

BEACH RD

Swanbridge

ST MARY'S WELL BAY RD

2

Sully Bay

CLIFF RD

LYNOS CRES VIEW

Sports Ground

Swanbridge Farm

Ball Rock

Ball Bay

Swanbridge Bay

Sully Sound

67

West Point

Sully Island

East Point

1

Bristol Channel

66

15 A 16 B 17 C

D   E   F

Golf
Course
CH

LAVERNOCK RD
B4267
BROCKHILL RISE
BIRCH LA
CARTER'S CL
CHERRY LA
CAYNHAM AVE
CRAVEN WLK
STANTON WAY
WHITCLIFFE DR
THE PADDOCKS

The
Stairs

Roundbush
Rocks   4

Cosmeston

UPPER COSMESTON
FARM

Ranny Bay   69

Dismantled Railway

Lavernock

FORT RD   Lavernock
Lavernock   Farm
Holiday   The
Camp   Cove
            Lavernock
            Point   68

                                                               3

                                                               2

                                        22

                              Flat Holm   Jetties

                        65   65   67

                           North West
                           Point   Foghorn
                                              Station   Jackdaw
                                                             Point

                           Bottleswell
                           Point   Lighthouse
                                                        Point

                                        22   1

                                                               66

EXPLANATION OF THE STREET INDEX REFERENCE SYSTEM

Street names are listed alphabetically and show the locality, the page number and a reference to the square in which the name falls on the map page.

Example:	Senghenydd St. Treo..94 B3

Senghenydd St | This is the full street name, which may have been abbreviated on the map.

Treo | This is the abbreviation for the town, village or locality in which the street falls.

94 | This is the page number of the map on which the street name appears.

B3 | The letter and figure indicate the square on the map in which the centre of the street falls..The square can be found at the junction of the vertical column carrying the appropriate letter and the horizontal row carrying the appropriate figure.

ABBREVIATIONS USED IN THE INDEX
Road Names

Approach	App	Green	Gn
Arcade	Arc	Grove	Gr
Avenue	Ave	Heights	Hts
Boulevard	Bvd	Industrial Estate	Ind Est
Buildings	Bldgs	Junction	Junc
Business Park	Bsns Pk	Lane	La
Business Centre	Bsns Ctr	North	N
Broadway	Bwy	Orchard	Orch
Causeway	Cswy	Parade	Par
Centre	Ctr	Park	Pk
Circle	Circ	Passage	Pas
Circus	Cir	Place	Pl
Close	Cl	Precinct	Prec
Common	Comm	Promenade	Prom
Corner	Cnr	Retail Park	Ret Pk
Cottages	Cotts	Road	Rd
Court	Ct	South	S
Courtyard	Ctyd	Square	Sq
Crescent	Cres	Stairs	Strs
Drive	Dr	Steps	Stps
Drove	Dro	Street,Saint	St
East	E	Terrace	Terr
Embankment	Emb	Trading Estate	Trad Est
Esplanade	Espl	Walk	Wlk
Estate	Est	West	W
Gardens	Gdns	Yard	Yd

Key to abbreviations of Town, Village and Rural locality names used in the index of street names.

Sully	Sully	226	A3
Penarth	Pen	216	C2
Barry	Barry	224	C3
Rhoose	Rhoose	223	D1
St Athan	St Ath	221	E2
Llancarfan	Ll'car	212	C1
Bonvilston	Bonv	201	D1
Dinas Powis	D Pow	216	A1
Michaelston-le-Pit	M-l-Pit	216	A4
Wenvoe	Wen	215	D3
St Nicholas	St Nic	201	F1
Llantrithyd	Ll'thyd	212	B3
St Mary Church	St M Ch	211	D2
Llanmaes	Ll'maes	220	B4
Llantwit Major	Ll' Maj	220	A3
Cardiff	Card	205	F2
Peterston-super-Ely	P-s-Ely	201	F3
Marshfield	Marsh	175	E1
Michaelston-y-Fedw	M-y-Fed	175	D3
Rhiwderin	Rhiwd	155	F2
St Donat's	St Don	218	C3
Pendoylan	Pendo	201	D3
Welsh St Donat's	W-St-D	199	F3
Llanharry	Ll'hry	183	E3
Pentyrch	Penty	186	B4
Church Village	Ch Vil	169	F4
Llantrisant	Ll'tris	168	C2
Cowbridge	Cowb	198	B1
Monknash	Monk	208	B1
Llysworney	Llys	197	F1
Wick	Wick	208	B3
St Brides Major	St B M	195	E1
Ewenny	Ewen	195	F4
Colwinston	Colw	197	D2
Penllyne	Penll	198	D3
Merthyr Mawr	Mer M	195	D4
St Mary Hill	St M H	181	F1
Porthcawl	Porthc	193	D4
Bridgend	Bridg	180	C3

Pyle	Pyle	161	D1
Cefn Cribwr	Ce Cr	162	A1
Pencoed	Penco	181	E4
Heol-y-Cyw	H-y-Cy	165	A3
Bryncoch	Brynco	164	A2
Tondu	Tondu	163	E3
Garth Place	Gar P	153	D2
Bedwas	Bedw	152	B4
Maesycwmmer	Maesy	101	D1
Caerphilly	Caer	152	B2
Pontypridd	Ponty	124	C1
Abertridwr	Aber	151	D4
Crosskeys	Cross	129	E2
St Brides Wentlooge	St B W	191	F2
Pontymister	Pontmi	129	F1
Abercarn	Aberca	129	D4
Ynysddu	Ynys	128	A3
Pontllanfraith	Pontll	101	F2
Pengam	Peng	101	E4
Taff's Well	T We	171	D2
Llanbradach	Ll'bra	126	C1
Llanharan	Ll'ha	167	D2
Tonyrefail	Tony	147	E2
Porth	Porth	122	C1
Ogmore Vale	Og Va	119	F1
Pontycymer	Pontcr	118	C2
Maesteg	Maest	117	D1
Margam	Marg	139	F2
Port Talbot	P Tal	113	D1
Glyncorrwg	Glyn	66	C2
Tonypandy	Tonypa	121	E3
Ynysybwl	Ynybw	97	F1
Tylorstown	Tylor	96	B2
Abercynon	Abercy	98	B2
Mountain Ash	M Ash	72	C2
Nelson	Nel	99	F2
Gelligaer	Gell	100	B3
Bargoed	Bar	75	F2
Treharris	Tre	99	D4

Bedlinog	Bed	74	A4
Deri	Deri	75	D4
New Tredegar	N Tre	54	C2
Oakdale	Oak	101	F4
Markham	Mark	76	B4
Merthyr Vale	Mer V	73	E2
Trealaw	Trea	122	A3
Ferndale	Fern	95	F4
Aberaman	Abera	71	E4
Aberdare	Aberd	50	B1
Treherbert	Trehe	68	C1
Bryn	Bryn	115	F3
Cwmavon	Cwma	114	B3
Ton-mawr	Ton	89	E3
Clyne	Clyne	64	B3
Resolven	Reso	44	B2
Tonna	Tonna	63	E1
Treorchy	Treo	94	C4
Ystrad	Yst	95	E2
Neath	Neath	87	E2
Bryn-coch	B-coch	62	B2
Swansea	Swan	110	B2
Skewen	Skew	86	B4
Neath Abbey	N Abb	87	D4
Llangyfelach	Ll'fel	59	D1
Pontlliw	Pont	58	A4
Penllergaer	Penga	58	A1
Loughor	Lough	56	C1
The Mumbles	T Mum	137	D3
Bishopston	Bish	135	F3
Upper Killay	U Kill	108	B3
Southgate	South	135	D3
Penmaen	Penma	134	A3
Oxwich	Ox	133	D1
Port-Eynon	P-Ey	157	D4
Rhossili	Rhos	130	B3
Llangennith	Ll'gen	102	C2
Llanrhidian	Ll'rh	105	D3
Pen-clawdd	Pen-cl	80	C2

Gowerton	Gow	82	D3
Llanelli	Ll'el	79	F4
Llangennech	Ll'ge	56	B4
Hendy	Hen	36	A2
Pontardulais	Pontar	36	B2
Craig-cefn-parc	Craig	39	D1
Clydach	Cly	60	C4
Allt-wen	A-wen	40	C2
Pontardawe	Pontdw	40	B3
Betws	Betws	19	D4
Glanaman	Glan	4	A4
Gwaun-Cae-Gurwen	G-C-G	5	D2
Brynamman	Bry	5	D4
Cwmllynfell	Cwmll	6	B3
Ystalyfera	Ystal	23	D3
Ystradgynlais	Ystra	8	A1
Blaengwrach	Blae	45	F4
Glyn-neath	G-nea	26	C1
Crynant	Cry	43	D3
Seven Sisters	Se Si	25	D3
Onllwyn	Onll	9	F1
Coelbren	Coel	9	F2
Ystradfellte	Ystraf	27	F4
Llanfrynach	Ll'fry	2	B4
Rhigos	Rhig	47	E4
Penywaun	Peny	49	D3
Hirwaun	Hir	48	C4
Llwydcoed	Llwy	49	F3
Cefn-coed-y-cymmer	C-c-y-c	31	F2
Merthyr Tydfil	Mer T	33	D2
Troedyrhiw	Troed	52	B1
Rhymney	Rhy	34	C2
Talybont-on-Usk	T-on-U	15	D4
Llangynidr	Ll'gy	15	F4
Trefil	Trefil	16	C3
Cwm	Cwm	55	F4
Tredegar	Tred	35	F4

230

Abbey Cl. T We
Ashford Cl. Ponty

Abbey Cl. T We 171 D2
Abbey Ct. Ch Vil 149 F1
Abbey Rd. Marg 139 E4
Abbey Rd. Pyle 161 E1
Abbeyville Ave. P Tal 138 B4
Abbeyville Ct. P Tal 113 E1
Abbot's Wlk. B-coch 87 E4
Abbott's Cl. Marg 139 F1
Aber Houses. Og Va 119 F2
Aber Rd. Og Va 119 F2
Aber St. Card 205 D1
Aber-Fawr Terr. Aber 151 D4
Aber-Ffrwd Rd. M Ash 72 B2
Aber-Nant Rd. Abera 50 A2
Aber-Rhondda Rd. Porth 122 C2
Aberafan Ctr. Marg 114 A1
Aberafan Rd. P Tal 113 F1
Aberaman Enterprise Park. Aberd 71 F4
Aberaman Park Ind Est. Abera 71 E3
Aberbran Rd. Card 188 B1
Abercedy. Pen-cl 81 D2
Abercerdin Rd. Og Va 146 A4
Aberclydach Pl. Cly 60 B4
Abercrave Terr. Coel 9 D3
Abercregan Rd. Glyn 90 C3
Abercwmboi-Isaf Rd. M Ash 72 A2
Abercynon Rd. Abercy 98 A3
Abercynon Rd. Abercy 98 B3
Abercynon Rd. Ponty 124 B3
Abercynon St. Card 205 D1
Aberdale Rd. G-nea 27 D1
Aberdare Rd. Abercy 98 B1
Aberdare Rd. Fern 95 F4
Aberdare Rd. G-nea 27 D1
Aberdare Rd. M Ash 72 A2
Aberdare Rd. Mer T 32 B1
Aberdaron Rd. Card 190 C3
Aberdore Rd. Card 188 B1
Aberdovey Cl. D pow 216 B2
Aberdovey St. Card 205 F3
Aberdulais Cres. Card 188 A1
Aberdulais Rd. Card 188 A1
Aberdyberthi St. Swan 84 B1
Aberfan Cres. Mer V 73 E2
Aberfan Fawr. Mer V 73 E2
Aberfan Rd. Mer V 73 E3
Aberfawr Rd. Aber 151 D4
Aberffrwd. Tred 35 E3
Abergarw Rd. Tondu 163 F3
Abergarw Trad Est. Brynco 164 A3
Abergele Cl. Card 190 C3
Abergele Rd. Card 190 C3
Abergelly Rd. Swan 83 E3
Abergwawr Pl. Abera 71 D4
Abergwawr St. Abera 71 E4
Abergwernffrwd Row. Ton 89 E3
Aberhenwaun Uchaf. Onll 25 E4
Aberllechau Rd. Tylor 122 B4
Abermorlais Terr. Mer T 32 B1
Abernant Cres. Mark 76 C4
Abernant Rd. G-C-G 5 D1
Abernant Rd. Mark 76 B4
Abernethy Cl. Card 191 D4
Abernethy Quay. Swan 110 B3
Abernethy Sq. Swan 110 C3
Aberpennar St. M Ash 72 B1
Aberporth Rd. Card 188 A1
Abertaf. Abercy 98 C2
Aberteifi Cl. Card 188 B1
Aberteifi Cres. Card 188 B1
Aberthaw Rd. Card 203 E3
Aberthin La. Cowb 199 D1
Aberthin Rd. Cowb 199 D1
Abertonllwyd St. Trehe 68 C1
Aberystwith St. Card 205 F3
Abingdon St. Barry 225 D4
Acacia Ave. Gell 100 C2
Acacia Ave. Mer T 32 B2
Acacia Ave. P Tal 113 E1
Acacia Cl. P Tal 113 E1
Acacia Rd. T Mum 137 D4
Acacia St. Ponty 150 A3
Acland Rd. Bridg 179 F3
Acorn Pl. P Tal 113 E4
Adam St. Card 205 D3
Adam Wlk. B-coch 87 D4
Adams Ave. Brynco 163 F2
Adams St. Tonypa 121 D4
Adamscroft Pl. Card 205 E3
Adamsdown La. Card 205 E3
Adamsdown Pl. Card 205 E3
Adamsdown Sq. Card 205 E3
Adare St. Bridg 179 F2
Adare St. Og Va 119 F2
Adare St. Og Va 146 A4
Adare St. P Tal 138 C4
Adare Terr. Tonypa 121 F3
Adare Terr. Treo 94 B4
Addison Ave. Ll'hry 183 D3
Addison Cres. Card 203 E3
Addison Pl. P Tal 138 C4
Addison Rd. Neath 87 E2
Addison Rd. P Tal 138 C4
Addison St. Peng 101 E4
Addison Way. Bedw 153 E3
Addoldy Rd. G-nea 26 C1
Adelaide Ct. Peng 101 E3
Adelaide Pl. Card 205 D1
Adelaide St. Card 205 D1
Adelaide St. Swan 110 B3
Adeline St. Card 205 F3
Adenfield Way. Rhoose 222 C1
Admirals Wlk. Swan 109 E3
Adrian Cl. Porth 192 C4
Ael-y- Bryn. Bridg 179 D3
Ael-y -bryn. Porth 123 E1
Ael-y-bryn. Aberd 49 E2
Ael-y-Bryn. Bed 99 E4
Ael-y-Bryn. Bedw 152 C3
Ael-y-Bryn. Caer 151 F3
Ael-y-Bryn. Card 187 D4
Ael-y-Bryn. Card 189 E2
Ael-y-Bryn. Ll'tris 169 D4
Ael-y-Bryn. Maest 91 D1
Ael-y-Bryn. P-s-Ely 201 F3
Ael-y-Bryn. Pen-cl 80 C2
Ael-y-Bryn. Penty 186 B4
Ael-y-Bryn. Pyle 177 D4
Ael-y-Bryn Rd. Swan 83 F2
Ael-y-Bryn. Rhy 34 B3
Ael-y-Bryn. Trehe 69 D1
Ael-y-bryn. Ystra 8 A1
Ael-y-Fro. Pontdw 40 B4
Aelfryn. Ll'hry 183 D3
Aelfryn Terr. Cwma 114 B3
Aelybryn. Ponty 124 A1
Aelybryn St. Deri 53 E4
Aeron Ct. Bar 76 A1
Aeron Pl. Bar 76 A1
Aeron Pl. Swan 85 D1
Aeron Terr. Mer T 51 F4
Afan Rd. Glyn 90 B2
Afan Terr. Cwma 115 D4
Afan Valley Cl. Neath 88 A3
Afan Valley Rd. Cwma 115 D4
Afan Valley Rd. Neath 88 A3
Afan Way. P Tal 113 E2
Afandale. P Tal 113 E2
Afon Cl. M-y-Fed 174 B2
Afon Fach. Pyle 161 D1
Afon Rd. Ll'ge 56 B4
Afon St. Ponty 123 E1
Afon Villas. Cwma 115 D4
Afon-Llan Gdns. Swan 83 E3
Afon-y-Felin. B-coch 63 E2
Africa Gdns. Card 188 C1
Agate St. Card 205 E3
Agent's Row. Aberd 50 B2
Agincourt Rd. Card 205 E4
Agnes St. Pen 216 C3
Aintree Dr. Card 203 F3
Alamein Rd. Swan 84 C2
Alaw Rd. Trea 122 A3
Alban Terr. Glyn 90 C3
Albany Cl. Swan 84 B2
Albany Ct. Pen 217 D2
Albany Rd. Card 205 E4
Albany Rd. Peng 101 F3
Albany Rd. Pontcr 118 C2
Albany St. Fern 96 A3
Albany St. M Ash 72 B1
Albert Cres. Pen 217 D2
Albert Ct. Pen 217 D2
Albert Rd. Pen 217 D2
Albert Rd. Ponty 149 D4
Albert Row. Swan 110 B3
Albert St. Abera 50 A1
Albert St. Barry 225 E3
Albert St. Card 204 B3
Albert St. Fern 96 A4
Albert St. M Ash 72 B1
Albert St. Maest 91 E1
Albert St. Yst 94 C3
Albert Terr. Maest 116 C2
Albert Wlk. Card 204 B3
Alberta Pl. Pen 217 D1
Alberta Rd. Pen 217 D1
Alberta St. Mer V 73 E3
Alberto Rd. Swan 85 D3
Albion Ind Est. Ponty 124 C3
Albion Pl. Pyle 161 E1
Albion Rd. P Tal 113 E3
Albion Road App. P Tal 113 E4
Albion St. Abera 71 D4
Albion St. Yst 95 D1
Albion Terr. Peng 101 F3
Alden Dr. Swan 83 E1
Aldenham Rd. Porthc 193 E4
Alder Ave. Ystra 23 E4
Alder Dr. Aberd 49 F1
Alder Gr. Mer T 32 B3
Alder Rd. Card 189 D1
Alder Rd. Ll'hry 183 D3
Alder Rd. Neath 88 A3
Alder Terr. Glyn 91 E2
Alder Way. Gow 82 B3
Alder Way. T Mum 136 C4
Alderbrook. Card 173 E1
Alderbrook Ct. Swan 83 F3
Aldergrove Cl. P Tal 113 F2
Aldergrove Ct. Porth 122 C3
Aldergrove Rd. Porth 122 C3
Alderman Cl. Peng 101 E4
Alderwood Cl. Card 190 C4
Alderwood Cl. Cry 24 A1
Alderwood Rd. T Mum 137 D4
Aldsworth Rd. Card 203 F4
Aldwych Cl. Card 172 C1
Aldwyn Rd. Swan 83 E1
Aled Way. St M Ch 221 E4
Alexander Cres. B-coch 62 C1
Alexander Ct. Caer 152 B2
Alexander Pl. Tred 35 F4
Alexander Pl. Troed 51 F2
Alexander Rd. B-coch 62 C1
Alexander Rd. Neath 87 E2
Alexander St. Card 205 D4
Alexander St. Rhy 54 A4
Alexandra Ave. Mer T 32 C2
Alexandra Cl. Mer T 32 C2
Alexandra Ct. Card 204 B3
Alexandra Pl. Abercy 98 C2
Alexandra Pl. Rhy 34 C3
Alexandra Rd. Card 204 B3
Alexandra Rd. Gall 101 D2
Alexandra Rd. Lough 57 D1
Alexandra Rd. Maest 91 D1
Alexandra Rd. Mer T 32 C2
Alexandra Rd. N Tre 54 C1
Alexandra Rd. Pontcr 118 C2
Alexandra Rd. Ponty 149 E4
Alexandra Rd. Swan 110 B4
Alexandra Rd. Ynys 127 F3
Alexandra Rd. Yst 95 D1
Alexandra St. P Tal 114 A1
Alexandra Terr. Aber 125 F2
Alexandra Terr. Abera 50 A1
Alexandra Terr. Abera 71 D2
Alexandra Terr. Ch Vil 169 E3
Alexandra Terr. M Ash 72 C2
Alexandra Terr. Mer T 51 F4
Alexandra Terr. Swan 109 F3
Alexandra Terr. Tred 35 F3
Alexandria Ct. Pen 217 D2
Alford Rd. Neath 87 F4
Alfred Rd. Swan 84 C3
Alfred St. Bar 76 A1
Alfred St. Card 189 D1
Alfred St. Maest 117 D2
Alfred St. Mer T 32 C2
Alfred St. Neath 87 F4
Alfred St. P Tal 113 F1
Alfred St. Rhy 54 B4
Alfred St. Tony 146 B3
Alfred St. Tonypa 122 A1
Alfred's Terr. T We 171 D2
Alfreda Rd. Card 187 F2
Alfreds Ct. Card 187 F2
Alice Pl. Abera 71 D2
Alice St. Card 205 D1
Alice St. Neath 87 E3
Alice St. Swan 84 A1
Alison Ct. Porthc 193 E4
All Saints Pl. Cwma 114 C3
All Saints Way. Bridg 163 E1
Allan Durst Cl. Card 187 E2
Allen Ct. Ll' Maj 220 A3
Allen St. M Ash 72 B2
Allens Ct. Card 189 E3
Allensbank Cres. Card 188 C1
Allensbank Rd. Card 188 C1
Allerton St. Card 204 C2
Allister St. Neath 87 F4
Alloy Court Est. Pontdw 40 C3
Allt Wen. Card 187 F4
Allt-Iago Rd. Pontar 36 B2
Allt-y-Graban Rd. Lough 57 E4
Allt-y-Graban Rd. Pontar 57 E4
Allt-y-Waun. Pontdw 40 B4
Alltacham Dr. Pontdw 40 C3
Alltmawr Rd. Card 189 E3
Alltwen Hill. A-wen 40 C2
Alltwen Ind Est. A-wen 41 D3
Alltygrug Farm Rd. Ystal 23 D4
Alltygrug Rd. Ystal 23 D4
Alltywerin. Pontdw 40 B3
Alma Cotts. Bedw 152 C4
Alma Houses. Maest 117 D1
Alma Pl. Yst 94 C3
Alma Rd. Card 189 E1
Alma Rd. Maest 117 D1
Alma St. Aberd 49 F2
Alma St. Bedw 154 A4
Alma St. Mer T 33 D3
Alma St. Mer T 51 F4
Alma St. Trehe 68 C1
Alma Terr. Maest 117 D1
Alma Terr. Marg 139 E3
Alma Terr. Mer T 33 D3
Alma Terr. Og Va 144 C4
Alma Terr. Tondu 163 E2
Almond Cl. Ch Vil 169 E3
Almond Dr. Card 173 F1
Almond Gr. Mer T 32 B2
Alpha House. Ponty 170 C4
Alpha Pl. P Tal 113 E4
Alpha Pl. Ponty 124 B1
Alpha St. Ponty 124 B1
Alphonso St. Mer T 33 D3
Althorp Dr. Sully 227 D4
Alun Rd. Swan 84 A1
Alwen Dr. Card 172 C2
Alyson Way. Penco 181 E4
Aman Ct. Abera 71 D2
Aman St. Abera 71 D2
Amber Cl. Card 189 F4
Amber Cl. P Tal 113 D1
Ambergate Dr. Card 173 F1
Amberheart Dr. Card 172 C2
Amberley Cl. Card 189 F4
Amberley Dr. T Mum 137 D2
Amberton Pl. Mer T 32 C2
Amberwood Cl. Card 173 F1
Amblecote Cl. Card 173 F1
Ambleside Ave. Card 189 D1
Ambleside Ct. Gell 100 C4
Ambleside. T Mum 137 D4
Ambrooke Cl. Card 173 F1
Amelia Terr. Trea 121 F4
America Pl. Porth 122 C2
Amesbury Rd. Card 189 E1
Amethyst Rd. Card 187 E1
Amherst St. Card 204 C1
Amman Rd. Bry 5 E4
Amman Terr. Bry 6 A4
Ammanford Rd. Glan 4 C3
Amos Hill. Tonypa 122 A2
Amroth Ct. Swan 84 A4
Amroth House. Card 188 A2
Amroth Rd. Card 203 E3
Amyas Cl. Card 204 C2
Anchor Ct. Card 205 D2
Anchor Ct. Swan 110 B3
Anchor Ind Est. Card 205 D2
Anchor St. T We 171 D2
Anchor Way. Pen 216 C3
Anderson La. South 135 D3
Anderson Pl. Card 205 E3
Anderson Terr. Tonypa 121 F3
Andrew Cres. Swan 60 A2
Andrew Rd. Pen 216 C3
Andrew's Rd. Card 187 F1
Andrews Cl. Bar 76 A1
Andrews Cl. Mer T 51 D4
Andrews Ct. Ll' Maj 220 A3
Andrews Ct. Ponty 149 E4
Androven Ct. Card 189 E3
Aneddfan. Cwma 114 C3
Aneurin Ave. Peng 101 D3
Aneurin Bevan Ave. Brynco 163 F3
Aneurin Bevan Ave. Gell 100 B3
Aneurin Bevan's Way. Maest 117 E1
Aneurin Cl. Swan 109 D3
Aneurin Cres. Mer T 51 F4
Aneurin Rd. Barry 225 D3
Aneurin Terr. Rhy 34 C3
Aneurin Way. Swan 109 D3
Angel La. Bar 76 A2
Angel Pl. Neath 87 F4
Angel St. Bridg 179 F2
Angel St. Neath 87 F4
Angel St. P Tal 113 F1
Angelina St. Card 205 D2
Angelton Cotts. Bridg 163 F1
Angelton Gn. Bridg 163 E1
Angle Pl. Card 172 B1
Anglesey Cl. Ch Vil 150 A1
Anglesey Cl. Ll' Maj 220 A4
Anglesey St. Card 204 B3
Anglesey Way. Porth 176 C1
Angleton Rd. Bridg 179 E4
Anglia Cl. Bridg 163 F1
Angus St. Card 189 E1
Angus St. Mer V 73 E3
Angus St. Troed 52 A1
Ann St. Abercy 98 B1
Ann St. Aberd 49 F2
Ann St. Card 204 B3
Ann St. Ponty 124 C3
Anstee Ct. Card 204 B3
Anthony Gr. Troed 51 F2
Anton Ct. Card 188 A3
Apex Bldgs. Card 205 D2
Apollo Cl. Card 172 C1
Apollo Way. Peng 101 E4
Appledore Pl. T Mum 136 C3
Appledore Rd. Card 188 B2
Applegrove. Ll'rh 104 B1
Appletree Ave. Porth 122 B2
Appletree Rd. Porth 122 B2
Applewood Cl. Card 205 E3
Approach Rd. Swan 84 B1
Aqueduct Terr. Cwma 89 D1
Aquilla Ct. Card 204 B4
Ar-y-Nant. Barry 225 D4
Arabella St. Card 189 D1
Aran St. Swan 84 C4
Arbroath Ct. Card 205 F4
Arbutus Cl. Mer T 32 B3
Arcade Terr. Glan 4 B4
Arch Hill. Cross 129 E3
Archer Cres. Card 203 E3
Archer Pl. Card 203 E3
Archer Pl. Pen 217 D2
Archer Rd. Card 203 E3
Archer Rd. Pen 217 D2
Archer St. Troed 52 B1
Archer St. Ynybw 97 F1
Archer Terr. Card 203 E3
Archer Terr. Pen 217 D1
Archview Ct. Card 189 D1
Arcot La. Pen 217 D2
Arcot Lane (North). Pen 217 D3
Arcot St. Pen 217 D2
Arden Way. Barry 225 E4
Ardmore Ave. Tonypa 121 F2
Ardwyn. Card 187 F4
Ardwyn Pl. Og Va 119 F1
Ardwyn Terr. Tonypa 121 F3
Ardwyn Terr. Yst 95 D1
Arennig Rd. Swan 84 A3
Arethusa Quay. Swan 110 B3
Arfonfab Cres. Ponty 150 A2
Arfryn. Peny 49 D3
Arfryn Pl. Mer T 51 F4
Arfryn Rd. Swan 109 F4
Arfryn Terr. Mer T 51 F4
Arfryn Terr. Tylor 96 A2
Argae La. D Pow 215 E1
Argoed Ave. Ll'ha 167 D2
Argoed Terr. Mer V 73 E3
Argyle St. Abercy 98 C2
Argyle St. Mer T 32 C1
Argyle St. Porth 122 C1
Argyle St. Swan 110 A3
Argyle St. Yst 94 C3
Argyle Terr. Trea 121 F4
Argyle Way. Card 203 F2
Argyll Ave. Lough 57 D1
Arlan Gwilli. Hen 36 A2
Arles Rd. Card 203 F3
Arlington Cres. Card 190 B3
Arlington Pl. Porth 192 C4
Arlington Rd. Porth 192 C4
Arlington Rd. Sully 226 A3
Armine Rd. Swan 83 F2
Army Pl. Yst 95 E2
Arnant Villas. Og Va 119 F3
Arno Rd. Barry 225 E4
Arnold Ave. Card 190 B4
Arnold St. M Ash 72 C2
Arnott's Pl. Aberd 49 F1
Arnside Rd. Card 189 E1
Arosfa Ave. Porthc 193 E4
Arran Cl. Ponty 149 D3
Arran Pl. Card 205 E4
Arran St. Card 205 E4
Arrol St. Card 205 E3
Arthur St. Barry 225 E3
Arthur St. Card 205 F4
Arthur St. Glyn 92 A3
Arthur St. M Ash 97 F4
Arthur St. Neath 87 F4
Arthur St. P Tal 114 A1
Arthur St. Rhy 54 B4
Arthur St. Tonypa 122 A1
Arthur St. Troed 52 A2
Arthur St. Ynys 128 A2
Arthur St. Yst 95 E2
Arthur Terr. Pontdw 40 C3
Arundel Pl. Card 204 B2
Arvonia Terr. Peng 101 D3
Arwelfa. Swan 59 E1
Ascot Cl. Card 203 F3
Ascot Dr. P Tal 113 F3
Asgog St. Card 205 E3
Ash Cres. Mer T 32 B2
Ash Ct. Oak 101 F3
Ash Gr. Barry 225 E4
Ash Gr. Bridg 179 D3
Ash Gr. C-c-y-c 32 A3
Ash Gr. Card 188 A3
Ash Gr. Ll'ha 183 F4
Ash Gr. Ll'hry 183 D3
Ash Gr. Lough 57 D2
Ash Gr. M Ash 97 F4
Ash Gr. Neath 88 A3
Ash Gr. Pen 216 C3
Ash Gr. Porthc 193 F4
Ash Gr. Swan 82 B2
Ash Gr. Swan 108 B4
Ash Gr. W St D 199 E4
Ash Gr. Wen 203 D1
Ash Gr. Yst 94 C3
Ash La. Ll'maes 221 D4
Ash Pl. Bar 75 F1
Ash Pl. Card 187 E1
Ash Plant Rd. St Ath 221 F1
Ash Rd. Troed 52 A1
Ash Sq. Ponty 150 A3
Ash St. Abera 71 F2
Ash St. Swan 85 D4
Ash St. Tony 146 A3
Ash Tree Cl. Card 187 D3
Ash Wlk. Ll'tris 168 B1
Ashbourne Cl. Aberd 49 E1
Ashbrook. Bridg 180 A3
Ashburnham Dr. T Mum 108 C1
Ashburton Ave. Card 190 B4
Ashby Rd. Sully 226 A3
Ashchurch Cl. Card 188 A3
Ashcroft Cres. Card 187 E1
Ashdale Rd. Tonypa 122 A1
Ashdene Cl. Card 187 E1
Ashdown Cl. Card 190 C4
Ashfield Ct. Card 190 C4
Ashford Cl. Ponty 124 B3

Ashgrove. Aberd 49 F2
Ashgrove. Bedw 152 C3
Ashgrove. D pow 216 A1
Ashgrove. Gell 100 C1
Ashgrove. Ll' maj 219 F3
Ashgrove. P Tal 113 E4
Ashgrove. Peng 101 F3
Ashgrove. Ponty 124 F3
Ashgrove Terr. Nel 99 F2
Ashgrove. Tre 98 C3
Ashgrove Villas. Bed 74 A4
Ashlea Dr. Mer T 32 C1
Ashleigh Cl. Swan 109 E2
Ashleigh Rd. Swan 109 E2
Ashleigh Terr. Skew 112 B4
Ashmount Bsns Pk. Swan 60 A1
Ashville. Tred 35 F3
Ashwood Cl. Peng 101 F3
Ashwood Ct. Card 205 E4
Ashwood Dr. A-wen 41 D3
Aspen Ave. Peng 101 F3
Aspen Cl. Card 190 C4
Aspen Way. Ch Vil 169 E3
Aspen Way. Neath 88 B3
Asquith St. Gall 101 D3
Aster Cl. Card 191 D4
Aster View. P Tal 113 E2
Astoria Ct. Card 172 C1
Atfield Cl. Card 189 F1
Athelstan Rd. Card 187 F2
Atlantic Cl. Swan 85 D3
Atlantic Pl. Barry 225 E4
Atlantic Way. Barry 225 D2
Atlantic Wharf. Card 205 E2
Atlas Pl. Card 204 B3
Atlas Rd. Card 204 B3
Atlee Terr. Maest 91 D1
Attlee Ave. P Tal 138 C4
Attlee Cl. Tred 35 E3
Attlee Ct. Caer 152 B2
Attlee Rd. Peng 101 F4
Attlee St. Brynco 163 F3
Attlee Way. Tred 35 F3
Aubrey Ave. Card 204 A4
Aubrey Rd. Porth 122 C1
Aubrey Rd. Tonypa 122 A2
Auburn Ave. P Tal 113 D1
Augusta Cres. Pen 217 D1
Augusta Rd. Pen 217 D1
Augusta St. Card 205 E3
Augusta St. Yst 95 D2
Augustus St. Ynybw 97 F1
Austen Cl. Card 190 B4
Austin Ave. Bridg 178 C2
Austin Ave. Bridg 179 F3
Austin Ave. Porthc 193 E4
Austin Cl. Porthc 193 E4
Austin St. M Ash 72 B2
Australia Rd. Card 188 C1
Australian Terr. Bridg 179 F3
Auxiliary Boiler House Rd.
    St Ath 221 F1
Avan St. Marg 114 A1
Avenue Cl. Gell 100 C1
Avenue De Clichy. Mer T 32 B1
Avenue Ind Pk. Card 190 A4
Avenue The. Bar 76 A1
Avenue The. Bedw 153 D3
Avenue The. Card 187 F2
Avenue The. Card 188 A1
Avenue The. Card 190 B1
Avenue The. Cwma 114 B3
Avenue The. Gall 101 D1
Avenue The. Ll'bra 126 C1
Avenue The. M Ash 72 A3
Avenue The. Neath 87 E2
Avenue The. Pontcr 118 C2
Avenue The. Ponty 124 B1
Avenue The. Tony 147 E3
Avenue The. Tre 98 C3
Avenue The. Tylor 122 B4
Avenue The. Ynys 101 F1
Averil Vivian Gr. Swan 109 F3
Avoca Pl. Card 204 C2
Avocet Ct. Barry 225 D3
Avon Cl. Barry 225 E4
Avon Cl. Pontll 101 E2
Avon Dale Terr. Glyn 91 E3
Avon St. Fern 95 F4
Avon St. G-nea 26 C1
Avon St. Glyn 91 E3
Avon Terr. Tylor 122 C4
Avondale. Abercy 98 B3
Avondale Cres. Card 205 D1
Avondale Gdns. Card 205 D1
Avondale Gdns S. Card 205 D1
Avondale Rd. Card 205 D1
Avondale Rd. Porth 123 D1
Avondale Rd. Yst 95 D1
Avondale Sq. Glyn 91 E3
Avondale St. Abercy 98 B3
Avonmuir Rd. Card 206 A4
Avonridge. Barry 225 D3
Avonridge. Card 172 B1
Awel Mor. Card 189 E2
Awelfryn. Ll'tris 149 D2
Awelfryn. Peny 49 D3
Awelfryn Villas. Mer T 32 C2

Axbridge Cres. Card 190 B3
Axminster Rd. Card 205 F4
Aylesbury Rd. Swan 109 F3
Ayron St. Fern 95 F3
Ayton Terr. Trea 121 F4
Azalea Cl. Card 189 E4

B Station Access Rd.
    St Ath 221 F1
Baber Cl. Card 189 F1
Bach Rd. P Tal 113 D2
Back Dr. Skew 86 A4
Bacton Ct. Card 188 A1
Bacton Rd. Card 188 A1
Baden Rd. Card 206 A3
Baden Terr. Mer T 32 C1
Bader Cl. Card 188 C3
Badminton Gdns. Swan 83 F3
Baglan Bay Shopping Centre.
    P Tal 113 E2
Baglan Cotts. Tondu 163 E4
Baglan Hts. P Tal 113 F4
Baglan St. Swan 111 D4
Baglan St. Trehe 94 A4
Baglan St. Treo 94 A4
Baglan St. Tylor 96 B1
Baglan St. Yst 94 C3
Baglan Way. P Tal 113 F2
Bagot St. Abercy 98 A3
Baiden Ave. Pyle 161 E1
Bailey Cl. Card 203 F4
Bailey St. Deri 54 A1
Bailey St. M Ash 72 B1
Bailey St. P Tal 114 A1
Bailey St. Tylor 122 C4
Bailey St. Yst 94 C2
Baker's La. Ll' maj 219 F4
Bakers Ct. Card 204 A4
Bakers Ct. Marsh 191 F4
Bakers Row. Card 205 D3
Bakers Way. Brynco 163 F2
Bakery La. Marsh 175 E1
Bala Cotts. Ystra 8 A2
Bala Rd. Card 188 A1
Balaclava Ct. Tonypa 121 F2
Balaclava Rd. Card 189 E1
Balaclava Rd. Mer T 33 D2
Balaclava Rd. Swan 61 D3
Balaclava St. Swan 110 C4
Baldwin Cl. Card 187 E2
Baldwin St. Bar 75 F2
Baldwin St. Bryn 115 F3
Baldwin's Cres. Skew 111 F3
Ball Cl. Card 190 A4
Ball La. Card 190 A3
Ball Rd. Card 190 A3
Ballarat. Penco 165 F1
Ballards Ct. Skew 86 C4
Ballas Cl. Pyle 177 D4
Balmoral Cl. Card 173 D1
Balmoral Pl. Ponty 149 D3
Bampton Rd. Card 190 B4
Banalog Terr. Mark 55 E1
Banastre Ave. Card 188 C1
Banc-yr-Allt. Bridg 179 D3
Banfield Terr. Lough 56 C1
Bangor Ct. Card 189 E1
Bangor La. Card 189 E1
Bangor St. Card 189 E1
Bangor St. Maest 117 D3
Bangor Terr. Maest 117 D3
Bank Cotts. Ystra 8 A2
Bank La. Tred 35 F4
Bank Rd. Ll'ge 56 B4
Bank Side. Neath 87 F4
Bank St. Maest 117 D2
Bank St. Tonypa 122 A2
Bank Terr. C-c-y-c 32 A2
Bankers Hill. Ce Cr 162 B2
Bankes St. Abera 50 A1
Bankside Cl. Card 172 C2
Banwell Pl. Card 190 B3
Banwell St. Swan 84 C4
Banwen La. A-wen 40 C2
Banwen Pl. G-C-G 5 D4
Banwy Rd. Swan 59 E1
Banwy Rd. Swan 84 B4
Baptist Row. Fern 95 F4
Baptist Sq. Fern 95 F4
Baptist Well Pl. Swan 84 B1
Baptist Well St. Swan 84 B1
Baran Rd. Pontdw 21 D1
Barberry Rise. Pen 216 C3
Barbrook Cl. Card 173 D1
Bardsey Ave. Swan 83 F4
Bardsey Cl. Porth 176 C1
Bardsey Cres. Card 172 C1
Bargoed Cl. Tre 99 D4
Bargoed St. Card 205 D2
Bargoed Terr. Tre 99 D4
Barkley St. Rhy 54 B4
Barmouth Rd. Card 190 A2
Barnabas Cl. Swan 82 C2
Barnard Ave. Card 203 F3
Barnardo St. Maest 117 D1
Barnes Ave. Bridg 179 D3

Barnstaple Rd. Card 190 B3
Barnwood Cres. Card 202 C2
Baron Cl. Pen 216 C2
Baron Rd. Pen 216 C2
Baron's Cl. Ll' Maj 220 A3
Baron's Court Rd. Card 189 E1
Baroness Pl. Pen 216 C2
Barquentine Pl. Card 205 E2
Barrack La. Card 205 D3
Barrack Row. Mer T 33 D3
Barrett St. Treo 94 A2
Barrington Rd. Card 188 A2
Barrington St. Mer V 73 E3
Barry Cl. Gell 100 C4
Barry Rd. G-C-G 5 D3
Barry Rd. Pen 216 C3
Barry Rd. Ponty 124 A1
Bartlett St. Caer 152 A1
Bartley Terr. Swan 84 C3
Basil Pl. Card 205 D4
Bassaleg Cl. Card 191 D4
Bassett Rd. Sully 226 A3
Bassett St. Abercy 98 C2
Bassett St. Barry 225 D3
Bassett St. Card 204 B3
Bassett St. Ponty 124 B1
Bastian Cl. Barry 225 E4
Batchelor Rd. Card 188 B1
Bath Ave. Swan 59 F1
Bath La. Swan 110 B3
Bath Rd. Swan 84 C4
Bath St. Marg 114 A1
Bath Villas. Swan 84 C4
Bathurst St. Swan 110 B3
Baton Ct. Card 188 B2
Battenberg St. Abercy 98 B3
Baxter Terr. Glyn 66 C2
Bay St. Swan 111 D4
Bay Tree Ave. Swan 109 D3
Bay View Cl. Skew 86 C3
Bay View Cres. Swan 110 A3
Bay View Gdns. Skew 86 C3
Bay View. Marg 114 B1
Bay View Rd. Porthc 193 E4
Bay View. Swan 110 C4
Bay View Terr. Swan 110 A3
Baylis Cl. Card 203 F1
Bayliss Rd. Brynco 163 F2
Baynton Cl. Card 187 F1
Bayside Rd. Card 205 E3
Bayswater Rd. Swan 109 E4
Baywood Ave. T Mum 137 D4
Beach La. Pen 217 D2
Beach Rd. Pen 217 D2
Beach Rd. Pen-cl 80 C2
Beach Rd. Porthc 193 E4
Beach Rd. Pyle 161 D1
Beach Rd. St B M 207 D4
Beach Rd. Sully 226 B2
Beach St. P Tal 138 C4
Beach St. Swan 110 A3
Beacon St. Card 204 B4
Beacons Pk. Hir 29 D3
Beacons The. Hir 48 B4
Beacons View. Neath 88 A3
Beaconsfield Ct. Swan 109 D4
Beaconsfield Rd. B-coch 62 C1
Beaconsfield Way. Swan 109 D4
Beadon St. M Ash 72 B1
Beale Cl. Card 187 F1
Beatrice Rd. Barry 225 D3
Beatrice Rd. Card 188 A2
Beatrice St. Glyn 92 B3
Beattie St. Swan 84 A1
Beatty Ave. Card 189 D3
Beatty Cl. Barry 225 D4
Beatty St. Gall 101 D3
Beauchamp St. Card 204 C3
Beaufort Ave. T Mum 137 D2
Beaufort Cl. T Mum 137 D2
Beaufort Ct. Swan 83 F3
Beaufort Ct. Swan 84 C3
Beaufort Dr. South 135 F4
Beaufort Gdns. South 135 F4
Beaufort Rd. Swan 84 C3
Beaufort Rd. Tred 35 F4
Beaufort Way. Rhoose 222 C1
Beaumaris Cl. Ch Vil 169 F1
Beaumaris Cl. Rhiwd 155 F2
Beaumaris Rd. Card 190 A2
Beaumont Cres. Swan 110 C4
Beaumont Ct. Pen 216 C2
Beckett St. M Ash 72 B2
Beckgrove Cl. Card 206 A4
Beda Rd. Card 204 B3
Bedavere Cl. Card 172 C1
Beddoe St. Abera 71 E4
Beddoe St. Tre 99 D3
Bedford Cl. Ce Cr 162 A1
Bedford Pl. Card 205 E4
Bedford Rd. Ce Cr 162 A2
Bedford St. Abera 71 E4
Bedford St. Card 205 D4
Bedford St. Swan 85 D1
Bedlinog Terr. Bed 74 A4
Bedlwyn Rd. N Tre 54 C2

Bedw Arian. Bridg 179 D3
Bedw Cl. Porth 122 C1
Bedw Rd. Bed 74 A4
Bedw Rd. Ponty 124 C2
Bedw St. Porth 122 C1
Bedwas Cl. Card 191 D4
Bedwas Pl. Pen 216 C2
Bedwas Rd. Bedw 152 B3
Bedwas Rd. Caer 152 B2
Bedwas St. Card 204 C2
Bedwellty Rd. Bar 76 A3
Bedwellty Rd. N Tre 54 C1
Bedwellty Rd. Peng 101 E4
Bedwlwyn Cl. Gell 100 C1
Bedwlwyn Rd. Gell 100 C1
Bedwlwyn St. Gell 100 C1
Beech Ave. Pontll 101 F2
Beech Cres. Lough 57 D2
Beech Ct. Bar 75 F1
Beech Ct. Card 171 E1
Beech Dr. Gell 100 C2
Beech Emb. Gell 100 C1
Beech Gr. Mer T 32 C2
Beech Gr. Porthc 193 E4
Beech House. Card 187 F4
Beech Pk. Colw 197 D2
Beech Rd. Card 203 D4
Beech Rd. Ll'hry 183 D3
Beech Rd. Pontcr 143 F4
Beech St. Fern 95 F3
Beech St. Tony 146 A3
Beech Terr. Abera 71 F2
Beech Tree Cl. Card 187 D3
Beech Tree La. Swan 109 E3
Beech Tree Way. Nel 99 F2
Beechcroft. Bed 99 E4
Beechcroft. Pontll 101 F3
Beecher Ave. Card 204 C1
Beecher Terr. Cross 129 E3
Beeches Cl The. Swan 109 F3
Beeches The. Bridg 179 F3
Beechfield Ave. Gall 101 D2
Beechgrove. Caer 152 B3
Beechgrove. Tre 98 C3
Beeching Way. Ch Vil 169 F1
Beechlea Cl. Ll'tris 184 B3
Beechwood Ave. Aberd 49 F1
Beechwood Ave. Bridg 179 E3
Beechwood Ave. C-c-y-c 32 A3
Beechwood Ave. Neath 87 E3
Beechwood Ave. Ynys 128 C2
Beechwood Dr. Ch Vil 169 E3
Beechwood Dr. Mer T 50 C4
Beechwood Dr. Pen 216 C1
Beechwood Gr. Penco 165 E1
Beechwood Rd. Marg 139 F2
Beechwood Rd. Swan 109 F3
Beechwood Rd. T We 171 D2
Beechwood St. Ponty 150 A3
Began Rd. Card 174 B2
Began Rd. M-y-Fed 174 B2
Beili Glas. Lough 56 C1
Beili Glas Rd. Peng 101 D3
Belgrave Cl. Card 172 C2
Belgrave Cl. Lough 57 D1
Belgrave Ct. Card 204 C3
Belgrave Ct. Swan 110 A3
Belgrave Gdns. Swan 110 A3
Belgrave La. Swan 110 A3
Belgrave Rd. Lough 57 D1
Belgrave St. Yst 95 D1
Belgrave Terr. Ponty 124 C2
Bell St. Aberd 49 F2
Belle View Terr. Barry 225 E4
Belle Vue. Tonypa 122 A2
Belle Vue. Aberd 49 F2
Belle Vue Cl. Pen 217 D2
Belle Vue Cres. Card 187 F2
Belle Vue. Pen-cl 80 C2
Belle Vue St. Tonypa 121 D4
Belle Vue Terr. Pen 217 D3
Belle Vue Terr. Ponty 149 F3
Belle Vue Way. Swan 110 B4
Bellevue Rd. T Mum 136 C3
Bellevue Terr. Mer V 73 E2
Bells Hill. Mer V 73 E2
Belmont Cl. Maest 117 D2
Belmont St. Barry 225 D3
Belmont Terr. Abera 71 E4
Belmont Terr. Porth 122 C1
Belmont Wlk. Card 205 D1
Belvedere Cres. Barry 225 D3
Belvedere Terr. Pontmi 129 F2
Belvoir Ct. Ll'tris 168 C1
Benbow Cl. Swan 109 E3
Bendrick Dr. South 134 C3
Bendrick Rd. Barry 225 E2
Benecrofte. Rhoose 223 D1
Benedict Cl. B-coch 87 D4
Benjamin Ct. Tred 35 D1
Bennett Ave. Bridg 180 B2
Bennett St. Bridg 180 B2
Bennett St. Swan 84 B2
Benson Rd. Pen-cl 80 C2
Benson St. Pen-cl 80 C2

Benson Terr. Pen-cl 80 C2
Benthall Pl. Swan 110 C4
Beresford Rd. Card 205 F4
Beresford Road La. Card 205 F4
Berkeley Cl. Swan 61 D1
Berkeley Ct. Card 189 D3
Berkeley Sq. Wen 203 D1
Berkley Cl. Rhiwd 155 F2
Berkley Dr. Pen 217 D2
Berkley Rd. Rhiwd 155 F2
Berkrolles Ave. St Ath 221 E2
Berllangron Cotts. Peng 76 C1
Berllanlwyd Ave. Mark 76 C4
Berllanlwyd St. Gell 100 C4
Berma Cl. T Mum 137 E2
Bernard Ave. Card 204 A3
Bernard St. Aberca 129 E4
Bernard St. Swan 109 F3
Berrington Villas. Bry 6 C3
Berry Ct. Ll' Maj 220 A3
Berry Pl. Card 187 E1
Berry Sq. Mer T 33 D2
Berrylands. P Tal 138 B4
Berrymead Rd. Card 189 D4
Bertha Pl. Marg 139 F2
Bertha Rd. Marg 139 F2
Bertha St. Ponty 149 F3
Berthlwyd. Penty 170 B1
Berthin St. Card 204 B4
Bertram St. Card 205 F4
Berw Rd. Ponty 124 B1
Berw Rd. Swan 110 A4
Berw Rd. Tonypa 121 F3
Berwedd-dy Cotts. Ponty 124 C2
Berwick Terr. Swan 110 B4
Berwyn Pl. Swan 84 A2
Beryl St. Cly 60 C4
Bessant Cl. Cowb 198 C1
Bessborough Dr. Card 204 C2
Bessemer Cl. Card 204 B1
Bessemer Close Workshops.
    Card 204 B1
Bessemer Rd. Card 204 B2
Bethania. Abercy 98 C2
Bethania Cl. Maest 117 D1
Bethania Hill. Tony 147 E1
Bethania Pl. Aberd 71 F4
Bethania Rd. Cly 60 B4
Bethania Row. Card 190 B4
Bethania Row. Og Va 119 F1
Bethania St. G-nea 27 D1
Bethania St. Maest 117 D1
Bethany La. T Mum 137 D4
Bethel Ave. Tred 35 F3
Bethel Pl. Hir 48 B4
Bethel Rd. G-nea 27 D1
Bethel Rd. Pen-cl 80 C2
Bethel Rd. Ystal 7 D1
Bethel Rd. Ystra 23 E4
Bethel St. Neath 113 E4
Bethel St. Ponty 149 D4
Bethesda Rd. Ponydw 41 D4
Bethesda St. Mer T 32 B1
Bethesda St. Porth 123 E1
Bethesda St. Swan 110 B4
Bethlehem Rd. Skew 86 C4
Bethuel St. Abera 50 A1
Bettisland. T Mum 136 C4
Bettws Rd. Swan 84 A2
Bettws-y-Coed Rd. Card 189 D4
Betws Rd. Pontcr 143 F1
Beulah Rd. Card 188 B4
Beulah St. Rhy 34 C2
Bevan Cl. Bedw 152 C3
Bevan Cres. Peng 101 E4
Bevan Rise. Bedw 152 C3
Bevan St. P Tal 138 C4
Bevan Way. Swan 82 C2
Bevan's Terr. Ton 89 D1
Bevans Row. Swan 111 D4
Bevans Terr. Swan 85 F3
Beverley Cl. Swan 83 F2
Beverley Gdns. Swan 83 F2
Beverley St. Barry 225 D4
Beverley St. Marg 139 D4
Bevin Ave. P Tal 138 B4
Bevin House. P Tal 138 B4
Bicester Rd. Barry 225 F3
Bideford Rd. Card 190 B3
Bill Harry Ct. Tred 35 E4
Billingham Cres. Mer T 32 C2
Bilton Rd. Neath 87 F4
Bingle La. St Ath 221 E3
Birch Cres. Ch Vil 169 E3
Birch Gr. Gell 100 C2
Birch Ct. Card 171 E1
Birch Gr. Bridg 179 D3
Birch Gr. Caer 152 B3
Birch Gr. Ch Vil 149 F1
Birch Gr. Ll'hry 183 D3
Birch Gr. Mer T 32 B3
Birch Gr. Swan 82 B2
Birch Hill. Card 171 E1
Birch La. Pen 217 D1
Birch Rd. Card 203 E4
Birch Rd. P Tal 113 E4
Birch Tree Cl. Swan 109 E3

232

Birch Wlk. Porth — Broomfield St. Caer

Birch Wlk. Porthc 193 E4
Birches The. M Ash 72 A3
Birchfield Cl. Ch Vil 150 A1
Birchfield Cres. Card 204 A3
Birchfield Rd. Pontdw 40 C3
Birchfield Rd. T Mum 136 C4
Birchgrove. Aberd 49 F1
Birchgrove. Bedw 152 C3
Birchgrove. N Tre 54 B2
Birchgrove. Ponty 149 E4
Birchgrove Rd. Card 188 B2
Birchgrove Rd. Swan 61 D2
Birchgrove. Rhiwd 155 F3
Birchgrove St. Porth 122 C2
Birchgrove. Tre 98 C3
Birchley. Ponty 149 E3
Birchway The. C-c-y-c 32 A3
Birchwood Ave. Ponty 149 F3
Birchwood Cl. B-coch 62 B3
Birchwood Cl. P Tal 113 F3
Birchwood Cl. Peng 101 F3
Birchwood Gdns. Card 188 B2
Birchwood La. Card 189 E2
Birchwood Pk. Card 188 B2
Birchwood Rd. Card 189 E2
Birkdale Cl. Card 191 D4
Birkdale Cl. T Mum 108 C1
Birmingham Mount. Swan 84 C3
Bishop Hannon Dr. Card 187 D1
Bishop Rd. Glan 4 B4
Bishop St. Card 204 C2
Bishop St. Tonypa 122 A2
Bishop's Gr. Swan 109 D3
Bishop's Rd. Card 188 A2
Bishop's Wlk. Swan 59 F1
Bishops' Ave. Card 203 F4
Bishops Cl. Card 188 A2
Bishops' Cl. Card 203 F4
Bishops Ct. Card 188 A2
Bishops Pl. Card 188 A2
Bishops' Pl. Card 203 F4
Bishops' Wlk. Card 203 F4
Bishopston Rd. Bish 135 F3
Bishopston Rd. Card 203 E2
Bishopswood. Bridg 180 B2
Bishwell Pk. Gow 82 B2
Bishwell Rd. Gow 82 B2
Bittern Ct. B-coch 62 C1
Bittern Way. Sully 227 D4
Black Oak Ct. Card 173 E1
Black Oak Rd. Card 189 E4
Black Rd. Ch Vil 149 D2
Blackberry Pl. M Ash 72 A3
Blackbird Rd. Ll' Maj 220 B3
Blackbirds Way. Card 190 B4
Blackfield Row. Ce Cr 162 C1
Blackhall Rd. St B M 195 E2
Blackhill Rd. Lough 57 D2
Blackhills La. South 107 F2
Blackhills La. U Kill 108 A2
Blackmill Rd. Brynco 164 A3
Blackmoor Pl. Card 190 B3
Blackstone St. Card 204 C3
Blackthorn Ave. Mer T 32 B3
Blackthorn Pl. Swan 83 D1
Blackvein Rd. Cross 129 E2
Blackweir Terr. Card 204 C4
Blackwell Cl. Barry 225 D3
Blackwood Rd. Pontll 101 F2
Blaen Cefn. Swan 85 E3
Blaen Cwm. Se Si 25 D3
Blaen Dewi. Wick 208 B3
Blaen Dowlais St. Mer T 33 E2
Blaen Ogwr Ct. Og Va 119 F3
Blaen Wern. Aberd 49 E2
Blaen-Nant-y-Groes Rd. Abera 50 C1
Blaen-y-Coed. Card 187 D3
Blaen-y-Coed. Card 188 B4
Blaen-y-cwm. Bar 76 A3
Blaen-y-Cwm Rd. Trehe 68 B2
Blaen-y-Cwm Terr. Trehe 68 C2
Blaen-y-Fro. Penco 165 F1
Blaen-y-Llyn. Ponty 150 A2
Blaen-y-Maes Dr. Swan 83 F3
Blaenafon Terr. Ton 89 E3
Blaenant St. Glyn 90 B2
Blaenavon Cl. Card 191 D4
Blaencaerau Est. Maest 91 E1
Blaencaerau Rd. Maest 91 E1
Blaencedi. Pen-cl 80 C2
Blaenclydach Pl. Card 204 C2
Blaenclydach St. Card 204 C2
Blaencoed. Swan 85 F4
Blaencwm Rd. Swan 86 A4
Blaengarw Rd. Pontcr 118 B4
Blaengwawr Cl. Abera 71 D4
Blaenlau St. Tonypa 121 F2
Blaenllechau Rd. Fern 96 A4
Blaenmorfa. Pontar 36 B2
Blaenogwr Terr. Og Va 119 F3
Blaenrhondda Rd. Trehe 68 B2
Blaenwern. B-coch 62 C1
Blagdon Cl. Card 190 A3
Blaina Cl. Card 190 C4
Blake St. Fern 70 A1
Blanch St. Tonypa 122 A1
Blanche St. Card 205 F4
Blanche St. Mer T 33 E2
Blanche St. Ponty 124 B1
Blandings Ct. Card 189 D3
Blandon Way. Card 188 A2
Blandy Terr. Og Va 119 F1
Blandy Terr. Og Va 119 F3
Blandy Terr. Pontcr 118 C2
Blandy Terr. Tony 121 E1
Blanthorn Ct. Card 187 F3
Blenheim Rd. Card 189 E1
Blethin Cl. Card 187 F2
Blodwen St. P Tal 113 F1
Blodwen Terr. Pen-cl 80 C2
Bloom St. Card 204 B4
Bloomfield Rd. Peng 101 E4
Bloss Terr. Porth 122 C1
Blosse Rd. Card 188 A1
Blosse St. Maest 117 D3
Blossom Dr. Card 173 D2
Blue Anchor Rd. Pen-cl 81 D2
Bluebell Dr. Card 190 B4
Blundell Ave. Porth 192 C3
Blyth Cl. Barry 215 D1
Board St. Rhy 34 C1
Boarlands The. P-Ey 157 D4
Bodalaw. Mer T 33 D2
Bodnant Cl. Card 190 C3
Bodringallt Terr. Yst 95 E2
Bodwenarth Rd. Ponty 124 C2
Bog Rd. Swan 85 F2
Bogey Rd. Mer T 52 A4
Bohun St. Swan 84 B2
Boi Cl. M Ash 72 A2
Boleyn Wlk. Card 189 E1
Bolgoed Rd. Pontar 36 C1
Bon-y-Maen Rd. Swan 85 D2
Bona Rd. Ll'Maj 209 E3
Boncath Rd. Card 188 A1
Bond St. Abera 50 A1
Bond St. Swan 110 A3
Bont Cl. Peng 101 D4
Bontnewydd Terr. Bed 99 E4
Bonville Terr. Swan 110 A3
Bonvilston Rd. Ponty 124 B1
Bonvilston Terr. Ponty 124 B1
Booker St. Card 205 F4
Boon Cl. Barry 225 D4
Boot The. Maesy 101 D1
Border Rd. P Tal 113 E2
Borough Cl. Cowb 198 C1
Borough Rd. Lough 56 C1
Borough St. P Tal 138 C4
Borrowdale Cl. Card 189 E1
Borth Rd. Card 190 B3
Bosco La. South 135 D2
Boswell Cl. Card 190 A4
Bosworth Rd. Skew 86 C4
Boulevard de Nantes. Card 205 D3
Bournville Terr. Tred 35 E4
Boverton Brook. Ll' Maj 220 B3
Boverton Ct. Ll' Maj 220 B3
Boverton Park Dr. Ll' Maj 220 B3
Boverton Rd. Ll' Maj 220 A3
Boverton St. Card 189 D1
Bow St. Wen 203 D1
Bowden Rd. Neath 87 F3
Bowen Ind Est. Bar 76 A1
Bowen St. Neath 87 E3
Bowen St. Swan 84 B1
Bower St. Pyle 161 E1
Bowham Ave. Bridg 179 F1
Bowls Cl. Caer 151 F3
Bowls La. Caer 151 E4
Bowls Terr. Caer 151 F3
Bowman's Way. Cowb 198 B1
Bowman's Well. Cowb 198 B1
Box Cotts. Tondu 163 E4
Box Rd. Lough 57 D4
Box Terr. Tondu 163 E4
Brachdy Cl. Card 190 A1
Brachdy La. Card 190 A1
Brachdy Rd. Card 190 A1
Bracken Pl. Card 187 E1
Bracken Rd. Marg 139 F2
Bracken Rd. Neath 87 F4
Bracken Rise. Abera 50 B1
Bracken Way. Bridg 163 F1
Brackla St. Bridg 179 F2
Brackla Street Ctr. Bridg 179 F2
Brackla Way. Bridg 180 B3
Bradenham Pl. Pen 217 D2
Bradfield Ave. Bridg 179 E3
Bradfield Rd. Bridg 179 E2
Bradford Pl. Pen 217 D2
Bradford St. Caer 152 A1
Bradford St. Card 205 D1
Bradley St. Abercy 98 B1
Bradley St. Card 205 F4
Braeval St. Card 205 D4
Bragdu. Penco 181 D4
Bragdy. C-c-y-c 14 B1
Brahms Ave. P Tal 113 D2
Braichycymer Rd. Pontcr 118 C2
Bramble Cl. Bridg 180 B2
Bramble Cl. Card 187 D1
Bramble Cl. Mer T 32 B2
Bramble Rise. Pen 216 C3
Bramblewood Cl. Card 172 C1
Bramblewood Cl. P Tal 113 F3
Brambling Dr. Card 172 C2
Bramley Dr. T Mum 136 C3
Bran Cl. Swan 85 E4
Brandon Cres. Swan 85 E3
Brandreth Rd. Card 189 D1
Brandy Cove Cl. T Mum 137 D2
Brandy Cove Rd. Bish 136 A3
Brangwyn Cl. Pen 216 C3
Brangwyn Cl. Swan 59 F1
Brangwyn Rd. Tred 35 E3
Bransby Rd. Tonypa 122 A2
Branwen Cl. Card 203 D1
Branwen Gdns. Swan 84 A1
Braunton Ave. Card 190 B3
Braunton Cres. Card 190 A3
Brayford Pl. Card 190 B4
Brayley Rd. Swan 59 F1
Breaksea Cl. Sully 226 A2
Brean Cl. Sully 226 B3
Brecon Cl. Hir 48 B4
Brecon Ct. Barry 225 D3
Brecon House. P Tal 138 B4
Brecon House. Pen 216 C1
Brecon House. Swan 110 C3
Brecon Pl. Abera 71 E4
Brecon Rd. Hir 48 B4
Brecon Rd. Mer T 32 B2
Brecon Rd. Pontdw 40 C3
Brecon Rd. Ystra 8 B3
Brecon Rise. Mer T 33 D4
Brecon St. Abera 71 E4
Brecon St. Card 204 B3
Brecon St. Ll' Maj 220 A4
Brecon Terr. Deri 75 D4
Brecon Terr. Trefil 16 C1
Brecon Way. Ch Vil 149 F1
Bredenbury Gdns. Porth 176 C1
Brendon Cl. Card 190 B3
Brendon View Cl. Rhoose 223 D1
Brenig Cl. Card 172 C2
Brenig Rd. Swan 84 A2
Brenroy Rd. Ll'Maj 209 E2
Brentwood Ct. Card 172 C1
Breon Rd. Sully 225 F3
Brewer St. Rhy 53 F4
Brewery La. Bridg 179 F3
Brewery La. C-c-y-c 32 A2
Brewery Terr. Tylor 122 B4
Brian Cres. Porth 192 C4
Brianne Dr. Card 172 C2
Briar Cl. Card 203 E4
Briar Dene. Swan 109 D3
Briar Rd. Aberd 71 F4
Briar Rd. P Tal 113 E1
Briar Way. Ch Vil 150 A1
Briar Way. Hir 48 B4
Briar's Ct. Swan 83 F3
Briarmeadow Dr. Card 172 C2
Briarwood Cl. B-coch 62 B2
Briarwood Dr. Card 189 E4
Briarwood Gdns. T Mum 136 B3
Briary Way. Bridg 180 B2
Brick Row. Maest 117 E1
Brick Row. Se Si 24 C3
Brick St. Glyn 66 C2
Brickfield Est. Mer T 51 F4
Brickyard Bsns Pk. Card 188 B1
Brickyard Cotts. Neath 87 F4
Brickyard Cotts. Ystra 8 B3
Brickyard Rd. Swan 83 F2
Bridge Houses. Ch Vil 169 E3
Bridge Rd. Aberd 71 F4
Bridge Rd. Card 174 B1
Bridge Rd. Card 187 F1
Bridge Rd. Ch Vil 150 B1
Bridge Rd. Cowb 210 B4
Bridge Rd. Swan 82 C2
Bridge St. Abera 50 A2
Bridge St. Bar 76 A3
Bridge St. Barry 225 D4
Bridge St. Card 188 A1
Bridge St. Card 205 D3
Bridge St. Cly 61 D3
Bridge St. Glyn 66 C2
Bridge St Ind Est. Tred 35 F3
Bridge St. Ll'ge 56 B4
Bridge St. Maest 117 D2
Bridge St. Marg 139 E4
Bridge St. Mer V 73 E3
Bridge St. Neath 87 F4
Bridge St. Og Va 144 C4
Bridge St. Pen 216 C3
Bridge St. Peng 101 F3
Bridge St. Pontcr 118 C3
Bridge St. Pontmi 129 F1
Bridge St. Ponty 124 B1
Bridge St. Ponty 149 F4
Bridge St. Porth 123 E2
Bridge St. Pyle 161 E1
Bridge St. Swan 84 B1
Bridge St. Tonypa 121 F3
Bridge St. Tred 35 F3
Bridge St. Troed 52 B1
Bridge St. Ynys 127 F3
Bridge St. Ystra 7 D1
Bridge Terr. M-y-Fed 175 D4
Bridge Terr. Marg 139 E4
Bridge View. Ynys 128 A2
Bridgefield St. Aber 151 D4
Bridgeman Ct. Pen 217 D2
Bridgeman Rd. Pen 217 D2
Bridgend Rd. Bridg 163 E1
Bridgend Rd. Ll'ha 166 C1
Bridgend Rd. Maest 117 E1
Bridgend Rd. Maest 142 B3
Bridgend Rd. Pontcr 118 C1
Bridgend Rd. Porthc 193 E4
Bridgend Rd. Tondu 163 E2
Bridgewater Rd. Sully 226 A3
Bridgwater Rd. Card 190 B3
Bridle Mews. T Mum 137 E2
Brierley La. Bridg 179 F1
Brierly Pl. Aberca 129 D4
Brig-y-Don Hill. St B M 194 B1
Brigantine Pl. Card 205 E2
Brigham Ct. Caer 151 E2
Bright St. Cross 129 E2
Brighton Rd. Lough 57 E1
Brindley Rd. Card 204 B1
Brisbane Ct. Peng 101 E3
Bristol St. Tondu 163 E2
Britannia Centre For Enterprise. Peng 76 A1
Britannia Rd. Card 205 E1
Britannia Rd. Swan 84 C3
Britannia St. Porth 123 D1
Britannia Terr. Peng 76 A1
Britannia Wlk. Peng 76 A1
Brithdir St. Card 188 C1
Brithwen Rd. Swan 82 B2
Brithweunydd Rd. Trea 122 A3
British Legion Dr. Card 190 A2
Briton Ferry Rd. Neath 87 F3
Brittania Pl. Fern 96 A3
Britten Rd. Pen 216 C1
Britway Ct. D pow 216 A2
Britway Rd. D pow 216 A2
Brixham. Pyle 177 D4
Bro Dawel. Ll'fel 59 E1
Bro Dawel. Ll'tris 184 A3
Bro Dawel. Swan 108 B4
Bro Dedwydd. Swan 108 B4
Bro Deg. Aberd 71 F4
Bro Dirion. Swan 108 B4
Bro Ryan. Glan 4 A4
Bro-Deg. Penco 181 E4
Bro-y-Fan. Caer 152 B3
Bro-y-Ffrwd. Mer T 31 F2
Broad Oak Way. Bridg 179 D3
Broad Pl. Card 204 B3
Broad Shoard The. Cowb 198 C1
Broad St. Card 204 B3
Broad St. Marg 139 E4
Broad St. Mer T 33 D3
Broad St. Mer T 51 E4
Broad View. Tondu 163 E3
Broadacre. Swan 108 B4
Broadacres. Card 204 B3
Broadfield Cl. Tonypa 122 A2
Broadfield Ct. Card 203 E2
Broadhaven. Card 204 B2
Broadlands Ct. Card 190 C4
Broadmead Cres. Bish 136 A3
Broadmead. Pontll 101 E2
Broadmead. Swan 108 B4
Broadoak Ct. Lough 56 C1
Broadparks. T Mum 136 C4
Broadstairs Rd. Card 204 B3
Broadview Cl. T Mum 137 D2
Broadview La. T Mum 137 D3
Broadway. Card 205 E4
Broadway. Cowb 198 C1
Broadway Gn. St Nic 202 A1
Broadway. Ponty 149 E4
Broadwell Cl. Card 190 C3
Brocastle Ave. Colw 180 C1
Brocastle Rd. Card 188 A3
Brock Hill Way. Pen 227 D4
Brock St. Barry 225 D4
Brockhampton Rd. Card 190 C4
Brockhill Rise. Pen 227 D4
Brodawel Cl. Ystraf 27 F2
Brodawel. Maest 117 D2
Brodawel. Mer T 51 F4
Brodawel. Neath 88 A3
Brodawel. Peny 49 D3
Brodawel. Ystraf 27 F2
Brodeg. Penty 186 B4
Brodorion Dr. Swan 59 F2
Brohedydd. Fern 70 A1
Brokesby Cl. Swan 85 D2
Brokesby Rd. Swan 85 D2
Brombil Ct. Marg 139 F2
Brombil Gdns. Marg 139 F2
Brombil St. Marg 139 E3
Bromfield Pl. Pen 217 D3
Bromfield St. Card 204 C1
Bromley Dr. Card 203 F3
Bromsgrove St. Card 204 C1
Bron Afon. Pont 58 A3
Bron Allt. Cry 43 D3
Bron Felen. Card 172 B1
Bron Haul. Aberd 71 F4
Bron Rhiw. Bedw 153 F4
Bron yr Allt. Ystal 23 D4
Bron-y-Bryn. Swan 108 C4
Bron-y-Deri. M Ash 72 C2
Bron-y-Garth. Gell 100 C4
Bron-y-Waun. Maest 117 E1
Bron-y-Wawr. Pyle 161 D1
Bronallt Terr. Abera 71 F2
Broncynon Terr. Aberd 49 E2
Brondeg Cres. Swan 84 A2
Brondeg La. A-wen 40 C2
Brondeg. Mer T 32 A1
Brondeg St. Tylor 96 A1
Brondeg. Swan 84 A2
Brondeg Terr. Aberd 49 F1
Bronhall. Ll'tris 168 B1
Bronhaul. Penty 186 B4
Bronheulog Terr. Troed 73 E4
Broniestyn Terr. Aberd 49 F2
Broniestyn Terr. Hir 48 B4
Bronllan. Swan 85 E3
Bronllwyn. Penty 186 A4
Bronllwyn Rd. Yst 95 D1
Bronllys. Peny 49 D3
Bronmynnyd. Aber 151 D3
Bronrhiw Ave. Caer 152 A1
Bronrhiw Fach. Caer 152 A1
Bronte Cl. Card 190 B4
Bronte Cres. Card 190 B4
Bronwydd Ave. Card 189 E1
Bronwydd Cl. Card 189 E1
Bronwydd Rd. Card 206 A4
Bronwydd. Swan 86 B4
Bronywawr. Pontdw 40 C3
Brook Ct. Card 203 F4
Brook La. St Nic 213 F4
Brook Pl. Yst 94 C3
Brook Rd. Card 188 A2
Brook Rd. Card 203 F4
Brook Row. Brynco 164 A3
Brook Row. Deri 53 E4
Brook St. Aber 151 D4
Brook St. Abera 71 E4
Brook St. Barry 225 D3
Brook St. Bridg 179 F3
Brook St. Card 204 C3
Brook St. Fern 70 A1
Brook St. Fern 95 F3
Brook St. M Ash 72 B1
Brook St. Marg 139 E4
Brook St. Ponty 149 F3
Brook St. Porth 122 C1
Brook St. Porth 123 D1
Brook St. Skew 86 C4
Brook St. Tonypa 122 A2
Brook St. Trehe 68 B2
Brook St. Treo 94 C3
Brook St. Yst 95 E1
Brook Terr. Ch Vil 149 F1
Brook Terr. G-C-G 5 E3
Brook Terr. Ll'ha 166 C2
Brook Terr. Ll'tris 168 C1
Brook Villas. Ll'ha 167 D2
Brook Villas. Ll'tris 168 C3
Brookbank Cl. Abera 50 B1
Brookdale Ct. Ch Vil 169 F4
Brookdale St. Neath 87 F3
Brookfield Ave. Barry 225 E4
Brookfield Ave. Rhy 35 D1
Brookfield. B-coch 62 A1
Brookfield Cl. Lough 56 C2
Brookfield Dr. Card 190 C3
Brookfield Park Rd. Cowb 198 C1
Brookfield Pl. Swan 83 F3
Brookfield. Ponty 124 A3
Brookfield. Ponty 124 C2
Brookfield Rd. Fern 95 E4
Brookfield Rd. Maest 117 E1
Brookland Terr. Og Va 119 F3
Brookland View. N Tre 54 C2
Brooklands Cl. Maesy 101 D1
Brooklands Cl. Mer T 32 B2
Brooklands Cl. Penga 82 A1
Brooklands. Nel 99 E3
Brooklands Terr. Aberca 129 E4
Brooklands Terr. Coel 9 D3
Brooklands Terr. Swan 110 A4
Brooklands Terr. Wen 202 C1
Brooklea Pk. Card 173 D1
Brooklyn Cl. Card 172 A1
Brooklyn Gdns. P Tal 113 E2
Brooklyn Gdns. T Mum 137 D3
Brooklyn Terr. T Mum 136 C3
Brookside. Ch Vil 150 A1
Brookside Cl. Caer 151 E2
Brookside Cl. Card 188 B3
Brookside Cl. P Tal 113 F3
Brookside Cl. Ponty 124 C2
Brookside. Colw 181 D1
Brookside Cres. Caer 152 B2
Brookside Ct. Card 188 A3
Brookside. D pow 216 A2
Brookside. Gow 82 B2
Brookvale Dr. Card 172 C2
Brookview Cl. Card 172 C1
Brookway. Ch Vil 150 A1
Brookway Cl. P Tal 113 F3
Broom Pl. Card 203 E4
Broomfield Cl. Ch Vil 150 A1
Broomfield St. Caer 152 A1

Broomhill. Marg 139 E4
Brotalwg. Tre 99 D4
Broughton Ave. Swan 83 F3
Broughton Pl. Barry 225 D4
Broughton Rd. Wick 208 B2
Brown St. Fern 96 A3
Brown St. Maest 116 C3
Browning Cl. Bridg 179 E3
Browning Cl. Card 190 A4
Browns Dr. South 135 D3
Bruce Knight Cl. Card ... 187 F1
Bruce Rd. Swan 83 D2
Bruce St. Card 189 D1
Bruce St. M Ash 72 B2
Brummell Dr. Penty 185 F3
Brunant Rd. Lough 57 D2
Brundall Cres. Card 203 D2
Brunel Cl. Barry 225 E4
Brunel Cl. Gell 100 C4
Brunel Cl. Tonna 63 E2
Brunel Cl. Swan 110 A4
Brunel Ind Est. Cwma ... 114 B2
Brunel St. Card 204 C3
Brunel Way. Swan 84 C2
Brunner Dr. Cly 39 F1
Brunswick St. Card 204 B3
Brunswick St. Mer T 32 B1
Brunswick St. Swan 110 A3
Bruton Pl. Card 188 A1
Brwyna Ave. P Tal 113 F1
Brwynen Las. B-coch 62 B1
Bryan Terr. Tonypa 95 E2
Bryanston Rd. Sully 225 F3
Brychan Pl. Mer T 32 B1
Brydges Pl. Card 205 D4
Brymbo Ave. Marg 139 E3
Bryn Aber. Aber 126 A1
Bryn Adar. Card 187 F4
Bryn Amlwg. Gell 100 C2
Bryn Aur. Ynybw 124 B3
Bryn Awel. Bedw 152 C3
Bryn Awel. Bridg 179 D3
Bryn Awel. Gall 101 D2
Bryn Awel. Neath 87 F3
Bryn Awel. Pontcr 143 F2
Bryn Awel. Ynybw 124 B3
Bryn Awelon. Aberd 71 F4
Bryn Awelon. Bridg 179 E3
Bryn Bach. Card 188 A4
Bryn Bach Cotts. Pontcr ... 143 E1
Bryn Bach Rd. Bry 5 D4
Bryn Bach Rd. Pont 37 D1
Bryn Bedd. Se Si 25 D3
Bryn Bedw. Porth 122 C1
Bryn Canol. Bedw 152 C3
Bryn Canol. Gell 100 C3
Bryn Carno. Rhy 34 C3
Bryn Carwyn. Mer T 33 D2
Bryn Castell. Card 187 D4
Bryn Catwg. B-coch 62 C1
Bryn Celyn. Card 189 F4
Bryn Celyn. Maest 117 D1
Bryn Celyn. Pontdw 40 B3
Bryn Celyn Rd. Card 189 F3
Bryn Celyn. Swan 86 A3
Bryn Cl. Bedw 152 C3
Bryn Cl. Gow 82 B2
Bryn Cl. Lough 57 D2
Bryn Coed. Glyn 91 F2
Bryn Cotts. Bryn 115 F3
Bryn Cotts. Pontcr 143 F4
Bryn Creigiau. Ll'tris 185 E4
Bryn Cres. Mark 76 C4
Bryn Crydd. Porth 122 B1
Bryn Deri. Bridg 179 D3
Bryn Derw. Ll'tris 169 D4
Bryn Derw Gdns. Swan ... 59 F1
Bryn Derwen. Aberd 49 E2
Bryn Derwen. Card 187 D4
Bryn Derwen. Pontdw 40 B3
Bryn Derwen. Swan 83 D1
Bryn Dinas View. Trea 122 A3
Bryn Eglur Rd. Swan 84 B2
Bryn Eglwys. Ll'ha 167 D2
Bryn Eglwys. Tonypa 122 A1
Bryn Eithin. Aberd 49 E2
Bryn Eithin. Gow 82 A3
Bryn Ffynnon. Porth 122 B1
Bryn Glas. Aberd 71 F4
Bryn Glas. Bedw 152 C4
Bryn Glas. Card 172 B1
Bryn Glas. Ce Cr 162 B1
Bryn Glas. Gell 100 C1
Bryn Glas. Ll'fel 59 E1
Bryn Golau. A-wen 40 C2
Bryn Golau. Gall 101 D2
Bryn Goleu. Bedw 152 C4
Bryn Golau Rd. Swan 83 F2
Bryn Golwg. Card 187 D4
Bryn Gorof. Ystra 23 E4
Bryn Gors. Tondu 163 F3
Bryn Gwyn Cl. Peny 49 D3
Bryn Haidd. Card 189 F4
Bryn Hawddgar. Cly 60 C4
Bryn Hedydd. Ll'fel 59 E1
Bryn Hedydd. Rhiwd 155 F2
Bryn Helyg. Swan 85 D3
Bryn Henllan. Ll'ha 166 B2

Bryn Henllan. Trehe 68 B2
Bryn Heol. Bedw 152 C3
Bryn Heulog. H-y-Cy 165 D3
Bryn Heulog Terr. Bedw ... 153 F4
Bryn Heulog. Trehe 69 D1
Bryn Hir. Aberd 71 F4
Bryn Hyfryd. Brynco 163 F2
Bryn Ifor. Caer 151 E3
Bryn Ifor. M Ash 72 B1
Bryn Ivor St. Trea 121 F4
Bryn Ivor. Trea 121 F4
Bryn La. Pontll 101 E2
Bryn Llawen. Pyle 161 E1
Bryn Llewelyn. A-wen 41 D2
Bryn Llidiard. Bridg 179 F4
Bryn Mair. Mer T 33 D2
Bryn Moreia. Llwy 49 F3
Bryn Morfa. Bridg 179 F3
Bryn Morfa. Swan 85 E3
Bryn Nant. Caer 151 E3
Bryn Nedd. Neath 87 F3
Bryn Olwg. Ponty 124 C1
Bryn Onnen. Hir 29 D2
Bryn Onnen. Pontdw 40 C3
Bryn Owain. Caer 151 F3
Bryn Pinwydden. Card ... 189 F4
Bryn Pobydd. Penco 181 E4
Bryn Rd. Bridg 180 C2
Bryn Rd. Cly 60 B4
Bryn Rd. Cwmll 6 B3
Bryn Rd. Glyn 66 C2
Bryn Rd. Lough 56 C1
Bryn Rd. Mark 76 B4
Bryn Rd. Neath 87 F3
Bryn Rd. Og Va 144 C4
Bryn Rd. Peng 101 E4
Bryn Rd. Pont 58 A4
Bryn Rd. Pontar 36 A2
Bryn Rd. Pontll 101 F2
Bryn Rd. Swan 82 C2
Bryn Rd. Swan 83 F2
Bryn Rd. Tondu 163 E3
Bryn Rd. Ystra 8 A1
Bryn Rhedyn. Ch Vil 149 F1
Bryn Rhedyn. Penco 181 E4
Bryn Rhedyn. Tony 147 D3
Bryn Rhedyn. Trehe 69 D1
Bryn Rhedyn. Ynybw 124 B3
Bryn. Rhig 47 E4
Bryn Rhodfa. Treo 94 B4
Bryn Rhos. Peny 49 D3
Bryn Rhosog. Lough 81 F4
Bryn Rhosyn. Card 187 D4
Bryn Rhosyn. Ll'fel 59 E1
Bryn Seion St. Rhy 34 B3
Bryn Siriol. Caer 151 E3
Bryn Siriol. Gell 100 C4
Bryn Siriol. Glyn 91 F2
Bryn Siriol. Penty 186 B4
Bryn Siriol. Pontcr 143 E1
Bryn Siriol. Swan 83 F2
Bryn St. Mer T 51 F4
Bryn Teg. Bar 75 F1
Bryn Teg. Bedw 152 C4
Bryn Teg. Caer 151 F3
Bryn Teg. Gall 101 D2
Bryn Teg. Neath 87 D2
Bryn Teg. Swan 85 F4
Bryn Terr. Aberd 49 E2
Bryn Terr. C-c-y-c 14 C2
Bryn Terr. Ce Cr 162 A1
Bryn Terr. Ch Vil 169 E4
Bryn Terr. Clyne 65 D4
Bryn Terr. Gall 101 D2
Bryn Terr. Ll'tris 183 F3
Bryn Terr. Maest 91 D1
Bryn Terr. Maest 143 D3
Bryn Terr. Pen-cl 81 F1
Bryn Terr. Penga 57 E1
Bryn Terr. Porth 122 C2
Bryn Terr. Swan 84 B2
Bryn Terr. T Mum 137 D2
Bryn Terr. Tonypa 121 E3
Bryn Terr. Tonypa 121 A2
Bryn Terr. Tylor 122 B4
Bryn The. Bedw 152 C3
Bryn The. Swan 109 E3
Bryn Tirion. Cly 60 C4
Bryn Vernel. Lough 56 C1
Bryn View Cl. Ll'rh 132 C4
Bryn Wyndham Terr. Trehe . 68 C2
Bryn y Gors. Ll'fel 59 D1
Bryn yr Ysgol. Caer 151 E3
Bryn-Amlwg Rd. Swan ... 83 F2
Bryn-Awelon Rd. Card ... 189 E4
Bryn-Bach Rd. Pont 37 F2
Bryn-Bedw St. Pontcr ... 118 C4
Bryn-Dedwydd. Neath ... 88 B3
Bryn-Dolwen. Bedw 152 C4
Bryn-du. Bridg 165 D1
Bryn-Eirw St. Porth 123 E1
Bryn-Glas Rd. Swan 83 F2
Bryn-Glas Terr. Pyle 161 D1
Bryn-Gwyn Rd. Card 189 E4

Bryn-Gwyn St. Bedw 152 B4
Bryn-Hedd. Tony 146 B3
Bryn-hyfryd Terr. Pontmi ... 129 F1
Bryn-Lloi Rd. Glan 4 A4
Bryn-Melyn St. Swan 84 B1
Bryn-onen Terr. Mer T 32 C2
Bryn-Rhedyn. Caer 152 B2
Bryn-Seton St. Mer T 33 D2
Bryn-Syfi Terr. Swan 110 B4
Bryn-teg Terr. Mer T 32 C1
Bryn-tywod. Ll'fel 59 D2
Bryn-y-Cae. Ll'ha 166 C1
Bryn-y-Don Rd. Swan 110 B4
Bryn-y-Fran Ave. Bedw ... 152 C3
Bryn-y-Grug. Ystal 23 D4
Bryn-y-mor Cres. Swan ... 110 A3
Bryn-Y-Mor. Pen-cl 81 E1
Bryn-y-Mor Rd. Gow 82 A3
Bryn-y-Mor Rd. Swan 110 A3
Bryn-y-mor. St Ath 221 E2
Bryn-y-Nant. Card 189 F3
Bryn-y-pwll. Bar 76 A2
Bryn-yr-Eglwys. Penty 186 B4
Bryn-yr-eglwys. Tony 146 B3
Brynaeron. Swan 82 B1
Brynafn Terr. Cwma 114 C2
Brynafon Rd. Lough 57 D2
Brynamlwg. Cly 39 F1
Brynamlwg. Ll'tris 184 B4
Brynamlwg Rd. Lough 57 D1
Brynamlwg. Tonypa 121 F3
Brynamman Rd. G-C-G 5 D3
Brynau Dr. T Mum 108 C1
Brynau Rd. Caer 152 A2
Brynau Rd. T We 171 D2
Brynau Wood. Neath 88 B3
Brynavon Terr. Gall 101 D2
Brynawel. Caer 151 E3
Brynawel Cl. Cry 43 D3
Brynawel Cres. Swan 84 B3
Brynawel. Cry 43 D3
Brynawel. Pontdw 40 C3
Brynawel Rd. Lough 57 D1
Brynawel Rd. Ystra 7 F1
Brynawel Terr. Bry 6 C3
Brynawel Villas. Ystra 8 A1
Brynawelon. Bry 6 B4
Brynawelon. Coel 57 D1
Brynawelon. Tonna 63 F2
Brynbala Way. Card 190 C3
Brynbedw Rd. Tylor 96 A2
Brynbrain. Bry 6 B4
Brynbryddan. Cwma 114 B3
Bryncae Ind Est. Ll'ha ... 166 C1
Bryncelyn. Ll'fel 59 E1
Bryncelyn. Nel 99 E2
Bryncerdin Rd. T Mum ... 136 C3
Bryncethin Rd. Glan 4 A4
Bryncoch Rd. Brynco 163 F2
Bryncoch. T We 171 D2
Bryncoed Terr. Aber 151 D4
Bryncoed Terr. Gell 100 C4
Bryncyn. Card 189 F4
Bryncynon. Hir 48 C4
Brynderi Cl. Penga 58 A1
Brynderwen Cl. Card 189 E2
Brynderwen Ct. Fern 95 F4
Brynderwen Rd. Ponty ... 124 C3
Brynderwen Rd. Tonypa ... 121 F2
Bryndolau. Swan 108 A4
Bryndu Rd. Pyle 161 E2
Bryndulais Ave. Se Si 24 C3
Bryndulais Row. Se Si 24 C4
Bryneglwys Ave. Porthc ... 193 E4
Bryneglwys Gdns. Porthc . 193 E4
Bryneinon Rd. Lough 57 D2
Bryneithin Terr. Swan 59 F1
Bryneithyn. Ystra 7 E1
Brynfa Terr. Pen-cl 80 C2
Brynfab Rd. Ponty 150 A3
Brynfedw. Bedw 152 C4
Brynfedw. Gell 100 C1
Brynfedwen St. Trehe 69 D1
Brynffrwd Cl. Bridg 180 C2
Brynfynnon Rd. Lough ... 57 D2
Brynfynnon Cl. Abera 50 A1
Brynfield Ct. T Mum 136 C2
Brynfield Rd. T Mum 136 C2
Bryngarn Rd. H-y-Cy 165 F2
Bryngelli Dr. Swan 84 B4
Bryngelli Rd. Swan 84 B4
Bryngelli Terr. Aber 151 D4
Bryngerwn Ave. Tre 99 D3
Bryngerwn Cotts. Tre 99 D3
Brynglas Ave. Cwma 114 B3
Brynglas Ave. Pontll 101 F2
Brynglas. B-coch 62 B2
Brynglas. Bridg 179 D2
Brynglas. Caer 151 E3
Brynglas. Rhy 53 F4
Brynglas St. Mer T 32 C2
Brynglas Terr. Maest 91 E1
Bryngolau. Bridg 179 D3
Bryngolau. Gar P 153 D2

Bryngolau. Lough 57 D1
Bryngolau. Tony 147 D3
Bryngoleu Cres. Fern 95 F4
Bryngoleu St. Peng 101 E4
Bryngoleu Terr. Pontll 101 F2
Bryngoleu Terr. Swan 109 E4
Bryngolwg. Aberd 71 F4
Bryngwastad Rd. Lough ... 57 D1
Bryngwennol. Ll'bra 127 D3
Bryngwyn Ave. Lough 82 B4
Bryngwyn. Caer 151 F1
Bryngwyn. Skew 86 B3
Bryngwyn St. Peng 101 E4
Bryngwyn St. Porth 122 C2
Bryngyrnos St. Bryn 115 F3
Brynhafod. Bryn 115 F3
Brynhafod Rd. Aber 151 D4
Brynhenwyeg. Ponty 123 F1
Brynheulog. Card 187 D4
Brynheulog. Card 189 F4
Brynheulog Ct. Tondu 163 E3
Brynheulog. Ll'ha 166 C2
Brynheulog Pl. Marg 139 E4
Brynheulog Rd. Glyn 91 E2
Brynheulog St. Gell 100 B3
Brynheulog St. Marg 139 E4
Brynheulog St. Mer T 32 C2
Brynheulog Terr. Cwma ... 114 B3
Brynheulog Terr. Cwmll ... 6 B3
Brynheulog Terr. Porth ... 122 C2
Brynheulog Terr. Tonypa .. 121 E3
Brynheulog Terr. Tylor 96 A3
Brynheulog. Tondu 163 F3
Brynheulog. Ystra 8 A1
Brynhill. Card 189 E3
Brynhill Terr. Ch Vil 149 F1
Brynhy Fryd. Tony 146 B3
Brynhyfrd. Rhy 35 D1
Brynhyfrd Terr. C-c-y-c ... 32 A2
Brynhyfryd. Abera 70 C2
Brynhyfryd Ave. Tonypa ... 122 A2
Brynhyfryd. Bedw 152 B4
Brynhyfryd. Caer 151 F2
Brynhyfryd. Card 187 D4
Brynhyfryd. G-nea 27 D1
Brynhyfryd. Ll'ge 56 A4
Brynhyfryd. Ll'tris 169 D4
Brynhyfryd Pl. Ponty 149 E4
Brynhyfryd. Pontcr 118 C2
Brynhyfryd. Pontcr 143 E2
Brynhyfryd Rd. Lough 57 D2
Brynhyfryd Rd. Marg 139 F2
Brynhyfryd Rd. Neath 87 D1
Brynhyfryd. Rhy 53 F4
Brynhyfryd Sq. Swan 84 B2
Brynhyfryd St. Mer T 32 C2
Brynhyfryd St. Pontll 101 F2
Brynhyfryd St. Swan 84 B2
Brynhyfryd St. Tonypa 121 E4
Brynhyfryd St. Treo 94 A4
Brynhyfryd Terr. Aber 125 F2
Brynhyfryd Terr. Bedw 154 A4
Brynhyfryd Terr. Fern 95 F3
Brynhyfryd Terr. Gell 100 C4
Brynhyfryd Terr. Ponty 124 A1
Brynhyfryd Terr. Se Si 25 D4
Brynhyfryd. Tonypa 121 F3
Brynhyfryd. Tylor 96 A2
Brynhyfryd Villas. Troed ... 73 E4
Bryniago. Pontar 36 C2
Bryniau Rd. Mer T 32 C1
Brynllefrith Cotts. Ch Vil .. 169 E3
Brynllwchwr Rd. Lough ... 81 F4
Brynllywarch. Maest 116 C1
Brynmair Cl. Abera 71 D3
Brynmair Rd. Abera 71 D3
Brynmair Terr. Mer T 32 C2
Brynmawr Pl. Maest 117 D2
Brynmawr. Pontcr 143 E2
Brynmead Cl. Swan 109 E4
Brynmead Ct. Swan 109 E4
Brynmill Ave. Swan 109 F3
Brynmill Cres. Swan 109 F3
Brynmill La. Swan 109 F3
Brynmill Terr. Swan 109 F3
Brynmorgrug. A-wen 41 D3
Brynmorlais St. Mer T 32 C2
Brynmynach Ave. Gell 100 C1
Brynna Rd. Cwma 114 B3
Brynna Rd. Ll'ha 166 A1
Brynna Rd. Ll'ha 166 C2
Brynnewydd Gdns. Swan .. 109 F3
Brynogwy Terr. Og Va 119 F3
Brynrhos Cres. Penga 58 A1
Brynsiriol. G-C-G 5 D3
Brynsiriol. Hir 48 C4
Brynsiriol. Neath 88 B3
Bryntaf. C-c-y-c 32 A2
Bryntaf. Mer V 51 F4
Bryntawe Hall Cl. Swan ... 60 B3
Bryntawe Rd. Swan 60 A2
Bryntawer Terr. Tonypa ... 121 E4
Brynteg Ave. Bridg 179 F2
Brynteg Ave. Pontll 101 F2
Brynteg Ave. Pyle 161 D1
Brynteg. Card 172 A1
Brynteg Cl. Card 189 E2

Brynteg. Cly 60 B4
Brynteg Gdns. Bridg 179 F1
Brynteg. H-y-Cy 165 D2
Brynteg La. Ll'tris 169 D3
Brynteg. Maest 116 C1
Brynteg Pl. Tre 99 D4
Brynteg Rd. Lough 57 D2
Brynteg. Se Si 24 C2
Brynteg St. Bryn 115 F3
Brynteg Terr. Deri 53 E4
Brynteg Terr. Fern 96 A3
Brynteg Terr. Mer V 73 E3
Brynteg Terr. N Tre 54 C1
Brynteg Terr. Tonypa 122 A2
Brynteg Terr. Tre 99 D4
Bryntirion. Abercy 98 A3
Bryntirion. Bedw 152 C4
Bryntirion. Caer 151 F3
Bryntirion. Card 188 B4
Bryntirion Cl. Bridg 179 E2
Bryntirion Cotts. Bridg ... 179 D2
Bryntirion Hill. Bridg 179 E2
Bryntirion Rd. Mer T 32 C1
Bryntirion St. Mer T 33 D3
Brynview Ave. Gell 100 C1
Brynwern St. Mer T 33 D3
Brynygroes Cotts. Ystra ... 7 F1
Brynymor Rd. Lough 56 C1
Bryony Cl. Mer T 51 F4
Brython Dr. Card 191 D4
Buarth-y- Capel. Ynybw ... 97 F1
Buckingham Cl. Card 173 D1
Buckingham Rd. Swan 85 D1
Buckley Cl. Card 187 E2
Buckley Cl. Trea 121 F4
Buckley Rd. Trea 121 F4
Bude Haven Terr. T Mum .. 137 D3
Bull Hill. St B M 195 E1
Bullfinch Rd. Ll' Maj 220 C3
Bullin's La. Swan 110 A4
Bullring. Ll'tris 168 B2
Bulrush Cl. Card 191 D3
Bungalow Ave. Porthc 193 D4
Bungalows The. Bridg 179 F3
Bungalows The. Gell 100 C1
Bungalows The. Og Va 119 F3
Bungalows The. Og Va 144 C4
Bungalows The. Og Va 146 A4
Bungalows The. Pontcr 144 A3
Bunker's Hill. Rhos 130 C3
Bunyan Ct. Card 190 B4
Burgess Pl. Card 204 C2
Burgesse Cres. Ll'tris 168 B1
Burgley Ct. Swan 83 F3
Burial La. Ll' maj 219 F3
Burke Ave. P Tal 138 C4
Burley Pl. St M Ch 221 E4
Burlington St. Barry 225 D3
Burlington Terr. Card 204 A4
Burman St. Swan 110 A4
Burn's Way. Ponty 149 D3
Burnaby St. Card 205 F3
Burne Jones Cl. Card 187 F1
Burnham Ave. Card 190 B4
Burnham Ave. Sully 226 A3
Burnham Ct. Card 190 B3
Burnham Dr. T Mum 136 C3
Burns Cl. Bedw 153 E3
Burns Cres. Bridg 179 E3
Burns Rd. P Tal 138 C4
Burns St. Abera 71 D2
Burnside Ct. Card 203 D4
Burnside. Neath 87 F3
Burrows Cl. South 135 D3
Burrows La. Ll'gen 102 B3
Burrows Pl. Swan 110 B3
Burrows Rd. Neath 87 D2
Burrows Rd. P Tal 113 E3
Burrows Rd. Skew 86 C3
Burrows Rd. Swan 110 A3
Burrows The. Porthc 193 F4
Burt Cl. Card 205 D1
Burt St. Card 205 D1
Burton Terr. Rhoose 222 A1
Bush Rd. M Ash 72 C1
Bush Rd. Swan 60 A1
Bush Row. Neath 87 E3
Bute Cres. Card 205 E1
Bute Espl. Card 205 D1
Bute La. Pen 217 D2
Bute Pl. Card 205 E1
Bute St. Abera 50 A1
Bute St. Card 171 C1
Bute St. Card 205 D2
Bute St. Trehe 69 D1
Bute St. Treo 94 B4
Bute Terr. Card 205 D3
Bute Terr. Hir 48 C4
Bute Terr. N Tre 76 A4
Butleigh Ave. Card 204 A4
Butterslade Gr. Swan 60 A2
Button Ride. St Nic 214 A4
Buttry Terr. Peng 101 D3
Butts The. Cowb 198 C1
Buxton Ct. Caer 152 B2
Bwl Rd. Nel 99 E2
Bwlch Cres. Neath 88 A2

Bwlch Rd. Card 203 E4
Bwlch Rd. Lough 56 C1
Bwlch Rd. Neath 88 A2
Bwlch y Gwyn. Craig 37 F1
Bwlch-y-clawdd Rd. Treo ... 94 A2
Bwllfa Cotts. Yst 95 D1
Bwllfa Rd. Aberd 49 D2
Bwllfa Rd. Swan 60 B3
Bwllfadare Terr. Aberd ... 49 D1
Bwrw Rd. Lough 81 E4
By Pass Rd. Bridg 179 E1
By-Ways Ct. Bridg 180 C2
Byass St. Marg 139 F2
Byng Morris Cl. Swan 109 D3
Byng St. Swan 84 B1
Byrd Cres. Pen 216 C1
Byron Ave. Bridg 179 E3
Byron Ave. Ll'tris 169 D3
Byron Ct. Pen 216 C1
Byron House. P Tal 138 B4
Byron Pl. Pen 216 C2
Byron Rd. Bar 76 A2
Byron St. Abera 71 D2
Byron St. Card 205 E4

Ca'r Pwll. D pow 216 A1
Caban Isaac Rd. Pen-cl ... 80 C2
Cadaxton Terr. B-coch ... 63 D1
Cadfan Rd. Swan 110 A4
Cadlan Bethel. Mer T 32 B1
Cadle Cl. Swan 83 F3
Cadle Cres. Swan 83 E3
Cadle Mill. Swan 83 F3
Cadle Pl. Swan 83 F3
Cadle-Dell Pl. Swan 83 F3
Cadle-Wood Rd. Swan 83 F3
Cadnant Cl. Card 172 B1
Cadoc Cres. Barry 225 E3
Cadogan Cl. Yst 95 D1
Cadogan St. Og Va 119 F3
Cadoxton Rd. B-coch 62 C1
Cadrawd Rd. Swan 84 A1
Cadvan Rd. Card 203 D3
Cadwaladr St. M Ash 72 B2
Cadwgan. Ll'tris 169 D3
Cadwgan Pl. Card 203 D3
Cadwgan Rd. Craig 39 D1
Cadwgan Terr. Porth 123 E1
Cae Bach. Bedw 153 F4
Cae Bach. Pontcr 144 A2
Cae Banc. Swan 109 E4
Cae Bedw. Caer 151 F4
Cae Bracla. Bridg 180 A3
Cae Brandi. Marsh 191 F4
Cae Bron. Bridg 180 A2
Cae Bryn. Bridg 179 E2
Cae Calch. Caer 151 F3
Cae Caradog. Caer 151 E3
Cae Coed. H-y-Cy 165 D3
Cae Crug. Ll'fel 59 D1
Cae Crwn. Swan 108 C4
Cae Dre St. Bridg 179 F2
Cae Du Mawr. Caer 151 F4
Cae Eithin. Ll'fel 59 D1
Cae Fardre. Ch Vil 149 F1
Cae Felin Parc. Hir 48 C4
Cae Ffynnon. Bridg 180 A3
Cae Ffynnon. Caer 151 F3
Cae Ffynnon. Ch Vil 149 F1
Cae Folland. Pen-cl 80 C2
Cae Forgan Cotts. Pontcr . 144 A2
Cae Garn. H-y-Cy 165 D3
Cae Garw. Card 172 B1
Cae Garw. D pow 216 A1
Cae Gethin. Caer 151 F3
Cae Glas. Barry 225 D4
Cae Glas. Caer 151 F3
Cae Glas. Deri 53 E4
Cae Glas. Ewen 195 F4
Cae Glas. Penco 181 F4
Cae Glas. Tonypa 122 A1
Cae Grawn. Gow 82 A3
Cae Gwyn Rd. Card 188 B3
Cae Leon. Barry 214 C1
Cae Lewis. Card 171 E1
Cae Llwyd. Caer 152 A3
Cae Lynch. Skew 86 C3
Cae Maen. Card 188 B2
Cae Maen Lloyd. Gell ... 100 C3
Cae Mansel Rd. Gow 82 A2
Cae Marchog. Caer 151 F3
Cae Mari Dwn. Mer T ... 32 C1
Cae Mawr Ind Est. Treo ... 94 C3
Cae Mawr Rd. Card 188 B4
Cae Mawr. Se Si 25 D3
Cae Morfa Rd. P Tal ... 113 E1
Cae Odin. Bridg 180 A3
Cae Pandy. Caer 152 A3
Cae Pant. Caer 151 F3
Cae Pen- y-Graig. Caer ... 151 F4
Cae Pentice. Ce Cr 162 A1
Cae Perllan. Bridg 180 A3
Cae Rex. Cowb 198 C1
Cae Rhos. Caer 152 A3
Cae Rhys Ddu Rd. Neath ... 88 A3
Cae Rowland St. Swan ... 84 C4
Cae Samson. Card 203 E2

Cae Siriol. Tylor 122 C3
Cae Siwsan. Bridg 180 A3
Cae Stumpie. Cowb 198 C1
Cae Syr Dafydd. Card ... 204 B4
Cae Talcen. Penco 165 F1
Cae Ty Mawr. Card 187 F2
Cae Yorath. Card 188 A3
Cae Ysgubor. Bridg 180 A2
Cae Ysgubor. Caer 151 F4
Cae Ysgubor. Gell 100 C3
Cae'r Berllan. Penco 165 F1
Cae'r Cynffig. Pyle 176 C4
Cae'r Efail. Penco 165 F1
Cae'r Fferm. Caer 151 F2
Cae'r Graig. Card 187 D4
Cae'r Hen Eglwys. Bridg ... 179 E3
Cae'r Odyn. D pow 216 A1
Cae'r Wern. Mer T 51 E4
Cae'r-llwyn Terr. Ynys ... 127 F4
Cae-Bricks Rd. Swan 84 A1
Cae-Bryn. Aber 151 D4
Cae-Bryn Ave. Swan 109 E3
Cae-groes Terr. B-coch ... 62 C1
Cae-Gwyn Rd. Pontar ... 36 B2
Cae-Is-Maen. Pontdw ... 40 B2
Cae-nan. Swan 60 A2
Cae-Pys Rd. Swan 84 B3
Caeau Duon. Penco 165 F1
Caebach Cl. Card 202 C2
Caecerrig Rd. Pontar 36 B3
Caeconna Rd. Swan 83 F3
Caedegar Rd. Ystra 7 F1
Caedelyn Rd. Card 188 A3
Caederwen Rd. Neath ... 87 F3
Caedraw Rd. Mer T 51 E4
Caedu Rd. Cwmll 6 B3
Caedu Rd. Og Va 119 F1
Caeglas Ave. Card 190 A2
Caeglas Rd. Card 190 B2
Caegwenith Clos. Tonna ... 63 D1
Caelbryn Terr. Tondu ... 163 E3
Caemaen St. Abercy 98 B3
Caemansel La. Gow 82 A2
Caemawr Gdns. Porth ... 122 C2
Caemawr Rd. Porth 122 C2
Caemawr Rd. Swan 84 C4
Caemawr Terr. Tony 122 A1
Caenant. Ponty 149 F3
Caenant Rd. Caer 152 A3
Caenant Terr. Skew 86 C4
Caenewydd Cl. Card 202 C2
Caepistyll St. Swan 84 B1
Caer Bont Ind Est. Ystra ... 8 B2
Caer Castell Pl. Card ... 190 B3
Caer Gymrig. Maest 117 E1
Caer Newydd. Bridg 180 B3
Caer St. Swan 110 B4
Caer Wenallt. Card 187 F4
Caer Wetral. Pyle 161 E1
Caer-Gynydd Rd. Swan ... 82 C2
Caeracca Villas. Mer T ... 33 D3
Caerau Cl. Card 203 D1
Caerau La. Card 203 D1
Caerau La. Penty 186 B4
Caerau La. Wen 203 E2
Caerau Park Cres. Card ... 203 E2
Caerau Park Pl. Card 203 E2
Caerau Park Rd. Card ... 203 E2
Caerau Rd. Card 203 E2
Caerau Rd. Maest 91 D1
Caerbragdy. Caer 152 A3
Caerhendy St. Mer T ... 32 C2
Caerleon Cl. Card 191 D4
Caerleon Ct. Caer 151 E2
Caerleon Rd. Card 188 B1
Caerleon Rd. D pow 216 B2
Caerllysi. Penco 181 D4
Caernarvon Cl. D pow ... 216 B2
Caernarvon Ct. Caer 151 E2
Caernarvon Dr. Rhiwd ... 155 F2
Caernarvon Gr. Mer T ... 31 F2
Caernarvon Pl. Peng 76 B1
Caernarvon Rd. Rhiwd ... 155 F2
Caernarvon Way. Card ... 190 B3
Caernarvon Way. Swan ... 85 D2
Caerphilly Ave. Swan ... 85 E2
Caerphilly Bsns Pk. Caer .. 152 B1
Caerphilly Cl. D pow 216 B2
Caerphilly Cl. Rhiwd 155 F2
Caerphilly Rd. Aber 125 F1
Caerphilly Rd. Card 188 B3
Caerphilly Rd. Gell 126 C4
Caerphilly Rd. Nel 99 F2
Caerphilly Rd. Ponty 151 E1
Caerphilly Rd. Ponty 170 C4
Caerphilly Rd. Ponty 171 D4
Caerphilly Rd. Rhiwd ... 155 F2
Caerphilly Rd. Tre 99 D3
Caerwent Rd. Card 203 D3
Caetyla Heol. Bridg 180 C2
Caewal Rd. Card 204 A4
Caewallis St. Bridg 179 F2
Caiach Terr. Bed 99 E3
Cairnmuir Rd. Card 205 F4
Cairo St. Trea 122 A3
Calderton Rd. Ll'tris ... 169 D3

Caldey Pl. Swan 83 F4
Caldicot Cl. Peng 76 B1
Caldicot Cl. Swan 85 E2
Caldicot Ct. Caer 151 E2
Caldicot Rd. Card 203 E2
Caldicot Rd. Swan 85 E2
Caldicott Cl. Ll'tris 169 D3
Caldwell Cl. Ll'tris 169 D3
Caldy Cl. Porth 176 C1
Caldy Rd. Card 188 A2
Caledfryn Way. Caer ... 151 E2
Calland St. Swan 84 C3
Callencroft Ct. T Mum ... 136 C3
Calvert Terr. Swan 110 A4
Camarthen Rd. Swan ... 83 F2
Cambell Ct. Barry 225 D2
Camberwell Ave. Bridg ... 179 E3
Cambourne Ave. Card ... 187 F3
Cambray Cl. Porth 192 C4
Cambria Rd. Card 203 D2
Cambrian Ave. Ll' Maj ... 220 A3
Cambrian Ave. Tony 146 B3
Cambrian Cl. Swan 85 D4
Cambrian Ind Pk. Tonypa . 121 E3
Cambrian Pl. Marg 139 E4
Cambrian Pl. Pontar 36 B2
Cambrian Pl. Ponty 149 F4
Cambrian Pl. Swan 110 C3
Cambrian Pl. Ystra 6 C2
Cambrian St. Deri 75 D4
Cambrian St. Mer T 32 B1
Cambrian St. Rhy 34 C3
Cambrian Terr. Trea 121 F4
Cambridge Cl. T Mum ... 137 D2
Cambridge Gdns. T Mum . 137 D2
Cambridge Rd. T Mum ... 137 D2
Cambridge St. Card 205 D1
Cambridge St. Swan 109 F4
Camellia Cl. Aberd 49 E2
Camellia Dr. Swan 59 F2
Camelot Way. Card 172 B1
Cameron Pl. Lough 57 D1
Cameron St. Card 205 F4
Camffrwd Way. Swan ... 60 B1
Camm's Cnr. D pow 216 B2
Camnant Rd. Onll 10 A1
Camona Dr. Swan 110 B3
Campbell Dr. Card 217 D4
Campbell St. Swan 110 B4
Campbell Terr. M Ash ... 72 B2
Campbell Terr. Trea 121 F4
Camperly Cl. Ll'tris 169 D3
Campion Pl. Card 187 E1
Campton Pl. Ll'tris 169 D3
Camrose Dr. Swan 82 C2
Camrose Rd. Card 203 E2
Can-yr-Aderyn. Swan ... 59 E1
Can-yr-Eos. Swan 59 F1
Canada Rd. Card 188 C1
Canal Par. Card 205 D2
Canal Rd. Aberd 71 F4
Canal Rd. Neath 87 E4
Canal Row. Troed 51 F2
Canal Side. B-coch 63 E2
Canal Terr. Ystal 23 D3
Canaston Ct. Card 203 E2
Canberra Cl. Oak 101 F4
Canberra Rd. Bridg 179 F3
Candleston Cl. Porth ... 176 C1
Candleston Pl. Swan ... 85 E2
Canning Ct. Yst 94 C2
Cannington Ave. Card ... 190 B3
Cannington Cl. Sully ... 226 A3
Cannisland Pk. South ... 107 E1
Cannon St. G-C-G 5 D4
Canolfan. Bridg 180 A2
Canon St. Abera 50 A1
Canonbie Cres. Mer V ... 73 E2
Canopus Cl. Card 190 B3
Canterbury Rd. Swan ... 109 F3
Canton Ct. Card 204 C3
Canton Wlk. Card 204 B3
Cantref Cl. Card 172 C2
Cantref Ct. Swan 83 F3
Capel Bethlehem. Mer T ... 32 B1
Capel Bldgs. Cly 60 C4
Capel Gwilym Rd. Card ... 172 B2
Capel Rd. Cly 60 C4
Capel St. Bar 76 A2
Capel-Ifan. Tony 147 E3
Capital Valley Ind Pk. Rhy . 34 C1
Captains Hill. Bed 99 E4
Caradoc Ave. Barry 225 D4
Caradoc Cl. Card 191 D4
Caradoc Rd. M Ash 72 B1
Caradoc St. Aberca 129 E4
Caradoc St. M Ash 72 B1
Caradoc St. Mer T 32 B1
Caradog Pl. Swan 110 A4
Caradog Rd. Bridg 180 B2
Caradog Rd. Tylor 96 A2
Caradog St. Marg 139 E4
Caraway Cl. Card 191 D4
Cardiff Centre Trad Est.
Card 205 D2
Cardiff Pl. Treo 94 B3
Cardiff Rd. Abera 71 E4
Cardiff Rd. Abercy 98 B1

Cardiff Rd. Bar 76 A2
Cardiff Rd. Barry 225 E3
Cardiff Rd. Caer 152 A1
Cardiff Rd. Card 203 D4
Cardiff Rd. Card 204 B4
Cardiff Rd. Cowb 199 D1
Cardiff Rd. D pow 216 A2
Cardiff Rd. Gal 101 D4
Cardiff Rd. Ll'tris 168 B1
Cardiff Rd. M Ash 72 C1
Cardiff Rd. Mer V 73 E2
Cardiff Rd. Penty 185 F3
Cardiff Rd. Ponty 150 A2
Cardiff Rd. T We 170 C3
Cardiff Rd. Tre 99 D3
Cardiff Rd. Tre 99 E4
Cardiff Rd. Troed 73 E4
Cardiff St. Abera 50 A1
Cardiff St. Og Va 119 F1
Cardiff St. Treo 94 B3
Cardiff St. Troed 51 F2
Cardiff Workshops. Card ... 205 E2
Cardigan Cl. Ch Vil 149 F1
Cardigan Cl. D pow 216 B2
Cardigan Cl. Porth 176 C1
Cardigan Cres. Ll' Maj ... 220 B3
Cardigan Cres. Swan ... 85 E3
Cardigan Ct. Card 204 B3
Cardigan House. P Tal ... 138 B4
Cardigan House. Pen ... 216 C1
Cardigan Rd. D pow 216 B2
Cardigan St. Card 204 B3
Cardigan Terr. Og Va ... 119 F3
Cardigan Way. Peng ... 76 B1
Cardinal Dr. Card 173 D2
Cardonnel Rd. Skew ... 86 C3
Carew Ct. Card 188 A3
Carew Gr. Mer T 31 F1
Carew Pl. Swan 85 E3
Carey Wlk. B-coch 87 E4
Cargill Cl. Ll'tris 169 D3
Carig Cres. Swan 84 A1
Carig Gdns. Swan 84 A1
Carisbrooke Way. Card ... 189 E2
Carling Ct. Card 203 D2
Carlisle St. Card 205 F3
Carlos St. Marg 114 A1
Carlton Cl. Card 172 C2
Carlton Cres. Ll'tris ... 169 D3
Carlton Pl. Cross 129 E3
Carlton Rd. Penfro 192 C4
Carlton Rd. Cly 39 F1
Carlton Terr. Cross ... 129 E3
Carlton Terr. Swan ... 110 B4
Carlton Terr. Troed ... 52 A1
Carlton Terr. Troed ... 73 E4
Carlyle St. Neath 87 E2
Carmarthen Cl. Ll' Maj ... 220 A3
Carmarthen Ct. Caer ... 151 E2
Carmarthen Ct. Card ... 204 B3
Carmarthen Dr. Ch Vil ... 149 F1
Carmarthen House. P Tal . 138 B4
Carmarthen House. Pen ... 216 C1
Carmarthen Rd. D pow ... 216 B2
Carmarthen Rd. Hen ... 36 A3
Carmarthen Rd. Swan ... 83 E3
Carmarthen St. Card ... 204 B3
Carmel Rd. Pont 57 F4
Carmel Rd. Swan 85 E3
Carmel St. Trehe 94 A4
Carmen St. Maest 117 D4
Carn Celyn. Ll'tris 169 D3
Carn-y-tyla Terr. Rhy ... 54 A4
Carne Ct. Ll' Maj 220 A3
Carne Ct. Yst 94 C3
Carne Terr. Llys 209 F4
Carnegie Dr. Card 189 D3
Carnglas Ave. Swan ... 109 E4
Carnglas Rd. Swan ... 109 E4
Carno Pl. Swan 84 B4
Carno St. Rhy 34 B3
Caroline Ave. Pyle 176 C4
Caroline St. Bridg 179 F2
Caroline St. Card 205 D3
Caroline St. Glyn 92 B3
Caroline St. Neath 87 E1
Caroline St. Tonypa ... 122 A1
Caroline St. Trehe 68 B3
Caroline Terr. Glyn ... 92 B3
Carreg Arwyn. Ll'hry ... 183 D3
Carreg Cennen Gdns. Swan . 85 D2
Carreg yr Afon. Ystal ... 22 C2
Carrog Rd. Swan 84 A3
Carshalton Rd. Ll'tris ... 169 D3
Carswell Cl. Ll'tris ... 169 D3
Carter Pl. Card 187 E1
Cartersford Pl. T Mum ... 137 D4
Cartref. Skew 86 C4
Cartwright Ct. Card ... 189 D1
Cartwright La. Card ... 203 D3
Caryl Terr. Swan 84 C3
Carys Cl. Card 203 D1
Carys Cl. Pen 216 C1
Caspian Cl. Card 190 C3
Castan Rd. Ll'tris 184 A4
Castell Cl. Swan 85 E4
Castell Ddu Rd. Lough ... 36 A1

Castell Meredith. Caer ... 152 B3
Castell Morgraig. Caer ... 152 B3
Castell Morlais. C-c-y-c ... 14 C2
Castell-y-Mynach Rd. Ll'tris ... 168 C4
Castellau Rd. Ll'tris ... 168 C4
Castle Acre. T Mum ... 137 D3
Castle Ave. Card 189 F1
Castle Ave. Pen 216 C1
Castle Ave. T Mum ... 137 D3
Castle Bailey St. Swan ... 110 B4
Castle Bldgs. Ponty ... 149 F3
Castle Cl. Cross 129 E3
Castle Cl. D pow 216 B2
Castle Cl. Ll' Maj 220 B3
Castle Cl. Penty 185 F4
Castle Cres. Card 190 A1
Castle Cres. T Mum ... 137 D3
Castle Ct. Ch Vil 149 F1
Castle Ct. D pow 216 B2
Castle Ct. Ll' maj 219 F3
Castle Ct. Maest 117 D2
Castle Ct. St M Ch ... 210 C3
Castle Dr. D pow 216 B2
Castle Dr. Neath 88 A3
Castle Fields. Rhy ... 34 C2
Castle Gn. Wen 203 F3
Castle Graig Rd. Swan ... 84 B3
Castle Hill. Card 203 D4
Castle Hill. Cowb 198 B3
Castle Hill Ct. Card ... 202 C4
Castle Hill. Gell 100 B3
Castle Ivor St. Ponty ... 124 A1
Castle La. Card 205 E4
Castle La. Cross 129 E3
Castle La. Swan 110 B4
Castle Meadows. Bridg ... 180 B4
Castle Prec. St M Ch ... 210 C4
Castle Rd. Card 171 E1
Castle Rd. Rhoose ... 222 B2
Castle Rd. Rhoose ... 223 D1
Castle Rd. T Mum ... 137 D3
Castle Rise. Card 190 A1
Castle Sq. Mer T 32 B1
Castle Sq. T Mum ... 137 D3
Castle St. Bridg 180 A1
Castle St. Caer 152 A2
Castle St. Card 205 D3
Castle St. Glyn 66 C2
Castle St. Ll' maj ... 219 F4
Castle St. Ll'tris 168 B2
Castle St. Lough 56 B1
Castle St. Maest 117 D2
Castle St. Mer T 32 B1
Castle St. Neath 87 F4
Castle St. P Tal 114 A1
Castle St. Peng 101 D4
Castle St. Ponty 149 F4
Castle St. Skew 86 C3
Castle St. Swan 110 B4
Castle St. T Mum ... 137 D3
Castle St. T We 171 D2
Castle St. Tred 35 F3
Castle St. Treo 94 B3
Castle St. Troed 52 A2
Castle View. Bridg ... 179 F3
Castle View. Caer ... 151 F3
Castle View. Card ... 187 E4
Castle View. Mer T ... 32 A1
Castle View. Neath ... 87 F4
Castle Yd. Mer T 32 B1
Castlefield Pl. Card ... 188 C1
Castleford Cl. Ll'tris ... 169 D3
Castleland St. Barry ... 225 D3
Castleton Ave. Trehe ... 68 B2
Castleton Rd. St Ath ... 221 E3
Caswell Ave. T Mum ... 136 C2
Caswell Bay Rd. Bish ... 136 A3
Caswell Chalets. T Mum ... 136 B3
Caswell Cl. Hir 48 B4
Caswell Dr. T Mum ... 136 B2
Caswell Rd. Bish 136 B2
Caswell Rd. Card 190 A2
Caswell Rd. T Mum ... 136 B2
Caswell St. Swan 110 A3
Cath Cob Cl. Card ... 190 C4
Cathan Cl. Swan 83 F3
Cathan Cres. Swan ... 83 F3
Cathays Terr. Card ... 205 D4
Cathedral Cl. Card ... 188 A1
Cathedral Ct. Card ... 188 A1
Cathedral Gn The. Card ... 188 A1
Cathedral Rd. Card ... 204 C4
Cathedral View. Card ... 188 A1
Cathedral Wlk. Card ... 205 D3
Catherine Cl. Troed ... 51 F2
Catherine Dr. Card ... 171 E1
Catherine Dr. Marsh ... 191 F4
Catherine Meazey Flats.
Pen 217 D3
Catherine St. Abera ... 50 A1
Catherine St. Card ... 205 D4
Catherine St. P Tal ... 113 F1
Catherine St. Ponty ... 124 B1
Catherine St. Swan ... 110 A3
Catherine St. Yst 95 D1
Catherine Terr. Porth ... 122 C1
Catkin Dr. Pen 216 C3

Cattwg Cotts. Ll'car 222 B4
Cattybrook Terr. Cwma 114 C3
Causeway Hill. Cowb 210 B4
Causeway The. Cowb 210 B4
Causeway The. Swan 109 F4
Cavan Row. Maest 117 D2
Cave St. Swan 84 A1
Cavell St. Glyn 66 C1
Cavendish Cl. Card 172 C1
Cavendish Pl. Ll'tris 169 D3
Cawley Pl. Barry 225 D4
Cawnpore St. Pen 216 C3
Caxton Pl. Card 190 A4
Caynham Ave. Pen 227 D4
Cecil Rd. Gow 82 B2
Cecil Rd. Lough 57 E1
Cecil St. Card 205 E4
Cecil St. Neath 87 E3
Cecil St. Swan 84 B2
Cedar Ave. Lough 57 D2
Cedar Cl. Aberd 49 F1
Cedar Cl. Gow 82 B2
Cedar Cl. Pontll 101 E2
Cedar Cres. Ch Vil 150 A1
Cedar Cres. T Mum 136 C4
Cedar Gdns. P Tal 113 E3
Cedar Gdns. Porthc 193 F4
Cedar Gr. Card 187 E1
Cedar House. Card 187 F3
Cedar La. Ponty 150 A3
Cedar Rd. Ll'maes 221 D4
Cedar Rd. Neath 87 F4
Cedar St. Blae 45 E4
Cedar Way. Gell 100 C1
Cedar Way. Mer T 32 B2
Cedar Way. Pen 216 C2
Cedric Cl. Swan 109 D3
Cefn Bryn. Porth 122 B1
Cefn Bychan. Penty 170 B1
Cefn Carfan Cotts. Brynco .. 164 C4
Cefn Carfan Rd. Brynco 164 B3
Cefn Carnau Rd. Card 188 C3
Cefn Coch. Card 187 D4
Cefn Coed Ave. Card 189 E2
Cefn Coed. Bridg 179 E3
Cefn Coed Cres. Swan 83 E1
Cefn Coed La. Bridg 179 E3
Cefn Ct. Peng 101 F4
Cefn Ffynon. Marg 139 F2
Cefn Gelli. Blae 45 E4
Cefn Glas. Swan 60 A2
Cefn Glas. Swan 109 D4
Cefn Glas. Tred 35 E4
Cefn Graig. Card 188 A4
Cefn Gwrgan Rd. Marg 139 F2
Cefn Helig. Swan 83 D1
Cefn Hengoed Rd. Swan ... 85 E2
Cefn Ilan. Aber 151 D3
Cefn Isaf. C-c-y-c 32 A2
Cefn La. Ponty 124 B3
Cefn La. Ponty 124 C3
Cefn Llan. Penty 186 B4
Cefn Llwyn. Swan 85 E3
Cefn Llywnau St. Gell 100 B2
Cefn Mably Rd. Card 173 E2
Cefn Mount. D pow 216 A2
Cefn Nant. Card 172 A1
Cefn Nant. Penco 165 E1
Cefn Onn Meadows. Card .. 172 C2
Cefn Parc. Tred 35 F3
Cefn Penuel. Penty 186 B4
Cefn Rd. Card 188 B2
Cefn Rd. Ce Cr 162 A1
Cefn Rd. Deri 75 E4
Cefn Rd. G-C-G 5 D2
Cefn Rd. Gall 101 D2
Cefn Rd. Peng 101 F4
Cefn Rd. Rhiwd 155 F3
Cefn Rd. Swan 60 C3
Cefn Rd. Swan 85 E2
Cefn Rd. Tylor 122 B4
Cefn Rhos. Tred 35 E3
Cefn Stylle Rd. Gell 81 F3
Cefn-Bryn-Brain. Bry 6 B4
Cefn-Coed Cres. Card 189 D2
Cefn-Coed Gdns. Card 189 D2
Cefn-Coed Rd. Card 189 D2
Cefn-Draw. Pen-cl 81 E1
Cefn-Fforest Ave. Peng 101 E4
Cefn-Glas Rd. Bridg 179 E3
Cefn-Parc. Skew 86 C3
Cefn-Pennar Rd. Aberd 72 A4
Cefn-Porth Rd. Card 173 F3
Cefn-Porth Rd. Gar P 173 F3
Cefn-Rhychdir Rd. N Tre ... 54 C2
Cefn-Saeson Cl. Neath 88 A3
Cefn-y-Lon. Caer 151 E3
Cefn-yr-Allt. B-coch 63 E2
Cefncoed Rd. Cwma 114 B3
Cefndon Terr. Cwma 114 B3
Cefndon Terr. Hir 48 C4
Cefnllan Rd. Pontdw 40 B3
Cefnpennar Rd. Aberd 72 A4
Cefnsaeson Rd. Swan 86 A4
Ceidrim Rd. Glan 4 B4
Ceiriog Cl. Barry 225 D4
Ceiriog Cl. Pen 216 C2

Ceiriog Cres. Ponty 149 F3
Ceiriog Dr. Caer 152 A2
Ceiriog Dr. Card 187 F4
Ceiriog Rd. Swan 110 A4
Celerity Dr. Card 205 E2
Celtic Gn. D pow 216 A2
Celtic Rd. Card 188 B2
Celtic Rd. Maest 117 E1
Celtic View. Bridg 163 F1
Celtic Way. Bedw 152 C3
Celtic Way. Rhoose 222 C1
Celyn Ave. Caer 152 A2
Celyn Ave. Card 189 D3
Celyn Cl. St M Ch 221 E4
Celyn Gr. Caer 152 A2
Celyn Gr. Card 189 E4
Celyn Isaf. Tony 147 E1
Cemaes Cres. Card 190 C3
Cemetery Rd. Abercy 98 B2
Cemetery Rd. Aberd 49 F2
Cemetery Rd. Bridg 179 F3
Cemetery Rd. G-C-G 5 D2
Cemetery Rd. Maest 117 E2
Cemetery Rd. Og Va 144 C4
Cemetery Rd. Ponty 149 F4
Cemetery Rd. Porth 122 B2
Cemetery Rd. Swan 84 B3
Cemetery Rd. T We 171 D2
Cemetery Rd. Treo 94 B4
Cenarth Dr. Abera 50 C1
Centenary Ct. Ll'tris 169 D3
Central Ave. Peng 101 E4
Central Bldgs. Bedw 153 D3
Central Houses. Bedw 152 C3
Central Link. Card 205 E2
Central Rd. Marg 139 E2
Central Rd. Marg 139 E3
Central Sq. Card 205 E2
Central St. Caer 151 F4
Central St. Gell 100 C1
Central Way. Sully 225 F3
Centre Ct. Ponty 170 C4
Centurion Ct. Card 203 E2
Century Park. Swan 85 D3
Cenydd Terr. Aber 125 F2
Cerdin Ave. Ll'tris 184 A4
Cerdinen Terr. Aberd 71 F4
Ceredig St. Troed 52 A2
Ceri Ave. Rhoose 223 D1
Ceri Rd. Rhoose 223 D1
Ceri Rd. Swan 83 F1
Ceridwen St. Fern 70 A1
Ceridwen St. M Ash 72 B1
Cerise Cl. P Tal 113 D2
Cfarthfa Ind Est. Mer T 32 B1
Chaddesley Terr. Swan 110 A4
Chain Rd. G-nea 45 E4
Chain Wlk. G-nea 26 C1
Chalfont Cl. Ll'tris 169 D3
Challacombe Pl. T Mum 136 C3
Chalvington Cl. Ll'tris 169 E3
Chamberlain Rd. Card 188 A2
Chamberlain Rd. Neath 87 E2
Chamberlain Row. D pow .. 216 B2
Chancery La. Card 204 B3
Chancery La. M Ash 72 B2
Chandlers Reach. Ch Vil ... 169 E3
Chandlery The. Trea 121 F4
Channel Ave. Porth 147 F4
Channel Cl. Rhoose 222 C1
Channel View. B-coch 62 B2
Channel View. Bridg 180 B2
Channel View. M-y-Fed 175 D2
Channel View. P Tal 138 B4
Channel View. Pen 217 D1
Channel View Rd. Card 204 C1
Channel View. Rhiwd 155 F2
Channel View. Swan 109 D3
Channel View. Swan 109 D3
Chantal Ave. Bridg 163 E1
Chantry Ct. Swan 83 F3
Chantry Rise. Pen 217 D1
Chantry The. Card 187 F1
Chapel Banks. Mer T 32 B1
Chapel Cl. Cowb 199 D2
Chapel Cl. D pow 216 B2
Chapel Cl. Troed 52 A2
Chapel Ct. Bedw 153 D4
Chapel Farm Terr. Aberca . 129 D4
Chapel Hill Cl. Ll'ha 166 C2
Chapel Hill. Ll'ha 166 C2
Chapel La. Pen 217 D3
Chapel Rd. Card 187 D4
Chapel Rd. Hir 29 D3
Chapel Rd. Monk 208 B1
Chapel Rd. N Tre 54 A3
Chapel Rd. Pen-cl 80 A1
Chapel Rd. Pen-cl 81 F1
Chapel Row. Card 190 B4
Chapel Row. D pow 216 B2
Chapel Row. Mer T 32 B1
Chapel St. Abera 71 E4
Chapel St. Bar 75 A3
Chapel St. Bed 74 A4
Chapel St. Bridg 179 F2
Chapel St. Card 204 A4
Chapel St. Deri 75 D4
Chapel St. Glyn 92 B3

Chapel St. N Tre 54 C2
Chapel St. Og Va 119 F3
Chapel St. Penga 57 E1
Chapel St. Pontcr 118 C2
Chapel St. Ponty 124 B1,
Chapel St. Ponty 149 F3/
Chapel St. Rhy 34 C1
Chapel St. Swan 84 B1
Chapel St. T Mum 137 D3
Chapel St. Tondu 163 F3
Chapel St. Tonypa 121 F3
Chapel St. Tonypa 122 A2
Chapel St. Trehe 68 A1
Chapel St. Trehe 68 B2
Chapel St. Treo 94 B3
Chapel St. Troed 51 F2
Chapel St. Troed 52 B1
Chapel St. Yst 95 D2
Chapel St. Yst 95 E2
Chapel Terr. Bryn 115 F3
Chapel Terr. Gell 100 C2
Chapel Terr. Rhiwd 155 F2
Chapel Terr. Tylor 122 C4
Chapel View. Ynys 128 A2
Chapel Wood. Card 189 F2
Chard Ave. Card 190 A3
Chargot Rd. Card 204 A4
Charles Ave. Penco 165 E1
Charles Ct. Lough 57 D1
Charles Row. Maest 117 D2
Charles St. Bridg 179 F3
Charles St. Caer 152 A2
Charles St. Card 205 D3
Charles St. N Tre 76 A4
Charles St. Neath 87 F4
Charles St. Ponty 124 A1
Charles St. Porth 122 C2
Charles St. Rhy 54 B4
Charles St. Skew 86 C4
Charles St. Tonypa 121 E3
Charles St. Trea 122 A3
Charles St. Tred 35 F4
Charles St. Trehe 94 A4
Charles St. Tylor 96 A2
Charlotte Pl. Barry 225 D3
Charlotte Sq. Card 188 B4
Charlotte St. Mer T 33 D2
Charlotte St. Pen 216 C3
Charnwood Ct. Card 189 D1
Charnwood Ct. Swan 85 E3
Charteris Cl. Pen 227 D4
Charteris Cres. Card 203 E3
Charteris Rd. Card 203 E3
Chartist Ind. Ll'tris 168 B2
Chartist Way. Peng 101 E4
Chartist Way. Tred 35 F4
Chartley Cl. Card 191 D4
Chartwell Ct. Penty 186 B4
Chartwell Dr. Card 173 D1
Chase The. Bridg 180 B2
Chase View. Mer T 32 C2
Chatham. Bedw 154 A4
Chatham St. Bedw 154 A4
Chatterton Sq. Card 216 C4
Chaucer Cl. Bridg 179 E3
Chaucer Cl. Card 190 B4
Chaucer Cl. Pen 216 C2
Chave Terr. Maesy 101 D1
Cheam Pl. Card 188 C4
Cheapside. Bridg 179 F2
Cheapside. Bridg 180 A1
Cheddar Cres. Card 190 A3
Chelhydra Wlk. Swan 110 B3
Chelsea Ave. Bridg 179 E4
Cheltenham Rd. Porth 192 C4
Cheltenham Terr. Bridg 179 F2
Chemical Rd. Swan 59 F1
Chemical Row. Ystal 23 D2
Chepstow Cl. Card 203 E2
Chepstow Cl. Mer T 31 F1
Chepstow Cl. Peng 76 B1
Chepstow St. Caer 151 E2
Chepstow Pl. Swan 85 E2
Chepstow Rd. Treo 94 B3
Cheriton Ave. Gell 100 C3
Cheriton Cres. Swan 83 F3
Cheriton Dr. Card 172 C1
Cheriton Gr. Ch Vil 150 A1
Cherry Cl. Card 187 D1
Cherry Cl. D pow 216 B1
Cherry Cl. Pen 227 D4
Cherry Dr. Aberd 49 E2
Cherry Gr. Mer T 32 C2
Cherry Gr. P Tal 113 F3
Cherry Gr. Swan 109 D2
Cherry Orchard Rd. Card .. 172 C2
Cherry Tree Ave. Porthc ... 193 F4
Cherry Tree Cl. Bedw 152 B2
Cherry Tree Cl. C-c-y-c 32 A3
Cherry Tree Cl. Card 173 D2
Cherry Tree Rd. Pontll 101 D2
Cherry Tree Way. Bed 99 E4
Cherry Tree Wlk. Ll'tris 168 B4
Cherry Trees. Mark 76 B4
Cherrydale Rd. Card 203 F3
Cherrydown Cl. Card 172 C1
Cherrywood Cl. Card 172 C1
Chervil Cl. Card 191 D4

Cherwell Cl. Card 187 E1
Cherwell Rd. Pen 216 C1
Cheshire Cl. Card 188 C3
Chesshyre St. Swan 109 F3
Chester Cl. Card 190 C3
Chester Cl. Mer T 31 F1
Chester Cl. Caer 151 E2
Chester Pl. Card 204 C2
Chester St. Card 204 C2
Chesterfield St. Barry 225 D4
Chesterton Rd. Card 190 A4
Chestnut Ave. Ll'maes 221 D4
Chestnut Ave. Lough 57 D2
Chestnut Ave. T Mum 136 C4
Chestnut Cl. Aberd 49 F1
Chestnut Cl. B-coch 62 B1
Chestnut Cl. D pow 216 A1
Chestnut Cl. Neath 88 A3
Chestnut Dr. Porthc 193 F4
Chestnut Gr. Barry 225 D3
Chestnut Gr. Pontll 101 F2
Chestnut Rd. Card 203 E4
Chestnut Rd. Neath 88 A3
Chestnut Rd. P Tal 113 F4
Chestnut St. Ponty 150 A3
Chestnut Tree Cl. Card 187 D3
Chestnut Way. Bridg 179 D3
Chestnut Way. Mer T 32 B3
Chestnut Way. Pen 216 C2
Chestnuts The. Ll'tris 184 B3
Cheviot Cl. Card 188 C4
Cheviot Cl. Swan 83 F2
Chevron St. Porth 122 C2
Chichester Rd. Pen 216 C3
Chichester Way. Card 203 F3
Chilcote St. Barry 225 D3
Chillcott Ave. Brynco 163 F3
Chiltern Cl. Card 188 C4
Chiltern Cl. Swan 83 F2
Chimney Rd. St Ath 221 F1
Chirk Gdns. Swan 85 E2
Chiswick Cl. Bridg 179 E3
Chopin Rd. P Tal 113 D2
Chorley Cl. Card 203 E4
Chorleywood Cl. Bridg 180 A2
Christchurch Rd. Oak 101 F4
Christchurch Rd. P Tal 113 E2
Christina St. Card 205 D2
Christina St. Swan 110 B4
Christopher Ct. Swan 85 D3
Christopher Rd. Maest 117 E2
Christopher Rd. Skew 86 C4
Christopher Rd. Swan 60 A2
Christopher Rise. Pont 58 A3
Christopher Terr. Mer T ... 51 F4
Chrome Ave. P Tal 113 D1
Chumleigh Cl. Card 190 A2
Church Acre. Bridg 180 B3
Church Ave. Llwy 49 F3
Church Ave. Pen 217 D2
Church Cl. B-coch 62 B2
Church Cl. Card 173 E2
Church Cl. Ch Vil 169 E3
Church Cl. St B M 194 B1
Church Cl. St B W 191 F3
Church Cl. Swan 85 E4
Church Cotts. M-l-Pit 216 A4
Church Cres. Blae 45 F4
Church Cres. P Tal 113 F3
Church Hill Cl. Cowb 210 B4
Church La. Bish 135 F4
Church La. Card 190 B4
Church La. G-C-G 5 D2
Church La. Ll' maj 219 F3
Church La. Marsh 175 E1
Church La. Nel 99 F2
Church La. P Tal 113 F3
Church La. Pen-cl 80 C1
Church La. St Ath 221 E1
Church La. T We 171 D4
Church Meadow. Ll' Maj ... 220 B3
Church Meadow. Ll'rh 104 B1
Church Park La. T Mum 137 D2
Church Pk. T Mum 137 D2
Church Pl. Bar 76 A2
Church Pl. Maest 117 D2
Church Pl. Neath 87 F4
Church Pl. Pontcr 118 C3
Church Pl. Porth 192 C3
Church Pl S. Pen 217 D3
Church Rd. A-wen 41 E3
Church Rd. Aber 150 C4
Church Rd. Barry 225 D4
Church Rd. Bridg 179 F2
Church Rd. Card 173 E2
Church Rd. Card 174 B1
Church Rd. Card 188 A2
Church Rd. Card 190 A4
Church Rd. Card 203 E2
Church Rd. Card 204 B3
Church Rd. Ch Vil 149 F1
Church Rd. Cowb 198 B1
Church Rd. Gell 100 B4
Church Rd. Hen 17 D1
Church Rd. Hir 29 D3
Church Rd. P Tal 113 F3
Church Rd. Pen 217 D2

Church Rd. Penty 186 B4
Church Rd. Pontar 36 B2
Church Rd. Pontdw 40 C4
Church Rd. Pontmi 129 F2
Church Rd. Ponty 124 C1
Church Rd. Ponydw 41 D4
Church Rd. Rhoose 223 D1
Church Rd. Se Si 24 C3
Church Rd. Swan 85 E4
Church Rd Terr. Pontmi 129 F2
Church Rd. Tonypa 122 A1
Church Rd. Wick 208 B3
Church Rd. Yst 95 D2
Church Rd. Ystal 23 D2
Church Rise. Wen 215 D3
Church Row. Aberd 49 F2
Church Row. Glan 4 B4
Church Row. Mer T 33 D2
Church Row. St Nic 201 F1
Church Sq. Cwma 114 C3
Church Sq. Ll'ge 56 A4
Church St. Abera 50 A1
Church St. Bar 75 F2
Church St. Bedw 152 C3
Church St. Bedw 154 A4
Church St. Card 205 D3
Church St. Cowb 198 C1
Church St. Fern 70 A1
Church St. Fern 95 F4
Church St. Gell 100 C1
Church St. Glyn 91 E2
Church St. Gow 82 A3
Church St. Ll' maj 219 F3
Church St. Ll'bra 126 C1
Church St. Ll'ha 166 B2
Church St. Ll'tris 168 B2
Church St. Llys 197 F1
Church St. M Ash 97 F4
Church St. Maest 91 D1
Church St. Maest 117 D2
Church St. Mer T 32 B1
Church St. Mer T 32 C1
Church St. Mer T 32 C2
Church St. Mer T 33 D2
Church St. Neath 87 D1
Church St. P Tal 114 A1
Church St. Pontcr 118 C2
Church St. Pontcr 118 C3
Church St. Pontdw 40 C3
Church St. Ponty 124 B1
Church St. Porthc 193 E4
Church St. Rhiwd 155 F3
Church St. Rhy ,,............. 34 C1
Church St. Rhy 34 C3
Church St. T We 171 D2
Church St. Tondu 163 E2
Church St. Tonypa 121 F3
Church St. Trea 121 F4
Church St. Tred 35 F4
Church St. Trehe 69 D1
Church St. Treo 94 A3
Church St. Troed 52 A1
Church St. Wick 208 B3
Church St. Ynybw 97 F1
Church St. Yst 95 D2
Church Terr. Barry 225 E4
Church Terr. Card 205 E4
Church Terr. Ll'ha 167 D2
Church Terr. Ll'thyd 211 E4
Church Terr. N Tre 54 C2
Church Terr. Og Va 119 F4
Church Terr. Pontcr 118 C3
Church Terr. St M Ch 211 D2
Church Terr. Tonypa 122 A1
Church Terr. Tylor 96 B2
Church Terr. Tylor 122 C3
Church View. Bridg 178 C2
Church View Cl. Ll'ha 166 B2
Church View. Cowb 198 B1
Church View. Ll'ha 166 B2
Church View. P Tal 113 F3
Church View. St Don 218 B4
Church View. Tylor 96 A1
Church Wlk. Porth 123 D2
Churchfield Cl. Gell 100 C3
Churchfield Row. Yst 95 D2
Churchfields. Barry 225 D4
Churchill Cl. Bridg 179 E2
Churchill Cl. Card 173 D2
Churchill Terr. Barry 225 E3
Churchill Way. Card 205 D3
Cil-Hendy. Ll'tris 184 B4
Cil-y-Coed. Swan 83 D2
Cildaudy Rd. Tondu 163 D4
Cilfedw. Card 187 D4
Cilfynydd Rd. Ponty 124 C3
Cilgerran Cres. Card 188 B4
Cilgerran Pl. Swan 85 E3
Cilgerran Way. Peng 76 C1
Cilhaul Terr. M Ash 72 B1
Cilhaul. Tre 99 D4
Cilmaengwyn. Ystal 22 B1
Cilonen Rd. Pen-cl 81 E1
Cilparc. Porthc 193 D4
Cilsanws La. C-c-y-c 31 F3
Cimla Cl. Neath 87 F3
Cimla Cres. Neath 88 A3
Cimla Rd. Neath 87 F3

Circle The. Pontll 101 F2
Circle The. Tred 35 F3
Circle Way E. Card 189 F3
Circle Way W. Card 189 E2
Citrine Ave. P Tal 113 D1
Citrine Cl. P Tal 113 D1
City Hall Rd. Card 205 D3
City Rd. Card 205 D4
City Rd. Pontcr 143 E1
Claerwen Cl. Abera 50 C1
Claerwen Dr. Card 189 D3
Claerwen. Gell 100 A3
Clan-yr-Afon. Ll'tris 184 A4
Clara St. Yst 94 C2
Clarbeston Rd. Card 188 A2
Clare Ct. Lough 56 C1
Clare Dr. Cowb 198 C1
Clare Gdns. Card 204 C3
Clare Pl. Card 204 C3
Clare Rd. Card 204 C2
Clare Rd. Treo 94 B3
Clare Rd. Ystal 23 D4
Clare St. Card 204 C3
Clare St. Mer T 51 F4
Clare St. Swan 84 B2
Claremont Ave. Card 190 A2
Claremont Cres. Card 190 A2
Claremont Dr. Tre 99 E3
Clarence Ct. Swan 110 B3
Clarence Emb. Card 205 D1
Clarence Pl. Card 205 D1
Clarence Pl. Pontmi 129 F1
Clarence Rd. Card 205 D1
Clarence St. M Ash 72 B1
Clarence St. Swan 110 B3
Clarence St. Yst 95 D2
Clarence Terr. Abera 71 E3
Clarence Terr. Swan 110 B3
Clarendon. Card 189 E3
Clarendon Rd. Card 189 E2
Clarendon Rd. Swan 109 E4
Clarice St. P Tal 113 F1
Clarion Cl. Swan 85 E4
Clarion Ct. Swan 85 E4
Clark St. Treo 94 B3
Clarke St. Card 203 F3
Clarke Way. Swan 85 E3
Clas Ael-y-Bryn. Ynybw 97 E2
Clas Cwm. Ynybw 124 B3
Clas Dyfrig. Card 188 A2
Clas Gabriel. Card 188 A2
Clas Heulog. Card 188 A2
Clas Illtyd. Card 188 B2
Clas Isan. Card 188 B2
Clas Odyn. Card 188 A2
Clas Teilo. Card 188 A2
Clas Ty Wern. Card 188 B3
Clas Ty'n-y-Cae. Card 188 B3
Clas Tynewydd. Card 188 A2
Clas Yorath. Card 188 A3
Clas-Ty-Gelli. Ynybw 124 B3
Clas-y-Bedw. Swan 82 C2
Clas-y-Dderwen. M Ash 72 C2
Clas-y-Deri. Swan 83 D2
Clas-yr-Onnen. Swan 83 D2
Clase Dr. Swan 59 E1
Clase Rd. Swan 85 D4
Clasemont Rd. Swan 59 E1
Claude Rd. Card 205 E4
Claude Rd. Caer 152 A1
Claude Rd. Card 205 E4
Claverton Cl. Ll'tris 169 D3
Claymore Pl. Card 217 D4
Clayton Cres. Ponty 124 B3
Clayton Rd. Hen 36 A2
Clayton St. Swan 84 B2
Clear Water. Card 189 D3
Clearway Ct. Card 188 A2
Clearwell Ct. Rhiwd 155 F2
Cleddau Cl. Card 191 D4
Cledwyn Terr. Aberd 49 F2
Clees La. Ystal 23 D3
Cleeve Dr. Card 188 C4
Clevedon Ave. Sully 226 A2
Clevedon Cl. Swan 109 F4
Clevedon Rd. Card 190 B3
Cleveland Ave. T Mum 137 E2
Clevis Cres. Porthc 193 E4
Clevis Hill. Porthc 193 E4
Clevis La. Porthc 193 E4
Clevisfield Ave. Porthc 193 E4
Cleviston Gdns. Porthc 193 E4
Cleviston Pk. Ll'ge 56 A3
Cliff Hill. Pen 217 D1
Cliff Par. Pen 217 D1
Cliff Pl. Card 204 A3
Cliff Rd. Pen 217 D1
Cliff Rd. Pong 101 F4
Cliff Side. Pen 217 D1
Cliff St. M Ash 72 B1
Cliff St. Pen 217 D3
Cliff Terr. Ponty 149 E4
Clifflands Cl. T Mum 136 C3
Clifford St. Neath 87 E3
Clifton Cres. Abera 71 E4
Clifton Ct. Aberd 49 F3
Clifton Ct. Card 205 E3

Clifton Ct. Swan 84 B3
Clifton Hill. Swan 110 B4
Clifton Mews. Card 205 E3
Clifton Row. Porth 123 D1
Clifton Row. Swan 110 B4
Clifton St. Card 205 E3
Clifton St. Pontmi 155 E4
Clifton St. Treo 94 B3
Clifton Terr. P Tal 114 A1
Clifton Terr. T Mum 137 E2
Clinton Rd. Pen 217 D1
Clipper Rd. Card 205 F2
Clive Cres. Pen 217 D2
Clive Ct. Card 204 A3
Clive La. Card 204 C1
Clive La. Pen 216 C3
Clive Mews. Card 204 A3
Clive Pl. Aberd 49 F2
Clive Pl. Card 205 E4
Clive Pl. Pen 217 D2
Clive Rd. Card 204 A3
Clive Rd. St Ath 221 E3
Clive St. Aber 125 F1
Clive St. Aberd 49 F2
Clive St. Caer 152 A1
Clive St. Card 204 C1
Clive Terr. Ynybw 97 F1
Clodien Ave. Card 188 C1
Cloisters The. Swan 110 A3
Clordir Rd. Pont 58 A4
Clos Afon Llan. Gow 82 B3
Clos Afon Tywi. Peng 101 E3
Clos Allt-y-Gog. Pontar 36 B2
Clos Alun. Ll'ha 166 B2
Clos Alyn. Card 173 F1
Clos Berriew. Card 188 A2
Clos Blean Crymlyn. Swan .. 85 F3
Clos Bron Iestyn. Ponty 124 A1
Clos Bryn Dafyd. Penga 58 B1
Clos Brynafon. Lough 56 C2
Clos Brynderi. Card 188 B4
Clos Brynmellyn. Card 187 D3
Clos Burlais. Swan 84 A1
Clos Cadno. Swan 59 F3
Clos Cae Fainc. Ll'ge 56 A4
Clos Cae Wal. Card 171 E1
Clos Caersalem. Swan 84 B4
Clos Caewal. Penty 170 B1
Clos Caradog. Ch Vil 169 E4
Clos Carolyn. Peng 101 E3
Clos Cas-Bach. Card 191 D3
Clos Cefn Bychan. Penty .. 170 B1
Clos Ceirw. Peng 101 E3
Clos Cemmaes. Card 188 A2
Clos Cilfwnwr. Penga 58 A2
Clos Claerwen. Peng 101 E3
Clos Coedydafarn. Card ... 173 E1
Clos Cornel. Card 188 A2
Clos Corris. Card 188 A2
Clos Creyr. Ch Vil 149 E1
Clos Cromwell. Card 172 B1
Clos Crucywel. Swan 60 A2
Clos Cwm Creunant. Card ... 149 F1
Clos Cwm Du. Card 173 F1
Clos Cwrt y Carne. Lough ... 57 D2
Clos Cynan. Swan 108 C4
Clos Cyncoed. Caer 151 E3
Clos Darran Las. Penty 185 F4
Clos Dyfnaint. Card 191 D3
Clos Ebol. Swan 59 F2
Clos Fach. Card 188 B4
Clos Glan Nant. Caer 152 A1
Clos Glanaber. Card 191 D3
Clos Glanlliw. Pont 58 A3
Clos Glas Llwch. Card 190 C3
Clos Gors Fawr. Lough 57 E3
Clos Gronw. Peng 101 E3
Clos Guto. Caer 152 B2
Clos Gwendraeth. Peng 101 E3
Clos Gwent. Ll'tris 168 B1
Clos Gwern-y-Mor. Card ... 190 C3
Clos Gwernen. Gow 82 B3
Clos Gwlad-yr-Haf. Card ... 191 D3
Clos Gwynedd. Ll'tris 168 C3
Clos Hafodyrynys. Card ... 190 C3
Clos Hafren. Card 191 D3
Clos Healy. Gow 82 A3
Clos Hendre. Card 188 B4
Clos Hereford. Ll'tris 168 B1
Clos Lancaster. Ll'tris 168 B1
Clos Leighton Davies. Gow .. 82 A3
Clos Leland. Ll'tris 168 B1
Clos Llandyfan. Lough 82 B4
Clos Llanfair. Wen 215 D3
Clos Llangefni. Ll'tris 168 C3
Clos Llewellyn. Penty 185 F3
Clos Maerun. Card 190 C3
Clos Maes Isaf. Ll'ge 56 B4
Clos Maes-y-mor. Card 191 D3
Clos Manmoel. Card 190 C3
Clos Marina. Gow 82 A3
Clos Meifod. Card 188 A2
Clos Melin Mynach. Lough .. 82 B4
Clos Menter. Card 188 B1
Clos Min yr Afon. Lough 56 C1
Clos Morgan Gruffydd.
   Aber 150 C4
Clos Morgan Owen. Gow 82 A3

Clos Nant Bran. Swan 61 D1
Clos Nant Ddu. Card 173 F1
Clos Nant Mwlan. Card 173 F1
Clos Nant y Cor. Card 173 F1
Clos Newydd. Card 187 F2
Clos Pantycosyn. Card 190 C3
Clos Pen Pant. Pontar 36 B2
Clos Pen y Banc. Swan 84 B4
Clos Pen y Clawdd. Card .. 190 C3
Clos Penderri. Penga 58 B1
Clos Pengelli. Lough 57 E4
Clos Penglyn. Penco 165 F1
Clos Pentyle. A-wen 40 A1
Clos Powys. Ll'tris 168 C3
Clos Rhandir. Lough 81 F4
Clos Rhymni. Swan 60 A2
Clos Sant Teilo. Ll'fel 59 D1
Clos Smyrna. Bridg 179 E4
Clos Synod. Card 188 A2
Clos Taf. Card 187 F1
Clos Tirfforddi. Penga 58 B1
Clos Ton Mawr. Card 172 B1
Clos Trafle. Gow 82 B3
Clos Trefin. Pontll 101 F2
Clos Tregare. Card 190 C3
Clos Treoda. Card 188 A3
Clos Ty Clyd. Card 187 F2
Clos Ty Mawr. Penga 58 A1
Clos Tygwyn. Cly 60 C4
Clos Tygwyn. Gow 82 A3
Clos Tyla Bach. Card 191 D4
Clos Tyrwen. Bedw 152 B3
Clos Vernon Watkins.
   Lough 57 D2
Clos Waun Wen. Ll'fel 59 D1
Clos William. Card 172 B1
Clos y Berllan. Card 191 D3
Clos y Bryn. Card 172 A1
Clos y Gwadd. Card 172 B2
Clos y Morfa. Lough 56 C2
Clos y Mynydd. Lough 56 C1
Clos y Nant. Card 203 E4
Clos y Nant. Lough 56 C1
Clos y Wern. Card 188 B4
Clos Ynys-y-Grug. Trea 121 F3
Clos yr Aer. Card 188 B4
Clos yr Hafod. Card 188 B4
Clos yr Orsaf. Swan 85 D4
Clos yr Wenallt. Card 172 A1
Clos-Mabon. Card 188 A4
Clos-y- Dyfrsi. Card 172 B2
Clos-y-Betws. Card 190 C3
Clos-y-Blaidd. Card 172 B2
Clos-y-Broch. Card 172 C2
Clos-y-Carlwm. Card 172 B2
Clos-y-Cedr. Caer 152 A3
Clos-y-Ceinach. Card 172 C2
Clos-y-Culfor. Card 190 C3
Clos-y-Cwarra. Card 202 C3
Clos-y-Deri. Porth 192 C4
Clos-y-Draenog. Card 172 C2
Clos-y-Gof. Card 202 C3
Clos-y-Grug. Porth 192 C4
Clos-y-Gweydd. Gow 82 A3
Clos-y-Maerdy. Lough 82 B4
Clos-y-Rhiw. Card 203 D2
Clos-y-Talcen. Bridg 179 E4
Clos-y-waun. Bridg 180 A3
Clos-y-Wern. Bridg 180 A3
Clos-y-Wiwer. Card 172 C2
Clos-yr- Eirin. Bridg 179 D3
Clos-yr-Ardd. Card 188 A4
Clos-yr-Eos. Pyle 176 C3
Clos-yr-Gornant. Card 191 D3
Clos-yr-Onnen. Card 191 D3
Clos-yr-Onnen. Ll' Maj 220 A3
Close The. Abera 50 A1
Close The. Bar 76 A1
Close The. Brynco 163 E2
Close The. Card 188 C4
Close The. Gell 100 C2
Close The. Ll'fel 59 E1
Close The. Lough 57 D1
Close The. Ponty 150 A3
Cloth Hall La. C-c-y-c 32 A3
Clovelly Cres. Card 190 A3
Clovelly Pl. T Mum 136 C3
Clover Gr. Card 187 E1
Clover Rd. Mer T 32 A3
Club La. Ystra 7 F1
Club Row. Yst 95 E2
Club St. Abera 71 D4
Clun Ave. Ll'tris 184 A4
Clun Cres. Ll'tris 184 A4
Clun Terr. Card 189 D1
Clwyd Ave. Abera 50 C1
Clwyd House. Card 189 E1
Clwyd. Pen 217 E3
Clwyd Rd. G-C-G 5 D2
Clwyd Rd. Swan 84 A3
Clwyd Way. St M Ch 221 E4
Clwyd -Wen. Gow 82 A3
Clydach Ave. Reso 44 B1
Clydach Cl. Ponty 124 B3
Clydach Rd. Craig 39 D1
Clydach Rd. Swan 60 B3
Clydach Rd. Tonypa 121 E4
Clydach Rd. Ynybw 97 F1

Clydach St. Card 205 D2
Clydach Terr. Ynybw 97 F1
Clyde Cl. Pontll 101 E2
Clyde St. Card 205 E3
Clydesmuir Rd. Card 205 F4
Clyndu St. Swan 84 C4
Clyne Cl. T Mum 108 C1
Clyne Cres. T Mum 108 C1
Clyne Ct. Swan 109 D3
Clyne Dr. T Mum 109 D1
Clyne Rd. Gell 100 C3
Clyne Terr. Clyne 64 B3
Clyne Valley Cotts. Swan .. 108 C3
Clyne Valley Rd. Swan 108 C3
Clyne View. Swan 108 C3
Clyngwyn Rd. Trehe 68 B2
Clyngwyn Rd. Ystal 23 D4
Clyngwyn Terr. Trehe 68 B2
Clynmaes Pl. Swan 83 F3
Clyro Ct. Swan 85 E2
Clyro Pl. Card 188 A2
Cnap Llwyd Rd. Swan 84 B3
Co-Operative St. Yst 94 C2
Coal Pit La. M-y-Fed 175 D2
Coal Pit La. Marsh 175 D2
Coal Plant Control Rd.
   St Ath 221 F1
Coalbrook Rd. Lough 57 E3
Coaster Pl. Card 205 F2
Coates Pl. Card 190 B4
Coates Rd. Pen 216 C1
Cobden Pl. Cross 129 E2
Cobden St. Abera 71 E3
Cobden St. Cross 129 E2
Cobham Cl. Lough 57 D2
Cobham Dr. Neath 88 B3
Cobol Rd. Card 191 D4
Coburn St. Card 205 D4
Coch-y-Cwm Rd. Swan .. 85 E1
Cockett Rd. Swan 83 E1
Coed Arhyd. Card 202 C2
Coed Arian. Card 188 A2
Coed Bach. Penco 181 E4
Coed Bychan Cres. Ll'ha .. 166 C2
Coed Cae. Caer 152 B2
Coed Cae. N Tre 54 C1
Coed Cae'r Odin. Bridg 179 D3
Coed Celyn Rd. Swan 109 D2
Coed Cochwyn Ave. Card . 172 C1
Coed Edeyrn. Card 189 E2
Coed Gethin. Caer 151 F4
Coed Glas Rd. Card 188 B4
Coed Helyg. Bridg 179 D3
Coed Isaf Rd. Ponty 149 D4
Coed Lan. Pen-cl 81 E1
Coed Leddyn. Caer 151 F3
Coed Main. Caer 152 B2
Coed Marsarnen. Colw 197 D2
Coed Mor. Swan 109 D3
Coed Parc Ct. Bridg 179 F2
Coed Parc. Cwma 114 B3
Coed Pwll. Caer 152 B2
Coed Tymaen. Bridg 179 E3
Coed y Llinos. Caer 151 F2
Coed y Wennol. Caer 151 F2
Coed yr Eos. Caer 151 F2
Coed yr Esgob. Ll'tris 168 B2
Coed yr Ynn. Card 188 B4
Coed-Cae-Ddu Rd. Pontll . 101 E2
Coed-Saeson Cres. Swan . 109 E4
Coed-y-Brain Rd. Ll'bra ... 151 F4
Coed-y-Gores. Card 189 F3
Coed-y-Graig. Penco 181 E4
Coed-y-Lan Rd. Ponty 124 B3
Coed-y-Llyn. Card 187 D4
Coed-y-Llyn. Card 189 D2
Coed-y-Pergwm. G-nea 26 C1
Coed-y-Pia. Ll'bra 127 D3
Coed-y-Rhaidyr. Ystraf 28 A3
Coed-yr-Haf. Gell 100 B1
Coedbach. Pontar 36 B2
Coedcae Bach. Mer T 33 E3
Coedcae. Gell 126 C4
Coedcae Ind Est. Ll'ha 167 F1
Coedcae La. Ll'ha 168 A1
Coedcae Rd. Aber 151 D4
Coedcae Rd. Porth 123 D2
Coedcae Row. Mer T 33 E3
Coedcae St. Card 204 C2
Coedcae Wlk. Peng 101 E4
Coedcae'r Cwrt. Mer T 51 F4
Coeden Dal. Card 189 F4
Coedffaldau. Cwmll 6 B2
Coedglas. Peny 49 D3
Coedlan. Ystra 23 E4
Coedpenmaen Rd. Ponty . 124 B1
Coedriglan Dr. Card 202 C2
Coedwig Pl. Swan 84 A2
Coedwig Villas. Porth 122 C3
Coedybrain Ct. Ll'bra 151 F4
Coedymoeth Rd. Bar 76 A3
Coegnant Cl. Bridg 180 A4
Coegnant Cotts. Maest 117 D4
Coegnant Rd. Maest 117 D3
Coffins Row. Mer T 32 B1
Cog Rd. Sully 226 A3
Cogan Ct. Pen 216 C3

Cogan Hill. Pen 216 C3
Cogan Pill Rd. Pen 216 C4
Cogan Terr. Card 205 D4
Coigne Terr. Barry 225 D3
Coity Cl. Card 191 D4
Coity Rd. Bridg 179 F3
Colbourne Rd. Ll'tris 169 D3
Colbourne Terr. Swan 84 B1
Colbourne Wlk. Card 204 B3
Colbren Sq. G-C-G 5 D2
Colchester Ave. Card 189 F1
Colchester Ct. Card 189 E1
Cold Stores Rd. Card 205 F1
Coldbrook Rd E. Barry 225 E4
Coldbrook Rd W. Barry 225 D4
Coldra Rd. Trehe 68 C2
Coldstream Terr. Card 204 C3
Cole Ct. Caer 152 B2
Coleford Dr. Card 190 C3
Colenso Rd. Rhy 34 C3
Colenso Terr. Tred 35 F3
Coleridge Ave. Pen 216 C2
Coleridge Cl. Bridg 179 E3
Coleridge Cres. Swan 108 C4
Coleridge Gdns. Bedw 153 F3
Coleridge Rd. Card 204 B1
Colhugh Cl. Ll' maj 219 E3
Colhugh Pk. Ll' maj 219 E3
Colhugh St. Ll' maj 219 E3
Colin Way. Card 203 F3
College Cl. Bridg 180 A2
College Cl. Card 188 A2
College Gdns. Ll' maj 219 F3
College Gn. Marg 139 F2
College Rd. Barry 188 A2
College Rd. Card 205 D4
College Row. Ystra 23 F4
College St. Abera 50 A1
College St. Ll' maj 219 F3
College St. Swan 110 B4
College Way Cardiff Rd.
   Ponty 149 F3
Collenna Rd. Tony 147 F3
Colliers Row. N Tre 54 B4
Colliery Rd. Bedw 152 C4
Colliery Rd. Ll'bra 126 C2
Colliery St. Ponty 123 E1
Collingdon Rd. Card 205 D2
Collins Cl. Trehe 68 C1
Collins' Row. Rhy 34 B4
Collins St. Neath 87 E2
Collins Terr. Ponty 149 F3
Collwyn Rd. Pyle 161 D1
Collwyn St. Tony 167 E4
Coltshill Dr. T Mum 136 C3
Colum Dr. Card 204 C4
Colum Pl. Card 204 C4
Colum Rd. Card 204 C4
Colum Terr. Card 204 C4
Columbus Cl. Barry 225 D4
Columbus Wlk. Card 205 D2
Column St. Sully 225 F3
Column St. Treo 94 B3
Colwill Rd. Card 188 A1
Colwinstone Cl. Card 188 A2
Colwinstone St. Card 188 A2
Colwyn Ave. Swan 85 E3
Colwyn House. Card 188 A2
Colwyn Rd. Card 190 B3
Colwyn Rd. Yst 95 D1
Coly Row. Bed 73 F4
Comet St. Card 205 E3
Comfrey Cl. Card 191 D4
Commerce Pl. Abera 71 E4
Commercial Bldgs. Ynys ... 128 A3
Commercial Pl. Abercy 98 A3
Commercial Pl. Pontcr 118 C2
Commercial Rd. Barry 225 D3
Commercial Rd. Bedw 153 E4
Commercial Rd. Bedw 154 A3
Commercial Rd. Marg 139 E3
Commercial Rd. Pontdw ... 40 B4
Commercial Rd. Reso 44 A1
Commercial Rd. Ynys 128 A3
Commercial St. Aber 125 F1
Commercial St. Aberd 50 A1
Commercial St. Bar 76 A1
Commercial St. Bar 76 A2
Commercial St. Bed 74 A4
Commercial St. Fern 96 A4
Commercial St. Gell 100 B4
Commercial St. Gell 100 C1
Commercial St. Glyn 66 C2
Commercial St. Glyn 92 B3
Commercial St. Ll' maj 219 F3
Commercial St. Ll'tris 169 D4
Commercial St. M Ash 72 B2
Commercial St. Maest 117 D2
Commercial St. N Tre 54 C2
Commercial St. Neath 87 F4
Commercial St. Nel 99 F2
Commercial St. Og Va 119 F1
Commercial St. Og Va 119 F3
Commercial St. Peng 101 E4
Commercial St. Pontll 101 F2
Commercial St. Pontmi 155 E4
Commercial St. Pyle 161 E1
Commercial St. Se Si 24 C3

Commercial St. Tred 35 F4
Commercial St. Ynys 128 A3
Commercial St. Ystal 23 D3
Commercial St. Ystra 7 F1
Commercial Terr. Tre 99 D3
Commerical St. Mer T 33 D2
Commin Cl. Mark 76 B4
Commin Rd. Bar 76 A3
Common Rd. Ponty 124 B1
Company St. Reso 44 A1
Compass Rd. Card 205 F1
Compass Row. Pontdw 40 B3
Compass St. Swan 84 B2
Compton Ave. Skew 86 C4
Compton Rd. Skew 87 D4
Compton Rd. Tonypa 121 F3
Compton St. Card 204 C2
Concorde Dr. Tony 147 F3
Conduit Pl. Marg 139 E4
Conduit St. Marg 139 E4
Conifer Ct. Card 203 D4
Coniston Rise. Abera 50 C1
Coniston Wlk. Swan 109 E4
Connaught Cl. Porth 176 C1
Connaught Rd. Card 205 A4
Connaught St. Marg 139 E4
Consort St. M Ash 72 C1
Constant Cl. Card 217 D4
Constant Rd. Marg 139 E3
Constellation St. Card 205 E3
Constitution Hill. Cowb 198 C1
Constitution Hill. Swan 110 A4
Convent St. Swan 84 B1
Convil Rd. Pontcr 118 C3
Conway Cl. D pow 216 B2
Conway Cl. Ponty 124 B3
Conway Cres. Ch Vil 149 F1
Conway Ct. Caer 151 E2
Conway Ct. Peng 76 B1
Conway Ct. Swan 84 A2
Conway Dr. Abera 50 C1
Conway Gr. Mer T 31 F1
Conway House. Card 188 A2
Conway Rd. Card 204 B4
Conway Rd. Swan 84 A2
Conway Rd. Treo 94 B3
Conybeare Rd. Sully 226 A3
Conybeare St. M Ash 72 B1
Cook Rd. Barry 215 D1
Cook Rees Ave. Neath 87 F3
Coombe-Tennant Ave.
  Skew 86 B4
Coombes Rd. Skew 86 C4
Coopers La. Cowb 198 C1
Coopers Yd. Card 205 D2
Copleston Rd. Card 188 A1
Coplestone St. M Ash 72 B1
Copley Cl. Bish 136 A4
Copley Lodge. Bish 136 A4
Copley St. M Ash 72 B2
Copper St. Card 205 E3
Copperfield Dr. Card 172 C1
Coppice The. Ch Vil 150 A1
Coppins The. Card 173 D2
Copse The. C-c-y-c 32 A4
Copthorne Way. Wen 202 C1
Cora St. Barry 225 D3
Corbett Cres. Caer 152 A1
Corbett Rd. Card 204 C4
Corbett Rd. Pen 216 B3
Corbett St. Og Va 119 F1
Corbett St. Trehe 69 D1
Corbetts La. Caer 152 A3
Corinthian Cl. Pen 216 B4
Cormorant Cl. Card 190 C4
Cormorant Way. T Mum 136 C3
Cornborough Lodge. Card . 189 E2
Cornelly Cl. Card 188 A2
Cornelly St. Card 188 A2
Corner House St. Llwy 49 F4
Cornerswell Pl. Pen 216 C2
Cornerswell Rd. Pen 216 C2
Cornfield Cl. Card 172 B1
Cornfield Rise. Bedw 152 B3
Cornflower Cl. Card 173 D2
Cornish Cl. Card 205 D1
Corntown Rd. Ewen 196 B4
Cornwall Pl. T Mum 137 D2
Cornwall Rd. Tonypa 122 A2
Cornwall St. Card 204 C2
Cornwood Cl. Card 187 D1
Coronation Ave. Glyn 91 E2
Coronation Ave. Reso 44 A1
Coronation Bldgs. Ynys ... 128 A2
Coronation Cres. Deri 53 E3
Coronation House. P Tal .. 138 B4
Coronation Pl. Cross 129 E4
Coronation Pl. Mer V 73 E3
Coronation Rd. Card 188 B2
Coronation Rd. Glan 4 B4
Coronation Rd. Maest 142 B3
Coronation Rd. Og Va 146 A4
Coronation Rd. Peng 101 F3
Coronation St. Barry 225 D2
Coronation St. Bedw 153 D3
Coronation St. Bryn 115 F3
Coronation St. Og Va 119 F2
Coronation St. Tondu 163 E2

Coronation St. Tonypa 122 A1
Coronation St. Tred 35 F3
Coronation Terr. Aber 125 F2
Coronation Terr. Maest ... 117 D3
Coronation Terr. Mer T 32 A1
Coronation Terr. Pen 217 D3
Coronation Terr. Ponty 124 C2
Coronation Terr. Porth 122 C3
Coronation Terr. Rhy 34 B3
Coronet Way. Swan 85 D4
Corporation Rd. Card 205 D1
Corporation Rd. Lough 56 C1
Corporation Rd. P Tal 139 D4
Corporation Rd. Swan 83 E2
Corporation St. Mer T 32 C1
Corrwg Ct. Glyn 66 C1
Corwen Cres. Card 188 A2
Cory Cres. P-s-Ely 201 F3
Cory Pl. Card 217 D4
Cory St. Reso 44 A1
Cory St. Swan 109 E3
Cory Way. Barry 225 D2
Coryton Cl. Card 187 F4
Coryton Cres. Card 187 F4
Coryton Dr. Card 187 F4
Coryton Rise. Card 187 F4
Cosheston Rd. Card 187 E1
Cosmeston Dr. Sully 227 D4
Cosmeston St. Card 188 C1
Cosslett Pl. Card 205 D1
Cotswold Ave. Card 173 D2
Cotswold Cl. Swan 83 F2
Cotswold Ct. Card 189 D3
Cotswold Rise. Barry 225 D3
Cottage Cl. Card 172 C1
Cottage Gdns. Bridg 178 C2
Cottesmore Way. Ll'tris ... 168 C1
Cottrell Rd. Card 188 A2
Cottrell Rd. Card 205 E4
Cottrell Sq. Barry 225 D4
Cottrell St. Mer V 73 E3
Council St. Mer T 32 C2
Cound Terr. Marg 139 E4
Coundley Cl. Peng 101 D3
Countess Pl. Pen 216 C2
Countisbury Ave. Card 190 B4
Court Cl. Card 188 B2
Court Cl. Ll' maj 219 F4
Court Colman Flats.
  Og Va 119 F4
Court Colman St. Og Va .. 119 F4
Court Cotts. Card 202 C3
Court Cres. Cowb 199 E2
Court Dr. Cowb 198 C4
Court Gdns. Rhiwd 155 F3
Court House St. Ponty 149 E4
Court Isha. Mer M 178 A1
Court Mews. Barry 225 D3
Court Newton. Barry 225 D3
Court Pl. Tonypa 121 F3
Court Rd. Barry 225 D3
Court Rd. Bridg 179 F2
Court Rd. Caer 151 F2
Court Rd. Card 188 B2
Court Rd. Maest 116 C2
Court St. Mer T 51 F4
Court St. Tonypa 121 F3
Court Terr. Ce Cr 162 B2
Court Terr. Mer T 51 F4
Court The. Bridg 180 C2
Court The. Card 173 D2
Court The. Card 205 E4
Court Wlk. B-coch 87 E4
Courtenay Rd. Barry 225 D3
Courtenay Rd. Card 205 F3
Courtenay St. Swan 84 B1
Courtfield Cl. Rhiwd 155 F3
Courtis Rd. Card 203 D3
Courtland Bldgs. Marg 139 D4
Courtland Pl. Marg 139 D4
Courtland Terr. Mer T 32 C1
Courtlands Way. Swan 83 F3
Courtyard The. Porth 176 C2
Cove Rd. P Tal 113 E1
Coveny St. Card 205 F3
Cowbridge By-Pass. Cowb 198 C2
Cowbridge Rd. Bridg 180 A1
Cowbridge Rd E. Card 204 B3
Cowbridge Rd. Ll'tris 168 A1
Cowbridge Rd. Ll'tris 183 F3
Cowbridge Rd. St Ath 221 E4
Cowbridge Rd. St M Ch ... 221 E4
Cowbridge Rd W. Card 203 D3
Cowbridge Rd. W St D 183 F2
Cowbridge St. Barry 225 D4
Cowell Rd. Glan 4 C3
Cowper Cl. Pen 216 C1
Cowper Pl. Card 205 E4
Cowslip Dr. Pen 216 C3
Coychurch Rd. Bridg 179 F2
Coychurch Rd. Bridg 180 A2
Coychurch Rd. Bridg 180 B2
Coychurch Rd. Bridg 181 D2
Coychurch Rd. Penco 181 D2
Coychurch Rise. Barry 225 D4

Coychurch Road Gdns.
  Bridg 179 F2
Coytrahen Cl. Bridg 180 A3
Crabapple Cl. Mer T 32 B3
Crabtree Rd. Trea 122 A3
Crabtree Wlk. C-c-y-c 32 A3
Crack Hill. Colw 197 D3
Crack Hill. Ewen 196 B4
Craddock St. Card 204 C3
Cradoc Rd. Card 188 B2
Cragside Cl. Card 190 C3
Craig Castell. Card 187 D4
Craig Cres. Porth 122 B1
Craig Isaf. Aberd 49 F1
Craig Nedd. G-nea 45 F4
Craig Rd. Neath 87 E1
Craig Terr. Swan 84 A2
Craig y Bwldan. Swan 108 C4
Craig y Fforest. Ponty 149 F3
Craig yr Allt. Card 172 A1
Craig-fryn Terr. Og Va 119 F4
Craig-y-Fan Terr. Glyn 91 E3
Craig-y-Haul Dr. Marsh ... 175 E2
Craig-y-Hendre. Bed 74 A4
Craig-y-Llyn Cres. Aberd .. 50 B1
Craig-yr-Eos Ave. St B M .. 194 B2
Craig-yr-Eos Rd. St B M ... 194 B1
Craiglas Cres. Peng 101 E4
Craiglee Dr. Card 205 D2
Craigmuir Rd. Card 205 F4
Cramic Way. Marg 139 D4
Cranbrook St. Card 205 D4
Cranfield Ct. Swan 83 F3
Cranleigh Rise. Card 190 A2
Cranmer Ct. Card 204 A4
Cranmer Ct. Swan 83 F3
Cranwell Cl. Card 187 F1
Craven Wlk. Pen 227 D4
Crawford Cl. Ll'tris 169 D3
Crawford Dr. Card 174 A1
Crawford Gn. P Tal 113 E4
Crawford Rd. P Tal 113 E4
Crawley Cl. Card 172 C2
Crawshay Dr. Ll' Maj 220 A4
Crawshay La. Card 205 D2
Crawshay St. Card 205 D2
Crawshay St. Hir 48 B4
Crawshay St. Ynybw 124 A4
Crawshay St. Yst 95 D2
Crediton Rd. Card 190 B3
Creidiol Rd. Swan 110 A4
Crescent Cl. Cowb 198 C1
Crescent Cott. Porth 176 C1
Crescent Ct. Card 189 E3
Crescent Rd. Brynco 163 F2
Crescent Rd. Caer 152 A2
Crescent Rd. G-C-G 5 D1
Crescent Rd. Pontmi 129 E2
Crescent St. Mer V 73 E2
Crescent The. Bedw 152 C3
Crescent The. Bedw 153 F4
Crescent The. Bridg 180 A2
Crescent The. Caer 151 F2
Crescent The. Card 203 E4
Crescent The. Cry 43 D3
Crescent The. Maesy 101 D1
Crescent The. Swan 83 F3
Crescent The. Tondu 163 E2
Crescent. Wen 203 D1
Cresselly Villas. M Ash 72 C2
Cresswell Cl. Card 191 D4
Cresswell Ct. Swan 84 B4
Cressy Rd. Card 189 E1
Crest Acre Cl. T Mum 136 C3
Creswell Rd. Neath 87 F4
Creswell Rd. Swan 84 B4
Cribarth. Coel 9 E4
Cribb's Row. Neath 87 F4
Cribbwr Sq. Pyle 161 E1
Cribyn-Du St. Ynybw 124 A4
Criccieth Cl. Peng 76 B1
Criccieth Ct. D pow 216 B2
Criccieth Gr. Mer T 31 F1
Criccieth Pl. Swan 85 E3
Criccieth Rd. Card 190 B2
Crichton St. Card 205 D2
Crichton St. Trehe 69 D1
Crichton St. Treo 94 B4
Crickhowell Pl. Swan 85 E3
Crickhowell Rd. Card 190 C3
Cricklewood Cl. Bridg 179 E3
Crimson Ave. P Tal 113 D1
Crimson Cl. P Tal 113 D1
Cripps Ave. Tred 35 E3
Crockett Pl. Ponty 124 A1
Crockherbtown La. Card .. 205 D3
Croes Cadarn. Card 173 F1
Croes Heol y Sblot. Ll'Maj . 209 D1
Croes Heol y Sblot. St Dan 209 D1
Croescadarn Cl. Card 190 A4
Croescadarn Rd. Card 173 F1
Croescade Rd. Ch Vil 169 D4
Croeserw Ind Est. Glyn 91 E2
Croesffyrddd. Ystra 23 E3
Croeso Sq. Peng 101 E4
Crofft-y-Genau Rd. Card .. 186 C1

Croffta. D pow 216 A1
Croft Cotts. C-c-y-c 14 C2
Croft Gdns. Sully 226 A3
Croft Goch Gdns. Pyle 161 E1
Croft Goch Rd. Pyle 161 E1
Croft John. Rhoose 222 C3
Croft La. St B M 207 D4
Croft St. Cowb 198 C1
Croft St. N Tre 54 C2
Croft St. Swan 110 B4
Croft Terr. Cowb 198 C1
Croft The. Lough 56 B1
Croft The. N Abb 87 D4
Croft The. Pontcr 143 E2
Croft The. Pontcr 144 A2
Crofta. Card 173 D1
Croftfield Cres. T Mum 136 C3
Crofton Dr. P Tal 113 F3
Crofts St. Card 205 E4
Crofty Ind Est. Pen-cl 80 A2
Crole St. Swan 110 A4
Cromer St. Abera 71 F2
Cromwell Ave. B-coch 62 C1
Cromwell Rd. B-coch 62 C1
Cromwell Rd Bungalows.
  Cross 129 E2
Cromwell Rd. Card 188 B2
Cromwell Rd. Pontmi 129 E2
Cromwell St. Mer T 32 B1
Cromwell St. Swan 110 A4
Cronin Ave. P Tal 138 C4
Crosby Yd. Bridg 179 F3
Cross Acre. T Mum 136 C4
Cross Blanche St. Mer T ... 32 A3
Cross Brook St. Trehe 68 B3
Cross Common Rd. D pow 216 A1
Cross Francis St. Mer T 33 D3
Cross Houlson St. Mer T ... 33 D3
Cross Ifor Terr. Mer T 33 D3
Cross Inn Rd. Ll'tris 168 C2
Cross King St. Mer T 33 D4
Cross Lake St. Fern 95 F3
Cross Mardy St. Mer T 33 D4
Cross Morgan St. Mer T 32 B1
Cross Morland St. Mer T ... 33 D3
Cross Pl. Card 188 C1
Cross Rd. Onll 10 A1
Cross Row. Tonypa 121 F2
Cross Row. Tonypa 121 F2
Cross St. Aber 125 F1
Cross St. Aber 151 D4
Cross St. Abera 50 A1
Cross St. Abercy 98 B3
Cross St. Bar 76 A1
Cross St. Bar 76 A3
Cross St. Barry 225 D3
Cross St. Bedw 152 C3
Cross St. Bridg 179 F2
Cross St. Card 171 E1
Cross St. Deri 75 D4
Cross St. Fern 95 F3
Cross St. Hir 48 B4
Cross St. Lough 57 E1
Cross St. M Ash 97 F4
Cross St. Maest 117 D2
Cross St. Marg 114 A1
Cross St. Mer V 73 E2
Cross St. N Tre 54 C1
Cross St. Pontar 36 B2
Cross St. Pontcr 118 B4
Cross St. Ponty 124 C1
Cross St. Porth 122 C1
Cross St. Porth 122 C2
Cross St. Reso 44 A1
Cross St. Rhy 34 C2
Cross St. Swan 84 B2
Cross St. Tondu 163 E3
Cross St. Tonypa 121 F2
Cross St. Tre 99 D4
Cross St. Tylor 122 C4
Cross St. Yst 95 E1
Cross St. Ystra 8 A2
Cross The. Ll'rh 105 D2
Cross Thomas St. Mer T ... 51 F4
Crossbrook St. Ponty 124 B1
Crossfield Ave. Porth 192 C4
Crossways Rd. Card 203 D3
Crossways St. Barry 225 D3
Crossways St. Ponty 124 B1
Crosswood St. Treo 94 C3
Crowbridge Rd. Ll' maj ... 219 F4
Crown Ave. Treo 94 B4
Crown Cotts. Ystra 7 F1
Crown Est. Pontll 101 E2
Crown Hill. Ch Vil 169 F1
Crown Hill Dr. Ch Vil 169 E1
Crown La. Pontll 101 E2
Crown Rd. Maest 117 E2
Crown Rd. Pyle 161 F2
Crown Row. Aberd 71 F4
Crown Row. Maest 117 D2
Crown St. Marg 114 A1
Crown St. Swan 84 C4
Crown Terr. Treo 94 B4
Crown Way. Card 188 C1
Crown Wlk. Bedw 154 A4

Croyde Ave. Card 190 B3
Crud-yr-Awel. B-coch 62 B1
Crud-yr-Awel. Lough 82 A4
Crumlin Dr. Card 191 D4
Crundale Cres. Card 188 C4
Crwys La. Barry 225 D4
Crwys Pl. Card 205 D4
Crwys Rd. Card 189 D1
Crwys Terr. Swan 84 A3
Cryddan Rd. Neath 87 F3
Crymlyn Parc. Skew 86 B3
Crymlyn Rd. Skew 86 A3
Crymlyn Rd. Swan 86 A3
Crymlyn St. Swan 111 D4
Crymlyn Terr. Swan 85 E1
Crynallt Rd. Neath 88 A3
Crynant Bsns Pk. Cry 43 D4
Crynant Cl. St M Ch 221 E4
Crystal Ave. Card 189 D3
Crystal Glen. Card 188 C3
Crystal Rise. Card 188 C3
Crystal St. Card 188 C3
Crystal Wood Rd. Card 188 C3
Cuckoo St. Pontcr 118 C1
Culfor Rd. Lough 81 F4
Culver Cl. Pen 216 C1
Cumberland St. Card 204 B3
Cumnock Pl. Card 205 E3
Cumnock Terr. Card 205 E3
Cumrae St. Card 205 E3
Cunard Row. Cwma 114 C3
Cunard Terr. Cwma 114 C3
Cunningham Cl. Card 189 D2
Cunningham Cl. Swan 109 E3
Curlew Cl. B-coch 62 C1
Curlew Cl. Card 188 A3
Curlew Cl. Porth 176 B1
Curlew Cres. Ll' Maj 220 B3
Curlew Rd. Porth 176 B1
Curll Ave. Card 188 C2
Curran Emb. Card 205 D2
Curran Rd. Card 205 D2
Curre St. Abera 71 E4
Curry Cl. Swan 108 C4
Curtis St. Neath 87 F3
Curwen Cl. Ton 88 C2
Curwen Terr. Pyle 176 C4
Curwen Terr. Ton 88 C2
Custom House Pl. Pen 217 D3
Customhouse St. Card 205 D2
Cuthbert St. Og Va 119 F1
Cuthbertson St. Neath 87 E2
Cwan-y-garw. Pontcr 118 C2
Cwm Alarch. M Ash 72 A2
Cwm Arian. Swan 60 A1
Cwm Bath Rd. Swan 59 F1
Cwm Chapel Rd. Swan 85 D2
Cwm Clyd. Swan 83 D2
Cwm Cotts. Pontcr 144 A2
Cwm Cuddy Villas. Rhiwd . 155 F2
Cwm Cwddy Dr. Rhiwd ... 155 F1
Cwm Dylan Cl. Rhiwd 155 F1
Cwm Eithin. Nel 99 E2
Cwm Farm La. Swan 109 E2
Cwm Farteg. Bryn 115 F2
Cwm Fedw. Bedw 154 A4
Cwm Ffoes. Ce Cr 162 B1
Cwm Glas. Tred 35 E4
Cwm Gwynlais. Card 187 E4
Cwm Isaac. Rhig 47 E4
Cwm Level Rd. Swan 84 B3
Cwm Nant. Neath 88 C2
Cwm Nant-Llwyd Rd.
  A-wen 41 E2
Cwm Nofydd. Card 188 A4
Cwm Rd. Bar 76 A3
Cwm Rd. Mark 76 C2
Cwm Rd. Swan 84 B1
Cwm Rhos View. Tred 35 F3
Cwm Tawe Rd. Ystra 8 A2
Cwm Terr. Swan 84 B1
Cwm y Dwr. Neath 87 E3
Cwm-clydach Cotts. B-coch 62 B2
Cwm-Hwnt. Rhig 47 D4
Cwm-y-Nant. Pontmi 155 D4
Cwm-yr-Wch. Swan 108 A4
Cwmaman Rd. Abera 71 E3
Cwmamman Rd. Glan 4 B4
Cwmavon Rd. Cwma 114 B2
Cwmbach Rd. Abera 50 B1
Cwmbach Rd. Aberd 71 F4
Cwmbach Rd. B-coch 62 C2
Cwmbach Rd. Swan 83 E2
Cwmcarn Cl. Card 190 C4
Cwmcarn Forest Dr.
  Aberca 129 E4
Cwmcarn Forest Dr. Cross 129 E3
Cwmcerwyn Cotts. Maest . 116 C1
Cwmclais Rd. Cwma 114 B3
Cwmclyd. Ystra 8 A2
Cwmdare St. Card 188 C1
Cwmdonkin Dr. Swan 110 A4
Cwmdonkin Terr. Swan ... 109 F4
Cwmdu Ind Est. Swan 83 F1
Cwmdu La. Maest 117 E2
Cwmdu Rd. Troed 52 A1
Cwmdu Rd. Ystal 22 B1

Cwmdu St. Maest

Cwmdu St. Maest 117 D2
Cwmgarw Rd. Bry 6 A4
Cwmgelli Cl. Swan 84 B3
Cwmgelli Dr. Swan 84 B3
Cwmgelli Rd. Swan 84 B4
Cwmgors Ind Est. G-C-G 5 D2
Cwmlan Terr. Swan 84 B2
Cwmnanthir Terr. G-C-G 5 E3
Cwmneol Pl. Abera 71 D2
Cwmneol St. Abera 71 D2
Cwmrhydyceirw Rd. Swan 59 F2
Cwmsaerbren St. Trehe 68 C1
Cwmsyfiog Rd. N Tre 76 A4
Cwmtawe Business Park.
    Pontdw 40 C3
Cwmynysmintan Rd. Llwy 49 E2
Cwndonkin Cl. Swan 110 A4
Cwrt Alun Lewis. Abera 71 C2
Cwrt Bryn Cynon. Abercy 98 B3
Cwrt Bryn Isaf. Rhig 47 E4
Cwrt Cefn. Card 173 D1
Cwrt Cilmeri. Swan 60 A1
Cwrt Deri. Card 188 A4
Cwrt Eglwys Newydd. Card 188 A3
Cwrt Faenor. Ll'tris 168 C3
Cwrt Fforest. M Ash 72 C1
Cwrt Glanrhyd. Rhig 47 E4
Cwrt Glanwern. Aberd 71 F4
Cwrt Glas. Card 188 C4
Cwrt Glyn. Ynybw 124 A4
Cwrt Gwalia. Og Va 119 F1
Cwrt Hendre. Peng 101 E4
Cwrt Hydd. Swan 59 F3
Cwrt Isaf. Swan 61 D1
Cwrt Llanddewi. Abera 71 E4
Cwrt Llanwonno. M Ash 72 B1
Cwrt Llwyn Fedwen. Swan .. 60 A1
Cwrt Llwynog. Swan 59 F2
Cwrt Pentre Bach. Card 191 D4
Cwrt Pentwyn. Ch Vil 169 D4
Cwrt Sart. Neath 87 E2
Cwrt Twyn-Rhyd. Rhig 47 E4
Cwrt Ty Mawr. Caer 152 B1
Cwrt Ty-Fferm. Ll'bra 151 F4
Cwrt y Garth. Ll'tris 169 D3
Cwrt y Waun. Ll'tris 169 D3
Cwrt y Waun. Peng 101 E4
Cwrt Ynysmeurig. Abercy ... 98 C1
Cwrt-Coch St. Bar 76 A3
Cwrt-Ty-Mynydd. Card 187 D3
Cwrt-ucha Terr. Marg 139 E4
Cwrt-y- Goedwig. Ch Vil ... 169 D4
Cwrt-y-Cadno. Ll' Maj 220 A4
Cwrt-y-Clafdy Rd. Skew 86 C4
Cwrt-y-Clafdy. Skew 86 C4
Cwrt-y-Fedw. Swan 61 D1
Cwrt-y-Felin. Wick 208 B3
Cwrt-y-Vil Rd. Pen 217 D2
Cwrt-y-Vil Road (Lower).
    Pen 217 D1
Cwrt-yr-Ala Ave. Card 203 D2
Cwrt-yr-Ala Rd. Card 203 E1
Cwrt-yr-Iolo. St M Ch 211 E1
Cwt Ty Mawr. Caer 152 A1
Cyd Terr. Clyne 64 A3
Cyfarthfa Rd. Mer T 32 B1
Cyfarthfa St. Card 205 E4
Cyfyng Rd. Ystal 23 D3
Cygnet Cl. Swan 108 C3
Cylla St. Gell 100 B3
Cymdda. Brynco 163 F2
Cymer Rd. Maest 91 D1
Cymmer Rd. Glyn 66 C1
Cymmer Rd. Porth 122 B2
Cymmer St. Card 204 C2
Cymric Cl. Card 203 E3
Cymric Cl. Penny 48 C3
Cyn-Coed Ave. Card 189 E3
Cyn-Coed Cres. Card 189 E3
Cyn-Coed Rd. Card 189 E3
Cynan Cl. Barry 225 D4
Cynan Cl. Ll'tris 169 D3
Cyncoed Ave. Card 189 E3
Cyncoed Cl. Swan 108 B4
Cyncoed Pl. Card 189 E3
Cyncoed Rd. Marg 139 F2
Cyncoed Rise. Card 189 E3
Cyncoed. Ynybw 97 F2
Cynllan Cott. Ll'ha 167 D1
Cynllwyndu Rd. Tylor 96 A2
Cynon Cl. Aberd 49 F2
Cynon Cl. Swan 85 D4
Cynon St. Abera 71 E3
Cynon Terr. Abercy 98 C1
Cynon Terr. M Ash 98 A4
Cynon Terr. Peny 48 C4
Cynon View. Ponty 124 C2
Cyntwell Ave. Card 203 D2
Cyntwell Cres. Card 203 D2
Cyntwell Pl. Card 203 D2
Cynwal Terr. Ystra 6 C1
Cypress Ave. T Mum 136 C4
Cypress Ct. Mer T 32 B3
Cypress Ct. Aberd 49 F2
Cypress Dr. Card 191 D4

Cypress Pl. Card 187 E1
Cypress St. Ponty 150 A3
Cyrch-y-Gwas Rd. Ponty ... 149 F4
Cyres St. Mer T 32 C2
Cyril St. Barry 225 D3
Cyril St. Card 205 E4

D C Griffiths Way. Neath 87 E3
Daffodil Cl. P Tal 113 E2
Dafolog Terr. N Tre 54 C2
Dafydd Pl. Barry 225 D4
Dahlia Cl. P Tal 113 E1
Daisy St. Card 204 A3
Dalcross St. Card 189 D1
Dale Ave. Card 188 B3
Dale Cl. Swan 83 D2
Dale House. Card 188 A2
Dale View. Ce Cr 162 B1
Daleside. Brynco 164 A3
Dalmuir Rd. Card 205 F4
Dalrymple St. P Tal 114 A1
Dalton Cl. P Tal 138 B4
Dalton Rd. P Tal 113 E1
Dalton St. Card 189 D1
Dan Caerlan. Ll'tris 168 C2
Dan y Bryn. Og Va 146 A4
Dan y Coed. Penco 181 E4
Dan y Cribyn. Ynybw 124 A4
Dan y Graig. Card 187 F4
Dan y Graig. Pontmi 129 F1
Dan y Graig Rd. Pontmi ... 129 F1
Dan y Graig. Rhy 54 A4
Dan yr Allt. Gow 82 A3
Dan yr Heol. Og Va 144 B2
Dan-y-Bryn Ave. Card 187 D3
Dan-y-bryn. Ce Cr 162 B2
Dan-y-Bryn Cl. Card 187 D3
Dan-y-Bryn. Maest 91 D1
Dan-y-Bryn. Og Va 119 F3
Dan-y-Bryn Rd. Marg 139 E4
Dan-y-Bryn. Tonna 63 E2
Dan-y-bryn Villas. Ponty .. 149 E4
Dan-y-Coed. C-c-y-c 14 C2
Dan-y-Coed Cl. Card 189 D3
Dan-y-Coed. Cwma 114 C3
Dan-y-Coed. Gell 100 C2
Dan-y-Coed. M Ash 72 C2
Dan-y-Coed. Og Va 144 C1
Dan-y-Coed Rd. Card 189 D3
Dan-y-Coed Rd. Swan 86 A4
Dan-y-Coed Rise. Bridg ... 180 A3
Dan-y-Coed Rise. Card 189 D3
Dan-y-coed. Ton 89 D3
Dan-y-coed. Tondu 163 E2
Dan-y-Coedcae Rd. Ponty . 149 D4
Dan-y-Craig Rd. Neath 87 F3
Dan-y-Darren. Ll'bra 127 D3
Dan-y-Deri La. C-c-y-c 32 A2
Dan-y-Felin. Ll'tris 168 B2
Dan-y-fron. Ystra 8 C3
Dan-y-Gaer Rd. Gell 100 B3
Dan-y-Graig. Aber 151 D4
Dan-y-Graig Rd. N Abb 87 D4
Dan-y-graig Terr. B-coch ... 63 D2
Dan-y-Lan. Tondu 163 E2
Dan-y-Parc. Swan 59 F1
Dan-y-Rhiw. Abera 71 D2
Dan-y-Allt Cl. Ponty 150 A3
Dan-yr-Heol. Card 189 D3
Dan-yr-Heol. Peny 49 D3
Dana Dr. Swan 109 E3
Dane St. Mer T 32 B1
Dane Terr. Mer T 32 B1
Danescourt Way. Card 187 F2
Daniel Hopkin Cl. Ll' maj . 219 F1
Daniel St. Abera 50 C1
Daniel St. Barry 225 D4
Daniel St. Card 189 D1
Daniell Cl. Sully 226 A3
Dantwyn Rd. Pontar 36 C3
Danybryn. Ll'tris 183 F3
Danybryn Rd. Lough 57 D1
Danycoed Terr. Tonypa 121 E4
Danycoed. Yst 95 F1
Danyderi St. Abera 71 E3
Danyderi Terr. Mer V 73 E3
Danyffynon. Marg 114 B1
Danygraig Ave. Porthc 193 F4
Danygraig. Bedw 153 D3
Danygraig Bungalows.
    Pontmi 129 F1
Danygraig. Cly 60 B4
Danygraig Cres. Ll'tris .. 168 B2
Danygraig Dr. Ll'tris 168 B2
Danygraig. Og Va 144 C3
Danygraig. P Tal 114 A1
Danygraig Rd. Ll'ha 167 D2
Danygraig Rd. Pontdw 40 B1
Danygraig Rd. Swan 111 D4
Danygraig. Ponty 149 D4
Danygraig Terr. Ll'ha 167 D2
Danygraig Terr. Tonypa .. 121 E4
Danygraig Terr. Tylor 122 C4
Danygraig. Yst 95 F1
Danygraig. Ystra 7 D1
Danylan Rd. Ponty 124 C1
Danyparc. Mer T 32 C1

Danywern Terr. Yst 95 E2
Daphne Cl. B-coch 62 C1
Daphne Rd. B-coch 62 C1
Darby Rd. Card 206 A2
Dare Ct. Aberd 49 E2
Dare Rd. Aberd 49 E2
Daren-Ddu Rd. Ponty 124 B2
Daren Cl. Maest 117 E1
Darran Pk. N Abb 61 F1
Darran Pk. Ponty 124 B2
Darran Rd. M Ash 72 B1
Darran Rd. Pontmi 129 F2
Darran St. Card 204 C4
Darran Terr. Fern 95 F3
Darren Bungalows. Pontcr . 118 C3
Darren Cl. Caer 152 B3
Darren Cl. Swan 198 B1
Darren Cl. N Abb 61 F1
Darren Ct. Ponty 124 B3
Darren Hill. Cowb 198 B1
Darren Las. Mer V 73 E1
Darren Rd. Neath 87 E2
Darren Rd. Ystal 23 D3
Darren Terr. Pontdw 40 A2
Darren View. Maest 142 B4
Darren View. Mer T 32 C1
Darren Wen. P Tal 113 F4
Dartford Pl. Swan 85 D1
Dartford Rd. Swan 85 D2
Darwin Rd. P Tal 138 C4
David Davies Rd. Barry ... 225 D2
David Price St. Abera 50 A1
David St. Aberd 49 E2
David St. Aberd 49 F2
David St. Barry 225 E4
David St. Bridg 180 C2
David St. Mer T 32 B1
David St. Peng 101 F3
David St. Pontcr 118 C4
David St. Swan 84 A1
David St. Tonypa 121 E4
David St. Tonypa 122 A2
David St. Trehe 68 B2
David St. Trehe 68 C1
David St. Treo 94 A2
David St. Wick 208 B3
David Williams Terr. Swan 111 E4
David's Ct. Ll'tris 184 A4
David's Terr. Swan 84 C4
Davies Ave. Bridg 179 F4
Davies Ave. Porth 176 C1
Davies Cl. Trea 122 B3
Davies Dr. Caer 151 F3
Davies Pl. Card 203 F4
Davies Pl. Tylor 122 C3
Davies Rd. Neath 87 F4
Davies Rd. Pontdw 40 C3
Davies Row. Hir 48 B4
Davies Row. Swan 84 B3
Davies St. Barry 225 D3
Davies St. Coel 9 D3
Davies St. Gell 100 C1
Davies St. Mer T 33 D1
Davies St. Peng 101 E4
Davies St. Porth 122 C2
Davies St. Swan 85 D4
Davies St. Tonypa 121 E3
Davies Terr. Maest 116 C3
Daviot Ct. Card 189 D1
Daviot St. Card 189 D1
Davis Ave. Brynco 164 A3
Davis St. Card 205 E3
Davis St. Swan 84 C3
Davis's Terr. Card 188 A3
Davnic Cl. Barry 225 D3
Dawlish Cl. T Mum 136 C3
Dderi Rd. Cwmll 6 B1
Ddol Rd. Swan 108 A4
De Berclos. Porth 192 C4
De Braose Cl. Card 187 E2
De Breos Dr. Porth 192 C4
De Burgh Pl. Card 204 C3
De Burgh St. Card 204 C3
De Clare Ct. Porth 192 C4
De Clare Ct. Ll' Maj 220 A3
De Croche Pl. Card 204 C3
De Granville Cl. Porth 192 C4
De La Beche Terr. Swan 59 F1
De Londres Cl. Porth 192 C4
De Turberville Cl. Porth .. 192 C4
De Winton St. Tonypa 121 F3
De Winton Terr. Ll'bra 126 C1
De Winton Terr. Trea 121 F4
De-Barri St. Ch Vil 149 F2
De-Breos St. Swan 109 F2
De-La Beche St. Swan 110 B4
De-La-Beche Rd. Swan 109 E3
Dean St. Abera 50 A1
Dean's Ct. Card 188 A1
Deans Cl. Card 204 A4
Dee Pl. Swan 60 A2
Deeley Rd. Ystal 23 D3
Deemuir Rd. Card 205 F4
Deepdale Cl. Card 189 D1
Deepdene Cl. Card 202 C3

Deepfield Cl. Card 202 C3
Deepslade Cl. South 135 D2
Deepwood Cl. Card 202 C3
Deere Cl. Card 203 D2
Deere Pl. Card 203 D2
Deere Rd. Card 203 D2
Deganwy Cl. Card 172 C1
Dehewydd Isaf. Ch Vil 169 E4
Dehewydd La. Ch Vil 169 E4
Deighton Cl. Tred 35 E4
Delfan. Ll'fel 59 E1
Delfan. Swan 85 F3
Delffordd. A-wen 41 D1
Delfryn. Llwy 49 F3
Delhi St. Swan 110 C4
Dell The. Bridg 178 C2
Dell The. Brynco 164 A2
Dell The. Card 190 B4
Dell The. Ch Vil 149 F2
Dell The. P Tal 113 E3
Dell The. Pont 57 F3
Dell The. Swan 108 C3
Delta St. Card 204 B3
Delwen Terr. Trehe 68 A1
Denbigh Cl. Ch Vil 149 F1
Denbigh Cl. Peng 76 C1
Denbigh Cres. Swan 60 A3
Denbigh Ct. Caer 151 E2
Denbigh Cl. Card 188 A3
Denbigh Ct. Pen 216 C1
Denbigh Dr. Ll' Maj 220 B3
Denbigh Rd. D pow 216 B2
Denbigh St. Card 204 B4
Denison Way. Card 202 C3
Denleigh Cl. Bar 75 F2
Dennis Pl. Brynco 164 A3
Denton Rd. Card 204 B3
Denver Rd. Swan 83 D3
Denys Cl. D pow 216 A2
Depot Rd. Abera 50 A1
Depot Rd. Cwma 114 C3
Deri Ave. Penco 181 E4
Deri Cl. Card 189 F1
Deri Ct. Penco 165 E1
Deri Rd. Card 189 E1
Deri St. Tylor 96 A1
Derllwyn Cl. Tondu 163 E3
Derllwyn Rd. Tondu 163 E3
Derlwyn. Peny 49 D3
Derlwyn St. N Tre 54 C2
Derlwyn. Swan 108 B4
Derw Rd. Pontdw 40 B2
Derwen Aur. Tylor 122 C3
Derwen Cl. Bridg 179 F4
Derwen Cl. Gell 100 C2
Derwen Cl. Peng 101 F4
Derwen Cl. Swan 82 B2
Derwen Ct. Card 189 E4
Derwen Deg. Pontdw 40 B3
Derwen Fawr Rd. Swan 109 D2
Derwen Rd. Bridg 179 F2
Derwen Rd. Card 189 E4
Derwen Rd. Ll'tris 184 A4
Derwen Rd. Pontdw 40 B2
Derwen Rd. Yst 95 E2
Derwen Rd. Ystra 7 F1
Derwendeg Ave. Gell 100 C2
Derwendeg Ave. Peng 101 E4
Derwendeg Ave. Ponty 124 B3
Derwent Cl. Card 172 C1
Derwent Dr. Abera 50 C1
Derwydd Ave. G-C-G 5 D2
Derwydd Rd. Tonypa 121 F3
Despenser Ave. Ll'tris ... 168 B1
Despenser Gdns. Card 204 C3
Despenser Pl. Card 204 C3
Despenser Rd. Sully 226 A3
Despenser St. Card 204 C3
Dessmuir Rd. Card 205 F4
Devon Pl. Card 204 C2
Devon Pl. T Mum 137 D2
Devon St. Card 204 C2
Devon Terr. Swan 110 A4
Devon View. Swan 109 D4
Devonshire Dr. Hir 48 B4
Devonshire Pl. Marg 139 E4
Dew Cres. Card 203 F2
Dew Rd. P Tal 113 E1
Dewi Ct. Card 204 A4
Dewi St. Ponty 124 C2
Dewi Terr. Swan 84 A1
Dewsbury Ct. Swan 110 B3
Diagonal Rd. St Ath 221 F1
Diamond St. Card 205 E3
Diana La. Card 189 D1
Diana St. Card 189 D1
Diana St. Troed 73 D4
Dickens Ave. Card 190 A4
Dickens Ave. P Tal 138 C4
Dickens Ct. Bedw 153 D4
Dickinson Cl. P Tal 113 D1
Dicksdale. T Mum 137 D2
Digby Cl. Card 187 F1
Digby La. Card 189 D1
Digby Rd. Neath 88 A4
Digby St. Barry 225 D3
Dillington Terr. M Ash 97 F4
Dillwyn Rd. Swan 109 E3

Dillwyn St. Swan 110 B3
Dilwyn Ave. Gell 100 C1
Dilwyn Gdns. Bridg 179 F1
Dilwyn Rd. Penga 57 F1
Dilwyn St. M Ash 97 F4
Dilys St. Trehe 68 B1
Dimbath Ave. Og Va 145 D2
Dimbath La. Og Va 145 D2
Dimlands Rd. Ll' maj 219 E3
Dinam Cl. Og Va 119 F3
Dinam Park Ave. Yst 94 C3
Dinam Rd. Swan 85 E1
Dinam St. Og Va 119 F3
Dinas Baglan Rd. P Tal ... 113 C2
Dinas Iasf Cotts. Tonypa . 122 A1
Dinas Isaf Ind Est. Tony . 122 A1
Dinas Pl. Card 204 C2
Dinas Rd. Pen 216 C1
Dinas Rd. Porth 122 A4
Dinas Rd. Tonypa 122 A3
Dinas St. Card 204 C2
Dinas St. Swan 84 C3
Dinas Terr. Ystraf 27 F1
Dingle La. Pen 217 D2
Dingle Rd. Pen 217 D1
Distillery Rd La. Ponty ... 123 F1
District St. Mer T 32 C2
Ditchling Ct. Pen 217 D1
Dixon St. Mer T 32 B1
Dixon's Pl. Pontmi 129 F1
Dobbins Rd. Barry 225 E4
Dochdwy Rd. Pen 216 C3
Dock Rd. Marg 139 D4
Dock St. Lough 81 E4
Dock St. Pen 216 C3
Dock St. Porth 192 C3
Dock View Rd. Barry 225 D3
Doddridge Way. Card 190 C2
Dodington Pl. Ponty 124 C1
Dogfield St. Card 189 D1
Dogo St. Card 204 B4
Dol Afon. Penco 181 F4
Dol Fran. Caer 152 B2
Dol Las. P Tal 113 F4
Dol y Paun. Caer 151 F1
Dol yr Eos. Caer 152 B2
Dol-Wen. Penco 165 F1
Dol-y-Coed. Swan 108 A4
Dol-y-Felin. Penty 185 E4
Dol-y-Felin St. Caer 152 A2
Dolau Ifan Ddu Terr. Og Va 144 C1
Dolawel. Bry 6 C3
Dolcoed. Llwy 49 F3
Dolcoed Terr. Tonna 63 E1
Dolfain. Ystra 8 A1
Dolgaer Houses. C-c-y-c ... 14 C2
Dolgellau Ave. Ch Vil 149 F1
Dolgoch Cl. Card 190 B3
Dolgoy Cl. T Mum 137 D4
Dolgwilym St. Tylor 96 B1
Dolgynog. Hir 29 D3
Dolphin Pl. P Tal 113 E2
Dolwen Rd. Card 188 A1
Dolwyddelan Cl. Peng 76 C1
Dombey Cl. Card 172 C1
Dominion Way. Card 205 F4
Donald St. Card 189 D1
Donald St. Nel 99 F2
Donald St. Troed 51 F2
Doniford Cl. Sully 226 A3
Donnen St. Marg 139 E3
Donnington Rd. Barry 225 F3
Dorchester Ave. Card 189 E1
Dorchester Ct. Card 189 E1
Dorchester Mansions. Card 187 F3
Dorothy St. Ponty 124 B1
Dorset St. Card 204 C2
Douglas Cl. Card 187 F1
Dove Rd. Swan 83 F4
Dovedale Cl. Card 189 D2
Dovedale St. Barry 225 D3
Dover St. St M Ash 72 B1
Dover St. Yst 95 D1
Dovey Cl. Card 190 B3
Dowlais Rd. Card 205 E2
Dowlais St. Aberd 49 F1
Dowlais Stables. Mer T 33 D2
Dowland Rd. Pen 216 C1
Dowlands Way. Card 190 A1
Down Leaze. Swan 83 E1
Down St. Cly 60 C4
Downfield Cl. Pen 216 C3
Downs Cl. Swan 83 F2
Downs Ct. Barry 215 D1
Downs The. Ll'rh 132 C4
Downs View Cl. Cowb 199 D2
Downs View. Cowb 199 D2
Downton Grange. Card 190 A1
Downton Rd. Card 190 A1
Downton Rise. Card 190 A1
Doyle Ave. Card 203 F4
Doyle Ct. Card 203 F4
Dragon Auto Cen. Swan 85 D2
Dragonfly Dr. Rhoose 223 D3
Drake Cl. St Ath 221 E4
Drake Wlk. Card 205 D2
Drangway. Ll' maj 219 F3

Dranllwyn Cl. Bedw 153 F4
Dranllwyn La. Bedw 153 F4
Drawlings Cl. Card 190 B4
Dring St. Swan 110 C4
Drive The. Bar 76 A1
Drive The. Card 203 E4
Drive The. D pow 216 B2
Drive The. Ll'tris 184 B3
Drive The. N Abb 87 D4
Drive The. Pontdw 40 B2
Drive The. South 135 D2
Drope Rd. Card 202 C2
Drope Terr. Wen 202 C2
Dros Col. Ll'hry 183 D3
Dros y Mor. Pen 217 D1
Druids Cl. T Mum 137 D3
Druids Cl. Treo 94 B3
Druids Gn. Cowb 198 C1
Druidstone Rd. Card 174 C1
Druidstone Rd. M-y-Fed 175 D2
Druidstone Way. Penga 58 A1
Drumau Cl. Skew 86 C4
Drumau Pk. Skew 86 C4
Drumau Rd. Skew 86 B4
Drumau Rd. Swan 86 B4
Drury Cl. Card 172 C1
Drusyln Rd. T Mum 136 C4
Drybrook Cl. Card 190 C3
Dryburgh Ave. Card 188 B3
Dryden Cl. Card 190 A4
Dryden Rd. Pen 216 C2
Drylla. D pow 216 A1
Drysgol Rd. Card 187 D3
Dryslwyn Cl. Penga 58 A1
Dudley St. Card 205 D1
Dudley St. Card 205 D1
Dudley St. Neath 87 F4
Duffryn Ave. Card 189 D3
Duffryn Cl. Bridg 181 D2
Duffryn Cl. Card 189 D3
Duffryn Cl. Gell 100 B4
Duffryn Cl. Tony 147 D3
Duffryn Cres. Ll'ha 166 C1
Duffryn House. D pow 216 B2
Duffryn La. St Nic 214 A4
Duffryn Rd. Card 189 C3
Duffryn Rd. Lough 57 D1
Duffryn Rd. Ynys 128 B2
Duffryn St. Card 205 D3
Duffryn St. Glyn 90 B2
Duffryn St. Rhy 53 F4
Duffryn Terr. Ch Vil 169 F4
Duffryn Terr. Ynys 128 C2
Duffryn View. Rhy 34 C2
Duffrynmadog. Maest 116 C3
Duffynmadog. Maest 116 C3
Dugdale Wlk. Card 204 B3
Duke St. Abera 50 A1
Duke St. Card 205 D3
Duke St. Maest 117 E1
Duke St. Marg 139 E3
Duke St. Ponty 149 F4
Duke St. Swan 110 A3
Duke St. Tred 35 F3
Duke Street Arc. Card 205 D3
Dukefield. Pen-cl 107 F4
Dukestown Rd. Tred 35 F4
Dulais Cl. B-coch 63 E2
Dulais Dr. B-coch 63 E2
Dulais Fach Rd. Tonna 63 E2
Dulais Gdns. Onll 9 E1
Dulais Gr. Swan 109 D3
Dulais Rd. Pontar 36 B2
Dulais Rd. Se Si 24 C2
Dulverton Ave. Card 190 B4
Dulverton Dr. Sully 226 A3
Dulwich Gdns. Card 204 B4
Dumballs Rd. Card 205 D2
Dumfries La. Card 205 D3
Dumfries Pl. Card 205 D3
Dumfries Pl. Ystal 23 F4
Dumfries St. Abera 50 A1
Dumfries St. Trehe 68 C1
Dumfries St. Treo 94 B4
Dummer Cl. Card 190 C4
Duncan Cl. Card 190 B3
Dunkery Cl. Card 190 A3
Dunlin Cl. Porth 192 B4
Dunns Cl. T Mum 137 D3
Dunns La. T Mum 137 D3
Dunns The. T Mum 137 D3
Dunraven Arc. Tonypa 121 F3
Dunraven Cl. D pow 216 B2
Dunraven Cl. Pen-cl 80 C2
Dunraven Cres. Ll'tris 168 A1
Dunraven Ct. Caer 151 F2
Dunraven Ct. Card 189 E1
Dunraven Ct. Porth 192 C4
Dunraven Pl. Bridg 179 F2
Dunraven Pl. Og Va 119 F2
Dunraven Pl. Og Va 146 A4
Dunraven Rd. Card 204 B2
Dunraven Rd. Swan 109 D4

Dunraven St. Blae 45 E4
Dunraven St. Bridg 180 A1
Dunraven St. Glyn 66 C2
Dunraven St. P Tal 114 A1
Dunraven St. Tondu 163 E2
Dunraven St. Tonypa 121 F3
Dunraven St. Trehe 68 C1
Dunraven Terr. Treo 94 B4
Dunsmuir Rd. Card 205 F3
Dunster Cl. T Mum 136 C3
Dunster Rd. Card 190 B4
Dunvant Ave. Clyne 64 C4
Dunvant Pl. Swan 110 B3
Dunvant Rd. Pen-cl 81 F1
Dunvant Rd. Swan 108 C4
Dunvant Sq. Swan 108 B4
Duport Cl. P Tal 113 E4
Dupre Rd. Swan 110 C4
Duraven Cotts. Bridg 179 F2
Durell St. Ll' maj 219 F3
Durham St. Mer T 32 A1
Durham St. Card 204 C2
Durleigh Cl. Card 190 B4
Durlston Cl. Card 187 F2
Duxford Cl. Card 187 E1
Dwr-y-Felin Rd. B-coch 62 B1
Dwyfor Rd. Glyn 91 E2
Dyfan Rd. Barry 225 D4
Dyfatty St. Swan 110 B4
Dyfed Ave. Swan 110 A4
Dyfed Cl. Swan 109 F4
Dyfed Dr. Caer 151 F3
Dyfed House. Card 189 E1
Dyfed. Pen 217 D3
Dyfed Rd. Neath 87 F4
Dyffryn Ave. Ponty 150 A3
Dyffryn Bach Terr. Ch Vil .. 169 F4
Dyffryn Cl. St Nic 202 A1
Dyffryn Cl. Swan 85 D4
Dyffryn Cres. P-s-Ely 201 F2
Dyffryn Cres. Ponty 150 A3
Dyffryn Gdns. Ponty 150 A3
Dyffryn. N Abb 62 A2
Dyffryn Pl. Maest 117 D4
Dyffryn Rd. A-wen 40 C2
Dyffryn Rd. Aberd 71 F4
Dyffryn Rd. B-coch 62 B2
Dyffryn Rd. M Ash 72 B2
Dyffryn Rd. Maest 91 D1
Dyffryn Rd. Marg 139 E4
Dyffryn Rd. Ponty 150 A3
Dyffryn Rd. Troed 52 A2
Dyffryn Row. Maest 116 C3
Dyffryn St. Abera 71 E3
Dyffryn St. Bar 76 A2
Dyffryn St. Gell 100 C2
Dyffryn St. M Ash 72 B2
Dyffryn Terr. N Tre 54 C2
Dyffryn Terr. Swan 60 A1
Dyffryn Terr. Tony 147 D3
Dyffryn View. B-coch 62 B3
Dyffryn-Aur Rd. Swan 85 F3
Dyfnallt Rd. Barry 225 D4
Dyfodwg St. Treo 94 B3
Dyfrig Cl. Card 203 F3
Dyfrig Cl. Ll' Maj 220 A4
Dyfrig Rd. Card 203 F3
Dyfrig St. Barry 225 D1
Dyfrig St. Card 204 C4
Dyke St. Mer T 51 F4
Dylan Ave. Ll'tris 169 D3
Dylan Ave. Peng 101 E4
Dylan Cl. Pen 216 C3
Dylan Cres. Barry 225 D4
Dylan Cres. P Tal 138 C4
Dylan Dr. Caer 152 A3
Dylan Pl. Card 205 E4
Dylan Rd. Swan 108 C4
Dyllas Ct. Porth 122 C1
Dyllas Rd. Porth 122 C1
Dynea Rd. Ponty 150 A2
Dynevor Ave. B-coch 62 B1
Dynevor Cl. Skew 86 C4
Dynevor Gr. Mer T 31 F1
Dynevor Pl. Swan 110 B4
Dynevor Rd. Card 189 E2
Dynevor Rd. Glan 4 B3
Dynevor Rd. Skew 86 C4
Dynevor Rd. Deri 53 E4
Dynevor St. Mer T 32 B1
Dynevor Terr. Nel 99 F2
Dynevor Terr. Pontdw 40 C3
Dynevor Way. Swan 86 B4
Dyrus Rd. Swan 84 C3
Dyserth Rd. Pen 216 C2

E F I Ind Est. Mer T 32 A2
Eagle La. Cowb 198 C1
Eagle Rd. Li' Maj 220 B3
Eagle St. Marg 139 D4
Eagle View. Bridg 180 B3
Eagles Pl. Swan 83 F3
Eaglesbush Cl. Neath 87 E2
Eagleswell Rd. Ll' Maj 220 A3
Earl La. Card 204 C1

Earl Rd. Marg 139 F3
Earl Rd. Pen 216 C2
Earl St. Card 204 C1
Earl St. Swan 84 B1
Earl St. Tred 35 E4
Earl's Court Rd. Card 189 E1
Earle Pl. Card 204 B3
Earls Court Pl. Card 189 E1
Earlswood Cl. G-nea 26 C1
Earlswood Ct. Card 189 D1
Earlswood Rd. Card 188 C4
East Ave. Aberd 49 F1
East Ave. Bedw 152 C3
East Ave. Caer 151 F2
East Ave. Ce Cr 162 A1
East Ave. Pyle 161 E1
East Bank Way. Swan 110 C4
East Bay Cl. Card 205 E3
East Burrows Rd. Swan 110 C3
East Canal Wharf. Card 205 D2
East Cliff. South 135 D2
East Crossways. Pontdw ... 40 C3
East Dr. St Don 218 C3
East Gr. Card 205 E3
East Grove La. Card 205 E3
East Moors Rd. Card 205 E2
East Rd. Barry 225 F3
East Rd. Gell 100 B3
East Rd. Marg 139 E2
East Rd. Tylor 96 B2
East Rise. Card 189 D4
East St. Bridg 180 C2
East St. Ll' maj 219 F3
East St. Marg 139 E4
East St. Mer T 33 D2
East St. Ponty 124 B1
East St. Tondu 163 E2
East St. Tonypa 121 E3
East St. Tylor 96 B2
East Tyndall St. Card 205 E3
East View. Caer 152 A1
East View. Llys 209 D4
East View. N Tre 55 D1
Eastbourne Ct. Barry 225 E4
Eastbourne Gr. Swan 109 E4
Eastbrook Cl. D pow 216 A2
Easterfield Dr. South 135 D2
Easterly Cl. Bridg 180 B3
Eastern Ave. Card 189 F1
Eastern Ave. Glyn 91 E2
Eastern Cl. Card 190 B4
Eastern Prom. Porthc 193 D3
Eastfield Ct. Ll'tris 168 C1
Eastgate. Cowb 198 C1
Eastland Cl. T Mum 136 C4
Eastland Pl. Neath 87 F3
Eastland Rd. Neath 87 F4
Eastlands Pk. Bish 136 A4
Eastmoor Park Cres.
  T Mum 136 C4
Eastview Terr. Bar 76 A2
Eaton Cres. Swan 110 A3
Eaton Rd. Swan 84 B2
Ebbw Cl. St M Ch 221 E4
Ebbw St. Pontmi 129 F1
Ebbw Vale Row. Cwma 114 C3
Ebenezer Cl. Bed 99 E4
Ebenezer Rd. Tonypa 121 F3
Ebenezer St. Aberd 49 F2
Ebenezer St. Ponty 149 F3
Ebenezer St. Swan 110 B4
Ebenezer Terr. Og Va 144 C2
Ebwy Ct. Card 203 E2
Eckley Rd. Sully 226 A3
Eclipse St. Card 205 E3
Eddystone Cl. Card 204 C2
Eden Ave. Swan 109 F4
Edgar St. Mer T 32 C2
Edgehill Ave. Card 172 B1
Edgehill Cl. P Tal 113 E4
Edgehill Ct. Card 172 B1
Edgehill. Peng 101 E4
Edgemoor Cl. U Kill 108 A3
Edgemoor Dr. U Kill 108 A3
Edgeware Rd. Swan 109 F4
Edinburgh Ct. Card 204 C3
Edington Ave. Card 188 C1
Edison Cres. Cly 39 F1
Edith Rd. D pow 216 A2
Edmond's Ct. Card 189 D1
Edmondes St. Tylor 96 B2
Edmondstown Rd. Porth ... 122 B1
Edmund Pl. Barry 225 D4
Edmund St. Porth 123 D2
Edmund St. Rhy 53 F4
Edward Cl. Mer T 32 C1
Edward Clarke Cl. Card 187 F1
Edward Nicholl Ct. Card 189 E1
Edward St. A-wen 41 D3
Edward St. Aberca 129 D4
Edward St. Abercy 98 C1
Edward St. Aberd 49 F2
Edward St. Barry 225 D4
Edward St. Bridg 179 F2
Edward St. Card 205 D3
Edward St. Fern 70 A1
Edward St. G-nea 27 D1
Edward St. Gell 126 C4

Edward St. Marg 114 A1
Edward St. Mer T 33 D4
Edward St. Neath 87 F3
Edward St. Peng 101 D3
Edward St. Porth 122 C2
Edward St. Tre 99 D3
Edward Stephens Terr.
  Troed 73 E4
Edward Terr. Aber 151 D4
Edward Terr. Tred 35 F3
Edward Thomas Cl. Gar P . 153 D2
Edwards St. Blae 45 E4
Edwards St. M Ash 72 C1
Edwards St. Trea 121 F3
Edwards Terr. Bed 74 A4
Edwards Terr. Reso 43 F1
Edwards Terr. Tre 99 D3
Edwardsville. Aberca 129 D4
Edwardsville. Tre 98 C3
Egerton St. Card 204 B3
Egham St. Card 204 B3
Eglwys Ave. Ponty 150 A3
Eglwys Fan. Rhy 34 C3
Eglwysian Rd. Aber 150 C3
Eglwysilan Rd. Ponty 150 B4
Egremont Rd. Card 189 D1
Egypt St. Ponty 149 E4
Egypt St. Trea 122 A3
Eiddwen Rd. Swan 84 A2
Eider Cl. Card 190 C4
Eiddon Cres. Barry 225 D4
Eifion Cl. Barry 225 D4
Eigen Cres. Swan 110 A4
Eighth Ave. Mer T 32 C3
Eighth Ave. Swan 59 E1
Eileen Pl. Trehe 68 C1
Eileen Rd. Swan 85 F4
Eileen Terr. Trehe 68 C1
Einon Ct. Penga 57 E1
Eirw Rd. Porth 123 D1
Eisteddfa Rd. Yst 95 F1
Eithen Cl. Card 172 C1
Eithen Pl. Porth 192 C3
Elaine Cl. Card 172 C1
Elan Cl. Swan 59 E1
Elan Cl. Abera 50 C1
Elan Rd. Card 189 D4
Elba Ave. Marg 139 E3
Elba Cres. Skew 111 F4
Elba St. Gow 82 B3
Elder Dr. Porthc 193 E4
Elder Rd. P Tal 113 E4
Elder St. Bridg 179 F2
Elder Wood Cl. Card 189 F2
Elderberry Rd. Card 187 D1
Eldon Ct. Card 204 C2
Eleanor Cl. Penco 181 D4
Eleanor Pl. Card 205 D1
Eleanor St. Tonypa 121 F3
Eleanor St. Trehe 69 D1
Eleven St. Sully 225 F3
Eleventh Ave. Mer T 32 C3
Elfed Ave. P Tal 138 B4
Elfed Ave. Pen 216 C2
Elfed Gn. Card 187 F1
Elfed Rd. Swan 110 A4
Elfed Way. Barry 225 D4
Elford Rd. Card 203 D3
Elgar Ave. P Tal 113 D1
Elgar Cl. Peng 101 E4
Elgar Cres. Card 190 B4
Elgar Rd. Pen 216 C1
Elgin St. Swan 84 A2
Elias Dr. B-coch 62 B2
Elias Rd. B-coch 62 B2
Elias St. Neath 87 F4
Elim St. Mer T 32 C2
Elizabeth Cl. Swan 60 A2
Elizabeth Maisonettes.
  Card 204 C2
Elizabeth Rd. Bridg 179 E3
Elizabeth St. Abera 50 A1
Elizabeth St. Abercy 98 B1
Elizabeth St. Tony 147 D1
Elizabeth St. Ystal 94 C3
Elizabethan Ct. Pen 216 C2
Ellen St. Card 205 D3
Ellen's Rd. Skew 86 B4
Ellesmere Ct. Card 190 B3
Elliot St. N Tre 54 C1
Ellwood Cl. Card 190 C3
Elm Cl. Sully 226 B2
Elm Cl. Swan 82 C1
Elm Cotts. Bridg 178 C2
Elm Cres. Bridg 179 D3
Elm Ct. Lough 57 D2
Elm Ct. Oak 101 F3
Elm Gr. Aberd 49 F1
Elm Gr. Barry 225 E4
Elm Gr. Caer 152 B3
Elm Gr. Hir 48 C4
Elm Gr. Ll'maes 221 D4
Elm Gr. Lough 57 D2
Elm Gr. Mer T 32 C3
Elm Grove La. D pow 216 A2
Elm Grove Pl. D pow 216 A2
Elm Grove Rd. D pow 216 A2
Elm House. Card 187 F3
Elm Rd. Ll'hry 183 D3

Elm Rd. Neath 87 D1
Elm Rd. Porthc 193 E4
Elm Rise. Brynco 163 F2
Elm St. Abera 71 F2
Elm St. Bar 76 A2
Elm St. Card 205 E4
Elm St. Fern 95 F4
Elm St. Ponty 150 A3
Elm St. Tony 146 A3
Elm St. Troed 52 A1
Elm Terr. Og Va 119 F1
Elmfield Cl. Card 190 C3
Elmgrove. Bedw 152 C3
Elmgrove Cl. Ponty 124 B3
Elmgrove Rd. Card 187 F2
Elmgrove Rd. T Mum 136 C4
Elmhurst Cres. Swan 110 C4
Elms Pk. Ll'tris 184 B3
Elms The. P-s-Ely 201 E3
Elmwood Ct. Card 205 E4
Elmwood Dr. Neath 87 E1
Elmwood Rd. P Tal 113 E3
Elmwood. Tred 35 F3
Elphin Cres. Swan 83 F1
Elphin Gdns. Swan 84 A1
Elphin Rd. Swan 83 F1
Elworthy Cl. Sully 226 A3
Elwy Cres. Swan 83 F1
Elwy Gdns. Swan 83 F1
Elwyn Dr. Mer T 51 F4
Elwyn St. Tony 167 E4
Ely Bridge Ind Est. Card 203 F3
Ely Ind Est. Tonypa 122 A1
Ely Rd. Card 204 A4
Ely St. Ll'tris 184 A4
Ely St. Tonypa 121 F3
Ely Valley Rd. Ll'tris 168 A3
Ely Valley Rd. Tony 147 E1
Emanuel Pl. Neath 87 E3
Emerald St. Card 205 E4
Emlyn Dr. Caer 152 A2
Emlyn Gdns. Swan 84 A1
Emlyn Rd. Swan 84 A1
Emlyn Terr. Swan 84 C3
Emlyn Terr. Tonypa 121 D3
Emmanuel Cl. Trehe 68 C1
Emmanuel Gdns. Swan 109 D2
Empire Ave. Blae 45 F4
Emroch St. Marg 139 F4
Emsworth Ct. Card 189 D3
Ena Ave. Neath 87 F4
Endeavour Cl. Bridg 180 B3
Endeavour Cl. P Tal 113 D2
Energlyn Cl. Caer 151 F2
Energlyn Terr. Caer 151 F3
Enfield Cl. Swan 59 F2
Enfield St. P Tal 138 C4
Enid Rd. Cly 60 C4
Enid St. Trea 122 A3
Ennerdale Cl. Card 189 D1
Enoch Morrell Cl. Troed 52 A1
Eppynt Rd. Swan 84 A2
Epsom Cl. Card 203 F3
Epstein Cl. Card 187 E1
Erasmus Terr. Maesy 101 D1
Erald Pl. Swan 109 F3
Ernest St. Mer T 51 F4
Erw Deg. Bridg 179 D3
Erw Fach. Ch Vil 149 E1
Erw Hir. Ll'tris 168 C2
Erw Ifan. Penco 181 E4
Erw Las. Card 188 A2
Erw Las. Mer T 32 A1
Erw Las. Peny 49 E3
Erw Wen. Card 188 A4
Erw Wen. Penco 181 E4
Erw Wen. Pyle 176 C4
Erw'r-Delyn Cl. Pen 216 B2
Eskdale Cl. Card 189 D2
Espalone. Bish 136 B3
Esplanade Ave. Porth 192 C3
Esplanade. Pen 217 D2
Esplanade. Porth 192 C3
Essex Terr. Swan 84 C3
Essich St. Card 189 E1
Esterling Dr. Porth 192 C4
Ethel St. Card 204 A3
Ethel St. Neath 87 E3
Etna Terr. Tony 146 B4
Eton Ct. Card 188 C3
Eton Rd. Card 204 B3
Eugene Cl. Card 191 D4
Eurgan Cl. Ll' maj 219 F3
Eurocast Trad Est. Card 187 F3
Eurwg Cres. Card 190 B4
Eustace Dr. Brynco 163 F2
Eva St. M Ash 72 B1
Eva St. Neath 87 F3
Evan St. Tre 99 D4
Evan's Rd. Neath 87 E3
Evans Houses. C-c-y-c 14 C2
Evans Sq. Ponty 124 C2
Evans St. Marg 114 B1
Evans St. Pyle 161 E2
Evans Terr. Abercy 98 C1
Evans Terr. Maest 117 D4
Evans Terr. Pyle 176 C4
Evans Terr. Swan 110 B4

Evans Terr. Trea 122 A3
Evans's Terr. Tonypa 121 E4
Evansfield Rd. Card 187 F2
Eveline Terr. Marg 139 D4
Evelyn Rd. Skew 86 C4
Evelyn St. Barry 225 D3
Evelyn St. Card 205 D1
Evenlode Ave. Pen 216 C1
Everard St. Barry 225 D3
Everard Way. Card 189 D2
Everest Ave. Card 172 C1
Everest Wlk. Card 172 C1
Evergreen Cotts. Pyle 176 B4
Evergreen Ct. Tony 147 F3
Eversley Rd. Swan 109 E3
Everswell Ave. Card 203 E4
Everswell Rd. Card 203 E4
Ewart Pl. Swan 84 B2
Ewbank Cl. Barry 225 E4
Ewenny Cl. Barry 225 D4
Ewenny Cl. Porth 176 C1
Ewenny Cross. Ewen 195 E4
Ewenny Ind Est. Bridg 180 B1
Ewenny Pl. Swan 84 B4
Ewenny Rd. Bridg 179 F1
Ewenny Rd. Card 189 D4
Ewenny Rd. Ewen 179 F1
Ewenny Rd. Maest 117 D1
Ewenny Rd. St B M 195 E1
Ewenny Rd. Wick 208 B4
Excalibur Dr. Card 172 C1
Excelsior Rd. Card 188 B1
Excelsior Terr. Fern 95 E4
Exchange Rd. Neath 87 E3
Exchange Rd. Pontmi 129 F2
Exchange St. Maest 116 C2
Exeter Cl. Mer T 32 A1
Exeter Mansions. Card 187 F3
Exford Cres. Card 190 A3
Exhibition Row. Llwy 49 F4
Eynon St. Penga 57 E1
Eyre St. Card 205 F3

Faber Way. Card 204 B2
Fabian Way. Swan 111 E4
Factory Houses. G-nea 26 C1
Factory La. A-wen 41 D3
Factory La. Ponty 149 D4
Factory Rd. Bar 75 F3
Factory Rd. Cly 60 B4
Factory Rd. Cowb 210 B4
Factory Terr. Tondu 163 E2
Fagwr Isaf. Craig 39 D1
Fagwr Pl. Swan 60 A1
Fagwr Rd. Craig 39 D1
Fair View Cl. Ll'tris 184 A4
Fair View Cl. Swan 85 F3
Fair View. Peng 101 E4
Fair View. Rhy 53 F4
Fair View. Tony 146 B4
Fair View. Tre 99 D3
Fairacre Cl. Card 172 C1
Fairbrook Cl. Card 188 A4
Fairfax Cres. Porth 192 C4
Fairfax Rd. Card 188 B3
Fairfield Ave. Card 204 A3
Fairfield Cl. Aberd 71 F4
Fairfield Cl. Card 203 F4
Fairfield Cl. Ll' Maj 220 A3
Fairfield Cl. Peng 101 F3
Fairfield Cl. Ponty 150 A2
Fairfield Cres. Ll' Maj 220 A3
Fairfield La. Ponty 150 A2
Fairfield. P Tal 113 F1
Fairfield. Pyle 177 D4
Fairfield Rd. Bridg 180 A1
Fairfield Rd. Glyn 91 E2
Fairfield Rd. Pen 216 C2
Fairfield Rise. Ll' Maj 220 A3
Fairfield Terr. Swan 110 A4
Fairfield. Tred 35 F4
Fairfield Way. Neath 87 F4
Fairford St. Barry 225 D4
Fairhaven Cl. Card 191 D4
Fairhaven Ct. T Mum 137 D3
Fairhill Dr. Ch Vil 150 A1
Fairhill Dr. P Tal 113 F2
Fairland Cl. Ll'tris 168 C2
Fairlawn Ct. Card 188 A1
Fairlawn Terr. Penco 181 E4
Fairlawns. Neath 87 D2
Fairleigh. M-I-Pit 215 F4
Fairleigh Rd. Card 204 B4
Fairmead Ct. Card 203 F4
Fairmeadow. Penty 170 B3
Fairmeadows. Maest 142 B4
Fairmound Pl. Ch Vil 170 A4
Fairoak Chase. Bridg 180 B2
Fairoak Cres. Aberd 49 F1
Fairoak Gr. Rhiwd 155 F1
Fairoak Mews. Card 189 D1
Fairoak Rd. Card 189 D1
Fairoaks. D pow 216 A2
Fairthorn Cl. Card 172 C2
Fairview Ave. P Tal 113 F1
Fairview Cl. Card 191 D4

Fairview Ct. Card 189 F4
Fairview Est. Mer T 31 F1
Fairview. Hir 29 E1
Fairview Houses. C-c-y-c 31 F3
Fairview. Ll'tris 169 D4
Fairview Rd. Ll'fel 59 E1
Fairview Terr. Abercy 98 C2
Fairview Terr. Mer T 51 F4
Fairview. Tonypa 122 A1
Fairwater Ave. Card 203 F4
Fairwater Cl. M-y-Fed 175 D3
Fairwater Gn. Card 203 E4
Fairwater Gr E. Card 203 F4
Fairwater Gr W. Card 203 F4
Fairwater Road. Card 203 F4
Fairwater Workshop. Card 203 F4
Fairway. Bar 75 F3
Fairway Dr. Caer 151 F3
Fairway Dr. Pontdw 40 B3
Fairway. P Tal 113 E1
Fairway The. Card 173 E1
Fairways Cres. Card 203 E4
Fairways. Pyle 176 C4
Fairways The. Peng 101 F4
Fairways View. Ll'tris 168 A2
Fairwood Cl. Card 187 F1
Fairwood Dr. P Tal 113 F3
Fairwood Rd. Card 187 F1
Fairwood Rd. Swan 108 B4
Fairwood Rd. T Mum 137 D4
Fairwood Terr. Gow 82 B3
Fairy Glen. Og Va 119 F2
Fairy Gr. Swan 108 C4
Fairyland. Neath 88 A4
Fairyland Rd. Neath 88 A4
Fairyland Rd. Tonna 63 D1
Falcon Dr. Neath 88 A2
Falcon Gr. Sully 227 D4
Falcon Pl. Swan 83 F4
Falcon Rd. Barry 225 E4
Falconwood Dr. Card 202 C3
Falfield Cl. Card 173 D1
Fanhaulog. Ll'tris 168 A1
Fanny St. Card 205 D4
Faraday Rd. Cly 39 F1
Fardre Cres. Ch Vil 149 F1
Fardre Ct. Ch Vil 149 F1
Farm Cl. Aber 151 D4
Farm Dr. Card 189 D2
Farm Dr. P Tal 113 E1
Farm Rd. A-wen 40 A1
Farm Rd. Abera 71 E3
Farm Rd. Caer 152 B2
Farm Rd. Ce Cr 162 C1
Farm Rd. Neath 87 E2
Farm Rd. Rhy 34 C1
Farm Rd. Yst 95 D1
Farm Terr. Mer T 32 A1
Farm Terr. N Tre 54 C2
Farm View. Peng 76 A1
Farmers Rd. B-coch 62 B3
Farmfield Ave. P Tal 113 E1
Farmhouse Way. Card 203 D2
Farmleigh. Card 190 A2
Farmville Rd. Card 205 F3
Farraday Dr. Gell 100 C4
Farteg Rd. Bryn 115 F3
Farthings The. Card 173 F1
Fault St. Swan 59 F1
Feeder Row. Aberca 129 E4
Felbridge Cl. Card 205 E2
Felin Fach. Card 188 A2
Felin Fran. Swan 60 C1
Felin Wen. Card 188 B4
Felindre Ave. Penco 181 F4
Felindre Rd. Ll'ha 181 F4
Felindre Rd. Penco 181 F4
Felinfach. Cwmll 6 C2
Fell St. Tre 99 D4
Felsted Cl. Card 173 F1
Fenbrook Cl. P Tal 113 E3
Fendrod Way. Swan 85 E4
Fennel Cl. Card 191 D4
Fennel Cl. Pen 216 C3
Fenton Pl. Pontcr 118 C1
Fenton Pl. Porth 192 C4
Fenviolet Cl. Card 191 D3
Fenwick Dr. Bridg 180 B3
Fenwick St. Tylor 122 B4
Fermoy Ct. Swan 83 F3
Fern Cres. Aberd 49 E1
Fern Hill. Yst 95 D1
Fern Pl. Card 203 E4
Fern St. Card 204 A3
Fern St. Og Va 144 C4
Fern St. Swan 84 A1
Fern Terr. Tonypa 121 E3
Ferndale Ct. Fern 95 F3
Ferndale Ind Est. Fern 95 E4
Ferndale Rd. Tylor 96 A1
Ferndale St. Card 204 C2
Fernfield. P Tal 113 F2
Fernhill Cl. Mer T 32 B3
Fernhill Cl. T Mum 109 D1
Fernhill Cl. Troed 52 B1
Fernhill. M Ash 72 A2
Fernhill Rd. Lough 57 D2

Fernhill Terr. N Tre 54 C2
Fernlea. Pontmi 129 F2
Ferntree Dr. Card 190 C4
Ferny Ct. Card 189 E1
Ferrara Sq. Swan 110 B3
Ferrier Ave. Card 187 E1
Ferrier's Row. Maest 117 D2
Ferry Rd. Card 216 C4
Ferry Rd. Lough 56 B1
Ferry Side. Swan 110 C3
Ferryboat Cl. Swan 85 D4
Festiniog Rd. Card 188 A1
Ffald Rd. Pyle 161 D1
Ffaldau Ind Est. Pontcr 118 C3
Ffaldau Terr. Fern 95 E4
Fferm Goch. St M H 181 F1
Fferm-y-Bryn. Gell 100 C1
Fferm-y-graig. St Ath 221 E2
Fforch-Dwm Rd. Ton 89 F3
Fforchaman Rd. Abera 71 D2
Fforchneol Row. Abera 71 D3
Fford Rhaglan. H-y-Cy 165 D3
Fford-yr-Ywen. Ch Vil 150 A1
Ffordd Abiah. Cly 60 C4
Ffordd Afan. Cwma 114 B3
Ffordd Alltwen. Gow 82 A3
Ffordd Aneurin Bevan.
  Swan 109 D4
Ffordd Beck. Gow 82 A4
Ffordd Bryngwyn. Lough 82 B4
Ffordd Brynheulog. Pontdw 40 B3
Ffordd Butler. Gow 82 A3
Ffordd Celyn. Card 188 A2
Ffordd Cwm Tawe. Swan 60 B3
Ffordd Cwm Tawe. Swan 84 C3
Ffordd Cynghordy. Swan 85 E4
Ffordd Cynore. Swan 83 E3
Ffordd Dawel. Swan 85 F3
Ffordd Ddu. Pyle 161 D1
Ffordd Dewi. Ll'fel 59 D1
Ffordd Dinas. Cwma 114 B3
Ffordd Dinefwr. Penty 185 F4
Ffordd Elin. Barry 225 D4
Ffordd Ellen. Craig 39 D1
Ffordd Emlyn. Ystal 23 D3
Ffordd Eynon Evans. Caer 151 E3
Ffordd Ganol. Bridg 180 A2
Ffordd Gerdinan. Ch Vil 150 A1
Ffordd Glandwr. Ystal 23 D3
Ffordd Gwyn. Swan 85 E4
Ffordd Las. Aber 151 D4
Ffordd Las. Card 187 D3
Ffordd Llundain. Swan 85 E4
Ffordd Llyffant. Swan 86 A4
Ffordd Newydd. Pyle 177 D4
Ffordd Parc Ynysderw.
  Pontdw 40 C2
Ffordd Pengam. Card 206 A4
Ffordd Silkin. Pontdw 40 C3
Ffordd Talfan. Lough 82 B4
Ffordd Taliesin. Swan 108 C4
Ffordd Talygarn. Ll'tris 184 A4
Ffordd Tollborth. Swan 85 E4
Ffordd y Bedol. Ynybw 124 B3
Ffordd y Brain. Swan 83 F3
Ffordd y Brenin. Card 205 D3
Ffordd y Frenhines. Marg 141 D4
Ffordd y Gamlas. Gow 82 A3
Ffordd y Goedwig. Pyle 161 E2
Ffordd y Mynach. Pyle 161 D1
Ffordd -y-Barcer. Card 202 C3
Ffordd yr Eglwys. Pyle 177 D4
Ffordd -yr-Afon. Bridg 179 D3
Ffordd-yr-Ysgol. P Tal 113 E1
Ffordd-y-Bryn. Swan 61 D1
Ffordd-y-Capel. Ch Vil 169 F3
Ffordd-y-Dderwyn. Bridg 179 E3
Ffordd-y-Gollen. Ch Vil 149 F1
Ffordd-y-Gyfraith. Tondu 162 C3
Ffordd-y-Mynnydd. Swan 86 A4
Ffordd-y-Parc. Bridg 180 A4
Ffordd-y-Parc. Swan 59 F1
Fforest Hill. B-coch 63 E2
Fforest Rd. Ll'hry 183 E2
Fforest Rd. M Ash 72 C2
Fforest Rd. W St D 183 E4
Ffos Cl. Nel 99 F2
Ffos Felen. Gow 82 A3
Ffos-y-Fran. Rhiwd 155 F1
Ffos-yr-Efail Terr. Pontar ... 36 B2
Ffos-yr-Hebog. Ll'bra 127 D3
Ffrwd Amos Cotts. Tonypa 121 F2
Ffrwd Cres. M Ash 72 B2
Ffrwd Rd. C-c-y-c 31 F3
Ffrwd St. Abera 71 E3
Ffrwd Terr. Abera 126 C1
Ffrwd Vale. B-coch 62 B1
Ffrwd-Wyllt St. Marg 139 E3
Ffrwdwyllt Cotts. Marg 139 E3
Ffwrwm Rd. Bedw 153 F4
Ffynnon Samlet. Swan 85 E4
Ffynnon Tudful. Mer T 32 B1
Ffynnon Wen. Pyle 161 D1
Ffynnon-Las. Yst 95 F1
Ffynnon-wen Terr. Peng 76 A1
Ffynnonbwla Rd. Aber 150 C2
Ffynon y Maen. Pyle 161 D1
Ffynone Cl. Swan 110 A4

Ffynone Dr. Swan 110 A4
Ffynone Rd. Swan 110 A4
Fiddlers Elbow. Tre 99 D2
Fidlas Ave. Card 189 D4
Fidlas Rd. Card 189 D4
Field Cl. Swan 60 A1
Field St. Bed 99 E4
Field St. Swan 84 B2
Field St. Tonypa 121 F2
Field Terr. Marg 139 E4
Field Terr. N Tre 54 C2
Field Terr. Penty 170 B1
Field View. Barry 225 D4
Field View Rd. Barry 225 D4
Field Way. Card 188 C3
Fieldfare Dr. Card 191 D3
Fielding Cl. Card 190 A4
Fields Ct. Card 204 B4
Fields Park Rd. Card 204 B4
Fields Park Terr. Cross 129 D3
Fields Rd. Pontmi 155 D4
Fields Rd. Tred 35 F3
Fife St. Abercy 98 C2
Fifth Ave. Hir 28 C1
Fifth Ave. Mer T 32 C3
Fifth Ave. Swan 59 E1
Finchley Rd. Card 203 F4
Finsbury Terr. Swan 109 F3
Fir Grove St. Yst 94 C3
Fir St. Fern 95 F4
Fir Tree Cl. Mer T 32 B3
Fir Tree Dr. Tre 99 D3
Firbank Terr. Ynys 128 A3
Firbanks Way. Ll'tris 168 A2
Firm St. Swan 110 B2
Firs Ave. Card 203 D4
Firs The. Porthc 193 F4
First Ave. Caer 151 F2
First Ave. Mer T 32 C3
First Ave. Swan 84 B4
Firtree Cl. Card 203 E4
Firwood Cl. B-coch 62 B3
Firwood Cl. Card 187 F2
Fishguard Cl. Card 189 D4
Fishguard Rd. Card 188 C4
Fishpond Rd. Card 190 A3
Fitzalan Ct. Card 205 D3
Fitzalan Pl. Card 205 E3
Fitzalan Rd. Card 205 E3
Fitzhamon Ct. Ll' Maj 220 A3
Fitzhamon Emb. Card 204 C3
Fitzhamon La. Card 204 C3
Fitzhamon Rd. Porth 192 C4
Fitzroy Lodge. Peng 101 E4
Fitzroy St. Card 205 D4
Fitzwilliam Cl. Ll'tris 168 C1
Five Bells Rd. Bridg 179 F2
Flanders Meadow. Ll' maj 219 F3
Flanders Rd. Ll' maj 219 F3
Flatholm Pl. Swan 83 F4
Flatholm Way. Porth 176 C1
Flats The. Card 188 C1
Flax Ct. Pen 216 C3
Flaxland Ave. Card 188 C2
Fleet St. Swan 110 A3
Fleet Way. Card 204 C1
Flemingston Rd. Ll'maes 221 E4
Fleur-De-Lys Ave. Pontll 101 F2
Flint Ave. Ll' Maj 220 A4
Flint House. P Tal 138 B4
Flint St. Card 205 C1
Flora St. Card 205 D4
Floral Ave. Peng 101 D4
Florence Gr. Caer 152 A1
Florence St. Card 205 F4
Florence St. Neath 87 F3
Florentia St. Card 189 D1
Flush Meadow. Ll' maj 219 F3
Fochriw Rd. Rhy 53 F4
Foel View Cl. Ch Vil 169 D4
Folland Ct. T Mum 109 D1
Folland Rd. Glan 4 B2
Fonmon Cres. Card 203 E3
Fonmon Park Rd. Rhoose 222 C1
Fonmon Rd. Rhoose 222 B1
Fonthill Pl. Card 204 C2
Fontigary Rd. Card 190 B2
Fontygary Rd. Rhoose 222 C1
Forbes St. Card 205 F4
Ford Rd. Ch Vil 150 B1
Ford Rd. Marg 114 A1
Ford Rd. Peng 101 D3
Ford Rd. Ponty 124 A1
Fordwell. Card 188 A1
Foreland Rd. Card 188 A3
Foreshore Rd. Card 205 F2
Forest Ave. Gell 100 C3
Forest Cl. Brynco 163 F3
Forest Ct. Card 204 B4
Forest Farm Rd. Card 187 D3
Forest Gr. Ponty 124 A1
Forest Hill. Pontll 101 F3
Forest Hills Dr. Ll'tris 168 A1
Forest Oak Cl. Card 173 E1
Forest Rd. Ll'tris 169 D3
Forest Rd. Ponty 149 F3

Forest Rd. Tre 99 D4
Forest View. Aberca 129 E4
Forest View. Card 203 E4
Forest View. Ll'tris 168 B1
Forest View. Neath 88 A2
Forest View. Ponty 124 B3
Forest View. Pyle 161 D1
Forest Wlk. Ll'tris 168 A1
Forge Cres. Rhy 34 C1
Forge Factory Est. Maest 116 C2
Forge Pl. Abera 50 A2
Forge Pl. Card 203 D2
Forge Rd. Bedw 154 B4
Forge Rd. Marg 114 A1
Forge Rd. Pen-cl 80 C1
Forge Row. Abera 71 E3
Forge St. Yst 95 D2
Forge Trip. Aberd 50 A2
Forge View. Abera 71 E3
Forge Way. Porth 192 C4
Forrest Rd. Card 204 A3
Forrest Rd. Pen 217 D1
Forrest St. Card 204 C1
Forrester's Cotts. Pontmi ... 129 F2
Forster Rd. Neath 87 F4
Forsythia Cl. Card 32 B3
Forsythia Dr. Card 189 D4
Fort Rd. Sully 227 D3
Fort St. Card 205 F4
Fortran Rd. Card 191 D4
Foster Dr. Card 189 F1
Foster St. Barry 225 D4
Fothergil Cres. Mer T 32 C1
Fothergill Rd. Blae 45 E4
Fothergill St. Abera 50 A2
Fothergill St. Mer T 32 C1
Fothergill St. Ponty 149 F4
Fothergills Rd. N Tre 54 C2
Founders Row. Llwy 49 F4
Foundry Pl. Ponty 124 B1
Foundry Pl. Porth 122 C4
Foundry Rd. Hir 48 B4
Foundry Rd. Neath 87 F3
Foundry Rd. Ponty 124 A1
Foundry Rd. Swan 85 D4
Foundry Rd. Trea 121 F3
Foundry Row. Skew 86 C4
Foundry View. Abera 71 E3
Fountain La. Card 191 D4
Fountain Rd. Tondu 163 D2
Fountain St. Fern 96 A3
Fountain St. M Ash 72 B2
Fountain St. Ponty 123 D2
Fountain Terr. Pontcr 143 E1
Four Acre. Ll' Maj 220 A4
Four Elms Ct. Card 205 E3
Four Elms Rd. Card 205 E4
Fouracres Cl. Barry 225 E4
Fourteenth Ave. Rhig 28 C1
Fourth Ave. Mer T 32 C3
Fourth Ave. Rhig 28 C1
Fourth Ave. Swan 59 E1
Fowler's Pl. Maest 117 C4
Fox Gr. Swan 83 D2
Fox Hollows. W St D 199 E3
Fox Russell Cl. Card 188 A1
Fox St. Card 205 F4
Fox St. M Ash 72 B2
Fox St. Tre 99 D4
Foxfields. Bridg 180 B2
Foxglove Cl. Card 203 D2
Foxglove Rise. Pen 216 C3
Foxhole Dr. South 135 D2
Foxhole Rd. Swan 84 C1
Foxhollows. Bridg 180 B3
Foxwood Cl. Rhiwd 155 F2
Frampton Ct. Lough 56 C1
Frampton Rd. Lough 57 D2
Francis Rd. Barry 215 D1
Francis Rd. Swan 59 F1
Francis St. Aber 150 C4
Francis St. Bar 76 A2
Francis St. Fern 96 A3
Francis St. Mer T 33 D3
Francis St. Peng 101 D3
Francis St. Pontdw 40 C2
Francis St. Ponty 150 A2
Francis St. Skew 86 C4
Francis St. Swan 110 A3
Francis St. Tony 147 D2
Francis St. Tonypa 121 D4
Francis Terr. Ponty 124 C2
Frank Rd. Card 203 E3
Franklen Rd. Card 188 B2
Franklen St. Card 204 C2
Frederick St. Aberd 49 F2
Frederick St. Card 205 D3
Frederick St. Fern 95 F3
Frederick St. P Tal 138 C4
Frederick St. Swan 84 B2
Free School Ct. Bridg 179 F2
Freeman St. Swan 84 B2
Fremington Pl. Card 190 B3
Freshmoor Rd. Card 205 F3
Frewer Ave. Card 187 E1
Friars The. Card 205 D3
Friary The. Card 205 D3
Frigate Rd. Card 205 E1

Froglane. Ll'gen 103 E4
Frogmore Ave. Swan 109 E3
Fron Heulog. Brdg 179 E3
Fron Terr. Ponty 124 C1
Fron-Wen Terr. Og Va 119 F2
Frondeg. Tred 35 E3
Fronheulog. Ponty 124 A1
Fronwen Terr. Mer T 32 C2
Frost Pl. Peng 101 E4
Fryatt St. Barry 225 D2
Fuller St. Pontdw 40 C3
Fullers Row. Swan 109 B1
Fulmar Cl. Card 190 C4
Fulmar Cl. Sully 227 D4
Fulmar Cl. T Mum 136 C4
Fulmar Rd. Porth 192 C4
Furnace Cl. Tylor 96 B1
Furnace Row. Troed 52 A1
Furnace St. Sully 225 F3
Furnace Terr. Neath 87 E3
Furness Cl. Card 203 D2
Furze Cres. Swan 59 E1
Furzeland Dr. B-coch 62 B2
Furzeland Dr. Swan 109 D3

Gabalfa Ave. Card 188 A1
Gabalfa Rd. Card 188 A1
Gabalfa Rd. Swan 109 D3
Gables The. Card 188 B3
Gables The. D pow 216 A1
Gadley's Terr. Glyn 66 C2
Gadlys Gdns. Abera 50 A1
Gadlys Rd. Abera 49 F1
Gadlys St. Aberd 49 F1
Gadlys Terr. Aberd 49 F1
Gadlys Uchaf. Aberd 49 F2
Gadwgan Rd. Treo 94 C3
Gaer Pl. Gell 100 B3
Gaerwen Cl. Card 188 B4
Gaffer's Row. Treo 94 A2
Gainsborough Ct. Pen 216 C3
Gainsborough Rd. Pen 216 C3
Gainsborough Rd. Tred 35 E3
Galahad Cl. Card 172 B1
Gallamuir Rd. Card 205 F4
Gallipoli Row. Marg 139 E3
Galltcwm Terr. Bryn 115 F2
Galon Uchaf Rd. Mer T 32 C2
Galston St. Card 205 E3
Gamlyn Terr. Penny 48 C3
Gardd Jolyon. Peng 101 E3
Garden City. Mer T 32 C2
Garden City. Rhy 34 C1
Garden Cl. Ll'bra 127 D1
Garden Cres. Lough 82 B4
Garden Ct. Bridg 180 B3
Garden St. Ll'bra 127 D1
Garden St. Mer T 33 D2
Garden St. Swan 110 B3
Garden Suburbs. Cross 129 E3
Gardeners La. Neath 87 F2
Gardenia Cl. Card 189 E4
Gardens The. Ynys 127 F3
Gardens The. Ystal 23 D3
Gardner Cl. Ponty 124 B3
Garesfield St. Card 205 E3
Gareth Cl. Card 172 B1
Garfield Ave. Bridg 179 F4
Garfield St. Peng 101 F3
Garn Rd. Maest 117 D1
Garngoch Ind Est. Penga ... 57 F1
Garngoch Terr. Lough 82 B4
Garnlwyd Cl. Swan 84 B4
Garnswllt Rd. Craig 18 A3
Garnswllt Rd. Pontar 17 F1
Garnwen Rd. Maest 116 C3
Garnwen Terr. Maest 116 C3
Garon Terr. Og Va 119 F4
Garreg Rd. Pontcr 118 C2
Garreg Side. Pontcr 118 C3
Garreg-Wen. Gell 100 B4
Garrick Dr. Card 172 C1
Garrod Ave. Swan 82 B1
Garth Ave. Maest 117 C1
Garth Ave. Ponty 124 B3
Garth Cl. Card 187 D4
Garth Cl. Gar P 153 D2
Garth Cotts. Mer T 32 C1
Garth Dr. Bridg 180 A4
Garth Est. Aber 150 C4
Garth Gr. Hir 29 E1
Garth La. Gar P 153 D2
Garth Lwyd. Caer 152 B3
Garth Olwg. Penty 170 C3
Garth Pl. Card 188 B1
Garth Rd. G-C-G 5 D2
Garth Rd. Swan 60 B2
Garth Rd. Swan 60 C3
Garth Rd. Trea 122 A3
Garth St. Card 205 D3
Garth St. Mer T 32 B1
Garth St. Pyle 161 E1
Garth St. Rhy 53 F4
Garth St. T We 171 D2
Garth St. Tony 167 E4
Garth Terr. Bed 74 A3
Garth Terr. Rhiwd 155 F1
Garth View. Bedw 152 B4

Garth View. Ch Vil 169 F4
Garth View. Ll'tris 169 D3
Garth View. Ponty 171 D4
Garth View. Swan 60 A2
Garth Wen. Trea 122 A3
Garwelht. Peny 49 D3
Garwfechan Rd. Pontcr 143 F4
Gas Rd. Ponty 124 B1
Gaskell Cl. Ll' Maj 220 B3
Gasworks Rd. Abera 71 E4
Gasworks Terr. Tondu 163 E3
Gate Rd. Bridg 180 B1
Gawain Cl. Card 172 B1
Geifr Rd. Marg 139 F3
Geiriol Gdns. Swan 83 F1
Geiriol Rd. Swan 83 F1
Gelert St. Swan 84 B3
Gelli Arael Rd. Tony 146 A3
Gelli Aur. Aberd 49 E2
Gelli Aur. B-coch 62 B1
Gelli Crossing. Yst 95 E2
Gelli Dawel. B-coch 62 B1
Gelli Dawel. Caer 151 F2
Gelli Deg. B-coch 62 B1
Gelli Deg. Caer 151 F3
Gelli Deg. Card 188 B4
Gelli Fron. Yst 95 D1
Gelli Gdns. Swan 84 A4
Gelli Hirion Ind Est. Ponty . 150 B2
Gelli Houses. Glyn 91 F3
Gelli Ind Est. Yst 95 E1
Gelli Ind. La. Pontll 101 F2
Gelli. Ll'hry 183 E3
Gelli Rd. Tonypa 121 F3
Gelli Rd. Tred 35 E4
Gelli Rd. Ynybw 98 A1
Gelli Rd. Yst 95 D1
Gelli St. Maest 117 D4
Gelli St. Swan 111 D4
Gelli Terr. Glyn 92 B3
Gelli Terr. Yst 95 E1
Gelli'r Haidd. Tony 147 D1
Gelli-deg. Mer T 32 A1
Gelli-Deg. St Maesy 101 D1
Gelli-Deg. Tony 147 D2
Gelli-Groes Rd. Pontll 101 F2
Gelli-Gynore. Penga 57 F1
Gelli-Ron. Gell 100 B4
Gelli-siriol Cotts. Maest ... 142 C3
Gelli-Unig Pl. Cross 129 E3
Gelli-unig Terr. Cross 129 E3
Gelliargwellt Rd. Gell 100 B3
Gelliaur. Penco 165 E1
Gellidawel Rd. G-nea 27 D1
Gellidawel Rd. Ponty 150 A3
Gellidderw. Pontdw 40 B3
Gellideg Cl. Maesy 101 E1
Gellidde Hts. Maesy 101 E1
Gellideg. Pontdw 40 B3
Gellideg Rd. Ponty 149 D4
Gellideg Rd. Ponty 150 B2
Gellifaelog Old Rd. Mer T ... 33 D2
Gellifaelog Terr. Mer T 33 D2
Gellifawr Rd. Swan 84 B4
Gellifeli Rd. Ll'ha 166 B2
Gelligaer Gdns. Card 188 C1
Gelligaer La. Card 188 C1
Gelligaer Rd. Gelli 99 F3
Gelligaer Rd. Gell 100 C3
Gelligaer St. Card 188 C1
Gelligaled Rd. Yst 95 E1
Gelligeiros. A-wen 41 D3
Gelliglas Rd. Swan 84 B4
Gelligron Est. Tony 147 D3
Gelligron Rd. Pontdw 40 B3
Gelligwyn Rd. Swan 84 B4
Gellihaf Rd. Peng 101 D3
Gellihyll Rd. Penga 57 F1
Gellionen Rd. Cly 39 F1
Gellionen Rd. Pontdw 40 A3
Gellionnen Cl. Cly 60 C4
Gelliwastad Gr. Ponty 124 B1
Gelliwastad Rd. Ponty 124 B1
Gelliwen St. Gell 100 B3
Gelliwion Rd. Ponty 148 C3
Gelliwion Woods. Ponty 149 D4
Gellyfowy Rd. Ponydw 41 D4
Gellygaer Rd. Gell 100 C2
Gelynis Terr. Card 187 D4
Gelynis Terr N. Card 187 D4
Gelynos Ave. Mark 76 C3
Gendros Ave E. Swan 84 A2
Gendros Ave W. Swan 83 F2
Gendros Cl. Swan 84 A2
Gendros Cres. Swan 84 A2
Gendros Dr. Swan 83 F2
Geoffrey Ashe Ct. Cowb ... 198 C1
Geoffrey St. Neath 87 F4
George Bank. T Mum 137 E2
George Cl. Penty 170 C2
George Manning Way. Gow 82 A2
George St. Abera 71 E4
George St. Aberca 129 E4
George St. Bar 76 A2
George St. Barry 225 D3

George St. Bed 74 A4
George St. Bridg 180 B2
George St. Card 205 E1
George St. Fern 96 A4
George St. Gell 100 C1
George St. Ll'tris 168 B2
George St. Maest 91 D1
George St. Marg 139 E4
George St. Mark 76 C3
George St. Mer T 33 D2
George St. N Tre 54 C2
George St. Neath 87 F3
George St. Peng 101 F4
George St. Pontdw 40 C3
George St. Porth 192 C4
George St. Swan 110 A3
George St. Tonypa 122 A2
George St. Trehe 94 A4
George St. Ynys 128 C2
George Terr. M Ash 97 F4
George Thomas Ave.
  Brynco 163 F3
George Thomas Cl. Porth . 192 C4
George's Row. Neath 87 D1
George's Terr. Tonypa 121 E4
Georges Cnr. Penty 170 A1
Georgetown Hill. Tred 35 F3
Georgetown Penty 170 C2
Georgetown Villas. Mer T ... 32 B1
Georgian Cl. Ll' Maj 220 A4
Georgian Cl. Porthc 193 D4
Georgian Way. Bridg 180 A2
Georgian Way. Card 188 C4
Geotre Bellaf Rd. Swan 108 B4
Ger y Afon. Ynybw 124 B3
Ger y Nant. Ll'ge 56 A4
Ger y Pant. Pontar 36 B2
Ger yr Afon. Glan 4 A4
Ger-Y -Parc. Swan 59 F1
Ger-y-Bont. Peny 49 D3
Ger-y-Coed. Bridg 180 B3
Ger-y-Ffrwd. Swan 85 F3
Ger-y-Llan. St Nic 202 A1
Ger-y-Llyn. Porthc 193 D4
Ger-y-Nant. Bridg 179 F3
Ger-y-Nant. G-nea 26 B1
Ger-y-Sedd. Bridg 180 B3
Ger-yr-afon. Abera 71 E4
Ger-yr-Afon. B-coch 63 E2
Ger-yr-Afon. G-C-G 5 D2
Ger-yr-Afon. Ystra 7 D1
Ger-yr-Eglwys. Hen 36 A2
Geraint Cl. Card 172 B1
Geraint House. Marg 139 F2
Geraint Pl. Barry 225 D4
Geraint's Way. Cowb 198 B1
Geraints Cl. Cowb 198 B1
Gerald St. P Tal 118 C4
Gerald St. Swan 84 B1
Gernant. Card 188 B4
Gernant La. Mer T 50 C4
Gerrard Ct. Card 204 C3
Gerretts Cl. Bish 136 A3
Gersanws. C-c-y-c 32 A3
Gertrude St. Abercy 98 C1
Gethin Cl. Swan 84 A2
Gethin Rd. Tonypa 121 F2
Gethin Rd. Treo 94 C3
Gethin St. Neath 87 D1
Gethin St. Troed 51 F2
Gethin Terr. Porth 123 D2
Gething St. Swan 110 B3
Giant's Grave Rd. Neath ... 87 D1
Gibbet's Hill. Penll 198 B2
Gibbons Way. Pyle 177 D4
Gibbonsdown Cl. Barry 225 D4
Gibbonsdown Rise. Barry . 225 D4
Gibbs Cl. Peng 101 E4
Gibson Cl. Card 188 C3
Gilar St. Mer T 51 F4
Gilbert La. D Pow 215 D1
Gilbert La. D Pow 215 E1
Gilbert Pl. Card 188 B1
Gilbert St. Barry 225 D4
Gilberts Cross. D Pow 215 E1
Gilbertscliffe. T Mum 136 C2
Gileston Rd. Card 204 B4
Gileston Rd. St Ath 221 E2
Gilfach Houses. Maest 141 F3
Gilfach. Penga 58 A1
Gilfach Rd. B-coch 62 C2
Gilfach Rd. Tony 147 D3
Gilfach Rd. Tonypa 121 F2
Gilfach Rd. Tonypa 121 F3
Gilfach St. Bar 76 A2
Gilfach-Cynon. Mer T 51 F4
Gillian Rd. Card 187 F1
Gilmour St. Tonypa 121 F3
Gilwern Cres. Card 172 C1
Glade The. Brynco 164 A2
Glade The. Porth 176 C1
Gladeside Cl. Card 172 C2
Gladstone Rd. Barry 225 D3
Gladstone St. Abera 71 E4
Gladstone St. Cross 129 D2
Gladstone St. M Ash 72 C1
Gladstone St. Maest 117 D2

Gladstone Terr. M Ash 72 C1
Gladstone Terr. Mer T 51 F4
Gladstone Terr. Rhy 34 B3
Gladys St. Card 205 D4
Gladys St. P Tal 113 F1
Gladys St. Tony 167 E4
Glais Rd. A-wen 40 B1
Glamorgan Cl. Li' Maj 220 A4
Glamorgan Ct. Abera 71 E4
Glamorgan St. Abera 71 E4
Glamorgan St. Card 204 B3
Glamorgan St. M Ash 97 F4
Glamorgan St. Swan 110 B3
Glamorgan Street Mews.
  Card 204 B3
Glamorgan Terr. Tony 122 A1
Glamorgan Terr. Tony 146 B4
Glamorgan Terr. Trea 121 F4
Glan Creigiau. Ll'tris 185 E4
Glan Dulais. Swan 108 B4
Glan Ely Cl. Card 203 E4
Glan Ffrwd. Caer 151 F3
Glan Ffrwd. Porth 122 B1
Glan Gwrelych. G-nea 27 D1
Glan Hafren. P Tal 113 E3
Glan Islwyn. Pontll 101 F2
Glan Llwyd. Pontar 36 B3
Glan Nant Rd. Bridg 179 E3
Glan Rd. Aberd 49 F1
Glan Rd. Porthc 193 D4
Glan y Lli. Pen-cl 81 D2
Glan yr Afon Rd. Pyle 161 E2
Glan yr Afon Rd. Swan 109 E4
Glan yr Avon. Ystal 23 D3
Glan-Ddu Rd. Peng 101 D3
Glan-Ddu Terr. Gell 101 D3
Glan-nant Row. Pontcr 143 E1
Glan-Nant St. Abera 50 A1
Glan-Pelenna. Ton 88 C2
Glan-Rhyd Rd. Pontdw 40 B2
Glan-Rhyd Rd. Ystra 23 E4
Glan-y-Fford. T We 171 D3
Glan-y-Llan. Pyle 177 D4
Glan-y-Llyn. Tonypa 121 E3
Glan-y-Mor Ave. Marg 139 F2
Glan-y-Mor Rd. Card 190 C3
Glan-y-Nant. Colw 181 D1
Glan-y-Nant Ct. Card 188 A3
Glan-y-Nant. Deri 53 E4
Glan-y-Nant. Penco 181 E4
Glan-y-Nant Rd. Card 188 A3
Glan-y-Nant. Rhy 34 C3
Glan-y-Nant Terr. Card 188 A3
Glan-y-Parc. Bridg 179 F2
Glan-y-Wern Rd. Swan 85 F4
Glan-yr-Afon Ct. Maest 117 D4
Glan-yr-Afon Gdns. Swan . 109 E3
Glan-yr-Afon. Maest 142 B4
Glan-yr-Afon. Mer V 73 E2
Glan-yr-Afon Rd. Marg 161 E2
Glan-yr-Afon. Rhy 34 B3
Glan-yr-afon. Treo 94 B4
Glan-yr-avon. N Tre 54 C2
Glan-yr-Ysgol. Ystal 23 D3
Glanafon Terr. Maest 117 D4
Glanaman Rd. Abera 70 C2
Glanant St. Hir 48 B4
Glanberis Terr. Pontcr 118 B4
Glanbran Rd. Swan 86 A4
Glanbrydan Ave. Swan 109 F3
Glancynon St. M Ash 72 C1
Glancynon Terr. Abera 71 E4
Glancynon Terr. Abercy 98 C2
Glandovery Terr. Tred 35 E4
Glandovey Gr. Card 190 C3
Glandwr Cres. Swan 84 B2
Glandwr Pl. Card 188 A2
Glandwr Terr. Trea 121 F1
Glandyffryn Cl. Marg 139 E4
Glanfelin. Ponty 150 A2
Glanffornwg. Bridg 179 F4
Glanffrwd Rd. Pontar 36 B3
Glanffrwd Terr. Ynybw 97 F1
Glanhowy Rd. Ynys 127 F4
Glanlay St. M Ash 97 F4
Glanllyn Rd. Swan 61 D3
Glanmor Cres. Swan 109 F4
Glanmor Cl. Swan 109 F4
Glanmor La. Swan 109 F4
Glanmor Park Rd. Swan ... 109 F4
Glanmor Rd. Swan 109 F4
Glanmor Terr. Pen-cl 80 C2
Glanmorfa. Gow 82 A3
Glanmorlais. Mer T 33 D4
Glanmuir Rd. Card 206 A4
Glannant Pl. Blae 45 E4
Glannant Rd. Og Va 146 A4
Glannant Rd. Swan 36 C3
Glannant Rise. Neath 88 B3
Glannant St. Blae 45 E4
Glannant St. Tonypa 121 F2
Glannant St. Ynys 128 A2
Glannant Terr. Blae 45 E4
Glannant Terr. Ystra 23 F4
Glannant Way. Neath 88 B3
Glanogwr Rd. Bridg 179 F2
Glanrhyd. Card 188 B4

Glanrhyd St. Abera 70 C2
Glanrhyd Terr. Lough 82 B4
Glanselsig Terr. Trehe 68 A1
Glantaff Rd. Troed 52 A1
Glantawe Pk. Ystra 23 E4
Glantawe Row. Ystra 23 F4
Glantawe St. Swan 85 D4
Glantwrch. Ystal 23 E4
Glanville Terr. Fern 95 E4
Glanymor La. Lough 56 C1
Glanymor. Ll' Maj 220 B3
Glanymor Park Dr. Lough ... 56 C1
Glanymor Rd. Lough 56 C1
Glanymor St. Neath 87 D2
Glanyrafon Cl. Penga 58 A1
Glanyrafon Rd. Penco 181 F4
Glanyrafon Rd. Pontar 36 B2
Glas Canol. Card 188 A2
Glas Cwm. C-c-y-c 14 C2
Glas Efail. Card 188 B4
Glas Fryn. Gell 100 C4
Glas Ifor. Card 188 B3
Glas-y-Pant. Card 187 F4
Glasbrook Pl. Swan 83 F3
Glasbrook Terr. M Ash 98 A4
Glasbury Rd. Swan 84 B4
Glasfryn. Aberd 49 E2
Glasfryn. Bridg 180 B2
Glasfryn Cl. Swan 83 F1
Glasfryn Rd. Pontar 36 B2
Glasfryn Sq. Pyle 161 D1
Glasfryn Terr. Lough 82 C4
Glasfryn Terr. Tylor 96 A2
Glasier Rd. Mer T 51 F4
Glaslyn Dr. Abera 50 C1
Glaslyn Pl. Swan 59 E1
Glastonbury Rd. Sully 226 A3
Glastonbury Terr. Card 190 A3
Glayn yr Afon. Bedw 154 A3
Glebe Pl. Card 188 C4
Glebe Rd. Lough 56 C1
Glebe St. Barry 225 D4
Glebe St. Bedw 152 C3
Glebe St. Pen 217 D3
Glebe The. Bish 136 A4
Glebeland Cl. Bridg 180 C2
Glebeland Pl. St Ath 221 E2
Glebeland St. B-coch 62 C1
Glebeland St. Mer T 32 B1
Glen Cl. M Ash 72 A2
Glen Coed. Maesy 101 D1
Glen Garw. Ponter 118 C3
Glen Rd. Neath 88 A4
Glen Rd. T Mum 136 C3
Glen The. Brynco 163 F2
Glen View. Bridg 179 F4
Glen View. Card 188 C3
Glen View. Gell 100 C1
Glen View. Maesy 101 D1
Glen View. Mark 55 E1
Glen View. Og Va 145 D2
Glen View St. Tonypa 121 E4
Glen View Terr. Deri 53 E3
Glen View Terr. P Tal 114 A1
Glenavon Cres. Porth 192 B4
Glenavon St. Glyn 91 D3
Glenavon St. P Tal 138 C4
Glenavon Terr. Og Va 119 F4
Glenavon Terr. Tony 146 B4
Glenboi. M Ash 72 A2
Glenbrook Dr. Barry 225 E4
Glenbrook. M Ash 72 A2
Glencoe St. Barry 225 D3
Glendale Ave. Card 172 C1
Glendale. B-coch 62 B2
Glendower Cl. Bridg 180 A3
Glendower St. Mer T 33 D3
Glenfield Cl. Swan 109 D4
Glengower Cl. T Mum 137 D3
Glenmount Way. Card 172 B1
Glenrhondda Ct. Trehe 68 C1
Glenrise Cl. Card 191 D4
Glenroy Ave. Swan 110 C4
Glenroy St. Card 205 E4
Glenside Ct. Card 189 E1
Glenside Rd. Swan 83 F3
Glenview. Bridg 163 E1
Glenview Terr. Ll'bra 127 D1
Glenview Terr. Ynys 127 F3
Glenville Rd. T Mum 137 D3
Glenwood. Card 189 E3
Glenwood Cl. Bridg 180 C2
Globe St. Swan 85 D4
Glossop Rd. Card 205 E3
Glossop Terr. Penco 181 E4
Gloucester Bldgs. Pontcr .. 118 C2
Gloucester Pl. Swan 110 C3
Gloucester Pl. T Mum 137 D2
Gloucester St. Abera 50 A1
Gloucester St. Card 204 C3
Gluepot Rd. Li'Maj 209 E2
Glyn Bargoed Rd. Bed 99 E4
Glyn Bedw. Ll'bra 127 D2
Glyn Coed. Fern 95 D4
Glyn Coed Rd. Card 189 E4
Glyn Collen. Card 190 A4
Glyn Collen. Ll'bra 127 D2
Glyn Cres. Swan 109 E1

Glyn Deri. Deri

Glyn Deri. Deri 54 A1
Glyn Derwen. Ll'bra 127 D2
Glyn Eiddew. Card 189 F4
Glyn Eiddew. Ll'bra 127 D2
Glyn Hirnant. Swan 60 A2
Glyn Llwyfen. Ll'bra 127 D2
Glyn Neath Rd. G-nea 44 B2
Glyn Neath Rd. Reso 44 A2
Glyn Rd. G-C-G 5 D4
Glyn Rhosyn. Card 189 F4
Glyn Simon Cl. Card 187 F1
Glyn St. Og Va 119 F1
Glyn St. P Tal 138 C4
Glyn St. Porth 122 C1
Glyn St. Rhy 54 A4
Glyn St. Swan 84 B1
Glyn St. Ynybw 124 A4
Glyn Teg. Pontcr 143 E1
Glyn Terr. Deri 53 E4
Glyn Terr. Tonypa 121 C1
Glyn Terr. Tred 35 F2
Glyn Terr. Ynys 128 A3
Glyn View. Tony 147 F3
Glyn-Dwr Ave. Ponty 149 F3
Glyn-Gaer Rd. Gell 100 C4
Glyn-Llwchwr Rd. Pontar ... 36 B2
Glyn-Meirch Rd. Pontdw ... 40 B2
Glyn-Mynach St. Ynybw ... 124 A4
Glyn-neath Village
  Workshops. G-nea 26 C1
Glyn-y-Coed Rd. Neath 87 F4
Glyn-y-mel. Penco 181 D4
Glynbridge Cl. Swan 214 C1
Glynbridge Gdns. Bridg ... 179 F3
Glyncoed Terr. Mer T 51 F4
Glyncoli Cl. Treo 94 B4
Glyncoli Rd. Treo 94 B3
Glyncollen Cres. Swan 60 A2
Glyncollen Dr. Swan 60 A2
Glyncornel Cl. Trea 121 F4
Glyncynwal Rd. Cwmll 6 C2
Glynderwen Cl. Swan 109 D2
Glynderwen Cres. Swan ... 109 D1
Glyndwr Ave. St Ath 221 E2
Glyndwr Pl. Swan 110 A4
Glyndwr Rd. Card 203 D3
Glyndwr Rd. Pen 216 C2
Glyndwr St. Marg 114 A1
Glyndwr St. Mer V 73 E3
Glyndyrus Cl. Troed 51 F3
Glynfach Rd. Porth 122 C1
Glyngwyn St. M Ash 72 C1
Glynhafod St. Abera 70 C2
Glynhir Rd. Pontar 36 B3
Glynleiros Gdns. B-coch 87 E4
Glynllan. Og Va 145 D2
Glynmarch St. Deri 75 D4
Glynmelyn Rd. G-nea 27 D2
Glynn Terr. Mer T 32 C1
Glynne St. Card 204 B3
Glynrhondda St. Card 205 D4
Glynrhondda St. Treo 94 B4
Glynrhosyn. Lough 57 D1
Glynstell Cl. Card 204 B3
Glynstell Rd. Porth 176 C1
Glynsyfi. N Tre 54 C1
Glyntaff Rd. Ponty 149 F4
Glynteg Rd. Pontar 36 B3
Gnoll Ave. Neath 87 F4
Gnoll Bank. Neath 88 A4
Gnoll Cres. Neath 87 F4
Gnoll Dr. Neath 87 F4
Gnoll Park Rd. Neath 87 F4
Gnoll Rd. Ystal 22 C1
Gnoll View. Neath 88 A4
Goat Mill Rd. Mer T 33 D2
Godfrey St. Card 205 E3
Godre'r Coed Rd. C-c-y-c ... 32 A2
Godre'r Coed. Swan 59 E1
Godre'r Fro. Pontdw 40 B4
Godreaman St. Abera 71 E3
Godrer Coed. Gell 100 C4
Godwin Cl. Card 187 E2
Goetre Bellaf Rd. Swan 108 B4
Goetre Fach Rd. Swan 108 B4
Goetre Fawr Rd. Swan 108 B4
Goitre Coed Isaf. Abercy 98 C2
Goitre La. Mer T 32 B3
Goitre-Coed Rd. Tre 99 D3
Golate. Card 205 D3
Gold St. Card 205 E3
Goldcrest Dr. Card 189 E4
Golden Ave. P Tal 113 D1
Golden Cl. T Mum 136 C4
Golden Gr. Swan 84 B3
Golden Lion Ter. Ystal 7 D1
Golden Terr. Maest 117 D2
Goldsmith Cl. Bridg 179 E3
Goldsmith Cl. Card 190 A4
Goleg-y-Fro. Bridg 180 A2
Golf Rd. P Tal 113 E1
Golwg Hafren. Swan 109 C4
Golwg y Graig. Cry 43 D3
Golwg y Mynydd. Ystal 23 D2
Golwg-y-Bryn. Onll 25 D4
Golwg-y-Cwn. G-C-G 5 D3
Golwg-y-Gamlas. B-coch ... 62 C1
Golwg-y-Mynydd. Rhy 34 C3

Golwg-yr-Afon. B-coch 63 E2
Golwg-yr-Afon. Ll'ge 56 A4
Gomer Gdns. Swan 84 A1
Gomer Rd. Swan 83 F1
Gonhill. T Mum 136 C4
Goodrich Ave. Caer 152 B1
Goodrich St. Caer 152 A1
Goodwick Rd. Card 190 B2
Goodwin St. Maest 117 D2
Goodwood Cl. Card 202 C2
Goole Rd. Swan 83 E3
Goose Island. Swan 110 B3
Goppa Rd. Pontar 36 C2
Gordon Cl. Peng 101 E3
Gordon Cres. P Tal 113 E1
Gordon Rd. Card 205 D4
Gordon Rd. P Tal 113 E1
Gordon Rd. Peng 101 F3
Gordon Rd. Porth 192 C3
Gordon St. Abera 71 D3
Gordon St. Yst 94 C2
Gordon Thomas Cl. Swan ... 84 B1
Gore Terr. Swan 110 B4
Gored Cotts. Clyne 64 C4
Gored Terr. Clyne 64 C4
Gorof Rd. Ystra 23 E4
Goronwy Rd. Swan 83 F1
Gors Goch Rd. G-C-G 5 D4
Gors Rd. Penga 58 A1
Gorsafle. Ystra 24 A4
Gorse La. G-C-G 5 D2
Gorse La. Swan 110 A3
Gorse Pl. Card 203 E4
Gorse Terr. N Tre 54 C2
Gorsedd Gardens Rd. Card 205 D3
Gorsedd St. M Ash 72 B1
Gorsedd Terr. Mer T 32 C1
Gorseinon Rd. Penga 57 F1
Gorslas. Pyle 160 C1
Gorslwyn Terr. G-C-G 5 D1
Gorsto Rd. Cwmll 6 B1
Gorsto Rd. G-C-G 5 D3
Gorwydd Rd. Gow 82 B2
Gorwl Flats. Og Va 119 F1
Gorwl Rd. Og Va 119 F1
Goscombe Dr. Pen 216 C3
Goscombe Pk. Ll'thyg 212 B4
Goshen Cl. Rhy 34 C2
Goshen Pk. Skew 86 C4
Goshen St. Rhy 34 C2
Gospel Hall Terr. Aberd 49 F2
Gough Ave. Ystra 23 E4
Gough Rd. Card 203 E3
Gough Rd. Ystal 23 D3
Gower Cres. P Tal 113 E4
Gower Davies Ct. Ynybw ... 124 A4
Gower Holiday Village.
  P-Ey 132 A2
Gower Pl. T Mum 137 D3
Gower Rd. Abera 50 C1
Gower Rd. Swan 108 B3
Gower Rd. U Kill 108 B3
Gower St. Card 189 D1
Gower St. Marg 139 E4
Gower St. Neath 87 E2
Gower Terr. Pen-cl 80 C2
Gower View Rd. Lough 57 D2
Gower's Bldgs. Neath 87 D1
Gowerton Rd. Pen-cl 81 D2
Gowerton Rd. Pen-cl 81 F1
Goya Pl. P Tal 138 B4
Goytre Cl. Marg 139 F4
Goytre Cres. Marg 139 F4
Goytre Rd. Marg 139 F4
Gradon Cl. Barry 225 E3
Grafog St. Swan 111 D4
Grafton Cl. Card 189 E2
Grafton Dr. Ll'tris 168 C1
Grafton Terr. Card 188 B3
Graham Ave. Bridg 163 E1
Graham Cl. Card 189 F1
Graham Ct. Caer 152 B2
Graham St. Swan 84 B1
Graham Terr. Skew 86 C4
Graham Way. Mer T 32 B1
Graham Wlk. Card 204 B3
Graig Ave. Abera 71 F3
Graig Ave. Marg 139 F2
Graig Ave. Ponty 149 D4
Graig Cl. Troed 51 F2
Graig Cotts. Ll'tris 184 B3
Graig Cres. Abera 71 F3
Graig Ddu Cotts. Porth 122 B2
Graig Ddu. Fern 95 D4
Graig Ddu Pl. Porth 122 B2
Graig Fach. Ponty 149 F4
Graig Hir. Card 187 D4
Graig Llwyn Rd. Card 173 F2
Graig Lwyd. Card 187 D4
Graig Newydd. Ystal 22 C2
Graig Parc. N Abb 62 A1
Graig Parc. N Abb 62 C1
Graig Pl. Aberd 49 F1
Graig Pl. Swan 110 B4
Graig Rd. A-wen 41 D3
Graig Rd. Card 173 D3
Graig Rd. Cly 61 D3
Graig Rd. G-C-G 4 C3

Graig Rd. Gell 100 C1
Graig Rd. Glyn 92 A3
Graig Rd. Pontdw 40 B2
Graig Rd. Skew 86 B4
Graig Rd. Swan 84 C4
Graig Rd. Troed 51 F2
Graig Rd. Tylor 122 C4
Graig Rd. Ystal 22 C1
Graig Row. Ce Cr 162 B1
Graig St. Aberd 49 F1
Graig St. M Ash 72 B2
Graig St. Ponty 149 E4
Graig St. Swan 110 B4
Graig St. Tylor 96 A1
Graig Terr. Aber 125 F2
Graig Terr. Abera 71 F3
Graig Terr. Bar 75 F3
Graig Terr. Bed 74 A4
Graig Terr. Fern 96 A3
Graig Terr. Mer T 33 D3
Graig Terr. Og Va 144 C1
Graig Terr. Ponty 149 E4
Graig Terr. Swan 110 B4
Graig The. Bridg 179 F2
Graig The. Ce Cr 162 B1
Graig Twrch. Ystal 7 D3
Graig View. Bedw 154 A4
Graig View. Card 173 D2
Graig View. Pontmi 129 F1
Graig View. Ynys 128 A3
Graig Wen. Card 187 D4
Graig Wen. Fern 95 D4
Graig y Darren. Ystal 23 D2
Graig y Pal. Cly 61 D3
Graig yr Wylan. Caer 151 F1
Graig Ysguthan. Cly 127 D3
Graig-Llwyn Rd. Card 173 F2
Graig-y-Bedw. N Tre 54 C2
Graig-y-Coed. Pen-cl 80 B2
Graig-y-Ddelw. Trehe 68 B2
Graig-y-Dderi. Cly 61 D3
Graig-yr-Eos Terr. Tonypa 122 A2
Graig-yr-Helfa Rd. Ponty ... 149 F4
Graigddu Rd. Tonypa 122 A2
Graiglas. Pontcr 144 A1
Graiglwyd. Aberd 49 E2
Graiglwyd Rd. Swan 109 F4
Graiglwyd Sq. Swan 109 F4
Graigola Rd. Cly 61 D3
Graigwen Cres. Aber 151 D4
Graigwen Parc. Ponty 124 A2
Graigwen Pl. Ponty 124 A1
Graigwen Rd. Ponty 124 A1
Graigwen Rd. Porth 122 C1
Graigymerched. Ystal 23 D3
Graigyrhesg Pl. Ponty 124 B2
Graigyrhesg Rd. Ponty 124 B2
Grampian Way. Swan 83 F2
Grand Ave. Card 203 E3
Grandison St. Neath 87 E1
Grandison St. Swan 84 B1
Grange Ave. Wen 215 D4
Grange Cl. Caer 151 F2
Grange Cl. Wen 215 D4
Grange Cres. Bridg 180 C2
Grange Cres. T Mum 137 D4
Grange Ct. Barry 225 E3
Grange Gdns. Card 204 C1
Grange Gdns. Ll' Maj 220 A3
Grange Hill. Peng 101 E3
Grange La. T Mum 137 D4
Grange Pl. Card 205 D1
Grange Rd. Marg 139 F1
Grange Rd. T Mum 137 D4
Grange St. Marg 139 E4
Grange Terr. Trea 121 F4
Grange The. Caer 151 F2
Grange The. Card 204 A4
Grangetown Link. Card 204 B1
Grangetown Link. Pen 216 C4
Granogwen Rd. Swan 84 B1
Grant's Cl. Card 187 E4
Grant's Field. Wen 202 B1
Grantham Cl. Card 187 F1
Granville Ave. Card 204 A4
Granville Rd. Swan 110 C4
Granville Terr. M Ash 72 B2
Grasholm Gdns. Swan 83 F4
Grassholm Way. Porth 176 B1
Grassmere Cl. Pen 216 C3
Grawen La. C-c-y-c 31 F3
Grawen. Mer T 32 B1
Grawen St. Porth 122 C2
Grawen Terr. Mer T 32 B1
Gray La. Card 204 B3
Gray St. Card 204 B3
Gray's Pl. Mer V 73 E2
Graylands The. Card 188 B3
Grays Gdns. Bedw 153 E3
Grays Wlk. Cowb 198 C1
Great St. Ponty 123 E1
Great Western Ave. Bridg . 179 F3
Great Western Cotts. Mark . 55 E1
Great Western Ct. Card 204 B3
Great Western La. Card 205 D1
Great Western Terr. Cwma 114 C3

Great Western Terr. Ll'tris . 168 A1
Greave Cl. Wen 215 D4
Greehill Ct. Card 188 A4
Greek Church St. Card 205 D2
Green Acre Dr. Tonypa 121 F3
Green Acre. Penty 185 F4
Green Ave The. Porth 192 C3
Green Bank Rd. T Mum ... 136 C4
Green Circ. Pyle 161 D1
Green Cl. T Mum 109 D1
Green Dragon La. Swan ... 110 B3
Green Farm Cl. Card 203 D2
Green Farm Rd. Card 203 D2
Green Field Terr. Pontcr ... 143 E1
Green Hill. Pontcr 118 C2
Green Hill. Yst 95 D2
Green La. Barry 225 E4
Green La. D Pow 226 A4
Green La. Ll' maj 219 E3
Green Lawns. Barry 225 D4
Green Meadow. Glyn 66 C2
Green Meadow Terr.
  Pontcr 144 A2
Green Meadows. Card 190 C3
Green Park St. P Tal 139 D4
Green Pk. Ll'tris 168 B1
Green Row. Bedw 153 F3
Green St. Aberd 49 F1
Green St. Bridg 179 F3
Green St. Card 204 C3
Green St. Neath 87 F4
Green St. P Tal 138 C4
Green St. Swan 85 D4
Green The. Brynco 163 F2
Green The. C-c-y-c 32 A3
Green The. Card 187 E3
Green The. M-I-Pit 204 A1
Green The. Neath 87 E4
Green The. Penco 181 F4
Green The. Pontll 101 E2
Green The. Rhy 54 B4
Green Wood Dr. Ch Vil 169 D2
Greenacre Dr. Bedw 152 B3
Greenacre Dr. Penco 181 E4
Greenacre Dr. Swan 61 D3
Greenacres. Barry 225 E4
Greenacres. Marg 140 A1
Greenacres. Pyle 176 C3
Greenbay Rd. Card 206 A3
Greenclose Rd. Card 188 B2
Greencroft Ave. Card 203 F3
Greendale Pl. Card 187 E4
Greenesway. Rhy 54 B4
Greenfield Ave. Card 188 B3
Greenfield Ave. Card 204 B4
Greenfield Ave. Marg 139 F2
Greenfield Ave. Ponty 124 B3
Greenfield Cl. Swan 85 F4
Greenfield Cres. Swan 85 F4
Greenfield Gdns. Troed 52 A2
Greenfield. N Tre 54 B2
Greenfield Pl. Aber 150 C4
Greenfield Pl. Lough 81 F4
Greenfield Rd. Card 188 B3
Greenfield Rd. Glan 4 B4
Greenfield St. Bar 76 A2
Greenfield St. Rhy 53 F4
Greenfield St. Tonypa 122 A2
Greenfield Terr. Abercy 98 C3
Greenfield Terr. Aberd 71 F4
Greenfield Terr. Brynco 164 C3
Greenfield Terr. M Ash 72 A3
Greenfield Terr. Maest 91 D1
Greenfield Terr. Maest 117 D2
Greenfield Terr. Maest 142 C3
Greenfield Terr. Mark 76 C2
Greenfield Terr. Mer T 33 D2
Greenfield Terr. Og Va 119 F1
Greenfield Terr. Pontcr 118 C2
Greenfield Terr. Pyle 176 C4
Greenfield Terr. Swan 84 B1
Greenfield Terr. Swan 85 E4
Greenfield Terr. Ynys 127 F3
Greenfield Way. Cowb 198 B3
Greenfield Way. Porth 176 C1
Greenfields Ave. Bridg 179 E2
Greenfields Terr. Swan 109 E4
Greenhaven Rise. Pen 216 C3
Greenhill Dr. Abera 71 E4
Greenhill Pl. Gell 100 B3
Greenhill St. Swan 84 C1
Greenlands Rd. Ll'tris 168 C2
Greenlawns. Card 189 E1
Greenmeadow Bungalows.
  Gall 101 D4
Greenmeadow. Ce Cr 162 A1
Greenmeadow Cl. D pow .. 216 A1
Greenmeadow Cl. Ponty .. 124 B3
Greenmeadow Cl. Ll'tris .. 168 C1
Greenmeadow Dr. Card ... 187 E4
Greenmeadow. Gar P 153 E3
Greenmeadow. Pontcr 143 E2
Greenmeadow. Rhy 54 B4
Greenmeadow Rd. Ynys .. 128 B2
Greenmeadow. Tonypa122 A1
Greenmeadows. Bridg 179 F3
Greenock Rd. Card 190 B2
Greenside. Cowb 198 C1

Groves Ave. T Mum

Greenway Ave. Card 190 B2
Greenway. Bedw 152 B3
Greenway Cl. Pen 216 B4
Greenway Ct. Barry 225 E4
Greenway Ct. Bedw 152 B3
Greenway Rd. Card 190 B3
Greenway Rd. Neath 87 F4
Greenway The. Skew 86 B2
Greenway Workshops.
  Bedw 152 B3
Greenways. Porthc 193 D4
Greenways. Swan 82 B2
Greenways The. Maest 117 D1
Greenwich Rd. Card 204 A4
Greenwood Ave. Maest ... 117 D1
Greenwood Cl. Bridg 179 F4
Greenwood Cl. Swan 109 E3
Greenwood Cl. Caer 152 B2
Greenwood Dr. Hir 48 C4
Greenwood Dr. Neath 88 B3
Greenwood La. Card 203 D4
Greenwood Pl. Swan 83 E3
Greenwood Rd. Card 187 F1
Greenwood Rd. Neath 87 E2
Greenwood Rd. P Tal 113 E4
Greenwood Rd. Peng 101 E4
Gregory Cl. Penco 181 D4
Grenfell Ave. Lough 57 D2
Grenfell Park Rd. Swan ... 110 C4
Grenfell Town. Swan 84 C2
Grenig Rd. Glan 4 A3
Grenville Rd. Card 205 E4
Gresford Cl. Card 190 B3
Gresham Pl. Tre 99 D3
Grey Cres. Gall 101 D3
Grey's Dr. Ll' Maj 220 A3
Grey's Pl. Llwy 49 F4
Greyfriars. Bridg 179 F3
Greyfriars Ct. Porthc 193 E4
Greyfriars Pl. Card 205 D3
Greyfriars Rd. Card 205 D3
Greys Terr. Swan 61 D1
Grieg Cl. P Tal 113 C2
Griffith John St. Swan 84 B1
Griffith St. Abera 50 A1
Griffith St. Fern 70 A1
Griffiths St. Gell 100 C1
Griffiths St. Yst 94 C2
Griffiths Terr. Maest 91 D1
Grimson Cl. Sully 226 A3
Gripoly Mills. Card 204 C1
Grisedale Cl. Card 189 D3
Groes Lon. Card 188 A4
Groes-Faen Terr. Deri 75 E3
Groes-Wen La. Marg 139 E2
Groeswen Dr. Caer 151 E2
Groeswen. Ll' maj 219 E4
Groeswen Rd. Aber 151 D2
Groeswen Rd. Caer 151 E2
Gron Ffordd. Card 172 A1
Gron Rd. G-C-G 5 D2
Grongaer Terr. Ponty 149 E4
Grosmont Cl. Peng 76 C1
Grosvenor Rd. Swan 109 E4
Grosvenor St. Card 204 A3
Grosvenor Terr. Maest 91 D1
Grouse St. Card 205 E4
Grove Est. Bedw 153 D4
Grove House Ct. Tylor 96 B3
Grove La. Neath 87 E3
Grove La. Skew 86 C4
Grove Pk. Mer T 32 B2
Grove Pl. Card 188 B3
Grove Pl. Marg 139 D4
Grove Pl. Pen 217 D2
Grove Pl. Swan 110 B4
Grove Place La. Pen 217 D2
Grove Rd. Bridg 179 F2
Grove Rd. Cly 39 E1
Grove Rd. Llys 209 D4
Grove Rd. Pontdw 40 C3
Grove Rd. Pontmi 129 F1
Grove St. Ll'bra 126 C1
Grove St. Lough 57 D2
Grove St. Maest 117 D1
Grove Terr. Aber 125 F1
Grove Terr. Abera 71 F3
Grove Terr. Bed 74 A4
Grove Terr. Ll'ha 166 C2
Grove Terr. Pen 217 D2
Grove Terr. Ynybw 124 A4
Grove The. Abera 50 A1
Grove The. Card 190 B2
Grove The. Deri 53 E4
Grove The. Mer T 32 B1
Grove The. Mer V 73 E3
Grove The. Pontll 101 F2
Grove The. Ponty 149 F3
Grove The. Swan 109 F4
Grove The. T Mum 137 D2
Grove Way. Card 190 B2
Grovefield Terr. Tonypa ... 121 F2
Groveland Rd. Card 188 B3
Grovenor Rd. Rhiwd 155 F2
Grover St. Ponty 149 D4
Grovers Cl. Ponty 124 B3
Groves Ave. T Mum 136 C2

Groves Rd. Neath

Groves Rd. Neath 87 F3
Gruffyd Dr. Caer 152 A3
Grwyne Terr. Mark 76 C2
Guardian Ind Est. Card 205 F4
Guenever Cl. Card 172 B1
Guest Cotts. Mer T 33 D3
Guest Rd. Card 205 F2
Guest St. Deri 53 E4
Guildford Cres. Card 205 D3
Guildford St. Card 205 D3
Guildhall Place. Card 205 D3
Guildhall Rd N. Swan 110 A3
Guildhall Rd S. Swan 110 A3
Gulliver's Cl. T Mum 137 D4
Gurnos Rd. Gow 82 A3
Gurnos Rd. Mer T 32 B2
Gurnos Rd. Ystal 23 E4
Gurnos Rd. Ystra 23 E4
Guthrie St. Barry 225 D3
Guy's Rd. Barry 225 D3
Gwaelod-y-garth Ind Est.
   Penty 171 D1
Gwaelodygarth Rd. Ponty 150 B1
Gwaelodygarth Cl. Mer T 32 B2
Gwaelodygarth Rd. Mer T .. 32 C2
Gwaelodygwaun Villas. Bar .. 76 A2
Gwalia Cl. Bridg 163 F1
Gwalia Cl. Penga 57 E1
Gwalia Cres. Penga 57 E1
Gwalia Ct. Cly 60 B4
Gwalia Ct. Swan 110 A3
Gwalia Gr. Ponty 149 F3
Gwalia Rd. Penco 181 F4
Gwalia Terr. Penga 57 E1
Gwar-y-Caeau. Marg 139 E4
Gwaun Bedw. Porth 122 C1
Gwaun Cl. Card 187 F2
Gwaun Coed. Card 180 A2
Gwaun Cotts. Ll'ha 183 D4
Gwaun Newydd. Caer 152 B2
Gwaun Rd. Ponty 149 F3
Gwaun-Bant. Pontcr 118 C2
Gwaun-Fro. Gell 100 B4
Gwaun-Hyfryd. Caer 152 B2
Gwaun-Ruperra Cl. Ll'tris .. 168 B2
Gwaun-Ruperra Rd. Ll'tris. 168 B2
Gwaun-y-groes. Ll'tris 168 C1
Gwaunfarren Cl. Mer T 32 C2
Gwaunfarren Gr. Mer T 32 C2
Gwaunfarren Rd. Mer T 32 C2
Gwaunmiskin Rd. Ll'tris ... 169 D3
Gwaunrhydd. Ll'tris 169 D3
Gwawr St. Abera 71 D4
Gwbert Cl. Card 190 C3
Gwelfor. Ce Cr 162 A1
Gwelfor. Swan 108 C4
Gwendoline Pl. Card 205 E3
Gwendoline Rd. Pontmi ... 129 F1
Gwendoline St. Card 205 E3
Gwendoline St. Mer T 32 C2
Gwendoline St. Og Va 119 F3
Gwendoline St. P Tal 114 A1
Gwendoline St. Pontcr 118 C3
Gwendoline St. Trehe 68 C1
Gwendoline Terr. Abercy 98 C2
Gwendoline Terr. Maest 142 A4
Gwendraeth Pl. Swan 85 D1
Gwenfo Dr. Wen 215 D4
Gwenfron Terr. Tonypa 122 A1
Gwenlais Rd. Pont 57 F4
Gwenllian St. Barry 225 E3
Gwenllian Terr. Ponty 149 F2
Gwennyth St. Card 189 D1
Gwent Ct. Peng 101 D3
Gwent Gdns. Swan 83 F1
Gwent Gr. Swan 109 D3
Gwent House. Card 189 E1
Gwent House. P Tal 138 B4
Gwent. Pen 217 E3
Gwent Rd. Card 203 D2
Gwent Rd. Ponty 150 B1
Gwent Rd. Swan 84 B4
Gwent Shopping Ctr. Tred .. 35 F4
Gwent Terr. Porth 122 C2
Gwent Way. Tred 35 E4
Gwern Ave. Aber 125 F1
Gwern Einon Rd. Swan 109 D2
Gwern Fadog Rd. Swan 60 A2
Gwern-Rhuddi Rd. Card ... 189 E4
Gwerna Cres. Maesy 101 D1
Gwernant. Cwmll 6 B3
Gwernifor St. M Ash 72 B1
Gwernllwyn Cl. Mer T 33 D2
Gwernllwyn Terr. Tylor 96 A2
Gwernllwynchwyth Rd.
   Swan 60 C1
Gwernllyn Rd. Mer T 33 D2
Gwernos. Swan 60 A1
Gwerthonor La. Bar 101 D4
Gwerthonor Pl. Bar 76 A1
Gwili Terr. Swan 84 A1
Gwilym Pl. Barry 225 D4
Gwilym Rd. Cwmll 6 B3
Gwilym St. Ch Vil 149 F2
Gwlad Du Gwyrdd. Tony ... 146 A3
Gwlad-y-Gan. Card 59 E1
Gwladys St. Mer T 32 C2
Gwladys St. Mer T 33 D4

Gwladys St. Peny 49 D3
Gwrhyd Rd. Cwmll 6 B1
Gwrhyd Rd. Pontdw 21 F2
Gwrhyd Rd. Ystal 22 A4
Gwydr Cres. Swan 109 F3
Gwydr Mews. Swan 109 F3
Gwydr Pl. Lough 56 B1
Gwydr Sq. Swan 109 F3
Gwydr Villas. Lough 56 B1
Gwylfa Rd. Swan 83 F1
Gwylym St. Swan 84 A1
Gwyn Cr. P Tal 139 D4
Gwyn Ct. P Tal 139 D4
Gwyn Dr. Caer 152 A2
Gwyn James Ct. Pen 216 C3
Gwyn St. A-wen 40 C2
Gwyn St. Ponty 149 F3
Gwyn Terr. Cry 43 D3
Gwyn Terr. P Tal 139 D4
Gwyn's Pl. A-wen 40 C2
Gwynant Cres. Card 189 D3
Gwyndy Rd. Swan 85 D1
Gwynedd Ave. Glyn 91 E2
Gwynedd Ave. Swan 83 F1
Gwynedd Gdns. Swan 110 A4
Gwynedd House. Card 189 E1
Gwynfe Rd. Lough 56 C2
Gwynfi St. Glyn 92 A3
Gwynfi St. Swan 84 B3
Gwynfi Terr. Ll'ha 167 D2
Gwynfor Rd. Swan 83 F1
Gwynfryn. Ch Vil 169 E4
Gwynfryn Rd. Pontar 36 B2
Gwynne Terr. Swan 111 D4
Gwynnes Cl. Mer T 32 C1
Gwyrddgoed. Pontdw 40 C3
Gwysfa Rd. Swan 60 A3
Gwysfryn. Ystra 6 C2
Gyfeillon Rd. Ponty 123 F1
Gynol Rd. Cwmll 6 B3
Gynor Ave. Tylor 122 C3
Gynor Pl. Tylor 122 C3
Gypsy La. Aber 151 E1
Gyrnosfa. Ystra 23 E4

Habershon St. Card 205 F3
Hackerford Rd. Card 189 E4
Hadfield Rd. Card 204 B1
Hadland Terr. T Mum 137 D3
Hadley House. Pen 216 C1
Hadrian's Cl. Gell 100 B4
Hael La. South 135 D2
Hafan Deg. Maest 142 B4
Hafan Deg. Penco 181 E4
Hafan Deg. Se Si 24 C3
Hafan Deg. Tondu 163 E2
Hafan Glyd. Cly 60 C4
Hafan y Don. Swan 108 C4
Hafan-Werdd. Caer 152 B3
Hafan-y-Bryn. Bridg 179 E2
Hafandeg. Llwy 49 F3
Hafnant. Swan 85 E3
Hafod Cl. Peng 101 D3
Hafod Decaf. Pyle 161 D1
Hafod La. Ponty 123 F2
Hafod Las. Penco 181 E4
Hafod Pk. Swan 84 B1
Hafod St. Card 204 C2
Hafod St. Swan 84 B1
Hafod The. Mer T 33 D3
Hafod Tudor Terr. Ynys ... 128 C2
Hafod Wen. Aberd 49 E2
Hafod Wen. Tony 147 E3
Hafod-y-Mynydd. Rhy 35 D2
Haford St. Marg 139 E4
Hafren Ct. Card 204 B4
Haig Pl. Card 203 D2
Haig Pl. Swan 83 F2
Hailey Ct. Card 187 F2
Haldane Ct. Caer 152 B2
Halifax Terr. Trehe 68 C2
Hall Cl. Pyle 177 D4
Hall Dr. Pyle 177 D4
Hall La. Pen-cl 80 B2
Hall St. Abera 50 A1
Hall St. Bry 5 E4
Hall St. Peng 101 F4
Hall St. Swan 84 B1
Hall's Rd. Cross 129 E3
Hallbank. T Mum 137 D2
Hallbank Terr. T Mum 137 D2
Halsbury Rd. Card 204 A4
Halswell St. Abercy 98 A3
Halt Cl. Rhig 28 B1
Halt Rd. Rhig 28 B1
Halton Cl. Pen 227 D4
Ham La E. Ll' Maj 220 A3
Ham La S. Ll' Maj 220 A3
Haman Pl. Gell 100 B3
Hamilton St. Card 204 C3
Hamilton St. M Ash 72 B2
Hamilton St. Swan 84 B2
Hamilton St. Troed 52 A2
Hamilton Terr. Maest 91 E1
Hammond Way. Card 189 F1
Hampstead Wlk. Card 202 C2
Hampton Court Rd. Card .. 189 F1
Hampton Cres E. Card 173 E1

Hampton Cres W. Card 173 E1
Hampton Ct. Card 189 E1
Hampton Rd. Card 188 B2
Hampton St. Mer T 51 F4
Hanbury Ct. Card 187 F3
Hanbury Rd. Bar 76 A2
Hanbury Sq. Bar 76 A2
Hanbury St. Gall 101 D4
Handel Ave. P Tal 113 D2
Handel Cl. Pen 216 C1
Hangman's Cross. Ox 132 C1
Hankey Pl. Mer T 51 F4
Hannah Cl. Card 188 C3
Hannah St. Barry 225 D3
Hannah St. Card 205 D2
Hannah St. Porth 122 C2
Hannants The. B-coch 87 E4
Hanover Cl. T Mum 137 D3
Hanover Ct. Barry 225 E4
Hanover Ct. Bridg 179 F3
Hanover Ct. Card 187 F3
Hanover Ct. Swan 109 E4
Hanover La. Swan 110 A4
Hanover St. Card 204 B3
Hanover St. Mer T 32 B1
Hanover St. Swan 110 A4
Hansom Pl. Card 204 C2
Harbour View Rd. Pen 217 D3
Harbour View Rd. Swan ... 111 D4
Harcombe Rd. Trea 122 A4
Harcourt Pl. Rhy 34 B3
Harcourt Rd. M Ash 72 B2
Harcourt St. Swan 110 A4
Harcourt Terr. Tred 35 F3
Harding Cl. Ll' Maj 220 B3
Hardingsdown La. Ll'gen .. 103 E2
Hardwicke St. Card 204 A4
Hardy Cl. Barry 225 D4
Hardy Pl. Card 205 E4
Harebell Cl. Swan 60 A2
Harford Cl. Card 187 F3
Harford St. Swan 109 E3
Harford Gdns. Tred 35 F4
Harford St. Tred 35 F4
Harle St. Neath 87 F4
Harlech Cl. D pow 216 B2
Harlech Cl. Peng 76 B1
Harlech Cl. Swan 109 D4
Harlech Cres. Swan 109 D4
Harlech Ct. Caer 151 E2
Harlech Ct. Card 188 A3
Harlech Dr. D pow 216 B2
Harlech Dr. Mer T 31 E2
Harlech Dr. Rhiwd 155 F2
Harlech House. Card 187 E3
Harlech Rd. Aberd 49 F1
Harlech Rd. Card 190 B2
Harlech St. G-C-G 5 F3
Harlequin Ct. Card 205 F4
Harlequin Rd. P Tal 113 F1
Harleyford Rd. Hen 36 A2
Harlington Rd. Swan 84 A1
Harold St. Card 205 F4
Harold St. Ll'ha 166 C1
Harold Wilson Ind Est.
   Caer 152 B1
Harpur St. Card 205 D2
Harries St. Swan 110 A4
Harriet St. Aberd 49 F2
Harriet St. Card 205 D4
Harriet St. Pen 216 C3
Harriet Town. Troed 52 A1
Harrington Ct. Card 203 D2
Harrington Pl. Swan 84 B1
Harrington St. Swan 84 B1
Harris Ave. Card 190 B2
Harris Rd. Cwmll 6 B3
Harris Row. C-c-y-c 14 C2
Harris St. Hir 48 B4
Harris St. Swan 84 C4
Harris View. M Ash 97 F4
Harrismith Rd. Card 189 E1
Harrison St. Mer T 32 C2
Harrison Way. Card 216 C4
Harrowby La. Card 205 D1
Harrowby Pl. Card 205 D1
Harrowby St. Card 205 D1
Harry Simpson House.
   Swan 110 C4
Harry St. Swan 59 F1
Hartfield Cl. Swan 109 D4
Hartland Rd. Card 190 A3
Hartley Pl. Card 204 C2
Hartshorn Ct. Caer 152 B2
Hartshorn Terr. Maest 91 D1
Harvey Cres. P Tal 138 C4
Harvey St. Barry 225 E3
Harvey St. Card 204 B3
Harvey St. Maest 117 D2
Hastings Ave. Pen 216 C2
Hastings Cl. Pen 216 C2
Hastings Pl. Pen 216 C2
Hatfield Ct. Swan 83 F3
Hathaway Pl. Barry 225 E4
Hatherleigh Dr. T Mum 136 C3
Hatherleigh Rd. Card 190 A2
Haul Bryn. Og Va 119 F3

Haul Fron. Tonypa 122 A1
Haul Fryn. Caer 187 F4
Haulfryn. Peny 49 D3
Haulfryn. Pontdw 40 C3
Haulfryn. Swan 61 D1
Haulfryn. Tondu 163 F3
Haulwen Rd. Gell 100 C4
Haulwen Rd. Swan 83 E1
Havant Cl. Rhoose 223 D1
Havard Rd. Aber 150 C4
Havard's Row. Rhy 34 C2
Havelock Pl. Card 204 C2
Havelock St. Card 205 D3
Haven Cl. Troed 52 A1
Haven The. Hir 48 B4
Haverford Way. Card 203 E2
Havergal Cl. T Mum 136 B2
Hawfinch Cl. Card 189 E4
Hawkhurst Ct. Porth 176 C1
Hawkstone Cl. T Mum 136 C4
Hawkwood Cl. Card 187 D1
Hawthorn Ave. Gell 100 C2
Hawthorn Ave. Lough 57 D1
Hawthorn Ave. Mer T 32 B2
Hawthorn Ave. Neath 87 F3
Hawthorn Ave. P Tal 113 E3
Hawthorn Ave. Pen 216 C2
Hawthorn Cl. Cwma 114 C2
Hawthorn Cl. D pow 216 A1
Hawthorn Cres. Ponty 150 A2
Hawthorn Dr. Bridg 180 C2
Hawthorn Dr. Pontll 101 F2
Hawthorn Dr. Pyle 176 C3
Hawthorn Hill. C-c-y-c 32 A4
Hawthorn Pl. Cross 129 E3
Hawthorn Pl. Porthc 193 E4
Hawthorn Rd E. Card 187 F2
Hawthorn Rd. Ll'hry 183 E3
Hawthorn Rd. Ponty 150 A2
Hawthorn Rd W. Card 187 F2
Hawthorn Rise. Aberd 49 E2
Hawthorn Terr. M Ash 97 F4
Hawthorn Villas. Ponty 150 A2
Hawthorn Villas. Ystra 7 F1
Hawthorn Way. Bridg 180 B2
Hawthorne Ave. Swan 109 F4
Hawthorne Rd. Nel 79 F1
Hawthorne Terr. Abera 50 A1
Hawthorns The. Card 189 F3
Hawthorns The. Mer T 33 D4
Haxby Ct. Card 205 E2
Hay's Cres. G-nea 27 D1
Haydn Terr. Mer T 32 C2
Hayes Bridge Rd. Card 205 D3
Hayes La. Barry 225 E4
Hayes Rd. Barry 225 F2
Hayes Rd. Sully 225 F2
Hayes The. Card 205 D3
Haywain Ct. Bridg 180 A2
Hazel Cl. Porthc 193 E4
Hazel Cl. Swan 109 D3
Hazel Ct. Tony 147 E3
Hazel Dr. Aberd 49 E1
Hazel Gr. Bedw 152 C3
Hazel Gr. Caer 152 B3
Hazel Gr. D pow 216 A1
Hazel Mead. Tondu 163 F3
Hazel Pl. Card 187 E1
Hazel Rd. Pen 216 C1
Hazel Rd. Swan 109 F4
Hazel Terr. M Ash 97 F4
Hazel Terr. Troed 52 A1
Hazel Tree Cl. Card 187 D3
Hazel Tree Way. Bridg 180 B3
Hazeldene Ave. Bridg 180 B2
Hazeldene Ave. Card 189 D1
Hazeldene. Ll'hry 183 D3
Hazelhurst Rd. Card 187 F2
Hazelmere Rd. Swan 109 E4
Hazeltree Copse. Pen-cl .. 80 A1
Hazelwell Rd. Porth 192 C4
Hazelwood Dr. Card 190 C4
Hazelwood Rd. Neath 87 F4
Hazelwood Row. Cwma ... 114 C3
Hazelwood. St B M 194 B1
Hazelwood Terr. Cwma 114 C2
Hazledene Cl. Barry 225 D4
Hazlitt Cl. Card 190 B4
Headland Cl. Bish 136 A3
Headland Rd. Bish 136 A3
Headland Rd. Swan 110 C4
Heads Of The Valleys
   Ind Est. Rhy 34 B2
Heads of the Valleys Rd.
   Hir 30 B1
Heads of the Valleys Rd.
   Mer T 31 E2
Heads Of The Valleys Rd.
   Mer T 33 E3
Heads Of The Valleys Rd.
   Rhy 34 B4
Heads Of The Valleys Rd.
   Trefil 16 C1
Hearts of Oak Cotts. Maest 117 D4
Heaselands Pl. Swan 108 A3
Heath Ave. Pen 216 B3

Heath Cl. Abera 50 B1
Heath Cl. T Mum 136 C3
Heath Cres. Ponty 124 A1
Heath Halt Rd. Card 189 D3
Heath Mead. Card 189 D3
Heath Park Ave. Card 189 D3
Heath Park Cres. Card 189 D2
Heath Park Dr. Card 189 D3
Heath Park La. Card 188 B2
Heath Park La. Card 189 D3
Heath Rd. Pontll 101 E2
Heath St. Card 204 C3
Heath Terr. Ponty 124 A1
Heath Terr. Tylor 122 C4
Heathbrook. Card 189 D3
Heathcliffe Cl. Card 190 B4
Heather Ave. Card 203 F3
Heather Cl. Brynco 163 F2
Heather Cres. Swan 109 D3
Heather Rd. Mer T 32 B3
Heather Way. Card 203 E4
Heather Way. Porth 123 D2
Heatherslade Cl. South ... 135 D2
Heatherslade Cl. T Mum .. 137 D2
Heatherslade Rd. G-nea .. 135 D2
Heathfield. Lough 57 D1
Heathfield Ave. G-nea 27 D1
Heathfield Cres. Ll'ha 166 C1
Heathfield Cl. G-nea 27 D1
Heathfield. Lough 57 D1
Heathfield Pl. Card 188 C1
Heathfield Rd. Card 188 C1
Heathfield Rd. Pontdw 40 C3
Heathfield. Swan 110 B4
Heathfield Wlk. Bar 76 A3
Heathlands. Gell 100 C1
Heathlands The. Tony 146 B3
Heathway. Card 188 C3
Heathwood Ct. Card 188 C3
Heathwood Gr. Card 189 D2
Heathwood Rd. Card 188 C3
Heathwood Rd. T Mum 137 D4
Hebbles La. Barry 225 D4
Hebron Rd. Cly 60 B4
Hebron Villas. Abercy 98 A3
Hedd Aberth. Onll 25 D4
Heddfaen N. Card 189 F4
Heddfaen S. Card 189 F4
Heddwch Cl. Mer T 33 D3
Hedel Rd. Card 204 A3
Hedgemoor. Bridg 180 B2
Hedreladus. Ystra 8 A1
Heilbronn Way. Marg 139 D4
Heilbronn Way. P Tal 114 A1
Hel Ton. Pyle 176 B4
Helen Pl. Card 205 E4
Helen St. Card 205 E4
Helen's Rd. Neath 87 E3
Helig Fan. Pyle 161 D1
Helwick Cl. T Mum 137 D3
Hemingway Rd. Card 205 E1
Hen Felin. Ystra 23 E4
Hen Parc Ave. U Kill 108 A3
Hen Parc La. U Kill 108 B2
Hendre Ave. Og Va 119 F2
Hendre. Caer 151 F3
Hendre Cl. Card 204 A4
Hendre Cl. Ll'ge 56 A4
Hendre Cres. Ll'ge 56 A4
Hendre Fawr. Rhig 47 D4
Hendre Gdns. Card 204 A4
Hendre Gwilym. Tonypa .. 121 F2
Hendre. Onll 9 F1
Hendre Owain. Swan 109 E4
Hendre Owen Rd. Glyn ... 90 B2
Hendre Pk. Ll'ge 56 A4
Hendre Rd. Aber 150 C4
Hendre Rd. Card 190 C3
Hendre Rd. Glan 4 B4
Hendre Rd. Hen 17 E4
Hendre Rd. Ll'ge 56 A4
Hendre Rd. Penco 181 D2
Hendre. Swan 108 B4
Hendre Terr. Tonypa 122 A2
Hendre-Foilan Rd. Swan .. 109 D4
Hendrecafn Rd. Tonypa ... 121 F2
Hendredenny Dr. Caer 151 E2
Hendrefadog St. Tylor 96 B2
Hendrefoilan Ave. Swan .. 109 D4
Hendrefoilan Cl. Swan 109 D4
Hendrefoilan Dr. Swan 109 D4
Hendrefoilan Student
   Village. Swan 109 D4
Hendreforgan Cres. Tony . 146 B3
Hendregwilym. Tonypa ... 121 F2
Hendremawr Cl. Swan 109 E4
Hendrewen Rd. Trehe 68 B1
Hendy Cl. Swan 109 D2
Hendy Rd. Pen-cl 80 C2
Hendy St. Card 189 D1
Henfaes Rd. Tonna 63 E1
Henfaes Terr. Tonna 63 E1
Hengoed Cl. Card 203 E2
Hengoed Cres. Gell 100 C2
Hengoed Hall Cl. Gell 100 C2
Hengoed Hall Dr. Gell 100 C2
Hengoed Parc. Gall 101 D2

Hengoed Parc. Gall

Hengoed Rd. Gell 100 C3
Henllys. Porth 147 F4
Henllys Rd. Card 189 E4
Hennage Dr. T Mum 109 D1
Henneuadd. Ystra 8 C3
Henrietta St. Swan 110 A3
Henry Richard St. Troed 73 E4
Henry St. Abera 71 E4
Henry St. Bar 75 F2
Henry St. Barry 225 E3
Henry St. Card 205 D2
Henry St. M Ash 72 B2
Henry St. Neath 87 F3
Henry St. Ponty 124 A1
Henshaw St. P Tal 138 C4
Hensol Rd. Ll'tris 184 B3
Hensol Villas. Pendo 184 C2
Henwysg Cl. Ponty 124 A1
Heol Aaron. Ystra 23 E4
Heol Adam. Gell 100 A4
Heol Adare. Tondu 163 E4
Heol Aer. Card 188 B4
Heol Alfred. Fern 95 D4
Heol Amlwch. Card 188 A2
Heol Aneurin Bevan. Rhy ... 34 C3
Heol Aneurin. Caer 151 F3
Heol Aneurin. Tony 147 E3
Heol Ap Pryce. Ll'tris 169 D3
Heol Aradur. Card 187 E2
Heol Arfryn. Pontcr 143 F1
Heol Awstin. Swan 83 F3
Heol Barri. Caer 151 F3
Heol Beddau. Caer 152 A1
Heol Bedw. Porth 122 C1
Heol Bedwas. Swan 61 D1
Heol Berllan. Caer 152 A3
Heol Berllan. Cry 43 D4
Heol Berry. Penty 171 D2
Heol Beulah. Ll'bra 151 F4
Heol Billingsley. Ponty 170 C4
Heol Blakemore. Card 187 F3
Heol Bonymaen. Mer T 33 D3
Heol Booker. Card 187 F3
Heol Bradford. Pontcr 143 F1
Heol Briallu. Swan 59 F1
Heol Brithdir. Swan 86 A4
Heol Briwnant. Card 172 A1
Heol Bro Wen. Caer 152 A3
Heol Broch. Swan 86 A4
Heol Brofiscin. Ll'tris 185 D4
Heol Bronallt. Hen 36 A3
Heol Bronwen. P Tal 113 F1
Heol Brychan. Bar 75 F2
Heol Brychan. Mer T 31 F2
Heol Brycyn. Swan 61 D1
Heol Bryn Fab. Nel 99 E2
Heol Bryn Glas. Ch Vil 169 E4
Heol Bryn Gwyn. Peny 49 D3
Heol Bryn Hebog. Mer T 31 F2
Heol Bryn Heulog. Ch Vil 169 E4
Heol Bryn Man. Mer T 31 F2
Heol Bryn Padell. Mer T 31 F2
Heol Bryn. Pyle 176 C4
Heol Bryn Seion. Onll 9 F1
Heol Bryn Selu. Mer T 31 F2
Heol Bryn-Gwyn. Glyn 66 C2
Heol Bryn-y-Gwyddyl.
Mer T 32 A2
Heol Bryncwils. Brynco 163 F2
Heol Bryncwtyn. Penco 181 E3
Heol Brynglas. Bridg 180 A3
Heol Brynglas. Card 188 A4
Heol Brynglas. Lough 82 A4
Heol Brynhyfryd. Ch Vil 169 D4
Heol Brynna. Neath 88 B3
Heol Brynnau. Aberd 49 E2
Heol Brynteg. Gell 126 C4
Heol Brynteg. Tony 147 D2
Heol Brython. Swan 108 A4
Heol By Eastwood. Bridg .. 180 B4
Heol Cadifor. Swan 84 A3
Heol Cadnawes. Swan 59 F2
Heol Cadrawd. Maest 142 B3
Heol Cae Celynnen. Caer . 152 A3
Heol Cae Copyn. Lough 56 C1
Heol Cae Fan Heulog.
Caer 152 A3
Heol Cae Glas. Brynco 163 F2
Heol Cae Gwyn. St B M 195 E1
Heol Cae Maen. Caer 152 A3
Heol Cae Rhosyn. Swan .. 61 D1
Heol Cae Tynewydd.
Lough 56 C1
Heol Cae-Defaid. Maest 117 E2
Heol Cae-Derwen. Bar 75 F2
Heol Cae-Glas. Swan 85 F3
Heol Caeglas. Tondu 163 E3
Heol Caerhys. Card 188 B4
Heol Caerlan. Ll'tris 168 C3
Heol Caerllion. Swan 60 A3
Heol Calfin. Swan 83 F2
Heol Cambrensis. Pyle 161 D1
Heol Camlan. Swan 61 D1
Heol Camlas. Cwma 114 C3
Heol Canola. Brynco 163 F2
Heol Capel. Tony 147 E3
Heol Cara Hir. Cry 43 D4

Heol Caradoc. Bar 75 F2
Heol Caradoc. Peny 49 E3
Heol Caredig. Tonna 63 E2
Heol Carnau. Card 203 E2
Heol Carne. Card 188 B2
Heol Carodog. Marg 139 E4
Heol Castell. Ce Cr 162 A1
Heol Castell Coety. Brigd .. 180 A4
Heol Cattwg. Card 188 A2
Heol Cattwg. Gell 100 B3
Heol Catwg. B-coch 62 B1
Heol Cawrdaf. Ll'tris 169 D3
Heol Cefn On. Card 173 D2
Heol Cefn Ydfa. Maest 116 C1
Heol Cefn Ydfa. Tondu 163 D4
Heol Cefni. Swan 84 C4
Heol Ceiriog. Tylor 96 B1
Heol Celyn. Gall 101 D2
Heol Celyn. Neath 88 A3
Heol Celynen. Ynybw 124 B3
Heol Ceri. Swan 82 B2
Heol Ceulanydd. Maest 91 D1
Heol Chappell. Card 187 F3
Heol Cleddau. Swan 82 B2
Heol Cledwyn. Swan 61 D1
Heol Clwyddau. Ll'tris 169 D3
Heol Clyd. Caer 151 E3
Heol Coch. Bridg 180 B3
Heol Coed Cae. Card 188 B2
Heol Coed Leyshon. Tondu 163 D4
Heol Coed. Swan 60 B3
Heol Coedcae. Bar 75 F2
Heol Coflorna. Tre 99 E3
Heol Coronial. Ll'tris 169 D4
Heol Creigiau. Ch Vil 169 E2
Heol Creigiau. Penty 169 E2
Heol Crochendy. Ponty 150 C1
Heol Croes Faen. Porth 176 C1
Heol Cronfa. Ponty 124 C2
Heol Crwys. Lough 57 D2
Heol Cwm Ifor. Caer 151 E3
Heol Cwm Mawr. Cwma ... 114 B3
Heol Cwrdy. Brynco 163 F2
Heol Cynan. Lough 57 D2
Heol Cynwyd. Maest 142 B3
Heol Dafydd. Ll'tris 184 A4
Heol Dalycopa. Swan 85 F3
Heol Daniel. Cwmll 6 B3
Heol Danyrodyn. Penty 170 B1
Heol Davies Andrews.
Tonna 63 D1
Heol Dderwen. Ch Vil 150 A1
Heol Ddeusant. Ll'tris 168 C3
Heol Ddu. Hen 17 F4
Heol Ddu. Swan 84 A4
Heol Ddu. Tony 148 B1
Heol Ddwr. Pontar 36 C4
Heol Deg. Ch Vil 150 A1
Heol Degwm. Pyle 176 C4
Heol Dennant. Card 203 F4
Heol Deri. Tony 147 D2
Heol Derlwyn. Card 188 A4
Heol Derw. Gell 100 C2
Heol Derwen. Neath 88 A3
Heol Deva. Card 203 E2
Heol Dewi. Gall 101 D1
Heol Dewi. Ll'ha 166 B2
Heol Dewi Sant. Penga 58 A1
Heol Dewi Sant. Pontcr 143 E2
Heol Dolfain. Swan 60 A2
Heol Dolwen. Card 188 B2
Heol Don. Card 187 F2
Heol Don Ct. Card 187 F2
Heol Dowlais. Ch Vil 169 F3
Heol Drewi. Pyle 176 C2
Heol Dulais. Swan 61 D1
Heol Dwyrain. Bridg 180 A2
Heol Dyddwr. Tonna 63 E2
Heol Dyfan. Swan 59 F2
Heol Dyfed. Card 188 B3
Heol Dyfed. Ll'tris 168 C3
Heol Dyfed. Lough 57 D2
Heol Dyfed. Maest 117 E1
Heol Dyfed. Peny 49 E3
Heol Dyfed. Tylor 96 A1
Heol Dyfodwg. Ll'tris 168 B2
Heol Dyhewydd. Ch Vil 169 D4
Heol Dylan. Lough 57 D2
Heol Dylan. Pyle 176 C4
Heol Dynys. Swan 83 F3
Heol Dywyll. Swan 60 B4
Heol Ebwy. Card 203 E2
Heol Edward Lewis. Gell .. 100 B3
Heol Edwards. Ponty 171 D4
Heol Eglwys. Bridg 163 E1
Heol Eglwys. Card 203 F2
Heol Eglwys. Coel 9 F2
Heol Eglwys Fair. Card 205 D3
Heol Eglwys. Ystra 7 F1
Heol Eirlys. Swan 59 F1
Heol Eithrim. Cly 60 B4
Heol Elfed. Lough 57 D2
Heol Elfed. Maest 117 E1
Heol Elfed. Swan 85 F3
Heol Emrys. Swan 84 A3
Heol Erwin. Card 172 B1
Heol Esgyn. Card 189 D3
Heol Esgyn. N Abb 62 A1

Heol Esgyn. Rhig 47 E4
Heol Evan Wynne. Rhy 34 C1
Heol Ewenny. Penco 181 E3
Heol Fach. Bar 75 F1
Heol Fach. Brynco 163 F2
Heol Fach. Caer 151 F2
Heol Fach. Ll'fel 59 D2
Heol Fach. Penco 181 E4
Heol Fach. Ponty 171 D4
Heol Fach. Porth 176 C4
Heol Fach. Swan 84 B3
Heol Faen. Maest 117 E1
Heol Faenor. Ll'tris 168 C3
Heol Fain. Brynco 163 F2
Heol Fain. Wick 208 A3
Heol Fair. Card 188 A1
Heol Fargoed. Bar 75 F1
Heol Fawr. Caer 151 E3
Heol Fawr. Card 205 D3
Heol Fawr. Nel 100 A1
Heol Fawr. Pyle 177 D4
Heol Fechan. Bridg 179 D3
Heol Fedw. Swan 59 F2
Heol Felen. Glan 4 B4
Heol Felyn Fach. Tondu 163 E3
Heol Fer. Caer 151 F3
Heol Ffaldau. Bridg 180 A3
Heol Fforest. Hen 36 A3
Heol Ffranc. Skew 86 B3
Heol Ffrwd Philip. Ch Vil ... 169 F3
Heol Ffynnon. Lough 56 C1
Heol Ffynnon Wen. Card 187 F4
Heol Frank. Swan 84 A3
Heol Gabriel. Card 188 B2
Heol Gadlys. Bridg 180 A4
Heol Gaer. Onll 10 A1
Heol Gam. Bridg 179 F1
Heol Gam. Penty 170 A1
Heol Ganol. Caer 151 F2
Heol Ganol. Og Va 119 F3
Heol Gelli Lenor. Maest 116 C1
Heol Gelynen. Bry 5 E4
Heol Gelynen. Peny 49 D3
Heol Gelynog. Ll'tris 169 D3
Heol Ger-y-Felin. Ll' Maj .. 220 A4
Heol Gerrig. Swan 84 B3
Heol Gethin. Gall 101 D2
Heol Giedd. Ystra 7 F2
Heol Glan-Nant. Swan 60 A2
Heol Glan-yr-Afon. Ynys 128 B2
Heol Glandulais. Card 173 F1
Heol Glanllechau. A-wen 40 C2
Heol Glannant. Pontcr 143 E2
Heol Glannant. Tonypa 122 A1
Heol Glasnant. Swan 108 C4
Heol Gledyr. Caer 152 A1
Heol Gleien. Ystra 7 D1
Heol Glyn. Caer 151 F3
Heol Glyn-Dyfal. Craig 37 F2
Heol Glyncoch. Tony 146 B3
Heol Glynderwen. A-wen ... 40 C2
Heol Glynderwen. B-coch .. 62 B1
Heol Glyndwr. Bridg 180 B3
Heol Goch. Penty 170 C1
Heol Godfrey. G-C-G 5 D4
Heol Goedog. Ce Cr 162 A1
Heol Goronwy. Tylor 96 B1
Heol Graig Wen. Caer 151 F3
Heol Graig-Felen. Cly 60 B4
Heol Groeswen. Ponty 150 B2
Heol Gron. Ystra 23 E4
Heol Gruffydd. Swan 83 F3
Heol Grug. Swan 59 F1
Heol Gwaun Rhos. Caer ... 152 A3
Heol Gwell. Swan 84 B3
Heol Gwenallt. Lough 57 D2
Heol Gwent. Card 188 B3
Heol Gwili. Lough 57 D2
Heol Gwili. Swan 85 F3
Heol Gwilym. Card 187 E1
Heol Gwrangfryn. Rhig 47 E4
Heol Gwrgan. Card 188 A3
Heol Gwrgan. Ll'tris 168 C3
Heol Gwyndaf. Card 188 C4
Heol Gwynedd. Card 188 B3
Heol Gwynno. Ll'tris 168 B2
Heol Gwyrosydd. Swan 84 A3
Heol Gwys. Cwmll 6 C2
Heol Hafdy. Swan 85 F4
Heol Harlech. Card 204 A4
Heol Haulfryn. Tony 147 D2
Heol Heddwch. N Abb 62 A1
Heol Heddwch. Se Si 25 D3
Heol Hen. Se Si 24 C3
Heol Hendre. B-coch 62 B3
Heol Hendre. Card 188 B4
Heol Hendy. Ll'tris 184 B4
Heol Henrhyd. Coel 10 A2
Heol Hensol. Ll'tris 169 D3
Heol Herbert. Reso 44 A1
Heol Hermas. Swan 84 A3
Heol Heulog. Og Va 146 A4
Heol Hir. Card 172 C1
Heol Hir. Card 172 C1
Heol Hir. G-C-G 5 D2
Heol Hopcyn John. Bridg .. 164 A1
Heol Horeb. Porth 122 C1
Heol Iago. Deri 53 E4

Heol Ida. Ll'tris 169 D4
Heol Iestyn. Card 188 A3
Heol Ifor. Card 188 B3
Heol Illtyd. B-coch 62 B1
Heol Illtyd. Ll'tris 168 B2
Heol Ioan. Tylor 96 A1
Heol Isaf. Bed 99 E4
Heol Isaf. Card 172 B1
Heol Isaf. Card 187 E3
Heol Isaf. Cwma 114 B3
Heol Isaf. Neath 88 B3
Heol Isaf. Nel 99 F2
Heol Isaf. Tony 147 E1
Heol Iscoed. Card 188 B4
Heol Iscoed. Ch Vil 169 F3
Heol Iscoed. Hen 36 A2
Heol Islwyn. Lough 57 D2
Heol Islwyn. Nel 99 F2
Heol Islwyn. Tony 147 E3
Heol Johnson. Ll'tris 168 B1
Heol Keir Hardie. Peny 49 D3
Heol Klockner. Rhy 34 B2
Heol Laethog. Brynco 164 C3
Heol Las. Bridg 164 C1
Heol Las. Brynco 164 C1
Heol Las Cotts. Brynco 164 C1
Heol Las Fawr. Cry 43 D4
Heol Las. Ll'bra 151 F4
Heol Las. Ll'tris 168 B2
Heol Las. Nel 100 A1
Heol Las. Penco 181 E4
Heol Las. Pontdw 21 F1
Heol Las. Ponydw 41 D4
Heol Las. Pyle 176 B4
Heol Las. Pyle 176 C4
Heol Las. St B W 191 E3
Heol Las Villas. Pyle 176 B4
Heol Las. Wick 208 A2
Heol Lewis. Caer 152 B3
Heol Lewis. Card 172 B1
Heol Llan. Brynco 164 C2
Heol Llan. Pyle 176 C4
Heol Llanbedr. P-s-Ely 201 F3
Heol Llangan. Card 188 A3
Heol Llangeinor. Pontcr 144 A2
Heol Llanishen Fach. Card 188 B4
Heol Llansantffraid. Brynco 163 F2
Heol Llechau. Tylor 96 B1
Heol Llidiard. St M H 181 F1
Heol Llwyn Brain. Mer T 32 A2
Heol Llwyn Celyn. B-coch .. 62 B1
Heol Llwyn Deri. Mer T 32 A2
Heol Llwyn Drysi. Mer T 32 A2
Heol Llwyn Golden. Mer T .. 32 A2
Heol Llwyn Onnen. Mer T .. 32 A2
Heol Llwyndyrus. Maest 142 B3
Heol Llwynon. B-coch 62 B1
Heol Llwynyffynnon. Pontcr 144 A2
Heol Llyswen. Nel 99 F2
Heol Mabon. Card 188 B4
Heol Mabon. Cwma 114 C3
Heol Mabon. Nel 99 E2
Heol Madoc. Card 188 B2
Heol Maendy. Brynco 163 F2
Heol Maendy. Pyle 176 C4
Heol Maes Eglwys. Swan .. 59 F2
Heol Maes Eiwrg. Card 191 D3
Heol Maes. Ll'ge 56 B4
Heol Maes y Cerrig. Lough .. 56 C1
Heol Maes-y-Dre. Ystra 7 F1
Heol Maes-y-Gelynen.
Swan 59 F1
Heol Maes-yr-Haf. Penco .. 181 E3
Heol Maesbryn. Lough 56 C1
Heol Mair. Bridg 163 F1
Heol Mair. Tylor 96 A1
Heol Mathew. Card 187 F3
Heol Merioneth. Ll' Maj 220 B3
Heol Merlin. Card 188 C4
Heol Meurig. Ystra 23 E3
Heol Miaren. Swan 59 F1
Heol Miles. Ll'tris 168 A1
Heol Miskin. Ll'tris 184 A4
Heol Morfa. Pyle 177 E4
Heol Morien. Nel 99 E2
Heol Mostyn. Pyle 161 E1
Heol Muston. Card 203 E3
Heol Mwrwg. Ll'ge 56 A4
Heol Mwyrdy. Ll'tris 168 C3
Heol Mynydd. Ch Vil 149 F1
Heol Mynydd. Ponty 125 D2
Heol Mynydd. W St D 199 F3
Heol Nant. Aberd 49 E2
Heol Nant Bran. Swan 61 D1
Heol Nant Caiach. Tre 99 D3
Heol Nant Castan. Card 188 A3
Heol Nant. Ch Vil 149 F1
Heol Nant Gelli. Swan 84 B3
Heol Nant. Ponty 125 D2
Heol Nant. Pyle 176 C4
Heol Nantgau. Mer T 32 A1
Heol Nedd. Blae 45 E4
Heol Nest. Card 188 B3
Heol Neuadd. Pyle 177 D4
Heol Newydd. Ce Cr 162 A1
Heol Newydd. Swan 83 F3
Heol Onnen. Pyle 176 C4

Heol Orchwy. Treo 94 B4
Heol Pandy. Pontcr 143 F1
Heol Pant Glas. Blae 45 E4
Heol Pant Gwyn. Ll'hry 183 E3
Heol Pant Ruthin. Penco .. 181 E3
Heol Pant y Dwr. Lough 56 C1
Heol Pant-y-Gored. Penty . 186 A4
Heol Pant-yr-Awel. Og Va . 144 B2
Heol Pant-yr-Yn. Card 187 F3
Heol Pantglas. Card 62 B3
Heol Pantycelyn. Card 187 F4
Heol Pantyderi. Card 203 E2
Heol Parc Glas. Mer T 31 F2
Heol Parc Maen. Mer T 32 A1
Heol Parc-y-Lan. Mer T 32 A2
Heol Pardoe. Ponty 150 C1
Heol Pen y Cae. Lough 56 C1
Heol Pen-Nant. Swan 60 B2
Heol Pen-Rhiw'r-Eglwys.
Mark 76 C3
Heol Pen-Tir-Garw. Swan .. 83 F3
Heol Pen-y-Beili. Lough 56 C1
Heol Pen-y-Bryn. Tylor 96 A1
Heol Pen-y-Coed. Neath .. 88 A3
Heol Pen-y-Foel. Ynybw ... 124 B3
Heol Pen-y-Parc. Ll'tris 168 B2
Heol Pen-y-Scallen. Lough . 56 C1
Heol Penallta. Gell 100 B3
Heol Penar. Swan 84 A3
Heol Pencarreg. Bar 75 F2
Heol Pencarreg. Card 188 A1
Heol Pencerdd. Maesf 117 E1
Heol Pendarren. Rhig 47 E4
Heol Penderyn. Bridg 180 B3
Heol Penderyn. N Abb 62 A1
Heol Pendyrus. Tylor 96 A2
Heol Penfelyn. Swan 59 F3
Heol Penhydd. Bryn 115 F3
Heol Penlan. Card 187 F3
Heol Penlan. N Abb 62 A1
Heol Penllwyn. Penty 170 A1
Heol Penmaen. Ll'tris 168 B2
Heol Pennar. Card 203 E2
Heol Penrhiw. M Ash 72 A3
Heol Penrhiw. Mer T 31 F2
Heol Pentre Bach. Lough .. 56 C1
Heol Pentre Felen. Ll'fel 59 E1
Heol Pentre. Maest 116 C1
Heol Pentre'r Cwrt. Ll' Maj . 220 A4
Heol Pentre'r Felin. Ll' Maj . 220 A4
Heol Pentwyn. Card 187 F3
Heol Pentwyn. Skew 86 B3
Heol Pentwyn. Tony 147 D2
Heol Pentyla. Brynco 163 E2
Heol Pentyla. Swan 85 F3
Heol Penyfai. Card 188 B2
Heol Peredur. Card 172 B1
Heol Persondy. Brynco 163 E2
Heol Persondy. Pontcr 143 E1
Heol Persondy. Tondu 163 E2
Heol Philip. Ystra 7 F1
Heol Phillip. A-wen 40 C2
Heol Pit-y-Ceiliogod. Peng . 76 B1
Heol Pit-y-Ceiliogod. Peng .. 76 C1
Heol Plas Isaf. Ll'ge 56 A4
Heol Pont George. Pyle 161 D1
Heol Pont y Seison. Gell .. 100 B1
Heol Pontprennau. Card .. 173 F1
Heol Powis. Card 188 B3
Heol Poyston. Card 203 E2
Heol Pwllypant. Caer 151 F3
Heol Pwllyplaca. Card 190 C3
Heol Pymmer. Tony 147 D2
Heol Rhayader. Card 187 F2
Heol Rhos Las. Mer T 32 A2
Heol Rhosyn. Swan 59 F1
Heol Rhuddos. Swan 86 A4
Heol Rhyd. Craig 39 D2
Heol Rhyd-Ddu-Fach. Bry .. 6 B4
Heol Rhyd-y-Bedd. Mer T ... 33 D3
Heol Rhys. Aberd 71 F4
Heol Richard Price. Pontcr 143 F2
Heol Robart. Ll'tris 184 A4
Heol S O Davies. Mer T 32 B1
Heol Saffrwm. Swan 59 F1
Heol Salem. Ch Vil 149 F1
Heol Sant Bridget. St B M . 195 E1
Heol Scwrfa. Mer T 32 A2
Heol Seddon. Card 187 E1
Heol Seion. Ll'ge 56 A4
Heol Serth. Caer 151 E3
Heol Seward. Ll'tris 168 C3
Heol Shon. Ce Cr 162 A1
Heol Shwlac. St B M 196 A1
Heol Shwlac. Wick 208 A4
Heol Siarl. Card 205 D3
Heol Silyn. Peny 49 E3
Heol Simonston. Bridg 180 B4
Heol Solva. Card 203 F2
Heol Spencer. Bridg 164 A2
Heol Spencer. Brynco 164 A2
Heol St Cattwg. Pendo 201 D3
Heol St Denys. Card 188 B3
Heol Sticil-y-Beddau. Ll'tris 168 B2
Heol Stradling. Card 188 A2
Heol Syr Lewis. Card 187 D4
Heol Syr William. Glyn 91 E2
Heol Tabor. Cwma 114 C3

Heol Tai Mawr. Mer T

Heol Tai Mawr. Mer T 32 A2
Heol Taliesin. Cwma 114 C3
Heol Tasker. Nel 99 E2
Heol Tawe. Ystra 9 D3
Heol Tegfryn. Pyle 161 D1
Heol Teifionydd. Tylor 96 A1
Heol Tewgoed. Cwma 114 C3
Heol Tir Coch. Ch Vil 169 F3
Heol Tir Du. Swan 60 A2
Heol Tir Gibbon. Caer 151 F3
Heol Tir Gwaidd. Tylor 96 A2
Heol Tir Ton. Ynys 128 A2
Heol Tir-y-Llan. Bar 76 A2
Heol Tirbach. Caer 151 E3
Heol Tircoed. Pont 58 A3
Heol Ton. Brynco 163 F2
Heol Ton. Tony 147 D2
Heol Tonmaen. Reso 44 B1
Heol Trane. Tony 147 D2
Heol Tre Dwr. Bridg 180 A1
Heol Trecastell. Caer 151 F1
Heol Tredeg. Cwmll 6 C2
Heol Treferig. Ll'tris 169 D3
Heol Treffynnon. Swan 60 A3
Heol Trefgarne. Card 203 E2
Heol Trefor. Swan 84 A3
Heol Treharne. Glyn 92 A3
Heol Treharne. Tondu 163 D4
Heol Trelai. Card 203 F2
Heol Trelales. Bridg 178 C2
Heol Trenewydd. Card 203 E2
Heol Treth. Pyle 161 E1
Heol Trewilliam. Tonypa 122 A1
Heol Trosserch. Ll'ge 56 A4
Heol Trostre. Card 190 C3
Heol Twrch. Ystal 7 D1
Heol Twrch. Ystra 7 D1
Heol Ty Aberaman. Abera 71 E3
Heol Ty Crwn. Caer 152 A3
Heol Ty Gwyn. B-coch 62 B2
Heol Ty Gwyn. Maest 116 C2
Heol Ty Maen. Ponty 150 B1
Heol Ty Mawr. Pendo 200 C3
Heol Ty Merchant. Caer 152 A3
Heol Ty Nant. Pontcr 144 A2
Heol Ty'n y Coed. Card 188 B4
Heol Ty'n-y-Cae. Card 188 B3
Heol Ty'n-y-Garn. Bridg 163 E1
Heol Ty-Gwyn. Ll'bra 127 D2
Heol Tydraw. Pyle 177 D4
Heol Tyle-Du. Treo 94 B4
Heol Tylluan. Swan 86 A4
Heol Tyllwyd. Tony 147 E3
Heol Tyn-y-Waun. Maest 142 B3
Heol Tynewydd. Peng 76 C2
Heol Tynygarn. Bridg 163 E1
Heol Tysant. Bridg 180 A4
Heol Tywith. Maest 117 D3
Heol Uchaf. Card 172 A1
Heol Uchaf. Gell 100 C2
Heol Uchaf. Hir 48 B4
Heol Uchaf. Neath 88 B3
Heol Uchaf. Nel 99 F2
Heol Uchaf. Peny 49 D3
Heol Undeb. Cwma 114 C3
Heol Undeb. Ll'tris 168 C3
Heol Urban. Card 187 F1
Heol Valentine. Cly 60 B4
Heol Wastadnant. Penco 181 E4
Heol Waun. Tony 147 D2
Heol Waun Waelod. Caer 151 F1
Heol Waun Wen. Ll'fel 59 D1
Heol Waun y Nant. Card 188 A2
Heol Wen. Card 188 A4
Heol Wernlas. Card 188 B2
Heol West Plas. Bridg 180 A4
Heol Wil Hopcyn. Maest 142 B3
Heol Will George. Swan 82 C2
Heol William Trigg. Pontcr .. 118 C3
Heol Wyllt. Pontar 36 C2
Heol y Barna. Pontar 36 C1
Heol y Beddau. Caer 152 A1
Heol y Bedw-Hirion. Bar 76 B2
Heol y Berllan. Pyle 161 D1
Heol y Bwlch. Cwma 114 B3
Heol y Caeau-Meinion.
   Peng 76 B2
Heol y Carnau. Caer 152 A3
Heol y Castell. Card 205 D3
Heol y Cawl. Llys 197 F1
Heol y Cefn. Bar 76 B1
Heol y Cefn. Peng 76 B1
Heol y Clun. Ll'tris 168 C3
Heol y Cnap. Swan 84 B3
Heol y Coed. Glyn 66 C2
Heol y Coed. Ll'tris 168 C3
Heol y Dderwen. Peng 101 E4
Heol y Delyn. Card 173 D1
Heol y Derw. Og Va 146 A4
Heol y Drudwen. Swan 59 F3
Heol y Dug. Card 205 D3
Heol y Felin. Hen 36 A3
Heol y Felin. Pontcr 143 F1
Heol y Felin. Se Si 25 D4
Heol y Ffynon. Neath 88 B3
Heol y Fran. Swan 59 F3
Heol y Frenhines. Card 205 D3
Heol y Frenhines. D pow 216 A1

Heol y Gamlas. Ponty 150 C1
Heol y Garn. Craig 18 B4
Heol y Garth. Gar P 153 D2
Heol y Glyn. Tony 147 E3
Heol y Glyn. Tre 99 E3
Heol y Gors. Card 188 B2
Heol y Gwydde. Coel 9 E3
Heol y Gyfraith. Ll'tris 168 B1
Heol y Moch. Maest 141 D4
Heol y Mynydd. Bar 75 F2
Heol y Mynydd. Craig 18 B3
Heol y Mynydd. Lough 57 E2
Heol y Nant. H-y-Cy 165 D3
Heol y Nantlais. Lough 57 D2
Heol y Parc. A-wen 40 C2
Heol y Pia. Caer 151 F2
Heol y Porth. Card 205 D3
Heol y Pwll. Ponty 170 C4
Heol y Rhosog. Card 190 B1
Heol y Stepsau. Ewen 196 A2
Heol y Twyn. Tylor 96 B1
Heol y Waun. Rhy 54 A4
Heol y Wern. Card 188 B4
Heol Ynysawdre. Brynco 163 F2
Heol yr Afon. Bridg 179 F4
Heol yr Eglwys. Bridg 180 B4
Heol yr Eglwys. Brynco 164 A3
Heol yr Eithen. Swan 60 A2
Heol yr Eryr. Swan 59 F3
Heol yr Odyn. Ponty 170 C4
Heol yr Wylan. Swan 59 F3
Heol yr Ysgol. Bridg 179 E3
Heol yr Ysgol. Bridg 180 B4
Heol-cae-Globe. Lough 81 F4
Heol-Cae-Gurwen. G-C-G 5 D2
Heol-Croeserw. Glyn 91 E2
Heol-Croesty. Penco 181 E3
Heol-Crwys. Cwma 114 C3
Heol-Fair. Porthc 193 D4
Heol-Jiwbili. Cwma 114 C3
Heol-Las. Cl. Swan 60 C1
Heol-Las. Swan 60 C1
Heol-pen-y-bryn. Caer 171 F3
Heol-Pen-y-Bryn. Card 171 F3
Heol-Tewdwr. Glyn 91 E2
Heol-Trelai. Card 203 D2
Heol-Ty-Cribwr. Bridg 179 D3
Heol-Ty-Maen. Bridg 179 D3
Heol-Uchaf. Rhy 34 C3
Heol-Wenallt. Blae 45 E4
Heol-y- Bryn. Ponty 150 A3
Heol-y- Coed. Ponty 171 D4
Heol-y- Dail. Ponty 179 D3
Heol-y-Bardd. Bridg 179 E2
Heol-y-Beddau. Ll'tris 169 D4
Heol-y-Beiliau. Ll'tris 168 B2
Heol-y-Berllan. Card 203 E2
Heol-y-Blodau. Bridg 179 D3
Heol-y-Bont. Card 188 B4
Heol-y-Bont. Tondu 163 F2
Heol-y-Broom. Pyle 176 C4
Heol-y-Bryn. Brynco 163 F2
Heol-y-Bryn. Card 188 A4
Heol-y-Bryn. Deri 53 E4
Heol-y-Bryn. Ll'tris 184 B4
Heol-y-Bryn. Maest 142 B3
Heol-y-Bryn. Penty 170 A1
Heol-y-Bryn. Rhig 47 E4
Heol-y-Bryn. Rhig 146 B3
Heol-y-Bryniau. Mer T 33 D4
Heol-y-Bwlch. Ll'el 56 A1
Heol-y-Bwnsi. Ponty 150 C1
Heol-y-Cadno. Card 172 A2
Heol-y-Cae. C-c-y-c 32 A2
Heol-y-Cae. Cly 60 B4
Heol-y-Cae. Pontar 36 C3
Heol-y-Capel. Bridg 180 C2
Heol-y-Capel. Porth 176 C1
Heol-y-Carw. Card 172 C2
Heol-y-Castell. Card 203 E3
Heol-y-Castell. Glyn 90 B2
Heol-y-Castell. Mer T 33 D4
Heol-y-Cawl. D pow 216 A2
Heol-y-Cawl. Ewen 196 B4
Heol-y-Coed. Card 188 A4
Heol-y-Coed. Ll' Maj 220 A3
Heol-y-Coed. Ll'tris 184 B4
Heol-y-Coed. Pontar 36 C3
Heol-y-Coed. Ynys 101 F1
Heol-y-Coedcae. Cwmll 6 B3
Heol-y-Craig. Cry 43 D3
Heol-y-Cwm. Caer 151 F1
Heol-y-Dderwen. Ponty 171 D4
Heol-y-Ddol. Caer 152 A3
Heol-y-De. Rhig 47 E4
Heol-y-Deiliaid. Marg 139 F1
Heol-y-Delyn Du. Bridg 179 D3
Heol-y-Deri. Card 188 A4
Heol-y-Deri. Ponty 124 A1
Heol-y-Deri. Swan 59 F2
Heol-y-Deryn. Glyn 66 C2
Heol-y-Dreflan. Caer 152 A3
Heol-y-Fagwr. Cly 39 F1
Heol-y-Fedw. Glyn 91 E2
Heol-y-Fedwen. Ch Vil 150 A1
Heol-y-fedwen. Og Va 119 D2
Heol-y-Felin. B-coch 62 B1

Heol-y-Felin. Blae 45 E4
Heol-y-Felin. Caer 151 F2
Heol-y-Felin. Card 188 B4
Heol-y-Felin. Card 203 F3
Heol-y-Felin. Gell 100 C3
Heol-y-Felin. Glyn 91 F3
Heol-y-Felin. H-y-Cy 165 D3
Heol-y-Felin. Ll' Maj 220 A3
Heol-y-Felin. Ll'tris 184 A4
Heol-y-Felin. Penga 58 A1
Heol-y-Fferm. Tondu 163 F3
Heol-y-Ffin. Bridg 179 E2
Heol-y-Fforest. Card 171 F2
Heol-y-Ffynnon. Ch Vil 169 F3
Heol-y-Ffynon. Tylor 96 A1
Heol-y-Foel. Ch Vil 149 F1
Heol-y-Foel. Cwma 114 B3
Heol-y-Foelas. Bridg 179 E3
Heol-y-Forlan. Card 188 A3
Heol-y-Frenhines. Bridg 179 E3
Heol-y-Fro. Ch Vil 169 E4
Heol-y-Fro. Ll' maj 219 F4
Heol-y-Gadarn. Glyn 90 C2
Heol-y-Gaer. Card 203 E2
Heol-y-Geifr. Ll'fel 59 D1
Heol-y-Gelli. Penco 181 E4
Heol-y-Gelli. Abera 71 D3
Heol-y-Gelli. Penga 57 F1
Heol-y-Gerddi. Penco 165 E1
Heol-y-Glo. Marg 161 E3
Heol-y-Glo. Tonna 63 F2
Heol-y-Glyn. G-nea 27 D1
Heol-y-Glyn. Glyn 91 E4
Heol-y-Goedlan. Cwmll 6 B2
Heol-y-Goedwig. Porthc 193 D4
Heol-y-Gog. Gow 82 A3
Heol-y-Gogledd. Caer 151 F3
Heol-y-Gors. Caer 152 A3
Heol-y-Gors. G-C-G 5 D1
Heol-y-Gors. Marg 160 B3
Heol-y-Gors. Ponty 171 D2
Heol-y-Gors. Swan 84 A1
Heol-y-Graig. Blae 45 E4
Heol-y-Graig. Cly 60 B4
Heol-y-Graig. Gell 126 C4
Heol-y-Graig. Ll'tris 168 B2
Heol-y-Graig. Porthc 193 E4
Heol-y-Graig. Rhig 28 B1
Heol-y-Graig. Tonna 63 E2
Heol-y-Graig. Tylor 96 A2
Heol-y-Groes. Bridg 179 F4
Heol-y-Groes. Penco 181 E4
Heol-y-Grug. Tony 146 B3
Heol-y-Gwrgan. Marg 139 F2
Heol-y-Llan. Lough 81 F4
Heol-y-Llwyna. A-wen 40 A1
Heol-y-Llwyni. Maest 117 E1
Heol-y-Maes. Ch Vil 169 E4
Heol-y-Maes. Pontar 36 B2
Heol-y-Mynach. Ynybw 97 F2
Heol-y-Mynydd. Aberd 49 F1
Heol-y-Mynydd. Brynco 163 F2
Heol-y-Mynydd. C-c-y-c 31 F3
Heol-y-Mynydd. Glyn 66 C2
Heol-y-Mynydd. Tony 146 B3
Heol-y-Mynydd. Yst 95 E2
Heol-y-Nant. B-coch 62 B1
Heol-y-Nant. Barry 225 D4
Heol-y-Nant. Bridg 179 E3
Heol-y-Nant. Brynco 163 F2
Heol-y-Nant. Caer 151 F2
Heol-y-Nant. Card 188 A3
Heol-y-Nant. Cly 60 A3
Heol-y-Nant. Glyn 92 A3
Heol-y-Nant. Llys 209 D4
Heol-y-Nant. Maest 117 E1
Heol-y-Nant. P Tal 113 F2
Heol-y-Nant. Penty 170 C2
Heol-y-Parc. Abera 50 B2
Heol-y-Parc. Caer 152 A2
Heol-y-Parc. Card 174 A2
Heol-y-Parc. Ch Vil 169 F3
Heol-y-Parc. Cwma 114 B3
Heol-y-Parc. Og Va 146 A4
Heol-y-Parc. Penty 186 A4
Heol-y-parc. Pont 58 A4
Heol-y-parc. Pyle 176 C4
Heol-y-Pavin. Card 188 A1
Heol-y-Plas. Hen 36 A3
Heol-y-Plwyf. Ynybw 97 F1
Heol-y-Rhedyn. Swan 59 F1
Heol-y-Rhos. Bridg 180 A3
Heol-y-Sarn. Ll'tris 168 B3
Heol-y-Sheet. Pyle 177 E3
Heol-y-Slough. St B M 195 D1
Heol-y-Splot. Pyle 177 E3
Heol-y-Twyn. Aberd 49 E2
Heol-y-Twyn. Pont 57 F4
Heol-y-Twyn. Rhy 34 C3
Heol-y-Tyla. Glyn 90 C2
Heol-y-Waun. Card 188 A2
Heol-y-Waun. Gell 100 B3
Heol-y-Waun. Pontar 36 B3
Heol-y-Waun. Se Si 25 D4
Heol-y-Waun. Tylor 96 A2
Heol-y-Wern. B-coch 62 B1
Heol-y-Wern. Caer 152 A3
Heol-y-Wern. Lough 81 F4

Heol-y-Wern. Nel 99 F2
Heol-yr-Afael. Glyn 90 C2
Heol-yr-Afon. Glyn 66 C2
Heol-yr-Afon. Tondu 163 E3
Heol-yr-Efail. Card 188 B4
Heol-yr-Enfys. Bridg 179 D3
Heol-yr-Eos. Penga 57 F1
Heol-yr-Haul. Ll'tris 185 E4
Heol-yr-Odyn. Card 203 D2
Heol-yr-Onen. Caer 151 F2
Heol-yr-Onnen. Bridg 179 D2
Heol-yr-Onnen. Penco 181 F4
Heol-yr-Orsedd. Marg 139 E3
Heol-yr-Ynys. Card 171 D1
Heol-yr-Ysgol. Maest 142 B3
Heol-yr-Ysgol. St B M 195 E1
Heol-yr-Ysgol. Tondu 163 E3
Heolaelfryn. Og Va 144 C2
Heolcae'r-Bont. Marg 159 F4
Heoldawe. Swan 9 D3
Heoldduu Ave. Bar 75 F2
Heolddu Cres. Bar 75 F2
Heolddu Dr. Bar 75 F2
Heolddu Gn. Bar 75 F2
Heolddu Gro. Bar 75 F2
Heolddu Rd. Bar 75 F2
Heolddu Rd. Pontll 101 F1
Heolganol. Brynco 163 F2
Heolgerrig. Mer T 32 A1
Heoltynton. Pontcr 144 A2
Heolyffin. A-wen 40 A1
Herbert Ave. Pontmi 155 E4
Herbert Cl. Marsh 191 F4
Herbert Dr. Caer 151 F3
Herbert March Cl. Card 187 E2
Herbert Rd. Neath 87 E3
Herbert St. Abera 50 A1
Herbert St. Abercy 98 C1
Herbert St. Barry 225 D4
Herbert St. Bridg 180 A3
Herbert St. Card 188 C1
Herbert St. Card 205 D2
Herbert St. N Tre 55 D1
Herbert St. Pontcr 118 C4
Herbert St. Pontdw 40 C2
Herbert St. Trehe 69 D1
Herbert St. Treo 94 B3
Herbert Terr. Pen 217 D2
Hereford St. Card 204 C2
Heritage Pk. Card 190 C4
Hermon Cl. Mer T 33 D1
Hermon Hill. Card 171 E1
Hermon Rd. Maest 117 D4
Hermon St. Treo 94 C3
Herne St. Neath 87 D1
Hernston La. Bridg 179 F1
Hernston La. Ewen 179 F1
Heron Rd. Card 190 B2
Herons Way. B-coch 62 C1
Herrick Pl. Bedw 153 E4
Heulwen Cl. Mer T 33 D3
Heulwen Clos. T We 171 F4
Hewell Ct. Card 204 C1
Hewell St. Card 204 C1
Hewell St. Pen 216 C3
Hewson St. Swan 110 A4
Hibbert Rd. Neath 87 F4
Hibiscus Ct. Ch Vil 169 E3
Hickman Rd. Pen 217 D2
Hickman St. Troed 52 A2
Hickory Ct. Card 205 E3
High Cl. Nel 99 F2
High Cnr. Penty 170 B1
High Croft Wlk. Card 190 A2
High Meadow. Ll' maj 219 F3
High Row. M Ash 72 B3
High St. A-wen 40 C2
High St. Aber 125 F1
High St. Aber 151 D4
High St. Abera 50 A1
High St. Bar 76 A2
High St. Bed 74 A4
High St. Bed 99 E4
High St. Blae 45 E4
High St. Bridg 178 C2
High St. C-c-y-c 32 A2
High St. Card 204 A4
High St. Card 205 D3
High St. Cly 60 C4
High St. Cowb 198 C1
High St. Cross 129 E3
High St. Cwma 114 B3
High St. Fern 95 F3
High St. G-nea 27 D1
High St. Glan 4 A4
High St. Glyn 92 B3
High St. H-y-Cy 165 D3
High St. Hir 48 B4
High St. Ll' maj 219 F4
High St. Ll'bra 126 C1
High St. Ll'tris 168 B2
High St. Ll'tris 183 F3
High St. Lough 57 E1
High St. Lough 57 E3
High St. M Ash 72 B2
High St. Maest 117 D4
High St. Marg 114 A1
High St. Mark 76 C3
High St. Mer T 32 B1

High St. Mer T 32 C2
High St. Mer T 33 E2
High St. Mer T 51 E4
High St. Mer T 51 F4
High St. N Tre 54 B3
High St. Neath 87 F4
High St. Nel 99 E2
High St. Og Va 119 F1
High St. Pen 217 D3
High St. Peng 76 C1
High St. Peng 101 D4
High St. Peng 101 F4
High St. Pontar 36 B3
High St. Pontcr 118 C2
High St. Pontdw 40 C3
High St. Ponty 149 E4
High St. Porth 122 C1
High St. Pyle 161 F1
High St. Rhy 34 C1
High St. Rhy 34 C2
High St. Se Si 24 C3
High St. Skew 86 C4
High St. Swan 110 B4
High St. Tony 146 B4
High St. Tony 147 E3
High St. Tonypa 121 D3
High St. Tred 35 F4
High St. Treo 94 C3
High St. Troed 51 F2
High St. Ynybw 97 F1
High St. Ynys 128 A3
High St. Ystraf 27 F2
High Street Arc. Card 205 D3
High Street Arc. Mer T 32 B1
High Trees. C-c-y-c 32 A4
High View. Bridg 180 A3
High View Gdns. Swan 109 D1
High View. Swan 84 B1
High View Way. Ponty 124 B3
Highbridge Cl. Sully 226 B2
Highbury Cl. Swan 84 A1
Highbury Cres. Bridg 179 E3
Highbury Dr. Peng 101 F3
Highbury Pl. Card 203 D2
Highbury Rd. Card 203 E3
Highcliffe Ct. T Mum 136 C2
Highdale Cl. Ll'tris 168 C1
Higher La. T Mum 137 D2
Highfield Ave. Bridg 179 F4
Highfield Ave. Porth 192 C3
Highfield Cl. B-coch 62 C1
Highfield Cl. Brynco 163 F2
Highfield Cl. Ch Vil 150 A1
Highfield Cl. D pow 216 B2
Highfield Cl. Pontmi 129 F1
Highfield Cl. Porth 192 C3
Highfield Cres. Bar 76 A3
Highfield Cres. Pontll 101 F2
Highfield Cl. Rhiwd 155 F2
Highfield. Fern 95 E4
Highfield Gdns. Rhiwd 155 F2
Highfield Ind Est. Fern 95 F4
Highfield La. Rhiwd 155 F2
Highfield. Lough 82 A4
Highfield. Pen 217 D2
Highfield Pl. Brynco 163 F2
Highfield Rd. Card 189 D2
Highfield Rd. Glan 4 C4
Highfield Rd. Neath 87 D1
Highfield Rd. Pontll 101 F2
Highfield Terr. Ponty 124 A1
Highfields. Bridg 180 A3
Highfields. Card 187 F1
Highfields Way. Peng 101 E3
Highland Ave. Brynco 164 A3
Highland Cl. Skew 86 C4
Highland Cres. Onll 10 A1
Highland Gdns. N Abb 62 A1
Highland Pl. Aberd 49 F1
Highland Pl. Bridg 179 F1
Highland Pl. Og Va 119 F1
Highland Terr. Peng 101 F4
Highland Terr. Pontar 36 C2
Highland View. Mer T 51 F4
Highlands. Card 190 A1
Highlands Cl. Tony 147 E3
Highlands. Tony 147 E3
Highmead Ave. T Mum 136 C3
Highmead Cl. T Mum 136 C3
Highmead. Pontll 101 E2
Highmead Rd. Card 203 E3
Highmoor. Swan 110 B3
Highpool Cl. T Mum 136 C3
Highpool La. T Mum 136 C3
Highview Rd. Pen 216 C3
Highwalls Ave. D pow 215 F2
Highwalls End. D pow 216 A2
Highwalls Rd. D pow 216 A2
Hilary Way. Porth 176 C1
Hilda St. Ponty 149 F3
Hiles Rd. Card 203 F3
Hill Crest. T Mum 137 D2
Hill Dr. Ch Vil 169 E4
Hill Head. Ll' maj 219 F3
Hill Rd. N Abb 87 D4
Hill Rd. Rhy 34 C1

Hill Rd. Rhy	54	B4	Hodges Row. Card	205	D2	Hospital Rd. Gell	100	B4	Ipswich Rd. Card	189	F1
Hill Side. M Ash	97	F4	Hodges Sq. Card	205	D2	Hospital Rd. P Tal	138	C4	Irene St. M Ash	97	F4
Hill Side St. Yst	94	C3	Hodges St. Mer T	32	C2	Hospital Rd. Penga	82	C4	Ireton Cl. Card	174	A1
Hill St. Abera	71	E4	Hodgson's Rd. Ystal	23	D2	Hospital Rd. Ponty	124	C1	Irfon St. Fern	95	F3
Hill St. Abercy	98	B1	Hoel Gellilodra. Pontcr	144	A2	Houlson St. Mer T	33	D3	Iris Cl. P Tal	113	E2
Hill St. Bar	75	F3	Hoel-y-Graig. Cwma	114	C4	Housman Cl. Card	190	B4	Iron Bridge Rd. Card	187	E4
Hill St. Barry	225	E3	Hoel-y-Nant. A-wen	41	D2	Howard Dr. Caer	152	A3	Iron Row. Tred	35	F3
Hill St. Clyne	64	C4	Hoel-y-Tyla. Glyn	90	B2	Howard Gdns. Card	205	E3	Iron St. Card	205	E3
Hill St. Deri	75	E4	Hogarth House. P Tal	138	B4	Howard Pl. Card	205	E3	Iron St. Tred	35	F3
Hill St. Fern	70	A1	Hogarth Pl. P Tal	138	B4	Howard St. Card	205	E3	Ironworks Rd. Hir	48	B4
Hill St. Gell	100	C1	Holborn Terr. Tonypa	121	F3	Howard St. Tonypa	121	D3	Is y Coed. Fern	95	E4
Hill St. Gow	82	A3	Holbrook Cl. Treo	94	B4	Howard St. Treo	94	B3	Is-Fryn. Rhy	34	C3
Hill St. Maest	117	D3	Holden Rd. Card	204	B1	Howard Terr. Card	205	E3	Is-y-Bryniau. Cwmll	6	B4
Hill St. Neath	87	E1	Holdings La. Penty	186	A3	Howardian Cl. Card	189	F1	Isaac's Pl. P Tal	138	C4
Hill St. Og Va	119	F1	Holford St. Abera	71	E4	Howel Rd. Neath	87	E2	Isfryn Ind Est. Og Va	144	C1
Hill St. Og Va	119	F3	Holford St. C-c-y-c	32	A2	Howell Cl. Mer T	32	B1	Island Farm Cl. Mer M	179	F1
Hill St. Swan	110	B4	Holford Terr. Aberd	49	E2	Howell Rd. Card	203	E3	Island Farm Rd. Mer M	179	F1
Hill St. T Mum	137	D3	Holgate Cl. Card	187	E2	Howell St. Og Va	119	F4	Island Mews. Marg	114	A1
Hill St. Tony	146	B3	Holland St. Marg	139	E4	Howell St. Ponty	124	C3	Islington St. Bridg	179	E3
Hill St. Tonypa	121	F2	Hollett Rd. Swan	84	B3	Howell's Cres. Card	204	A4	Islwyn Cl. Peng	101	D4
Hill St. Trehe	68	C1	Hollies The. Bridg	180	B2	Howell's Row. Abera	71	E3	Islwyn Cl. Ynys	127	F3
Hill St. Troed	52	A1	Hollies The. Ll'tris	184	A3	Howells Rd. Swan	108	B4	Islwyn Dr. Caer	152	A2
Hill Terr. Fern	96	A3	Hollies The. Tre	99	E3	Hubert Dr. Bridg	179	F4	Islwyn Mynydd Cl. Pontll	101	E2
Hill Terr. P Tal	114	A1	Hollies The. Marsh	191	F4	Hughes St. M Ash	72	C1	Islwyn Rd. Swan	110	A4
Hill Terr. Pen	216	C3	Hollies The. Mer T	32	A1	Hughes St. Tonypa	121	F2	Islwyn Rd. Ynys	128	C2
Hill Terr. Wen	214	C4	Hollins The. Neath	88	A3	Hughs Cl. Card	187	E2	Islwyn St. Ynys	128	A2
Hill View. Bridg	179	D3	Holly Dr. Aberd	49	E2	Hugon Dr. Card	189	F1	Islwyn Terr. Porth	122	B2
Hill View. Card	203	E4	Holly Gr. Card	173	D2	Humphrey St. Swan	110	A4	Islwyn Terr. Tred	35	F3
Hill View Cres. Swan	84	B4	Holly Pl. Peng	101	F4	Humphreys Terr. Maest	117	D4	Islwyn Way. Barry	225	E4
Hill View. Gall	101	D1	Holly Rd. Card	203	E4	Hunt Cl. Card	172	C1	Islwyn Workshops. Pontmi	155	F4
Hill View. Ll'tris	169	D3	Holly Rd. Neath	88	A3	Hunt Pl. Barry	225	E3	Isyrhos. Ystra	8	B2
Hill View. Penco	181	D4	Holly Row. M Ash	97	F4	Hunter St. Barry	225	E3	Ivey Pl. Swan	110	B4
Hill View. Pontcr	118	C2	Holly St. Pontdw	40	C3	Hunter St. Card	205	D1	Ivor Cl. Ll'tris	184	A3
Hill View. Pontll	101	F2	Holly St. Ponty	150	A3	Hunter St. Neath	87	E1	Ivor St. Aberca	129	E4
Hill View. Pyle	161	E1	Holly St. Tony	146	A3	Hunters Ridge. Bridg	180	B3	Ivor St. Maest	117	D1
Hill View. Skew	112	A4	Holly Terr. Card	188	A1	Hunters Ridge. Card	189	D2	Ivor St. Mer T	33	D2
Hill View. Tred	35	F3	Holly Terr. Troed	52	A1	Huntingdon Dr. Card	174	A1	Ivor St. Peng	101	D3
Hill View. Ynys	128	A2	Holly Way. Mer T	32	B2	Huntingdon Way. Swan	109	D4	Ivor St. Pontcr	118	C2
Hill's St. Card	205	D3	Holly Wlk. Porthc	193	F4	Huntington Cl. T Mum	137	D4	Ivor St. Ponty	123	E1
Hill-Snook Rd. Card	203	E4	Hollybush Cl. Ch Vil	150	A1	Huntington St. T Mum	137	D4	Ivor St. Yst	95	E2
Hillary Cl. Card	172	C1	Hollybush Cl. Card	189	E3	Huntsmans Cove. T Mum	136	C4	Ivorites Row. G-nea	27	D1
Hillary Mews. Barry	225	D3	Hollybush Dr. Swan	109	D4	Huntsmead Cl. Card	172	C2	Ivy Ave. Neath	88	A4
Hillary Rise. Barry	225	D3	Hollybush Est. Card	187	F4	Hurford Cres. Ponty	124	A1	Ivy Row. N Tre	76	A4
Hillary Rise. Cross	129	E3	Hollybush Gr. Porth	123	D2	Hurford Pl. Card	189	E4	Ivy St. Card	204	A4
Hillbrook Cl. Abera	71	D4	Hollybush Hts. Card	189	E4	Hurford St. Ponty	149	D4	Ivy St. Pen	217	D2
Hillbrook Cl. Swan	82	B2	Hollybush Rd. Card	189	E3	Hurman St. Card	205	D1	Ivy Terr. Ponty	124	A1
Hillcot Cl. Card	173	D1	Hollybush Rise. Card	189	E3	Huron Cres. Card	189	D2	Ivydale. Card	173	D2
Hillcrest Ave. Abera	71	E4	Hollybush Terr. Ch Vil	150	A1	Hurst Gr. Abera	50	A2			
Hillcrest. Bridg	163	E1	Hollybush Wlk. Rhiwd	155	F2	Hutchwns Cl. Porth	192	B4	Jack-y-Ddu Bank. Neath	87	D1
Hillcrest Cl. Card	172	C2	Hollycroft Cl. Card	203	F3	Hydrangea Cl. Card	189	E4	Jackson Cl. Rhoose	223	D1
Hillcrest Dr. Porth	122	C1	Holmes St. Barry	225	D3	Hylton Terr. Bed	74	A4	Jackson Rd. Card	203	D3
Hillcrest. Ll'ha	166	C2	Holmesdale Ct. Card	204	C1	Hywel Cres. Barry	225	D3	Jacrow Sq. Card	203	E2
Hillcrest. Mer T	32	C4	Holmesdale St. Card	204	C1				Jade Cl. Card	173	D2
Hillcrest View. Fern	95	E4	Holmeside. Card	173	D2	Ian's Wlk. Swan	60	A2	James Cl. Brynco	163	F2
Hillcroft Cres. Glyn	91	E2	Holms Ct. Sully	226	A3	Idris Davies Pl. Rhy	34	C1	James Cl. Peng	101	D3
Hillfort Cl. Card	203	E2	Holmview Ct. Card	190	B3	Idris Pl. Bridg	179	F4	James Cl. Swan	85	E3
Hillgrove. T Mum	136	C2	Holmwood. Ch Vil	169	E3	Idris Terr. Swan	84	C3	James Pl. Ponty	149	F4
Hillrise. Card	189	E3	Holmwood Cl. Card	189	E2	Idwal Pl. Swan	84	A3	James' Rd. Pontcr	118	C3
Hillrise Pk. Cly	60	B4	Holton Rd. Barry	225	D3	Idwal St. Neath	88	A4	James St. Abera	71	E3
Hillsboro. Bridg	179	E3	Holts Field. Bish	136	B3	Iestyn Dr. Penco	165	E1	James St. Aberd	49	F2
Hillsboro Pl. Porth	192	C3	Holyhead Cl. Caer	151	E2	Iestyn St. Aberd	49	F2	James St. Bar	76	A2
Hillside. Aberd	49	E2	Holyrood Terr. Trea	121	F4	Iestyn Cl. Card	204	B4	James St. Barry	225	E3
Hillside Ave. Aber	150	C4	Holywell Rd. Ch Vil	150	A1	Iestynian Ave. Card	204	B4	James St. Bedw	153	D4
Hillside Ave. Ll'ha	167	D2	Homelands Rd. Card	188	B3	Ifor Hael Rd. Rhiwd	155	F3	James St. Card	205	D1
Hillside Ave. Mark	76	B4	Homelong House. Card	188	C4	Ifor Jones Ct. Card	189	E3	James St. Fern	70	A1
Hillside. Bridg	163	E1	Homerton St. Abercy	98	A3	Ifor St. M Ash	72	B1	James St. Ll'bra	126	C1
Hillside. Caer	152	A4	Homeside House. Pen	217	D2	Ilan Ave. Ponty	149	F3	James St. M Ash	72	C1
Hillside Cl. Barry	225	E3	Homfray St. Maest	117	D3	Ilan Rd. Aber	151	D4	James St. Marg	139	E4
Hillside Cl. Mer V	73	E3	Honddu Pl. Swan	59	E1	Ilchester Rd. Card	190	B3	James St. Mark	76	B4
Hillside Cl. Trea	121	F4	Honeysuckle Cl. Card	203	E4	Ilex Cl. Card	188	C4	James St. Mer T	51	F4
Hillside Cres. Swan	110	A4	Honeysuckle Cl. Mer T	32	B3	Ilfracombe Cres. Card	190	B3	James St. N Tre	54	C2
Hillside Ct. Card	189	E1	Honeysuckle Way. Bridg	180	B3	Illtyd Ave. Ll' Maj	220	A3	James St. N Tre	55	D1
Hillside Ct. Ch Vil	169	E3	Hong Kong Terr. Brynco	164	A2	Illtyd Rd. Card	203	D3	James St. Pontar	36	B2
Hillside. Deri	53	E4	Honiton Rd. Card	190	B4	Illtyd St. Neath	88	A4	James St. Pontdw	40	B3
Hillside Gdns. Bar	75	F1	Hoo St. Neath	87	E1	Illtyd St. Ponty	149	D4	James St. Ponty	149	F4
Hillside Gn. Bridg	163	E1	Hoo St. Swan	111	D4	Illtyd St. Treo	94	B3	James St. Porth	192	C3
Hillside. Neath	87	F3	Hookland Rd. Porthc	193	E4	Ilminster Cl. Barry	225	D3	James St. Tonypa	122	A2
Hillside. Og Va	144	B2	Hope Ave. Tondu	163	E2	Ilminster St. Barry	225	D3	James St. Tred	35	F3
Hillside Pk. Bar	75	F1	Hope St. Card	205	D2	Ilston Way. T Mum	137	D4	James St. Treo	94	C3
Hillside Rd. Tony	147	E3	Hopkin St. P Tal	113	F1	Ilton Rd. Card	189	E1	James St. Ystra	8	A2
Hillside Terr. Bedw	152	C3	Hopkin St. Pontdw	40	C3	Imperial Bldgs. Card	205	D3	James St. Ystra	23	F4
Hillside Terr. Deri	54	A1	Hopkin St. Trehe	94	A4	Imperial Bldgs. Card	205	D3	James Terr. Gall	101	D1
Hillside Terr. Gell	100	B1	Hopkins St. Swan	84	B2	Imperial Ct. Abercy	98	C1	James Terr. Tonypa	121	F2
Hillside Terr. Og Va	144	B2	Hopkins Terr. Glyn	90	C3	Inchmarnock St. Card	205	E3	James Terr. Tylor	122	C3
Hillside Terr. Peng	101	F4	Hopkinstown Rd. Ponty	124	A1	Incline Rd. Abera	50	C1	Jamesville. Aberca	129	D4
Hillside Terr. Ponty	124	B1	Hopyard Meadow. Cowb	198	B3	Incline Row. Marg	139	E3	Janet St. Card	205	F3
Hillside Terr. Trea	121	F4	Horace Terr. Ll'bra	151	F4	Incline Side. Mer T	52	A4	Janet St. Ponty	149	F3
Hillside Terr. Tylor	122	B4	Horeb Cl. Mer T	32	C2	Incline Top. Abercy	98	C2	Jasmin Cl. P Tal	113	E2
Hillside Terr. Yst	95	D1	Horeb Rd. Swan	84	C4	Inglefield Ave. Card	188	C1	Jasmine Cl. Mer T	32	B3
Hillside View. Bar	75	F1	Horeb St. Mer T	50	C4	Inkerman Row. Marg	139	E3	Jasmine Cl. Swan	109	D4
Hillside View. Ponty	124	A1	Horeb St. Treo	94	B3	Inkerman St. Swan	110	C4	Jasmine Dr. Card	191	D4
Hilltop Ave. Ponty	124	C2	Horeb Terr. Llwy	49	F4	Inkerman Terr. Tred	35	E3	Jasper Cl. Card	187	F1
Hilltop Cl. P Tal	113	F3	Horizon Park. Swan	85	D3	Insole Cl. Card	203	F4	Jeffrey St. M Ash	72	B2
Hilltop Cl. Tre	99	D3	Hornbeam Cl. Card	191	D4	Insole Gdns. Card	204	A4	Jellicoe Gdns. Card	189	D3
Hilltop Cres. Ponty	124	C1	Hornbeam Cl. Mer T	32	B3	Insole Gr E. Card	203	F4	Jenkin St. Abera	50	A1
Hillview Terr. Marg	139	E4	Hornbeam Cl. Neath	88	B3	Insole Gr W. Card	203	F4	Jenkin St. Abera	71	E3
Hilton Pl. Card	187	F2	Hornbeam Wlk. Rhiwd	155	F2	Insole Pl. Card	204	A4	Jenkin St. Abercy	98	C2
Hinton St. Card	205	F3	Hornchurch Cl. Card	187	F1	Institute Pl. Trea	121	F4	Jenkin St. Barry	225	D4
Hirst Cres. Card	187	E1	Horner St. Gall	101	D3	Institute Rd. Trea	121	F4	Jenkin St. Bridg	179	E2
Hirwain Pl. Tylor	96	B2	Horsefair Rd. Colw	180	C1	Institute St. Fern	70	A1	Jenkin St. Maesy	101	D1
Hirwain Terr. Mer T	32	C2	Horton St. Swan	110	B4	Instow Pl. Card	190	B3	Jenkins Rd. Neath	87	D1
Hirwaun Rd. Aberd	49	F2	Horton Way. Sully	225	F3	Inter Valley Rd. Onll	26	C4	Jenkins Rd. Skew	87	D4
Hirwaun Rd. Peny	49	D3	Horwood Cl. Card	205	D4	Inter-Valley Rd. G-nea	27	E3	Jenkins Row. Deri	75	E4
Hlside Dr. Cowb	198	C1	Hosea Row. Swan	84	B2	Inverleith Terr. Trea	121	F4	Jenkins Row. Rhy	34	C2
Hoddinotts Houses. Yst	95	D3	Hosea Terr. Swan	84	B2	Inverness Pl. Card	189	D1	Jenkins St. Ponty	124	A1
Hodges Cres. Peng	76	A1				Iolo Pl. Barry	225	F3	Jenkins St. Porth	122	C3
						Iorwerth St. Swan	84	B1	Jenkins Terr. Glyn	92	B3

Jenkins Terr. Maest	142	E3
Jenkins Terr. Marg	139	E4
Jenner St. Barry	225	E3
Jericho Rd. Swan	110	C3
Jerry's La. Bedw	152	B4
Jersey Rd. Glyn	92	B3
Jersey Rd. Swan	85	E3
Jersey Row. Cwma	114	C3
Jersey St. Marg	114	B1
Jersey St. Swan	84	B1
Jersey Terr. Cwma	114	C3
Jersey Terr. Neath	87	D1
Jerusalem St. Rhy	34	C2
Jesmond Dene. T We	171	D2
Jestyn Cl. Card	202	C2
Jestyn Cl. D pow	216	A2
Jestyn St. Porth	122	C2
Jevan Cl. Card	187	E2
Jewel St. Barry	225	E3
Jim Driscoll Way. Card	205	D1
Job's La. C-c-y-c	31	F2
Jockey St. Swan	110	B4
John Morgan Cl. Card	187	F2
John Penry Cres. Swan	84	A3
John Pl. Ponty	149	F3
John St. Abera	50	A1
John St. Abera	71	F2
John St. Aberca	129	E4
John St. Bar	75	F2
John St. Barry	225	E3
John St. Card	205	D3
John St. Ce Cr	162	B1
John St. Hir	48	C2
John St. M Ash	72	C1
John St. Maest	116	C3
John St. Mark	76	C4
John St. Mer T	32	B1
John St. Og Va	119	F3
John St. P Tal	114	A1
John St. Pen	217	D2
John St. Ponty	149	F3
John St. Porth	122	C2
John St. Porth	192	C3
John St. Reso	44	A1
John St. Swan	83	E1
John St. Swan	110	B4
John St. T Mum	137	D2
John St. Tre	99	D3
John St. Trehe	69	D1
John St. Tylor	122	C3
John St. Ynys	127	F3
John St. Yst	94	C3
John's Hill. St Ath	221	E3
John's Terr. Ton	89	E3
Johnathans Terr. Ponty	124	C3
Johns La. Card	188	A1
Johnson Pk. Hir	48	C4
Johnston Rd. Card	172	B1
Joiners Rd. Pen-cl	81	E1
Jolly Rd. Glan	4	C3
Jones Pl. Ponty	124	C1
Jones St. M Ash	72	C1
Jones St. Mer T	33	D3
Jones St. N Tre	54	C2
Jones St. Pontdw	40	C3
Jones St. Ponty	124	C3
Jones St. Tonypa	121	E3
Jones St. Treo	94	A4
Jones Terr. Mer T	32	C1
Jones Terr. Swan	110	B4
Jonquil Cl. Card	191	D4
Joseph Davies' Cl. Swan	84	B1
Joseph Parry Cl. Pen	216	C3
Joseph Row. Pyle	161	E2
Joseph St. Marg	114	A1
Joslin Rd. Bridg	180	A4
Joslin Terr. Bridg	180	A4
Jowett Ave. Mer T	51	F4
Jubilee Cres. Bridg	180	A2
Jubilee Cres. Brynco	163	F2
Jubilee Cres. Skew	86	C4
Jubilee Gdns. Porth	177	D1
Jubilee Ind Est. Card	205	E3
Jubilee La. Lough	56	C1
Jubilee La. Lough	82	A4
Jubilee La. Pen	217	D2
Jubilee Rd. Abera	71	E3
Jubilee Rd. Bridg	180	A2
Jubilee Rd. N Tre	55	D1
Jubilee St. Card	204	C2
Jubilee St. Ll'ha	166	C1
Julian Terr. P Tal	113	F1
Julian's Cl. Gell	100	B4
Julian's Way. Pyle	177	D4
Junction Lock Rd. Card	205	E1
Junction Terr. Card	187	E3
Juniper Cl. Swan	109	D4
Justin Cl. Card	189	E2
Kames Pl. Card	205	E3
Kane Cl. Card	188	C4
Katie St. Pontcr	118	C4
Keats Cl. Bridg	179	E3
Keats Gr. Swan	108	C4
Keble St. Bedw	153	E4
Keen Rd. Card	205	E2

Keen's Pl. Brynco

Keen's Pl. Brynco 163 F2
Keir Hardie Rd. Maest 116 C1
Keir Hardie Rd. P Tal 113 E4
Keith St. Tylor 96 A2
Kelston Cl. Card 187 F3
Kelston Pl. Card 187 F3
Kelston Rd. Card 187 F3
Kelvin Rd. Card 189 D1
Kelvin Rd. Cly 39 E1
Kemble St. Swan 109 F3
Kemeys Rd. Rhoose 223 D1
Kemps Covert. St Don 218 C3
Kemys Pl. Card 188 B2
Kemys Way. Swan 85 D4
Kendal Cl. Abera 50 B1
Kendle Dr. Swan 109 E4
Kendon Ct. Hir 48 B4
Kenfig Cotts. Porth 176 C1
Kenfig Ind Est. Marg 160 A2
Kenfig Pl. Swan 85 D1
Kenfig Rd. Card 188 B2
Kenilworth Ct. Card 203 F4
Kenilworth Ct. P Tal 113 F3
Kenilworth Pl. T Mum 137 C4
Kenilworth Rd. Barry 225 D3
Kenley Cl. Card 187 F1
Kenmuir Rd. Card 205 F4
Kennard St. Yst 94 C1
Kennedy Cl. Ll'tris 169 D4
Kennedy Dr. Penco 181 E4
Kennel Row. Neath 87 D1
Kennerleigh Rd. Card 190 A2
Kenneth Treasure Ct. Card 190 B4
Kennington Cl. Card 172 C1
Kennington Cl. Swan 108 B3
Kenry St. Og Va 146 A4
Kenry St. Tonypa 121 F3
Kenry St. Treo 94 A4
Kensington Ave. Card 204 A3
Kensington Dr. Bridg 179 E3
Kensington Dr. Porth 123 D1
Kenson Cl. Rhoose 222 C1
Kenson Hill. Rhoose 222 C3
Kent Rd. Bridg 180 A2
Kent St. Card 204 C1
Kenway Ave. Neath 87 F3
Kenwood Rd. Card 203 D3
Kenyon Rd. Card 206 A4
Keppoch St. Card 205 E4
Kern Cl. P Tal 113 D2
Kerrigan Cl. Card 187 E1
Kerrycroy St. Card 205 E3
Kestrel Cl. B-coch 62 C1
Kestrel Cl. Bridg 180 B2
Kestrel Cl. Card 189 E4
Kestrel View. Gell 100 C2
Kestrel Way. Sully 227 D4
Keswick Ave. Card 189 D2
Keteringham Cl. Sully 226 A3
Kewstoke Ave. Card 190 A3
Kewstoke Pl. Card 190 A3
Keyes Ave. Card 189 D3
Keynsham Rd. Card 188 B3
Keyston Rd. Card 187 F1
Khartoum Terr. Onll 9 F1
Kidwelly Cl. Peng 76 C1
Kidwelly Cl. Caer 151 E2
Kidwelly Gr. Mer T 31 F1
Kilcattan St. Card 205 E3
Kildare St. Swan 84 B2
Kilfield Rd. Bish 136 A3
Kilgetty Cl. Card 203 D1
Kilgetty House. Card 188 A2
Killan Rd. Swan 108 A4
Killgetty Ct. Card 203 D4
Kiln St. Abera 71 E4
Kilvey Rd. Swan 84 C1
Kilvey Terr. Swan 110 C4
Kimberley Cl. Swan 109 E4
Kimberley Ct. Bridg 180 A2
Kimberley Rd. Card 189 E1
Kimberley Rd. Swan 109 E4
Kimberley Terr. Card 188 C4
Kimberley Terr. Tred 35 F3
Kimberley Way. Porth 122 C1
Kincraig St. Card 205 D4
King Edward Ave. Caer 152 A1
King Edward Rd. G-C-G 5 F2
King Edward St. Mer T 32 B1
King Edward St. Pontcr 118 C3
King Edward Terr. Rhy 34 C2
King Edward Vii Ave. Card 205 D4
King Edward's Rd. Swan .. 110 A3
King George Ct. Swan 109 D2
King George V Drive E.
  Card 188 C2
King George V Drive N.
  Card 188 C2
King George V Drive W.
  Card 188 C2
King St. Aber 151 D4
King St. Abera 71 E4
King St. Abercy 98 C2
King St. Aberd 49 E2
King St. Fern 96 A3
King St. M Ash 97 F4
King St. Marg 114 B1
King St. Mer T 33 D3

King St. Neath 87 F4
King St. Pen 217 D3
King St. Ponty 149 F3
King St. Rhy 34 C1
King St. Swan 110 B4
King St. T We 171 D2
King St. Ynys 128 A2
King St. Yst 95 D1
King Wood Cl. Card 189 F1
King's Ave. Card 187 E3
King's Head Rd. Swan 83 F2
King's Hill. Gall 101 D2
King's Hill. Porthc 193 D4
King's Rd. Card 187 E3
King's Rd. Card 204 B3
King's Rd. Swan 110 C4
Kingarth St. Card 205 E3
Kingcraft St. M Ash 72 B1
Kingdon-Owen Rd. Neath ... 87 F3
Kingfisher Cl. Card 190 C4
Kingfisher Sq. Ll' Maj 220 B3
Kingrosia Pk. Cly 61 D4
Kings Ave. Rhy 34 C3
Kings La. Swan 110 B4
Kings Rd. Card 204 B4
Kings Rd. T Mum 137 D2
Kings Ride. D Pow 215 F2
Kings Terr. Maest 116 C3
Kingsacre. Ch Vil 169 E3
Kingsbridge Bsns Pk.
  Lough 82 B4
Kingsbury Ct. Llwy 49 F3
Kingsbury Pl. Abera 71 D2
Kingsbury Pl. Llwy 49 F3
Kingsland Cres. Barry 225 D2
Kingsland Rd. Card 187 F2
Kingsland Rd. Card 204 A3
Kingsland Terr. Ponty 149 F4
Kingsley Cl. Sully 226 A3
Kingsley Pl. Aber 125 F1
Kingsley Terr. Mer T 32 C1
Kingsley Terr. Mer V 73 E2
Kingston Cl. Card 204 B3
Kingston Rd. Swan 109 E4
Kingsway. Bridg 180 C2
Kingsway. Card 205 D3
Kingsway. Swan 83 E2
Kingsway The. Swan 110 B4
Kingswood Cl. Ewen 195 F4
Kingswood Ct. Card 189 D1
Kingswood. Ponty 149 D4
Kinley St. Swan 110 C4
Kipling Cl. Card 190 A4
Kipling Cl. Pen 216 C3
Kipling Gdns. Bridg 179 E3
Kirkby Ct. Card 205 E2
Kirkhouse St. Ponty 149 D4
Kirkland Ct. Card 189 E1
Kirkwall Ct. Card 205 F4
Kirton Cl. Card 187 F1
Kitchener Rd. Card 204 B3
Kittiwake Cl. Porth 192 B4
Kittle Gn. South 135 F4
Kittle Hill La. South 135 F4
Knelston Pl. Swan 83 F4
Knight St. M Ash 72 B2
Knight St. P Tal 114 A1
Knights Rd. Marg 139 F2
Knights Terr. Abercy 98 C2
Knightswell Cl. Card 203 D1
Knightswell Rd. Card 203 D2
Knoll Ave. Swan 109 F3
Knoll Terr. Tonypa 121 E4
Knowbury Ave. Pen 227 D4
Knox Rd. Card 205 D3
Knox St. Marg 139 F2
Knoyle Dr. Swan 84 B4
Knoyle St. Swan 84 B4
Kyfts La. Ll'gen 103 E3
Kyle Ave. Card 188 B3
Kyle Cres. Card 188 B3
Kymin Rd. Pen 217 D2
Kymin Terr. Pen 217 D2
Kyveilog St. Card 204 B4

Laburnam Ave. Tred 35 E4
Laburnam La. C-c-y-c 32 A3
Laburnam Terr. Troed 52 A1
Laburnam Way. Pen 216 C2
Laburnham Pl. Swan 109 D3
Laburnum Ave. P Tal 113 F4
Laburnum Cl. Mer T 32 B2
Laburnum Ct. Ponty 150 A2
Laburnum Dr. Aberd 49 E2
Laburnum Dr. Porthc 193 F4
Laburnum Gr. Pontll 101 F2
Laburnum Pl. Card 203 E4
Laburnum Terr. Ponty 150 A3
Laburnum Way. D pow 216 A1
Lady Housty Ave. T Mum .. 136 C3
Lady Jane St. P Tal 138 C4
Lady Margaret Ct. Card 189 F1
Lady Margaret's Terr. Card 205 E3
Lady Mary Rd. Card 189 D2
Lady Tyler Terr. Rhy 34 C2
Ladysmith Rd. Card 189 E1
Ladysmith Rd. Peng 101 D3
Ladysmith Terr. Tred 35 F3

Laing St. Pyle 161 E1
Lake Dr. Cowb 198 C1
Lake Rd. P Tal 138 C4
Lake Road E. Card 189 D2
Lake Road N. Card 189 D3
Lake Road W. Card 189 D3
Lake St. Fern 95 F3
Lake View Cl. Card 189 D2
Lake View Ct. Card 189 D2
Lakeside Dr. Card 189 D3
Lakeside Gdns. Mer T 32 A2
Lakeside. Swan 85 D3
Lakeview Cl. Porthc 193 D4
Laleston Cl. Barry 225 D4
Laleston Cl. Card 203 E2
Laleston Cl. Porth 176 C1
Laleston Ct. Bridg 178 C3
Lamb And Flag Cotts. Ystra .. 8 B3
Lamb Rd. Hir 29 D3
Lambert Terr. Aberd 49 F1
Lamberton Way. Card 205 E3
Lambourne Cres. Card 188 C4
Lambourne Dr. T Mum 136 C3
Lambs Well Cl. T Mum 137 D2
Lamby Ind Pk. Card 190 B1
Lamby Way. Card 190 A1
Lamby Way Workshops.
  Card 190 B1
Lan Cl. Ponty 124 A1
Lan Coed. Swan 85 E3
Lan Deri. Swan 85 E3
Lan Manor. Swan 84 C4
Lan St. Swan 59 F1
Lan-y-Parc. Nel 99 F2
Lancaster Cl. G-nea 26 C1
Lancaster Cl. Swan 83 E3
Lancaster Dr. Ch Vil 169 E4
Lancaster St. Mer T 32 B1
Landeg St. Swan 84 C3
Landimore Pl. Swan 83 F3
Landor Ave. Swan 108 C4
Landor Dr. Lough 56 B1
Landore Ave. Marg 139 F2
Landraw Rd. Ponty 124 A1
Landsdowne Cl. Swan 83 E2
Landwade Cl. Card 203 E4
Lane The. Gow 81 F3
Lane The. Ll' maj 219 F2
Lane The. Wen 202 B1
Lanelay Cl. Ll'tris 168 A1
Lanelay Cres. Ponty 124 A1
Lanelay Pk. Ll'tris 168 A1
Lanelay Rd. Ll'tris 168 A1
Lanelay Terr. Ponty 149 D4
Langcliff Pk. T Mum 137 E2
Langcross Cotts. M-I-Pit ... 204 A1
Langdale Cl. Card 189 E1
Langdon Rd. Swan 110 C4
Langer Way. Cly 39 F1
Langham Way. Card 204 C2
Langland Bay Rd. T Mum .. 136 C2
Langland Cl. Hir 48 B4
Langland Cl. T Mum 137 D2
Langland Court Rd. T Mum 136 C2
Langland Rd. Card 190 B2
Langland Rd. T Mum 137 D2
Langland Terr. Swan 109 F3
Langland Villas. T Mum 137 D2
Langlands Rd. Barry 225 E4
Langport Ave. Card 190 B3
Lanhydrock Cl. Card 190 C3
Lanpark Rd. Ponty 124 B1
Lansbury Ave. Gell 100 C2
Lansbury Ave. Marg 139 F3
Lansbury Cl. Caer 151 F3
Lansbury Cl. Maest 116 C1
Lansbury Cres. Maest 116 C1
Lansbury Rd. Mer T 32 A2
Lansdale Dr. Ch Vil 150 A1
Lansdown. T Mum 136 C2
Lansdowne Ave. Card 188 B3
Lansdowne Ave E. Card 204 B3
Lansdowne Ave W. Card 204 A3
Lansdowne Rd. Card 204 B3
Lanwern Rd. Ponty 149 D4
Lanwood Rd. Ponty 124 A1
Lapwing Cl. Porth 192 B4
Lapwing Cl. Sully 227 D4
Larch Cl. Mer T 32 B3
Larch Cl. Neath 88 B3
Larch Cl. Porthc 193 F4
Larch Ct. Card 171 E1
Larch Gr. Caer 152 B3
Larch Gr. Card 173 D2
Larch House. Card 187 F4
Larches The. W St D 199 E4
Larchwood. Wen 215 D3
Lark Pl. Swan 83 F4
Lark Rise. Bridg 180 B4
Larkfield Ave. Abera 50 B1
Larkhill. P Tal 113 F4
Larkspur Cl. B-coch 62 C1
Larkspur Dr. T Mum 136 C4
Larkwood Ave. Pen 217 D1
Latimer Ct. Swan 83 F3
Latt The. Neath 87 F4
Lauderdale Rd. G-C-G 5 F3
Laugharne Ave. Card 190 B2

Laugharne Ct. Swan 109 D3
Laugharne Rd. Card 190 B2
Launcelot Cres. Card 172 C1
Laundry Rd. Ponty 124 A1
Laura St. Barry 225 E3
Laura St. Ponty 149 E4
Laureate Cl. Card 190 A4
Laurel Ave. P Tal 113 F3
Laurel Ave. Ponty 150 A3
Laurel Cl. Aberd 49 E2
Laurel Cl. Brynco 163 F2
Laurel Ct. Bedw 152 C4
Laurel Ct. Card 203 E4
Laurel Dr. Pontll 101 F2
Laurel Dr. Swan 82 B2
Laurel Pl. Swan 109 D3
Laurel Rd. Rhiwd 155 F2
Laureldene. Ll'hry 183 D3
Laurels The. Ll'ha 167 D1
Lauriston Cl. Card 203 E1
Lauriston Pk. Card 203 E1
Lavender Cl. Bridg 180 B3
Lavender Gr. Card 203 E4
Lavender Rd. Mer T 32 A3
Lavernock Rd. Pen 216 C1
Lavernock Rd. Sully 226 C3
Law St. Ce Cr 162 B2
Lawn Terr. Ponty 149 F4
Lawn Terr. Rhy 34 C2
Lawrence Ave. Mark 76 B4
Lawrence Ave. Peny 49 D3
Lawrence Cl. Bridg 179 F3
Lawrence St. Caer 152 A2
Lawrenny Ave. Card 204 B2
Laytonia Ave. Card 188 C1
Le Pouliguen Way. Ll' Maj .. 220 A3
Le Sor Hill. P-s-Ely 201 F3
Le-Breos Ave. Swan 109 F3
Le-Breos. T Mum 108 C1
Lead St. Card 205 E3
Leamington Rd. Card 188 A3
Leckwith Ave. Card 204 B3
Leckwith Cl. Card 204 B2
Leckwith Ct. Bridg 179 E2
Leckwith Pl. Card 204 B3
Leckwith Rd. Card 204 B2
Leckwith Rd. M-l-Pit 204 B1
Leckwith Rd. Pen 216 B4
Lee Cl. Card 189 E2
Lee Cl. D pow 216 A2
Lee Ct. Card 172 B1
Lee Rd. Barry 225 D2
Lee St. Ponty 124 A1
Lee St. Swan 110 C4
Legion's Way. Gell 100 A4
Leicester Sq. Gell 100 C4
Leigh Cl. Ll' Maj 220 B3
Leigh Terr. Tre 99 D3
Leighton Rees Cl. Ynybw ... 97 F1
Lennox Gn. Barry 225 E3
Leoline Cl. Cowb 198 B1
Leon Ave. T We 171 D2
Leonard St. Neath 87 F4
Leonard St. Peng 101 D3
Leslie St. P Tal 113 F1
Leslie Terr. Porth 123 D2
Letterston Rd. Card 190 B3
Letton Rd. Card 205 D2
Lettons Way. D pow 216 A2
Letty St. Card 205 D4
Leven Cl. Card 189 D3
Lewis Arms Row. Tony ... 122 A1
Lewis Ave. Bridg 179 F3
Lewis Ave. Cwmll 6 B4
Lewis Ave. Peng 101 F4
Lewis Dr. Caer 151 F3
Lewis Pl. Porth 122 C1
Lewis Pl. Porth 192 C4
Lewis Rd. Card 205 F2
Lewis Rd. Cry 43 D3
Lewis Rd. Maest 117 D3
Lewis Rd. Neath 87 F3
Lewis Rd. Pen 216 B4
Lewis Sq. Troed 51 F3
Lewis St. Abera 71 E4
Lewis St. Bar 76 A3
Lewis St. Bed 74 A4
Lewis St. Bedw 154 A4
Lewis St. Card 204 C3
Lewis St. Ch Vil 169 E4
Lewis St. Gell 100 C1
Lewis St. Ll'tris 184 A4
Lewis St. M Ash 72 B2
Lewis St. Peng 101 F4
Lewis St. Ponty 149 E4
Lewis St. Ponty 149 E4
Lewis St. Porth 123 E1
Lewis St. Swan 109 E3
Lewis St. Swan 110 C4
Lewis St. Ton 89 D1
Lewis St. Tonypa 122 A2
Lewis St. Yst 94 C1
Lewis Terr. Li'bra 126 C1
Lewis Terr. Mer T 32 C1
Lewis Terr. Ponty 124 B1
Lewis Terr. Porth 123 D2

Lewis Terr. Reso 43 F1
Lewis Terr. Tylor 122 B4
Lewis's Terr. Mer T 32 A1
Leydene Cl. Pontmi 129 F2
Leyshan Wlk. T Mum 136 C4
Leyshon Rd. G-C-G 5 D3
Leyshon Rd. Pontdw 40 C3
Leyshon St. Ponty 149 D4
Leyshon Terr. Porth 123 D1
Lias Rd. Porth 192 C3
Lias St. Bridg 179 F2
Libanus Rd. Lough 57 E1
Libanus Rd. Peng 101 F3
Libanus St. Mer T 33 D3
Library Cl. Ponty 150 A3
Library Cl. Yst 95 D2
Library La. Marg 139 E3
Library Rd. Maest 91 D1
Library Rd. Ponty 124 B1
Library Rd. Tonypa 121 F2
Library St. Card 204 B3
Lido Houses. P Tal 138 B4
Lifeboat Rd. Porth 192 C3
Lilac Cl. Card 187 E1
Lilac Cl. T Mum 136 C4
Lilac Dr. Ch Vil 169 E3
Lilac Gr. P Tal 113 F4
Lilburne Cl. Card 174 A1
Lilian Rd. Peng 101 F3
Lilian St. P Tal 113 F1
Lilliput La. T Mum 137 D4
Lily St. Card 205 E4
Lime Cl. Card 187 E2
Lime Gr. Card 187 D1
Lime Gr. Ll'maes 221 D4
Lime Gr. Mer T 32 B2
Lime Gr. Neath 88 A3
Lime Gr. Pontll 101 F2
Lime Gr. Swan 108 B4
Lime St. Fern 95 F3
Lime St. Lough 57 E1
Lime St. Ponty 150 A3
Lime Tree Way. Porthc ... 193 F4
Limebourne Ct. Card 188 A2
Limekiln Rd. T Mum 137 D3
Limes Ct. Cowb 198 C1
Limes The. Cowb 198 C1
Limeslade Cl. Card 203 F4
Limeslade Cl. Hir 48 B4
Limeslade Cl. T Mum 137 E2
Limeslade Dr. T Mum 137 E2
Limewood Ct. Card 190 C4
Lincoln Ct. Card 189 E3
Lincoln St. Card 204 A3
Lincoln St. Porth 122 C1
Linden Ave. Card 189 E1
Linden Ave. T Mum 137 D4
Linden Cl. B-coch 62 B2
Linden Cres. Aberd 49 E1
Linden Cl. Ll'hry 183 D3
Linden Gr. Caer 152 B3
Linden Gr. Card 190 A2
Linden Way. C-c-y-c 32 A4
Linden Way. Porthc 193 F4
Lindsay Cl. Penco 181 E4
Lindsay Ct. Bridg 180 A1
Lindway Ct. Card 204 A4
Lingfield Ave. P Tal 113 E1
Lingfield Ave. P Tal 113 F1
Lingholm Ct. Card 190 C3
Link The. Swan 109 D3
Links Ct. T Mum 136 C2
Linkside Dr. South 135 D3
Linkside. T Mum 136 C2
Linnet Cl. Card 189 E4
Linnet Way. Bridg 180 B3
Lion St. Swan 84 B1
Lion Way. Swan 85 D4
Lionel Rd. Card 204 A3
Lionel Terr. Ponty 149 F3
Lisburn Rd. Gell 100 C1
Lisburn Rise. Hir 48 B4
Lisnagarvey Ct. Card 187 F4
Lister Ave. P Tal 113 F1
Lisvane Ho. Card 173 D1
Lisvane Rd. Card 173 D1
Lisvane St. Card 188 C1
Litchard Bungalows. Bridg 179 F4
Litchard Cross. Bridg 179 F4
Litchard Hill. Bridg 179 F4
Litchard Ind Est. Bridg ... 180 A4
Litchard Pk. Bridg 179 F4
Litchard Rise. Bridg 179 F4
Litchard Terr. Bridg 179 F4
Litchfield Ct. Card 204 C2
Little Ave. P-s-Ely 201 F3
Little Dock St. Pen 216 C3
Little Frederick St. Card ... 205 D3
Little Gam St. Swan 110 B3
Little London. Ystra 8 B3
Little Mill. Card 188 A2
Little Moors Hill. Barry ... 225 E3
Little Orch. D pow 216 B2
Little Station Rd. Pyle ... 161 F2
Little Wind St. Abera 50 A1
Little Wind St. Swan 110 B3
Little Woods. Abercy 98 B1
Littlecroft Ave. Card 203 F3

Littlecroft Ave. Card

Street	Page	Grid
Littleton St. Card	204	C3
Livingstone Way. St M Ch .	221	E4
Llan Rd. Maest	142	A3
Llan-yr-Eos. Nel	99	F2
Llanarth Cl. Bedw	154	A3
Llanarth Sq. Pontmi	155	D4
Llanarth St. Bedw	154	A4
Llanarth St. Ynys	128	C2
Llanbad. Ll'ha	166	B2
Llanbedr Rd. Card	203	F4
Llanberis Cl. Ch Vil	149	F1
Llanbleddian Gdns. Card ..	205	D4
Llanbradach St. Card	204	C2
Llanbradach St. Ponty	124	A1
Llanbryn Gdns. Ll'ha	166	C2
Llancaiach Rd. Card	188	A2
Llancaiach View. Nel	99	F3
Llancayo Pk. Bar	75	F3
Llancayo St. Bar	75	F3
Llandaff Chase. Card	187	F1
Llandaff Cl. Pen	217	D1
Llandaff Rd. Card	204	B3
Llandaff Sq. Card	190	B4
Llandaff Way. Porth	147	F4
Llanddewi St. Abera	71	E4
Llandegfedd Cl. Card	172	C2
Llandeilo Rd. Glan	4	C4
Llandennis Ave. Card	189	D3
Llandennis Gn. Card	189	D3
Llandennis Rd. Card	189	D3
Llandetty Rd. Card	203	F4
Llandilo Cl. D pow	216	B2
Llandinam Cres. Card	188	A1
Llandogo Rd. Card	190	C4
Llandough Hill. Pen	216	B4
Llandough St. Card	205	D4
Llandough Trad Est. Pen ..	216	B4
Llandovery Cl. Card	203	E2
Llandow House. Barry	215	D1
Llandow Rd. Card	203	E3
Llandraw Ct. Ponty	124	A1
Llandraw Woods. Ponty	149	D4
Llandudno Rd. Card	190	B2
Llandyfrig Cl. D pow	216	B2
Llanedeyrn Cl. Card	189	F2
Llanedeyrn Dr. Card	189	F2
Llanedeyrn Rd. Card	189	F2
Llanedi Rd. Hen	36	A4
Llanerch Cres. Lough	57	D2
Llanerch Goed. Ch Vil	149	E1
Llanerch Rd. Swan	85	D1
Llanerch Rd. Swan	108	B4
Llanenwrrg Way. Card	190	C4
Llanfabon Ct. Ponty	124	C2
Llanfabon Dr. Bedw	152	C2
Llanfabon Rd. Nel	99	E1
Llanfaes. Ystra	23	F4
Llanfair Gdns. T Mum	137	D3
Llanfair Hill. Yst	95	D1
Llanfair Rd. Card	204	B4
Llanfair Rd. Ponty	149	D4
Llanfair Rd. Tonypa	122	A2
Llanfedw Cl. Caer	152	C3
Llanfoist Cl. Yst	95	D2
Llangattock Rd. Card	203	F4
Llangefni Pl. Card	172	C1
Llangeinor Rd. Tondu	163	F3
Llangeinor Terr. Og Va	144	C3
Llangewydd Rd. Brigg	179	E3
Llangorse Rd. Abera	50	C1
Llangorse Rd. Aberd	50	C1
Llangorse Rd. Card	189	E4
Llangorse Rd. Swan	84	A3
Llangranog Pl. Card	172	B1
Llangranog Rd. Card	172	C1
Llangwm Pl. Card	190	B2
Llangwm. Swan	83	F3
Llangwm Way. Porth	192	C4
Llangybi Cl. Card	202	C2
Llangyfelach Rd. Swan	84	B3
Llangyfelach St. Swan	84	B1
Llangynidr Rd. Card	203	F4
Llanharan Villas. Pontcr	118	C1
Llanharran Terr. Og Va	119	F3
Llanharry Rd. Ll'ha	183	D4
Llanharry Rd. Ll'hry	183	E3
Llanidloes Rd. Card	188	A1
Llanina Gr. Card	190	C3
Llanishen Cl. Card	188	C4
Llanishen Ct. Card	188	C1
Llanllienwen Cl. Swan	60	A2
Llanllienwen Rd. Swan	60	A2
Llanmaes Rd. Ll' Maj	220	A4
Llanmaes St. Card	204	C1
Llanmihangel Rd. Cowb	210	B4
Llanmihangel Rise. Cowb .	210	B4
Llanmorlais Rd. Card	188	B1
Llannant Rd. Lough	56	C3
Llanofer Rd. Glyn	91	E2
Llanon Rd. Card	172	C1
Llanover Ave. Pontll	101	F2
Llanover Rd. Card	202	C2
Llanover Rd. Ponty	124	B1
Llanover St. Barry	225	D3
Llanover St. Ponty	124	B1
Llanquian Cl. Cowb	198	C1
Llanquian Rd. Cowb	199	E2
Llanrumney Ave. Card	190	A3
Llansamlet Ind Est. Swan	84	C3
Llansannor Dr. Card	205	E2
Llansawel Cres. Neath	87	D2
Llansawel. Neath	87	E1
Llanstephan Rd. Card	190	B2
Llantarnam Rd. Card	188	B1
Llantrisant Bsns Pk. Ll'tris .	168	B3
Llantrisant Rd. Card	186	B2
Llantrisant Rd. Ch Vil	169	E3
Llantrisant Rd. Ll'tris	149	D3
Llantrisant Rd. Ll'tris	168	C4
Llantrisant Rd. Ll'tris	169	E3
Llantrisant Rd. Ponty	149	D3
Llantrisant Rd. Tony	147	E3
Llantrisant Rise. Card	187	F1
Llantrissant St. Card	204	C4
Llantrithyd Rd. Ll'thyd	211	E4
Llantwit Gardens Cl. St Ath	221	E3
Llantwit Major Rd. Ll'Maj	209	F3
Llantwit Rd. Ll' Maj	220	C3
Llantwit Rd. Neath	88	A4
Llantwit Rd. Ponty	149	F3
Llantwit Rd. St Ath	221	E3
Llantwit Rd. Wick	208	B3
Llantwit St. Barry	225	D4
Llantwit St. Card	205	D4
Llanwern Rd. Card	203	E3
Llanwonno Cl. Ponty	124	A1
Llanwonno Rd. Abera	71	D2
Llanwonno Rd. M Ash	72	B1
Llanwonno Rd. Ponty	124	A1
Llanwonno Rd. Tylor	96	B1
Llanwonno Rd. Tylor	122	C3
Llanyrnewydd. Pen-cl	80	C2
Lle Canol. Glyn	66	C2
Lle Hyfryd. Llwy	49	F3
Llest Terr. Ch Vil	169	E3
Lletai Ave. Penco	181	F4
Lletty Dafydd. Clyne	64	C3
Llettyharri. Marg	114	B1
Llewellyn Ave. B-coch	62	B1
Llewellyn Ave. Card	203	D3
Llewellyn Cl. Marg	139	E4
Llewellyn Dr. Bridg	163	E1
Llewellyn Dr. Caer	152	A2
Llewellyn Pl. Yst	95	D2
Llewellyn St. Penga	57	F1
Llewellyn St. Aberd	49	F2
Llewellyn St. Barry	225	D3
Llewellyn St. G-nea	27	D1
Llewellyn St. Mer T	32	B1
Llewellyn St. Neath	87	F3
Llewellyn St. P Tal	114	A1
Llewellyn St. Tony	146	B3
Llewellyn St. Tonypa	121	F2
Llewellyn St. Trehe	68	B1
Llewellyn St. Tylor	96	A1
Llewellyn St. Yst	94	C3
Llewellyn Terr. Trea	121	F4
Llewellyn Terr. Trea	122	A3
Llewellyn Terr. Ynybw	97	F1
Llewellyn's Rd. Marg	139	D4
Llewelyn Circ. Swan	110	A4
Llewelyn Park Dr. Swan	84	C4
Llewelyn St. Bar	76	A1
Llewelyn St. Mer T	33	D3
Llewelyn St. Og Va	119	F4
Llewelyn St. Ponty	124	A1
Llewelyn St. Swan	109	E3
Llewitha Terr. Lough	83	D3
Lloyd Ave. Card	203	F4
Lloyd Rd. Swan	84	B3
Lloyd St. A-wen	40	A1
Lloyd St. Maest	91	D4
Lloyd St. Yst	95	D2
Lloyd's Terr. Glyn	91	E2
Lloyds Terr. Mer T	32	C2
Lluest. Ystra	8	A1
Llwncelyn Cl. Mer T	51	E4
Llwyd Coed. Card	171	F1
Llwyd y Berth. Caer	151	F1
Llwydarth Cotts. Maest	117	D1
Llwydarth Rd. Maest	117	E1
Llwydcoed Rd. Llwy	49	F3
Llwyfen St. Mer T	32	B1
Llwyn Afang. Swan	59	F3
Llwyn Arosfa. Swan	109	E4
Llwyn Bedw. Penco	181	E4
Llwyn Bedw. Swan	83	E2
Llwyn Berry. Mer T	32	B1
Llwyn Brwydrau. Swan	86	A3
Llwyn Bryn Melyn. Card	187	D3
Llwyn Castan. Card	189	F4
Llwyn Celyn. Swan	83	E2
Llwyn Deri Cl. Rhiwd	155	F1
Llwyn Derw. Pontdw	40	C2
Llwyn Derw. Swan	83	E3
Llwyn Derwen. Pyle	176	C4
Llwyn Dic Penderyn. Mer T .	32	B1
Llwyn Drysgol. Card	187	D3
Llwyn Eithin. Caer	152	B3
Llwyn Eithin. Swan	83	E2
Llwyn Grug. Card	188	B2
Llwyn Gwern. Penco	181	E4
Llwyn Gwyn. Ll'hry	183	D3
Llwyn Helyg. Swan	83	E3
Llwyn Mallt. Card	187	E4
Llwyn Mawr Cl. Swan	109	D4
Llwyn Mawr Rd. Swan	109	D4
Llwyn On. Pyle	177	D4
Llwyn On. Swan	83	E2
Llwyn Onn. Card	172	A1
Llwyn Onn. Gell	100	C4
Llwyn Onn. Hir	29	D2
Llwyn Onn. Ll'hry	183	F4
Llwyn Rd. G-C-G	5	D1
Llwyn Rhosyn. Swan	109	D4
Llwyn Rhosyn. Card	188	B4
Llwyn y Bioden. Swan	59	F3
Llwyn y Gog. Swan	59	F3
Llwyn y Golomen. Swan	60	A3
Llwyn y Pia Rd. Card	173	D2
Llwyn yr Hebog. Swan	60	A3
Llwyn yr Iar. Swan	60	A3
Llwyn-Bach Terr. Mark	55	E1
Llwyn-Crwn Rd. Swan	85	E4
Llwyn-nant. G-C-G	21	D4
Llwyn-On Cl. Caer	151	F2
Llwyn-On St. Caer	151	F2
Llwyn-y-Bryn. Skew	86	B3
Llwyn-y-Gelynen. Mer T	51	E4
Llwyn-y-Grant Pl. Card	189	E1
Llwyn-y-Grant Rd. Card	189	E1
Llwyn-y-Grant Terr. Card ..	189	E1
Llwyn-y-Mor. T Mum	136	C2
Llwyn-yr-Eos. Swan	59	F1
Llwyn-yr-Eos. Troed	51	F2
Llwynbrain Terr. Ll'ha	167	D2
Llwyncarw. Swan	59	F3
Llwyncelyn Ave. Pontar	36	B2
Llwyncelyn Parc. Porth	123	D2
Llwyncelyn. Pontcr	143	F2
Llwyncelyn Rd. G-C-G	5	D2
Llwyncelyn Rd. Porth	123	D2
Llwyncelyn Terr. Coel	9	F2
Llwyncelyn Terr. Nel	99	E2
Llwyncethin Rd. Swan	84	A2
Llwyncrwn Rd. Ll'tris	168	C3
Llwynderi. Peny	49	D3
Llwynderw Ave. Maest	117	E2
Llwynderw Cl. T Mum	109	D1
Llwynderw Dr. T Mum	137	D4
Llwynderw. Lough	57	D1
Llwynderw. Pen-cl	81	F1
Llwynderw Rd. Card	188	B2
Llwynfedw Gdns. Card	188	B3
Llwynfedw Rd. Card	188	B3
Llwynfen Rd. Ll'tris	184	A4
Llwynmadoc St. Ponty	124	A1
Llwynon. Cly	39	F1
Llwynon. Cry	43	D3
Llwynpennau Cotts. Ll'tris .	185	E3
Llwynypia Rd. Trea	121	F4
Llwynypia Terr. Trea	121	F4
Llygad-yr-Haul. B-coch	62	B1
Llygad-yr-Haul. G-nea	26	B1
Llyn Cl. Card	189	D3
Llyn Cres. Fern	95	F3
Llynfa Rd. Pen-cl	81	D2
Llynfi La. Bridg	179	F3
Llynfi La. Maest	117	D2
Llynfi St. Bridg	179	F2
Llynfi St. Tondu	163	E3
Llynfi View. Maest	117	D4
Llys Aneirin. Lough	82	B4
Llys Baldwin. Gow	82	A3
Llys Briallen. Bridg	180	B3
Llys Brynteg. Lough	57	D2
Llys Cambria. Ll'bra	151	F4
Llys Caradog. Penty	185	E4
Llys Catwg. G-nea	45	F4
Llys Celyn. Ch Vil	150	A1
Llys Coed Derw. Ch Vil	169	E4
Llys Coed. Ynybw	124	B3
Llys Corrwg. Ponty	150	B3
Llys Cynon. Hir	48	C4
Llys Derwen. Ynybw	124	B3
Llys Dewi Dinefwr. Penty ..	185	F4
Llys Dewi. Ll' maj	219	F4
Llys Dewi Sant. Lough	57	E1
Llys Dol. Swan	60	A1
Llys Dulais. Cry	43	D3
Llys Dwfnant. Clyne	64	C4
Llys Dwrgi. Swan	86	A4
Llys Dyfodwg. Ll' maj	219	F4
Llys Dyfodwg. Penty	185	F3
Llys Dyfrig. Ll'tris	185	E3
Llys Elba. Gow	82	A3
Llys Faen. Bridg	179	F3
Llys Felin. B-coch	63	E4
Llys Felin Newydd. Swan	85	E3
Llys Garth. Ch Vil	149	E1
Llys Ger y Llan. Pontar	36	B2
Llys Glanrafon. Pontdw	40	C2
Llys Groeswen. Marg	139	E3
Llys Gwalia. Penga	57	F1
Llys Gwernen. Swan	59	F1
Llys Gwyn. Bridg	179	F3
Llys Gwyn. Maest	117	D3
Llys Gwynfaen. Lough	56	C2
Llys Gwynfryn. B-coch	62	B3
Llys Gwynno. Penty	185	F3
Llys Hafn. T We	171	D2
Llys Hebog. Swan	86	A4
Llys Hebron. Yst	95	D2
Llys Illtyd. Penty	185	E4
Llys Llywelyn. Ch Vil	169	E4
Llys Maelwg. Ll'tris	168	B1
Llys Nant Fer. G-C-G	5	D3
Llys Nant Glas. M Ash	98	A4
Llys Nant Pandy. Caer	152	A2
Llys Nedd. B-coch	62	B1
Llys Penpant. Ll'fel	59	E1
Llys Pentre. Swan	84	B2
Llys Pum Cyfair. Card	188	B1
Llys Sant Teilo. Ll'fel	59	D1
Llys Steffan. Ll' maj	219	F4
Llys Tal-y-Bont Rd. Card ..	188	C1
Llys Teilo. Ll' maj	219	F4
Llys Teilo. Ll'tris	168	B1
Llys Teilo. Penty	185	F3
Llys Trerobant. Ynybw	124	A4
Llys Tripp. Penty	171	D2
Llys Tudful. Penty	185	F4
Llys Tylcha Fawr. Tony	147	E3
Llys Wenallt. Tonna	63	F2
Llys Wern. B-coch	62	B1
Llys y Brenin. Lough	82	A4
Llys y Fedwen. Caer	152	B3
Llys-y-Coed. Lough	56	B1
Llys-y-Fedwen. Caer	152	B2
Llys-y-Felin. Swan	84	B2
Llys-y-Fran. Bridg	179	D3
Llys-Coed. Swan	61	D1
Llys-Gwyn Terr. Pontar	36	B2
Llys-le-Breos. T Mum	108	C1
Llys-Teg. Swan	108	B4
Llys-Uchaf. Swan	86	A4
Llys-y-Bryn. Swan	86	A4
Llys yr Efail. Tony	147	E3
Llys-y-Nant (Brook Court).		
Neath	87	E2
Lon Alfa. Swan	108	C4
Lon Bedwen. Swan	109	E4
Lon Beili Glas. G-C-G	5	D2
Lon Brydwen. Lough	57	D1
Lon Brynawel. Swan	85	F3
Lon Bryngwyn. Swan	109	F4
Lon Brynneuadd. G-C-G	5	D3
Lon Brynteg. B-coch	62	B1
Lon Cadog. Swan	109	F4
Lon Cae Banc. Swan	109	E4
Lon Camlad. Swan	109	F4
Lon Caron. Swan	109	F4
Lon Carreg Bica. Swan	86	A4
Lon Catwg. A-wen	41	D3
Lon Cedwyn. Swan	109	F4
Lon Cefn Mably. Rhoose ..	222	C1
Lon Claerwen. Swan	84	C4
Lon Coed Bran. Swan	109	F4
Lon Coed Parc. Swan	109	F4
Lon Cothi. Swan	83	F1
Lon Cwmgwyn. Swan	109	E4
Lon Cynfor. Swan	109	F4
Lon Cynlais. Swan	109	F4
Lon Dan-y-Coed. Swan	109	F4
Lon Derw. Swan	109	F4
Lon Draenen. Swan	109	F4
Lon Draenog. Swan	59	F3
Lon Einon. Penga	57	F1
Lon Eithrym. Cly	60	B4
Lon Enfys. Swan	85	F3
Lon Fach. Caer	151	F1
Lon Fach. Card	188	A4
Lon Fawr. Caer	151	F1
Lon Gaer. Penga	57	F1
Lon Ganol. Card	188	A4
Lon Ger-y-Coed. Swan	109	F4
Lon Glynfelin. N Abb	62	A1
Lon Gwendraeth. Swan	84	C4
Lon Gwernen. Swan	59	F1
Lon Gwili. Swan	109	F4
Lon Gwladys. Penga	57	F1
Lon Gwynfryn. Swan	109	F4
Lon Hafren. Caer	151	F1
Lon Hafren. Swan	84	C4
Lon Heddwch. Craig	39	D1
Lon Heddwch. Swan	85	F3
Lon Helygen. Ynybw	124	B3
Lon Heulog. Ponty	150	A2
Lon Heulog. Tondu	163	E3
Lon Hir. A-wen	40	C2
Lon Illtyd. Swan	109	F4
Lon Iorwg. Swan	109	E4
Lon Irfon. Swan	83	E1
Lon Isa. Card	188	A4
Lon Isaf. Caer	151	F1
Lon Ithon. Swan	84	C4
Lon Killan. Swan	108	B4
Lon Las. Llwy	49	E3
Lon Madoc. Card	188	B2
Lon Mafon. Swan	109	E4
Lon Masarn. Swan	109	E4
Lon Mefus. Swan	109	E4
Lon Menai. Swan	61	D1
Lon Nedd. Swan	84	C4
Lon Ogwen. Swan	61	D1
Lon Olchfa. Swan	109	D3
Lon Owain. Card	203	D2
Lon Pen-y-Coed. Swan	83	F1
Lon Penfro. Swan	60	A2
Lon Penllyn. Card	188	A3
Lon Pennant. Peng	76	C1
Lon Robin Goch. Caer	151	F2
Lon Sawdde. Swan	84	C4
Lon Tanyrallt. A-wen	40	C2
Lon Teify. Swan	83	F1
Lon Towy. Swan	83	E1
Lon Ty'n-y-Cae. Card	188	B3
Lon Tyr Haul. Swan	85	F3
Lon Ucha. Card	188	A4
Lon Uchaf. Caer	151	F1
Lon y Fran. Caer	151	F2
Lon y Nant. Card	188	B4
Lon y Tresglen. Caer	151	F2
Lon yr Odyn. Caer	152	B2
Lon yr Ysgol. Ll'ge	56	B4
Lon-Od-Nant. Ll' Maj	220	A3
Lon-Werdd. Card	203	D3
Lon-Werdd Cl. Card	203	D3
Lon-y-Barri. Caer	151	F3
Lon-y-Bryn. G-nea	27	D1
Lon-y-Bugail. Bridg	179	D2
Lon-y-Cariadon. Pyle	161	D1
Lon-y-Castell. Card	203	E2
Lon-y-Celyn. Card	187	F3
Lon-y-Celyn. Nel	99	E2
Lon-y-Coed. Bridg	179	D3
Lon-y-Coed. Pontdw	40	B3
Lon-y-Dail. Card	188	A4
Lon-y-Dderwen. Card	188	A4
Lon-y-Dderwen. Nel	99	E2
Lon-y-ddraenen. Caer	151	F1
Lon-y-Deri. Caer	151	F1
Lon-y-Deri. Card	188	A4
Lon-y-Felin. Craig	18	B4
Lon-y-Felin. M Ash	72	A3
Lon-y-Ffin. Card	203	D3
Lon-y-Fro. Penty	186	B4
Lon-y-Garwa. Caer	151	F1
Lon-y-Gors. Caer	151	F1
Lon-y-Groes. Card	188	B2
Lon-y-Llwyn. Nel	99	E2
Lon-y-Llyn. Caer	151	F1
Lon-y-Mynydd. Card	188	B4
Lon-y-Nant. G-nea	27	D1
Lon-y-Parc. Card	188	A3
Lon-y-Parc. Maest	91	D1
Lon-y-Rhedyn. Caer	151	F1
Lon-y-Rhyd. Card	188	A4
Lon-y-Twyn. Caer	152	A1
Lon-y-Waun. Caer	151	F1
Lon-y-Wern. A-wen	40	C2
Lon-y-Wern. Caer	151	F1
Lon-y-Winci. Card	188	A4
Lon-yr-Afon. Bridg	127	D1
Lon-yr-Awel. Ll'tris	184	A4
Lon-yr-Efail. Card	203	D2
Lon-yr-Eglwys. St B M	195	E1
Lon-yr-Ysgol. A-wen	41	D2
Lon-Ysgubor. Card	188	A4
Loncaeau Porth. Card	172	B1
Londeg. Pontdw	40	B3
London Rd. Cwma	114	B2
London Rd. Neath	87	F4
London Rd. Cwma	114	B2
London St. M Ash	72	B2
Lone Rd. Cly	39	E1
Long Acre. Bish	136	A3
Long Acre Ct. Bish	136	A3
Long Acre Ct. Porth	176	B1
Long Acre Dr. Porth	176	C1
Long Acre. Pyle	176	C4
Long House Cl. Card	173	D1
Long Meadow Dr. Barry	225	D4
Long Oaks Ave. Swan	109	F3
Long Oaks Ct. Swan	109	F4
Long Ridge. Swan	84	B1
Long Row. Fern	95	F4
Long Row. N Tre	54	C1
Long Shepherds Dr.		
T Mum	136	B2
Long St. Ystra	8	A2
Long View Ct. Swan	84	B4

Long View Rd. Swan 59 E1
Long Vue Rd. P Tal 113 E1
Longacre Cl. Barry 225 E4
Longacre Cl. Ll'tris 168 C1
Longcross St. Card 205 E3
Longfellow Dr. Bridg 179 E3
Longfellow Gdns. Bedw 153 E4
Longfield Ct. Hir 48 B4
Longford Cres. Swan 111 D4
Longford La. N Abb 62 A1
Longford Rd. N Abb 62 A1
Longlands Cl. Pyle 161 D1
Longleat Cl. Card 173 D1
Longmeadow Dr. D pow 216 A1
Longmede Pk. Rhig 28 B1
Longreach Cl. Card 202 C2
Longships Rd. Card 217 F4
Longspears Ave. Card 188 C2
Longwood Dr. Card 187 E4
Lonlas Ave. Skew 86 B4
Lonlas Village Workshops.
      Skew 86 B4
Lonsdale Rd. Card 189 F2
Lord St. Abera 71 E4
Lord St. Pen 217 D3
Lorraine Cl. P Tal 113 E1
Lothian Cres. Card 189 E2
Loudoun Sq. Card 205 D2
Lougher Gdns. Porth 192 C3
Lougher Pl. Pyle 176 C4
Lougher Pl. St Ath 221 E2
Loughor Comm. Lough 57 D1
Loughor Rd. Lough 82 A4
Loughor Row. Porth 176 C1
Louisa Pl. Card 205 D1
Louise Cl. Clyne 64 C4
Louise Ct. Card 187 F2
Love La. Card 205 D3
Love La. Cowb 198 C1
Low Row. M Ash 72 B3
Lower Acre. Card 203 D2
Lower Adare St. Porth 118 C2
Lower Alma Pl. Yst 95 D2
Lower Alma Terr. Ponty 149 E4
Lower Bailey St. Tylor 122 C4
Lower Brooklands. Coel 9 D3
Lower Brynhyfryd Terr.
      Aber 125 F1
Lower Cathedral Rd. Card .. 204 C3
Lower Church St. Pontcr ... 118 C2
Lower Colbren Rd. G-C-G 5 D2
Lower Coronation St. Tred .. 35 F3
Lower Cross St. Hir 48 B4
Lower Cross St. N Tre 54 B2
Lower Edward St. Mer T 32 B1
Lower Forest Level. M Ash . 72 C1
Lower Glyn-Gwyn St.
      Bedw 153 D3
Lower Guthrie St. Barry 225 D3
Lower Holmes St. Barry 225 E3
Lower James St. Mark 76 C2
Lower Llansantffraid Rd.
      Brynco 163 E2
Lower Morel St. Barry 225 D3
Lower Mount Pleasant.
      Troed 52 B1
Lower Pantteg. Ystal 23 D2
Lower Pyke St. Barry 225 D3
Lower Rd. N Tre 55 D1
Lower Row. Mer T 33 D3
Lower Row. Rhy 34 B4
Lower Salisbury St. Tred ... 35 F3
Lower St. Abera 71 E4
Lower Station Rd. Glan 4 B4
Lower Station St. Abera 71 E4
Lower Terr. Treo 94 B3
Lower Terr. Tylor 96 B1
Lower Thomas St. Mer T 32 C1
Lower Union St. Mer T 33 D2
Lower Vaynor Rd. C-c-y-c ... 32 A3
Lower Wern Rd. Ystal 23 D3
Lowerdale Cl. Ll'tris 168 C1
Lowfield Dr. Card 172 C1
Lowland Dr. Ch Vil 150 A1
Lowndes Cl. Rhiwd 155 F2
Lowther Rd. Card 205 D4
Lucania Bldgs. Marg 139 E4
Lucas Cl. Barry 225 E4
Lucas Rd. Swan 61 D3
Lucas St. Card 189 D1
Lucknow St. Card 204 C2
Lucy Rd. Skew 86 B4
Ludlow Cl. Card 205 D1
Ludlow La. Pen 217 D2
Ludlow St. Caer 152 A1
Ludlow St. Card 204 C1
Ludlow St. Pen 217 D2
Lundy Cl. Card 188 C4
Lundy Cl. Porth 176 C1
Lundy Dr. T Mum 136 C4
Lunnon Cl. Penma 134 C4
Lupin Cl. Mer T 32 A3
Lupin Cl. Mer T 32 B3
Lupin Cl. P Tal 113 E2
Luther La. Mer T 32 C1
Luther St. Mer T 51 F4

Luton St. Fern 95 F4
Luton St. Treo 94 B3
Lydford Ave. Swan 110 C4
Lydford Cl. Card 188 A3
Lydstep Cres. Card 188 A1
Lydstep Flats. Card 188 A1
Lydstep House. Card 188 A2
Lydwood Cl. Bedw 154 A4
Lyle St. M Ash 72 B2
Lynch Blosse Cl. Card 187 F1
Lyncroft Cl. Card 188 B4
Lynden. Ystra 7 E1
Lyndhurst St. Card 204 B3
Lyndhurst St. M Ash 72 B2
Lynmouth Cres. Card 190 A2
Lynmouth Dr. Sully 226 A2
Lynn Davies Ave. Og Va ... 144 C3
Lynn St. Swan 84 A1
Lynsdale Rd. Swan 84 B2
Lynton Cl. Card 190 A2
Lynton Cl. Sully 226 A3
Lynton Ct. T Mum 136 C3
Lynton Pl. Card 190 A2
Lynton Terr. Card 190 A2
Lynwood Ct. Card 187 D3
Lynwood Ct. Card 205 E4
Lyon Cl. Card 204 B1
Lyon's Pl. Reso 44 B1
Lyric Way. Card 172 C1

Maberly Ct. Card 189 D4
Mabon Cl. Lough 56 C2
Macaulay Ave. Card 190 A4
Macdonald Ave. Penco 181 E4
Macdonald Cl. Card 203 D2
Macdonald Rd. Card 203 D2
Mace La. Treo 94 A4
Machen Cl. Card 191 D4
Machen Pl. Card 204 C3
Machen St. Card 204 C2
Machen St. Pen 216 C2
Machen St. Pontmi 129 F1
Mackintosh Pl. Card 189 D1
Mackintosh Rd. Ponty 124 B1
Mackintosh St. Mer V 73 E3
Mackintosh Terr. Bed 99 E3
Mackworth Dr. Neath 88 B3
Mackworth Rd. Porthc 193 D4
Mackworth St. Bridg 179 F3
Mackworth Terr. Swan 110 C4
Maddocks Pl. Bridg 179 F2
Maddox St. Tonypa 121 E3
Madeline St. Tylor 96 A1
Madeline St. Yst 94 C3
Madoc Cl. Bridg 180 A3
Madoc Cl. D pow 216 B2
Madoc Pl. Swan 110 B3
Madoc Rd. Card 205 F3
Madoc St. Ponty 149 E4
Madoc St. Swan 110 B3
Madog Cl. Tylor 96 A2
Maelfa. Card 189 F2
Maelgwyn Terr. Aberd 49 F1
Maelog Cl. Ll'tris 184 A4
Maelog Pl. Card 188 C1
Maelog Rd. Card 188 B2
Maen Dy. Mer T 32 A1
Maen Ganol. Bed 99 E4
Maen Gilfach. Bed 74 B1
Maendy Rd. Cowb 199 D2
Maengwyn. Ystal 22 B1
Maerdy Heol. Caer 152 B2
Maerdy La. Card 173 E1
Maerdy Rd. Aberd 70 C4
Maerdy Rd. Betws 18 B4
Maerdy Rd. Fern 70 A1
Maerdy Rd Ind Est. Fern ... 95 E4
Maerdy Road Flats. Fern ... 70 A1
Maerdy View. Rhy 35 D1
Maerdypark. Penco 181 E3
Maes Bedw. Porth 122 C1
Maes Briallu. Caer 152 B2
Maes Briallu. Swan 85 F4
Maes Bryn. Bridg 179 D3
Maes Brynna. Aberd 49 E2
Maes Collen. Swan 59 F2
Maes Dafydd. Lough 82 A4
Maes Ganol. Ponty 150 B2
Maes Gareth Edwards.
      G-C-G 5 D3
Maes Glas. Caer 152 B1
Maes Glas. Card 188 A2
Maes Glas. Ce Cr 162 A1
Maes Glas. Lough 57 D1
Maes Glas. Tondu 163 F3
Maes Glas. Tred 35 F4
Maes Glas. Ynybw 124 B3
Maes Gollen. Penty 185 F4
Maes Gwair. Bridg 179 D3
Maes Gwyn. B-coch 63 D2
Maes Gwyn. Caer 152 A1
Maes Hir. Caer 151 F3
Maes Hyfryd. Aberd 71 F4
Maes Lloi. Cowb 199 D2
Maes Maddock. Lough 57 D1
Maes Maelwg. Ll'tris 168 C3
Maes Melyn St. Marg 139 E3

Maes Pwll. Clyne 64 B3
Maes Rhedyn. P Tal 113 E3
Maes Rhosyn. A-wen 41 D2
Maes Sant Teilo. Ll'fel 59 D1
Maes St. Swan 110 C4
Maes Talcen. Bridg 180 A3
Maes Teg. Pontar 36 B3
Maes Trane. Ll'tris 169 D3
Maes Trisant. Ll'tris 168 B1
Maes Ty-canol. P Tal 113 F3
Maes Uchaf. Ponty 150 B2
Maes Watford. Caer 171 F4
Maes y Coed. Card 188 A4
Maes y Deri. Bry 5 A4
Maes y Drudwen. Caer 151 F1
Maes y Fedwen. Swan 59 F2
Maes y Felin. Swan 83 E3
Maes y Fron. Glan 4 B4
Maes y Gollen. Swan 109 D3
Maes y Gwernen Cl. Swan ... 59 F2
Maes y Gwernen Dr. Swan ... 59 F2
Maes y Meillion. Swan 85 F4
Maes y Parc. Card 188 A3
Maes y Parc. Swan 83 E3
Maes y Rhedyn. Fern 95 D4
Maes y Siglen. Caer 151 F2
Maes yr Awel. Card 187 D3
Maes yr Awel. Ponty 150 B2
Maes yr Awel. Swan 85 F4
Maes yr Haf. Card 187 F4
Maes yr Haf. Llwy 49 F3
Maes- yr-Helyg. Llwy 49 F3
Maes-Deri. Swan 85 E3
Maes-Gwyn St. P Tal 138 C4
Maes-Gwyn. Ton 89 D3
Maes-Lan. Swan 85 F3
Maes-Mawr Rd. Cry 43 D3
Maes-y-Bedw. Bed 73 F4
Maes-y-Bettws. Cwma 115 D4
Maes-y-Bryn. Card 187 D4
Maes-y-Bryn. Colw 197 D2
Maes-y-Bryn Rd. Card 174 A2
Maes-y-Bryn. Swan 59 F1
Maes-y-Bryn. Tony 147 E3
Maes-y-coed. Aberd 49 E2
Maes-y-Coed. Bed 99 E3
Maes-y-Coed. Lough 82 A4
Maes-y-Coed Rd. Card 188 C3
Maes-y-Coed. Swan 59 F1
Maes-y-Crochan. Card 191 D4
Maes-y-Cwm St. Barry 225 D3
Maes-y-Cwrt Terr. Marg ... 139 E4
Maes-y-Dderwen. Gell 100 B4
Maes-y-Dderwen. Ll'fel 59 D1
Maes-y-Dderwen. Maest 117 D3
Maes-y-Dderwen. Penty 185 F3
Maes-y-Dderwen. Swan 86 A3
Maes-y-deri. Abera 71 E3
Maes-y-Deri. B-coch 63 E3
Maes-y-Deri. Card 188 A4
Maes-y-Deri Cl. Penco 181 E4
Maes-y-Deri. Ponty 124 A1
Maes-y-Dre. G-nea 45 F4
Maes-y-Felin. Bridg 179 F4
Maes-y-Felin. Caer 152 A2
Maes-y-Felin. Card 188 A3
Maes-y-Felin. Llys 209 D4
Maes-y-Felin. Ponty 150 A2
Maes-y-Ffynnon Cl. Neath .. 87 F3
Maes-y-ffynnon La. Abera .. 71 D4
Maes-y-Ffynnon. Mer T 33 D2
Maes-y-Ffynon. Bonv 201 D1
Maes-y-Ffynon. G-nea 26 C1
Maes-y-garreg. C-c-y-c 31 F2
Maes-y-Glyn. G-C-G 5 D4
Maes-y-Graig St. Bar 76 A1
Maes-y-Grufydd Rd. Swan .. 109 E4
Maes-y-Gwrnen Rd. Swan ... 59 F2
Maes-y-Nant. Penty 185 E4
Maes-y-Parc. Cwma 114 C3
Maes-y-Pergwm. G-nea 26 C1
Maes-y-Rhedyn. Ll'tris 168 A2
Maes-y-Rhedyn. Penty 185 F3
Maes-y-Sarn. Penty 170 A1
Maes-y-Tyra. Reso 44 B1
Maes-y-Wern. Penco 181 E4
Maes-yr Haf. Pen-cl 80 C2
Maes-yr-Afon. Bedw 152 B3
Maes-yr-afon. Ll'tris 184 A3
Maes-yr-Awel. Maest 91 D1
Maes-yr-Efail. Lough 57 D1
Maes-yr-Efail. Swan 108 B4
Maes-yr-Eglwys. G-nea 26 C1
Maes-yr-Eithin. Swan 61 D1
Maes-yr-Haf Rd. Neath 87 F4
Maes-yr-Haf Rd. Pyle 177 D4
Maes-yr-Haf. Rhy 35 D2
Maes-yr-Haf. Swan 85 F3
Maes-yr-Hafod. Penty 185 F4
Maes-yr-Haul. Tondu 163 F3
Maes-yr-Onen. Nel 99 E2
Maes-yr-Onnen. Penty 185 F3
Maes-yr-Onnen. Swan 60 A2
Maescynog. Ystra 23 F4
Maescynon. Hir 48 C4
Maesglas. Bridg 179 E3
Maesglas. Cwma 114 B3
Maesglas. Pontcr 143 F1

Maesglas. Pyle 161 E1
Maesglas Rd. Swan 84 A2
Maesgwyn. Aberd 49 E2
Maesgwyn Dr. Pontar 36 B2
Maesgwyn Rd. Pontar 36 B2
Maesgwynne. C-c-y-c 32 A2
Maeslan. A-wen 41 D2
Maesmelyn. Aberd 49 E2
Maespica Rd. Ystra 7 D1
Maestaf St. Troed 52 A2
Maesteg Cres. Ch Vil 150 A1
Maesteg Gdns. Ch Vil 150 A1
Maesteg Gr. Ch Vil 150 A1
Maesteg Rd. Bryn 115 F3
Maesteg Rd. Glyn 91 E3
Maesteg Rd. Glyn 91 E3
Maesteg Rd. Maest 142 B4
Maesteg Rd. Tondu 163 E3
Maesteg Row. Maest 117 D1
Maesteg St. Swan 110 C4
Maesybedol. Glan 4 B4
Maesycoed Rd. Ponty 124 A1
Maesycoed. Ystal 22 B1
Maesycoed Terr. Gell 100 B1
Maesycwm. Ystra 7 F1
Maesydderwen. Ystra 23 F4
Maesyfelin Cres. Ll'tris .. 184 A4
Maesyffynon Rd. Abera 71 D4
Maesyffynon Terr. Trea 122 A3
Maesyfron. Ystra 8 C3
Maesyrhaf Pl. Lough 57 D1
Maesyrhendre. Glan 4 B4
Maesywerin. G-C-G 5 B3
Mafeking Rd. Card 189 E1
Mafeking Terr. Tred 35 F3
Magazine St. Maest 117 D4
Magellan Cl. Barry 225 D4
Magnolia Cl. Card 189 E4
Magnolia Cl. Mer T 32 B3
Magnolia Cl. Porth 123 D2
Magnolia Dr. Peng 101 F3
Magnolia Way. Ch Vil 169 E3
Magpie Rd. Ll' Maj 220 B3
Maiden St. Maest 142 B4
Maillard's Haven. Pen 217 D1
Main Access Rd. St Ath 221 F1
Main Ave. Bridg 180 A4
Main Ave. Card 189 F1
Main Ave. P-s-Ely 201 F3
Main Ave. Ponty 150 B1
Main Rd. Abercy 98 A3
Main Rd. B-coch 62 B2
Main Rd. B-coch 62 C1
Main Rd. B-coch 62 D2
Main Rd. B-coch 63 E3
Main Rd. Ch Vil 150 A1
Main Rd. Cry 43 D4
Main Rd. Ll'tris 168 C2
Main Rd. Maesy 101 D1
Main Rd. Onll 10 A1
Main Rd. Penty 170 C2
Main Rd. St B M 194 B2
Main Rd. Ton 89 D1
Main St. Barry 225 D4
Maindee Rd. Ynys 128 A3
Maindy Cres. Yst 94 C2
Maindy Croft. Yst 94 C2
Maindy Ct. Ch Vil 149 F1
Maindy Gr. Yst 94 C2
Maindy Rd. Card 188 C1
Maindy Rd. Yst 94 C2
Mainwaring Terr. Swan 84 B1
Maitland Pl. Card 204 C2
Maitland St. Card 188 C1
Major Rd. Card 204 B3
Major St. Swan 84 B1
Malborough Ct. Card 189 E1
Maldwyn St. Card 204 B4
Malefant St. Card 189 D1
Maliphant St. Swan 84 B1
Mallard Cl. Card 190 C4
Mallard Way. Porth 192 B4
Mallard Way. Sully 227 D4
Mallards Reach. Marsh 175 E1
Mallory Cl. St M Ch 221 E4
Malmsmead Rd. Card 190 B4
Malpas Cl. Card 190 C4
Malt Hall. Ll'rh 105 D3
Maltings The. Card 173 F1
Malus Ave. Ch Vil 169 E3
Malvern Dr. Card 188 C4
Malvern Terr. Swan 109 F3
Man-Moel Rd. Mark 55 F3
Manchester Pl. Hir 48 B4
Mandeg. Bed 99 E3
Mandela Ave. Bridg 180 A3
Mandeville Rd. Card 204 C3
Mandeville Rd. Peng 101 F3
Mandeville St. Card 204 C3
Manest St. Rhy 34 C2
Mangoed. Peny 49 D3
Manitoba Cl. Card 199 E3
Manley Cl. Tony 147 E3
Mannsmann Cl. Swan 85 E4
Manod Rd. Card 188 A1
Manor Chase. Ll'tris 169 D3
Manor Cl. Card 188 A3

Manor Ct. Card 188 A3
Manor Ct. Ch Vil 149 F1
Manor Ct. Ewen 195 F4
Manor Dr. Bridg 180 C2
Manor Dr. G-nea 26 B1
Manor Gr. Porthc 193 E4
Manor Hill. Ll'tris 184 B4
Manor Pk. Li' Maj 220 A3
Manor Pk. Ll'ha 166 A1
Manor Rd. Pontll 101 F2
Manor Rd. Swan 84 B2
Manor Rise. Card 188 B2
Manor St. Card 188 C1
Manor St. Marg 139 E4
Manor Way. Card 188 B3
Manor Way. Neath 87 E2
Manorbier Cl. Ch Vil 149 F1
Manorbier Cl. D pow 216 B2
Manorbier Cl. Peng 76 B1
Manorbier Cres. Card 190 B2
Mansel Cl. Gow 82 A3
Mansel Dr. Bish 136 B3
Mansel Rd. Swan 85 D2
Mansel St. Gow 82 A3
Mansel St. Marg 139 D4
Mansel St. Neath 87 E1
Mansel St. Swan 110 B4
Manselfield Rd. Bish 136 B3
Mansell Ave. Card 202 C2
Manselton Rd. Swan 84 A2
Mansfield St. Card 204 C3
Manston Cl. Card 187 F1
Maple Ave. P Tal 113 F4
Maple Cl. Barry 225 D4
Maple Cl. Ll'hry 183 D3
Maple Cl. Lough 57 D2
Maple Cl. Mer T 32 B2
Maple Cl. Neath 88 B3
Maple Cl. Pontll 101 E2
Maple Cres. C-c-y-c 32 A3
Maple Cres. Swan 109 F4
Maple Ct. Tony 147 E3
Maple Dr. Aberd 49 E1
Maple Dr. Bridg 180 C2
Maple Dr. Swan 82 B2
Maple Gr. Swan 109 F3
Maple Rd. Card 187 D1
Maple Rd. Pen 216 C2
Maple St. Ponty 150 A3
Maple Terr. Abera 71 F2
Maple Terr. Maest 117 D1
Maple Tree Cl. Card 187 D3
Maple Wlk. Porthc 193 F4
Maplewood Ave. Card 187 F2
Maplewood Cl. B-coch 62 B2
March Hywel. A-wen 41 D2
March Hywel. B-coch 63 E3
Marchwood Cl. Card 190 B3
Marcross Rd. Card 203 D2
Mardy Cl. Mer T 152 B2
Mardy Cres. Caer 152 B2
Mardy Ct. Card 204 C2
Mardy Rd. Card 190 C1
Mardy St. Card 204 C2
Mardy St. Mer T 33 D1
Mardy Terr. Mer T 51 F4
Margam Ave. Swan 85 D4
Margam Cl. St M Ch 221 E4
Margam House. Bridg 179 E2
Margam Rd. Marg 139 F2
Margam Row. Pyle 161 E2
Margam St. Glyn 91 D3
Margam St. Maest 117 D4
Margaret Ave. Barry 214 C1
Margaret St. Abera 71 E3
Margaret St. Abercy 98 C1
Margaret St. Aberd 49 F2
Margaret St. B-coch 62 B2
Margaret St. Bar 76 A1
Margaret St. Marg 114 B1
Margaret St. Mer T 32 B1
Margaret St. Ponty 123 F1
Margaret St. Porth 123 E1
Margaret St. Swan 111 D4
Margaret St. Trehe 68 C1
Margaret St. Tylor 122 B4
Margaret St. Yst 94 C3
Margaret Terr. Glyn 92 B3
Margaret Terr. Swan 111 D4
Margaret's Cl. Neath 87 D1
Maria Ct. Card 205 D2
Maria St. Card 205 D2
Marian St. Pontcr 118 C4
Marian St. Tonypa 121 D4
Marianwen St. Peng 101 E4
Marigold Cl. Mer T 32 B3
Marigold Ct. Bridg 180 B3
Marigold Pl. Se Si 25 D4
Marine Bldgs. Pen 217 D3
Marine Cl. P Tal 113 E1
Marine Dr. P Tal 113 E1
Marine Dr. St B M 194 B2
Marine House. Skew 112 B4
Marine Par. Pen 217 D1
Marine Terr. Porth 192 C3

Marine Wlk. St B M 194 B2
Marine Wlk. Swan 110 B3
Mariner St. Swan 110 B4
Mariner's Hts. Pen 217 D3
Marion Ct. Card 173 D1
Marion St. Card 205 F3
Marionville Gdns. Card 203 F4
Maritime Ind Est. Ponty ... 149 D4
Maritime Rd. Card 205 E1
Maritime Rd. Marg 139 D4
Maritime St. Ponty 149 D4
Maritime Terr. Ponty 149 D4
Marjorie St. Tonypa 122 A2
Mark St. Card 204 C3
Market Pl. Card 204 B3
Market Pl. Card 204 B3
Market Rd. Card 204 B3
Market Sq. Mer T 32 B1
Market St. Abera 50 A1
Market St. Bridg 179 F2
Market St. Caer 152 A1
Market St. Card 171 E1
Market St. Mer T 33 D2
Market St. Ponty 124 B1
Market St. Swan 84 C4
Market St. Tred 35 F3
Markham Terr. Mark 76 B4
Marl Ct. Card 204 C1
Marland House. Card 205 D3
Marlas Cl. Pyle 161 D1
Marlas Rd. Pyle 161 D1
Marlborough Cl. Barry 225 E4
Marlborough Cl. Ch Vil 169 E3
Marlborough Rd. Card 205 E4
Marlborough Rd. Lough 82 A4
Marlborough Rd. Swan 109 F3
Marlborough Terr. Card 204 C4
Marloes Ct. Swan 83 F3
Marloes Rd. Card 203 D3
Marlpit La. Porth 177 D1
Marne St. Aberca 129 D4
Marquis Cl. Barry 225 E4
Marsden St. Swan 84 B1
Marsh St. P Tal 113 F1
Marshall Cl. Card 187 F1
Marshall Cres. Mer T 32 C3
Marshfield Ave. Pyle 161 D1
Marshfield Ct. Pontll 101 F1
Marshfield Ct. Tony 147 E3
Marshfield Rd. Fern 95 E4
Marshfield Rd. Marsh 175 E1
Marshfield Rd. Neath 87 E3
Martell St. Swan 83 F2
Martin Cl. Mer T 32 A1
Martin Cres. Tony 147 E3
Martin Rd. Card 206 A2
Martin St. Cly 60 B4
Martin St. Swan 84 C4
Martin's La. Abercy 98 C1
Martin's Terr. Abercy 98 C1
Martindale Cl. Tred 35 E4
Martins Row. Deri 53 E4
Martyn's Ave. Se Si 24 C3
Marwyn Gdns. Bar 75 F1
Mary Ann St. Card 205 D3
Mary St. Abera 50 A1
Mary St. Abera 71 F2
Mary St. Bed 74 A4
Mary St. Bedw 153 D4
Mary St. Card 187 F1
Mary St. Cry 43 D3
Mary St. Glyn 92 B3
Mary St. M Ash 72 C1
Mary St. Mer T 33 D2
Mary St. Mer T 51 F4
Mary St. Neath 87 E4
Mary St. Ponty 124 C3
Mary St. Porth 122 C2
Mary St. Porth 192 C4
Mary St. Tre 99 D3
Mary St. Trehe 69 D1
Mary Twill La. T Mum 136 C2
Maryland Rd. Pontmi 155 D4
Maryport Rd. Card 189 D1
Marysfield Cl. Marsh 175 F1
Masefield Mews. Bridg 179 E3
Masefield Rd. Pen 216 C2
Masefield Way. Ponty 150 A3
Mason St. Abera 71 E4
Masonic St. Mer T 51 E4
Matexa St. Yst 94 C2
Mathews Terr. Ll'tris 149 D2
Mathias Cl. Card 189 F1
Matthew Rd. Rhoose 222 C1
Matthew St. Swan 110 B4
Matthew Terr. D pow 216 B2
Matthews' St. Glyn 66 C2
Mattie Collins Way The.
  Treo 94 B3
Maughan Terr. Pen 217 D3
Maureen Ave. Card 203 F3
Mavis Gr. Card 188 B3
Mawrbryn Cl. Card 191 D4
Maximin Rd. Marg 139 F2
Maxton Ct. Caer 152 B2
Maxwell Rd. Card 190 B2
Maxwell St. Fern 95 F3
Mayals Ave. T Mum 109 D1

Mayals Gn. T Mum 108 C1
Mayals Rd. T Mum 109 D1
Mayberry Rd. P Tal 113 E4
Mayfair Dr. Card 172 C2
Mayfair. Wen 203 D1
Mayfield Ave. Bridg 178 C2
Mayfield Ave. Card 204 A3
Mayfield Ave. Porthc 193 E4
Mayfield Pl. Ll'tris 168 C1
Mayfield Rd. Ponty 124 A1
Mayfield St. Marg 139 E4
Mayfield Terr. Swan 84 A2
Mayflower Ave. Card 172 B1
Mayflower Cl. Swan 109 D3
Mayhill Cl. Card 172 C2
Mayhill Gdns. Swan 84 A1
Mayhill Rd. Swan 84 A1
Maynard Ct. Card 204 A4
Maytree Ave. T Mum 136 C4
Maytree Cl. Lough 56 C1
Maytree Cl. Swan 84 B4
Maywood. Ll'ha 166 B2
McCale Ave. Card 203 F4
McDonnel Rd. Bar 75 F2
McGregor Row. Maest 117 D2
McLaren Cotts. Rhy 54 B4
McRitchie Pl. Swan 83 F2
Mead The. Swan 108 B4
Meadow Ave. Pyle 161 E1
Meadow Cl. Bridg 180 C2
Meadow Cl. Card 189 E4
Meadow Cl. Hir 48 C4
Meadow Cl. Ll'ha 166 C2
Meadow Cl. M Ash 72 A2
Meadow Cl. Peng 101 D3
Meadow Cres. Caer 152 A1
Meadow Cres. Ch Vil 150 A1
Meadow Cres. Pontmi 155 D4
Meadow Croft. Rhoose 223 D1
Meadow Ct. St B M 195 E2
Meadow Dr. Lough 56 C1
Meadow La. Hir 48 B4
Meadow La. Pen 217 D1
Meadow La. Porthc 193 D4
Meadow Rd. Neath 87 E3
Meadow Rise. Brynco 163 F2
Meadow Rise. Ll'ha 166 C2
Meadow Rise. Swan 109 E2
Meadow St. Bridg 179 F3
Meadow St. Card 204 B4
Meadow St. Cwma 114 C3
Meadow St. Maest 117 D2
Meadow St. Og Va 119 F1
Meadow St. Pontcr 118 C2
Meadow St. Ponty 149 F3
Meadow St. Pyle 176 C4
Meadow St. Swan 84 A1
Meadow St. Tondu 163 E2
Meadow St. Tony 146 A3
Meadow Sweet Dr. Card ... 191 D3
Meadow Terr. N Tre 54 C2
Meadow The. W St D 199 E4
Meadow Vale. Barry 225 E4
Meadow View. Barry 225 E4
Meadow View. Bedw 152 B4
Meadow View Ct. Sully 226 A3
Meadow View. Og Va 144 C1
Meadow View. St B W 191 F3
Meadow View. Swan 108 B4
Meadow Wlk. Yst 95 D2
Meadowbank Cl. Abera 50 B1
Meadowbank Ct. Card 187 E1
Meadowcroft. South 135 D3
Meadowlark Cl. Card 190 C4
Meadows The. Ewen 196 A4
Meadows, The. Neath 88 B3
Meadows The. Penll 198 A3
Meadowside. Pen 216 B2
Meadvale Rd. Card 190 B3
Medart Pl. Cross 129 E2
Medart St. Cross 129 E2
Megan St. Swan 84 A1
Meini Tirion. Bridg 179 D3
Meirion Cl. Barry 225 D4
Meirion Pl. Card 206 A3
Meirion St. Aberd 49 F2
Meirwen Dr. Card 203 D1
Melbourne Ct. Card 188 A3
Melbourne Ct. Peng 101 E3
Melbourne Rd. Card 188 C4
Melbourne Terr. Ll'ha 166 B2
Melcorn Dr. T Mum 136 C3
Meliden La. Pen 216 C2
Meliden Rd. Pen 216 C2
Melin St. Ynys 128 A2
Melingriffith Dr. Card 187 E3
Mellte Ave. Ystraf 27 F2
Melrose Ave. Card 189 E1
Melrose Cl. Card 190 C4
Melrose Cl. Swan 85 D4
Melrose Cl. Card 189 E1
Melrose Ct. Card 204 B4
Melrose St. Barry 225 D3
Melton Dr. Bridg 179 F1
Melville Ave. Card 190 C4
Melville Cl. Barry 214 C1
Melville Terr. Caer 152 A2
Melyn Cl. Neath 87 E3

Melyn St. Glyn 66 C2
Menai Ave. Glyn 91 E2
Menai Cl. Ch Vil 149 F1
Menai Way. Card 190 B3
Mendip Cl. Swan 83 E2
Mendip Rd. Card 190 A3
Mendip View. Barry 225 E3
Merchant St. Abera 50 A1
Merchant St. Rhy 34 C1
Merches Gdns. Card 204 C2
Merches Pl. Card 204 C2
Mercia Rd. Card 205 F3
Mercies The. Porthc 193 D4
Meredith Rd. Card 205 F3
Merevale. D Pow 215 F2
Merfield Cl. Brynco 163 F2
Merganser Cl. Porth 192 C4
Merion St. Tonypa 122 A1
Merlin Cl. Card 172 C1
Merlin Cl. Ponty 124 A1
Merlin Cl. Porth 192 C4
Merlin Cl. Sully 227 D4
Merlin Cres. Bridg 179 E3
Merlin Cres. Swan 109 F4
Merlin Pl. Barry 225 D4
Merrick Cotts. St Nic 201 F1
Mersey Cl. Pontll 101 E2
Merthyr Rd. Card 187 E4
Merthyr Rd. Card 188 A2
Merthyr Rd. Card 188 B2
Merthyr Rd. G-nea 27 E1
Merthyr Rd. Hir 48 B4
Merthyr Rd. Llwy 49 F4
Merthyr Rd. Mer T 32 C2
Merthyr Rd. Ponty 124 B1
Merthyr Rd. Rhy 16 C1
Merthyr Rd. Trefil 16 C1
Merthyr Rd. Troed 52 A2
Merthyr St. Card 204 C4
Merthyr St. Ll'tris 184 A4
Merthyrmawr Rd. Bridg 179 F1
Merthyrmawr Rd. Bridg 179 F2
Merthyrmawr Rd. Mer M ... 179 E1
Merthyrmawr Rd. Mer M ... 195 D4
Mervinian Cl. Card 205 E2
Mervyn Rd. Card 188 A2
Mervyn Rd. Card 205 F3
Mervyn St. Mer V 73 E3
Mervyn St. Ponty 149 F3
Mervyn Terr. Cwma 114 B3
Mervyn Way. Penco 181 D4
Metal St. Card 205 E3
Metcalfe St. Maest 117 E3
Meteor St. Card 205 E3
Methodist La. Ll' maj 219 F3
Metz Cotts. Ystra 8 A2
Mew St. Neath 87 F4
Mews The. Aberca 129 D4
Mewslade Ave. Swan 83 F3
Meyler St. Tony 147 D1
Meyrick Rd. Card 203 D2
Meyrick Villas. Mer T 32 B2
Meyricks Row. Tonypa 122 A1
Michael's Field. T Mum 137 E2
Michael's Rd. Trehe 68 A1
Michaelston Cl. Barry 225 D4
Michaelston Ct. Card 202 C2
Michaelston Rd. Card 202 C3
Michaelstone Terr. Cwma ... 114 B2
Michelston Ct. Card 203 E2
Michna St. P Tal 113 F1
Middle Rd. Swan 83 E3
Middle Row. Fern 95 F4
Middle Row. M Ash 72 B3
Middle Row. Rhy 34 B4
Middle St. Ponty 124 B1
Middle St. Tonypa 121 F2
Middle Terr. Tylor 96 B1
Middlecroft La. Bish 135 F4
Middlegate Ct. Cowb 198 C1
Middleton St. Glyn 92 B3
Middleton St. Neath 87 E1
Middleton St. Swan 110 C4
Midland Pl. Swan 85 E4
Midland Rd. Swan 85 E4
Midland Terr. Ystra 23 E3
Miers St. Swan 110 C4
Mikado St. Tonypa 121 F2
Milborough Rd. Ystal 23 D4
Milbourne Cl. Mer T 51 F4
Milbourne St. Abercy 98 A3
Milbourne St. Tonypa 122 A2
Milbourne Terr. Mer T 51 F4
Milburn Cl. Rhoose 222 C1
Mildred St. Ll'tris 169 D4
Mile End Row. Neath 87 E3
Miles Ct. Penty 171 D2
Miles La. Bish 136 B3
Miles Rd. Swan 84 B2
Miles St. Fern 70 A1
Miles St. Mer T 32 B1
Milford Cl. Ch Vil 149 F1
Milford House. Card 188 A2
Milford Way. Swan 83 F3
Mill Brook. P Tal 113 E3
Mill Cl. Card 173 D1
Mill Cl. D pow 216 A2
Mill Cotts. Card 188 B1

Mill Cotts. Ll'ha 166 B2
Mill Gdns. T Mum 109 D1
Mill La. Bridg 179 F3
Mill La. Card 190 B4
Mill La. Card 204 A4
Mill La. Card 205 D3
Mill La. Ll'bra 126 C3
Mill La. Ll'rh 105 D3
Mill La. Marsh 175 E2
Mill La. T Mum 109 D1
Mill Lay La. Ll' Maj 220 A3
Mill Pk. Cowb 198 C1
Mill Pl. Card 203 F3
Mill Race. Ll'tris 184 B3
Mill Rd. B-coch 62 B1
Mill Rd. Caer 152 A2
Mill Rd. Card 171 E1
Mill Rd. Card 173 D1
Mill Rd. D pow 216 A2
Mill Rd. Deri 75 D4
Mill Rd. M Ash 72 B2
Mill Rd. Ynybw 97 D3
Mill Row. A-wen 40 C2
Mill St. Aberd 49 F2
Mill St. Gow 82 A3
Mill St. Lough 57 E1
Mill St. Maest 142 B4
Mill St. Pen-cl 80 C2
Mill St. Pontmi 155 D4
Mill St. Ponty 124 A1
Mill St. Ponty 124 B1
Mill St. Tony 147 D2
Mill St. Tre 99 E3
Mill St. Ynys 128 A2
Mill St. Yst 95 E1
Mill Terr. G-nea 26 C1
Mill The. Ll'ha 167 D2
Mill View. Maest 117 E1
Milland Rd. Neath 87 E4
Millands Cl. T Mum 136 B3
Millbrook Cl. D pow 216 A2
Millbrook Hts. D pow 216 A2
Millbrook Pk. Card 173 D2
Millbrook Rd. D pow 216 A2
Millbrook St. Swan 84 B3
Millcroft Ct. St M Ch 211 D2
Miller's Ct. Swan 83 F3
Millers Ave. Brynco 163 F3
Millfield. Bridg 179 F3
Millfield. Card 173 D2
Millfield Cl. Card 190 C3
Millfield Cl. Swan 109 D3
Millfield. Ll'tris 184 A4
Millfield Dr. Cowb 198 C1
Millgate. Card 173 D1
Millheath Dr. Card 173 D1
Millicent St. Card 205 D3
Millrace Cl. Card 173 D1
Millwood. Card 173 D2
Millwood St. Swan 84 B2
Milton Cl. Bar 76 A2
Milton Cl. Ll' Maj 220 A3
Milton Cl. Ll'tris 169 D3
Milton Dr. Bridg 179 E3
Milton Pl. Bedw 153 E4
Milton Pl. Card 203 F4
Milton Pl. Mer T 51 F4
Milton Rd. Pen 216 C2
Milton St. Abera 71 D2
Milton St. Card 205 E4
Milton Terr. N Tre 54 C1
Milton Terr. Swan 110 B4
Milverton Rd. Card 190 B4
Milward Rd. Barry 225 D3
Min y Coed. Neath 88 A3
Min-y-Coed. Bridg 180 B3
Min-y-Coed. Card 187 D4
Min-y-Coed. G-nea 26 C1
Min-y-Nant. Card 188 A4
Min-y-Nant. Penco 181 E4
Min-y-rhos. Ystra 8 A2
Minafon. Card 172 A1
Minavon. Card 188 A3
Minehead Ave. Sully 226 A3
Minehead Rd. Card 190 B3
Miners Row. Llwy 49 F3
Minerva St. Bridg 179 F3
Minffrwd Cl. Penco 165 F1
Minffrwd Rd. Penco 165 F1
Minister St. Card 205 D4
Minny St. Card 205 D4
Minorca. Gar P 175 D4
Minsmere Cl. Card 191 D4
Minster Cl. Barry 225 D4
Minster Cl. Swan 85 D4
Minyffordd. Ystal 23 D3
Minyrafon Rd. Cly 39 E1
Minyrafon. Ystal 23 D3
Mirador Cres. Swan 110 A3
Miskin Cres. Ll'tris 184 A4
Miskin Rd. M Ash 72 C1
Miskin Rd. Trea 121 D3
Miskin St. Card 205 D4
Miskin St. Trehe 68 C1
Miskin Terr. M Ash 72 C1
Mission Rd. Maest 117 E1

Misty Hills Cl. Pen-cl 81 E1
Mitchell Cres. Mer T 32 C3
Mitchell Ct. Tonypa 121 F3
Mitchell Terr. Ponty 149 E4
Miterdale Cl. Card 189 D2
Mitre Ct. Card 188 A1
Mitre Pl. Card 188 A1
Mixen Cl. T Mum 136 C3
Modern Cotts. Mer T 32 C1
Moel Fryn. Caer 151 E3
Moel Gilau. Pontcr 143 E3
Moira Pl. Card 205 E3
Moira St. Card 205 E3
Moira Terr. Card 205 E3
Moira Terr. Og Va 119 F1
Mona Cl. Swan 85 D3
Mona Pl. Card 205 F4
Mona St. Abera 50 A1
Monastery Rd. N Abb 87 D4
Monger St. Swan 84 B1
Monica St. Maest 117 D1
Monk St. Abera 50 A1
Monk's Cl. Pyle 161 D1
Monksland Rd. P-Ey 132 A2
Monkstone Cl. Pen 216 C1
Monkstone Rise. Card 190 B3
Monkton Cl. Card 203 E4
Monmouth Cl. Ch Vil 149 F1
Monmouth Ct. Caer 151 E2
Monmouth Dr. Mer T 31 F1
Monmouth House. Pen 216 C1
Monmouth Pl. Swan 60 A3
Monmouth St. Card 204 C2
Monmouth St. M Ash 97 F4
Monmouth View. Ll'bra 127 D1
Monmouth Way. Ll' Maj ... 220 A4
Montana Pl. Swan 84 B2
Montclaire Ave. Peng 101 F3
Monterey St. Swan 84 B2
Montgomery St. Card 189 E1
Monthermer Rd. Card 189 D1
Monton Terr. Swan 111 D4
Montpellier Terr. Swan 110 A4
Moor King Cl. Card 191 D3
Moor La. Ll'gen 102 C2
Moor La. Porth 176 C2
Moor Rd. Colw 180 C1
Moor Rd. P Tal 113 E2
Moorby Ct. Card 205 D2
Moordale Rd. Card 205 D1
Moore Cl. Card 203 E3
Moore Rd. Card 203 D3
Moore's Row. Deri 53 E4
Moorland Ave. T Mum 136 C3
Moorland Cl. Hir 48 C4
Moorland Cres. Ll'tris 169 D4
Moorland Hts. Ponty 149 F4
Moorland Rd. Bar 75 F2
Moorland Rd. Card 205 F3
Moorland Rd. Neath 87 F3
Moorland Rd. P Tal 138 B4
Moorland Rd. P Tal 138 C2
Moorlands. Onll 10 A1
Moorlands Rd. Bridg 179 F1
Moors La. Card 205 E3
Moorside Rd. T Mum 136 C4
Moorside Villas. Coel 9 F2
Moorview Cl. Swan 83 F2
Moorview Rd. Swan 83 F2
Morawel. Swan 85 E3
Morel St. Barry 225 D3
Morfa Ave. Marg 139 E3
Morfa Cres. Card 190 C3
Morfa Glas. G-nea 26 C1
Morfa La. Wen 215 D3
Morfa Rd. Marg 139 E2
Morfa Rd. Swan 84 C1
Morfa St. Bridg 179 F3
Morfydd St. Swan 84 C4
Morgan Arc. Card 205 D3
Morgan Ct. Trea 95 F1
Morgan Flats. Caer 152 A2
Morgan St. Aberd 49 F1
Morgan St. Barry 225 D3
Morgan St. Caer 152 A2
Morgan St. Card 205 D3
Morgan St. Coel 9 D3
Morgan St. Ll'bra 126 C1
Morgan St. M Ash 72 C1
Morgan St. Mer T 32 B1
Morgan St. Mer T 33 D2
Morgan St. N Tre 54 C2
Morgan St. Pontdw 40 B1
Morgan St. Ponty 124 B1
Morgan St. Porth 122 C2
Morgan St. Swan 84 B1
Morgan St. Tred 35 F3
Morgan Terr. Porth 122 C2
Morgan Terr. Tred 35 E3
Morgan Terr. Treo 94 A2
Morgan's Pl. Brynco 164 A3
Morgan's Rd. Neath 87 E3
Morgan's Terr. Neath 87 E2
Morgan's Terr. Ton 89 D1
Morgannwg St. Ponty 123 E1
Morganwg House. P Tal ... 138 B4
Moriah Pl. Llwy 49 F3
Moriah Pl. Pyle 161 D1

251

Moriah Rd. Swan

Oak Ct. Pen

Moriah Rd. Swan 84 B3
Moriah St. Bed 74 A4
Moriah St. Mer T 32 B1
Moriah St. Rhy 34 C1
Morien Cres. Ponty 149 F3
Morlais Cl. Mer T 31 F2
Morlais Ct. Caer 151 E2
Morlais Rd. Ll'ge 56 A4
Morlais Rd. Marg 139 F2
Morlais Rd. Swan 84 A3
Morlais St. Barry 225 E3
Morlais St. Card 189 D1
Morlais St. Mer T 33 D3
Morlais St. Troed 52 A2
Morningside Wlk. Barry 214 C1
Morrell St. Mer T 51 F4
Morris Ave. Card 172 B1
Morris Ave. M Ash 97 F4
Morris Finer Cl. Card 203 F3
Morris La. Swan 110 C4
Morris St. Abera 71 D2
Morris St. Maest 117 D2
Morris St. Swan 85 D4
Morris St. Trehe 69 D1
Morris Terr. Fern 95 F4
Morris Terr. Penga 83 D3
Morrison Cres. P Tal 113 E1
Morrison Ct. P Tal 113 E1
Morrison Rd. P Tal 113 E1
Morrison St. Peng 101 F4
Morriston Pl. G-C-G 5 E2
Morse Row. Brynco 163 F2
Mortimer Rd. Card 204 B4
Morton Terr. Tonypa 121 D4
Moss Row. Aberd 50 A2
Mostyn Cl. Ll'ha 166 B2
Mostyn Rd. Card 203 D2
Mostyn St. Abera 71 F2
Mound Rd. Ponty 149 D4
Mount Cres. Penga 57 F1
Mount Cres. Swan 59 E1
Mount Earl. Bridg 179 F1
Mount Earl Cl. Bridg 179 F1
Mount Hill St. Abera 71 E4
Mount Libanus St. Trehe 69 D1
Mount Pleasant Ave. Card 190 B3
Mount Pleasant. Bar 75 F3
Mount Pleasant. Barry 225 D3
Mount Pleasant. Bed 74 A4
Mount Pleasant. Bridg 163 E1
Mount Pleasant. Bridg 179 D3
Mount Pleasant Cotts. M Ash 72 C1
Mount Pleasant Cotts. Pontcr 144 A3
Mount Pleasant Dr. Swan 110 B4
Mount Pleasant. Gow 82 A2
Mount Pleasant La. Card 190 B3
Mount Pleasant. Maesy 101 D1
Mount Pleasant. Mer T 32 A1
Mount Pleasant Pl. M Ash 72 C1
Mount Pleasant. Pontcr 118 C2
Mount Pleasant. Pontcr 118 C4
Mount Pleasant. Porth 123 E1
Mount Pleasant Rd. Porth 122 C2
Mount Pleasant Rd. Porth 177 E2
Mount Pleasant St. Aberd 49 F2
Mount Pleasant St. Bar 76 A3
Mount Pleasant St. Mer T 33 D3
Mount Pleasant. Swan 110 B4
Mount Pleasant Terr. Cross 129 E3
Mount Pleasant Terr. M Ash 72 C1
Mount Pleasant. Tondu 163 E2
Mount Pleasant. Tonna 63 E1
Mount Pleasant. Ynys 128 A3
Mount Rd. D pow 216 A2
Mount Rd. Rhig 28 A1
Mount St. Abera 71 E4
Mount St Denys. Card 173 D2
Mount St. Gow 82 A3
Mount St. Mer T 32 B1
Mount St. Rhy 34 C1
Mount St. Swan 59 F1
Mount St. Tred 35 F4
Mount Stuart Sq. Card 205 D1
Mount The. Card 204 B4
Mount The. D pow 216 A2
Mount View. Mer T 33 D1
Mount View. Mer V 73 E1
Mount View Terr. P Tal 114 A1
Mountain Ash Rd. Abercy 98 C2
Mountain Rd. Abera 71 D2
Mountain Rd. Bedw 152 B4
Mountain Rd. Caer 152 A1
Mountain Rd. Craig 39 E1
Mountain Rd. P Tal 114 A1
Mountain Rd. Penty 170 B1
Mountain Rd. Tonypa 122 A1
Mountain Row. Fern 95 F4
Mountain View. Aber 151 D4
Mountain View. Bedw 153 F4
Mountain View. Caer 152 A3
Mountain View. Mark 76 B4
Mountain View. Neath 87 D2
Mountain View. Ponty 149 F3
Mountain View. Pyle 177 D4
Mountain View. Trea 121 F4
Mountain View. Trehe 68 C1
Mountain Way. Nel 99 F1
Mountbatten Cl. Card 189 D3
Mountbatten Ct. Swan 83 F3
Mountbatten Rd. Barry 215 D1
Mountbatten. Rhy 34 C2
Mountjoy Ave. Pen 216 C2
Mountjoy Cl. Pen 216 C2
Mountjoy Cres. Pen 216 C2
Mountjoy La. Pen 216 C2
Mountjoy Pl. Pen 216 C2
Moxon St. Barry 225 E3
Moy Rd. Card 205 D4
Moy Rd. Mer V 73 D3
Moy Rd. T We 171 D2
Mozart Ct. P Tal 113 D2
Mozart Dr. P Tal 113 D2
Muirfield Dr. T Mum 108 C1
Muirton Rd. Card 205 F3
Mulberry Ave. T Mum 136 C4
Mulgrave Way. T Mum 109 D1
Mullins Ave. Card 190 B3
Mumbles Bay Ct. T Mum 109 D1
Mumbles Rd. Swan 109 E2
Mumbles Rd. T Mum 137 E2
Mundy Pl. Card 205 D4
Mur Gwyn. Card 188 B4
Murch Cres. D pow 216 B2
Murch Rd. D pow 216 B2
Muriel Terr. Bed 74 A4
Muriel Terr. Mer T 33 E3
Murlande Way. Rhoose 223 E1
Murray Wlk. Card 204 B3
Murrayfield Cl. Swan 83 E2
Murrayfield Rd. Card 188 B3
Murrells Cl. Ch Vil 169 E3
Murton La. T Mum 136 B3
Museum Ave. Card 205 D4
Museum Pl. Card 205 D4
Mwyndy Terr. Ll'tris 184 C4
Mydam La. Lough 57 D1
Mylo-Griffiths Cl. Card 187 F2
Mynach Clos. Gell 100 C4
Mynachdy Rd. Card 188 B1
Mynachdy Rd. Ynybw 97 E2
Mynydd Garnllwyd Rd. Swan 84 B4
Mynydd Gelli Wastad Rd. Swan 59 F3
Mynydd-Newydd Rd. Swan 84 A4
Mynydd-yr-Eos. Tonypa 122 A2
Myrddin Gdns. Swan 85 D2
Myrddin Rd. Swan 85 D2
Myrtle Cl. Pen 216 C2
Myrtle Gr. Barry 225 E4
Myrtle Gr. Gell 100 C2
Myrtle Gr. Swan 109 F4
Myrtle Hill. Pontar 36 B3
Myrtle. Pen-cl 80 C2
Myrtle Rd. Lough 82 B4
Myrtle Rd. Neath 88 A3
Myrtle Terr. T Mum 137 D2
Mysydd Rd. Swan 84 B2
Mysydd Terr. Swan 84 B2

Nailsea Ct. Sully 226 B3
Nant Canna. Colw 181 D1
Nant Celyn. Ch Vil 170 A3
Nant Ddu. Caer 152 A1
Nant Eirin. Tony 147 D2
Nant Ffornwg. Bridg 179 D3
Nant Gwineu Rd. Glan 4 C4
Nant Gwyn. Bed 99 E3
Nant Gwyn. Porth 122 B1
Nant Hir. G-nea 26 B1
Nant Isaf. Wen 215 D4
Nant Lais. Bridg 179 E3
Nant Meyn Terr. Tony 147 E1
Nant Morlais. Mer T 33 D3
Nant The. Deri 53 E4
Nant Walla. Card 188 B4
Nant y Dowlais. Card 202 C2
Nant y Felin. Ch Vil 169 F3
Nant y Felin. Gar P 154 B2
Nant y Garth. Penty 170 C2
Nant y Hwyad. Caer 151 F2
Nant y Pepra. Card 202 C2
Nant y Plac. Card 202 C2
Nant y Rhos. Card 202 C2
Nant yr Arthur. Card 202 C2
Nant yr Eglwys. G-C-G 5 E3
Nant-cae'r-efael. Coel 9 E3
Nant-Fawr Cl. Card 189 D3
Nant-Fawr Cres. Card 189 D3
Nant-Fawr Rd. Card 189 D3
Nant-y-Coed. Troed 52 A1
Nant-y-Dall Ave. Ponty 150 A2
Nant-y-Drope. Card 202 C2
Nant-y-Fedw. Abercy 98 B3
Nant-y-Fedw Rd. Glyn 91 E2
Nant-y-Ffyddlon. Gell 100 B4
Nant-y-Ffynnon. Bridg 180 A3
Nant-y-Gleisiad. Reso 44 A1
Nant-y-Gwyddon Rd. Yst 95 E1
Nant-y-moel Row. Og Va 119 F4
Nant-y-Mynydd. Onll 25 E4
Nant-yr-Adar. Bridg 179 D3
Nant-yr-Adar. Ll' Maj 220 A3
Nant-yr-Ely. Card 202 C2
Nantcarn Rd. Aberca 129 E4
Nantddu Terr. Tre 98 C3
Nantgarw Rd. Caer 151 F1
Nantgwyddon Cl. Yst 95 E1
Nantgwyn. Aberd 49 E2
Nantgwyn St. Tonypa 121 F2
Nanthir Lodge. Pontcr 118 C3
Nanthir Rd. Pontcr 118 C3
Nantlais. Ewen 196 A4
Nantong Way. Swan 84 C2
Nantyboda. Bryn 115 F2
Nantyffin N. Swan 85 E4
Nantyffin Rd. Pontar 36 B2
Nantyffin Rd. Swan 85 E4
Nantyffin S. Swan 85 E3
Nantyffyllon Terr. Maest 116 C3
Nantygwenith St. Mer T 32 B1
Nantyrychain Terr. Pontcr 118 C1
Napier Cl. Bridg 180 A2
Napier St. Bedw 154 A4
Napier St. M Ash 72 B1
Narberth Ct. Caer 151 E2
Narberth House. Card 188 A2
Narberth Rd. Card 203 E3
Naseby Cl. Card 173 F1
Nash St. Abercy 98 B1
Nash View. Penll 197 F2
Navigation Cl. Tre 99 E4
Navigation Rd. Pontmi 129 F2
Navigation St. Bedw 153 D4
Navigation St. M Ash 72 B2
Navigation Terr. Maest 91 D1
Navigation Villas. M Ash 72 C1
Navigation Yd. M Ash 72 C2
Neath Abbey Bsns Pk. N Abb 87 D4
Neath Abbey Rd. B-coch 87 E4
Neath Abbey Rd. N Abb 87 D4
Neath Rd. B-coch 62 B3
Neath Rd. Bryn 115 E4
Neath Rd. Cry 43 D3
Neath Rd. Cwma 115 E4
Neath Rd. Maest 116 C2
Neath Rd. Reso 43 F1
Neath Rd. Swan 84 C2
Neath Rd. Tonna 63 D1
Neath Rd. Ystra 24 A4
Neath Road. A-wen 62 B4
Neath St. Card 205 F3
Nebo Est. Yst 95 E2
Nelson Rd. Barry 225 D4
Nelson St. Abera 71 D3
Nelson St. Swan 110 B3
Nelson Terr. N Tre 54 C1
Neol St. Abera 71 D2
Nesta Rd. Card 204 A3
Nettlefold Rd. Card 205 E2
Neuadd Rd. G-C-G 4 C4
Neuadda Cl. Rhiwd 155 F1
Neuaddwen St. Bar 76 A3
Neville Pl. Card 204 C3
Neville Rd. Bridg 179 F1
Neville Rd. Porthc 193 D4
Neville St. Card 204 C3
Neville Terr. Aberd 49 F1
Nevills Cl. Gow 82 B3
Nevin Cres. Card 190 B2
Nevin House. Card 188 A2
New Barn. Ll' maes 210 C1
New Bridge. Bridg 179 F2
New Bryn Terr. Tylor 122 B4
New Bryngwyn St. Peng 101 D3
New Castle St. Mer T 32 C1
New Ceidrim Rd. Glan 4 B4
New Century St. Trea 122 A3
New Chapel St. Treo 94 B3
New Church St. C-c-y-c 32 A3
New Cotts. Bridg 179 E4
New Cut Rd. Swan 110 B4
New Forest View. Cowb 199 D1
New Henry St. Neath 87 E3
New House Ct. Barry 225 D4
New Houses. Mer T 33 D3
New Inn Pl. Reso 44 A2
New Inn Rd. Mer M 179 E1
New King St. Yst 95 D1
New Mill Cnr. Ll'tris 184 B3
New Mill Rd. Swan 109 D3
New Orchard St. Swan 110 B4
New Park Cres. Ponty 149 F4
New Park Rd. Cross 129 E2
New Park Terr. Ponty 149 F3
New Quarr Rd. Swan 84 B3
New Rd. A-wen 40 A1
New Rd. A-wen 41 D2
New Rd. Abercy 98 B3
New Rd. B-coch 63 E3
New Rd. Bry 6 C3
New Rd. Card 190 A1
New Rd. Cwmll 6 C3
New Rd. Deri 75 E4
New Rd. G-C-G 5 D3
New Rd. Gall 101 D2
New Rd. Ll'ha 166 B1
New Rd. Lough 57 E3
New Rd. M Ash 72 B2
New Rd. Mark 76 C2
New Rd. Mer T 33 D2
New Rd. N Abb 87 D4
New Rd. Pen-cl 80 A2
New Rd. Pontar 36 A2
New Rd. Ponydw 41 D4
New Rd. Porthc 193 D4
New Rd. Pyle 161 E2
New Rd. Skew 86 B1
New Rd. Skew 87 D4
New Rd. Swan 60 C1
New Rd. Swan 83 E1
New Rd. Swan 84 B3
New Rd. Tondu 163 D3
New Rd. Ynybw 124 A4
New Rd. Ynys 128 B2
New Row. Bedw 153 F3
New School Rd. Glan 4 B4
New St. Abera 71 E3
New St. Abercy 98 B1
New St. Bridg 180 A1
New St. Caer 151 F3
New St. Fern 96 A3
New St. G-nea 27 D1
New St. P Tal 114 A1
New St. Pontcr 118 C1
New St. Swan 110 B4
New St. Tondu 163 E2
New St. Tonna 63 E2
New St. Trehe 68 C2
New St. Ystal 23 D2
New Tynybedw St. Treo 94 C3
New Villas. Abera 71 D2
New Well La. T Mum 136 C3
New Zealand Rd. Card 188 C1
Newborough Ave. Card 188 C4
Newbridge Gdns. Bridg 179 F2
Newbridge Rd. Ll'tris 168 C2
Newbridge Rd. P Tal 138 C4
Newby Ct. Card 205 D2
Newcastle Hill. Bridg 179 F2
Newell Rd. Skew 86 C4
Newent Rd. Card 190 C3
Newfoundland Rd. Card 188 C1
Newgale Pl. Card 203 E2
Newgate House. Card 188 A2
Newlands Ave. Bridg 180 A4
Newlands Cl. Pyle 161 E1
Newlands Ct. Card 173 D1
Newlands. P Tal 113 F3
Newmarket Wlk. Mer T 32 B1
Newminster Rd. Card 205 F4
Newnham Cres. Swan 109 F4
Newport Rd. Aberca 129 D4
Newport Rd. Bedw 153 E3
Newport Rd. Card 190 B3
Newport Rd. Card 205 E4
Newport Rd. Mark 55 E3
Newport Rd. Pontll 101 F2
Newport Rd. Pontmi 155 E4
Newport Road La. Card 205 E3
Newport St. Card 205 D1
Newton Ave. P Tal 113 F1
Newton Cl. Gell 100 C4
Newton Nottage Rd. Porthc 193 E4
Newton Rd. Card 190 C1
Newton Rd. Card 204 B2
Newton Rd. Cly 39 E1
Newton Rd. T Mum 136 C3
Newton Rd. T Mum 137 D3
Newton St. Barry 225 D3
Newton St. Swan 110 B4
Newton St. Troed 51 F2
Newton Villas. T Mum 136 C3
Newtown Ind Est. Cross 129 D2
Newydd Ct. Card 187 E4
Neyland Cl. Ch Vil 149 F1
Neyland House. Card 188 A2
Neyland Pl. Card 203 E2
Niagara St. Ponty 149 E4
Nibloe Terr. Mer T 32 C2
Nicander Par. Swan 110 A4
Nicander Pl. Swan 110 A4
Nicholas Rd. Swan 61 D3
Nicholl Ct. Ll' Maj 220 A3
Nicholl St. Swan 110 A3
Nicholls Ave. Porthc 193 D4
Nicholls Rd. Tondu 163 E4
Nicholson Webb Cl. Card 187 E2
Nidum Cl. B-coch 87 E4
Nightingale Pl. D pow 216 B2
Nightingale St. Troed 51 F2
Nightingale's Bush. Ponty 149 E4
Nile Rd. Trea 122 A3
Nile St. Ponty 149 E4
Nine Mile Point Rd. Ynys 128 C2
Ninian Park Rd. Card 204 C3
Ninian Rd. Card 189 D1
Ninian St. Trehe 69 D1
Ninian St. Treo 94 B4
Ninth Ave. Hir 29 D1
Ninth Ave. Mer T 32 C3
Ninth Ave. Swan 59 E1
Nith St. Abera 50 A1
Nixon Terr. Swan 60 A1
Nixonville. Mer T 73 E2
Nobel Ave. P Tal 113 F1
Nolton Arc. Bridg 179 F2
Nolton Ct. Swan 83 F3
Nolton Pl. Bridg 179 F2
Nolton St. Bridg 179 F2
Nora St. Card 205 E3
Norbury Ave. Card 203 F4
Norbury Ct. Card 203 F4
Norbury Rd. Card 203 F4
Nordale Ct. Card 188 C4
Nordale Rd. Ll' Maj 220 A3
Nordale Rise. Barry 225 E3
Norfolk St. Card 204 A3
Norfolk St. Swan 110 A4
Norman Cotts. M-l-Pit 216 A4
Norman Rd. Card 188 A2
Norman St. Card 205 D4
Norman St. P Tal 114 A1
Norman Terr. Mer T 32 B1
Normandy Rd. Swan 84 C2
Norris Cl. Pen 216 B3
Norseman Cl. Rhoose 222 C1
North Ave. Aberd 49 F1
North Ave. Maesy 101 D1
North Ave. Pyle 161 E1
North Blackvein Ind Est. Ynys 129 D2
North Church St. Card 205 D2
North Clive St. Card 204 C2
North Edward St. Card 205 D3
North Hill Rd. Swan 110 B4
North Hills La. Penma 134 B3
North Luton Pl. Card 205 E3
North Mead. Brynco 163 F2
North Morgan St. Card 204 C3
North Park Rd. Card 205 F3
North Rd. Bar 75 F2
North Rd. Barry 225 F3
North Rd. Bridg 180 B2
North Rd. Card 188 B2
North Rd. Cowb 198 C1
North Rd. Cross 129 E3
North Rd. Fern 95 F4
North Rd. Gell 100 C3
North Rd. Lough 56 C1
North Rd. Og Va 119 F1
North Rd. Porth 122 C2
North Rd. St Ath 221 F1
North Rise. Card 173 D1
North St. Abercy 98 C2
North St. Card 204 C2
North St. Maest 91 D1
North St. Marg 139 E4
North St. Mer T 32 C2
North St. Mer T 33 D2
North St. Ponty 124 B1
North Terr. Fern 70 A1
North Terr. Tonypa 121 E3
North View. T We 171 D2
North View Terr. Abera 71 E3
North View Terr. Caer 152 A1
North Wall Rd. St Ath 221 F1
Northam Ave. Card 190 A3
Northampton La. Swan 110 B4
Northcliffe Dr. Pen 217 D3
Northcote La. Card 205 D4
Northcote St. Card 205 D4
Northcote Terr. Barry 225 E3
Northern Ave. Card 188 A3
Northeron. T Mum 136 C4
Northlands. Card 190 A1
Northlands Pk. Bish 136 A4
Northumberland St. Card 204 B3
Northway. Bish 136 A4
Northway Ct. Bish 136 A4
Northways. Porthc 193 D4
Norton Ave. Card 188 B2
Norton Ave. T Mum 137 D3
Norton Dr. South 135 D3
Norton La. South 135 D4
Norton Rd. Glyn 67 D2
Norton Rd. T Mum 137 D3
Norton Terr. Glyn 66 C2
Norwich Rd. Card 189 F1
Norwood. Card 172 C1
Norwood Cres. Barry 225 E4
Norwood Ct. Card 205 E4
Nottage Mead. Porth 176 C1
Nottage Meadows. Porth 176 C1
Nottage Mews. T Mum 136 C2
Nottage Rd. Card 203 E2
Nottage Rd. T Mum 136 C2
Nottingham St. Card 204 A3
Notts Gdns. Swan 109 F4
Nuns Cres. Ponty 124 A1
Nursery Cres. Rhy 35 D1
Nursery Gdns. Bridg 179 F4
Nursery Rd. Glyn 66 C1
Nursery Rise. Bedw 152 B4
Nursery Terr. Tred 35 F4
Nurses Cnr. Pen-cl 80 C2
Nurston Cl. Rhoose 222 C1
Nydfa Rd. Peng 101 D4
Nythbran Terr. Porth 123 D2

O'Donnell Rd. Barry 225 D4
Oak Cl. Ll'tris 168 B1
Oak Ct. Card 171 E1
Oak Ct. Oak 101 F3
Oak Ct. Pen 216 C1

252
Oak Dr. Swan
Park Pl. Brynco

Oak Dr. Swan 82 B2
Oak Gr. Ll'maes 221 D4
Oak Gr. Neath 88 A3
Oak Hill Pk. Skew 86 C4
Oak House. Card 187 F4
Oak La. Bedw 154 A3
Oak Pl. Bar 75 F1
Oak Rd. Ll'hry 183 D3
Oak Rd. Mer T 32 B2
Oak Rd. Rhiwd 155 F3
Oak Ridge. Og Va 144 C1
Oak Ridge. Swan 109 D3
Oak St. Abera 50 A1
Oak St. Fern 95 F4
Oak St. Lough 82 B4
Oak St. Peng 101 F4
Oak St. Ponty 150 A3
Oak St. Tondu 163 E2
Oak St. Tony 146 B3
Oak St. Tonypa 121 D4
Oak St. Trehe 94 A4
Oak St. Yst 95 D1
Oak Terr. Abera 71 F2
Oak Terr. Cross 129 E3
Oak Terr. Ll'bra 126 C1
Oak Terr. M Ash 97 F4
Oak Terr. Og Va 119 F1
Oak Terr. Peng 101 D3
Oak Terr. Tondu 163 E4
Oak Tree Ave. Swan 109 E3
Oak Tree Cl. Card 187 D3
Oak Tree Ct. Bridg 180 B3
Oak Way. Brynco 163 F2
Oak Wlk. Swan 109 E3
Oak Wood Ave. Card 189 F2
Oakdale Rd. Tonypa 122 A1
Oakdale Terr. Tonypa 122 A1
Oakdene Cl. Card 189 E2
Oakdene Cl. P Tal 113 F3
Oakdene. Swan 108 B4
Oakengates. Porthc 193 E4
Oakfield Bungalows. Ponty 150 A2
Oakfield Cres. Ch Vil 150 A1
Oakfield Gdns. Bedw 154 A3
Oakfield Rd. Glan 4 B4
Oakfield Rd. Pontdw 40 C3
Oakfield Rd. Tred 35 F3
Oakfield St. Card 205 E4
Oakfield St. Gell 100 C1
Oakfield St. Ll'bra 127 D2
Oakfield St. Mer V 73 E3
Oakfield St. Pontar 36 B2
Oakfield Terr. Og Va 119 F3
Oakfield Terr. Trea 121 F4
Oakford Cl. Card 173 F1
Oakland Cl. Swan 61 D3
Oakland Cres. Ponty 124 C2
Oakland Dr. B-coch 62 B2
Oakland Rd. T Mum 137 D2
Oakland St. Bed 74 A3
Oakland St. M Ash 72 C1
Oakland Terr. Fern 96 A3
Oakland Terr. Ponty 124 C2
Oakland Terr. Rhy 34 C3
Oakland Terr. Tre 99 D4
Oakland Villas. Og Va 119 F3
Oaklands Ave. Bridg 179 E2
Oaklands. Bar 75 F1
Oaklands Bsns Pk. Fern 96 A3
Oaklands Cl. Bridg 179 E2
Oaklands Cl. Card 190 C4
Oaklands Ct. T Mum 109 D1
Oaklands Dr. Bridg 179 E2
Oaklands Dr. Yst 95 D2
Oaklands. Marg 114 B1
Oaklands. Mer V 73 E2
Oaklands Park Dr. Rhiwd 155 F2
Oaklands Rd. Bridg 179 E2
Oaklands Rd. Pont 58 A3
Oaklands Rise. Bridg 179 E2
Oaklands. T Mum 136 C3
Oaklands Terr. Swan 110 A4
Oakleafe Dr. Card 173 F1
Oakleigh Rd. Lough 56 C1
Oakley Pl. Card 204 C1
Oakley Terr. Tonypa 122 A1
Oakmead Cl. Card 173 F1
Oakmeadow Ct. Card 190 C4
Oakmeadow Dr. Card 190 C3
Oakridge. Card 172 C1
Oaks End Cl. Gell 100 C4
Oaks The. Bedw 154 A3
Oaks The. Card 173 D1
Oaks The. Ch Vil 169 E4
Oaks The. Tre 99 E3
Oakway. Card 203 E4
Oakwood Ave. Cwma 115 D4
Oakwood Cl. Pen 216 C3
Oakwood Dr. Maest 117 E1
Oakwood House. Cwma 115 D4
Oakwood. Maest 117 E1
Oakwood Pl. Marg 114 B1
Oakwood Rd. Marg 139 D4
Oakwood Rd. Neath 87 F4
Oakwood Rd. Swan 109 F3
Oakwood St. Marg 139 D4
Oakwood St. Ponty 149 F3
Oban St. Barry 225 D3
Ocean Cres. Swan 110 B3
Ocean House Rd. St Ath 221 F1
Ocean St. Treo 94 A2
Ocean View Cl. Swan 109 D2
Ocean Way. Card 205 E2
Ocean Way. P Tal 113 E1
Ochr-y-Waun Rd. Cwmll 6 B3
Oddfellows' St. Bridg 179 F2
Oddfellows St. G-nea 27 D1
Oddfellows' St. Ystra 7 F1
Odessa St. Mer T 33 D3
Odet Ct. Card 187 F4
Odo St. Swan 84 B1
Odyn's Fee. Rhoose 222 C1
Office Row. Ystal 23 D3
Office St. Porth 122 C2
Ogilvie Terr. Deri 54 A1
Ogmore Cres. Bridg 180 A2
Ogmore Ct. Bridg 179 E1
Ogmore Ct. Caer 151 E2
Ogmore Ct. Og Va 119 F1
Ogmore Dr. Porth 176 C1
Ogmore Pl. Barry 225 D4
Ogmore Rd. Card 203 E2
Ogmore Rd. Ewen 195 E4
Ogmore Rd. Swan 85 D1
Ogmore Terr. Bridg 179 F2
Ogmore Terr. Brynco 164 A3
Ogmore Terr. Og Va 119 F3
Ogwen Dr. Card 189 E3
Ogwr Ent Ctr. Tondu 163 E3
Ogwy St. Og Va 119 F3
Okehampton Ave. Card 190 B4
Olchfa Cl. Swan 109 D3
Olchfa La. Swan 109 D4
Old Bakery Ct. Penty 170 B1
Old Brithweunydd Rd. Trea 122 A3
Old Chapel Rd. C-c-y-c 32 A2
Old Church La. Maesy 101 D2
Old Church Rd. Card 188 A3
Old Church St. C-c-y-c 32 A2
Old Clipper Rd. Card 205 F2
Old Farm La. Penty 185 F4
Old Farm Mews. D pow 216 A2
Old Furnace House. Neath 87 E3
Old Garden Ct. Card 187 D3
Old Hill. Card 190 B3
Old Kittle Rd. South 135 F4
Old Llanharan Rd. Ll'ha 166 B1
Old Malt House. D pow 216 A2
Old Market Pl. Cwma 114 B3
Old Market St. Neath 87 F4
Old Market. Wen 215 D3
Old Mill La. Mer T 32 B1
Old Mill Rd. Card 173 D1
Old Nantgarw Rd. Ponty 151 E1
Old Newport Rd. Card 190 C4
Old Parish Rd. Gall 101 D2
Old Parish Rd. Og Va 144 C1
Old Parish Rd. Ynybw 124 A4
Old Park Rd. Marg 160 B4
Old Park Terr. Ponty 149 F4
Old Pen-Rhys Rd. Yst 95 E1
Old Rd. N Abb 87 D4
Old Rd. Neath 87 E2
Old Rd. P Tal 113 E4
Old Rd. Ponydw 41 D4
Old Rd. Skew 87 D4
Old School Cl. Mer T 32 B1
Old School Ct. Cross 129 E3
Old School Grange. Gell 100 C1
Old School Rd. Porth 192 C3
Old St. Tonypa 121 E3
Old Stone Rd. Glyn 66 C2
Old Tavern. Pontcr 144 A2
Old Vicarage Cl. Card 188 C4
Old Vicarage Cl. Peng 101 D4
Old Village La. Porth 176 C1
Old Wern Rd. Ystal 23 D3
Old Winch Fawr Rd. Mer T 31 F1
Oldmill Rd. Barry 225 E4
Oldway. Bish 136 A3
Oldwell Ct. Card 189 E1
Olive Branch Cres. Neath 87 D2
Olive Rd. T Mum 136 C4
Olive St. P Tal 114 A1
Olive Terr. Porth 122 B1
Oliver Jones Cres. Tred 35 E4
Oliver St. Ponty 124 A1
Oliver Terr. Ponty 149 F3
Ollivant Cl. Card 187 E2
Onllwyn Rd. Onll 9 E1
Onslow Terr. Tondu 163 E3
Ontario Way. Card 189 E3
Orange Gr. Card 187 E1
Orbit St. Card 205 E3
Orchard Castle. Card 172 C1
Orchard Cl. Ll' maes 210 A2
Orchard Cl. Ll' Maj 220 B3
Orchard Cl. Marsh 191 E4
Orchard Cl. Mer V 73 E3
Orchard Cl. P-Ey 157 D4
Orchard Cl. Penco 165 F1
Orchard Cl. Porth 123 D2
Orchard Cl. Wen 215 D4
Orchard Cres. D pow 216 A2
Orchard Ct. Card 172 C2
Orchard Dr. Card 188 A3
Orchard Dr. Pen-cl 81 E1
Orchard Dr. Ponty 124 B3
Orchard Dr. Porthc 193 F4
Orchard Gr. Card 187 D4
Orchard Gr. Penga 58 A1
Orchard La. Peng 76 A1
Orchard Lodge. Ll' Maj 220 B3
Orchard Pk. Card 190 B4
Orchard Pl. Card 204 B3
Orchard Rise. Pen 216 C2
Orchard St. N Tre 54 C2
Orchard St. Neath 87 F4
Orchard St. Pontdw 40 C3
Orchard St. Swan 110 B4
Orchard Terr. Pen-cl 105 F4
Orchard The. Cowb 199 D2
Orchard The. T Mum 136 C3
Orchard Way. St Ath 221 E2
Orchid Cl. Card 191 D3
Orchid Cl. Gell 100 C3
Orchid Cl. P Tal 113 E1
Ordell St. Card 205 E3
Oregano Cl. Card 191 D4
Ormes Rd. Skew 86 C4
Ormond St. Neath 87 E2
Ormonde Cl. Card 189 F2
Ormsby Terr. Swan 111 D4
Orpheus Rd. Swan 60 A2
Osborne Cl. Bridg 163 F1
Osborne Sq. Card 204 C2
Osborne St. Neath 87 F4
Osborne Terr. Og Va 119 F3
Osborne Terr. Swan 109 F3
Osprey Cl. B-coch 62 C1
Osprey Cl. Card 190 C4
Osprey Cl. Sully 227 D4
Osprey Cl. T Mum 136 C4
Osprey Dr. Neath 88 A3
Osterley St. Neath 87 E1
Osterley St. Swan 111 D4
Oswestry Cl. Card 190 B2
Other St. Ynybw 97 F1
Othery Pl. Card 190 B4
Oval The. Mer T 32 C1
Overdene. Pontll 101 F2
Overland Cl. T Mum 137 D2
Overland Rd. T Mum 137 D2
Overton Cl. Porth 192 C4
Overton St. Mer T 33 D3
Ovington Terr. Card 204 A4
Owain Cl. Card 189 E2
Owain Cl. Pen 216 C2
Owain Ct. St Ath 221 E2
Owen St. Ponty 150 A2
Owen's Ct. Card 188 B2
Owen's La. Ystal 22 C2
Owen's Pl. P Tal 113 E1
Owen's Row. Neath 87 D1
Owls Lodge La. T Mum 108 C1
Oxford Arc. Card 205 D3
Oxford Ct. Og Va 119 F1
Oxford La. Card 205 E3
Oxford St. Aberd 49 F1
Oxford St. Card 205 E4
Oxford St. Fern 70 A1
Oxford St. Gell 100 B4
Oxford St. M Ash 72 B2
Oxford St. Pontcr 118 C2
Oxford St. Ponty 149 F3
Oxford St. Ponty 170 C4
Oxford Street. Swan 110 B3
Oxwich Cl. Card 203 F4
Oxwich Cl. Gell 100 C3
Oxwich Ct. Swan 85 D3
Oxwich Leisure Pk. Ox 133 D1
Oyster Bend. Sully 226 A2
Oystermouth Ct. T Mum 137 D3
Oystermouth Rd. Swan 110 B3
Ozanam Ct. Swan 83 F3

Pace Cl. Card 187 E1
Packers Rd. Porth 122 C2
Padarn Cl. Card 189 D3
Paddock Pl. Barry 225 D4
Paddock The. Card 173 D2
Paddock The. Card 189 E1
Paddock The. Cowb 199 D1
Paddock The. T Mum 137 D4
Paddocks Cres. Ll'tris 183 F3
Paddocks The. Abera 71 E4
Paddocks The. Ch Vil 149 E1
Paddocks The. Ll'tris 185 E3
Paddocks The. Pen 217 D1
Paddocks The. Peng 76 C1
Paddocks The. Tony 147 E3
Padley's Cl. Maest 117 E1
Page St. Swan 110 A4
Paget La. Card 204 C2
Paget Pl. Pen 217 D3
Paget Rd. Pen 217 D3
Paget St. Card 204 C1
Paget St. Ynybw 97 F1
Paget Terr. Pen 217 D3
Painter's Row. Treo 94 A4
Palace Ave. Card 204 A4
Palace Ct. Card 189 D3
Palace Rd. Card 204 A4
Palalwyf Ave. Ll'tris 184 A4
Pale Rd. Skew 86 C3
Palleg Rd. Ystra 7 E1
Palm Rd. Mer T 32 B3
Palmer Pl. Peng 101 E4
Palmer St. Barry 225 E4
Palmers Row. Porth 122 C1
Palmerston Rd. Barry 225 E3
Palmerston Trad Est. Barry 225 E4
Palmerston Workshops. Barry 225 E4
Palmyra Ct. T Mum 137 D3
Pamela St. M Ash 72 B1
Pandy Cl. Mer T 32 A2
Pandy Cres. Pyle 161 D1
Pandy La. Bedw 154 A4
Pandy Pk. Tondu 163 E2
Pandy Rd. Bedw 152 B4
Pandy Rd. Tondu 163 E2
Pandy View. Bed 99 E3
Pandy View. Cross 129 E3
Pandy View. Neath 88 A2
Pandy-Mawr Rd. Bedw 152 B4
Pangbourne Cl. Porth 176 C1
Pant Bach. Pyle 161 D1
Pant Celydd. Marg 139 F2
Pant Cl. Mer T 33 D4
Pant Cl. St B M 195 E2
Pant Glas. Card 190 A4
Pant Glas Cl. Bedw 152 C3
Pant Glas Ct. Rhiwd 155 F1
Pant Glas Ind Est. Bedw 152 C3
Pant Glas. Ll'bra 127 D2
Pant Glas. Penco 181 E4
Pant Gwyn. Swan 109 E3
Pant Hirgoed. Penco 165 E1
Pant Hirwaun. Brynco 164 C2
Pant Hirwaun. H-y-Cy 165 D2
Pant Howel Ddu. Neath 87 F1
Pant Howellddu. Neath 87 E2
Pant Lasau Rd. Swan 59 E2
Pant Morfa. Porthc 193 D4
Pant Rd. Mer T 33 D3
Pant St. Bar 76 A3
Pant St. Pontcr 118 C1
Pant St. Swan 111 D4
Pant Tawel La. Card 186 C3
Pant y Brwyn. Bry 6 C3
Pant y Dwr. Pen-cl 81 E1
Pant y Fedwen. G-C-G 5 D2
Pant yr Helys. Swan 83 D3
Pant-Bach Rd. Card 188 B3
Pant-Du Rd. Ponty 125 D3
Pant-y-Blawd Rd. Swan 60 A1
Pant-y-Blawd Rd. Swan 85 E4
Pant-y-Blodau. Ll'fel 59 D1
Pant-y-brad. Tony 147 F2
Pant-y-Celyn Pl. St Ath 221 E2
Pant-y-Celyn Rd. Swan 109 F4
Pant-y-Cerdin. Aberd 71 F4
Pant-y-Coed. Ll'car 222 A4
Pant-y-Deri Cl. Card 203 E2
Pant-y-Fedwen. Abera 71 E3
Pant-y-Felin Rd. Pontar 36 B3
Pant-y-Ffynnon. Penco 165 F1
Pant-y-Gog. Pontcr 118 C1
Pant-y-gwand Row. Ystal 23 D3
Pant-y-Pistyll. Pontdw 40 B2
Pant-y-Sais. Skew 86 B1
Pant-y-Seren. Tony 147 D1
Pant-yr-Arian La. P Tal 113 F3
Pant-yr-Awel. Og Va 144 C2
Pant-yr-Eos. Abera 50 B2
Pantanas. Tre 99 D3
Pantaquesta Cotts. Ll'tris 184 B3
Pantbach Ave. Card 188 B2
Pantbach House. Card 188 B3
Pantbach. Penty 186 B4
Pantbach Pl. Card 188 B2
Panteg Cl. Card 202 C2
Panteg. Penty 186 B4
Pantglas Fawr. Mer V 73 E3
Pantglas. Lough 57 D1
Pantglas. Penty 186 B4
Pantglas Rd. Mer V 73 E3
Pantglas View. Bedw 152 C3
Pantgwynlais. Card 171 E1
Pantiago Rd. Pontar 36 B2
Pantile Row. Glyn 66 C2
Pantmawr Ct. Card 187 F4
Pantmawr Rd. Card 187 F4
Pantycefn Rd. Mark 76 B4
Pantycelyn Dr. Caer 151 F3
Pantycelyn. Lough 57 D1
Pantycelyn Rd. Pen 216 B3
Pantycelyn St. Gell 100 C1
Pantycelynen. Mer T 32 B1
Pantyffyn Rd. Mer T 32 C1
Pantyffynnon Terr. Ystal 23 D2
Pantyffynnon Rd. Ystra 23 F4
Pantyfid Rd. Bar 76 A3
Pantygraigwen Rd. Ponty 124 A1
Pantygwydr Rd. Swan 109 F3
Pantyrheol. Neath 87 E2
Paper Mill Rd. Card 204 A3
Parade. Ponty 124 B1
Parade The. Card 187 F2
Parade The. Card 205 E3
Parade The. Ch Vil 169 F4
Parade The. D pow 216 B2
Parade The. Fern 95 F4
Parade The. Mer T 32 C1
Parade The. Neath 87 F4
Parade The. Porth 122 C2
Parade The. Yst 94 C2
Parc Andrew. Skew 86 C3
Parc Ave. Caer 152 B3
Parc Ave. Swan 84 C3
Parc Ave. Swan 84 C4
Parc Bryn. Skew 86 C3
Parc Castell-y-Mynach. Penty 185 F4
Parc Cotts. Aber 125 F1
Parc Cotts. Bridge 164 A1
Parc Cres. Colw 180 C1
Parc Crymlyn. Skew 86 B3
Parc Glas. Aberd 49 E2
Parc Glas. Skew 86 C3
Parc Hafod. Card 187 F3
Parc Hendy Cres. Pen-cl 80 C2
Parc Landwr. Swan 85 D3
Parc Mawr Cl. Penga 58 A1
Parc Newydd. Ll'tris 168 B1
Parc Newydd. Neath 87 D2
Parc Onen. Skew 86 C3
Parc Pontypandy. Caer 152 B3
Parc Rd. Swan 84 C3
Parc Terr. Aber 125 F1
Parc Terr. Swan 84 C4
Parc The. Ewen 179 F1
Parc Ty Glas. Card 188 C4
Parc Wenallt. Tre 99 D4
Parc Wern Rd. Swan 109 F4
Parc Wern. Skew 86 C3
Parc Wood. St Don 218 C3
Parc-y-bont. Brynco 163 F3
Parc-y-Bryn. Ch Vil 169 E4
Parc-y-Bryn. Marg 139 F4
Parc-y-Bryn. Penty 185 E4
Parc-y-Coed. Penty 185 F4
Parc-y-Delyn. Ll'fel 59 E1
Parc-y-Deri. Skew 86 C3
Parc-y-duc Terr. Swan 84 C4
Parc-y-Felin. Penty 185 E4
Parc-y-Fro. Penty 185 F4
Parc-y-Nant. Ponty 171 D4
Parc-y-Rhos. Penco 181 E4
Parc-yr-Helig Rd. Swan 86 A4
Parcau Ave. Bridg 179 E2
Parcau Rd. Bridg 179 E2
Parcyfelin St. Caer 152 A2
Parfitt Cl. Tylor 96 A2
Parfitt Pl. Peng 101 E4
Parfitt Terr. Mer T 51 F4
Parish Rd. Blae 45 F4
Parish Rd. Ll'tris 169 D4
Park Ave. Bedw 152 C3
Park Ave. Card 187 F3
Park Ave. G-nea 26 C1
Park Ave. Og Va 144 C4
Park Ave. Porth 192 C4
Park Ave. Rhiwd 155 F3
Park Ave. Skew 86 B4
Park Ave. T Mum 137 D2
Park Ave. Wen 203 D1
Park Cl. Lough 57 D1
Park Cl. Pontar 36 B2
Park Cl. Ponty 149 E3
Park Cl. Swan 59 F1
Park Cl. Swan 85 D2
Park Cl. Trehe 68 C1
Park Court Rd. Bridg 179 E2
Park Cres. Bar 75 F2
Park Cres. Card 187 F3
Park Cres. Ll'tris 184 A4
Park Cres. Porth 122 C2
Park Cres. Skew 86 B4
Park Cres. Tre 99 D4
Park Cres. Treo 94 B3
Park Ct. Aberca 129 D4
Park Ct. Bridg 179 E2
Park Dr. Bar 75 F2
Park Dr. Skew 86 B4
Park Dr. Swan 109 F4
Park End Ct. Card 189 D3
Park End La. Card 189 D3
Park Field. Tonna 63 E2
Park Gr. Aberd 49 F2
Park Gr. Card 205 D4
Park Hill. M Ash 72 B2
Park Hill. M Ash 72 C1
Park Hill. Tred 35 E3
Park Homes. Pontmi 155 E4
Park La. Aberd 49 F2
Park La. Caer 152 A1
Park La. Card 187 F3
Park La. Card 205 D3
Park La. G-C-G 5 D4
Park La. Gell 100 B1
Park La. Glyn 92 B3
Park La. Ll'ge 56 B4
Park La. Ll'tris 185 D4
Park La. T We 170 C2
Park La. Tre 99 D3
Park Pl. Bar 76 A1
Park Pl. Brynco 163 F2

253
Park Pl. Card
Penyard Rd. N Abb

Park Pl. Card 205 D4
Park Pl. Cross 129 E3
Park Pl. Ponty 124 C3
Park Pl. Swan 109 F3
Park Pl. Tred 35 F3
Park Pl. Trehe 68 C1
Park Pl. Troed 73 D4
Park Prospect. Ponty 124 A1
Park Rd. Abera 71 E4
Park Rd. Abercy 98 C2
Park Rd. Bar 75 F2
Park Rd. Card 187 D3
Park Rd. Card 187 F3
Park Rd. Cly 60 C4
Park Rd. D pow 216 A2
Park Rd. Fern 70 A1
Park Rd. Fern 96 A3
Park Rd. Gow 82 B2
Park Rd. Lough 57 D1
Park Rd. Maesy 101 D1
Park Rd. Pen 217 D2
Park Rd. Pen-cl 80 C2
Park Rd. Pontmi 129 F1
Park Rd. South 135 D3
Park Rd. Swan 60 B2
Park Rd. Tondu 163 E2
Park Rd. Tonypa 122 A2
Park Rd. Treo 94 A2
Park Row Gdns. Mer T 32 B2
Park Row. Tred 35 F3
Park Side La. Ponty 124 B1
Park St. Aberca 129 E4
Park St. Abercy 98 B1
Park St. Bridg 179 F2
Park St. Card 205 D3
Park St. Cross 129 D3
Park St. G-C-G 5 D4
Park St. Glyn 66 C1
Park St. M Ash 97 F4
Park St. Maest 117 D1
Park St. Marg 139 E4
Park St. Neath 87 F4
Park St. Og Va 119 F3
Park St. Pontcr 118 C2
Park St. Ponty 149 F4
Park St. Porth 122 B2
Park St. Pyle 161 E1
Park St. Skew 87 D4
Park St. Swan 110 B4
Park St. T Mum 137 D3
Park St. Tonna 63 E2
Park St. Tonypa 121 D3
Park St. Tylor 96 A2
Park Terr. Bed 99 E3
Park Terr. Ll'ha 166 C2
Park Terr. Mer T 32 B1
Park Terr. Oak 101 F3
Park Terr. Pontar 36 B1
Park Terr. Swan 84 B1
Park Terr. Tondu 163 D3
Park Terr. Treo 94 A3
Park The. Swan 109 D4
Park The. Tre 99 D4
Park View. Abera 71 D2
Park View. Abercy 98 C2
Park View. Bar 75 F2
Park View. Bridg 179 D3
Park View. Bridg 180 C2
Park View Bungalows. Oak 101 F4
Park View. Cross 129 D3
Park View Ct. Card 188 A3
Park View Ct. Card 204 C3
Park View. Ll'bra 126 C1
Park View. Ll'ha 167 D1
Park View. Ll'tris 168 B2
Park View. Maest 117 E1
Park View. Marg 139 E4
Park View Terr. Abera 50 A2
Park View Terr. Abera 71 F3
Park View Terr. Swan 109 E3
Park View. Tondu 163 D3
Park View. Tred 35 E3
Park View. Tylor 96 B2
Park View. Tylor 122 C4
Park View. Yst 95 D2
Park Way. Swan 109 D3
Parkdale View. Ll'tris 168 C1
Parker Pl. Card 203 D2
Parker Rd. Card 203 D2
Parkfield Pl. Card 188 C1
Parkfield Rd. Abera 50 B1
Parkfields. Bridg 179 E4
Parkfields Rd. Bridg 179 E2
Parkhill Rd. Swan 84 B3
Parkhill Terr. Swan 84 B3
Parkland Cres. Tony 147 E3
Parkland Rd. Tony 147 E3
Parklands. Ewen 196 A4
Parklands. Peng 101 F4
Parklands View. Swan 109 D3
Parkside Ct. Card 204 B3
Parkstone Ave. Card 190 C4
Parkville. Tred 35 F3
Parkwall Rd. Card 174 A2
Parkwood Dr. Rhiwd 155 F1
Parkwood. Gow 82 B2
Parr Ave. Neath 87 F4
Parracombe Cl. Card 190 B4
Parracombe Cres. Card 190 B4
Parry Cl. B-coch 87 D4
Parry Rd. P Tal 113 D2
Parry Rd. Swan 59 F1
Parry St. Card 204 B3
Parry St. Tylor 96 A1
Parry St. Yst 95 D2
Parrys Dr. Abercy 98 B3
Parsons La. Tonna 63 E1
Partridge Ave. Trea 121 F4
Partridge La. Card 205 E4
Partridge Rd. Card 205 E4
Partridge Rd. Ll' Maj 220 C3
Partridge Sq. Trea 121 F4
Partridge St. Yst 95 D2
Pascal Cl. Card 191 D4
Pascall Ct. Card 205 E4
Pascoes Ave. Bridg 179 F3
Pastoral Way. Swan 109 D4
Patagonia Wlk. Swan 110 B3
Patch The. Ll'hry 183 D3
Patchway Cres. Card 190 A2
Patmore Cl. Penty 170 C2
Patterdale Cl. Card 189 D1
Pavaland Cl. Card 190 C3
Paviland Pl. Swan 83 F3
Pavilion Ct. Porth 192 C4
Pavin Ct. Card 188 A1
Paxton Cl. Gell 100 C4
Paxton Dr. Swan 110 B3
Paxton St. Swan 110 B3
Payne St. Neath 87 E3
Peach Pl. Card 203 E4
Pearce's Ct. C-c-y-c 32 A3
Pearl Pl. Card 205 E3
Pearl St. Card 205 E3
Pearl St. Cly 60 C4
Pearson Cres. Ponty 124 B3
Pearson St. Card 205 E4
Pease La. Mer T 51 F4
Peckham Cl. Card 187 E2
Pedair Erw Rd. Card 188 B3
Pedrog Terr. Swan 84 A1
Pegler St. Swan 84 B2
Pelican St. Ystra 7 F1
Pell St. Swan 110 B4
Pellau Rd. Marg 139 F3
Pellett St. Card 205 D3
Pembrey House. Card 188 A2
Pembridge Dr. Pen 216 C3
Pembroke Cl. Ch Vil 149 F1
Pembroke Cl. D pow 216 B2
Pembroke Cl. Mer T 31 F1
Pembroke Cl. Peng 76 B1
Pembroke Cres. Ll'ha 168 A3
Pembroke Ct. Caer 151 E2
Pembroke Ct. Card 188 A3
Pembroke House. P Tal 138 B4
Pembroke Pl. Ll' Maj 220 A3
Pembroke Pl. Mer T 32 C2
Pembroke Rd. Card 204 B3
Pembroke St. Abera 50 A1
Pembroke St. Swan 84 A2
Pembroke St. Troed 52 B1
Pembroke Terr. Og Va 119 F4
Pembroke Terr. P Tal 138 C4
Pembroke Terr. Pen 217 D3
Pembrook Mews. Card 204 A3
Pembrook St. Ll'ha 147 D1
Pen Coed Isaf Rd. Ll'el 56 A2
Pen Darren. Porth 122 B1
Pen Dinas. Porth 122 A2
Pen Gurnos. Mer T 32 B3
Pen Gwern. Penco 165 E1
Pen Heol-Shenkyn. Peng 76 B3
Pen Isa Coed. Swan 110 C4
Pen Locks. Tre 99 D3
Pen Onnen. Bridg 180 B3
Pen Parcau. Pontcr 143 E2
Pen Tyntyla. Tylor 96 A1
Pen y Dre. Porth 147 E4
Pen y Groes Gr. Rhiwd 155 F1
Pen y Groes. Ll'tris 185 D4
Pen y Maes. Ll'fel 59 E1
Pen y Morfa. Pen-cl 81 D2
Pen y Mynydd. Pontcr 143 E2
Pen y Pant. Og Va 144 C3
Pen-Cae-Crwn Rd. Lough 57 D2
Pen-Cefn-Arda Rd. Lough 57 D2
Pen-Hill Rd. Card 204 B4
Pen-Hydd St. Cwma 89 D1
Pen-Llwyn Ave. Pontll 101 F2
Pen-Llwyn-March Rd. Swan 84 A2
Pen-Pentre. Cry 43 D3
Pen-Pych Cl. Trehe 68 B2
Pen-Twyn Rd. Glyn 90 A2
Pen-Twyn Rd. Treo 94 C2
Pen-y-Banc. Bridg 180 A2
Pen-y-Banc. Cwma 115 D4
Pen-y-Banc. Porth 122 B1
Pen-y-Banc. Se Si 24 C3
Pen-y-bont. Cry 24 A1
Pen-y-Bont. Gell 100 B4
Pen-y-Bryn. Bridg 179 E3
Pen-y-Bryn. Caer 151 F3
Pen-y-Bryn Cl. Penga 58 A1
Pen-y-Bryn. Cwmll 6 B3
Pen-y-Bryn. Glyn 91 E2
Pen-y-Bryn. Maest 117 D4
Pen-y-Bryn. Neath 87 F3
Pen-y-Bryn Pl. Card 188 C1
Pen-y-Bryn. Ponty 124 B3
Pen-y-Bryn Rd. Card 188 C1
Pen-y-Bryn Rd. Card 189 E4
Pen-y-Bryn. Se Si 25 D3
Pen-y-Bryn. Skew 86 C3
Pen-y-bryn Terr. Pontll 101 E2
Pen-y-Bryn. Tonna 63 E2
Pen-y-Bryn View. Brynco 163 F2
Pen-y-Bryn Way. Card 188 C1
Pen-y-bryn. Ystra 8 A1
Pen-y-Cae. Caer 152 B3
Pen-y-Cae. Gell 126 C4
Pen-y-Cae La. Lough 56 C1
Pen-y-Cae Rd. Marg 139 E4
Pen-y-Cefn. Card 172 B1
Pen-y-Craig. Gell 100 C4
Pen-y-Craig Rd. Bry 6 C3
Pen-y-Cwarel Rd. Ynys 127 F4
Pen-y-cwm. Penty 170 B1
Pen-y-Cwm. Rhy 35 D1
Pen-y-Darren Cl. Ponty 124 B1
Pen-y-Dre. Caer 151 F4
Pen-y-Dre. Card 188 A3
Pen-y-Dre. Gow 82 A2
Pen-y-Dre. Mer T 32 B3
Pen-y-Dre. Neath 87 F4
Pen-y-Dre. Rhy 34 C3
Pen-y-Fan. Swan 85 F3
Pen-y-Ffordd. Pyle 177 D4
Pen-y-Fro. Aberd 49 E2
Pen-y-Fro Cl. Swan 82 A1
Pen-y-Fro. Penco 165 E1
Pen-y-Garn. C-c-y-c 14 C1
Pen-y-Graig Rd. A-wen 40 C2
Pen-y-Graig Rd. Swan 110 A4
Pen-y-Groes Ave. Card 188 B4
Pen-y-Groes. Caer 151 F3
Pen-y-Groes Rd. Card 188 B4
Pen-y-Heol. Skew 86 B2
Pen-y-lan Ct. Card 189 E2
Pen-y-Lan. Pen-cl 80 C2
Pen-y-Lan Pl. Card 189 E1
Pen-y-Lan Rd. Card 189 E1
Pen-y-Lan Rd. Cowb 199 D2
Pen-y-Lan Terr. Card 189 E1
Pen-y-Mead. Pontll 101 E2
Pen-y-Mor Rd. Swan 84 B3
Pen-y-Mynydd. Glyn 91 E2
Pen-y-parc. Ll'tris 169 D4
Pen-y-Peel Rd. Card 204 B3
Pen-y-Rhiw. Cwmll 6 B1
Pen-y-Rhiw. Yst 95 E2
Pen-y-Turnpike Cotts.
D pow 216 A2
Pen-y-Turnpike Rd. D pow 216 A3
Pen-y-Turnpike Rd. Pen 216 B3
Pen-y-Wain La. Card 189 D1
Pen-y-Wain Pl. Card 189 D1
Pen-y-Wain Rd. Card 189 D1
Pen-y-Waun. D pow 216 A2
Pen-y-Waun. Penty 170 B1
Pen-y-Werlod Rd. Mark 76 B4
Pen-y-werlod Terr. Mark 76 B4
Pen-y-Wern. Glyn 91 F2
Pen-y-Wern Rd. Cly 60 C4
Pen-y-Wern Terr. Swan 84 B2
Pen-yr-Alley Ave. Skew 86 C3
Pen-yr-Allt. Caer 171 F4
Pen-yr-Allt. Ystal 23 D4
Pen-yr-Eglwys. Ch Vil 149 E1
Pen-yr-Grug. Ystal 23 D4
Pen-yr-Heol. Bridg 163 E1
Pen-yr-Heol Dr. Swan 109 D4
Pen-yr-Heol. Penty 49 D3
Pen-yr-Heol. Pyle 177 D4
Pen-yr-Heol. Skew 86 C3
Pen-yr-Yrfa. Swan 59 E1
Pen-yr-Ysgol. Maest 117 D1
Penallt. Swan 108 C4
Penallta Rd. Gell 100 C2
Penally Rd. Card 203 F2
Penarth Dock Ind Est. Pen 217 D3
Penarth Head La. Pen 217 D2
Penarth Rd. Card 204 C1
Penarth Rd. Pen 216 C3
Penbryn Rd. Skew 86 C4
Penbryn Terr. Gell 100 B3
Penbryn Terr. Swan 109 F3
Penbryn Villas. Mer T 32 C2
Pencader Rd. Card 203 F3
Pencaerfenni La. Pen-cl 80 A2
Pencaerfenni Pk. Pen-cl 80 A2
Pencai Terr. Treo 94 B3
Pencerrig St. Ll'bra 126 C1
Pencerrig St. Ponty 124 A1
Pencisely Cres. Card 204 A4
Pencisely Rd. Card 204 A4
Pencisely Rise. Card 204 A4
Pencisley Ave. Card 204 A4
Penclawdd. Caer 152 B3
Penclawdd Rd. Gow 81 E3
Pencoed Ave. Peng 101 E4
Pencoed Ave. Ponty 124 C1
Pencoed. Swan 108 C4
Pencoed. Tred 35 E3
Pencoedtre Rd. Barry 215 D1
Pencoedtre Rd. Barry 225 D4
Pencwmdu. Ystal 22 A1
Pendarren St. Aberd 49 F2
Pendarren St. Gell 100 C4
Pendarren. Ystal 22 A1
Pendarvis St. P Tal 113 F1
Pendarvis Terr. P Tal 138 C4
Pendderi Rd. Ll'el 56 A2
Penderry Rd. Swan 84 A2
Penderyn Ave. Marg 139 F3
Penderyn Rd. Glyn 91 E2
Pendinas. Card 188 A1
Pendine House. Card 188 A2
Pendine Rd. Card 203 F3
Pendoylan Cl. Barry 225 D4
Pendoylan Ct. Card 203 E2
Pendoylan Ct. Card 203 F3
Pendragon Cl. Card 172 B1
Pendraw Pl. Card 189 D3
Pendre. Bridg 179 F4
Pendre. Card 188 A1
Pendre Cres. Ll'ha 166 C2
Pendrill St. Neath 87 E3
Pendwyallt Rd. Card 187 F4
Pendyris St. Card 204 C2
Penfai Rd. Tondu 163 E1
Penffordd. Penty 186 B4
Penfilia Rd. Swan 84 B2
Penfilia Terr. Swan 84 B2
Penford Ct. Card 205 D4
Pengam Rd. Card 205 F4
Pengam Rd. Gell 100 C1
Pengam Rd. Gell 100 C4
Pengam Rd. Peng 76 A1
Pengam St. Gall 101 D4
Pengham Rd. Bar 76 A1
Pengorof Ct. Ystra 7 F1
Pengors Rd. Ll'fel 59 D1
Pengry Rd. Lough 56 C1
Pengwern Rd. Card 203 F3
Pengwern Rd. Swan 84 B4
Penheol Ely Rd. Ponty 124 C1
Penheolferthyr. Mer T 51 F4
Penhevad St. Card 204 C1
Penhill Cl. Card 204 B4
Penhydd House. Cwma 115 D4
Penhydd Rd. Glyn 91 E2
Penhydd-waelod Cotts.
Bryn 115 E2
Peniel Green Rd. Swan 85 F4
Peniel Rd. Swan 84 B3
Penlan Cres. Swan 109 F4
Penlan Fach. Swan 84 B2
Penlan Gr. Swan 84 A3
Penlan. Ll'ge 56 A3
Penlan Rd. Lough 56 C1
Penlan Rd. Pen 216 B3
Penlan Rd. Skew 86 B4
Penlan Rd. Swan 84 B3
Penlan Rise. Pen 216 B3
Penlan St. Troed 52 A2
Penlan Terr. Swan 84 B3
Penlan View. Mer T 51 E4
Penlline Ct. Card 188 A3
Penlline Rd. Card 188 A3
Penlline St. Card 205 D4
Penllwyn La. Bedw 153 E4
Penllwyn La. Pontll 101 F2
Penllwyn St. Ynys 128 A2
Penllwyn Terr. Pontll 101 F2
Penllwyn Wlk. Bedw 153 E4
Penllwyngwent Ind Est.
Og Va 119 F2
Penllwyngwyn Farm Dr.
Ll'ge 56 A3
Penllwyngwyn Rd. Ll'ge 56 A3
Penllyn. Cwma 114 C3
Penllyn Rd. Card 204 B3
Penmachno. Swan 59 E1
Penmaen Cl. Gell 100 C3
Penmaen Terr. Swan 110 A4
Penmaen Wlk. Card 202 C2
Penmaes. Penty 186 B4
Penmaesglas Terr. Tonypa 121 F2
Penmain St. Porth 122 C2
Penmark Gn. Card 203 D2
Penmark Rd. Card 203 D2
Penmark Row. Hir 48 B4
Penmynydd. Lough 57 D1
Penmynydd Rd. Swan 84 A3
Penn St. Tre 99 D4
Pennant Cres. Card 189 E3
Pennard Dr. South 135 D3
Pennard Pl. Card 188 B2
Pennard Rd. South 135 E3
Pennard St. Swan 84 B2
Pennine Cl. Card 188 C4
Pennine Cl. Swan 83 F2
Pennsylvania. Card 189 E3
Pennyroyal Cl. Card 191 D4
Penparlas. Porth 122 B2
Penpisgah Rd. Tonypa 121 F2
Penplas Rd. Ll'fel 59 D1
Penplas Rd. Swan 84 A4
Penplas Shopping Ctr.
Swan 83 F3
Penprysg Rd. Penco 165 F1
Penrhiw Goch. P Tal 113 E4
Penrhiw La. Bedw 154 A4
Penrhiw Rd. Ponty 149 D4
Penrhiw Rd. Swan 59 E1
Penrhiw Rd. Yst 95 D1
Penrhiw St. Bryn 115 F3
Penrhiw-Fer Rd. Tony 147 D4
Penrhiwceiber Rd. M Ash 97 F4
Penrhiwgwynt Rd. Porth 122 C2
Penrhiwiau. A-wen 40 C2
Penrhiwtyn St. Neath 87 E2
Penrhos. Card 187 D4
Penrhos Cres. Card 190 B2
Penrhos. Lough 57 D1
Penrhos Pl. Swan 83 F2
Penrhyn Ave. Swan 84 A2
Penrhyn Cl. Card 190 C3
Penrhyn Ct. Swan 60 A2
Penrhyn St. Marg 139 E3
Penrhyn Terr. N Tre 54 C2
Penrhys Ave. Tylor 96 A1
Penrhys Rd. Tylor 96 A1
Penrhys Rd. Yst 95 F1
Penrhys Uchaf. Tylor 96 A1
Penrice Ct. Swan 85 D3
Penrice St. Swan 59 F1
Penry St. Mer T 32 B1
Penryce Ct. Swan 110 B3
Pensalem Rd. Swan 84 A3
Pensarn Rd. Card 190 C3
Penscynor. B-coch 63 D2
Penshannel. N Abb 61 F1
Pensidan View. Rhiwd 155 F1
Pent-Lee. Card 189 F4
Pentewan Cl. Swan 60 A2
Pentland Cl. Card 188 B4
Pentre Afan. P Tal 113 E2
Pentre Banadl. Swan 108 C4
Pentre Fedwen. Neath 88 A3
Pentre Gdns. Card 204 C2
Pentre Howell. Penco 181 F4
Pentre Mawr Rd. Swan 84 B1
Pentre Pl. Card 204 C2
Pentre Pl. Pyle 161 E1
Pentre Rd. Fern 70 A1
Pentre Rd. Lough 36 B1
Pentre Rd. Pontar 36 B1
Pentre Rd. Yst 95 D3
Pentre St. Card 204 C2
Pentre St. G-nea 26 C1
Pentre Tai Rd. Rhiwd 155 F3
Pentre-Chwyth Rd. Swan 84 C1
Pentre-Dwr Rd. Swan 85 F3
Pentre-Gethin Rd. Swan 84 A1
Pentre-Guinea Rd. Swan 110 C4
Pentre-Poeth Cl. Rhiwd 155 F1
Pentre-Poeth Rd. Rhiwd 155 F1
Pentre-Treharne Hill. Swan 84 B2
Pentre-Treharne Rd. Swan 84 B2
Pentrebach Rd. Mer T 51 F3
Pentrebach Rd. Ponty 149 F4
Pentrebane Rd. Card 187 E1
Pentrebane St. Caer 152 A1
Pentrebane St. Card 204 C1
Pentrebeili Pl. Og Va 144 C3
Pentrebeili Terr. Og Va 144 C3
Pentregethin Rd. Swan 83 F3
Pentremalwed Rd. Swan 84 C4
Pentrepoeth Rd. Swan 59 F1
Pentrepoeth School Rd.
Swan 60 A1
Pentwyn Ave. Abercy 98 A3
Pentwyn Ave. Peng 101 F4
Pentwyn. B-coch 62 A2
Pentwyn Baglan Rd. P Tal 113 F3
Pentwyn. Caer 151 F3
Pentwyn. Card 187 D3
Pentwyn Cl. Peny 49 D3
Pentwyn Cotts. Card 191 F4
Pentwyn Cotts. Ll'ha 167 D2
Pentwyn Ct. Card 188 A4
Pentwyn Ct. Peng 101 F4
Pentwyn Deintyr. Tre 99 D2
Pentwyn Dr. Card 189 F4
Pentwyn Dr. P Tal 113 F3
Pentwyn Isaf. Caer 151 F3
Pentwyn. N Abb 62 A2
Pentwyn. Pen-cl 81 F1
Pentwyn Rd. Card 189 F4
Pentwyn Rd. Nel 99 E2
Pentwyn Rd. Penco 165 F1
Pentwyn Rd. Peng 101 F4
Pentwyn Rd. Reso 44 B1
Pentwyn Rd. Ystal 23 D4
Pentwyn Terr. Marsh 191 F4
Pentwyn Villas. Mer T 32 B2
Pentwyngwyn Rd. Gar P 153 D2
Pentyla. Maest 116 C2
Pentyla Rd. Swan 109 F4
Pentyla-Baglan Rd. P Tal 114 A1
Pentyrch St. Card 188 C1
Penuel Cl. Lough 57 D1
Penuel La. Ponty 124 B1
Penuel Rd. Penty 186 B4
Penuel St. Mer T 51 F4
Penyard Rd. Hir 48 B4
Penyard Rd. Mer T 32 C1
Penyard Rd. N Abb 87 D4

Penybanc La. Lough   **Protheroe Ave. Bridg**

Penybanc La. Lough 57 D2
Penybont Rd. Penco 181 F4
Penybryn Ave. Peng 101 E4
Penybryn. Pontcr 118 C2
Penybryn Rd. Lough 57 D1
Penybryn Rd. M Ash 97 F4
Penybryn Rd. Tondu 163 F3
Penybryn St. Aberd 49 F1
Penybryn St. Tony 146 B3
Penybryn Terr. M Ash 97 F4
Penybryn Terr. Tondu 163 F3
Penycoedcae Rd. Ll'tris 148 C1
Penydarren Dr. Card 187 F3
Penydarren Gdns. Mer T 32 C1
Penydarren Pk. Mer T 32 C1
Penydarren Rd. Mer T 32 C1
Penydre Rd. Cly 39 F1
Penyfai Rd. Bridg 163 E1
Penyffordd. Caer 151 F2
Penygarn Rd. Card 203 E3
Penygarn Rd. Hen 17 F4
Penygarn Terr. Maest 117 D1
Penygraig. Caer 172 A1
Penygraig Rd. Tonypa 121 F2
Penygraig Terr. Ynybw 97 F1
Penylan Ave. Porth 192 C4
Penylan. Bridg 179 F4
Penylan Cl. Porth 192 C4
Penylan Oval. Card 189 C4
Penylan Rd. Mark 76 C3
Penylan Rd. Penco 165 F1
Penylan Rd. Ponty 149 D4
Penylan Rd. St B M 195 E1
Penyrallt Ave. Bridg 179 F4
Penyrallt. Glan 4 C3
Penyralltwen Pk. A-wen 41 D2
Penyrheol Rd. Lough 57 D2
Penyrheol Terr. Llys 209 F4
Penywaun. Ch Vil 169 F3
Penywern Rd. B-coch 62 C1
Penywern. Ystal 23 D4
Penywlrod. Gell 100 B4
Pepys Cres. Card 190 A3
Percival Cl. Card 172 B1
Perclose. D pow 216 A2
Percy Rd. Glyn 90 A2
Percy Smith Rd. Ll' Maj 220 B3
Percy St. Card 205 D2
Pergwm St. Trea 122 A3
Peris Rd. Swan 84 A3
Pernhill Terr. Tre 99 D4
Perrington Villas. Brynco .. 164 C2
Perrots Cl. Card 203 F4
Perrott Pl. Tre 99 D3
Perrott St. Tre 99 D3
Perry Cl. Neath 87 E1
Persondy La. Card 202 C3
Perth Ct. Peng 101 E3
Perthi-Gleision Cres. Mer V . 73 E2
Perthlwyd. Peny 49 D3
Peter St. Swan 84 B1
Peter Terr. Swan 84 B1
Petherton Pl. Card 190 B3
Pethybridge Rd. Card 203 E3
Petrel Cl. Sully 227 D4
Pheasant Rd. A-wen 40 A1
Philadelphia Cl. Barry 225 E4
Philadelphia La. Swan 84 B1
Philadelphia Rd. Porth 192 C4
Philip Ave. Bridg 179 E3
Philip Cl. Card 188 B3
Philip Row. Aberd 71 F4
Philip St. Abera 50 A2
Philip St. Card 204 B3
Philippa Freeth Ct. Barry . 225 D2
Phillip St. M Ash 72 B2
Phillip St. Pontmi 129 F1
Phillip St. Ponty 149 D4
Phillip St. Swan 84 B1
Phillip's Wlk. Rhy 34 C3
Phillips Par. Swan 110 A3
Phillips St. N Tre 54 C1
Phillips Terr. Aber 125 F2
Phillips Terr. Porth 123 E4
Philog Cl. Card 188 B2
Philog The. Card 188 B2
Phoenix Ave. Marg 139 E3
Phoenix Bsns Pk. Swan 85 E4
Phoenix Est. Card 188 B3
Phoenix Way. Swan 85 D3
Phyllis Ave. Bridg 179 F2
Phyllis St. Swan 84 A1
Phyllis St. Troed 52 B1
Piccadilly. Cowb 210 B4
Piccadilly Sq. Caer 152 A2
Picket Mead Rd. T Mum 136 C3
Picketston Cl. Ll'maes 221 D4
Pickwick Cl. Card 172 C1
Picton Arc. Swan 110 B3
Picton Ave. Bridg 179 F1
Picton Ave. Porth 192 C3
Picton Cl. Bridg 180 A1
Picton Ct. Ll' Maj 220 A4
Picton Gdns. Bridg 180 A1
Picton La. Swan 110 B3
Picton Pl. Card 204 B3

Picton Rd. Skew 86 C4
Picton St. Maest 117 D3
Picton St. Pyle 161 E2
Picton St. Rhy 34 C1
Picton St. Tred 35 F4
Picton Terr. Ll'ha 167 D2
Picton Terr. Rhy 34 C1
Picton Terr. Swan 110 B4
Picton Wlk. Card 204 B3
Pier Cl. P Tal 113 E1
Pier St. Swan 110 C4
Pier Way. P Tal 113 E1
Piercefield Pl. Card 205 E3
Pil-y-Cynffig. Pyle 177 D4
Pilgrim's Cl. B-coch 87 E4
Pill St. Pen 216 C3
Pill Terr. Neath 87 D1
Pilton Pl. Card 188 B1
Pine Cl. Mer T 32 B3
Pine Cl. Porthc 193 E4
Pine Cres. Swan 59 F1
Pine Ct. Card 171 E1
Pine Ct. Ch Vil 169 E3
Pine Gr. Ll'tris 168 A2
Pine Gr. Gell 100 C1
Pine Gr. Neath 88 A3
Pine St. Fern 95 F4
Pine Tree Cl. Card 187 D4
Pine Tree Way. Nel 99 F1
Pine Valley. Cwma 114 B3
Pine Walk Dr. Porth 123 D1
Pine Wood Cres. Card 189 F2
Pineacre Cl. Swan 109 E3
Pinecrest Dr. Card 172 C2
Pinehurst Rd. Card 203 E4
Pines The. B-coch 63 D2
Pines The. Card 188 A3
Pines The. Hir 48 C4
Pinetree Ct. Swan 109 E3
Pineway. Swan 84 B3
Pintail Cl. Porth 176 B1
Pioneer Terr. Ynys 128 A2
Piper Cl. Card 187 E1
Pisgah St. Pyle 161 E1
Pit St. Maest 117 E1
Pitman La. Card 204 C3
Pitman St. Card 204 C3
Pittmedden Cl. Card 190 C4
Pittsburgh St. Swan 83 F4
Plane Gr. Mer T 32 B3
Plane St. Ponty 150 A3
Planet St. Card 205 E3
Plantagenet St. Card 204 C3
Plantation Cl. Mer T 32 C2
Plantation Gdns. Abercy 98 C2
Plantation Rd. Abercy 98 B2
Plantation Terr. Deri 53 E4
Plantation Terr. Rhy 34 C1
Plas Cadwgan. Penga 58 A1
Plas Cae Llwyd. Ll'bra 126 C1
Plas Croeso. Lough 57 D1
Plas Cwm Parc. Aber 125 F1
Plas Essyllt. D pow 216 A2
Plas Grug. Caer 151 F1
Plas Heddwch. Pyle 177 D4
Plas Kenfig. Pyle 176 C4
Plas Melin. Card 187 F2
Plas Morlais. Pyle 177 D4
Plas Nant. Aber 151 D4
Plas Newydd. Card 188 A2
Plas Newydd. Lough 57 E3
Plas Newydd. Swan 108 A4
Plas Pamir. Pen 217 D3
Plas Phillips. Caer 151 F2
Plas Rd. A-wen 41 E2
Plas Rd. Lough 57 E3
Plas Rd. Peng 101 D3
Plas St Andresse. Pen 217 D3
Plas St Pol De Leon. Pen .. 217 D3
Plas Taliesin. Pen 217 D3
Plas Terr. Peng 101 D3
Plas Thomas. Caer 151 F2
Plas Treoda. Card 188 A2
Plas Tymawr. Bridg 179 E4
Plas y Biswail. Card 190 C3
Plas y Coed Ave. Swan 84 C4
Plas y Coed Rd. Swan 84 C4
Plas y Delyn. Card 173 D2
Plas-Cadwgan Rd. Swan 60 B3
Plas-Mawr Rd. Card 203 E4
Plas-Newydd. P Tal 113 E2
Plas-y-coed. Card 189 D2
Plas-y-Fedwen. Ynybw 124 B3
Plas-y-Fforest. Penga 58 B1
Plas-y-Llan. Card 188 A3
Plasbach. Card 203 E4

Plasdraw Ave. Abera 50 A1
Plasdraw Pl. Abera 50 A1
Plasdraw Rd. Abera 50 A1
Plasgwyn. Pontar 36 B2
Plasgwyn Terr. Peng 101 D3
Plasmarl Ind Est. Swan 84 C3
Plasmarl. Llwy 49 E3
Plasmarl Terr. Swan 84 C3
Plasnewydd Pl. Card 205 E4
Plasnewydd Rd. Card 205 D4
Plasnewydd Sq. Card 205 E4
Plasnewydd St. Maest 117 D2
Plassey Sq. Pen 217 D3
Plassey St. Pen 217 D2
Plasturton Ave. Card 204 B4
Plasturton Gdns. Card 204 B3
Plasturton Pl. Card 204 C3
Plasturtwn. Ll'bra 127 D2
Plascyoed. Ystra 7 F1
Play-y-Fforest. Hen 36 A3
Players Ave. Cly 60 B4
Pleasant Cl. Lough 56 C2
Pleasant Hill. Fern 96 A3
Pleasant Pl. Caer 151 F3
Pleasant Rd. Penga 57 F1
Pleasant Rd. Tonypa 121 F2
Pleasant Row. Swan 84 B2
Pleasant St. Swan 59 F1
Pleasant St. Swan 110 B4
Pleasant St. Yst 94 C2
Pleasant Terr. Tonypa 121 D4
Pleasant Terr. Yst 95 E2
Pleasant View. Bed 74 A4
Pleasant View. Ce Cr 162 A1
Pleasant View. Deri 53 E4
Pleasant View. Glyn 91 E3
Pleasant View. Ll'tris 169 D3
Pleasant View. Maest 91 D1
Pleasant View. Maesy 101 D1
Pleasant View. N Tre 54 C1
Pleasant View. Peng 101 F4
Pleasant View. Ponty 124 B1
Pleasant View. Porth 123 E1
Pleasant View St. Abera 71 E3
Pleasant View Terr. Swan .. 84 B2
Pleasant View Terr. Swan . 110 B4
Pleasant View. Tondu 163 E2
Pleasant View. Tondu 163 F3
Pleasant View. Tony 147 D4
Pleasant View. Tre 99 D3
Pleasant View. Tylor 96 A1
Pleasant View. Tylor 122 B4
Pleasant View. Ynybw 97 F2
Pleasant View. Yst 95 D2
Pleasantview St. Mer T 32 B1
Plough Rd. Swan 84 B2
Plover Cl. Swan 84 B4
Plover Way. Sully 227 D4
Plumley Cl. Pyle 176 C4
Plunch La. T Mum 137 E2
Plunch Rd. T Mum 137 D2
Plymouth Dr. Card 187 E3
Plymouth Rd. Pen 217 D1
Plymouth Rd. Ponty 124 A1
Plymouth St. Mer T 51 F4
Plymouth St. Swan 110 B3
Plymouth Wood Cl. Card ... 203 E3
Plymouth Wood Cres. Card 203 E3
Plymouth Wood Rd. Card .. 203 E3
Pobbles Cl. South 135 D2
Pochin Cres. Tred 35 F2
Pochin Houses. Tred 55 E3
Poets Cl. Ponty 150 A3
Pomeroy St. Card 205 D1
Pommergelli Rd. Card 187 F2
Pond Mawr. Maest 117 E1
Pond Pl. Aberd 71 F4
Pond Row. Aberca 129 D4
Pont Aur. Ystra 23 D1
Pont George Rd. Marg 161 D2
Pont Newydd. Penco 181 D3
Pont St. Marg 139 E4
Pont-y-Capel Rd. C-c-y-c ... 32 A2
Pont-y-cob Rd. Gow 81 F3
Pont-y-Glasdwr. Swan 84 B1
Pont-y-Shoot. Swan 84 B3
Pontalun Cl. Barry 225 D4
Pontardawe Rd. Cly 61 D4
Pontardawe Rd. Pontar 21 D3
Pontardulais Ind Est. Pontar 36 B3
Pontardulais Rd. Hen 17 E4
Pontardulais Rd. Ll'ge 56 B4
Pontardulais Rd. Lough 57 E2
Pontardulais Rd. Swan 83 E3
Pontardulais Workshops.
Pontar 36 B3
Pontcanna Ct. Card 204 B4
Pontcanna Pl. Card 204 B4
Pontcanna St. Card 204 B4
Pontcynon Terr. Abercy 98 B2
Pontfaen. Card 189 E4
Pontgam Terr. Ynys 127 F4
Pontlottyn Rd. Deri 53 E4
Pontmorlais W. Mer T 32 B1
Pontneathvaughan Rd.
G-nea 27 D1
Pontneathvaughan Rd.
Ystraf 27 F2

Pontpren. Hir 29 E2
Pontrhondda Ave. Trea 95 F1
Pontrhondda Rd. Trea 95 F1
Pontrilas Cl. Card 202 C2
Pontsarn Cl. C-c-y-c 32 B4
Pontshonnorton Rd. Ponty .. 124 C2
Pontycapel Rd. C-c-y-c 32 A2
Pontygwindy Rd. Caer 152 A3
Pontymason Cl. Rhiwd 155 F4
Pontymason Ct. Rhiwd 155 F4
Pontymason La. Rhiwd 155 F4
Pontypandy La. Caer 152 A3
Pontypridd Rd. Porth 122 C2
Pontypridd St. Barry 225 D3
Poplar Ave. Porthc 193 D4
Poplar Cl. Card 187 E1
Poplar Cl. Swan 109 D4
Poplar Cres. Porthc 193 D4
Poplar Ct. Barry 225 D4
Poplar House. Card 187 F3
Poplar Pl. C-c-y-c 32 A4
Poplar Rd. Caer 152 B1
Poplar Rd. Card 203 E4
Poplar Rd. Ponty 150 A3
Poplar Rd. Porthc 193 D4
Poplar Rd. Tred 35 F3
Poplar St. Troed 52 B1
Poplar Way. Mer T 32 B3
Poplars Ave. Neath 88 A3
Poplars. P Tal 113 F1
Poplars The. Cross 129 E2
Poplars The. M Ash 72 B2
Poplars The. M Ash 72 C2
Poppy Cl. P Tal 113 E2
Poppyfield Cl. Card 190 C3
Porcher Ave. Ponty 124 B3
Porlock Dr. Sully 226 A3
Porlock Rd. Card 190 B4
Porset Cl. Caer 152 B1
Porset Dr. Caer 152 B1
Porset Row. Bedw 152 B1
Port Madoc Rd. Card 190 C3
Port Mews. Barry 214 C1
Port Rd E. Barry 214 C1
Port Rd. Rhoose 222 B2
Port Rd. Rhoose 223 F2
Port Rd. Wen 202 C1
Port Rd. Wen 215 D2
Port Talbot Ind Est. Marg .. 139 D4
Port Talbot Pl. Swan 83 F3
Port Talbot Workshops.
P Tal 138 C2
Port Tennant Rd. Swan 111 D4
Port Terr. Maest 117 D2
Portfield Cres. Card 188 C4
Porth Pl. Porth 122 C2
Porth St. Porth 122 C2
Porth y Waun. Gow 82 A3
Porth-y-Green Cl. Cowb 198 C1
Porthamal Ct. Card 188 B3
Porthamal Gdns. Card 188 B3
Porthamal Rd. Card 188 B3
Porthcawl Rd. Card 203 E2
Porthcawl Rd. Pyle 176 C3
Porthkerry Pl. Card 188 B1
Porthkerry Rd. Rhoose 223 E1
Portia Terr. Swan 110 B4
Portland Cl. Pen 217 D1
Portland Pl. Card 173 D1
Portland Pl. Peng 101 E3
Portland St. Swan 110 B4
Portmanmoor Rd. Card 205 F2
Portmanmoor Rd Ind Est.
Card 205 F2
Portmanmoor Road La.
Card 205 F3
Portmead Ave. Swan 83 F4
Portmead Pl. Swan 83 F4
Portreeve Cl. Ll'tris 168 B1
Portway. Bish 136 A4
Portway The. Porth 192 A4
Post Gwynne. Marsh 191 E4
Post Office La. Mer T 32 B1
Post Office Row. Tonypa .. 121 F3
Potters Gn. Brynco 163 F2
Pottery Rd. Gell 100 C3
Pound Hill. Marsh 175 F3
Pound La. Wen 214 C3
Powderham Dr. Card 204 C2
Powell St. Bed 74 A4
Powell St. Gall 101 D3
Powell St. Swan 110 B4
Powell's Terr. N Tre 54 C2
Powells Pl. Porth 122 C2
Powis Cl. Peng 76 B1
Powis View. Barry 225 A4
Powys Ave. Swan 110 A4
Powys Cl. D pow 216 B2
Powys Dr. D pow 216 A2
Powys Gdns. D pow 216 B2
Powys Gdns. Swan 109 F4
Powys House. Card 189 E1
Powys Pl. D pow 216 B2
Powys Pl. Ponty 149 F2
Powys Rd. Pen 216 C1
Powys Rd. Ponty 150 B1

Precinct The. Porth 176 C1
Prendergast Pl. Card 203 E2
Prescelli Rd. Swan 84 A3
Prescelly Rd. Glyn 91 E2
Prescilla Terr. Bed 99 E4
Prestatyn Rd. Card 190 B3
Presteign Ave. Ch Vil 149 F1
Preswylfa Ct. Bridg 179 F1
Preswylfa St. Card 204 A4
Pretoria Rd. Tony 147 E3
Pretoria St. Pontcr 118 C3
Pretoria Terr. Tred 35 F3
Prettyman Dr. Skew 86 B3
Price Ave. Barry 225 D4
Price St. Abera 50 A1
Price St. C-c-y-c 32 A2
Price St. Rhy 34 C3
Price St. Yst 94 C3
Price's Pl. Aberd 49 F1
Price's Row. Coel 9 F2
Prichard St. Tony 147 E3
Priest Rd. Card 205 E4
Primrose Bank. B-coch 62 A3
Primrose Cl. Bridg 180 B3
Primrose Cl. Card 190 A1
Primrose Cl. Cowb 199 D5
Primrose Cl. Mer T 33 D3
Primrose Cl. Nel 99 F2
Primrose Ct. Tony 147 E3
Primrose Hill. Aberd 49 F2
Primrose Hill. Cowb 199 D1
Primrose Hill. Mer T 51 F4
Primrose Hill. Swan 110 A4
Primrose La. A-wen 41 D1
Primrose La. Pontdw 40 B3
Primrose Rd. Neath 87 E2
Primrose Row. Pontdw 40 B3
Primrose St. Swan 110 A4
Primrose St. Tonypa 121 F3
Primrose Terr. Abera 71 E4
Primrose Terr. Porth 123 E2
Prince Charles Ct. Pen 217 D3
Prince Charles Hospl.
Mer T 32 B3
Prince Edward House. Pen . 217 D3
Prince Leopold St. Card ... 205 E3
Prince Llewellyn House.
Pen 217 D3
Prince Of Wales Dr. Neath .. 87 D1
Prince Of Wales Rd. Swan . 110 B4
Prince Rd. Pyle 161 E2
Prince Rhodry House. Pen . 217 D3
Prince's St. Fern 95 F4
Prince's St. Trehe 69 C4
Prince's St. Treo 94 C3
Princes Ave. Caer 152 A1
Princes Ct. Card 205 D3
Princes St. Card 205 E4
Princes Rise. Caer 152 A1
Princes Way. Bridg 180 A2
Princess Louise Rd. Trea .. 121 F3
Princess Margaret Way
The. P Tal 138 B4
Princess of Wales Ct. Swan 85 E3
Princess St. Lough 57 D1
Princess St. Maest 117 D1
Princess St. Ponty 149 F4
Princess Way. Bridg 180 A2
Princess Way. Swan 110 B3
Prior St. Marg 114 A1
Priors Cres. Swan 108 A4
Priors Town. Ll'gen 102 C2
Priors Way. Swan 108 A4
Priory Ave. Ewen 179 F1
Priory Cl. Ewen 179 F1
Priory Cl. Ponty 124 A1
Priory Gdns. Barry 225 D4
Priory Gdns. Bridg 179 F1
Priory Oak. Bridg 180 A2
Priory Rd. Bridg 179 F1
Priory Terr. Maest 116 C2
Pritchard Cl. Card 187 F1
Pritchard St. Tre 99 D4
Pritchard Terr. N Tre 54 C2
Pritchards Terr. Peng 101 D2
Promenade. Swan 110 B4
Promenade Terr. T Mum ... 137 D2
Promenade The. Pen-cl 80 B2
Promenade The. Tred 35 F3
Prospect Dr. Card 203 F4
Prospect Pl. Abera 71 D2
Prospect Pl. Cwmll 6 B3
Prospect Pl. Maest 142 B3
Prospect Pl. Og Va 119 F1
Prospect Pl. Pontcr 54 A4
Prospect Pl. Rhy 34 A4
Prospect Pl. Swan 109 E4
Prospect Pl. Tred 35 F3
Prospect Pl. Treo 94 C3
Prospect Pl. Tylor 96 B2
Prospect Pl. Ystal 23 D3
Prosser St. M Ash 72 C1
Prosser St. Tre 99 D3
Prosser's Terr. Glyn 91 E3
Protheroe Ave. Bridg 179 E4

Protheroe St. Fern

Protheroe St. Fern 96 A3
Protheroe St. Maest 91 D1
Provident Cotts. Maesy 101 D1
Pryce St. M Ash 72 B2
Pryce St. Yst 95 D2
Pryderi Foopath. Swan 110 A4
Prydwen Rd. Swan 83 D2
Pugsley Gdns. Brynco 163 F2
Pum Erw Rd. Card 188 B3
Pump House Rd. St Ath 221 F1
Purbeck St. Card 204 B3
Purcell Ave. P Tal 113 D2
Purcell Rd. Card 190 B4
Purcell Rd. Pen 216 C1
Purple Cl. P Tal 113 D2
Pwll Mawr Ave. Card 190 B2
Pwll Melyn. Penco 165 E1
Pwll St. Swan 84 B2
Pwll y Min Cres. P-s-Ely 201 F3
Pwll-Evan-Ddu. Bridg 180 B4
Pwll-Gwaun Rd. Ponty 124 A1
Pwll-y-Domen Rd. Swan 84 A2
Pwll-y-Glaw. Cwrna 115 D4
Pwll-y-Waun. Porthc 193 D4
Pwllcarn Terr. Pontcr 118 C4
Pwlldu La. Bish 135 F2
Pwllfa Pl. Abera 70 C2
Pwllfa Rd. Abera 71 D2
Pwllglas Rd. Peng 101 E4
Pwllheli Cl. Card 190 B4
Pwllhelyg. Card 187 E4
Pwllmawr Ct. Card 190 B1
Pwllmelin Rd. Card 203 F4
Pwllmelin Rd. Card 187 F1
Pwllygath St. Pyle 161 E1
Pyke St. Barry 225 D3
Pyle Cross. Pyle 161 D1
Pyle Inn Way. Pyle 161 D1
Pyle Rd. Bish 136 A3
Pyle Rd. Card 203 E2
Pyle Rd. Porth 177 D1
Pyle Rd. Pyle 161 D1
Pytchley Cl. Ll'tris 168 C1

Qakford Pl. Swan 83 E3
Quadrangle The. Brynco ... 163 F2
Quadrangle The. Pyle 161 D1
Quadrant Ctr. Swan 110 B3
Quadrant The. Swan 109 F3
Quar Rd. Neath 87 F3
Quarella. Bridg 179 F3
Quarella Cres. Bridg 179 F3
Quarella Rd. Bridg 179 F3
Quarella St. Barry 225 D3
Quarr Dr. Cly 60 B4
Quarr Rd. Cly 60 B4
Quarr Rd. Pontdw 40 C3
Quarry Cl. Card 203 E4
Quarry Cotts. M Ash 72 B2
Quarry Cres. Card 203 E4
Quarry Dale. Card 190 A1
Quarry Hill Cl. Ponty 124 A1
Quarry Pl. G-C-G 5 D3
Quarry Rd. M Ash 72 B2
Quarry Rd. Ponty 124 A1
Quarry Rd. Tonna 63 E1
Quarry Row. Mer T 32 B1
Quarry St. Ponty 170 C4
Quarry St. Swan 110 B4
Quarry St. Tylor 96 A2
Quay Par. Swan 110 C4
Quay Rd. Neath 87 F4
Quay St. Card 205 D3
Queen Anne Sq. Card 204 C4
Queen Charlotte Dr. Penty 185 F3
Queen St. Abera 71 E4
Queen St. Aberd 49 E2
Queen St. Bridg 179 E1
Queen St. Card 171 E1
Queen St. Card 205 D4
Queen St. Glyn 66 C2
Queen St. Maest 117 D2
Queen St. Marg 114 A1
Queen St. Mer T 33 D3
Queen St. Neath 87 F4
Queen St. Pontcr 118 C4
Queen St. Ponty 149 F3
Queen St. Rhy 34 C1
Queen St. Ton 89 D1
Queen St. Tondu 163 F3
Queen St. Yst 94 C3
Queen St. Yst 95 D2
Queen Street Back Rd.
    Neath 87 F4
Queen Victoria St. Tred 35 E3
Queen Wood Cl. Card 189 E2
Queen's Ave. Brynco 163 F2
Queen's Ave. Lough 57 D1
Queen's Ave. Porthc 193 D4
Queen's Cres. Rhy 34 C3
Queen's Rd. Mer T 32 C1
Queen's Rd. N Tre 54 C1
Queen's Rd. Pen 217 D1
Queen's Rd. Skew 86 C4
Queen's Rd. T Mum 137 D3
Queen's Terr. Troed 73 E4
Queens Arc. Card 205 D3

Queens Ct The. P Tal 138 B4
Queens Dr. Ch Vil 169 E3
Queens Dr. Wen 203 D1
Queens Rd. Bridg 180 B1
Queens Rd. Bridg 180 B2
Queens Rd. Glyn 91 E2
Queens Rd S. Card 217 E4
Queens Rd. Swan 109 E3
Queens Way. Barry 225 D2
Queens West. Card 205 D3
Queens Way. Barry 225 D2
Queensberry Rd. Card 189 F2
Queensway. Ponty 171 D4
Queensway. Swan 83 E2
Queenwood. Card 189 F2
Quentin St. Card 188 C1

Rachel Cl. Card 187 E2
Rachel St. Abera 50 A1
Radcliff Wlk. W St D 199 E4
Radnor Ct. Card 204 B3
Radnor Dr. Ch Vil 149 F1
Radnor Dr. Swan 60 A2
Radnor House. P Tal 138 B4
Radnor House. Pen 216 C1
Radnor House. Swan 110 C3
Radnor Rd. Card 204 B3
Radnor Rd. Ll' Maj 220 B3
Radnor Way. Porth 147 E4
Radyr Ave. T Mum 108 C1
Radyr Court Cl. Card 187 F1
Radyr Court Rd. Card 187 F1
Radyr Court Rd. Card 187 F2
Radyr Court Rise. Card 187 F1
Radyr Court Shopping
    Prec. Card 187 F2
Radyr Farm Rd. Card 187 E2
Radyr Pl. Card 188 B1
Radyr Rd. Card 187 F2
Raglan Cl. Card 191 D4
Raglan Cl. D pow 216 B2
Raglan Cl. Peng 76 B1
Raglan Ct. Caer 151 E2
Raglan Ct. Card 189 E1
Raglan Gr. Mer T 31 F2
Raglan Rd. Gall 101 D2
Raglan Rd. Swan 109 A3
Raglan Terr. Pontmi 129 F2
Raglande Ct. Ll' Maj 220 A3
Railway Cotts. Ynys 128 C2
Railway Cres. Card 205 E3
Railway Cres. Glyn 91 D3
Railway Houses. Rhoose ... 222 B1
Railway Houses. Tred 55 D4
Railway Row. Pontcr 143 E1
Railway Side. Porth 122 B2
Railway St. Aberd 49 F2
Railway St. Bed 99 E4
Railway St. Card 188 C1
Railway St. Pontmi 129 F1
Railway St. Pontmi 129 F2
Railway Terr. Bar 76 A1
Railway Terr. Brynco 164 C3
Railway Terr. Caer 152 A1
Railway Terr. Card 171 E1
Railway Terr. Card 204 B3
Railway Terr. Cwmll 6 B3
Railway Terr. D pow 216 B2
Railway Terr. Deri 53 E4
Railway Terr. Hir 29 E1
Railway Terr. Lough 57 E1
Railway Terr. M Ash 98 A4
Railway Terr. Maest 91 D1
Railway Terr. Mark 55 E2
Railway Terr. Mer T 51 F1
Railway Terr. N Tre 54 B2
Railway Terr. Neath 87 E1
Railway Terr. Og Va 119 F1
Railway Terr. Pen 217 D2
Railway Terr. Pontcr 118 B4
Railway Terr. Pontcr 118 C2
Railway Terr. Pyle 177 D3
Railway Terr. Reso 44 A1
Railway Terr. Skew 86 C4
Railway Terr. Swan 83 F2
Railway Terr. Ton 89 E3
Railway Terr. Tonypa 121 E3
Railway Terr. Tonypa 121 F3
Railway Terr. Tre 99 E4
Railway Terr. Treo 94 A2
Railway Terr. Tylor 122 C3
Railway Terr. Yst 95 D2
Railway Terr. Ystra 24 A4
Railway View. Tonypa 122 A1
Railway View. Trea 95 F1
Railway View. Tred 35 F4
Raisdale Rd. Pen 217 D1
Raldan Cl. Barry 225 D4
Raleigh Cl. Swan 109 E3
Raleigh Wlk. Card 205 D2
Ralph St. Ponty 124 B1
Ramah St. Treo 94 B4
Rambler Cl. Card 172 C2
Ramping Rd. Aberca 129 E4
Ramsay Rd. Cly 39 F1
Ramsden St. Rhy 34 C1
Ramsey Cl. Porth 176 B1

Ramsey Dr. Swan 59 E1
Ramsey Pl. Swan 83 F4
Rannoch Dr. Card 189 E3
Raphael Ave. Bridg 180 B3
Rathbone Terr. Maest 91 D1
Raven Cl. Bridg 180 A2
Raven Way. Sully 227 D4
Ravenhill Rd. Swan 83 F2
Ravenhill St. Yst 95 D1
Ravens Court Cl. Card 189 F1
Ravens Ct. Neath 88 A3
Ravens Wlk. T Mum 136 C3
Ravensbrook. Card 187 D4
Ravensfield. Gow 82 B2
Ravenshoe Rd. Barry 225 E4
Ravenswood Cl. B-coch 62 C1
Ravenswood Ct. Pontmi ... 129 F2
Rawden Mews. Card 204 C3
Rawden Pl. Card 204 C3
Rawlinson Terr. Tred 35 F3
Raymond Terr. Ponty 149 F3
Readers La. Rhoose 223 D1
Readers Way. Rhoose 223 D1
Recorder St. Swan 110 B3
Rectory Cl. Brynco 163 F2
Rectory Cl. Caer 152 A1
Rectory Cl. Lough 56 C1
Rectory Cl. Mer T 33 D3
Rectory Cl. Wen 215 D3
Rectory Dr. St Ath 221 E3
Rectory Gdns. Bedw 152 C4
Rectory Gdns. Bedw 154 A4
Rectory Rd. Barry 225 D3
Rectory Rd. Bedw 152 C4
Rectory Rd. Caer 152 A1
Rectory Rd. Card 204 B3
Rectory Rd. Gell 100 B4
Rectory Rd. Neath 87 F4
Rectory Rd. Pen 217 D1
Rectory Rd. St Ath 221 E3
Rectory Road La. Pen 217 D2
Red Brink Ct. Card 203 E3
Red House Cl. Card 203 E3
Red House Cres. Card 203 E3
Red House Pl. Card 203 E3
Red House Rd. Card 203 E3
Red Lion Cotts. Bonv 201 D1
Red Roofs Cl. Ll'ha 166 A1
Redbrink Cres. Barry 225 D1
Redbrook Ave. Bedw 153 D3
Redbrook Ct. Caer 152 A1
Redcliffe Ave. Card 204 A3
Redgate Terr. Ll'tris 185 E4
Redfield St. Yst 95 E1
Redhill Cl. Hir 48 B4
Redlands Ave. Pen 216 C2
Redlands Cl. Penco 181 E4
Redlands Rd. Pen 216 C2
Redlaver St. Card 204 C2
Redrose Hill. Yst 95 D2
Redshank Cl. Porth 192 B4
Redway Rd. Bonv 200 C1
Redway Rd. Ll'thyd 200 C1
Redwell Ct. Card 189 E1
Redwood Cl. B-coch 62 B3
Redwood Cl. Card 190 C4
Redwood Cl. Ll' Maj 220 B3
Redwood Ct. Card 188 C4
Redwood Dr. Aberd 49 E2
Redwood Dr. Ch Vil 169 E3
Redwood Rd. T Mum 136 C4
Reece's Terr. Aberca 129 E4
Rees Ct. Ll' Maj 220 A3
Rees Pl. Neath 87 F4
Rees Pl. Yst 94 C3
Rees Row. Brynco 163 F2
Rees St. Mer T 33 D3
Rees St. Mer T 51 F4
Rees St. P Tal 114 A1
Rees St. Tonypa 122 A1
Rees St. Treo 94 C3
Rees St. Yst 95 D1
Rees Terr. Ll'bra 126 C1
Rees Terr. Ponty 149 F3
Reform St. Rhy 53 F4
Regency Cl. Ll' Maj 220 A4
Regent Ave. Wen 203 D1
Regent St. Abera 71 E4
Regent St E. Neath 87 E1
Regent St. Mer T 33 D3
Regent St. Treo 94 C3
Regent St W. Neath 87 D1
Regina Terr. Card 204 A4
Reginald St. Marg 114 B1
Reginald St. Swan 111 D1
Reigate Cl. Card 172 C2
Reigit La. Bish 136 B3
Relf Rd. Card 190 B2
Rembrant Pl. P Tal 113 F1
Rennie St. Card 204 C1
Rest Bay Cl. Porth 192 B4
Restway Ct. Card 187 F2
Restways Cl. Card 187 E1
Restways. Porth 192 C4
Retford Ct. Card 188 B2
Retreat The. Bridg 179 F1
Retreat The. Brynco 163 F2
Retreat The. Card 189 E1

Retreat The. Porth 176 C1
Retreat The. Pyle 161 E1
Reynallt Pl. Porth 192 C4
Reynolds Cl. Pyle 176 C4
Rhanallt St. Marg 139 E3
Rheidol Ave. Swan 84 B4
Rheidol Cl. Abera 50 C1
Rheidol Cl. Card 189 D4
Rheidol Cl. Treo 94 A4
Rheidol Ct. Swan 84 B4
Rheola Ave. Reso 44 A1
Rheola St. M Ash 98 A4
Rheolau Terr. Porth 123 E1
Rhestr Fawr. Ystra 7 F1
Rhianfa Gdns. Swan 110 A4
Rhianfa La. Swan 110 A4
Rhiannon Cl. Card 172 B1
Rhigos Gdns. Card 188 C1
Rhigos Rd. Hir 48 A4
Rhigos Rd. Hir 48 B4
Rhigos Rd. Rhig 28 B1
Rhigos Rd. Trehe 68 C3
Rhiw Cae Mawr. Bridg 180 A3
Rhiw Cantcrion. Deri 53 F3
Rhiw Ceris. Aberd 71 F4
Rhiw Ctr The. Bridg 179 F2
Rhiw Fach. Caer 151 F3
Rhiw Felin. Ponty 150 A3
Rhiw Las. Bridg 180 B3
Rhiw Llech View. Glyn 91 F2
Rhiw Tremaen. Bridg 180 A3
Rhiw'r Ddar. T We 171 D3
Rhiwamoth St. Bar 76 A3
Rhiwbina Hill. Card 171 F2
Rhiwddar House. T We 171 D2
Rhiwderyn Cl. Card 202 C2
Rhiwderyn. Swan 86 A4
Rhiwfawr Rd. Ystra 7 D1
Rhiwfer. Nel 99 E2
Rhiwgarn. Porth 147 F4
Rhiwglyn Rd. Og Va 144 C4
Rhiwlas. B-coch 62 B1
Rhiwlas. Card 172 B1
Rhiwlas. Swan 108 C4
Rhiwsaeson Rd. Ll'tris 169 D1
Rhodes Ave. P Tal 113 F1
Rhodfa Bryn Rhos. Glan 4 A2
Rhodfa Fadog. Swan 60 A2
Rhodfa Ganol. Deri 53 E4
Rhodfa Newydd. Aberd 71 F4
Rhodfa Terr. Troed 52 B1
Rhodfa'r Brain. Swan 83 F3
Rhodfa'r Dryw. Swan 59 F3
Rhodfa'r Eos. Swan 60 A3
Rhodfa'r. Mer T 33 D4
Rhodfa'r Wennol. Swan 60 A3
Rhodfa'r Wiwer. Hen 36 A3
Rhododendron Cl. Card 189 E4
Rhondda Fechan Farm.
    Fern 95 F4
Rhondda Rd. Fern 95 F4
Rhondda Rd. Ponty 124 A1
Rhondda St. Swan 110 A4
Rhondda Terr. Fern 95 F3
Rhondda Terr. Trea 121 F3
Rhoose Rd. Rhoose 223 D1
Rhos Ave. Gell 100 C4
Rhos Cotts. Cry 23 F2
Rhos Dyfed. Abera 71 D4
Rhos Helyg. Caer 152 B2
Rhos Llan. Card 188 B4
Rhos Nathan Wyn. Abera ... 71 D4
Rhos Rd. Swan 83 F2
Rhos St. Caer 152 A3
Rhos-y-Bettws. Gell 100 B4
Rhoshyfryd. Hir 29 D3
Rhosili Rd. Gell 100 C3
Rhosnewydd Terr. Peng 101 E2
Rhossili Cl. Hir 48 B4
Rhossily Ave. Card 190 B2
Rhossily Rd. Card 190 B2
Rhosyn Gwyn. N Tre 54 C1
Rhuddlan Cl. Rhiwd 155 F2
Rhuddlan Ct. Caer 151 E2
Rhuddlan Way. D pow 216 B2
Rhych Ave. Porthc 193 D3
Rhyd Cotts. Bridge 163 F1
Rhyd Wen. Bry 6 A4
Rhyd y Fenni. Pen-cl 80 A2
Rhyd y Nant. Ll'tris 184 A1
Rhyd y Polan. Lough 57 D1
Rhyd-Hir. N Abb 62 A1
Rhyd-y-Coed. Swan 86 A4
Rhyd-y-Defaid Dr. Swan 109 D3
Rhyd-y-Felin. Swan 85 F3
Rhyd-y-Glyn. Swan 85 F3
Rhyd-y-Gwern. Caer 152 C3
Rhyd-y-Nant. Penco 165 E1
Rhyd-y-Pandy Rd. Craig 59 F4
Rhyd-y-Penau Cl. Card 189 D3
Rhyd-y-Penau Rd. Card 189 D4
Rhyd-y-Pennau. B-coch 62 B1
Rhyd-yr-Helyg. Ponty 170 C4

Rhyd-yr-Helyg. Swan 109 E3
Rhydarw Terr. Coel 9 F4
Rhyddings Park Rd. Swan . 109 F3
Rhyddings Terr. Swan 109 F3
Rhyddwen Rd. Craig 39 D1
Rhydfach. Troed 52 A2
Rhydhelig Ave. Card 188 C2
Rhydwen. Ystra 23 F3
Rhygoes St. Card 188 C1
Rhyl Rd. Card 190 B2
Rhymney Cl. Pontll 101 E2
Rhymney Ct. Card 205 D4
Rhymney River Bridge Rd.
    Card 190 A1
Rhymney St. Card 205 D4
Rhymney Terr. Caer 152 A1
Rhymney Terr. Card 205 D4
Rhys Rd. Peng 101 E3
Rhys St. Trea 121 F3
Rhys St. Tylor 122 B4
Rialto Ct. Card 188 A3
Rice St. Bridg 179 F2
Rice St. Marg 139 E4
Richard Lewis Cl. Card 187 F1
Richard St. Abera 71 F2
Richard St. Fern 95 D4
Richard St. Pontcr 118 C2
Richard St. Ponty 124 C3
Richard St. Swan 84 B1
Richard's Pl. Swan 110 B4
Richard's Terr. Aberd 71 F4
Richards Pl. Card 205 E4
Richards St. Card 205 D4
Richards Terr. Bed 99 E4
Richards Terr. Card 205 E4
Richards Terr. Tonypa 121 F3
Richardson Rd. Swan 110 A3
Richardson St. Pontdw 40 B2
Richardson St. Swan 110 A3
Richley Cl. P Tal 113 F3
Richmomd Terr. Aberd 50 A2
Richmond Cl. Ll'bra 151 F4
Richmond Cres. Card 205 D4
Richmond Ct. Card 205 D4
Richmond Ct. Swan 110 A4
Richmond Dr. Hir 29 E1
Richmond Pk. Lough 56 C1
Richmond Pk. Ystra 8 A1
Richmond Pl. Marg 139 E3
Richmond Rd. Lough 56 C1
Richmond Rd. M Ash 72 B2
Richmond Rd. Swan 110 A4
Richmond St. Neath 87 F4
Richmond Terr. Tred 35 F3
Richmond Villas. Swan 110 A4
Richmond Way. Swan 83 F3
Richs Rd. Card 188 B2
Rickards St. Ponty 149 E4
Rickards St. Porth 122 C4
Rickards Terr. Ponty 149 E4
Ridge Acre. Swan 109 E2
Ridge The. Swan 109 E3
Ridgeway. Bedw 153 D3
Ridgeway Cl. Ponty 123 A1
Ridgeway Pl. Ch Vil 150 A1
Ridgeway Rd. Card 190 A2
Ridgeway. Swan 108 B3
Ridgewood Gdns. Neath 88 A2
Ridings The. Ch Vil 150 A1
Ridley Way. Bish 136 A3
Rifleman St. Pontmi 129 F2
Rifleman's Row. Swan 84 C1
Rinastone Ct. Card 203 F4
Ringwood Cres. St M Ch ... 221 E4
Rink The. Mer T 32 C1
Risca Cl. Card 190 C4
Risca Rd. Cross 129 E2
Risca Rd. Pontmi 155 F4
Risca Rd. Rhiwd 155 F4
Rise The. Card 173 D1
Rise The. Ch Vil 149 F1
Rise The. Mer T 33 D4
Rise The. Peng 101 D4
Rise The. Ponty 150 B2
Rise The. Tylor 122 B3
Rise The. Yst 95 D1
Ritson St. Neath 87 E1
River Dale. Card 203 E3
River Glade. Penty 171 D2
River Rd. Rhy 34 C1
River St. Maest 117 D2
River St. Og Va 119 F1
River St. Ponty 149 F4
River St. Yst 95 E2
River Terr. Hen 36 A2
River Terr. Peng 101 D4
River Terr. Porth 122 C2
River Terr. Treo 94 B3
River View. Card 188 A1
River View Ct. Card 187 F1
River View. Tonypa 121 F3
River Wlk. Cowb 198 C1
River Wlk. Ll' maj 219 F2
River's Edge. Ll'tris 184 A4
Riverside. Card 188 A1
Riversdale Rd. T Mum 136 C3

256
Riverside. B-coch
St Nicholas Ct. Caer

Riverside. B-coch 63 E2
Riverside Cl. Mer V 73 E3
Riverside Cotts. Tondu 163 E4
Riverside Ct. Aber 125 F1
Riverside Dr. Neath 87 F4
Riverside Flats. Og Va 144 C4
Riverside Gdns. G-nea 27 D1
Riverside. Hir 48 C4
Riverside Ind Pk. Ch Vil 150 B1
Riverside. Pen-cl 80 A1
Riverside Pk. Mer T 32 B1
Riverside Pl. Barry 225 E3
Riverside St. T We 170 C3
Riverside Terr. Bedw 153 F3
Riverside Terr. Card 203 F3
Riverside. Tondu 163 E2
Riverside Villas. Porth 122 B2
Road No 1. P Tal 113 D2
Road No 2. P Tal 113 E3
Road No 3. P Tal 113 D3
Roath Court Pl. Card 205 E4
Roath Court Rd. Card 205 E4
Roath Dock Rd. Card 205 F2
Robert Owen Gdns. Swan 111 D4
Robert St. Barry 225 D3
Robert St. Card 189 D1
Robert St. Card 203 F3
Robert St. G-nea 26 C1
Robert St. Ll'ha 166 C1
Robert St. Swan 84 B2
Robert St. Ynybw 124 A4
Robert St. Yst 94 C2
Roberts Ave. Mer T 32 C3
Roberts Cl. G-nea 26 C1
Roberts Cl. St Ath 221 E3
Roberts La. Mer T 32 B1
Roberts Rd. Swan 110 C3
Roberts Terr. Tred 35 F3
Robin Cl. Card 189 E4
Robin Hill. D pow 216 A1
Robin Rd. Swan 83 F4
Robins Hill. Bridg 180 B2
Robins La. Barry 225 D4
Robinswood Cl. Pen 217 D1
Robinswood Cres. Pen 217 D1
Roche Cres. Card 187 E1
Rochester Mansions. Card 187 F3
Rock Chwyth Rd. A-wen 40 C2
Rock Cottages. Bridge 163 E1
Rock Cotts. Ponty 124 A1
Rock. Cwma 115 D4
Rock Dr. Yst 95 D1
Rock Houses. Tre 99 D3
Rock La. C-c-y-c 32 A2
Rock St. G-nea 26 C1
Rock St. M Ash 72 B1
Rock St. Tondu 163 E2
Rock Terr. Swan 59 F1
Rock Terr. Ynybw 97 F1
Rock View. Tre 98 C3
Rockfield Terr. Neath 87 E3
Rockfields Cl. Porth 176 C1
Rockfields Cres. Porth 176 C1
Rockfields. Porth 176 C1
Rockhill. T Mum 137 D3
Rockingham Terr. Neath 87 E1
Rockingstone Terr. Ponty 149 F4
Rockland Terr. Swan 84 B1
Rockleigh Ave. Bar 76 A3
Rockrose Way. Pen 216 C3
Rockwood Rd. T We 171 D2
Roden Ct. Card 205 E4
Rodericks Terr. Tre 99 D3
Rodney St. Swan 110 A3
Rofton Bungalows. Cwma 114 C3
Rogart Terr. Ponty 124 B2
Roger St. Swan 84 A4
Roger's La. Bridg 178 C2
Rogersmoor Cl. Pen 217 D1
Rogerstone Cl. Card 190 C4
Roland St. Card 205 D2
Rolls Ave. Gell 100 C4
Rolls St. Card 204 B3
Roman Bridge Cl. T Mum 109 D1
Roman Cl. Card 203 E2
Roman Ct. T Mum 109 D1
Roman Rd. Onll 26 A4
Roman Ridge. Gell 100 A4
Roman Way. B-coch 87 E4
Romilly Bldgs. Barry 225 D2
Romilly Cres. Card 204 B3
Romilly Pl. Card 204 B3
Romilly Rd. Card 204 B3
Romilly Rd. Rhoose 223 D1
Romilly Rd W. Card 204 A4
Romney House. P Tal 138 B4
Romney Rd. P Tal 138 B4
Romney Wlk. Pen 216 C3
Rompney Terr. Card 190 A1
Ronald Pl. Card 203 E3
Rook Cl. Ll' Maj 220 B3
Rookery Wood. Sully 226 A3
Rookwood Ave. Card 187 F1
Rookwood Cl. Card 187 F1
Rookwood Cl. Mer T 32 B2
Rookwood Cl. Neath 87 F4
Rookwood St. Card 204 C2
Rope Walk Terr. Neath 87 F4
Roper Cl. Card 187 E1
Roperwright Cl. Gow 82 A3
Ropewalk The. Neath 87 F4
Rose Cott. H-y-Cy 165 D2
Rose Cotts. Pen-cl 79 F1
Rose Cotts. Pontcr 144 A2
Rose Cotts. Ponty 124 A1
Rose Hill. Swan 110 A4
Rose Row. Aberd 71 F4
Rose St. Card 205 E4
Rose Terr. Ll'ha 166 C1
Rose Terr. Pontcr 143 E1
Rosebery Pl. Pen 217 D2
Rosebery Terr. Swan 84 C3
Rosedale Cl. Card 203 E4
Rosedale Terr. Trea 121 F4
Rosehill Terr. Swan 110 A4
Rosehill Terr. Tony 121 E1
Roseland Rd. Swan 82 C2
Roseland Terr. Swan 110 C4
Rosemary Cl. Swan 83 D1
Rosemary Ct. Swan 59 F1
Rosemary St. Card 205 D3
Rosemount Pl. Card 188 B2
Rosewarne Cl. Swan 82 C2
Rosewood Ave. P Tal 113 F3
Rosewood Cl. B-coch 62 B2
Rosewood Cl. Card 173 D2
Ross Cl. Ponty 149 D3
Rosser St. Fern 96 A3
Rosser St. Neath 87 F4
Rosser St. Ponty 149 D4
Rosser Terr. B-coch 63 E2
Rosser's Field. T Mum 137 E2
Rosset Cl. Card 190 C3
Rossetti Cl. Card 187 F2
Rotherslade Rd. T Mum 136 C2
Round Wood. Card 189 F3
Round Wood Cl. Card 189 F2
Roundel Cl. Card 172 C2
Rover Way. Card 205 F2
Row The. Gar P 154 B2
Row The. Lough 57 D4
Rowan Ave. Swan 109 D4
Rowan Cl. Lough 57 D2
Rowan Cl. M Ash 72 C2
Rowan Cl. Nel 99 F2
Rowan Cl. Pen 217 D1
Rowan Cl. Penco 181 E4
Rowan Cl. Ponty 149 D3
Rowan Cl. Swan 108 B3
Rowan Ct. Aberd 49 E1
Rowan Ct. Card 204 A4
Rowan Ct. Ll'hry 183 D3
Rowan Dr. Porthc 193 F4
Rowan Gr. Ll'maes 221 D4
Rowan House. Pen 216 C3
Rowan Rise. C-c-y-c 32 A3
Rowan Way. Card 173 D2
Rowan Way. Mer T 32 B2
Rowan's La. Brynco 164 A3
Rowans The. Bridg 180 B2
Rowena Ct. Card 203 E4
Rowland Terr. Og Va 119 F3
Rowlands Cotts. Bryn 115 F3
Rowley Terr. Fern 70 A1
Rowling St. Tonypa 122 A2
Roxburgh Garden Ct. Pen 217 D2
Roxby Ct. Card 205 D2
Royal Arc. Card 205 D3
Royal Bldgs. Pen 217 D2
Royal Cl. Pen 217 D3
Royal Cotts. Fern 95 D4
Royal Cres. Mer T 32 C2
Royal Oak. Bedw 154 A3
Royal Oak Cl. Bedw 154 A3
Royal Oak Rd. Swan 109 D2
Royal Stuart La. Card 205 D1
Royal Terr. Trea 122 A3
Royce Cl. Gell 100 C4
Royde Cl. Card 202 C2
Ruby St. Card 205 E3
Rudry Cl. Caer 152 C3
Rudry Rd. Caer 152 B3
Rudry Rd. Card 173 E3
Rudry Rd. Gar P 173 E3
Rudry St. Card 204 C2
Rudry St. Pen 216 C2
Rufus Lewis Ave. Lough 57 D2
Rugby Ave. Neath 87 F4
Rugby Rd. Reso 44 A1
Ruggles Terr. Swan 59 E1
Runcorn Cl. Barry 225 E4
Runcorn Cl. Card 190 B4
Runnymede. Swan 109 F4
Runway Rd. Card 206 A4
Ruperra Ct. Ponty 124 B1
Ruperra St. Ll'tris 168 B2
Ruperra St. N Tre 54 C2
Rural Way. Swan 109 D4
Rushbrook Cl. Card 187 F2
Rushfield Gdns. Bridg 180 A3
Rushmere Rd. Pontll 101 F2
Rushwind Cl. T Mum 136 C3
Rushwind Mews. T Mum 136 C3
Ruskin Ave. P Tal 138 C4
Ruskin Cl. Card 190 A4
Ruskin St. Neath 87 D2
Russell Cl. Rhiwd 155 F2
Russell St. Card 205 D4
Russell St. Mer T 33 D2
Russell St. N Tre 55 D1
Russell St. Swan 110 A3
Russet Cl. P Tal 113 D2
Rustic Cl. Swan 109 D4
Rusticana Ct. Card 188 B3
Ruth St. Bar 75 F2
Ruthin Ct. Bridg 180 C2
Ruthin Gdns. Card 205 D4
Ruthin Way. Ch Vil 150 A1
Rutland St. Card 204 C2
Ryan's Cl. B-coch 87 E4
Ryder St. Card 204 C3

Sable Ave. P Tal 113 D1
Sable Cl. Card 173 D2
Sable Cl. P Tal 113 D1
Sachville Ave. Card 188 C2
Saddler St. Swan 84 B2
Saffron Dr. Card 191 D4
St Aarons Dr. Ll'ha 166 C2
St Agatha Rd. Card 188 C2
St Agnes Rd. Card 188 B2
St Aidan Cres. Card 188 B2
St Aidan's Rise. Barry 225 E3
St Aiden Dr. Swan 108 B3
St Alban Ave. Card 188 B2
St Alban's Rd. Swan 109 F3
St Alban's Rd. Trehe 68 B2
St Alban's Terr. Marg 139 E3
St Alban's Terr. Trehe 68 C2
St Ambrose Cl. D pow 216 A1
St Ambrose Rd. Card 188 C2
St Andrew's Cl. Ponty 149 D3
St Andrew's Cl. T Mum 108 C1
St Andrew's Cres. Card 205 D3
St Andrew's La. Card 205 D3
St Andrew's Pl. Card 205 D3
St Andrew's Rd. Bridg 179 F4
St Andrew's Rd. D Pow 215 E2
St Andrew's Rd. Wen 215 E2
St Andrews Cl. Ch Vil 169 E3
St Andrews Cl. T Mum 108 C1
St Andrews Ct. Tonypa 121 F3
St Andrews Dr. Pontll 101 F3
St Angela Rd. Card 188 C2
St Ann St. Bar 75 F1
St Ann's Ct. Barry 225 D4
St Anne's Ave. Pen 216 C1
St Anne's Cl. T Mum 137 D2
St Anne's Cres. Bar 76 A1
St Anne's Cres. Porthc 193 E4
St Anne's Dr. Tonna 63 E1
St Anne's Gdns. Maesy 101 D1
St Anne's Terr. Tonna 63 E1
St Annes Ct. Ll'tris 183 F3
St Annes Dr. Ch Vil 169 E3
St Annes Gdns. Aber 151 D4
St Annes Rd. Peng 101 E4
St Anthony Rd. Card 188 C2
St Arvans Cres. Card 190 C4
St Asaph Cl. Card 188 C3
St Asaph Dr. P Tal 113 E1
St Asaph's Way. Caer 152 A1
St Asaphs Ct. P Tal 113 E1
St Athan Rd. Ll'thyd 211 D3
St Athan's Ct. Caer 151 F1
St Augustine Rd. Card 188 C2
St Augustine's Cres. Pen 217 D3
St Augustine's Pl. Pen 217 D3
St Augustine's Rd. Pen 217 D3
St Baruch Cl. D pow 216 A1
St Benedict Cres. Card 188 C2
St Bleddian Cl. Cowb 198 B1
St Bride's Cl. Porth 176 C1
St Bride's Rd. Card 202 C4
St Bride's Rd. Ewen 195 F4
St Bride's Rd. P-s-Ely 202 B4
St Bride's Rd. Tondu 163 E2
St Bride's Way. Barry 225 D4
St Brides Cl. Pontar 36 B2
St Brides Ct. Card 203 E2
St Brides Pl. P-s-Ely 202 A4
St Brides Rd. Wick 208 B3
St Brigid Rd. Card 188 C3
St Brioc Rd. Card 188 C3
St Cadoc Rd. Card 188 C3
St Cadoc's Ave. D pow 216 A1
St Cadoc's Rise. Barry 225 E4
St Catherine's Cl. Bedw 152 B3
St Catherine's Ct. Cross 129 D2
St Catherine's Rd. P Tal 113 F3
St Catherines Mews. Card 204 B4
St Cattwg's Ave. Gell 100 B3
St Cattwg Wlk. T Mum 109 D1
St Cenydd Cl. Caer 151 F2
St Cenydd Rd. Caer 151 F2
St Cenydd Rd. Card 188 C3
St Cenydd Rd. Swan 83 F3
St Christopher Dr. Swan 108 B3
St Christopher's Dr. Caer 151 F1
St Christopher's Rd. Bridg 179 F4
St Christopher's Rd. Porthc 193 E4
St Christophers Ct. Bridg 180 A4
St Clares. Rhy 34 C1
St Clears Cl. Caer 152 A1
St Clears Pl. Swan 84 A4
St Curig's Cl. Rhoose 223 D1
St Cynwyd's Ave. Maest 117 D1
St Cyres Cl. Pen 216 C2
St Cyres Rd. Pen 216 C2
St David Ave. D pow 216 A2
St David Dr. Swan 108 B4
St David St. Pontcr 118 C2
St David St. Yst 95 D2
St David's Ave. Ll' Maj 220 A3
St David's Ave. Oak 101 F4
St David's Cl. Bridg 179 F4
St David's Cl. Gell 100 C4
St David's Cl. Hen 36 A2
St David's Cl. Lough 56 C1
St David's Cl. Mer T 31 F1
St David's Cl. Ponty 170 C4
St David's Cl. Yst 94 C2
St David's Cres. Pen 216 B2
St David's Ct. Card 204 C3
St David's Ct. Marsh 175 F1
St David's Dr. Bedw 153 E3
St David's Market. Card 205 D3
St David's Pl. Ll'tris 168 C2
St David's Pl. Maest 117 D1
St David's Pl. Swan 110 B3
St David's Rd. Bridg 179 E3
St David's Rd. Card 188 A2
St David's Rd. Maesy 101 D1
St David's Rd. P Tal 138 C4
St David's Rd. Peng 101 D4
St David's Rd. Ystal 23 E3
St David's Sq. Swan 110 B3
St David's St. Neath 87 F4
St David's Way. Caer 151 F1
St David's Way. Card 205 D3
St David's Way. Porthc 193 D4
St Davids Cl. Bridg 180 B3
St Davids Cl. Penga 58 A1
St Davids Cl. Porth 147 E4
St Davids Cl. Rhy 34 C2
St Davids Cres. Card 203 E3
St Davids House. Card 205 D3
St Davids Rd. G-C-G 5 E3
St Davids Rd. Ll'tris 184 B3
St Davids Rd. Swan 85 D4
St Davids Rd. Ystal 23 E3
St Deinols Cl. Peng 101 D3
St Denis Rd. Card 188 C3
St Dogmael's Ave. Card 188 C4
St Donat's Ave. Swan 109 D4
St Donat's Cl. Mer T 31 F1
St Donat's Ct. Caer 151 F1
St Donats Cl. D pow 216 B2
St Donats Ct. Card 203 E2
St Donats Rd. Card 204 B2
St Dyfrig Cl. D pow 216 A1
St Dyfrig Rd. Pen 216 C1
St Edeyrn's Rd. Card 189 E3
St Edeyrns Cl. Card 189 E3
St Edeyrns House. Card 189 E3
St Edwen Gdns. Card 188 C3
St Elmo Ave. Swan 110 C4
St Fagan's St. Card 204 C1
St Fagans Cl. Card 203 F4
St Fagans Ct. Card 202 C2
St Fagans Dr. Card 203 D4
St Fagans Gr. Mer T 31 F2
St Fagans Rd. Card 203 E4
St Fagans Rise. Card 203 E4
St Fagans St. Caer 152 A1
St Francis Ct. Card 188 A3
St Francis Rd. Bridg 179 F4
St Francis Rd. Card 188 A3
St Garmon Rd. Pen 216 C1
St George's Ave. Bridg 179 F4
St George's Terr. Ll'rh 104 C1
St Georges Ct. Tred 35 F4
St Georges Rd. Card 188 B2
St Germans Mews. Card 205 E3
St Gildas Rd. Card 188 C3
St Govans Pl. Swan 82 B2
St Gowan Ave. Card 188 C3
St Gwladys Ave. Bar 75 F3
St Gwladys Ct. Bar 75 F2
St Gwynnos Cl. D pow 216 A2
St Helen's Ave. Swan 110 A3
St Helen's Cres. Swan 110 A3
St Helen's Ct. Caer 151 F1
St Helen's Rd. Card 188 B2
St Helen's Rd. Swan 110 A3
St Helier Dr. P Tal 113 D2
St Hilary Dr. Swan 108 B4
St Ilan's Way. Caer 152 A1
St Illtyd Cl. D pow 216 A1
St Illtyd Rd. Ch Vil 149 F1
St Illtyd's Cl. P Tal 113 F3
St Illtyd's Cres. Swan 111 D4
St Illtyd's Dr. P Tal 113 F3
St Illtyd's Rd. Bridg 179 E3
St Illtyds Cl. Bridg 180 B3
St Ina Rd. Card 188 C3
St Isan Rd. Card 188 C3
St James Cl. Caer 152 C3
St James Cl. Maesy 101 D1
St James' Cres. Pyle 161 D1
St James Ct. Pen 216 C1
St James Gdns. Swan 110 A4
St James Mews. Card 204 B4
St James Pk. Bridg 180 B2
St James Way. Tred 35 F3
St James Way. Tred 35 F4
St James's Cres. Swan 110 A3
St John St. Aberd 49 F2
St John St. Card 205 D3
St John St. Og Va 144 C4
St John's Cl. Cowb 198 C1
St John's Cl. Maest 117 E1
St John's Cres. Card 188 A3
St John's Cres. Card 204 B3
St John's Cres. Rhiwd 155 F3
St John's Ct. Card 204 B3
St John's Dr. Penco 181 E4
St John's Dr. Porthc 193 E4
St John's Gr. Mer T 32 C2
St John's La. Nel 99 E2
St John's Pl. Card 188 A3
St John's Pl. Rhoose 222 C1
St John's Rd. Bridg 179 E3
St John's Rd. Cly 60 C4
St John's Rd. Swan 84 A2
St John's Rd. Tony 147 E3
St John's St. Porth 122 C1
St John's Terr. N Abb 87 D4
St John's View. St Ath 221 E3
St Johns Dr. Pontll 101 F3
St Johns Dr. Yst 94 C2
St Joseph's Terr. Abera 71 D2
St Judes Cl. Swan 84 B4
St Julian Cl. Barry 225 E4
St Julian's Ct. Caer 151 F1
St Julius Cres. Ll'ha 166 C2
St Katherines Ct. Swan 85 E3
St Kitts Pl. P Tal 113 E1
St Lawrence Ct. Swan 84 A4
St Leger Cres. Swan 110 C4
St Leonard's Rd. Bridg 179 E2
St Luke's Ave. Pen 216 C1
St Luke's Ave. Ponty 150 A2
St Luke's Cl. Ll'ha 166 C2
St Luke's Cl. Mer T 33 D3
St Luke's Rd. Porth 123 D2
St Lukes Ct. Swan 85 E3
St Lythan Cl. D pow 216 A1
St Lythan Ct. Card 203 E4
St Maddock's Cl. Bridg 180 B3
St Malo Rd. Card 188 C3
St Margaret Cross. Mer T 32 B1
St Margaret's Ave. Peng 101 E4
St Margaret's Ave. Skew 112 B4
St Margaret's Cl. Card 188 A3
St Margaret's Cres. Card 205 E4
St Margaret's Pk. Card 203 F3
St Margaret's Pl. Card 188 A3
St Margaret's Rd. Caer 151 F1
St Margaret's Rd. Card 188 A3
St Margarets Cl. Caer 152 C3
St Marie St. Bridg 179 F2
St Mark's Ave. Card 188 C2
St Mark's Cl. Ll'ha 166 C2
St Mark's Gdns. Card 188 C2
St Mark's Rd. Pen 216 C1
St Mark's Villas. Ponty 124 A1
St Martin's Cl. Pen 216 C1
St Martin's Cres. Caer 152 A1
St Martin's Rd. Caer 152 A1
St Martins Cres. Card 188 C4
St Mary Pl. P Tal 114 A1
St Mary St. Bar 76 A1
St Mary St. Bed 99 E4
St Mary St. Card 205 D3
St Mary St. P Tal 114 A1
St Mary St. Pontmi 129 F2
St Mary St. Swan 110 B3
St Mary's Ave. Barry 225 D3
St Mary's Cl. Blae 45 F4
St Mary's Cl. Mer T 32 B2
St Mary's Cl. Neath 87 D1
St Mary's Cl. Trehe 69 D1
St Mary's Cres. Maest 117 E1
St Mary's Ct. Porthc 193 E4
St Mary's Rd. Card 188 A3
St Mary's Rd. Pontll 101 F2
St Mary's Rd. Ponydw 41 D4
St Mary's Sq. Swan 110 B3
St Mary's St. Bedw 152 B3
St Mary's View. Bridg 181 D2
St Mary's Well Bay Rd. Sully 226 C2
St Marys Cl. Card 203 E2
St Mellons Bsns Pk. Card 191 D4
St Mellons Cl. Caer 151 F1
St Mellons Rd. Card 173 F1
St Mellons Rd. Marsh 191 E4
St Michael's Ave. Pontar 36 A2
St Michael's Ave. Ponty 149 E4
St Michael's Cl. Card 171 E1
St Michael's Cl. St Ath 221 E3
St Michael's Rd. Card 204 A4
St Michael's Rd. Maest 117 D2
St Michael's Rd. Porthc 193 E4
St Michael's Way. Bridg 180 B3
St Michaels Cl. M-I-Pit 216 A4
St Nicholas Cl. D pow 216 A1
St Nicholas Cl. Swan 82 C2
St Nicholas Ct. Caer 151 F1

St Nicholas Ct. Card

St Nicholas Ct. Card 189 F4
St Nicholas Ct. Card 203 E2
St Nicholas Rd. Swan 108 C3
St Nicholas Rd. Bridg 179 F4
St Nicholas Sq. Card 110 C3
St Non's Cl. Bridg 180 B3
St Oswald's Rd. Barry 225 E4
St Owains Cres. W St D 199 E4
St Patrick's Dr. Bridg 179 F4
St Paul's Ave. Pen 216 C1
St Paul's Ct. Card 188 A1
St Paul's Rd. P Tal 138 C4
St Paul's Terr. Lough 82 B4
St Peter's Ave. Swan 83 E2
St Peter's Cl. Ll'ha 166 C2
St Peter's Rd. Pen 216 C1
St Peter's Rd. T Mum 136 C2
St Peter's Terr. Swan 83 F1
St Peters Cl. Abera 71 F2
St Peters Dr. Pontll 101 F3
St Pierre Cl. Card 191 D4
St Quentin's Terr. Cowb 198 B1
St Quentins Cl. Swan 198 C1
St Quentins Hill. Cowb 198 B1
St Rhidian Dr. Swan 108 B4
St Rhidian Rd. Swan 83 F3
St Sannan Rd. Pontll 101 E2
St Stephen's Ave. Yst 94 C3
St Stephens Dr. Penco 165 E1
St Tanwg Rd. Card 188 C3
St Teilo Cl. D pow 216 A2
St Teilo St. Pontar 36 B2
St Teilo's Cl. Pontll 101 F3
St Teilo's Ct. Bish 135 F3
St Teilo's Ct. Card 205 E4
St Teilo's Rd. Bridg 179 E3
St Teilo's Way. Caer 151 F1
St Theodore's Way. Brynco 163 F3
St Tudor's View. Peng 101 F3
St Tydfil's Ave. Mer T 32 C1
St Vincent Cres. Swan 110 B3
St Winifred's Rd. Bridg 179 E3
St Winifreds Cl. D pow 216 A1
Salem Cotts. Tred 35 F4
Salem La. Ch Vil 149 F1
Salem Rd. Cwma 114 C3
Salem Rd. Swan 84 B3
Salem Terr. Trea 121 F4
Salisbury Ave. Pen 216 C2
Salisbury Cl. Mer T 31 F1
Salisbury Cl. P-Ey 132 A2
Salisbury Cl. Pen 216 C1
Salisbury Ct. Pen 216 C2
Salisbury Rd. Card 205 D4
Salisbury Rd. Maest 116 C2
Salisbury St. Cross 129 E2
Salisbury Terr. Abercy 98 B1
Salisbury Terr. N Tre 55 D1
Salmon Cl. Card 189 F1
Salmons Wood. Penll 198 A4
Salop Pl. Pen 217 D3
Salop St. Caer 152 A1
Salop St. Pen 217 D2
Saltoun St. Marg 139 F2
Salubrious Pl. Swan 110 B3
Salvia Cl. Card 191 D4
Salway Ave. Peng 76 A1
Sambucus Ave. Ll'Maj 209 E2
Samlet Rd. Swan 85 E4
Samlet Shopping Ctr. Swan 85 E4
Samuel Cres. Swan 84 A2
Samuels Rd. Cwmll 6 B3
Sanatorium Rd. Card 204 A3
Sanctuary Ct. Card 203 D1
Sanctuary The. Card 203 D1
Sand La. Neath 113 E4
Sand St. Mer T 32 B1
Sandbrook Rd. Card 191 D3
Sanderling Cl. Porth 192 B4
Sanderling Dr. Card 190 C4
Sandfields Rd. P Tal 113 E1
Sandfields Rd. Tondu 163 E2
Sandon St. Card 205 D3
Sandown Rd. P Tal 138 C4
Sandpiper Cl. Card 190 C4
Sandpiper Cl. P Tal 113 E1
Sandpiper Rd. Porth 176 B1
Sandringham Cl. Lough 82 A4
Sandringham Rd. Card 189 E1
Sandwick Ct. Card 189 E4
Sandy La. Porthc 193 D4
Sandy La. South 134 C3
Sandy Ridge. P Tal 113 E1
Sandybank Rd. Yst 95 E2
Sandymeers. Porthc 193 D4
Sannan St. Bar 76 A3
Sanquahar St. Card 205 E3
Sansom St. Pontmi 129 F2
Sapele Dr. Card 205 E3
Sapphire St. Card 205 E4
Sarah St. Mer V 73 E3
Sardis Cl. Swan 82 C2
Sardis Rd. Ponty 149 D4
Sardis Rd. Ponty 149 E4
Sarlou Cl. T Mum 137 D2
Sarn Helen. Ystraf 10 C2
Sarn Hill. Brynco 163 F2

Sarn Pl. Pontmi 129 F2
Sarnfan Baglan Rd. P Tal . 113 F2
Saron Cl. Lough 56 C2
Saron St. Ponty 149 F4
Saunders Rd. Card 205 D2
Saunders Way. Swan 109 D3
Saundersfoot Cl. Card 203 E2
Saville Cl. Og Va 119 F2
Sawel Terr. Hen 36 A2
Saxon St. Mer T 32 B1
Scales Houses. Llwy 49 F3
Scarborough Rd. Ponty 124 C1
Scarlet Ave. P Tal 113 D1
School La. Penty 170 C2
School La. Pontdw 40 C3
School La. Ponty 150 A2
School Pl. H-y-Cy 165 E3
School Rd. Bry 6 B4
School Rd. Cry 43 D4
School Rd. Glyn 91 E3
School Rd. Ll'tris 184 C4
School Rd. Maest 117 D1
School Rd. Neath 87 E3
School Rd. Og Va 119 F1
School Rd. Onll 26 A4
School Rd. Pyle 161 E2
School Rd. Skew 86 B1
School Rd. Swan 61 D3
School Rd. Tonna 63 E1
School Rd. Troed 52 B1
School Rd. Ystal 23 D3
School Rd. Ystra 23 E4
School St. Aber 125 F2
School St. Abera 71 F3
School St. Bar 76 A3
School St. Blae 45 E4
School St. Card 205 D2
School St. Cwma 89 D1
School St. Deri 75 D4
School St. Fern 70 A1
School St. Fern 95 F4
School St. G-C-G 5 D4
School St. Ll'bara 151 F4
School St. Ll'tris 168 B2
School St. Ll'tris 184 A4
School St. N Tre 54 B2
School St. N Tre 54 C1
School St. N Tre 55 D1
School St. Peng 101 D3
School St. Porth 122 C1
School St. Porth 122 C2
School St. Rhy 34 C1
School St. Tony 147 E3
School St. Tonypa 122 A1
School St. Trehe 68 A1
School St. Tylor 96 A1
School St. Yst 95 D2
School Terr. Cwma 114 C3
School Terr. Ll'ha 166 C2
School Terr. Pontcr 118 C2
School Terr. Pontcr 118 C3
School Terr. Pyle 176 C4
School Terr. Rhiwd 155 F3
School Terr. Trea 121 F4
School Terr. Tylor 122 B4
Schooner Way. Card 205 E2
Scotch St. Glyn 92 B3
Scott Cl. Bridg 179 E3
Scott Cl. St M Ch 221 E4
Scott Ct. Card 189 D2
Scott Rd. Card 205 D3
Scott St. Trehe 68 C1
Scranton Cl. Porth 122 C1
Scutari Row. Marg 139 E3
Scwd-yr-Afon. B-coch 63 E2
Sea Breeze. P Tal 113 E1
Sea View. Ce Cr 161 F1
Sea View. H-y-Cy 165 D3
Sea View. Pen-cl 80 C2
Sea View Terr. Barry 225 E4
Sea View Terr. P Tal 114 A1
Sea View Terr. Swan 84 B1
Seabank Ct. Porth 192 C4
Seabank. Pen 217 D2
Seabrook Pl. P Tal 138 C4
Seager Dr. Card 216 C4
Seagull Cl. Porth 176 C1
Seal Pit Rd. St Ath 221 F1
Sealands Dr. T Mum 137 E2
Seaton St. Ponty 124 A1
Seaton's Pl. Ponty 124 A1
Seaview Ct. Pen 217 D2
Seaview Dr. St B M 194 B2
Seaview Ind Est. Card 205 F3
Seaview Pl. Ll' Maj 220 A3
Seaview. Swan 85 E1
Seawall Rd. Card 206 A3
Seaward Ave. P Tal 113 E1
Seaward Cl. P Tal 113 E1
Seaway Par. P Tal 113 E1
Sebastopol St. Swan 110 C4
Second Ave. Caer 151 F2
Second Ave. Card 189 F1
Second Ave. Mer T 32 C3
Second Ave. Swan 84 B4
Sedd Goch. Bridg 180 A2
Sedgemoor Rd. Card 190 B4
Selina Rd. Abercy 98 B3

Senghennydd Pl. Card 205 D4
Senghennydd St. Treo 94 B3
Senny Pl. Swan 60 A3
Sepia Cl. P Tal 113 D1
Serecold Ave. Skew 86 B3
Sevenoaks Rd. Card 203 D3
Sevenoaks St. Card 204 C1
Seventeenth Ave. Rhig 28 B1
Seventh Ave. Mer T 32 C3
Seventh Ave. Swan 59 E1
Severn Cres. P Tal 113 E1
Severn Gr. Card 204 B4
Severn Rd. Card 204 B3
Severn Rd. Ch Vil 150 B1
Severn Rd. Pontll 101 E2
Severn Rd. Porth 192 C4
Severn Rd. Swan 84 B4
Seward St. Mer T 32 C2
Seymour Ave. Ll'ha 167 D2
Seymour St. Abera 50 A1
Seymour St. Card 205 F3
Seymour St. M Ash 72 B2
Seys Cl. Cowb 198 B1
Seys Ct. Ll' Maj 220 A4
Shackleton Cl. St Ath 221 E4
Shady Rd. Yst 95 D1
Shaftesbury Cl. Card 172 C2
Shakespeare Ave. Bridg 179 E3
Shakespeare Ave. Pen 216 C2
Shakespeare Cl. Card 205 D4
Shakespeare Dr. Ll' Maj 220 A3
Shakespeare Rise. Ponty .. 150 A3
Shakespeare St. Card 205 E4
Shamrock Rd. Card 203 E4
Shannon Cl. Pontll 101 E2
Sharpe Cl. Card 189 F1
Sharpsburgh Pl. Swan 84 B2
Shaw Cl. Card 190 A4
Shaw St. Gow 82 A3
Shears Rd. Card 203 F4
Shearwater Cl. Porth 192 B4
Shearwater Cl. Sully 227 D4
Shearwater Cl. T Mum 136 C4
Sheen Ct. Gell 100 C1
Sheerwater Cl. Card 190 C4
Shelburn Cl. Card 204 C2
Shelley Cl. Bar 76 A2
Shelley Cres. Pen 216 C2
Shelley Ct. Bedw 153 E4
Shelley Dr. Bridg 179 E3
Shelley Wlk. Ponty 150 A3
Shelone Rd. Neath 87 D1
Shelone Terr. Neath 87 E2
Shepherd's Rd. Swan 84 C2
Shepherds Terr. Lough 57 D2
Sheppard St. Ponty 124 A1
Sherborne Ave. Card 189 E4
Sherborne Wlk. T Mum 109 D1
Sheridan Cl. Card 190 A4
Sherringham Dr. T Mum 136 C3
Sherwood Ct. Card 187 E1
Sherwood St. Trea 95 F1
Shingrig Rd. Nel 99 F2
Ship La. Card 205 E1
Shirdale Cl. Maesy 101 D1
Shire Ct. Tre 99 E3
Shirley Cl. Barry 225 E4
Shirley Dr. Mer T 31 F1
Shirley Rd. Card 189 D1
Shoemakers' Row. Maest . 117 D2
Shop Houses. Llwy 49 F3
Shop Row. Tred 35 F3
Short St. Cly 39 E1
Short St. Neath 87 E2
Short St. Swan 110 B4
Shrewsbury Ave. Porth 147 E4
Siding Terr. Skew 86 B4
Siemens Cl. Swan 85 D3
Siloam Hill. Bedw 153 F4
Siloh Cres. Swan 84 B2
Siloh Rd. Swan 84 B2
Silver Ave. P Tal 113 D1
Silver Birch Cl. Card 188 A3
Silver Cl. P Tal 113 D2
Silver Cl. T Mum 136 C4
Silver St. Card 205 E3
Silver St. Cross 129 E3
Silverhill Cl. Ponty 124 C2
Silverstone Cl. Card 190 B4
Silverton Dr. Ll'tris 168 C1
Simon St. Tonypa 122 A1
Simpson's Way. Pyle 161 D1
Sinclair Dr. Card 189 F1
Singleton Rd. Card 205 F3
Singleton St. Swan 110 B3
Sinnatts The. B-coch 87 E4
Sion Pl. Aberd 71 F4
Sion St. Ponty 124 B1
Sion Terr. Aberd 71 F4
Sir Alfred Owen Way. Caer 152 A3
Sir Ivor Pl. D pow 216 B1
Sir Ivor's Rd. Pontll 101 E2
Sir Stafford Cl. Caer 152 B3
Sirhowy Hill Industrial
  Estate. Tred 35 F4
Sitwell Way. P Tal 138 C4
Six Bells Est. Mer T 32 A1
Sixteenth Ave. Rhig 28 B1

Sixth Ave. Mer T 32 C3
Sixth Ave. Swan 59 E1
Skaithmuir Rd. Card 205 F4
Skelmuir Rd. Card 205 F4
Skenfrith Cl. Peng 76 C1
Sker Ct. Porth 176 C1
Sker Wlk. Porth 176 C1
Sketty Ave. Swan 109 E4
Sketty La. Swan 109 E2
Sketty Park Cl. Swan 109 E3
Sketty Park Dr. Swan 109 D3
Sketty Park Rd. Swan 109 E3
Sketty Rd. Swan 109 F3
Skinner St. Swan 84 B1
Skokholm Cl. Porth 176 C1
Skomer Cl. Porth 176 B1
Skomer Pl. Swan 83 E4
Skomer Rd. Barry 225 D4
Slade Cl. Cowb 198 C1
Slade Cl. Sully 226 A3
Slade Gdns. T Mum 136 C3
Slade Rd. T Mum 136 C3
Slate St. Swan 84 C4
Slocombe Trust Cotts.
  Card 204 A4
Slon La. St B M 194 B1
Sloper Rd. Card 204 B2
Smallwood Rd. P Tal 113 F3
Smeaton Cl. Rhoose 222 C1
Smeaton St. Card 204 C3
Smith Row. St Nic 201 F1
Smith Row. Tony 122 A1
Smith St. Maest 116 C2
Smith St. Yst 95 D1
Smith's Ave. Rhig 28 A1
Smith's Rd. Swan 61 D1
Smithfield Rd. Pontdw 40 C3
Smithies Ave. Sully 226 A2
Smyrna Cotts. Marg 139 E3
Smyrna St. Swan 84 C3
Sneyd St. Card 204 B4
Snipe St. Card 205 E4
Snow Terr. Ystra 23 F3
Snowden Ct. Caer 152 B2
Snowden Rd. Card 203 D3
Snowdon Dr. Swan 83 E2
Soar Cl. Lough 56 C1
Soar Terr. Swan 60 A1
Soberton Ave. Card 188 C1
Solent Cl. Pontll 101 E2
Solent Rd. Barry 225 E4
Solva Ave. Card 189 D4
Solva Rd. Swan 84 B4
Somerset Cl. C-c-y-c 32 A3
Somerset Ct. Card 190 B4
Somerset La. C-c-y-c 32 A3
Somerset Pl. Cwma 114 C2
Somerset Pl. Mer T 32 C1
Somerset St. Swan 110 C3
Somerset Rd. T Mum 137 D2
Somerset St. Card 204 C2
Somerset St. Marg 139 E3
Somerset View. St B M 194 B1
Somerset View. Sully 226 A2
Somerville Ct. Swan 109 F4
Sophia Cl. Card 204 C3
Sophia's Wlk. Card 204 C3
South Ave. Aberd 49 F1
South Ave. Glyn 91 E2
South Cl. Bish 136 A3
South Cl. Penco 181 E4
South Clive St. Card 204 C1
South Cornelly Ind Est.
  Pyle 177 D3
South Cross Way. P Tal 113 E1
South Dr. Ll'tris 168 C2
South Loudoun Pl. Card 205 E3
South Luton Pl. Card 205 E3
South Morgan Pl. Card 204 C3
South Pandy Rd. Caer 152 A3
South Par. Maest 117 D2
South Park Rd. Card 205 F3
South Pl. Bridg 179 F2
South Pl. Porth 192 C4
South Prospect. Swan 110 B4
South Rd. Bridg 180 B1
South Rd. Gell 100 B3
South Rd. St Ath 221 F1
South Rd. Sully 226 A3
South Rise. Card 173 D1
South St. Abercy 98 B1
South St. Bar 75 D4
South St. Bridg 179 F2
South St. Marg 139 E4
South St. Mer T 33 D2
South St. Ponty 124 B1
South St. Tylor 122 C4
South Terr. C-c-y-c 32 A2
South Terr. St B M 195 D1
South View Dr. Card 190 B3
South View. Ll'ha 166 C1
South View. Mer V 73 E1
South View. Penco 181 E4
South View. Penga 57 E1
South View. Pyle 161 E1
South View Rd. Peng 101 D3
South View. Rhoose 223 D1
South View. T We 171 D2

Stacey Rd. Card

South View. Troed 52 B1
Southall Ave. Skew 86 C3
Southall St. Ll'ha 166 B2
Southcourt Rd. Card 189 E1
Southcross Rd. P Tal 113 E1
Southdown Rd. P Tal 113 E1
Southdown View. P Tal 113 E2
Southend Terr. Rhy 53 F4
Southend. Tred 35 F2
Southern St. Caer 152 A1
Southern Way. Card 205 F4
Southerndown Ave. T Mum 108 C1
Southerndown Rd. St B M . 195 E1
Southey St. Card 205 E4
Southgate Ave. Ll'tris 168 C2
Southgate Rd. South 135 D2
Southgate St. Neath 87 F3
Southlands Dr. T Mum 136 C3
Southminster Rd. Card 205 F4
Southra. D pow 216 A1
Southville Rd. P Tal 113 E1
Southward La. T Mum 136 C2
Spelter Site. Maest 117 D4
Spencer Dr. Pen 216 B4
Spencer La. Ponty 150 A2
Spencer Pl. Ponty 150 A2
Spencer St. Abera 71 D2
Spencer St. Card 189 D1
Spencer St. Swan 84 B2
Spencer Terr. Ystra 23 E4
Spencer's Row. Card 188 A1
Spinney Cl. Card 203 E3
Spinney The. Bridg 180 B2
Spinney The. Card 173 D1
Spinney The. Pontll 101 E2
Spinney The. Swan 109 D3
Spion Kop. Og Va 119 F1
Spionkop Rd. Swan 60 B3
Spires Wlk. Barry 225 D4
Spitzkop. Ll' maj 219 F3
Splott Ind Est. Card 205 F3
Splott Rd. Card 205 F3
Spoonbill Cl. Porth 176 C1
Spring Gardens Pl. Card 205 F4
Spring Gardens Terr.
  Card 205 F4
Spring Gdns. Penga 57 E1
Spring Gdns. Skew 86 C4
Spring Gr. Card 172 C1
Spring Meadow Rd. Card .. 190 B1
Spring St. Barry 225 E3
Spring St. Mer T 33 D3
Spring Terr. Swan 110 A3
Springbourne Cl. Gow 82 B2
Springfield Ave. Porth 192 B4
Springfield Ave. U Kill 108 A3
Springfield Cl. Aberd 71 F4
Springfield Cl. Gow 82 A3
Springfield Cl. Rhiwd 155 E2
Springfield Cl. Wen 215 D3
Springfield Ct. Ch Vil 149 F1
Springfield Dr. Abercy 98 C2
Springfield Gdns. Card 187 D4
Springfield La. Bridg 180 B2
Springfield La. Rhiwd 155 E2
Springfield. Maesy 101 D1
Springfield Pl. Card 204 B3
Springfield Rd. Fern 70 A1
Springfield Rd. Pontmi 155 D4
Springfield Rd. Rhiwd 155 E2
Springfield Rd. Skew 86 C4
Springfield Rd. Tony 147 E3
Springfield Rise. Barry 225 D4
Springfield St. Swan 59 F1
Springfield Terr. Mark 55 E1
Springfield Terr. Neath 87 F3
Springfield Terr. Nel 99 F2
Springfield Terr. P Tal 114 A1
Springfield Terr. Ponty 149 F3
Springfield. Tylor 122 C4
Springfields. Marsh 175 E1
Springhurst Cl. Card 187 F4
Springwood. Card 189 E3
Spruce Cl. Card 205 E3
Spruce Tree Gr. Mer T 32 B2
Square The. Aber 150 C4
Square The. Bedw 152 C3
Square The. Bridg 178 C3
Square The. Bridg 179 F3
Square The. Brynco 164 A3
Square The. Cry 43 D3
Square The. D pow 216 A2
Square The. Gall 101 D4
Square The. Ll'ha 167 D2
Square The. Ll'tris 168 C4
Square The. Nel 99 F2
Square The. N Tre 54 B2
Square The. Penco 181 E4
Square The. Porth 192 C3
Square The. Tony 147 D2
Square The. Tre 99 D4
Squire Cl. Swan 110 B3
Squire Dr. Brynco 163 F3
Squire St. Llys 197 F1
Squires Row. Trea 122 A3
Stable La. Tred 35 F3
Stables Ct. Mer T 33 D2
Stacey Rd. Card 205 E4

Stacey Rd. D pow 216 A2
Stadium Cl. Card 204 C1
Stadwen Rd. Swan 85 F4
Stafford Comm. Lough 82 B4
Stafford Rd. Card 204 C2
Stag La. Ll' maj 219 F3
Stag St. Aberd 49 F2
Stag Terr. Reso 43 F1
Staines St. Card 204 A4
Stair St. P Tal 113 F1
Stallcourt Ave. Card 205 E4
Stallcourt Ave. Ll' maj 219 F3
Stallcourt Cl. Card 189 F1
Stallcourt Cl. Cowb 198 B1
Stallcourt Rd. Marg 139 F2
Standard Rd. Bedw 153 D3
Standard Terr. Tylor 122 C4
Standard View. Tylor 122 C4
Standard Villas. Bedw 153 D4
Standert Terr. Se Si 25 D3
Stanley Dr. Caer 151 F3
Stanley Pl. B-coch 62 C1
Stanley Pl. Swan 110 B4
Stanley Rd. Skew 86 C4
Stanley Rd. Yst 95 D1
Stanley Sq. Tylor 96 B1
Stanley St. Aber 125 F1
Stanley St. G-C-G 5 D2
Stanley St. Peng 101 F4
Stanley St. T Mum 137 D3
Stanley St. Ynys 128 A2
Stanley Terr. Swan 110 B4
Stanton Way. Mer T 227 D4
Stanway Pl. Card 203 D3
Stanway Rd. Card 203 E3
Stanwell Cres. Pen 217 D3
Stanwell Rd. Pen 217 D2
Stapleton Pl. Card 84 C4
Star La. Penty 186 B3
Star St. Card 205 E3
Starbuck St. Gar P 153 D2
Starling Rd. Ll' Maj 220 B3
Station App. Ll'tris 184 A4
Station App. Pen 217 D2
Station App. Tondu 163 E3
Station Bldgs. Pontll 101 F2
Station Hill. Bridg 179 F2
Station Hill. Maest 117 D2
Station Houses. Penty 185 F4
Station Pl. Pontmi 129 F1
Station Rd. Abercy 98 C1
Station Rd. B-coch 63 E2
Station Rd. Bar 76 A3
Station Rd. Bry 5 E4
Station Rd. C-c-y-c 32 A2
Station Rd. Card 187 E3
Station Rd. Card 187 F2
Station Rd. Card 188 C4
Station Rd. Ch Vil 169 F4
Station Rd. Coel 9 D3
Station Rd. Coel 10 A2
Station Rd. Cry 43 D3
Station Rd. D pow 216 A2
Station Rd E. Wen 215 D4
Station Rd. Fern 70 A1
Station Rd. Fern 96 A4
Station Rd. Gall 101 D4
Station Rd. Gell 100 C1
Station Rd. Glan 4 A4
Station Rd. Glyn 91 E3
Station Rd. Glyn 92 B3
Station Rd. Gow 82 B3
Station Rd. Hen 36 A3
Station Rd. Hir 48 B4
Station Rd. Ll' maj 219 F3
Station Rd. Ll'bra 126 C1
Station Rd. Ll'el 56 A2
Station Rd. Ll'ge 56 B4
Station Rd. Lough 57 E3
Station Rd. Lough 81 E4
Station Rd. Maest 142 C3
Station Rd. Marg 139 D4
Station Rd. Mer T 33 D3
Station Rd. N Tre 55 D1
Station Rd. Neath 87 E2
Station Rd. Og Va 119 F4
Station Rd. Pen 217 D2
Station Rd. Pen-cl 80 B1
Station Rd. Pen-cl 80 C2
Station Rd. Pontmi 129 F1
Station Rd. Pyle 161 E2
Station Rd. Rhoose 223 D1
Station Rd. Rhy 54 B4
Station Rd. Se Si 25 D3
Station Rd. Skew 86 C4
Station Rd. Swan 61 D3
Station Rd. Swan 83 F2
Station Rd. Swan 84 B2
Station Rd. Swan 85 F4
Station Rd. Ton 89 D1
Station Rd. Tony 147 D3
Station Rd. Trea 122 A3
Station Rd. Treo 94 B3
Station Rd. Tylor 96 B1
Station Rd W. Wen 215 D3
Station Row. N Tre 54 C2
Station Row. Pontcr 143 F4

Station St. Abera 50 A1
Station St. Barry 225 D2
Station St. Bedw 154 A4
Station St. Maest 117 D2
Station St. Pontcr 118 C3
Station St. Porth 122 C2
Station St. Rhy 34 C1
Station St. Tonypa 121 F2
Station St. Trehe 68 C1
Station St. Tylor 122 C3
Station Terr. Aber 125 F1
Station Terr. Abera 71 D3
Station Terr. Bed 74 A4
Station Terr. Bryn 115 F2
Station Terr. Caer 151 F2
Station Terr. Caer 152 A1
Station Terr. Card 203 F3
Station Terr. Card 205 D3
Station Terr. Ch Vil 169 E4
Station Terr. Deri 53 E4
Station Terr. Ll'hry 183 E3
Station Terr. Ll'tris 184 A4
Station Terr. M Ash 97 F4
Station Terr. Maest 117 D4
Station Terr. Mer T 33 E3
Station Terr. Mer V 73 E2
Station Terr. Nel 99 F2
Station Terr. P Tal 138 C4
Station Terr. P-s-Ely 201 E3
Station Terr. Pen 217 D2
Station Terr. Pen-cl 80 C2
Station Terr. Rhoose 222 A1
Station Terr. Trea 121 F4
Station Terr. Trehe 68 C1
Station Yd. Bedw 152 B4
Steep St. Pen 217 D3
Steepholm Cl. Porth 176 C1
Stella Cl. Card 172 C2
Stembridge Ave. Swan 83 F3
Stenhousemuir Pl. Card .. 205 F4
Stephen's Terr. Abercy 98 C2
Stephenson Ct. Card 205 E4
Stephenson Rd. Swan 108 C3
Stephenson St. Card 204 C3
Stepney Rd. Glan 4 C4
Stepney Rd. Swan 82 C2
Stepney St. Swan 83 E1
Stepney St. Swan 84 A1
Sterry Rd. Gow 82 A3
Stewart Rd. Rhoose 223 D1
Stirling Rd. Card 203 D2
Stockland St. Caer 152 A1
Stockland St. Card 204 C2
Stockton Way. Tred 35 E4
Stocktonville. Tred 35 E4
Stonechat Cl. Card 191 D3
Stonechat Cl. Porth 176 B1
Stoneleigh Ct. Card 204 B4
Stonewell Ct. Card 189 E1
Stony La. Ewen 196 A3
Stormy La. Pyle 176 C4
Storrar Pl. Card 206 A4
Storrar Rd. Card 206 A4
Stow Hill. Ponty 149 E4
Stradling Cl. Brynco 163 F2
Stradling Cl. Cowb 198 B1
Stradling Cl. Sully 226 A3
Stradling Pl. Ll' Maj 220 A3
Stradmore Cl. T We 170 C3
Strand. Fern 95 F3
Strand Row. Swan 110 B4
Strand St. M Ash 72 C1
Strand. Swan 110 B4
Strand The. Ll' maj 219 F3
Strand The. Pontcr 118 C4
Stratford Dr. Porth 192 C4
Stratford Gn. Barry 225 E4
Strathnairn St. Card 205 D4
Strathy Rd. Card 191 D4
Stratton Way. B-coch 87 E4
Strauss Rd. P Tal 113 D1
Strawberry Pl. Swan 59 F1
Stream St. M Ash 72 B1
Street No 17. P Tal 113 D2
Street No 19. P Tal 113 D3
Street No 21. P Tal 113 D3
Stuart Cl. Card 216 B4
Stuart Cl. P Tal 113 D2
Stuart St. Abera 50 A1
Stuart St. Card 205 D1
Stuart St. Ll'tris 184 A4
Stuart St. Mer T 32 B1
Stuart St. Rhy 34 C1
Stuart St. Trehe 68 C1
Stuart St. Treo 94 B4
Stuart Terr. Ll'tris 168 A1
Sturmi Way. Pyle 161 E1
Sturminster Rd. Card 205 F4
Subway Rd. Barry 225 D2
Sudcroft St. Card 204 B2
Suffolk Cl. Porth 192 C4
Suffolk Pl. Og Va 119 F1
Suffolk Pl. Porth 192 C4
Suffolk St. Bridg 179 F2
Sullivan Cl. Card 190 B4
Sullivan Cl. Pen 216 C1
Sully Moor Rd. Barry 225 F3
Sully Moors Rd. Sully 225 F3
Sully Pl. Pen 217 D2

Sully Rd. D Pow 226 B4
Sully Rd. Pen 216 B2
Sully Rd. Sully 226 B4
Sully Terr. Pen 217 D1
Sully View. D Pow 225 F4
Summer Pl. Swan 85 F4
Summerau Ct. Card 204 B4
Summercliffe Chalet Pk.
  T Mum 136 B2
Summerfield Ave. Card .. 188 C1
Summerfield Ct. Card 188 A2
Summerfield Ct. Card 188 B3
Summerfield Ct. Trea 122 A3
Summerfield Dr. Ll'tris 168 C1
Summerfield Dr. Porth 176 C1
Summerfield Hall La.
  Maesy 101 D2
Summerfield Hall La. Peng 101 D2
Summerfield La. Bedw 153 D3
Summerfield Pl. Card 188 B3
Summerfield Pl. Neath 87 F4
Summerfield Terr. Mer T .. 32 C2
Summerfield Terr. Peng 101 D3
Summerhill Cl. Card 191 D4
Summerland Cl. Pen 216 B3
Summerland Cres. Pen 216 B3
Summerland La. T Mum .. 136 C3
Summerland Pk. U Kill 108 A3
Summerwood Cl. Card 203 D4
Sumner Cl. Card 187 F1
Sun St. Card 205 E3
Sundew Cl. Card 187 E1
Sundew Cl. Pen 216 C3
Sunningdale Ave. T Mum 108 C1
Sunningdale. Caer 151 F1
Sunningdale Cl. Card 189 D2
Sunningdale Dr. Lough 57 D2
Sunningdale Rd. P Tal 113 F3
Sunny Bank. Aber 151 D4
Sunny Bank. Glyn 66 C2
Sunny Bank. M Ash 97 F4
Sunny Bank. Og Va 119 F1
Sunny Bank Terr. Bedw 154 A4
Sunny Bank. Tonypa 121 E4
Sunny Bank. Tonypa 122 A1
Sunny Bank. Tre 99 D3
Sunny Bank. Treo 94 B3
Sunny Bank. Tylor 122 C3
Sunny Cres. Glyn 91 E2
Sunny Hill. Fern 70 A1
Sunny Hill. Rhy 35 D1
Sunny Mount. P Tal 113 E3
Sunny Rd. P Tal 138 B4
Sunny Side. Ponty 124 A1
Sunny View Terr. Mark 76 C2
Sunnybank Cl. T Mum 136 C4
Sunnybank Ct. Bridg 180 B3
Sunnybank. D pow 216 B2
Sunnybank. Mer T 32 B1
Sunnybank. N Tre 54 C2
Sunnybank Pl. P Tal 138 B4
Sunnybank. Pyle 161 D1
Sunnybank Rd. P Tal 138 B4
Sunnybank Rd. Peng 101 F4
Sunnybank. Rhiwd 155 F1
Sunnybank St. Abera 71 D4
Sunnybrook Ct. Card 187 E1
Sunnycroft Cl. D pow 216 A2
Sunnycroft La. D pow 216 A1
Sunnycroft Rd. P Tal 113 F3
Sunnycroft Rise. D pow 216 A1
Sunnyland Cres. Skew 86 C4
Sunnyside. Og Va 144 C4
Sunnyside Rd. Bridg 179 F2
Sunnyside Terr. Glyn 91 E3
Sunnyview. Tred 35 E4
Surrey St. Card 204 A3
Susannah Pl. Tre 99 D3
Sussex St. Card 204 C2
Sutherland Mansions. Card 187 F3
Sutton La. St B M 194 B2
Sutton Rd. Ll'Maj 209 E3
Sutton Rd. Llys 209 E3
Sutton Rd. St B M 194 B2
Sutton Rise. St B M 194 B2
Sw yr Eos. Ystal 23 F4
Swallowhurst Cl. Card 202 C2
Swan Ct. Swan 108 C3
Swan La. Ystal 23 E4
Swan Rd. P Tal 113 E4
Swan St. Ll'tris 168 B2
Swan St. Mer T 51 E4
Swan St. P Tal 113 E4
Swan St. Swan 110 B4
Swanage Cl. Card 191 D4
Swanbridge Gr. Sully 226 B2
Swanbridge Rd. Sully 226 B3
Swanfield. Ystal 23 E4
Swansea Ind Est. Swan .. 83 E2
Swansea Rd. Hir 48 C4
Swansea Rd. Ll'fel 59 D1
Swansea Rd. Lough 82 B4
Swansea Rd. Mer T 31 F2
Swansea Rd. Penga 58 A1
Swansea Rd. Penga 83 E4
Swansea Rd. Pont 58 A2
Swansea Rd. Pontdw 40 B2

Swansea Rd. Swan 82 C2
Swansea St. Card 205 F3
Sway Rd. Swan 60 A1
Sweet Briar La. T Mum 137 D4
Sweetwater Pk. C-c-y-c 32 A4
Sweetwells Cotts. Pontcr .. 143 F4
Sweldon Cl. Card 203 D2
Swift Bsns Ctr The. Card .. 205 E3
Swift Cl. Card 190 A4
Swinton St. Card 205 F3
Switch House Rd. St Ath .. 221 F1
Swn y Mor. St B M 195 D1
Swn yr Afon. Og Va 144 C3
Swn-yr-Mor. P Tal 113 E1
Swn-yr-Nant. Ch Vil 149 F1
Swn-yr-Nant. Cry 43 D4
Swn-yr-Nant. Penco 165 E1
Swn-yr-nant. Ystra 7 D1
Swn-yr-Afon. B-coch 63 E2
Swn-yr-afon. C-c-y-c 32 A2
Swn-yr-Afon. Pyle 161 F2
Swn-yr-Afon. Tony 146 A4
Swn-yr-Afon. Yst 95 D2
Swn-yr-Nant. Gell 100 B4
Sybil St. Cly 60 C4
Sycamore Ave. Ll'maes .. 221 D4
Sycamore Ave. Neath 88 A3
Sycamore Ave. Porthc 193 E4
Sycamore Ave. Pyle 161 E1
Sycamore Ave. Tred 35 E4
Sycamore Cl. Aberd 49 E2
Sycamore Cl. Bridg 179 F4
Sycamore Cl. D pow 216 A1
Sycamore Cl. Pen 216 C3
Sycamore Cl. Swan 109 D4
Sycamore Cres. Barry 225 D4
Sycamore Cres. C-c-y-c .. 32 A3
Sycamore Cres. P Tal 113 E4
Sycamore Cross. Bonv 201 E1
Sycamore Ct. Bar 75 F1
Sycamore Dr. Trea 122 A3
Sycamore House. Card 187 F3
Sycamore Pl. Card 203 E4
Sycamore Rd. Ll'hry 183 D3
Sycamore Rd. Mer T 32 C2
Sycamore Rd. T Mum 137 D4
Sycamore St. Ponty 150 A3
Sycamore St. T We 171 D2
Sycamore Tree Cl. Card .. 187 D3
Sychbant Ave. Maest 117 D1
Sydney Ct. Peng 101 E3
Sydney St. Swan 84 B2
Sylvan Cl. Card 187 F1
Sylvan Way. Swan 109 E4
Sylvia Terr. Swan 84 B2
Symmons St. Swan 84 B1
Syndicate Terr. Ynys 128 A2
Syon Park Cl. Card 191 D4
Syphon St. Porth 122 C2
Syr David's Ave. Card 204 A4
System St. Card 205 E3

Tabernacle Rd. Glan 4 A4
Tabernacle St. Skew 86 C4
Tabernacle St. Swan 84 B2
Tabernacle Terr. Cwma 114 B3
Tabernacle Terr. Pen-cl 80 B2
Tabor Pl. Maest 117 D2
Tabor Rd. Maesy 101 D1
Tabor St. T We 171 D2
Taf Houses.
  C-c-y-c 14 C2
Tafarnaubach Ind Est. Rhy . 16 C1
Tafarnaubach Ind Est. Trefil 16 C1
Taff Bsns Ctr. Ch Vil 150 B2
Taff Cotts. Ll'tris 168 C1
Taff Cotts. Trea 121 F4
Taff Emb. Card 204 C2
Taff Glen View. Mer T 51 F4
Taff St. Card 171 E1
Taff St. Card 205 D3
Taff St. Fern 95 F4
Taff St. Mer V 73 E2
Taff St. Ponty 124 B1
Taff St. Trehe 68 C1
Taff Terr. Abercy 98 B1
Taff Terr. Card 187 E3
Taff Terr. Card 205 D1
Taff Terr. Tonypa 121 E4
Taff Vale Flats. Ponty 149 E4
Taff Vale Prec. Ponty 124 B1
Taff Vale. Tre 98 C3
Taffs Fall Rd. Ch Vil 150 B1
Taffs Mead Emb. Card 204 C2
Taffs Mead Rd. Ch Vil 150 B1
Tafwys Wlk. Caer 152 A2
Tai Bach. Troed 52 A2
Tai Gwalia. Ystra 6 C1
Tai Mawr Rd. Mer T 32 A2
Tai Newydd. Ponty 150 A2
Tai Newydd. Ynybw 97 F1
Tai Penyard. Mer T 32 C1
Tai Siriol. Nel 99 E2
Tai Ysgol Fach. Mer T 50 C1
Tai'r Heol. Ponty 124 C1
Tai'r Twynau. Mer T 33 D4

Tai'r Ynys Fawr. Cwma 89 E1
Tai'r-Heol. Gell 100 B4
Tai-yr-Efail. Mer T 33 D4
Taicanol. Cwma 114 C3
Taillwyd Rd. B-coch 87 D4
Taillwyd Rd. N Abb 62 A1
Tair Croes. Ewen 196 B3
Tair Erw Rd. Card 188 B3
Tair Onen Forest Nursery.
  W st D 200 B1
Tair Waun Pl. Maest 116 C2
Tairfelin. Bridg 179 F4
Talana Terr. Maest 91 D1
Talbot Cl. Ll'tris 168 B2
Talbot Gn. Gow 82 B3
Talbot Rd. Ll'tris 168 B2
Talbot Rd. Marg 139 E4
Talbot Rd. Neath 87 F3
Talbot Rd. Penga 57 F1
Talbot Rd. Pyle 161 E2
Talbot Rd. Skew 86 C3
Talbot Sq. Mer T 32 C2
Talbot St. Card 204 C3
Talbot St. Gow 82 A3
Talbot St. Maest 117 D2
Talbot Terr. Maest 117 D2
Talbot Terr. St M Ch 211 D2
Talcennau Rd. Marg 139 E4
Taldwyn Terr. Troed 52 B1
Talfan Rd. Swan 85 D2
Talgarth St. Maest 117 E1
Taliesin Cl. Penco 165 D1
Taliesin Pl. Lough 56 B1
Taliesyn Rd. Swan 110 A4
Tall Oaks. Penco 165 D1
Talley Rd. Swan 84 A3
Tallis St. Treo 94 A3
Talworth St. Card 205 E4
Talybont Rd. Card 203 E3
Talycopa Ct. Swan 85 F3
Talyfan Cl. Cowb 198 C1
Talyfan. Ll'ha 167 D2
Talygarn Cl. Ll'tris 183 F3
Talygarn Dr. Ll'tris 183 F3
Talygarn St. Card 188 C1
Talywern. Ll'ge 56 A4
Tamar Cl. Pontll 101 E2
Tan y Bryn. Fern 95 D4
Tan y Marian. Fern 95 D4
Tan y Marian Rd. Swan .. 110 A4
Tan-y-Bryn. Aber 126 A1
Tan-y-Bryn. Ll'ha 166 B2
Tan-y-Bryn. Ll'tris 169 D4
Tan-y-Bryn. Penco 165 F1
Tan-y-Bryn. Porth 122 B1
Tan-y-bryn. Rhy 35 D1
Tan-y-bryn St. Abera 50 A1
Tan-y-bryn Terr. Pen-cl 80 C2
Tan-y-Farteg. Ystra 23 F4
Tan-y-Fron. Treo 94 B3
Tan-y-Geli. Glan 4 B4
Tan-y-graig. Ystra 8 B3
Tan-y-Groes Pl. Marg 139 E4
Tan-y-Groes St. Marg 139 E4
Tan-y-Lan Terr. Swan 84 C4
Tan-y-Llan Terr. Rhy 34 C2
Tan-y-Lon. Cly 39 E1
Tan-y-Pych. Trehe 68 B2
Tan-y-Rhiw. Se Si 25 D3
Tanglewood Cl. Card 173 D1
Tangmere Dr. Card 187 E1
Tank Farm Way. Barry 225 E3
Tanyard Pl. Abera 71 D4
Tanybryn. M Ash 97 F4
Tanybryn Pl. Mer T 32 C2
Tanybryn. Pontmi 155 E4
Tanybryn Terr. Tylor 122 B4
Tanycoed Rd. Cly 39 F1
Tanycoed St. M Ash 97 F4
Tanycoed Terr. Abera 71 F2
Tandarren. Ystal 22 B1
Tanygarth. Ystra 8 C3
Tanyrallt Ave. Bridg 179 F4
Tanyrallt. Cly 39 E1
Tanyrallt. Ystra 8 C3
Tanyrhiw Rd. Reso 44 B1
Tanywaun. Ystra 8 B2
Tanywern La. Ystal 23 D4
Tanyyrallt Ave. Bridg 179 F4
Tapley Cl. Card 203 E2
Taplow Terr. Swan 84 C1
Tarran Workshops. Bridg .. 179 F2
Tarren Terr. Cwma 115 D4
Tarrws Cl. Wen 215 D4
Tarwick Dr. Card 190 C3
Tatem Dr. Card 203 E4
Tathan Cres. St Ath 221 E3
Taunton Ave. Card 190 B3
Taunton Cres. Card 190 B3
Tavern-y-Coed. Ch Vil 150 A2
Tavistock Rd. Swan 109 F4
Tavistock Swan 109 E4
Tavistock St. Card 205 D4
Tawe Bsns Village. Swan .. 85 D3
Tawe Pk. Ystra 23 F4
Tawe Pl. Cly 60 C4
Tawe Rd. Swan 85 F4

259

Tawe St. Swan Ty-Coch Rd. Swan

Tawe St. Swan 85 D4
Tawe Terr. Pontdw 40 C2
Tawe View Cres. Swan 59 F1
Tawelfan. Nel 99 F2
Tawelfan. Ystra 7 F2
Tawelfryn. C-c-y-c 31 F3
Taylor Rd. Bridg 179 F4
Taylor St. Pontmi 129 F2
Taylor's Row. Neath 87 E3
Taymuir Rd. Card 205 F4
Teal Cl. Porth 192 C4
Teal St. Card 205 F4
Tealham Dr. Card 191 D4
Teamans Row. Card 187 D4
Teasel Ave. Pen 216 C3
Technology Dr. Mer M 179 F1
Tedder Cl. Card 188 C4
Teg Fan. Skew 86 C3
Tegfan. Caer 151 F2
Tegfan. Card 204 B3
Tegfan Cl. Card 188 C4
Tegfan. Fern 95 E4
Tegfan. Ll'tris 184 A3
Tegfan. Swan 85 F3
Tegid Rd. Swan 84 A1
Teifi Pl. Card 203 E3
Teify Cres. Og Va 119 F4
Teilo Cres. Swan 110 A4
Teilo St. Card 204 B4
Telelkebir Rd. Ponty 124 A1
Telford Cl. Gell 100 C4
Telford St. Card 204 C3
Telor-y-Coed. Ll'bra 127 D3
Telyn Aur. Swan 59 F1
Temperance Ct. Penty 170 A1
Temperance Hill. Pontmi 129 F2
Temperance Pl. Ponty 124 B1
Temple St. Maest 117 D2
Temple St. Swan 110 B4
Templeton Ave. Card 172 C1
Templeton Cl. Card 172 C1
Ten Acre Wood. Marg 140 A1
Tenby Cl. D pow 216 B2
Tenby Ct. Caer 151 E2
Tenby House. Card 188 A2
Tennyson Cl. Ponty 150 A3
Tennyson Dr. Bridg 179 E3
Tennyson Rd. Pen 216 C2
Tennyson Terr. N Tre 54 C1
Tennyson Way. Ll' Maj 220 A3
Tennyson Way. Swan 108 C4
Tensing Cl. Card 172 C1
Tensing Terr. Barry 225 D3
Tenth Ave. Mer T 32 C3
Tenth Ave. Swan 59 E1
Terfyn Ynysawdre. Pontcr 163 F2
Tern Cl. Card 190 C4
Tern Rd. Porth 192 B4
Terrace Rd. Swan 110 A4
Terrace The. Penty 185 F4
Terrace The. Rhy 34 C2
Tewdrig Cl. Ll' maj 219 F3
Tewkesbury Pl. Card 189 D1
Tewkesbury St. Card 189 D1
Thackeray Cres. Card 190 A4
Thames Cl. Pontll 101 E2
Thaw Cl. Rhoose 222 C1
Theobald Rd. Card 204 B3
Theodora St. Card 205 F4
Theodore Rd. Marg 139 E4
Thesiger St. Card 205 D4
Third Ave. Caer 151 F2
Third Ave. Mer T 32 C3
Third Ave. Swan 59 E1
Thirlemere Terr. Aberd 71 F4
Thirteenth Ave. Bridg 28 C1
Thistle Terr. Tonypa 121 F3
Thistle Way. Card 204 F4
Thistleboon Dr. T Mum 137 E2
Thistleboon Gdns. T Mum 137 D2
Thistleboon Rd. T Mum 137 D2
Thomas Cres. Pyle 177 D4
Thomas Davies Ct. Card 190 A2
Thomas Ellis Way. Tred 35 F4
Thomas Fields. Rhy 34 C2
Thomas' Pl. Porth 122 C1
Thomas Row. Swan 110 B4
Thomas St. Aber 151 D4
Thomas St. Abera 50 A2
Thomas St. Bar 76 A1
Thomas St. Bar 76 A3
Thomas St. Bedw 153 D3
Thomas St. Card 204 C2
Thomas St. Fern 70 A1
Thomas St. Ll'bra 126 C1
Thomas St. M Ash 72 C1
Thomas St. Maesy 101 D1
Thomas St. Mer V 73 E2
Thomas St. N Tre 54 C2
Thomas St. Neath 87 E1
Thomas St. Nel 99 F2
Thomas St. P Tal 113 F1
Thomas St. Pontdw 40 C3
Thomas St. Ponty 124 B1
Thomas St. Swan 110 B3
Thomas St. Swan 110 C4
Thomas St. Tony 146 B3
Thomas St. Tonypa 121 E3
Thomas St. Tonypa 121 F2
Thomas St. Tre 99 D3
Thomas St. Yst 95 D3
Thomas Terr. Reso 44 A1
Thomas Terr. Swan 84 C3
Thomas's Pl. Tylor 122 C4
Thomasville. Caer 151 F3
Thompson Ave. Card 204 A4
Thompson Ct. Card 204 B3
Thompson Ct. Lough 82 B4
Thompson Pl. Card 204 A4
Thompson St. Ponty 124 A1
Thompson St. Ynybw 124 A4
Thompson Villas. Ynybw 124 A4
Thorburn Cl. Neath 87 F4
Thorley Cl. Card 189 D2
Thorn Gr. Pen 227 D4
Thornaby Ct. Card 205 D2
Thornbury Cl. Card 188 B3
Thornbury Cl. Mer T 31 F1
Thornbury Cl. P Tal 113 F2
Thorncombe Rd. Peng 101 F3
Thorney Rd. P Tal 113 E4
Thornhill Ct. Card 188 B4
Thornhill Gdns. Rhiwd 155 F4
Thornhill Rd. Card 172 B2
Thornhill St. Card 204 B3
Thornhill Way. Rhiwd 155 F3
Thornton Cres. Pontcr 118 C1
Thornwood Cl. Card 172 C2
Thornwood Pl. Tre 99 D3
Thornwood. Tre 99 D3
Three Arches Ave. Card 189 D3
Three Cliffs Dr. South 135 D3
Three Elms Cl. Gell 100 C2
Three Oaks Cl. Bedw 152 B4
Three Salmon St. Mer T 51 E4
Thrush Cl. Card 191 D3
Thurston Rd. Ponty 124 B1
Thurston St. Abercy 98 C2
Thurston St. Card 204 B3
Tichbourne St. T Mum 137 D2
Tidenham Rd. Card 203 E2
Timbers Sq. Card 205 E4
Timbre Pl. P Tal 113 E1
Timothy Pl. Aberd 71 E4
Timothy Rees Cl. Card 187 E2
Tin St. Card 205 E3
Tingle La. Ewen 196 A4
Tintagel Cl. Card 172 B1
Tintern Cl. St M Ch 221 E4
Tintern St. Card 204 B3
Tir Bach Rd. Ynys 101 F1
Tir Coed. Caer 151 F3
Tir John North Rd. Swan 111 E4
Tir Meibion La. Ll'tris 168 B2
Tir Morfa Rd. P Tal 113 D1
Tir Newydd. Pyle 177 D4
Tir y Waun. Ystra 8 A1
Tir-afon Ct. Ll'tris 184 A4
Tir-y-Berth St. Gall 101 D3
Tir-y-Cwm La. Pontmi 129 F1
Tir-y-Cwm Rd. Pontmi 129 F1
Tirbach Rd. Ystal 23 E4
Tirfounder Rd. Aberd 71 F4
Tirgof. Ll'ge 56 A4
Tirmynydd. Lough 57 D1
Tirpenry St. Swan 60 A1
Tirycoed Rd. Glan 4 A4
Titan Rd. Card 205 E2
Tiverton Dr. Card 190 A2
Toftingall Ave. Card 188 B3
Tollgate Cl. Caer 152 B3
Tollgate Cl. Card 204 B1
Tollgate Rd. Marg 139 F2
Ton Glas. Bridg 179 D3
Ton Glas. Pyle 161 D1
Ton Hywel. Porth 122 B1
Ton Rhosyn. Bridg 180 A3
Ton Row. Yst 95 D2
Ton Teg. Penco 181 E4
Ton y Felin. Ponty 150 A3
Ton-Coch Terr. M Ash 72 A3
Ton-Mawr Rd. Ton 89 D3
Ton-y-Felin Rd. Caer 152 A2
Ton-y-Groes. Penco 181 F4
Ton-yr-Ywen Ave. Card 188 C3
Tonclwyda. Clyne 64 B3
Tondu Rd. Bridg 179 F3
Tonna Rd. Maest 117 D4
Tonna Uchaf. Tonna 63 E2
Tonteg Cl. Ch Vil 150 A1
Tonteg Rd. Ch Vil 150 A2
Tontine St. Swan 110 B4
Tonypandy Enterprise Ctr.
Trea 121 F4
Tonyrefail Rd. Ponty 148 C3
Topaz St. Card 205 E3
Tor View. Bedw 152 B4
Tor View. Penma 134 A3
Torbay Terr. Rhoose 223 D1
Toronto Ave. Marg 139 F2
Toronto Cl. Oak 101 F4
Torrens Dr. Card 189 D2
Torrington Rd. Card 190 B4
Torrington Rd. Swan 84 A2
Torymynydd. P Tal 113 E4
Tower Cl. Bridg 180 A2
Tower Ct. Swan 85 D4
Tower Hill. Pen 217 D2
Tower Rd. Hir 48 B4
Tower Rd. Rhig 48 B4
Tower Rd. St Ath 221 F1
Tower St. Ponty 149 E4
Tower Way. Sully 225 F3
Towers The. Hir 48 B4
Town Hall Sq. Cowb 198 C1
Town Mill Rd. Cowb 198 C1
Town Wall. Card 205 D3
Townhill Gdns. Swan 109 F4
Townhill Rd. Swan 109 F4
Towy Rd. Card 189 D4
Towyn Rd. Card 190 B2
Towyn Way. Ch Vil 150 A1
Trade La. Card 205 D2
Trade St. Card 205 D2
Traethmelyn. P Tal 113 D2
Trafalgar Ct. Card 189 E1
Trafalgar Pl. Swan 109 F3
Trafalgar Rd. Card 205 E4
Trafalgar St. Pontmi 155 D4
Trafalgar Terr. Yst 95 E1
Trahearne Ct. B-coch 87 E4
Traherne Dr. Card 202 C2
Trallwn Pl. Swan 85 F3
Trallwn Rd. Swan 85 F3
Tram Rd. Pontll 101 F2
Tram Road Side. Tre 99 D2
Tram Road Side. Tre 99 D3
Tramroad La. Mer T 32 C2
Tramroad Side. Mer T 32 B1
Tramroad Side N. Mer T 32 C1
Tramroad Side S. Mer T 51 F4
Tramroad Terr. Mer T 32 C1
Tramway. Peny 48 C4
Tramway Rd. A-wen 41 D3
Tramway Side. G-nea 27 E1
Trap Well. Caer 152 B3
Travis Way. Porth 176 C1
Trawler Rd. Swan 110 B3
Traws Fynydd. Bridg 180 A2
Tre Edwards. Rhy 34 B3
Tre Gwilym. Aberd 71 F4
Tre Telynog. Aberd 71 F4
Tre-banog Ter. Hir 29 D2
Tre-Beferad. Ll' Maj 220 B3
Tre-Ifor. Llwy 49 F4
Tre-Lyn La. Peng 101 D3
Tre-Pit Rd. Wick 208 A3
Tre-York St. Rhy 34 C2
Trealaw Rd. Trea 121 F3
Treasure St. Treo 94 B4
Trebanog Cl. Card 190 C3
Trebanog Cres. Card 190 C3
Trebanog Rd. Porth 122 B1
Treborth Rd. Card 190 C3
Trecastle. Ll'hry 183 E3
Trecenydd Ind Est. Caer 151 F2
Trecinon Rd. Card 190 C3
Tredegar Ave. Ll'ha 166 C2
Tredegar Cl. Ll'ha 166 C2
Tredegar Ct. Card 187 F3
Tredegar Flats. Bedw 153 F4
Tredegar Rd. Lough 57 E1
Tredegar Rd. N Tre 54 C2
Tredegar St. Card 205 D3
Tredegar St. Cross 129 D2
Tredegar St. Pontmi 129 F1
Tredegar St. Rhiwd 155 F2
Tredegar Terr. Bar 76 A2
Tredegar Terr. Cross 129 D2
Tredegar Terr. Pontmi 129 F1
Tredelerch Rd. Card 190 A1
Tredogan Rd. Rhoose 223 D2
Tredomen Terr. Gell 100 B1
Tredomen Villas. Gell 100 B1
Tree Tops Ave. Peng 101 F4
Treetops Cl. Card 187 D1
Trefaser Cres. Card 190 C3
Trefelin. Aberd 49 F2
Trefelin Cres. Marg 114 B1
Trefelin St. Marg 114 B1
Treforest Ct. Ponty 149 F3
Treforest Ind Est. Ch Vil 150 A2
Treforgan Rd. Cry 24 A1
Tregarne Cl. Swan 59 F2
Tregaron House. Marg 139 F2
Tregaron Rd. Card 203 D3
Tregarth Cl. Penty 185 E4
Tregarth Ct. Penty 185 E4
Tregelles Ct. Swan 60 A2
Tregelles Rd. N Abb 62 A1
Tregwilym Rd. Rhiwd 155 F3
Trehafod Rd. Porth 123 E1
Treharne Dr. Bridg 163 E1
Treharne Flats. Ponty 150 A3
Treharne Rd. Barry 225 D4
Treharne Rd. Maest 91 D1
Treharne Rd. Swan 59 F1
Treharne Rd. Tre 98 C3
Treharne Row. Maest 117 D2
Treharne Row. Pontcr 143 F4
Treharne St. Mer V 73 E3
Treharne St. Treo 94 A2
Treharne St. Yst 94 C2
Treharne Terr. Tre 98 C3
Treharris St. Card 205 E4
Treherbert St. Card 204 C4
Trelai Ct. Card 203 E2
Trelawney Ave. Card 190 A2
Trelawney Cres. Card 190 A2
Trelys Cl. Peng 101 D3
Trem y Bryn. Bridg 179 F4
Trem y Mor. Pen-cl 80 A1
Trem-y-Cwm. Ll'tris 169 D3
Trem-y-Glyn. Porth 122 B1
Trem-y-Mor. Bridg 180 A2
Trem-y-Mynydd. Trehe 68 C1
Tremadoc Wlk. Card 190 C3
Tremains Ct. Bridg 180 A2
Tremains Rd. Bridg 179 F2
Tremgarth. Bridg 179 F3
Trenant. Peny 48 C4
Trenchard Dr. Card 188 C3
Treneol. Abera 71 D3
Trenewyd Rd. Card 190 C3
Trenewydd Rise. Neath 87 F3
Trenos Gdns. Ll'ha 166 B1
Trenos Pl. Ll'ha 166 C1
Treoda Ct. Card 188 A3
Treoes Rd. Bridg 180 C2
Treorchy Ind Est. Treo 94 C3
Treorky St. Card 205 D4
Treowen Ave. Pontll 101 F2
Tresigin Rd. Card 190 C3
Tresilian Cl. Ll' maj 219 F3
Tresillian Terr. Card 205 D2
Tresillian Way. Card 205 D2
Tressilian Pl. Abercy 98 B1
Trevallen Ave. Neath 88 A3
Trevelyan Ct. Caer 152 B2
Trevelyan Ct. Ll' Maj 220 A4
Trevethick St. Card 204 C3
Trevethick St. Mer T 32 C1
Trevithick Gdns. Mer T 51 F4
Trevor Cl. Mer T 33 D4
Trevor St. Abera 50 A1
Trevor St. Treo 94 B4
Trewartha Ct. Card 188 A3
Trewaun. Peny 48 C4
Trewen Rd. Swan 61 D1
Trews Field Ind Site. Bridg 179 F3
Trewyddfa Common. Swan 84 C3
Trewyddfa Gdns. Swan 84 C3
Trewyddfa Rd. Swan 84 C3
Trewyddfa Terr. Swan 84 C3
Triangle. C-c-y-c 32 A2
Triangle The. Bridg 180 A2
Triangle The. M Ash 72 B2
Tribute Ave. Aberca 129 E4
Tridwr Rd. Aber 150 C4
Trinity Cl. Gell 100 C1
Trinity Cl. Pontar 36 B2
Trinity Cl. T Mum 137 D3
Trinity Ct. P Tal 113 E1
Trinity Hill. Cross 129 E3
Trinity La. Pen-cl 80 B2
Trinity Pl. Pontar 36 B2
Trinity Pl. Swan 110 B4
Trinity Rd. Tonypa 121 F3
Trinity St. Card 205 D3
Trinity St. Lough 57 E1
Trip Terr. Yst 95 D3
Triscombe Dr. Card 187 F1
Tristram Cl. Card 172 B1
Troad-y-bryn. Coel 9 E3
Troed y Rhiw. Card 172 A1
Troed-y-Bryn. Caer 151 F3
Troed-y-Garth. Penty 170 A1
Troed-y-rhiw Cotts. Maest 142 A4
Troed-y-Rhiw Rd. M Ash 72 C2
Troed-y-Rhiw Rd. Ynys 128 C2
Troed-y-Rhiw. Swan 85 F3
Troed-y-rhiw. Ystra 8 B3
Troedpennar Terr. Abercy 98 C2
Troedrhiw-trwyn. Ponty 123 F1
Troedyrhiw. Gell 126 C4
Troedyrhiw Rd. Porth 122 C2
Troedyrhiw Terr. Treo 94 C3
Trosnant Cres. Gell 100 B3
Trowbridge Gn. Card 190 C3
Trowbridge Rd. Card 190 C2
Tucker St. Neath 87 E2
Tudno Pl. Swan 83 F3
Tudor Ave. Hir 48 B4
Tudor Cl. Card 203 E4
Tudor Cl. Mer V 73 E2
Tudor Cl. Pen 217 D1
Tudor Ct. Bish 136 A3
Tudor Ct. Card 188 B3
Tudor Dr. Pontcr 143 F1
Tudor Est. Maest 91 D1
Tudor Gdns. Bedw 153 F3
Tudor La. Card 204 C2
Tudor Pl. Ll' Maj 220 A3
Tudor Rd. Swan 84 B3
Tudor Rd. Yst 95 D1
Tudor St. Card 204 C2
Tudor St. Fern 95 F3
Tudor St. Marg 114 A1
Tudor St. Ponty 150 A2
Tudor St. Ystra 23 E4
Tudor Terr. Aberd 49 F2
Tudor Terr. Mer T 32 B1
Tudor Way. Bish 136 A4
Tudor Way. Ch Vil 169 E3
Tudors The. Card 189 E1
Tulloch St. Card 189 E1
Tummel Cl. Card 189 E3
Tumulus Way. Ll'Maj 209 E2
Turberville Cres. Bridg 163 F1
Turberville Pl. Card 204 B3
Turberville Rd. Porth 122 C3
Turberville St. Maest 117 E1
Turberville St. Trea 95 F1
Turberville Terr. Tonypa 121 F2
Turbine Annexe Rd. St Ath 221 F1
Turkey St. Ll' maj 219 F4
Turner Rd. Card 204 A3
Turnham Gn. Card 189 F1
Turnpike Cl. D pow 216 A2
Turnstone Ct. P Tal 113 E1
Turnstone Rd. Porth 176 C1
Tuscan Cl. Pen 216 B4
Twchwyn Garth. Colw 197 F4
Tweedsmuir Rd. Card 205 F4
Twelfth Ave. Mer T 32 C3
Twll-yn-y-Wal Rd. Marg 139 F2
Twyn Bedw. Porth 122 C1
Twyn Bedw Rd. Cly 60 B4
Twyn Carno. Rhy 34 C3
Twyn Gdns. Peng 101 E4
Twyn Gwyn Rd. Tonypa 122 A2
Twyn. Peng 101 D3
Twyn Rd. Gell 126 C4
Twyn Teg. B-coch 62 B1
Twyn The. Caer 152 A1
Twyn yr Eglwys. Colw 196 C2
Twyn-Gwyn Rd. Ynys 128 A3
Twyn-y-Fedwen. Card 188 B2
Twyn-y-Gored. Cwma 115 D4
Twyn-yr-Eos. Trehe 69 D1
Twyn-yr-Ynys. Cwma 115 D4
Twyn-yr-Ysgol. Ystal 23 D4
Twyncarmel. Mer T 31 F1
Twyncarn Rd. Cross 129 D3
Twyncarn Terr. Aberca 129 D4
Twyncyn. D Pow 215 F2
Twyni Teg. Swan 108 C4
Twyniago. Pontar 36 B2
Twynrefail Pl. G-C-G 5 D2
Twynyffald Rd. Peng 101 E4
Twynygarreg. Tre 99 D4
Twynyrodyn Rd. Mer T 51 F4
Ty Bryncoch. T We 171 D2
Ty Canol La. Bedw 153 F4
Ty Canol. Porth 176 C1
Ty Cerrig. Barry 225 D4
Ty Cerrig. Card 189 F4
Ty Coch. Rhy 34 C3
Ty Dawel. Tony 147 E3
Ty Ddewi. Yst 95 D1
Ty Dewi Sant. Swan 83 F2
Ty Draw. Ch Vil 149 F1
Ty Draw La. Pyle 176 C3
Ty Fry. Aberd 49 F1
Ty Fry Rd. Bar 76 A2
Ty Fry Rd. Ce Cr 162 A1
Ty Glas Ave. Card 188 C4
Ty Gwenfo. Barry 225 E3
Ty Gwyn Cl. H-y-Cy 165 D3
Ty Gwyn. Gow 82 B3
Ty Isaf. Ll'hry 183 D3
Ty Llunfan. Tony 146 B4
Ty Llwyd Parc. Tre 99 E3
Ty Maur Uchaf. Ponty 123 F1
Ty Mawr La. Marsh 175 F1
Ty Mawr Parc. Ponty 123 F1
Ty Merchant. Penco 165 F1
Ty Nant. Bridg 179 E3
Ty Nant. Caer 151 F2
Ty Newydd. Card 188 A2
Ty Newydd. Gar P 153 E3
Ty Parc Cl. Card 187 E2
Ty Rhiw. T We 171 D2
Ty Segur. Neath 87 F3
Ty'n y Wern. Tony 147 E1
Ty'n yr Heol. Tondu 163 F3
Ty'n-y-Bonau Rd. Pontar 36 B3
Ty'n-y-Cae Gr. Card 188 B3
Ty'n-y-Coed La. Card 189 D1
Ty'n-y-Coed Pl. Card 189 D1
Ty'n-y-coed Terr. Brynco 163 F2
Ty'n-y-Craig. Cry 42 C3
Ty'n-y-Graig Rd. Ll'bra 126 C1
Ty'n-y-Pant Rd. Pontdw 40 B3
Ty'n-y-Parc Rd. Card 188 A3
Ty'n-y-Pwll Rd. Card 188 A3
Ty'n-yr-Heol Rd. B-coch 62 B2
Ty'r Felin. Swan 83 F3
Ty'r Fran. Swan 61 D1
Ty'r Maes. Swan 83 F3
Ty'r Waun. Ponty 171 D4
Ty'r-Groes Dr. Marg 139 F2
Ty'r-Owen Row. Cwma 114 B3
Ty'rfelin St. M Ash 97 F4
Ty-Canol La. Bedw 153 D4
Ty-Cefn Rd. Card 203 E3
Ty-Coch Cl. Rhiwd 155 F1
Ty-coch Maisonettes. Swan 109 E4
Ty-Coch Rd. Card 203 E1
Ty-Coch Rd. Swan 109 E4

Ty-Draw Cres. Swan ... 85 D1
Ty-Draw Hill. Marg ... 114 B1
Ty-Draw. Llys ... 209 D4
Ty-Draw Pl. Card ... 189 E1
Ty-Draw Pl. Marg ... 139 D4
Ty-Draw Pl. Swan ... 85 D1
Ty-Draw Rd. Abera ... 50 B1
Ty-Draw Rd. Card ... 173 F1
Ty-Draw Rd. Swan ... 85 E1
Ty-Draw St. Marg ... 139 D4
Ty-Drwa Pl. Aberd ... 50 B1
Ty-Fry Ave. Card ... 190 A2
Ty-Fry Cl. Card ... 190 B2
Ty-Fry Cl. Tondu ... 163 F4
Ty-Fry Gdns. Card ... 190 B2
Ty-Fry Rd. Card ... 190 A2
Ty-Fry Rd. Marg ... 139 F2
Ty-Glas Rd. Card ... 188 C4
Ty-Gwyn Ave. Card ... 189 E1
Ty-Gwyn Cres. Card ... 189 E2
Ty-Gwyn Rd. Card ... 188 B4
Ty-Gwyn Rd. Card ... 189 E1
Ty-Isaf. Caer ... 151 D4
Ty-Isaf Cres. Pontmi ... 155 D4
Ty-Isaf Park Circ. Pontmi ... 155 E4
Ty-Isaf Park Cres. Pontmi ... 155 E4
Ty-Isaf Park Rd. Pontmi ... 155 E4
Ty-Isaf Park Villas. Pontmi ... 155 D4
Ty-Isaf Rd. Ce Cr ... 162 A1
Ty-Isha Terr. Peng ... 101 E4
Ty-Llwyd Wlk. Bar ... 76 A3
Ty-Mawr Ave. Card ... 190 A1
Ty-Mawr Rd. Card ... 187 F2
Ty-Mawr Rd. Card ... 190 A1
Ty-Mawr Rd. Ponty ... 123 F1
Ty-myrtwydd. Lough ... 81 F4
Ty-Nant. Gell ... 100 B4
Ty-Nant Rd. Card ... 187 D4
Ty-nant Rd. Penty ... 171 D1
Ty-Nant St. Card ... 204 C2
Ty-Pica Dr. Wen ... 215 D4
Ty-To-Maen Cl. Card ... 190 C4
Ty-to-maen. Ll'car ... 212 C1
Ty-Wern Ave. Card ... 188 B3
Ty-Wern Rd. Card ... 188 B3
Tybryn Terr. Penco ... 181 D4
Tycoch Ave. Bridg ... 180 B4
Tycribwr Hill. Tondu ... 163 D2
Tyderwen. Maest ... 117 D4
Tydfil Pl. Card ... 189 D1
Tydfil Rd. Bedw ... 152 B4
Tydfil St. Barry ... 225 D3
Tydfil Terr. Troed ... 52 B1
Tydraw Cres. Pyle ... 177 D4
Tydraw Terr. Trehe ... 68 C2
Tydvil Cl. Bed ... 99 F3
Tyfica Cres. Ponty ... 124 B1
Tyfica Rd. Ponty ... 124 B1
Tygwyn Rd. Ch Vil ... 149 F1
Tygwyn Rd. Cly ... 60 C4
Tygwyn Rd. Ponty ... 124 C1
Tygwyn Rd. Swan ... 60 B1
Tygwyn St. Mer T ... 32 C2
Tyisaf Rd. Yst ... 95 D2
Tyla Glas. Caer ... 171 F4
Tyla Gwyn. Ponty ... 170 C4
Tyla La. M-y-Fed ... 175 D2
Tyla La. Marsh ... 175 D2
Tyla Rd. Neath ... 87 E2
Tyla Rhosyr. Cowb ... 198 B1
Tyla Teg. Card ... 187 F4
Tyla-Gwyn. Gell ... 100 B4
Tylacelyn Rd. Tonypa ... 121 F2
Tylacoch. Ll'hry ... 183 E3
Tylacoch Pl. Treo ... 94 B3
Tylagarw Terr. Ll'hry ... 183 F4
Tylcha Fach Bungalows.
  Tony ... 147 E1
Tylcha Fach Cl. Tony ... 147 E1
Tylcha Fach Terr. Tony ... 147 E1
Tylcha Fach. Tony ... 147 E1
Tylcha Isaf. Tony ... 147 E1
Tylcha Wen Cl. Tony ... 147 D2
Tylcha Wen Terr. Tony ... 147 D2
Tyle Garw. Ll'hry ... 183 F4
Tyle Glas. Pyle ... 177 D4
Tyle House Cl. Ll'maes ... 220 A4
Tyle Mali. Llys ... 197 F1
Tyle Teg. Cly ... 60 B4
Tyle-Fforest. Trehe ... 69 D1
Tyle-Rackland. Wick ... 208 B4
Tyler St. Card ... 205 F4
Tyllwyd. A-wen ... 40 C1
Tyllwyd. B-coch ... 62 A3
Tyllwyd St. Mer T ... 32 C2
Tymaen Cres. Cwma ... 114 C3
Tymaen Terr. Cwma ... 114 C3
Tymawr Cl. Card ... 190 A1
Tymawr Cl. W St D ... 199 E4
Tymawr St. Swan ... 111 D4
Tymawr Terr. Ponty ... 124 A1
Tymeinwr Ave. Pontcr ... 118 A3
Tymynydd Cl. Card ... 187 D3
Tyn-y-Banwen Rd. Tre ... 98 C3
Tyn-y-Bettws Cl. Pontcr ... 143 F1
Tyn-y-Cae. A-wen ... 40 C2

Tyn-y-Cae Rd. Swan ... 85 E4
Tyn-y-Caeau La. Porth ... 177 E1
Tyn-y-Coed Ffordd. Cly ... 61 D2
Tyn-y-Coed. Gell ... 100 C1
Tyn-y-Coedcae. Trehe ... 69 D1
Tyn-y-Cwm Rd. Pontmi ... 155 E4
Tyn-y-twr. P Tal ... 113 F3
Tyn-y-Waun. Pontcr ... 143 F2
Tyn-y-Waun Rd. Swan ... 85 F3
Tynant. Card ... 188 A2
Tynant Rd. Ll'tris ... 169 D4
Tynant Rd. Penty ... 185 E4
Tyndall St. Card ... 205 D2
Tyneside Rd. Card ... 205 E1
Tynewydd Dr. Marsh ... 175 E2
Tynewydd Row. Og Va ... 119 F1
Tynewydd Sq. Porth ... 122 C2
Tynewydd St. Rhy ... 53 F4
Tynrheol Flats. Neath ... 88 A3
Tyntaldwyn Rd. Troed ... 52 B1
Tynton Rd. Bridg ... 179 F3
Tyntyla Ave. Yst ... 95 F1
Tyntyla Pk. Yst ... 95 F1
Tyntyla Rd. Yst ... 95 F1
Tyntyla Terr. Yst ... 95 E2
Tynybedw St. Treo ... 94 C3
Tynybedw Terr. Treo ... 94 C3
Tynybryn Rd. Tony ... 147 D2
Tynycai Pl. Tonypa ... 121 F2
Tynycoed Cres. Peng ... 101 E4
Tynycoed Terr. Mer T ... 32 C2
Tynycymmer Cl. Porth ... 122 C2
Tynygraig Terr. Ll'bra ... 126 C1
Tynywaun. Yst ... 95 E2
Tynywern Terr. Bedw ... 153 D4
Tynywern Villas. Bedw ... 153 D4
Typica Cotts. Ponty ... 123 F1
Tyr Halen Row. P Tal ... 113 E3
Tyr Onen. P Tal ... 113 E3
Tyr Waun. Deri ... 53 E4
Tyr Winch Rd. Card ... 190 B4
Tyrisha Ave. Lough ... 57 E3
Tyrisha Rd. Lough ... 57 E3
Tyrwhitt Cres. Card ... 189 D3
Tytalwyn Ave. Pyle ... 161 E1
Tythegston Cl. Porth ... 176 C1
Tywith Cotts. Maest ... 117 D4
Tywyn Cl. P Tal ... 138 C4
Tywyn Cres. P Tal ... 138 C4

Ullswater Ave. Card ... 189 D2
Ullswater Cres. Swan ... 84 C4
Underhill Dr. Ch Vil ... 150 A1
Underhill La. Ox ... 157 E4
Underhill Mansions. Card ... 187 F3
Underwood Ave. Maesy ... 101 D1
Underwood. Caer ... 152 A1
Underwood Rd. B-coch ... 63 D2
Underwood Terr. Aber ... 151 D4
Underwood Terr. Ponty ... 124 A1
Union Pl. Mer T ... 32 C1
Union Pl. Tylor ... 96 A2
Union St. Aberd ... 49 F2
Union St. Fern ... 95 F3
Union St. M Ash ... 72 B2
Union St. Maest ... 116 C3
Union St. Mer T ... 32 C1
Union St. Ponty ... 149 E4
Union St. Rhy ... 34 C1
Union St. Swan ... 110 B3
Union St. Tred ... 35 E3
Union St. Yst ... 95 D2
Union Terr. Mer T ... 32 C1
Unity St. Aberd ... 49 F1
Universal St. Card ... 204 C2
University Pl. Card ... 205 F3
Uphill Cl. Sully ... 226 A3
Uphill Rd. Card ... 190 A3
Upland Rd. Neath ... 87 F3
Uplands Cres. Pen ... 216 C3
Uplands Cres. Swan ... 110 A3
Uplands Ct. Rhiwd ... 155 F3
Uplands Dr. Maest ... 116 C3
Uplands. G-C-G ... 5 D2
Uplands. Gow ... 82 A3
Uplands Rd. Card ... 190 A1
Uplands Rd. Pontdw ... 40 B2
Uplands Terr. Swan ... 84 C4
Uplands Terr. Swan ... 109 F3
Uplands The. Card ... 187 E3
Uplands The. Marg ... 114 B1
Uplands The. Rhiwd ... 155 F3
Uplands The. Ton ... 89 D3
Uplands. Yst ... 95 D2
Upper Alma Pl. Yst ... 94 C3
Upper Alma Terr. Ponty ... 149 E4
Upper Boat Ind Pk. Ponty ... 150 B2
Upper Canning St. Swan ... 94 C2
Upper Capel St. Bar ... 75 F2
Upper Church Pk. T Mum ... 137 D2
Upper Church St. Bar ... 75 F2
Upper Church St. Ponty ... 124 B1
Upper Colbren Rd. G-C-G ... 5 D2
Upper Colliers' Row. Mer T ... 32 A1
Upper Cosmeston Farm.
  Sully ... 227 D4

Upper Cross St. Tred ... 54 B2
Upper Edward St. Mer T ... 32 B1
Upper Elizabeth St. Mer T ... 33 D2
Upper Fforest Way. Swan ... 60 A1
Upper Forest Level. M Ash ... 72 C1
Upper Francis St. Aber ... 150 C4
Upper Gendros Cres. Swan ... 84 A2
Upper Gertrude St. Swan ... 98 C1
Upper Glyn Gwyn St. Bedw ... 153 D4
Upper Gynor Pl. Tylor ... 122 C3
Upper Heathfield Rd.
  Pontdw ... 40 C3
Upper High St. Bar ... 76 A3
Upper High St. Bed ... 74 A4
Upper High St. C-c-y-c ... 31 F3
Upper High St. Rhy ... 34 C3
Upper James St. Mark ... 76 C2
Upper Kincraig St. Card ... 205 E4
Upper King's Head Rd.
  Swan ... 83 F2
Upper Law St. Ce Cr ... 162 B3
Upper Meadow. Card ... 203 D2
Upper Mill Rd. Pontar ... 36 B2
Upper North Rd. Bar ... 75 F3
Upper Rd. N Tre ... 55 D1
Upper Regent St. Aber ... 50 A1
Upper Row. Mer T ... 33 D3
Upper Salisbury St. Tred ... 35 F3
Upper St Alban's Rd. Trehe ... 68 B2
Upper Station Rd. Glan ... 4 B4
Upper Strand. Swan ... 84 B1
Upper Taff St. Trehe ... 68 C1
Upper Terr. Tylor ... 96 B1
Upper Thomas St. Mer T ... 32 C1
Upper Trelyn Rd. Pontll ... 101 E2
Upper Ty'n-y-Parc Terr.
  Card ... 188 A3
Upper Union St. Mer T ... 33 D2
Upper Vaughan St. Ponty ... 124 A1
Upper West End. Marg ... 139 E4
Upper Wood St. Bar ... 75 F2
Uppercliff Cl. Pen ... 217 E3
Uppercliff Dr. Pen ... 217 E3
Upton Pl. Ll'tris ... 169 D3
Upton St. Glyn ... 92 B3
Upton St. Porth ... 122 C2
Upton Terr. Swan ... 111 D4
Upton Terr. Tonypa ... 121 F2
Urban St. Mer T ... 32 C2
Usk Ct. Card ... 188 A3
Usk Rd. Bar ... 75 F3
Usk Rd. Card ... 189 D4
Uskley Ct. Card ... 190 C3
Uxilla Terr. Bridg ... 180 A2

Vachell Ct. Ll' Maj ... 220 A3
Vachell Rd. Card ... 203 E3
Vaendre Cl. Card ... 175 D1
Vaindre Cl. Card ... 191 D4
Vaindre Dr. Card ... 191 D4
Vaindre La. Card ... 190 C4
Vaindre La. Card ... 191 D4
Valarian Cl. Card ... 191 D3
Vale Ct. D pow ... 216 A2
Vale Gdns. Ponty ... 124 A1
Vale Of Neath Rd. Swan ... 111 D4
Vale Rd. Card ... 205 F4
Vale Terr. Tred ... 35 F2
Vale View. Bar ... 75 F1
Vale View. Bridg ... 180 B3
Vale View. Brynco ... 163 F2
Vale View Cl. Pen ... 216 B3
Vale View Cres. Pen ... 216 B3
Vale View. Ll'ha ... 166 C2
Vale View. Maesy ... 101 D1
Vale View. Og Va ... 144 C4
Vale View. Pontmi ... 129 F1
Vale View Rd. Oak ... 101 F1
Vale View Terr. M Ash ... 97 F4
Vale View. Tonypa ... 122 A2
Vale View. Ystraf ... 27 F2
Valeview Terr. Og Va ... 119 F4
Valley View. Gell ... 100 C3
Valley View. Neath ... 88 A3
Valley View. Pontll ... 101 F2
Valley View St. Abera ... 71 E3
Valley View. Swan ... 109 D3
Valley Way. Swan ... 85 D3
Van Rd. Caer ... 152 B1
Van St. Card ... 204 C2
Van Terr. Caer ... 152 B1
Vancouver Dr. Oak ... 101 F4
Vanewood Ct. T Mum ... 137 E2
Vanfield Cl. Caer ... 152 B1
Vardre Rd. Cly ... 60 C4
Varna Terr. Marg ... 139 E4
Varteg Rd. Ystal ... 23 D3
Vaughan Ave. Card ... 204 A4
Vaughan Ave. Reso ... 44 A1
Vaughan Cl. P Tal ... 114 A1
Vaughan Pl. Lough ... 56 C1
Vaughan St. Mer T ... 33 D2
Vaughan St. Ponty ... 124 A1
Vaynor La. C-c-y-c ... 32 A3
Vaynor Rd. C-c-y-c ... 32 A3
Vaynor St. Porth ... 122 C2
Velindre Ct. Card ... 187 F3

Velindre Pl. Card ... 187 F3
Velindre Rd. Card ... 187 F3
Velindre St. Marg ... 114 A1
Venables Cl. Swan ... 83 E1
Vennaway La. South ... 135 E4
Venosa Trad Est. Caer ... 152 B2
Vensland. Bish ... 136 A3
Ventnor Pl. Card ... 188 B1
Venwood Cl. Wen ... 215 D3
Vera Rd. Cly ... 60 C4
Verbena Cl. Card ... 191 D4
Verdi Rd. P Tal ... 113 D1
Vere Pl. Bar ... 76 A1
Vere St. Bar ... 76 A1
Vere St. Barry ... 225 E3
Vere St. Card ... 205 E4
Verig St. Swan ... 84 B2
Verland Cl. Card ... 204 A4
Verland Way. Penco ... 181 E4
Verlands The. Cowb ... 198 B1
Verlon Cl. D Pow ... 225 F4
Vernoa Pl. Barry ... 225 E4
Vernon Cl. Mer T ... 32 C1
Vernon Cl. Pont ... 58 A3
Vernon Pl. Neath ... 87 D1
Vernon Rd. Porthc ... 193 D4
Vernon St. Bridg ... 180 A3
Vernon St. Neath ... 87 E1
Vernon St. Swan ... 84 B1
Versil Terr. Lough ... 81 F4
Viaduct Rd. Barry ... 225 D2
Vicarage Cl. Bar ... 75 F2
Vicarage Cl. Tony ... 147 E3
Vicarage Cl. Tonypa ... 122 A2
Vicarage Cl. Yst ... 95 E2
Vicarage Ct. Ch Vil ... 149 F1
Vicarage Dr. Pontdw ... 40 C3
Vicarage Gdns. Marsh ... 175 E1
Vicarage Gdns. Rhiwd ... 155 F3
Vicarage La. Bar ... 75 F2
Vicarage La. Swan ... 84 A1
Vicarage Rd. Glan ... 4 B4
Vicarage Rd. Swan ... 59 F1
Vicarage Rd. Tonypa ... 122 A2
Vicarage Rd. Tylor ... 122 C3
Vicarage Terr. Maest ... 116 C2
Vicarage Terr. Swan ... 110 C4
Vicarage Terr. Treo ... 94 A3
Victor St. M Ash ... 72 B1
Victoria Ave. Card ... 204 A3
Victoria Ave. Pen ... 217 D2
Victoria Ave. Porth ... 192 C3
Victoria Ave. T Mum ... 137 D3
Victoria Bldgs. Tondu ... 163 E4
Victoria Ct. T Mum ... 136 B2
Victoria Gdns. Neath ... 87 F4
Victoria Park Rd. Barry ... 225 E3
Victoria Park Rd E. Card ... 204 A3
Victoria Park Rd W. Card ... 204 A3
Victoria Pl. Bar ... 76 A1
Victoria Quay. Swan ... 110 B3
Victoria Rd. Card ... 188 A3
Victoria Rd. Lough ... 82 B4
Victoria Rd. Maesy ... 101 D2
Victoria Rd. P Tal ... 138 C4
Victoria Rd. Pen ... 217 D2
Victoria Rd. Pen-cl ... 80 C2
Victoria Rd. Peng ... 101 D2
Victoria Rd. Pyle ... 161 E2
Victoria Rd. Rhy ... 34 C2
Victoria Rd. Swan ... 82 C2
Victoria Rd. Swan ... 110 B3
Victoria Row. Pen-cl ... 80 C2
Victoria Sq. Abera ... 50 A1
Victoria Sq. Pen ... 217 D2
Victoria St. Ll'bra ... 127 D2
Victoria St. M Ash ... 72 C1
Victoria St. Maest ... 91 D1
Victoria St. Mer T ... 32 B1
Victoria St. Mer T ... 33 D3
Victoria St. Mer V ... 73 E3
Victoria St. Neath ... 87 D1
Victoria St. Pontcr ... 118 C2
Victoria St. Swan ... 109 F4
Victoria St. Tre ... 99 D3
Victoria St. Trea ... 122 A3
Victoria St. Trehe ... 68 C1
Victoria St. Tylor ... 122 B4
Victoria St. Yst ... 95 D2
Victoria St. Yst ... 95 E2
Victoria Terr. Cwma ... 114 B3
Victoria Terr. Pyle ... 161 D1
Victoria Terr. Swan ... 110 A3
Victoria Terr. Tre ... 99 D3
Victoria Terr. Tred ... 35 F3
Victory Ave. Porth ... 122 C2
View Rd. Cly ... 60 B4
Viking Pl. Card ... 205 F1
Viking Way. Swan ... 85 D3
Villa Terr. Swan ... 84 B3
Village Cl. B-coch ... 62 B2
Village Ct. Pyle ... 161 E1
Village Farm. Bonv ... 201 D1
Village Farm Ind Est. Pyle ... 161 E1
Village Farm Rd. Pyle ... 177 E4
Village Gdns. P Tal ... 113 E2

Village La. T Mum ... 137 D2
Villas The. Mark ... 76 B4
Villiers Ct. Neath ... 87 D1
Villiers Rd. Glyn ... 92 B3
Villiers Rd. Skew ... 87 D4
Villiers St. Marg ... 114 B1
Villiers St. Neath ... 87 E1
Villiers St. Swan ... 84 B1
Vincent Cl. Barry ... 225 E4
Vincent Pl. Mer T ... 32 B1
Vincent Rd. Card ... 203 E4
Vincent St. Swan ... 110 A3
Vine Row. Ystal ... 23 D3
Vintin Terr. Porthc ... 193 D4
Viola Rd. P Tal ... 113 E1
Violet Pl. Card ... 188 B2
Violet Row. Card ... 205 D4
Violet St. Abera ... 71 D4
Virgil St. Card ... 204 C2
Virginia Cl. Caer ... 152 A2
Vishwell Rd. Card ... 204 A4
Vishwell Rd. Wen ... 215 D3
Vista Ct. Pen ... 217 D3
Vista Rise. Card ... 187 E1
Vivian Ct. P Tal ... 138 C4
Vivian Ct. Swan ... 109 E4
Vivian Park Dr. P Tal ... 113 E1
Vivian Rd. Swan ... 109 E4
Vivian St. Swan ... 84 B1
Vivian St. Tylor ... 96 A2
Vivian Terr. P Tal ... 113 F1
Volunteer St. Yst ... 94 C3
Voss Park Cl. Ll' Maj ... 220 A3
Voss Park Dr. Ll' Maj ... 220 A3
Voylart Cl. Swan ... 108 B4
Voylart Rd. Swan ... 108 B4
Vulcan Rd. Mer T ... 32 B1

Wade Ave. Ystal ... 23 D3
Wagner Rd. P Tal ... 113 D2
Wagtail Rd. Ll' Maj ... 220 C3
Waldhof Ct. Swan ... 83 F4
Walford Pl. Card ... 204 B3
Walk Farm Dr. Marsh ... 175 D2
Walk The. Abera ... 50 A2
Walk The. Card ... 190 A2
Walk The. Card ... 205 D3
Walk The. Gell ... 100 C1
Walk The. Mer T ... 32 B1
Walker Rd. Card ... 205 F3
Wallace Rd. Neath ... 87 F3
Wallace Rd. Swan ... 110 C4
Wallhead Rd. Mer T ... 51 F4
Wallis Dr. Gell ... 100 C4
Walnut Cl. T Mum ... 136 C4
Walnut Gr. Ll'maes ... 221 D4
Walnut Tree Cl. Card ... 187 D4
Walnut Way. Mer T ... 32 C2
Walpole Cl. Card ... 190 B4
Walsh St. Abercy ... 98 A3
Walston Cl. Wen ... 215 D4
Walston Rd. Wen ... 215 D3
Walter Conway Ave. Tred ... 35 E2
Walter Rd. Swan ... 110 A3
Walter St. Abercy ... 98 C1
Walter St. Mer T ... 33 D3
Walter St. Rhy ... 54 A4
Walter St. Tred ... 35 F2
Walter's Rd. Neath ... 87 E3
Walter's Terr. Mer T ... 51 F4
Walter's Terr. Rhy ... 54 A4
Walters Cres. T Mum ... 137 D3
Walters La. Ll'gen ... 102 C2
Walters Rd. Bridg ... 179 E2
Walters Rd. Cwmll ... 6 B3
Walters Rd. Og Va ... 144 C4
Walters Rd. Ponty ... 149 D4
Walters Rd. Swan ... 60 C1
Walters Row. Swan ... 108 B4
Walters St. Fern ... 95 F4
Walters St. Swan ... 84 B2
Walters St. Swan ... 84 C4
Waltham Cl. Swan ... 84 B4
Walton Pl. Card ... 204 B2
Wanderers Cres. Card ... 203 D2
Warlow Cl. St Ath ... 221 E2
Warlow St. Mer T ... 51 F4
Warn's Terr. Rhy ... 54 A4
Warne St. Peng ... 101 D3
Warren Cl. Bridg ... 180 B2
Warren Cl. Ponty ... 150 A3
Warren Dr. Caer ... 152 A1
Warren Evens Ct. Card ... 188 A3
Warren Hill. Neath ... 87 D1
Warren Terr. Bed ... 99 E3
Warwick Cres. Porth ... 192 C4
Warwick Pl. Card ... 204 C2
Warwick Pl. T Mum ... 137 D4
Warwick Rd. Card ... 109 D2
Warwick St. Card ... 204 C2
Wasdale Cl. Card ... 189 D1
Washford Ave. Card ... 190 B4
Washington St. Swan ... 84 B2
Watchet Cl. Card ... 190 A3
Water Avens Cl. Card ... 191 D3
Water La. Swan ... 85 D4
Water St. Bridg ... 179 F2
Water St. G-C-G ... 5 D2

Water St. Marg 160 B3
Water St. Monk 208 B1
Water St. Neath 87 F4
Water St. Og Va 144 C4
Water St. P Tal 139 D4
Water St. Pontar 36 A2
Water St. Pontar 36 B2
Waterfall Cotts. Marg 139 E3
Waterfall Rd. Reso 65 D4
Waterford Cl. Card 204 C2
Waterhall Rd. Card 187 E1
Waterhall Rd. Pyle 161 E2
Waterhouse Dr. Card 204 C2
Waterloo Cl. Card 205 F4
Waterloo Gdns. Card 205 E4
Waterloo Pl. Aberd 49 F2
Waterloo Pl. Gar P 153 E3
Waterloo Pl. Swan 109 F3
Waterloo Rd. Card 189 E1
Waterloo St. Abera 50 C1
Waterloo Terr. Rhy 53 F4
Waterloo Terrace Rd.
      Gar P 153 E3
Waterston Ct. Card 188 A1
Waterston Rd. Card 188 A1
Waterton La. Bridg 180 C1
Waterton Rd. Bridg 180 B1
Waterton Rd. Bridg 180 C2
Watery La. Cowb 199 E2
Watford Cl. Caer 151 F1
Watford Rd. Caer 171 F4
Watford Rd. Card 205 F4
Watford Rise. Caer 152 A1
Watkin St. Swan 110 B4
Watkins Terr. Ystra 8 B2
Watson Rd. Card 188 A1
Watson Row. Deri 75 D4
Watson St. Barry 225 D3
Watson Terr. Deri 75 D4
Watton Cl. Card 188 C4
Waun Ave. Glyn 66 C1
Waun Bant Rd. Pyle 161 E1
Waun Borfa Rd. Peng 101 E4
Waun Cl. Lough 81 F4
Waun Dafydd Farm. Ce Cr 162 B1
Waun Daniel. A-wen 41 D1
Waun Erw. Caer 152 A3
Waun Fach. Card 189 F4
Waun Fach Terr. Og Va .. 119 F3
Waun Ganol St. Caer 152 A2
Waun Goch. Gell 100 C3
Waun Goch Terr. Og Va .. 119 F3
Waun Gyrlais. Ystra 8 A2
Waun Las. B-coch 62 B1
Waun Lee Ct. Card 189 F4
Waun Lwyd Terr. Og Va .. 119 F3
Waun Newydd. H-y-Cy 165 D3
Waun Penlan. Pontdw 40 B4
Waun Rd. Lough 81 F4
Waun Rd. Swan 59 F1
Waun Rd. Tonypa 121 E3
Waun Rhydd. Gell 100 B3
Waun St. Glyn 92 B3
Waun The. Cwma 114 C3
Waun Wen. Cwma 114 C3
Waun Wen. Porth 147 E4
Waun Wen Terr. Og Va ... 119 F3
Waun y Felin. Pen-cl 81 D2
Waun-Fawr Rd. Card 188 B3
Waun-Gron Cl. Swan 84 B3
Waun-Gron Rd. Card 204 A4
Waun-Gron Rd. Swan 84 B3
Waun-Wen Rd. Swan 84 B1
Waun-Wen Terr. Swan 84 B1
Waun-y-Groes Ave. Card . 188 B4
Waun-y-Groes Rd. Card .. 188 B4
Waunarlwydd Rd. Swan ... 83 D1
Waunfach Flats. Caer 152 A2
Waunfach. Pontcr 143 F2
Waunfach St. Caer 152 A2
Waunfain. Caer 151 F3
Waunfawr Gdns. Cross 129 E2
Waunfawr Park Rd. Cross . 129 E2
Waunfawr Rd. Cross 129 E2
Waunfawr Terr. Cross 129 E2
Waungron. Cly 60 B4
Waungron. G-nea 27 D1
Waungron. Pontcr 143 F2
Waunlelsion. G-C-G 5 D3
Waunllwyn Cres. Peng 101 E4
Waunlon. Porthc 193 E4
Waunrhydd Rd. Tony 147 D3
Waunscil Ave. Bridg 180 A2
Wauntreoda Rd. Card 188 B2
Wavell Cl. Card 188 C3
Waverley Av. Pyle 216 C3
Waverley Ct. Barry 225 D2
Waverley Dr. T Mum 137 D3
Waverley Sq. Card 205 D1
Waverley St. Cly 60 B4
Waverly Cl. Cly 60 C4
Wayne St. Aberd 49 F2
Wayne St. Porth 122 C2
Wayne St. Porth 123 E1
Weatheral St. Abera 50 A1
Weavers Rd. Ystra 24 A4
Webb Pl. P Tal 138 C4
Webbons Way. Swan 83 F1

Webster St. Tre 99 D4
Wedal Rd. Card 189 D1
Wedgewood Ct. Caer 152 B2
Wedmore Rd. Card 204 C2
Weekes Cl. Card 190 B4
Weig Fach La. Swan 83 E2
Weig Gdns. Swan 84 A2
Weig La. Swan 83 F2
Weig Rd. Swan 83 F2
Welby Rd. Card 204 B3
Welcome La. Swan 110 B4
Welfare Ave. Bryn 115 F3
Well Field. Swan 108 C4
Well La. St Nic 201 F1
Well Pl. Abera 50 B1
Well Rd. Abera 71 E4
Well Rd. Rhoose 222 A1
Well St. Abercy 98 B1
Well St. Bridg 178 C2
Well St. C-c-y-c 32 A2
Well St. Mer T 32 B1
Well St. Porth 192 C3
Well The. Bridg 178 C2
Well Wood Cl. Card 189 F1
Wellfield Ave. Neath 87 F3
Wellfield Ave. Porthc 193 D4
Wellfield. Bish 135 F3
Wellfield Cl. Lough 57 D1
Wellfield. Clyne 65 D4
Wellfield Cres. Porthc 193 D4
Wellfield Ct. Ch Vil 149 F1
Wellfield Ct. Marsh 191 E4
Wellfield. Ll'tris 169 D4
Wellfield Pl. Card 205 E4
Wellfield Pl. G-nea 26 C1
Wellfield Rd. Marsh 191 E4
Wellfield Rd. P Tal 114 A1
Wellfield Sq. Neath 87 F3
Wellington Ct. Card 204 C3
Wellington Mews. Card ... 204 C3
Wellington Pl. P Tal 138 C4
Wellington St. Aberd 49 F2
Wellington St. Card 171 E1
Wellington St. Card 204 B3
Wellington St. Swan 110 B3
Wellington Terr. N Tre 54 C1
Wellington Way. Rhy 34 C1
Wellingtonia Cl. Mer T 32 B3
Wellpark. Ll'gen 102 C2
Wellright Rd. Card 203 E4
Wells Cl. P Tal 113 F3
Wells Rd. P Tal 113 F3
Wells St. Card 204 C3
Wellwood. Card 189 F2
Wellwood Dr. D pow 216 A1
Welwyn Rd. Card 188 B3
Wembley Ave. Onll 9 F1
Wembley. Neath 87 E2
Wembley Rd. Card 204 B3
Wembley Rd. Ystal 23 D3
Wenallt Ct. Abera 50 A2
Wenallt Cl. Card 188 A4
Wenallt Rd. Abera 50 A2
Wenallt Rd. Card 172 A2
Wenallt Rd. Tonna 63 E1
Wengraig Rd. Trea 121 F3
Wenham Pl. Neath 87 F4
Wentlloog Rd. Card 190 C2
Wentlloog Rd. St B W 191 D1
Wentloog Cl. Card 190 A2
Wentloog Ct. Card 190 A2
Wentworth Cl. Card 191 D4
Wentworth Cl. Rhiwd 155 F2
Wentworth Cres. T Mum .. 108 C1
Wentworth La. Card 191 D4
Wenvoe Cl. Wen 215 D3
Wenvoe Ct. Card 203 E2
Weobley Ct. Swan 83 F3
Werfa Cl. Abera 50 B2
Werfa La. Abera 50 B2
Werfa St. Card 189 D1
Wern Cres. Nel 99 F2
Wern Cres. Skew 86 C3
Wern Ddu. Brynco 163 E2
Wern Deg. Penco 181 E4
Wern Fawr La. Card 190 C4
Wern Fawr Rd. H-y-Cy 165 F3
Wern Fawr Rd. Swan 111 E4
Wern Fraith. B-coch 62 B1
Wern Gethin La. Card 190 C3
Wern Goch E. Card 189 F3
Wern Goch W. Card 189 F3
Wern Isaf. Mer T 33 E3
Wern La. Mer T 51 E4
Wern Rd. C-c-y-c 32 A2
Wern Rd. Glan 4 B4
Wern Rd. Marg 139 D2
Wern Rd. Pen-cl 80 B1
Wern Rd. Skew 86 C4
Wern Rd. Swan 84 B2
Wern Rd. Tonypa 121 F3
Wern Rd. Ystal 23 D3
Wern St. Mer T 33 D3
Wern St. Tonypa 121 D4
Wern Tarw Houses. H-y-Cy 165 F4
Wern Terr. Glyn 91 E2
Wern Terr. Rhiwd 155 F1
Wern Terr. Swan 111 E4

Wern View. Ton 89 D1
Wern-Ddu Row. Caer 152 C1
Wernddu Ct. Caer 152 B1
Werngoch Rd. Card 189 E3
Wernlys Rd. Bridg 163 E1
Wernwood Rd. Ystal 23 D3
Wesley Ave. Rhoose 222 C1
Wesley Bldgs. Bedw 153 F4
Wesley Cl. Mer T 33 D2
Wesley Ct. Card 190 B3
Wesley Ct. D pow 216 A2
Wesley Hill. Bedw 153 F4
Wesley Pl. Marg 139 E3
Wesley Pl. Mer V 73 E2
Wesley Pl. Pontmi 129 F1
Wesley Pl. Yst 95 D2
Wesley Rd. Peng 101 F4
Wesley St. Abercy 98 B1
Wesley St. Ll' maj 219 F3
Wesley St. Maest 91 D1
Wessex Cl. Card 204 A3
West Acre. Ll'maes 220 A4
West Ave. Caer 151 F2
West Ave. Ce Cr 162 A1
West Ave. Maesy 101 D1
West Bute St. Card 205 E1
West Canal Wharf. Card .. 205 D2
West Cl. Card 205 D1
West Cliff. South 135 D2
West Crossways. Pontdw . 40 B3
West Dr. Porth 192 C3
West Dr. St Don 218 C3
West End Ave. Porth 176 C1
West End. Marg 139 E3
West End Terr. Ll' maj 219 F3
West Farm Cl. St B M 194 B1
West Farm Rd. St B M 194 C1
West Gr. Card 205 D3
West Gr. Mer T 32 B2
West Hill. Tred 35 E4
West House Rd. Bridg 179 E2
West Lee. Card 204 C3
West Luton Pl. Card 205 E3
West Mound Cres. Ch Vil . 150 A1
West Orchard Cres. Card . 204 A4
West Point Ind Est. Pen ... 216 B4
West Rd. Bridg 179 E2
West Rd. Card 187 F2
West Rd. Gell 100 B3
West Rd. Porth 176 C1
West Rhonnda. Pontcr 143 F4
West Rise. Card 189 D4
West St. Abercy 98 C2
West St. Bar 75 F2
West St. Ll' maj 219 F3
West St. Lough 57 D1
West St. Maest 117 D1
West St. Ponty 124 B1
West St. Tondu 163 E2
West St. Wick 208 B2
West Taff St. Porth 122 C2
West Terr. Pen 217 D2
West Town. Ll'gen 102 C2
West View Cres. Bed 99 E3
West View. Pontcr 143 F1
West View. T We 171 D2
West View Villas. Bar 76 A2
West Way. Swan 110 B3
West Wharf Rd. Card 205 D2
West-end Town. Ll' maj .. 219 F3
Westbourne Cres. Card ... 187 F2
Westbourne Ct. Barry 225 E4
Westbourne Ct. Card 190 B1
Westbourne Ct. Porth 192 C4
Westbourne Gr. Swan 109 E4
Westbourne Pl. Mer T 51 E4
Westbourne Pl. Porth 192 C4
Westbourne Pl. T Mum ... 137 D2
Westbourne Rd. Card 187 F2
Westbourne Rd. Neath 87 E2
Westbourne Rd. Pen 217 D1
Westbourne Rd. Swan 109 E4
Westbourne Terr. Ll'ha 166 C1
Westbury Cl. Barry 225 D4
Westbury Houses. Tony ... 146 B4
Westbury St. Swan 110 A3
Westbury Terr. Card 204 A4
Westcliff Mews. T Mum ... 137 E2
Westcliff. T Mum 137 E2
Westcross Ave. T Mum ... 137 D3
Westcross La. T Mum 136 C4
Westdale Rd. Swan 83 E4
Western Ave. Bridg 180 B2
Western Ave. Card 188 B1
Western Ave. Card 204 A4
Western Ave N. Card 188 B1
Western Ave. P Tal 113 E4
Western Bsns Ctr. Card ... 203 F3
Western Cl. T Mum 137 D2
Western Ct. Bridg 179 E2
Western Dr. Bar 75 F1
Western Dr. Card 188 B1
Western Dr. Tred 35 E4
Western Ind Est. Caer 151 F1
Western La. T Mum 137 D2

Western Rd. Pontdw 40 B2
Western Rd. Swan 60 B3
Western St. Ponty 123 E1
Western St. Swan 110 A3
Western Terr. Cross 129 D3
Western Terr. Glyn 92 B3
Western Terr. Swan 84 B2
Western Terr. Ynys 128 A2
Westernmoor Cotts. Neath .. 87 F3
Westernmoor Rd. Neath .. 87 F3
Westfa Rd. Swan 109 F4
Westfield Ave. Bridg 179 E4
Westfedale Ave. Card 188 B3
Westfield Cres. Card 189 E4
Westfield Ct. Ll'tris 168 C1
Westfield Rd. Card 188 B2
Westfield Rd. Ponty 124 B3
Westfield Rd. Swan 82 B2
Westgate Cl. Porth 176 C1
Westgate. Cowb 198 B1
Westgate St. Card 205 D3
Westgil Pen Ffordd. Peng . 101 E3
Westhill Dr. Ll'tris 168 C1
Westhill St. Ll' maj 219 F3
Westland Ave. T Mum 136 C4
Westland Cl. Lough 56 C1
Westlands. P Tal 113 E2
Westminster Cres. Card .. 189 E4
Westminster Dr. Card 189 E4
Westminster Dr. Sully 226 A3
Westminster Way. Bridg .. 179 E3
Westmoreland St. Card ... 204 B3
Weston Ave. Sully 226 A2
Weston Rd. Card 190 A3
Weston Rd. Tonypa 122 A1
Weston Sq. Barry 225 E3
Weston St. Barry 225 D3
Weston Terr. Treo 94 A2
Weston Terr. Tylor 122 C3
Westonbirt Cl. Card 190 C3
Westport Ave. T Mum 108 C1
Westra. D Pow 215 F1
Westside Rd. Aber 125 F1
Westview Terr. Bedw 152 B3
Westville Rd. Card 189 E1
Westville. Rhy 54 A4
Westville Wlk. Card 189 E1
Westward Cl. Bridg 179 D3
Westward Cl. T Mum 109 D1
Westward Pl. Bridg 179 D3
Westwinds Cl. Swan 82 C2
Westwinds Ct. Card 172 B1
Westwinds. T Mum 136 C2
Westwood Dr. Tre 99 D3
Wharf St. Card 205 D2
Wharfedale Rd. Card 189 F4
Wharton Cl. Rhoose 222 C1
Wharton St. Card 205 D3
Wheate Cl The. Rhoose .. 223 D1
Wheatfield Terr. Swan 84 B1
Wheatley Ave. P Tal 138 C4
Wheatley Pl. Mer T 51 F4
Wheatley Rd. Card 203 E3
Wheatley Rd. Neath 87 E2
Wheatsheaf Dr. Swan 84 B3
Wheatsheaf La. Mer T 32 B1
Whimbrels The. Porth 192 B4
Whinchat Cl. Card 191 D4
Whitaker Rd. Card 206 A4
Whitchurch Pl. Card 189 D1
Whitchurch Rd. Card 188 C1
Whitcliffe Dr. Pen 227 D4
Whitcombe St. Abera 50 A1
White Barn Rd. Card 188 B4
White Cl. P Tal 113 D2
White Cross La. Caer 151 F2
White Gates Cl. Skew 87 D4
White Gro. T Mum 136 C4
White Hart Cotts. Maest .. 142 A3
White Hart Dr. Bedw 153 F4
White Oaks Dr. Card 190 C4
White Rose Way. N Tre ... 54 C1
White St. Caer 152 A1
White St. Mer T 33 D3
White St. Swan 110 A4
White Walls. Swan 110 B3
Whiteacre Cl. Card 172 C1
Whitebeam Cl. Mer T 32 B3
Whitefield Cl. G-nea 26 C1
Whitefield Rd. Card 188 A1
Whitefield St. Yst 94 C2
Whiteford Rd. Swan 83 F3
Whitegates. T Mum 109 D1
Whitehall Ave. Card 190 A2
Whitehall Cl. Wen 214 C4
Whitehall Par. Card 190 A2
Whitehall Pl. Card 190 A2
Whitehall Rd. Card 187 F1
Whiterock Ave. Ponty 124 A1
Whiterock Cl. Ponty 124 A1
Whiterock Dr. Ponty 124 A1
Whitesands Rd. Card 172 B1
Whiteshell Dr. T Mum 136 C2
Whitestone Ave. Bish 136 A3
Whitestone Cl. T Mum 136 C3
Whitestone La. T Mum 136 C3

Whitestone Rd. Bish 136 A3
Whitethorn Dr. Bridg 180 A2
Whitethorn Pl. Swan 109 D3
Whitethorn Way. Marsh ... 191 F4
Whiteways. Ll' Maj 220 A4
Whitland Cl. Card 187 E1
Whitland Cl. Swan 83 F3
Whitland Cres. Card 187 F1
Whitland House. Card 188 A2
Whitley Rd. Lough 56 C1
Whitmuir Rd. Card 205 F4
Whittan Cl. Rhoose 222 C1
Whitting St. G-nea 27 D1
Whitting Terr. Tylor 122 C3
Whittington St. Neath 87 F3
Whittington St. Tonna 63 E2
Whittington Terr. Penga ... 57 E1
Whittle Rd. Card 204 B2
Whitworth Ct. Card 204 C2
Whitworth Terr. Tred 35 F3
Wick Rd. Ewen 196 A2
Wick Rd. Ll' maj 219 F4
Wick Rd. St B M 195 E1
Wicken Cl. Card 191 D4
Widecombe Dr. Card 190 A2
Widgeon Cl. Porth 176 C1
Wigan Terr. Brynco 164 A3
Wigmore Cl. Card 172 C1
Wild Gardens Rd. Card ... 189 D3
Wild Mill La. Bridg 179 F4
Wildbrook. Marg 139 E4
Wilden Ave. Marg 139 E3
Wilfred Brook Ho. Card ... 204 C1
Wilfred St. Barry 225 D3
Wilkins Terr. Caer 151 F3
Wilks Row. Swan 110 B4
Willesden Rd. Bridg 179 E3
Willet Cl. Neath 87 F4
William Bowen Cl. Gow ... 82 A3
William Cl. Swan 110 B3
William Forbes Bungalows.
      Bar 76 A3
William Harris Bungalows.
      Aber 151 D4
William Morris Gdns. Swan 111 D4
William St. A-wen 40 A1
William St. Aber 151 D4
William St. Abera 71 F2
William St. Abercy 98 C1
William St. Bar 76 A1
William St. Bar 76 A2
William St. Bedw 153 D3
William St. Card .... 204 BA
William St. Gall 101 D3
William St. Mer T 32 B1
William St. Pontcr 118 C2
William St. Ponty 124 C3
William St. Swan 110 B3
William St. T Mum 137 D3
William St. Tylor 122 C3
William St. Ynys 128 A2
William St. Yst 95 E2
William St. Ystra 23 F4
William's St. Marg 55 E2
Williams Ave. Reso 44 A1
Williams Church Terr.
      Tondu 163 F3
Williams Cres. Brynco 163 F3
Williams Pl. Mer T 32 C2
Williams Pl. Ponty 150 B2
Williams Pl. Pontcr 122 C2
Williams St. Ll'ha 166 B2
Williams St. Peng 101 F4
Williams St. Pontar 36 B2
Williams St. Trea 121 F4
Williams St. Trehe 68 C1
Williams Terr. Tre 99 D4
Williams Way. Card 205 D2
Williamstown. Mer T 32 B1
Willie Seager Memorial
      Homes. Card 189 F1
Williton Rd. Card 190 B4
Willow Bank. Gow 82 B3
Willow Cl. Bridg 180 C2
Willow Cl. Pen 216 C2
Willow Cl. Porthc 193 F4
Willow Ct. Card 205 E4
Willow Dr. Oak 101 F3
Willow Gr. Aberd 49 F1
Willow Gr. Card 191 D4
Willow Gr. P Tal 113 F3
Willow Herb Cl. Card 191 D3
Willow Rd. Ll'hry 183 E3
Willow Rd. Mer T 32 B3
Willow Rise. Gell 100 B4
Willow St. Ponty 150 A3
Willow Terr. M Ash 97 F4
Willow Tree Cl. Card 186 C3
Willow Way. P Tal 113 E3
Willow Wlk. Neath 88 B3
Willowbrook Dr. Card 190 C3
Willowbrook Factory Units.
      Card 190 C1
Willowbrook Gdns. T Mum 108 C1
Willowdale Cl. Card 203 E4
Willowdale Rd. Card 203 E4
Willowdene Way. Card 191 D4

Willowfield Ct. Card

Willowfield Ct. Card ... 189 E3
Willowford The. Ponty ... 170 C4
Willowmere. Pen ... 216 B4
Willows Ave. Card ... 205 F3
Willows Cres. Barry ... 225 D4
Willows Pl. Swan ... 110 B4
Willows The. Bedw ... 152 C4
Willows The. Bridg ... 178 C2
Willows The. Bridg ... 180 A2
Willowtube Ct. Brynco ... 163 F2
Wilmot St. Neath ... 87 F3
Wilson Pl. Card ... 203 E2
Wilson Rd. Card ... 203 D3
Wilson St. Card ... 205 F4
Wimble Wood Cl. T Mum ... 137 D4
Wimborne Cres. Sully ... 226 A3
Wimborne Rd. Barry ... 225 E3
Wimborne Rd. Penco ... 165 F1
Wimborne St. Mer T ... 33 D3
Wimbourne Cl. Ll' maj ... 219 F3
Wimbourne Cres. Penco ... 165 F1
Wimbourne Terr. Gell ... 75 D1
Wimmerfield Ave. Swan ... 108 C4
Wimmerfield Cl. Swan ... 108 C4
Wimmerfield Cres. Swan ... 108 C4
Wimmerfield Dr. Swan ... 108 C4
Winch Fawr Pk. Mer T ... 31 F1
Winch Fawr Rd. Mer T ... 31 F1
Winchester Ave. Card ... 189 C1
Wind Rd. Ystra ... 23 E4
Wind Road Ind Est. Ystra ... 23 E4
Wind St. Abera ... 50 A1
Wind St. Bridg ... 178 C3
Wind St. Fern ... 96 A4
Wind St. Neath ... 87 F4
Wind St. Swan ... 110 B4
Wind St. Tylor ... 122 C3
Windermere Ave. Card ... 189 D2
Windermere Cl. Abera ... 50 B1
Windermere Rd. Swan ... 84 C4
Windflower Cl. Card ... 191 D4
Windhover Cl. Card ... 191 D3
Windlass Ct. Card ... 205 E2
Windmill Cl. Card ... 172 C1
Windmill Cl. Ll' Maj ... 220 A4
Windmill La. Cowb ... 198 C1
Windmill La. Ll' Maj ... 220 A4
Windmill Terr. Swan ... 110 C4
Windrush Pl. Card ... 203 E4
Windsor Ave. Card ... 187 E3
Windsor Cl. Card ... 187 D3
Windsor Cl. Ll' Maj ... 220 A3
Windsor Cres. Card ... 187 E3
Windsor Ct. Card ... 205 E3
Windsor Ct. Pen ... 217 D2
Windsor Ct. Swan ... 110 B4
Windsor Ct. Ynybw ... 97 F1
Windsor Espl. Card ... 205 D1
Windsor Gdns. Card ... 203 F3
Windsor Gdns. Ll'tris ... 169 C4
Windsor Gn. Card ... 203 F3
Windsor Gr. Card ... 187 D3
Windsor La. Card ... 217 D3
Windsor La. Pen ... 217 D3
Windsor Mews. Card ... 205 E3
Windsor Pl. Aber ... 125 F1
Windsor Pl. Aber ... 150 C4
Windsor Pl. Card ... 205 D3
Windsor Pl. Mer T ... 33 D3
Windsor Pl. Pen ... 217 D2
Windsor Pl. T Mum ... 137 D3
Windsor Pl. Tre ... 99 D3
Windsor Pl. Ynybw ... 97 F1
Windsor Pl. Ynybw ... 98 A1
Windsor Pl. Yst ... 94 C2
Windsor Rd. Card ... 187 E3
Windsor Rd. Card ... 205 E3
Windsor Rd. M Ash ... 72 B1
Windsor Rd. Neath ... 87 F4
Windsor Rd. Pen ... 216 C3
Windsor Rd. Ponty ... 149 F4
Windsor Rd. Porth ... 192 C4
Windsor Rd. Tre ... 98 C3
Windsor St. Aberd ... 49 F2
Windsor St. Caer ... 152 A1
Windsor St. Swan ... 109 F4
Windsor St. Trehe ... 68 C1
Windsor St. Treo ... 94 B3
Windsor St. Troed ... 52 A1
Windsor St. Yst ... 94 C3
Windsor Terr. Aberd ... 50 B2
Windsor Terr. Card ... 205 D1
Windsor Terr. Mer T ... 51 F4
Windsor Terr. Pen ... 217 D2
Windsor Terr. Penga ... 57 E1
Windsor Terrace La. Pen ... 217 D2
Windsor Village. P Tal ... 113 E2
Windway Ave. Card ... 204 A4
Windway Rd. Card ... 204 A4
Windyridge. D pow ... 216 B1
Wine St. Ll' maj ... 219 F3
Wine St. Rhy ... 34 C1
Wingate Dr. Card ... 188 C3
Wingfield Ave. Ll'tris ... 168 C4
Wingfield Cl. Ponty ... 124 C1
Wingfield Cres. Ll'bra ... 127 D2
Wingfield Rd. Card ... 188 A2

Wingfield Rise. Tre ... 99 D3
Wingfield St. Mer V ... 73 E3
Wingfield Terr. Tre ... 99 D3
Winifred Rd. Skew ... 86 C4
Winifred St. M Ash ... 97 F4
Winifred St. Mer T ... 33 D3
Winnipeg Dr. Card ... 189 E3
Winsford Rd. Sully ... 226 B3
Winslade Ave. Neath ... 147 E3
Winsor Ct. Ll'tris ... 184 A4
Winston Ave. Wen ... 203 D1
Winston St. Swan ... 110 B4
Witherdene Rd. Tylor ... 96 B1
Withy Pk. Bish ... 136 A3
Withycombe Rd. Card ... 190 B4
Witla Court Rd. Card ... 190 B3
Wolfe Cl. Barry ... 225 E4
Wolffe Cl. Cowb ... 198 B1
Wolfs Castle Ave. Card ... 172 C1
Womanby St. Card ... 205 D3
Wood Cl. Card ... 173 D1
Wood Cl. Neath ... 87 E2
Wood Cl. Rhiwd ... 155 F4
Wood Rd. Ponty ... 149 F4
Wood St. Aberca ... 129 D4
Wood St. Bar ... 76 A2
Wood St. Card ... 205 D2
Wood St. Fern ... 70 A1
Wood St. Fern ... 95 F4
Wood St. Maest ... 117 D1
Wood St. Marg ... 139 E3
Wood St. Pen ... 217 D2
Wood St. Pontcr ... 118 C2
Wood St. Ponty ... 124 C3
Wood St. Tony ... 146 A3
Wood View. Neath ... 88 A3
Woodbine Pl. Peng ... 101 F4
Woodbine Rd. Peng ... 101 F4
Woodburn Dr. T Mum ... 137 D3
Woodcock St. Card ... 205 E4
Woodcote. Swan ... 108 B3
Woodfield Ave. Card ... 187 E2
Woodfield Ave. Pont ... 58 A3
Woodfield Bldgs. Porth ... 122 C2
Woodfield Cross. Tred ... 35 F2
Woodfield Park Cres. Oak ... 101 F3
Woodfield Rd. Ll'tris ... 168 A1
Woodfield Rd. Tred ... 35 F1
Woodfield St. Ll'ha ... 166 C1
Woodfield St. Marg ... 139 E3
Woodfield St. Swan ... 60 A1
Woodfield Terr. M Ash ... 97 F4
Woodfield Terr. Porth ... 122 C2
Woodfield Terr. Porth ... 123 E1
Woodford Cl. Card ... 187 F1
Woodford House. Ll' maj ... 219 F3
Woodford Rd. Swan ... 83 F4
Woodham Rd. Barry ... 225 D2
Woodland Ave. Marg ... 139 F2
Woodland Ave. Penco ... 181 E4
Woodland Ave. Porthc ... 193 D4
Woodland Ave. T Mum ... 136 C4
Woodland Cl. Neath ... 87 D2
Woodland Cl. Pontcr ... 143 F1
Woodland Cl. Skew ... 86 C4
Woodland Cotts. Bed ... 74 A4
Woodland Cres. Abercy ... 98 C2
Woodland Cres. Card ... 189 E2
Woodland Cres. Penty ... 185 F4
Woodland Dr. Rhiwd ... 155 F2
Woodland Dr. Rhiwd ... 155 F4
Woodland Pk. G-nea ... 27 D1
Woodland Pk. Hir ... 29 D2
Woodland Pl. Bar ... 76 A1
Woodland Pl. Bed ... 74 A4
Woodland Pl. Card ... 205 E4
Woodland Pl. Gell ... 100 C2
Woodland Pl. Mer T ... 32 C1
Woodland Pl. Pen ... 217 D2
Woodland Pl. Peng ... 101 D4
Woodland Pl. Pyle ... 177 D4
Woodland Rd. Bry ... 6 C3
Woodland Rd. Card ... 187 F2
Woodland Rd. Cry ... 43 D3
Woodland Rd. Glyn ... 66 C2
Woodland Rd. Ll'tris ... 169 D3
Woodland Rd. M Ash ... 72 B2
Woodland Rd. Neath ... 87 F4
Woodland Rd. Skew ... 86 C4
Woodland Rd. Tylor ... 96 A1
Woodland Rise. Bridg ... 163 E1
Woodland Row. Cwma ... 114 B3
Woodland St. M Ash ... 72 B2
Woodland St. Pontdw ... 40 C3
Woodland Terr. Aber ... 125 F2
Woodland Terr. Aber ... 150 C4
Woodland Terr. Abera ... 71 E3
Woodland Terr. Ll'ha ... 183 F4
Woodland Terr. M Ash ... 72 B2
Woodland Terr. Mark ... 76 C2
Woodland Terr. Mer T ... 32 C1
Woodland Terr. N Tre ... 54 B3
Woodland Terr. Og Va ... 144 B2
Woodland Terr. Ponty ... 149 D4
Woodland Terr. Treo ... 94 A2
Woodland Terr. Treo ... 94 B4
Woodland Vale. Treo ... 94 B4

Woodland View. Ynys ... 128 C2
Woodland Way. Brynco ... 163 F2
Woodlands Ave. Tre ... 99 D4
Woodlands. Ch Vil ... 169 D4
Woodlands Cl. Cowb ... 198 B1
Woodlands Cres. Tre ... 99 D3
Woodlands Park Dr. B-coch 62 C1
Woodlands Park Dr. Card ... 203 D2
Woodlands Pk. Penco ... 181 E4
Woodlands Pk. Pyle ... 161 F1
Woodlands Rd. Lough ... 56 C1
Woodlands Rise. Bridg ... 179 E2
Woodlands St. Og Va ... 119 F2
Woodlands Terr. Gow ... 82 B3
Woodlands Terr. Maest ... 91 D1
Woodlands Terr. Reso ... 44 B1
Woodlands Terr. Swan ... 110 A4
Woodlands The. Bridg ... 180 B3
Woodlands The. Card ... 173 D1
Woodlands Workshop
  Centre. Ll'ha ... 184 A4
Woodlawn Way. Card ... 172 C1
Woodmans Terr. Ystal ... 23 D3
Woodpecker Sq. Ll' Maj ... 220 C3
Woodridge Ct. T Mum ... 136 C2
Woodside Ave. Bridg ... 179 F4
Woodside Ave. Neath ... 87 F4
Woodside Ave. Swan ... 108 C3
Woodside. B-coch ... 63 D2
Woodside Cl. Bish ... 136 A3
Woodside Cl. Swan ... 108 C3
Woodside Cres. Cly ... 60 B4
Woodside Ct. Card ... 173 D1
Woodstock Gdns. Penco ... 165 E1
Woodstock Mews. Cowb ... 198 C1
Woodvale Ave. Card ... 189 E4
Woodview. Gow ... 82 B2
Woodview. Ll'ha ... 166 B2
Woodview Pl. Swan ... 83 F3
Woodville Ct. Card ... 205 D4
Woodville Rd. Card ... 205 D4
Woodville Rd. T Mum ... 137 D2
Woodville St. Pontar ... 36 B3
Woodville Terr. Mark ... 76 C3
Woodward Ave. Cross ... 129 D2
Woodward Rd. Cross ... 129 E2
Woolacombe Ave. Card ... 190 B3
Woolaston Ave. Card ... 189 E3
Woollacott Dr. T Mum ... 136 B3
Woollacott Mews. T Mum ... 136 B3
Woolmer Cl. Card ... 187 E1
Woosnnam Cl. Card ... 189 F1
Worcester Cl. Mer T ... 32 A1
Worcester Ct. Card ... 204 C1
Worcester Dr. T Mum ... 137 D2
Worcester Pl. Swan ... 110 B4
Worcester Rd. T Mum ... 137 D2
Worcester St. Card ... 204 C1
Wordsworth Ave. Bridg ... 179 E3
Wordsworth Ave. Card ... 205 E4
Wordsworth Ave. Pen ... 216 C2
Wordsworth Cl. Ll' Maj ... 220 A3
Wordsworth Gdns. Ponty ... 150 A2
Wordsworth St. Abera ... 71 D2
Wordsworth St. Swan ... 110 B4
Working St. Card ... 205 D3
Worle Ave. Card ... 190 A3
Worle Pl. Card ... 190 A3
Wren Ave. Neath ... 88 A3
Wren Bank. Neath ... 87 D1
Wren Cl. Bridg ... 180 B2
Wren Cl. Card ... 191 D3
Wren Rd. Ll' Maj ... 220 C3
Wrexham Ct. Card ... 190 C3
Wrgant Pl. Fern ... 70 A1
Wroughton Pl. Card ... 203 F3
Wychtree St. Swan ... 85 D4
Wychwood Cl. T Mum ... 137 D2
Wyeverne Rd. Card ... 205 D4
Wyfan Pl. Card ... 188 B1
Wyncliffe Rd. Card ... 190 A4
Wynd St. Barry ... 225 D3
Wyndham Arc. Card ... 205 D3
Wyndham Cl. Bridg ... 180 B3
Wyndham Cl. Pontar ... 36 B2
Wyndham Cres. Abera ... 71 E3
Wyndham Cres. Bridg ... 179 F1
Wyndham Cres. Card ... 204 B3
Wyndham Ct. Abera ... 71 E4
Wyndham Ct. Swan ... 85 E4
Wyndham House. Bridg ... 179 F2
Wyndham Park Way.
  P-s-Ely ... 201 F3
Wyndham Pl. Card ... 204 C3
Wyndham Rd. Card ... 204 B3
Wyndham St. Barry ... 225 D3
Wyndham St. Bedw ... 154 A4
Wyndham St. Bridg ... 179 F2
Wyndham St. Card ... 171 E1
Wyndham St. Card ... 204 C3
Wyndham St. Marg ... 139 E4
Wyndham St. Mer T ... 33 D2
Wyndham St. Og Va ... 119 F2
Wyndham St. Og Va ... 146 A4
Wyndham St. Porth ... 122 C1
Wyndham St. Swan ... 110 A3
Wyndham St. Tonypa ... 121 F2
Wyndham St. Trehe ... 68 C1

Wyndham St. Troed ... 52 B1
Wyndham St. Yst ... 95 D1
Wyndham Terr. Card ... 189 D2
Wyngarth. Swan ... 85 E3
Wynnstay Cl. Card ... 204 C2
Wynter Ct. Swan ... 84 B3
Wyon Cl. Card ... 187 E2
Wyvern Ave. P Tal ... 113 E1

Y Berllan. Ll'fel ... 59 E1
Y Berllan. Neath ... 88 A3
Y Berllan. Swan ... 108 B4
Y Berllan. Ystra ... 23 E4
Y Cilgant. Caer ... 151 F3
Y Clos. Cwmll ... 6 B3
Y Deri. Ch Vil ... 169 E3
Y Dolau. Ll'fel ... 59 E1
Y Dolydd. Caer ... 151 F1
Y Garn. Penga ... 58 A1
Y Garth. Aberd ... 49 E2
Y Gefnen. Swan ... 85 F3
Y Gilfach. Ystal ... 23 D4
Y Gilwern. Ystal ... 23 D3
Y Glyn. Maesy ... 101 D1
Y Glyn. Swan ... 108 B4
Y Goedlan. Cwmll ... 6 C2
Y Goedwig. Card ... 188 A4
Y Gorlan. Swan ... 108 B4
Y Groes. Brynco ... 163 F2
Y Groes. Card ... 188 A4
Y Gwernydd. Swan ... 60 C3
Y Lan. Penco ... 165 F1
Y Llest. Bridg ... 163 E1
Y Llwyni. Ll'fel ... 59 E1
Y Parc. Ll'tris ... 185 D4
Y Waun Fach. Ll'fel ... 59 D1
Y Waun. Ynybw ... 97 F1
Y Wern. Pontcr ... 143 F2
Y-Wern. Ll'fel ... 59 D1
Yalton. T Mum ... 136 C4
Yeo St. Reso ... 44 A1
Yew Cl. Mer T ... 32 B3
Yew Gr. Oak ... 101 F3
Yew St. Bar ... 76 A3
Yew St. Mer T ... 51 F4
Yew St. T We ... 171 D2
Yew St. Troed ... 52 B1
Yew Tree Cl. Colw ... 197 D2
Yew Tree Ct. Card ... 189 E1
Yewtree Cl. Card ... 203 E4
Yewtree Gr. Ll'maes ... 221 D4
Ymyl-yr-Afon. B-coch ... 63 E2
Ynisarwed Terr. Reso ... 64 B4
Yniscedwyn Rd. Ystra ... 23 F4
Ynisderw Rd. Pontdw ... 40 C2
Ynisisaf Cotts. Ystra ... 8 A2
Ynisydarren Rd. Ystal ... 23 D3
Yntsafan Terr. Cwma ... 114 C3
Ynys Cadwyn. G-nea ... 45 F4
Ynys Cl. Ponty ... 149 F3
Ynys Ct. Glyn ... 66 C1
Ynys Fach Ave. Reso ... 44 B1
Ynys Fawr Ave. Reso ... 44 B1
Ynys Glyd St. Gell ... 126 C4
Ynys Hir. Ynybw ... 124 B4
Ynys Las. Nel ... 99 E2
Ynys Nedd. Reso ... 44 B1
Ynys Newydd Rd. Swan ... 109 D2
Ynys Park Cotts. Yst ... 95 D2
Ynys St. Marg ... 114 B3
Ynys St. Tylor ... 122 C4
Ynys Terr. Ponty ... 149 F3
Ynys y Bont Cotts. Bry ... 6 C3
Ynys-bydafau. Ystra ... 8 B3
Ynys-cedwyn Lodge. Ystra . 23 E4
Ynys-Gau Rd. Yst ... 95 E2
Ynys-Gyfeillon Rd. Ponty .. 124 B1
Ynys-Lee. Cwma ... 114 C2
Ynys-Lwyd Rd. Abera ... 71 E4
Ynys-Lwyd St. Abera ... 50 A1
Ynys-Meudwy Rd. Ponydw . 41 D4
Ynys-Penllwch Rd. Cly ... 60 C4
Ynys-Penllwch Rd. Swan ... 61 D3
Ynys-y-gwial. Ystra ... 7 E3
Ynys-y-Mond Rd. A-wen ... 40 C1
Ynys-y-Mond Rd. Cly ... 61 D4
Ynys-y-Nos Ave. G-nea ... 27 E1
Ynys-yr-Afon. Clyne ... 64 B3
Ynysallan Rd. Swan ... 60 B2
Ynysangharad Rd. Ponty ... 124 B1
Ynysbryn Cl. Ll'tris ... 168 B2
Ynyscedwyn Ind Est. Ystra . 23 F4
Ynyscorrwg Rd. Ponty ... 150 A2
Ynyscynon Rd. Trea ... 121 F4
Ynyscynon St. Abera ... 50 B1
Ynyscynon Terr. Aberd ... 50 B1
Ynysddu. Ll'ha ... 184 A4
Ynysfeio Ave. Trehe ... 69 D1
Ynyshir Rd. Tylor ... 122 C4
Ynyslas Cres. G-nea ... 27 D1
Ynyslas. Porthc ... 193 D4
Ynyslyn Rd. Ponty ... 150 A2
Ynysmaerdy Terr. Ll'ha ... 168 A3
Ynysmeurig Rd. Abercy ... 98 C1
Ynysawel Fach. Mer V ... 73 E3
Ynystawe Rd. Swan ... 60 B3
Ynysteg. Tondu ... 163 F3
Ynyswen. Coel ... 9 E4

Ynyswen Ind Est. Treo ... 94 A4
Ynysygwas Hill. Cwma ... 114 C2
Ynysygwas Terr. Cwma ... 114 C2
Ynysymaerdy Rd. Neath ... 87 E2
Yorath Rd. Card ... 188 A3
York Cl. Mer T ... 32 A1
York Cl. Swan ... 110 B3
York Dr. Ch Vil ... 169 E3
York Mansions. Card ... 187 F3
York Pl. Aberca ... 129 D4
York Pl. Bridg ... 179 F2
York Pl. Card ... 204 C1
York Pl. Marg ... 139 E4
York Pl. Pontmi ... 129 F2
York Rd. Bridg ... 180 A1
York St. Abera ... 71 E3
York St. Card ... 204 B3
York St. M Ash ... 72 B1
York St. Porth ... 122 C2
York St. Swan ... 110 B3
York Terr. Tred ... 35 F3
Yr Allt. Ll'tris ... 168 B2
Yr Efail. Colw ... 181 D1
Yr Elain. Swan ... 108 B4
Yr Hafan. Pontcr ... 118 C1
Yr Hafod. Ll'fel ... 59 E1
Yr Hendre. Ponty ... 171 D4
Yr Ynys. Pyle ... 161 D1
Yr Ysfa. Maest ... 117 D1
Yr-Hen-Lawnt. Tonypa ... 121 F2
Yryswen Terr. Cry ... 24 A1
Ysgol St. Swan ... 111 D4
Ysgubor Fach. Bedw ... 153 F4
Ysgubor Fach St. Swan ... 84 B1
Ysguthan Rd. P Tal ... 138 C4
Yspitty Rd. Ll'nel ... 56 A1
Ystad Celyn. Maest ... 117 D1
Ystadwaun. Penco ... 165 E1
Ysticl-Garu. Llys ... 209 F4
Ysticlau Rd. Se Si ... 25 D4
Ystrad Bldgs. Bedw ... 153 D3
Ystrad Cl. Card ... 191 D4
Ystrad Einon. Lough ... 57 D1
Ystrad Fawr. Bridg ... 179 E3
Ystrad Ifor. Og Va ... 144 C3
Ystrad Rd. Swan ... 83 D2
Ystrad Rd. Yst ... 95 D2
Ystrad St. Card ... 205 D1
Ystrad Terr. Yst ... 95 D2
Ystrad-fawr Villas. Ystra ... 8 A1
Ystradbarwig Terr. Ch Vil .. 169 E3
Ystwyth Pl. Swan ... 59 E1

Zig-Zag Rd. Porth ... 177 D1
Zig-Zag Rd. Porthc ... 193 D4
Zinc St. Card ... 205 E3
Zion Terr. Tonypa ... 121 F3
Zoar Ave. Maest ... 117 D2
Zoar Pl. Maest ... 117 D2
Zoar Rd. Neath ... 87 F4
Zoar Rd. Ystal ... 23 D3
Zoar Terr. Tre ... 99 D3
Zouch St. Swan ... 84 B2

ORDNANCE SURVEY

STREET ATLASES

The Ordnance Survey / Philip's Street Atlases provide unique and definitive mapping of entire counties

Street Atlases available

- Berkshire
- Bristol and Avon
- Buckinghamshire
- Cardiff
- Cheshire
- Derbyshire
- Edinburgh
- East Essex
- West Essex
- Glasgow
- North Hampshire
- South Hampshire
- Hertfordshire
- East Kent
- West Kent
- Nottinghamshire
- Oxfordshire
- Staffordshire
- Surrey
- East Sussex
- West Sussex
- Warwickshire

The Street Atlases are revised and updated on a regular basis and new titles are added to the series. Many counties are now available in full-size hardback and softback editions as well as handy pocket-size versions. All contain Ordnance Survey mapping except Surrey which is by Philip's

The series is available from all good bookshops or by mail order direct from the publisher. However, the order form opposite may not reflect the complete range of titles available so it is advisable to check by telephone before placing your order. Payment can be made by credit card or cheque / postal order in the following ways:

By phone
Phone your order through on our special Credit Card Hotline on 01933 414000. Speak to our customer service team during office hours (9am to 5pm) or leave a message on the answering machine, quoting T512N99C, your full credit card number plus expiry date and your full name and address

By post
Simply fill out the order form opposite (you may photocopy it) and send it to: Cash Sales Department, Reed Book Services, PO Box 5, Rushden, Northants, NN10 6YX